The Promise of Sociology

The Promise of Sociology

CLASSICAL APPROACHES TO CONTEMPORARY SOCIETY

Second Edition

ROB BEAMISH

UNIVERSITY OF TORONTO PRESS

LIBRARY AND ARCHIVES CANADA CATALOGUING IN PUBLICATION

Beamish, Rob B. (Rob Barker), 1949–, author
    The promise of sociology : classical approaches to contemporary society / Rob Beamish.—
Second edition.

Includes bibliographical references and index.
Issued in print and electronic formats.

ISBN 978-1-4426-3404-6 (paperback).—ISBN 978-1-4426-3405-3 (hardback).—ISBN
978-1-4426-3406-0 (html).—ISBN 978-1-4426-3407-7 (pdf).

1. Sociology—Textbooks. 2. Sociology—Philosophy—Textbooks. 3. Popular culture—
Textbooks. I. Title.

HM586.B432016   301   C2016-903393-7   C2016-903394-5

We welcome comments and suggestions regarding any aspect of our publications—please
feel free to contact us at news@utphighereducation.com or visit our Internet site at
www.utppublishing.com.

North America
5201 Dufferin Street
North York, Ontario, Canada, M3H 5T8

2250 Military Road
Tonawanda, New York, USA, 14150

ORDERS PHONE: 1–800–565–9523
ORDERS FAX: 1–800–221–9985
ORDERS E-MAIL: utpbooks@utpress.utoronto.ca

UK, Ireland, and continental Europe
NBN International
Estover Road, Plymouth, PL6 7PY, UK
ORDERS PHONE: 44 (0) 1752 202301
ORDERS FAX: 44 (0) 1752 202333
ORDERS E-MAIL: enquiries@nbninternational.
com

Every effort has been made to contact copyright holders; in the event of an error or omission,
please notify the publisher.

The University of Toronto Press acknowledges the financial support for its publishing activities
of the Government of Canada through the Canada Book Fund.

Printed in the United States of America

To the students

CONTENTS

Preface ix

Introduction xv

Part One   Why Think Sociologically?

1. Visions and Profiles of Students Today 3
2. Generation Z and the Promise of Sociology 27
3. The Light of Reason:
    Higher Education's Challenges 59

Part Two   The Classical Tradition

4. Marx and the Dialectic of Dynamic, Unstable Social
    Formations 85
5. Marx, the *Communist Manifesto*, and Modernity 121
6. From Descartes to Durkheim:
    Toward a Science of Society 139
7. Durkheim and the Systematic Study of Social Facts 165
8. Weber and the Interpretive Understanding of Social
    Action 183
9. The Spirit of Capitalism, Modernity, and the
    Postmodern World 203

Part Three   Sociology and Contemporary Popular Culture

10. Culture and Critique 235
11. The Dialectics of Popular Culture 261
12. Rock 'n' Roll as Complex Culture 293
13. The Promise of Sociology 321

Glossary of Key Terms and Names 327
Bibliography 357
Index 379

PREFACE

The positive reception that *The Promise of Sociology*'s first edition received from students, reviewers, and other instructors easily surpassed my expectations for a book that differed so much from what has become the "standard" format for introductory texts in the social sciences. In addition, my own success with the book as an instructional tool also affirmed the approach I had taken in structuring the text and the ideas it contained. Rewarding as those feelings were, however, over the past five years, I have become acutely aware of several ways I could improve *The Promise* and warmly welcomed the invitation to produce a revised edition.

First, certain parts of the text had to be updated to keep abreast of the times. We live in a changing world. Today's first year students are no longer part of the Millennial generation—they constitute "Generation Z," and although they share many of the Millennials' generational traits, they also represent a different type of student than the last cohort. As a result, I have made extensive revisions to Part I, which now consists of three chapters rather than two. There is an up-to-date profile of today's students, a more detailed analysis of their expectations for the university experience, and a discussion of higher education today—the challenges it poses for undergraduate students and how their relationship to information and knowledge must change if they are to profit fully from their experiences and be prepared to succeed in the work world they will soon enter.

The changes to Part II streamline the presentation of material that students found too drawn out and allow me to highlight the themes that run through the work of Marx, Durkheim, and Weber more than in the earlier edition. In the section on Marx, for example, I get to the main points regarding his approach to grasping the complexity of the modern world more directly. The chapter on Durkheim has a more extensive discussion of "collective representations" than in the first edition, demonstrating this idea's importance more than before as well as how it shares some similarities with Marx's and Weber's thought. The Weber section has been streamlined considerably, and there is a clearer indication of how his work engages with that of Marx and Durkheim.

As in Part I, I have changed the material in Part III significantly. There are now four chapters instead of three: "Culture and Critique," "The Dialectics of Popular Culture," "Rock 'n' Roll as Complex Culture," and the conclusion "The Promise of Sociology."

"Culture and Critique" still presents both a history of the complex term "culture" and the concerns cultural critics have voiced about the demise of culture throughout the twentieth and early twenty-first century. The chapter ends with a Weberian "pure type" construction of culture as a form of critique. That pure type is used in the next two chapters to examine the emergence of popular culture in the post–World War II period and is applied to two case studies. The first case study focuses on the early work of Bob Dylan and the second on rock and roll.

Despite these changes, the same three fundamental principles informing the first edition continue to shape this one.

The first principle stems from advice given to me 35 years ago as I began to organize my first introduction to sociology course: never underestimate students' abilities. Although many think the education system has been "dumbed down" over the past 20 or more years to meet the needs of an emergent mass education system catering to increasingly disinterested but demanding student-consumers, my experiences as an instructor—confirmed by recent students' comments on *The Promise of Sociology*—suggest that today's highly capable students thrive on intellectual challenges. For me, the remarks that doyen of sociology Charles Page made during the dramatic expansionary period of North America's postsecondary education systems remain as pertinent now as they were then. As departments sought to increase their influence and prestige through larger enrolments, Page cautioned sociologists that they should resist what he saw as a dangerous temptation:

> [I]n the hands of instructors primarily devoted to empire-building, sociology, perhaps more than any other subject, lends itself to exploitation for the sake of popularity. At its worst, sociology can be a "gut" course, or a gossip column on social life providing spicy entertainment and mass appeal, or both, drawing to its classes in large numbers the lazy and the mediocre. At its best, sociology is a demanding study, the intellectual peer of any, and sufficiently challenging to attract superior students. These are extremes, of course, between which most sociologists ply their teaching trade. Many of them no doubt compromise. But if they are to discourage invidious comparison and, more importantly, raise the intellectual standards of their field, they should risk the dangers of limited popularity by offering sociology's richest goods. (Page 1959:591)

In view of today's neoliberal funding policies, the pressure to increase student enrolment at the expense of intellectual rigour may be stronger than ever. But I have found that meeting the "Page standard" still brings the greatest rewards for students and instructors seeking the best university experience possible. The systematic study of the social world is complex and difficult; if that were not the case, we would not need sociology. Students deserve the opportunity to struggle with the intricate complexity of the world they are inheriting, so they can create genuine, effective change. Most important, superior students thrive on rising to the challenge of mastering "sociology's richest goods."

The second principle is the overwhelming significance of socio-historical context. The easiest students to teach are those entering the postsecondary education system later in life or returning to it as "mature students." Students who have a wealth of life experiences behind them tend to grasp sociology and the sociological frame of reference quickly and easily because they can see from their own lives how one's social location at a particular point in time influences one's perception of the world fundamentally.

The corollary is that younger students, with far fewer life experiences and much less appreciation for historical time, have more difficulty grasping the main features of sociology. As a result, there is a temptation for instructors to focus exclusively on the contemporary and the popular, on what is familiar, so that students will find immediate relevance and interest in sociology. Like Page, I have never found that a sound teaching strategy.

Good sociology requires the examination of how people's immediate experiences (their personal biographies) intersect with history and social structure. And one cannot adequately grasp the immediate without knowing what happened before. As a result, I continually strive to place every topic, issue, and problem within a broader socio-historical context. This means my course is inescapably informed by social history—more to the point, it is structured so that students must begin to appreciate social history because it is so critical to good sociology.

Almost every issue I cover begins with a context that predates the year in which the majority of today's students were born. At first, some find it frustrating: who cares what happened in 1968? But, as they proceed through the course, what is almost intuitive to the mature student becomes automatic for younger students as well. Social context becomes a powerful departure point for how students examine their immediate, everyday life experiences. Not only does 1968 become relevant, but 1776, 1789, 1848, 1912, 1945, 1989, 2008, and numerous other signposts take on real meaning as the context for a fuller understanding of today's world. Despite the resistance and impatience of youth, holding firm on the importance of socio-historical context is a principle that has paid many dividends over my career in the lecture hall.

The final principle is to enjoy the freedom sociology brings to human life. I do not know how often students think of enjoyment, freedom, and sociology in the same sentence, but they all belong together. Sometimes sociology is work, sometimes it represents an obstacle to taking the day or night off from study, but, in the end, learning about the social world should bring excitement, satisfaction, and accomplishment—all feelings that one can enjoy. The best experience, however, is freedom—the freedom to explore, discover, and learn; the freedom to disagree, dispute, and reject. Sociology provides a framework that facilitates all of these freedoms and their enjoyment.

Rules are almost always associated with constraint—something is ruled out. But rules also enable. Without the rules of language, people could not communicate; without the informal rules of social interaction, we would never know how to proceed in social situations. Sociology is the same.

The sociological frame of reference rules out some forms of knowledge and inquiry. Sociology, for example, rejects mysticism as a form of explanation; it rejects tradition as the sole basis for legitimate action. As the discussions of Émile Durkheim and Max Weber in the text emphasize, sociologists must adhere to some very specific rules and criteria to achieve the goals of genuine scholarly inquiry. But, as much as those rules constrain, they also enable. Sociology's rules allow those who employ the sociological frame of reference to explore the world in a very open, systematic, and critical fashion. Enjoying the freedom sociology offers is the final principle I always keep in mind as I introduce students to what Auguste Comte called "the queen of the sciences."

Although many friends and colleagues have contributed over the years to what emerges in this book, there are four groups of people, in particular, whom I want to recognize and thank.

Bill Munn, a long-serving tutor-marker for the online section of introductory sociology at Queen's University, and Christina Salavantis, the Teaching-Assistant Coordinator for the Department of Sociology at Queen's, were central to the development of the first edition of *The Promise*, and their contributions to this edition have been invaluable. I have also benefitted enormously from Isabel Macquarrie's meticulous reading of this edition. Izzy's strengths as an outstanding graduate student and a meticulous young scholar, as well as her experiences as a teaching assistant, working directly with students in my course, have led to numerous small but vital adjustments to the text. In addition, Izzy drafted the "Questions for Review and Further Reflection" found at the end of each chapter.

Although I have lived much of the history of rock and roll, I am indebted to Hannah Bennett, Nicole Hills, Izzy, and the members of Jack the Lads—Paddy Beirne, Julian Lee, and Will Macquarrie—for all their insight into the contemporary scene. Their deep appreciation for the subtle sounds that really make rock and roll reach one's soul has been invaluable in writing Chapter 12.

I want to thank the anonymous reviewers of drafts for the first edition of this text and the students and instructors who gave me feedback over the past five years so that this revised edition could build on the strengths and overcome the weaknesses of the first edition.

Anne Brackenbury knows how much I have valued the support she offered in the completion of the first edition, and I want to express my gratitude to her for the encouragement and patience she demonstrated in the production of this new edition. Anne took a risk in originally supporting an introductory text that differs so much from the norm, and her confidence that others were sure to find the book stimulating and that, with some refining, it could reach a wider audience bolstered my own belief in continuing to pursue the "Page standard." I deeply appreciate all she has done to make *The Promise of Sociology* what it has become today.

Karen Taylor's careful attention to detail and fine aesthetic sense of the English language contributed significantly to the success of the first edition; this revision is equally in her debt for all the skill and patience she has invested in bringing its prose to life. In both editions, Karen's contributions went well beyond ensuring that this was a clean, clear, tight text. The suggestions she offered on the basis of her own knowledge and genuine interest in the material covered, along with her wonderful feel for words, have added immeasurably to the text each time it has gone to publication.

Last, but certainly not least, I want to once again thank Nada for her unfailing support of this project and of all the countless hours I have invested in its creation, many of which I could have spent enjoying time with her. Our lives have changed since the first edition, as Travis and Ryan have now established themselves in their own careers and households, and while our perspectives have had to adjust, I treasure Nada's ongoing support for all that is entailed in my commitment to sociology as a calling, and I value it as deeply today as when we first began our journey through life together.

Despite these debts, I want to dedicate this book to the students—past, present, and future—who have followed or will one day read the arguments and ideas presented in this text. It is my firm hope that they, too, will discover not only the liberating freedom and passion that Karl Marx, Émile Durkheim, Max Weber, C. Wright Mills, and ensuing generations of sociologists have found in the systematic study of the social world but also the same sense of commitment to making this world safer, more equitable, just, and intrinsically rewarding than ever before.

Rob Beamish, Kingston

INTRODUCTION

Sociology should be one of the most interesting, challenging, and intellectually liberating courses of study that a student can pursue. Sociologists focus on a broad range of issues that cover everything from the most mundane aspects of people's everyday lives through to concerns about globalization, the concentration of international power, war and famine, and the social processes that degrade the environment.

Good sociology provides a much-needed corrective to the taken-for-granted understandings people have about the world around them. It seeks to provide more comprehensive knowledge about issues that affect individuals, groups, local communities, nations, regions of the world, or the global population as a whole. Sociological analyses can help policy makers and everyday women and men change their own lives and the lives of others. Learning to think sociologically can be a life-altering experience, but it is not easy to become a good sociologist.

In the same way that an Olympic sprinter dedicates hour upon hour to heavy training for a decade or more in order to cover 100 metres in one one-hundredth of a second less than the record, students must complete a lengthy, sometimes difficult, and frequently solitary learning process before they are ready to change the world through a sophisticated sociological understanding of the problems they seek to address. An introductory sociology course and an introductory text are just two resources that will assist students in this long and occasionally arduous but ultimately exciting and highly rewarding journey.

There are times when studying sociology is work, but most often it is fascinating and sometimes even empowering. Becoming a good sociologist requires learning a certain vocabulary and building specific skills; the process of gaining and refining both is easier for some than for others. Similarly, some terms, ideas, or skills are mastered quickly while others require time, concentrated effort, and the will to understand the complexities of sociology and social life. It is, however, the total package that counts, and the rewards for mastering the terminology, skills, and knowledge required to become a good sociologist are deeply satisfying at a personal level and of significant consequence at an interpersonal and broader social level.

The Sociological Frame of Reference

To help students begin the sociological journey, I have written this book to meet four main objectives. The first is to introduce students to what C. Wright Mills (1959) calls "the sociological imagination." Even though each person is a highly knowledgeable, sophisticated human agent who draws upon a vast wealth of social knowledge, that does not mean people think sociologically. On the contrary, even though many feel they have an almost intuitive familiarity with sociology, the taken-for-granted "stocks of knowledge at hand" they use in their daily activities are significantly different from the theories and methods that sociologists routinely employ to understand social life critically (Schutz [1932] 1967:78).

An exploration of how one thinks sociologically is the first and foremost task facing students and their instructor in an introductory course. In many respects, this entire book is designed to introduce students to the sociological frame of reference and to help them refine and consolidate that particular perspective as they cover the material presented in each chapter.

To help reach that objective and in contrast to the quick overview provided in most introductory texts, a full chapter of this book is dedicated to exploring Mills's conception of the sociological imagination in detail. That framework is brought to life by using it to explore the experiences today's first year students will encounter in the postsecondary education system. There are two reasons for choosing today's university students as the focal point for an elaboration of the sociological imagination.

First, people are interested in themselves, and there is a lot to know about today's students, including many aspects of their lives about which they may not even be aware. Thus, having students read about themselves is an ideal way to introduce them to the key elements in Mills's framework.

Second, and of greater importance, the opening chapter provides an excellent opportunity for students to learn, from a sociological vantage point, about the strengths they possess and the challenges they will face in their university experience. The discussion provides an opportunity for students to assess critically what they can achieve in their studies and how they might best achieve those goals.

The second major objective for every introductory text and instructor is to provide students with a focused introduction to the discipline.

Unfortunately, no introductory course or text can cover everything; they are always selective. In making difficult choices, an instructor and the author of a text must try to ensure that the core areas and issues are covered while also exposing students to a meaningful range of the areas of inquiry that sociologists address.

There is also the question of breadth of coverage versus depth of analysis. One can cover a broad range of issues without going into too much detail or one can tackle a narrower range of material in greater depth. Unfortunately, there is not a perfect balancing point because some students will prefer broader coverage while others want greater depth; in a large class, it is impossible to meet the desires of every student. At the same time, instructors' views on what the correct balance is will vary. This book emphasizes an in-depth discussion of a few strategically selected themes and issues.

The Promise of Sociology is written to stand alone as an introduction to modern sociological thinking and the classical tradition. I use it in the first term of a two-term course. In the second term, students build on the foundation created here to explore more contemporary sociological theories as they survey a wider range of substantive topics. But *The Promise* can also be used in conjunction with one of the many introductory readers in sociology to give students that same broad understanding of the discipline and the issues sociologists tackle.

The Promise of Sociology, it is worth noting, can also be used in a fourth year, capstone course, or by graduate students wanting to reinvigorate their passion for sociology. In 1976, when I was a master's student, my supervisor handed me a copy of Peter Berger's (1963) *Invitation to Sociology* and said I should read it. I politely explained that I already had, in my introductory course. He replied, "Of course you have, but you'll be surprised how much Berger has learned in the past four years." As students at Queen's have emphasized to me on numerous occasions, *The Promise of Sociology* served them as a vitally important resource throughout their undergraduate programs—even when they majored in something other than sociology. Students in classical theory courses, upper year students, and graduate students who read *The Promise* will capture nuance that a first year student may miss, or they will appreciate insights that they had not noticed when reading the book for the first time.

Irrespective of how the book is used, it presents more material than a student new to sociology can fully internalize during a first year course. Becoming a sociologist takes time. Claude Henri de Rouvroy, comte de Saint-Simon; Auguste Comte; Karl Marx; Émile Durkheim; and Max Weber—to name five thinkers relevant to sociology—did not make great contributions to the discipline until they had read extensively and amassed considerable knowledge. And their labours were not always easy. Scholarship is demanding work—it is time consuming and labour intensive.

Writing to his daughter Jenny in 1867 after publishing the first volume of *Das Kapital*, Marx remarks on some of the frustrations and disappointments that scholars face:

> You are surely convinced, my dear child, that I love books a great deal because I must annoy you with how much time I spend with them. But you would be wrong. I am a machine, condemned to devour them and then throw them, in an altered form, on the dung hill of history. (Quoted in Marx and Engels 1999:2)

Here is a very personal glimpse into the demanding and, at times, disheartening life of a committed scholar; it is also a sentiment that many students feel during their studies—"There is just too much to read!" is a frustration and fear that every student, instructor, and scholar feels at one time or another.

The reality is that becoming a sociologist takes time, concentration, and a good deal of critical reading and sifting. No one expects a first year student to devour books at the same rate as Marx or Weber, but reading widely—reading with discipline every day—is the first step toward gaining a fully rewarding university education. The old adage that completing even the longest journey requires putting one foot in front of the other over and over again is true for scholars as much as it is for explorers—consistent effort over time brings the greatest rewards for both.

SOCIOLOGY AS A PASSION

The text's third objective is to convey the passion that sociologists feel for their discipline. It is not easy to project passion in an introductory text—particularly because students learn better when they are calmly focused on the ideas and concepts before them rather than emotionally stimulated, agitated, and even provoked by that material. Most often, instructors are more successful in transmitting their passion for sociology through their lectures, but there are ways in which this text tries to stimulate a passion for sociology.

Mills, Marx, Durkheim, and Weber—all featured in this text—wanted to do more than simply understand the world in a systematic manner; they also wanted to change it. Sociology is not an "academic" discipline in the negative, "ivory tower" sense of the word. From its emergence as a discipline, sociology has been used by conservatives, reformers, and revolutionaries to support particular social and political goals. Sociology is a discipline of and for change.

Sociological passion is also represented in the texture of some of the material and arguments included in this book. Some might think it unnecessary to quote so extensively from different sociologists' works or to include so many terms in the original French or German, but engaging directly with original sources places students in contact with thinkers' texts and ideas as they are developed. The direct engagement and dialogue between students and texts is the epitome of higher learning. At the same time, as each new generation of students wrestles with the meaning of classical texts, these writings are given new life and renewed significance. As a 17-year-old student at the University of Bonn, Marx understood Hegel's *Philosophy of Right* very differently than some of his professors or other established university authorities. Marx's fresh reading of Hegel, along with all-night debates with members of the Trier Tavern Club, changed the way Marx and some of his fellow students thought about the world around them. This radical critique of classical texts should not remain confined to the nineteenth century— students today should engage passionately with classical texts from the perspective of the present as they seek to improve the world in which they live.

CITIZENS OF THE WORLD

This text's final objective is to further the same goal that animated Mills's sociology. In *The Sociological Imagination*, Mills (1959) points out that ordinary men and women "often feel that their private lives are a series of traps" (p. 3). They feel constrained by "the private orbits in which they live; their visions and their powers are limited to the close-up scenes of job, family, neighborhood" (Mills 1959:3). In other aspects of their lives, ordinary men and women feel they are merely spectators. "What they need, and what they feel they need," Mills (1959) argues, "is a quality of mind that will help them to use information and to develop reason in order to achieve lucid summaries of what is going on in the world and what may be happening within themselves" (p. 5). What they require, Mills continues, is the sociological imagination to "understand the larger historical scene" and how it directly affects them and the lives of people around them.

Not every student who takes an introductory course in sociology or reads an introductory text will become a sociologist. But they all become citizens of the world. So they all need to be able to observe, analyse, and judge social actions and social relations. Mills (1960) discusses these and other benefits of sociology at the end of his introduction to *Images of Man: The Classic Tradition in Sociological Thinking*:

> Reading sociology should increase our awareness of the imperial reach of social worlds into the intimacies of our very self. Such awareness, of course, is the cultural goal of all learning as well as of much art. For all humanistic disciplines, if properly cultivated, help us to transcend the moral sloth and the intellectual rigidities that constitute most of everyday life in every society of which we know.

Sociological reflection is only one way of carrying on this cultural struggle, but surely today it is among the most direct of ways. Through such reflection, we become aware of our own "common sense" as being itself a social phenomenon to be examined and understood. One cuts beneath it, locating it within a particular nation or class or race at a particular period of history.... Classic sociology contains an enormous variety of conception, value, and method, and its relevance to the life-ways of the individual and to the ways of history-making in our epoch is obvious and immediate. This is why it is central to contemporary cultural work, and among the most valuable legacies of Western civilization. (P. 17)

The Promise of Sociology will help students who read it carefully, critically, and reflectively begin to cultivate sociology's unique awareness and insights, so they can better understand and shape the contemporary world. It is an extremely ambitious objective, but it is also a small, reasonable, and realistic one. Why? Mills (1960) notes that the sociological frame of reference can begin with "the acquisition of a vocabulary that is adequate for clear social reflection":

Such a vocabulary need not be very extensive. In fact, I should say that only some twenty or so pivotal terms are essential. (P. 17)

This text suggests some words that a student might include in a vocabulary "adequate for clear social reflection." Determining their adequacy and considering others is something that students and their instructors may choose to explore together further.

An Overview of the Text

In preparing this new edition, I have made the connections among the chapters more explicit than before. The main conceptual themes running through this text are the same as those identified and emphasized by every leading sociologist today (see, for example, Alexander 1982; Bourdieu [1980] 1990; Castells 2010; Giddens 1984; Habermas [1981] 1984, [1985] 1987; Latour 2005; Luhmann [1984] 1995; Münch 1987). Those major ideas centre on human agency, social structure, meaning, history, culture, power, and change (although the complexity of each concept is masked by the apparent simplicity of the noun denoting it). These concepts first emerged in the work of the sociologists comprising the classical tradition although the terms were not always identified in the same way that they are now. Thus, one of the themes running through this text is an examination of not only how classical sociologists identified and established the basic domain of sociology—"[recursive] social practices ordered across space and time" (Giddens 1984:2)—but also how the classical tradition remains important for contemporary sociological thinking.

To begin introducing sociology, the sociological perspective, and the classical tradition, Part 1 focuses directly on the students who will be reading this book. Chapter 1 develops a collective portrait of today's students. It shows that they are heavily reliant upon digital information and the Internet and are deeply embedded in an e-culture that they continuously rely upon and interact with through ubiquitous smartphones, tablets, and computers. Upon entering university, however, today's students quickly experience the tensions and contradictions that exist between the information sources they have used throughout their lives and those that dominate the world of higher education.

To understand these experiences and the students sociologically, Chapter 2 introduces Mills's conception of the "sociological imagination"—a perspective that draws directly from sociology's classical roots and opens the way to a full appreciation of a sociological frame of reference. Employing the three sets of questions that guide Mills's approach, the chapter presents material from the work of a number of scholars who have systematically studied the nature and impact of the contemporary social world on the youth of today. The discussion draws heavily from Manuel Castells's *The Information Age: Economy, Society and Culture* (2010); Marshall McLuhan's *The Gutenberg Galaxy* (1962) and *Understanding Media* (1964); Nicholas Carr's *The Shallows* (2011); and Howard Gardner and Katie Davis's *The App Generation* (2014), as well as from other smaller studies. These sources help to provide a more comprehensive context and deeper sociological understanding of the challenges today's students face in higher education and how well prepared they are to face this crucial phase in their lives. The chapter also reflects on how colleges and universities have adapted to the demands of the information age and the needs of today's students as they prepare for the work world lying ahead.

Chapter 3 continues the study of the postsecondary experience by looking at the idea of the university and how it has been contested and changed over time, especially from the latter third of the twentieth century into the present. Despite the challenges that currently exist within higher education, it still stands as the greatest opportunity for students to expand their intellectual horizons and profit deeply from their studies. Much of that growth can begin by following the principles of "intellectual craftsmanship" that Mills discusses at length in several of his works. The chapter provides students with an opportunity to reflect critically upon all that a postsecondary education might hold out for them as they begin their university studies.

The six chapters that constitute Part II—"The Classical Tradition"— introduce students to the three dominant macrosociological perspectives of classical sociology as they were developed by Marx, Durkheim, and Weber. There are three fundamental reasons for the depth and breadth of focus given to these three thinkers.

First, the ideas of Marx, Durkheim and Weber were shaped by the events and social circumstances that fundamentally changed the lives of humanity around the globe—they lived through a period that Karl Polanyi (1944) has aptly called "the great transformation." Writing during the emergence and consolidation of industrial capitalism in the early period of modernity, Marx, Durkheim, and Weber directly witnessed the profound changes that were taking place in England and western Europe. And they could draw important contrasts between their social worlds and earlier social formations while memories and interpretations of recently past times were still vivid and avidly debated by scholars, politicians, and people in the street (Giddens 1971, 1976). In short, all three thinkers wrote during a period that was highly conducive to developing the sociological frame of reference, and each of them did so with tremendous depth and insight.

Second, Marx, Durkheim, and Weber are complex, synthetic thinkers. Although introductory texts traditionally provide brief overviews of their work, a student can better grasp and understand their perspectives when given the opportunity to explore their ideas at some length. Although the precise details may fade from memory over time, the overall framework will remain vivid and alive when a student has the opportunity to work through some of the complexity of their perspectives rather than trying to memorize simplified summaries of Marx, Durkheim, or Weber "in a box."

Finally, the work of each of these early sociological thinkers was central to the development of sociology in the period after World War II. Their ideas shaped the discipline when it was becoming increasingly influential in people's lives and firmly established within higher education. At the same time, even as postmodernist perspectives have grown in influence, Marx, Durkheim, and Weber remain key reference points (and foils) for those engaged in sociological thought today.

The writings of Marx, discussed in Chapters 4 and 5, and of Durkheim, presented in Chapters 6 and 7, have features in common. But each scholar's work constitutes a unique perspective within the classical tradition. (Some argue that their positions are diametrically opposed, although the analysis presented here differs from that interpretation.) While Durkheim identifies institutionalized collective representations as the main focal point for sociology, Marx emphasizes that the social relations of production within which people produce (and tend to reproduce) their lives should be the departure point for understanding social life. Durkheim tends to focus on the integrating aspects of societies while Marx seeks to highlight the often invisible but inescapably important tensions and contradictions in different social formations. Both Marx and Durkheim address the ongoing presence of social change, and both think their work can contribute to the improve-ment of people's lives.

Weber's work also engages in very important ways with that of Marx and Durkheim. As Chapter 8 indicates, Weber's emphasis upon sociology as the comprehensive study of social action contrasts with Durkheim's work, which was heavily influenced by the positivist tradition within French social thought, in general, and the legacy of Saint-Simon and Comte, in particular. At the same time, however, Durkheim's approach to sociology was influenced by German sociological thought, and there are important aspects of his work that complement or reinforce some of Weber's fundamental conceptions and perceptions of social life.

With respect to Marx, Weber is frequently credited with overturning much of Marx's critique of capitalist society. However, Weber is best under-stood as engaging in a debate with Marx's legacy (including various distortions of Marx's positions by his successors) and as complementing critical aspects of Marx's contributions to sociology. Writing during the first two decades of the twentieth century and dealing, in particular, with the realities of German social and political life in the period between World War I and World War II, Weber faced many social and political challenges. As the material in Chapter 9 demonstrates, the issues Weber addressed helped make his contributions to sociology among the most significant and enduring, even though a school of Weberian sociology never developed during or after his lifetime. More than Marx or Durkheim, who both focus far more on the "structural" aspects of social life, Weber fleshes out the subjective aspects of human agency and how social meaning affects social practices across space and time.

Part III—"Sociology and Contemporary Popular Culture"—draws upon the ideas developed in the first two parts of the book and, in many ways, brings the book full circle. Part I addresses the everyday life-world of today's students; it involves an intensive study of e-culture and its impact upon those who consume it. Chapter 10 returns to the study of culture. This time the text overviews the changing meaning of the word "culture" and its significance to social life as a whole. The discussion then turns to a variety of concerns that different cultural critics, public intellectuals, and sociologists expressed about the apparent demise of culture in the age of mass production and mass consumption that followed the end of World War II. By synthesizing these critiques of mass or popular culture and fears about its stultifying impact upon those who consume it on an ongoing basis, one can construct what Weber termed a "pure type" or "ideal type" construct of culture. The pure type construct of culture developed at the end of Chapter 10 serves as the basis for a Weberian analysis of popular culture through the two short case studies found in Chapters 11 and 12.

The first case study centres on Bob Dylan's early folk phase. It includes a short history of folk music, an outline of the different influences that shaped

Dylan's sound and lyrics, and a discussion of the nature and composition of his first four albums. The chapter ends with an assessment of Dylan's early work in comparison to the pure or ideal construct of culture developed in Chapter 10. A short history of rock and roll is the focus of the case study completed in Chapter 12.

The discussion of popular culture through those two case studies illustrates how sociology can move beyond one's ordinary stocks of everyday knowledge to a much deeper appreciation of how social life is shaped and conditions the present and future. At the same time, these two case studies, like the opening discussion about the impact that a deep immersion in e-culture has upon the current and future prospects of today's students, demonstrate why a comprehensive, critical understanding of what might appear to be trivial aspects of everyday life is so essential to understanding and improving people's lives in the twenty-first century.

Chapter 13 brings the material covered in the text to a conclusion. It draws the key ideas together while also pointing to how students might develop their sociological imagination further and to the issues upon which they might concentrate.

PART ONE

Why Think Sociologically?

1

VISIONS AND PROFILES OF STUDENTS TODAY

Main Objectives

This chapter will

1. Introduce students to the idea of generational cohorts, and develop profiles of "Generation X," "the Millennials," and their own cohort, "Generation Z."
2. Consider, in some detail, the relationship of the Millennials and Generation Z to "print culture" and "e-culture"—and the impact this relationship may have on their university experience.
3. Introduce students to Michael Wesch's use of YouTube to develop a deeper understanding of the strengths and limitations of digital media and the Internet for teaching and learning in higher education.

When an instructor in a first year course enters the lecture hall, she or he usually looks out on a large lecture theatre, about two-thirds full, with students still flowing in looking for places to sit—choosing, as much as possible, to avoid the first couple of rows. At one level, year after year, the students look the same: they are young, filled with energy, enthusiasm, and vitality. They are either engaged in animated conversation or searching for a familiar face in the great expanse of the lecture hall. At the same time, no matter how much they try to mask it, as the beginning of their first lecture approaches, the students are nervous and begin to feel a growing sense of trepidation as the room fills, the conversational volume rises, and the instructor makes her or his final preparations before beginning the lecture.

Despite superficial similarities, today's students are not at all like the undergraduates with whom the instructor—even a young one—attended university. Their high-school experience was different, the work world that they anticipate entering holds considerable uncertainty, and, most important, the everyday life-world within which today's students are growing and maturing differs fundamentally from their instructor's.

From 1998 onwards, Beloit College in Beloit, Wisconsin has produced—and trademarked—"The Beloit College Mindset List." The list can serve as a useful one-way mirror for an instructor to look through and unobtrusively "observe" the incoming students she or he will teach each fall. Drawing upon the Beloit lists, scholarly research, and some popular commentaries on the current generation of students entering colleges and universities in the recent past, this chapter opens with a rough outline of first year students as a whole.[1] An introduction of the main features of Mills's "sociological imagination" follows. That discussion begins to establish a sociological framework through which a more detailed and analytical discussion of today's students takes place, one contrasting first year students' and university instructors' perceptions and expectations of the nature and types of knowledge and skills that are central to a successful postsecondary education.

Generations X, Y, and Z

The **Beloit College Mindset List** is an interesting idea—even an inspired one. The list provides an insightful sketch of the collective biography of the students entering postsecondary institutions each year. Although the list's generalizations do not apply to all students entering colleges and universities in the United States and Canada, they do capture the important "cultural touchstones that shape the lives of students entering college [each fall]" (Beloit College 2015a). The list for the class of 2019 notes that its members

> will enter college with high technology an increasing factor in how and even what they learn.... They will encounter difficult discussions about privilege, race, and sexual assault on campus. They may think of the "last century" as the twentieth, not the nineteenth, so they will need ever wider perspectives about the burgeoning mass of information that will be heading their way. And they will need a keen ability to decipher what is the same and what has changed with respect to many of these issues. (Beloit College 2015g)

---

1 There are two important points to note. First, this sketch is a broad typification of students entering higher education; not every student reflects all of the characteristics noted. However, there are identifiable traits of this generation of students that constitute an overall profile of the cohort. Second, the discussion is not designed to blame or praise students, teachers, parents, or others for the profile that is presented—the objective is simply to establish a general profile, to examine critically why it includes particular traits and not others, and to suggest some of the implications this has for first year university students and their instructors.

The general snapshot of the class of 2018 is less insightful. The class of 2018 arrives on campus "with a grasp of their surroundings quite distinct from that of their mentors. Born in 1996, they have always had The Daily Show to set them straight, always been able to secure immediate approval and endorsement for their ideas through 'likes' on their Facebook page, and have rarely heard the term 'bi-partisan agreement'" (Beloit 2015f). The basic essentials about the class of 2017 are, however, worth considering.

> [T]hese digital natives will already be well-connected to each other. They are more likely to have borrowed money for college than their Boomer parents were, and while their parents foresee four years of school, the students are pretty sure it will be longer than that. Members of this year's first year class, most of them born in 1995, will search for the academic majors reported to lead to good-paying jobs, and most of them will take a few courses taught at a distant university by a professor they will never meet.
>
> The use of smart phones in class may indicate they are reading the assignment they should have read last night, or they may be recording every minute of their college experience … or they may be texting the person next to them. (Beloit 2015e)

The characteristics of some of the other recent classes merit attention partly because they already seem so dated but also for the insight they provide into the life experiences that have also shaped today's incoming students. Here is a quick profile of the class entering university when the first edition of *The Promise of Sociology* was published:

> This year's entering college class of 2015 was born just as the Internet took everyone onto the information highway and as Amazon began its relentless flow of books and everything else into their lives. Members of this year's freshman class, most of them born in 1993, are the first generation to grow up taking the word "online" for granted and for whom crossing the digital divide has redefined research, original sources and access to information, changing the central experiences and methods in their lives. They have come of age as women assumed command of U.S. Navy ships, altar girls served routinely at Catholic Mass, and when everything from parents analyzing childhood maladies to their breaking up with boyfriends and girlfriends, sometimes quite publicly, have been accomplished on the Internet. (Beloit 2015d)

A year earlier, the Beloit College Mindset List points out that the class of 2014 "will be armed with iPhones and BlackBerries, on which making a phone call will be only one of many, many functions they will perform" (Beloit 2015c).

More important, these students "will now be awash with a computerized technology that will not distinguish information and knowledge. So it will be up to their professors to help them. A generation accustomed to instant access will need to acquire the patience of scholarship. They will discover how to research information in books and journals and not just on-line."

The class of 2013, heading off to university in 2009 still experienced "the economic anxiety that marked their first two years of life just as it has marked their last two years of high school." It is the first class Beloit identifies with texting. With their parents worrying about retirement and health, students of the class of 2013 "can turn to technology and text a friend: 'Momdad still worried bout stocks. urs 2? PAW PCM [parents are watching; please call me]'" (Beloit 2015b). It is also in 2009 that Beloit (2015b) notes the widespread adoption and integration of different digital technologies: "Members of the class of 2013 won't be surprised when they can charge a latté on their cell phone and curl up in the corner to read a textbook on an electronic screen. The migration of once independent media—radio, TV, videos and CDs—to the computer has never amazed them."

Taken together, the Beloit lists of the past eight years provide important insights into today's students. First, much has changed since students began reading *The Promise of Sociology* in 2011. It is the students of the class of 2015, those entering postsecondary education in 2011, that the list (2015d) first identifies as having been "born just as the Internet took everyone on the information highway." In many cases, four years is a short period of time, but it is an eternity when associated with the Internet and digital technology. The most recent sketch of students, which relates to those entering university in 2015, captures that sense of quantum change by noting how much "high technology" and "the burgeoning mass of information that will head their way" will affect "how and even what [students] learn" (Beloit College 2015g). Similarly, today's "digital natives" are "already well-connected to each other" and using smartphones for such a vast array of activities that the comment on how the class of 2014, "armed with iPhones and BlackBerries," will use them for more than just making a call seems an unnecessary observation in today's context (compare Beloit College 2015e and 2015c). The observation that the students of 2013 "won't be surprised" at being able to use a smartphone to "charge a latté," stream videos and music, or keep in continuous touch with friends close by or around the globe also seems very outdated today (Beloit College 2015b). The stresses today's students feel, the economic uncertainty they experience, and the necessity of their facing "difficult discussions about privilege, race, and sexual assault on campus" have not altered as much as the technological environment; these socio-economic factors remain as salient to the postsecondary experience of the most recent incoming class as they were for the class of 2015. The commitment to succeed on their own, the drive to find good-paying jobs, and the realization that postsecondary education may extend beyond the four years of an honours degree might distinguish the class of 2019 from some of the first readers of *The Promise of Sociology*, but economic uncertainty, family stress, and the merits of postsecondary education are also highlighted for the class of 2013.

One critical theme, noted for the class of 2014, holds for students beginning their postsecondary education today—and for all the cohorts in between. It concerns the information students customarily access and use versus the types of information that they will require to succeed in the more demanding environment of higher education. Students accustomed to instant access to information, much of which is contradictory, presented without evidence, and unfiltered by experts or even by a concern for objectivity, will need to acquire "the patience of scholarship." They will need to discover not only the media of traditional research—how to find information in books, scholarly journals, and primary sources—but also its methods. How do scholars in a particular field assess and compare information, design and test hypotheses, or present and support a claim? Thus, the role professors will have to play to help students distinguish between "information and knowledge" is as relevant now as it was in 2010, when the class of 2014 entered university (Beloit College 2015c). Today's students "will need ever wider perspectives" to critically assess and use "the burgeoning mass of information that will be heading their way," and those perspectives will take time and work to develop (Beloit College 2015g).

STUDYING GENERATIONS OF STUDENTS

In the short time that *The Promise of Sociology* has been in print, students' goals and their attitudes toward and approaches to higher education have changed—according to popular perceptions at least (see Levit 2015). Most of the students who will read this edition of *The Promise* were born after 1998. They are members of what many are identifying as "Generation Z," distinguishing them from "Generation Y" or the Millennials, who were the main readers of the first edition. As the Beloit lists demonstrate, four characteristics of today's students stand out: the predominant role the Internet and computers have played throughout their lives; the extensive use of smartphones in almost every aspect of daily activities; *instant, fingertip* access to information "24/7"; and an addiction-like need for online information and interaction through several social media platforms. Other scholarship confirms the Beloit characterization of Generation Z, but before this chapter introduces that material, it considers how these typifications of generations have evolved.

The scholarly identification and study of generations is an involved undertaking, but the idea of different generations and how they relate to each other is well established in popular culture.[2] In the post–World War II period, one often hears of three generational cohorts—the "Baby Boom Generation," identified by the explosion in the birth rate following the war; the "Baby Bust Generation," associated with the dip in the birth rate beginning in the early 1960s; and the "Echo Boom Generation," born during the rising birth rate in the early to mid-1980s (see Foot 1996; Masnick 2012).

Reflecting what many regard as a rapidly changing world, contemporary popular culture breaks those large classifications into smaller cohorts to capture dramatic differences that seem to occur with greater rapidity in the latter decades of the twentieth century. The Boomers (1945 to the early 1960s) remain a huge cohort, the size of which influences almost every aspect of its members' lives and those of adjacent cohorts. The next generation—frequently identified as "Generation X" (early 1960s to 1981)—is socially and culturally quite distinct from the Boomers. It is followed by "Generation Y" (better known as the "Millennials," 1982 to 1995) and then by Generation Z (1996 to the present), the newest generational cohort, which possesses many characteristics in common with Generation Y but has unique traits of its own.

GENERATION X

The **Generation X** label may originate with Madison Avenue advertisers trying to identify and target a new generation of consumers, but it is Canadian Douglas Coupland's 1991 novel *Generation X: Tales for an Accelerated Culture* that establishes the generation's popularized persona. Coupland (1991) presents "Gen X" as conflicted. Its middle-class members are born into material comfort and have parents holding high expectations for them, but their jobs, career paths, and futures are also blocked by those same Boomers who "won in a genetic lottery ... sheerly by dent of [their] having been born at the right time in history" (p. 20). Although their parents want them to live "the American Dream" of hard-won success, individuality, and material comfort, "Gen Xers"—just as many of their parents had in the 1960s—view that dream as the worship of materialism, greed, and self-promotion. By the early 1990s, Neil Howe and William Strauss (1992) note, Gen Xers are pursuing lives "of physical frenzy and spiritual numbness, a revelry of pop, a pursuit of high-tech, guiltless fun." The reasons for their malaise, Howe and Strauss argue, lie in the generation's collective biography.

> Trace the life cycle to date of Americans [and Canadians] born in 1961. They were among the first babies people took pills not to have. During the 1967 Summer of Love they were the kindergartners who paid the price for

---

2   See Burnett (2010) for a detailed discussion of how generations are constructed and what those constructions imply. See also Howe and Strauss (1991).

America's new divorce epidemic. In 1970 they were fourth-graders trying to learn arithmetic amid the chaos of open classrooms and New Math curricula. In 1973 they were the bell-bottomed sixth-graders who got their first real-life civics lesson watching the Watergate hearings on TV. Through the late 1970s they were the teenage mall-hoppers who spawned the Valley Girls and other flagrantly non-Boomer youth trends. In 1979 they were the graduating seniors of Carter-era malaise who registered record-low SAT scores and record-high crime and drug-abuse rates. (Pt II, para. 6)

Trapped in the wake of the Boomers, Gen Xers can only find a "McJob"—a term Coupland (1992) coins to signify a "low-pay, low-prestige, low-dignity, low-benefit, no-future job in the service sector. Frequently considered a satisfying career choice by people who have never held one" (p. 5). If they are lucky, they might find work outside the service industry in "veal-fattening pens"—"[s]mall cramped office workstations built of fabric-covered disassemblable wall partitions and inhabited by junior staff members. Named after the small preslaughter cubicles used by the cattle industry" (p. 20).

Although it describes why the novel's main characters—Dag, Andy, and Claire—decide to move to Palm Springs, the following passage symbolically captures the fate of Gen X in the early 1990s:

> We live small lives on the periphery; we are marginalized and there's a great deal in which we choose not to participate. We wanted silence and we have that silence now. We arrived here speckled in sores and zits, our colons so tied in knots that we never thought we'd have a bowel movement again. Our systems had stopped working, jammed with the odor of copy machines, Wite-Out, the smell of bond paper, and the endless stress of pointless jobs done grudgingly to little applause. We had compulsions that made us confuse shopping with creativity, to take downers and assume that merely renting a video on a Saturday night was enough. But now that we live in the desert, things are much, *much* better. (P. 11; see also Howe and Strauss 1992)

Tracking Gen X further into the life cycle shows some important changes. Now in their 30s and 40s, Gen Xers are, in fact, a well-educated cohort (43 per cent have baccalaureate degrees) with a high employment rate (85 per cent hold jobs), working long hours (70 per cent work and commute 40 or more hours per week) in largely satisfying occupations (see Miller 2011). Gen Xers are more involved with their children than the Boomers were and, ironically, have expectations for their children similar to those they rejected when their Boomer parents held them for the Xers themselves.

Critical to what follows, the members of Gen X are the first to have their childhood influenced by the Internet, as most middle-class Gen Xers had computers in their households as they grew up. Gen X lies at the transition between what Neil Postman (1985) identifies as "The Age of Television" and what Manuel Castells (2000) labels "The Network Society."

GENERATION Y OR THE MILLENNIALS

Born between 1982 and 1995, **Generation Y** is sometimes referred to as the "Echo Boomers," the "Boomlet," the "Nexters," the "Nintendo Generation," the "Digital Generation," or the "Net Generation," although its members prefer to be called the **Millennials** because they all reached 18 in the new millennium (Howe and Strauss 2000:12). In North America, the Millennials are a larger cohort than the Baby Boomers. Like Gen X, the Millennials are characterized by contradictions.

In *Millennials Rising*, Howe and Strauss (2000) paint this generation in stark contrast to Gen Xers. The Millennials are a "found" generation "born in an era when Americans [and Canadians] began expressing more positive attitudes about children" (p. 7); they are the "Echo Boom" representing a birth-rate reversal from the 1970s. The Millennials are optimists; they are cooperative team players who trust and respect authority. Coming from small, close families, the Millennials view their parents positively and tend to share their values and worldview. Howe and Strauss (2000) emphasize that the Millennials are "*the most watched over generation in memory*" (p. 9). Parental planning, involvement, supervision, and advocacy began before conception; extended through childcare arrangements, school selection, and enrichment opportunities; and included specifically chosen extracurricular activities, test coaches, and a heavy emphasis on all aspects of personal safety.

Although "helicopter parents" did serve as vital, positive influences, their hovering has had its costs.[3] Despite their high self-esteem, the Millennials rely heavily on adults for direction, reassurance, and confirmation. They have difficulty budgeting their time on their own, and they have a sense of entitlement that makes it difficult for them to be self-reflective and self-critical. In their study, *Ivory Tower Blues: A University System in Crisis*, James Côté and Anton Allahar (2007:108–14) identify the Millennials' lack of engagement as one of the most significant problems facing instructors, university administrators, parents, and students themselves. Data from *The American Freshman*, an annual publication of the Cooperative Institutional Research Program, show that in 2011 only 39.5 per cent of students entering four-year colleges and universities spent six or more hours per week studying or doing homework (Pryor, DeAngelo et al. 2011:8). In contrast, in 1987, 47 per cent

---

3 The term "helicopter parents" is commonly used to describe those who, like helicopters, "hover closely overhead, rarely out of reach whether their children need them or not" (cited in Côté and Allahar 2007:138; see pp. 138–46 for a sympathetic account of helicopter parents).

of students spend six or more hours studying and doing homework (Pryor, Hurtado et al. 2007:14). The figure is at its lowest in 2005, with only 31.9 per cent studying and doing homework six or more hours per week—so the trend has actually reversed in recent years.

Despite Millennials spending less than an hour a day on homework in high school, their grades remained high; almost half (49.7 per cent) of first year students in 2011 earned "A"-range averages in high school (Pryor, DeAngelo et al. 2011:19). To gain some perspective on grade inflation, we just have to note that, in 1966, only 19.4 per cent of first year students had high school averages in the "A" range. By 1985, it was 28.7 per cent and in 2006, 45 per cent (Pryor, Hurtado et al. 2007:54–55).

In *Ready or Not, Here Life Comes*, based on his clinical work at the University of North Carolina's Center for the Study of Development and Learning, Melvin Levine (2005) argues that students entering university "are not equipped with a durable work temperament, having been submerged in a culture that stresses instant rewards instead of patient, tenacious, sustained mental effort and the ability to delay gratification for the sake of eventual self-fulfillment" (p. 7). In other words, the Millennials "have grown up in an era that infiltrates them with unfettered pleasure, heavy layers of over-protection, and heaps of questionably justified feedback" (quoted in Côté and Allahar 2007:99).

The result is that the Millennials have difficulty charting their own paths in life, determining their own real ambitions and genuine strengths, and appraising realistically their personal worth, ability, and values. The university then confounds students as professors pose questions about complex issues, questions requiring time and prolonged effort if students are to propose even provisional answers. Often for the first time, students face situations where there is not one correct answer—but there are certainly wrong answers and even poorly researched and presented answers that are potentially correct. To make matters worse, professors assess the answer and not the time, struggle, and effort needed to arrive at a provisional end point. The best university instructors assign work that requires students to manage their time independently, prioritize the information they have collected, and integrate it into a cohesive, coherent whole—that is not a familiar experience for many students within the current high-school system (Côté and Allahar 2007:136–37). It is a challenge—for some so formidable that they simply disengage.

The Millennial generation is the first one to grow up completely surrounded by digital media. As the first "Digital Natives," to use Marc Prensky's (2001) term, the Millennials

> are used to receiving information really fast. They like to parallel process and multi-task. They prefer their graphics *before* their text rather than the opposite. They prefer random access (like hypertext). They function

best when networked. They thrive on instant gratification and frequent rewards. They prefer games to "serious" work. (P. 2)

Because of their direct and immediate access to so much information, the Millennials are politically aware but less sceptical and far less engaged than their parents at a similar age (Broadbent Institute 2015; Mitchell, Gottfried, and Matsa 2015:6). Part of the reason is the way information reaches them, as disconnected bits rather than systematic news located within a broader context—61 per cent of Millennials use Facebook as their primary news source (Mitchell, Gottfried, and Matsa 2015:2).

The Millennials, like the Gen Xers, have a weaker sense of history than the Boomers. The difference is partly because of changes in emphasis in secondary school curricula, as well as in the approach to educating this particular generation. Of at least equal importance is the way the Millennials consume information.

Although the Millennials were actively encouraged to read at a younger age than their parents and were read to far more than the Boomers, from a larger and richer body of engaging children's literature, because they are always pressed for time in fully scheduled lives, have information bombarding them continuously, and feel pressured to be connected to their peers (sometimes around the globe), reading becomes just one of numerous activities to be touched on each day. As the Millennials reached their teens, multi-tasking became a survival strategy. With so much "requiring" attention, difficulty in establishing priorities, and no time to reflect and consider, the Millennials habitually try to do everything at top speed. As a result, they frequently do things superficially, and Nike's "just do it" has changed from a branding slogan to part of their inner being (see Carr 2011). Equally important, because Millennials are digital natives, the neural pathways in the brain used for reading were developed in a very different way than in any previous generation, leading to reading patterns that are quite distracted (Carr 2011; Rose 2013; Wolf 2011).

GENERATION Z

As early as 2010, Sherry Posnick-Goodwin (2010) described **Generation Z** to the California Teachers' Association:

They'd rather text than talk. They prefer to communicate online—often with friends they have never met. They don't spend much time outdoors unless adults organize activities for them. They can't imagine life without cell phones. They have never known a world without technology or terrorism or Columbine. They prefer computers to books and want instant results. They are growing up in an economic depression and are under tremendous pressure to succeed. Mostly they are growing up fast, and exhibiting behavior far beyond their years. (P. 8)

Today's students share a good deal with their Millennial peers, but popular culture already portrays Generation Z as "the opposite or extreme versions of Millennials" (Sparks & Honey 2014:2).[4] Much of the discussion about and description of "Gen Z" seems to stem from the motive of targeting this generation of consumers. One such description, *Gen Z: Digital in Their DNA*, was produced by the New York marketing and communication firm J. Walter Thompson Company—or JWT, as it has branded itself (see JWT 2012).[5] In June 2014, the New York advertising agency Sparks & Honey also created a rather comprehensive and well-documented slide presentation, "Meet Generation Z: Forget Everything You Learned about Millennials." However, academic researchers, too, have focused on this generation.

Even though most of the research and commentary is American based, Canadian media have also given Gen Z a high profile. A month after the Sparks & Honey description, Anne Kingston's (2014) "Get Ready for Generation Z" was the feature article in *Maclean's* magazine. The cover included this provocative claim, which was splashed across the photo of a young, entrepreneurial looking "Zer" in a dark suit, white shirt, and tie: "They're smarter than boomers and way more ambitious than millennials. Brace yourselves for the ultimate generation war."

In September, as part of its "We Day" coverage and publicity, *The Globe and Mail* featured "Generation Z: The Kids Who'll Save the World?" (White 2014).[6] In the main story, Shelly White (2014) notes that Gen Z is comprised of

kids growing up in an era of global economic turmoil and climate change. Despite their youth, the digitally sophisticated, socially conscious high achievers emerging from this group are causing some people to wonder: Is this the generation that will solve the world's problems? (P. E1)

---

4 The Sparks & Honey presentation consists of 54 different PowerPoint slides; the numbers in the following Sparks & Honey references are to the appropriate slide rather than to page numbers.

5 The JWT document is also now available for download only as a SlideShare presentation. Citations refer to slides rather than pages.

6 We Day began in Canada on October 17, 2007, at Toronto's Ricoh Coliseum and has since become an annual event in Canada, the United States, and the United Kingdom. Initiated by the children's charity Free the Children: "WE Day is an annual series of stadium-sized events that brings together world-renowned speakers and performers—from Malala Yousafzai and Martin Sheen to Demi Lovato—with tens of thousands of youth to kick-start a year of action through We Act. You can't buy a ticket to WE Day—you earn it by taking on one local and one global action" (Free the Children 2016). "More than a one-day event," another description downloadable from the website continues, "We Day is connected to the year-long We Act program, which offers educational resources and campaigns to help young people turn the day's inspiration into sustained action. We Day and We Act are cause inclusive, empowering young people to find their passion and create the change they want to see" (Free the Children 2014).

Clearly some people hold extremely high expectations for the newest entrants into postsecondary education!

The reactions to the JWT and Sparks & Honey presentations and later press coverage and analyses run the gamut from praising the presentations for their important insight to their complete rejection as mere branding exercises. Nevertheless, although branding, advertising, and commercial interests may motivate the rush to identify Generation Z and its characteristics, the material produced in the exercise does offer important insight into students entering universities and colleges today.

The members of Gen Z are the children of Gen Xers, the "baby bust" generation. They are growing up in small families and experience less "helicopter parenting," leading to more self-directed problem solving and personal confidence (Sparks & Honey 2014:20). Like the Millennials, they are close to their parents and carry considerable influence in family decisions: 74 per cent of their mothers say that, even in their early teens, "Gen Zers" make their own clothing choices, 69 per cent indicate Zers take part in family entertainment choices, 65 per cent indicate Zers are included in vacation decisions, more than half say their Gen Z children influence technology choices, and 32 per cent note that Zers even have a say in home furnishing purchases (Sparks & Honey 2014:4).

Gen Z participates in an education system that fosters differentiated instruction. Being educated in small classes that have always involved "mainstreaming" and classmates with increasingly diverse racial and cultural backgrounds helps Zers develop a strong sense of inclusiveness (Eagan et al. 2014:2–3; Sparks & Honey 2014:15). Most important, the members of Gen Z do not approach learning in the same manner as did earlier generations.

Gen Zers are more engaged with their academic work than the Millennials although they also benefit from the grade inflation trends of the last 30 years. In contrast to the 39.5 per cent of the Millennials in 2011 who spent six or more hours a week studying or doing homework, in 2014, 42.9 per cent of Gen Zers made that commitment (Pryor, DeAngelo et al. 2011:8; Eagan et al. 2014:38). And this work has yielded results: 49.7 per cent of Millennials entering college in 2011 reported "A"-range averages in high school while 58.7 per cent of Gen Zers entering college in 2015 reported achieving those grades (Pryor, DeAngelo et al. 2011:19; Eagan et al. 2015:31). The 2014 survey from *The American Freshman* also shows that today's students have considerable self-confidence and greater assurance in their academic ability, creativity, and drive to achieve than the Millennials had (Eagan et al. 2014:42). As a result, almost a third (32 per cent) of Gen Zers anticipate that they will complete a university degree program beyond the bachelor's degree (e.g., a master's, doctoral, law, or medical degree).

Fully immersed in a digital world from birth, Gen Z is more connected to the outside world than even the Millennials. They will know, for example, what paintings hang in the Louvre through a number of digital platforms even though they may never travel to Paris. Various "push" notifications from Twitter, Facebook, Instagram, Pinterest, Tinder, and other sites keep Zers instantly in touch with everything that they feel is relevant to their lives (Posnick-Goodwin 2010). Not surprisingly, more than half of Gen Z members use YouTube and other social media as the bases for researching their assignments, multi-tasking across as many as five screens while they work (Sparks & Honey 2014:27–28; see also Posnick-Goodwin 2010:11–12).

Don Tapscott (2008), the author of *Grown Up Digital: How the Net Generation Is Changing Your World*, views Gen Z's involvement with technology with great enthusiasm. Tapscott argues that there is not a generation gap between the Zers and their parents (to say nothing of the distance between Zers and the Boomers) but *a generation lap*: "kids are lapping their parents on a digital track" (cited in White 2014:E5). The information presented by Sparks & Honey and emanating from the Pew Research Center, an independent, Washington-based think tank that tracks social issues, public opinion, and demographic trends shaping the world, certainly confirms Gen Z's digital expertise as well as the widening gap between their information practices and those of the Boomers, Gen X, and even the Millennials (see Duggan et al. 2015; Lenhart 2015).

With 41 per cent of Zers on their computers for more than three hours a day in activities not related to school or work (compared to 22 per cent in 2004) and with their preference for streaming information via Twitch and Ustream or communicating through Skype or FaceTime, this generation is deeply immersed in digital media and the Internet (Gardner and Davis 2014; Sparks & Honey 2014:37, 41). The Pew Research Center reports that, in 2015, 92 per cent of teens report being online daily and 24 per cent are online "almost constantly" (Lenhart 2015:2). Such a high online presence is facilitated by the widespread possession and use of mobile devices; almost 73 per cent of Gen Zers have access to smartphones and another 15 per cent have a basic phone (only 12 per cent do without a mobile phone).

The Pew research shows that Facebook is still the most popular and frequently used social media platform (71 per cent of teens between 13 and 17 use it) with Instagram (52 per cent), Snapchat (41 per cent), Twitter (33 per cent), Google (33 per cent), Vine (24 per cent), and Tumblr (14 per cent) providing supporting platforms. Although Facebook remains the most popular platform and its use among Gen Z users increased slightly between 2013 and 2014, according to Pew, in the same period, Instagram grew dramatically (from 37 per cent to 53 per cent) with Twitter (31 per cent to 37 per cent) and Pinterest (27 per cent to 34) increasing moderately (Duggan et al. 2015:5–8). The Sparks & Honey (2014:35) presentation indicates a similar profile showing Facebook in decline, Twitter falling slightly, and Instagram growing.

Instead of asking "how many times a day do Zers use their smartphones" the better question is "when are Gen Zers *not* using their phones?" A typical Gen Zer wakes up to the phone's alarm, hits snooze a few times before finally relenting, and then begins a day of constant connection via the mobile smartphone. Ninety per cent of teens with smartphones exchange texts, and a typical teen sends and receives almost 100 texts per day through messaging apps such as Kik or WhatsApp (Lenhart 2015:4–5; Posnick-Goodwin 2010:13). Checking the time, surfing the Internet, listening to music, streaming YouTube, and having 5 to 10 phone conversations each day in diverse and public locations, a typical Gen Zer chats on or uses a smartphone while walking along the sidewalk or sitting quietly in a coffee shop or in the library or even in class (surreptitiously, of course). These usual daily activities give us some insight into the centrality of the smartphone to the Gen Zers' life-world. As JWT (2012) notes,

> This group is addicted to their mobile device. With phone saturation reaching 83% of American kids by the time they reach middle school [grades six to eight]—according to 2011 research from Bridgewater University—the mobile is an omnipresent and indispensable tool. As these kids grow up, it will become deeply integrated into their daily lives: an Everything Hub that enables socializing, shopping and surfing the Web, with geolocation services supplying information on nearby friends, relevant deals and amenities. (Slide 23)

The extensive use of text messages has an important impact on how Zers learn to express themselves. Members of Gen Z prefer to use symbols, emoticons, and pictures to carry on rapid-fire, multi-directional communication, sacrificing precision and clarity for speed. Being connected and in the loop is crucial (Sparks & Honey 2014:33–34). Because of young people's extensive use of smartphones for communication, almost 70 per cent of teachers feel their students put little effort into developing writing skills (Sparks & Honey 2014:33–34). "When I'm writing an essay," a high school student notes, "I put in abbreviated words that I use in text messages. It's a habit from using computers a lot" (cited in Posnick-Goodwin 2010:14).

Sparks & Honey (2014) note that "Gen Z are the ultimate consumers of snack media. They communicate in bite sizes. Research studies suggest that their brains have evolved to process more information at faster speeds, and are cognitively more nimble to handle bigger mental challenges. But, getting and keeping their attention is challenging" (p. 29). This means that Gen Zers' attention spans are short (now 8 seconds, down from 12 in 2000), and 11 per cent are diagnosed with ADHD (up from 7.8 per cent in 2003). Many Gen Zers exhibit what John Raley, a clinical professor at Harvard Medical School, terms "acquired attention deficit disorder" (cited in Posnick-Goodwin 2010:11).

But Generation Z is also growing up in a post–9/11 world, constantly reminded of terrorism and wars around the globe, with more than 75 per cent worrying about world hunger and humankind's negative impact on the planet. In addition, living in the long shadow of the 2008 recession, the 2015 downturn in the Chinese economy, the impact of sustained drought in the major areas of fruit and vegetable production, the impact of falling oil prices on the Canadian economy as a whole, and the collapse of many American oil producers rippling across the entire economy, Zers worry about jobs and the economy. They also see from their parents' and older siblings' struggles that traditional choices do not guarantee success (Sparks & Honey 2014:23, 14; see also JWT 2012:20, 29). Almost 80 per cent worry about what jobs they can hold when they graduate, 74 per cent have concerns about their academic performance, and 62 per cent worry about the college or university that will accept them when they graduate from high school. Between 45 and 60 per cent of Gen Zers are anxious about how attractive they are, their popularity, success outside school, real-world and online bullying, and how many friends they have (JWT 2012:18).

> Gen Z were developing their personalities and life skills in a socio-economic environment marked by chaos, uncertainty, volatility and complexity. Blockbusters like The Hunger Games and Divergent depict teens being slaughtered. No wonder Gen Z developed coping mechanisms and a certain resourcefulness. (Sparks & Honey 2014:13)

Sanjay Khanna, the inaugural Resident Futurist at Massey College—one of Canada's leading interdisciplinary institutions housed at the University of Toronto—says members of this generation are "GenStressed" because their awareness of world issues exceeds their ability to see viable solutions. "Global economic uncertainty combined with climate change will make it tough for them to believe their quality of life will improve enough via their digital skills alone" (cited in White 2014:E5).

Despite their potential stress levels, Zers believe in themselves and in what individuals can accomplish. The 2008 election of Barack Obama as president of the United States—with his message of "Yes we can!"—and the 2015 election of Justin Trudeau—who promised "*real* change"—underscore their belief that individuals make their own history, irrespective of the conditions they inherit. As a result, the members of Gen Z are driven; more than 80 per cent believe they work harder than their peers (Sparks & Honey 2014:7). Their circumstances seem to foster a strongly independent, entrepreneurial spirit (42 per cent of high school students plan to start their own business). And Zers exude confidence: almost 40 per cent agree with the statement "I will invent something that changes the world" (Sparks & Honey 2014:24, 25; see also Kingston 2014; White 2014).

Sparks & Honey (2014) offer a list of 20 items to assist corporations wanting to "connect with Generation Z." The list provides a quick, at-a-glance portrait of Gen Z:

1. Depict them as diverse (ethnically, sexually, fashionably)
2. Talk in images: emojis, symbols, pictures, videos
3. Communicate more frequently in shorter bursts of "snackable content"
4. Don't talk down … talk to them as adults, even about global topics
5. Assume they have opinions and are vocal, influencing family decisions
6. Make stuff—or help Gen Z make stuff (they're industrious)
7. Tap into their entrepreneurial spirit
8. Be humble
9. Give them control and preference settings
10. Collaborate with them—and help them collaborate with others
11. Tell your story across multiple screens
12. Live stream with them—or give them live streaming access
13. Optimize your search results (they do their Internet research)
14. Talk to them about value (they care about the cost of things)
15. Include a social cause that they can fight for
16. Have your house in order (in terms of sustainability)
17. Help them build expertise … they want to be experts
18. Tease (think: ephemeral, puzzles, surprises and games)
19. Feed their curiosity
20. Feed them (Slides 48–49)

YOUTUBE—VISIONS OF STUDENTS TODAY

YouTube is a mind-boggling repository of digital video that Millennials and Zers use extensively. How much information is there? In 2009, more than 20 hours of video were uploaded to YouTube every minute. By 2013, that was 100 hours per minute, and, by 2014, 300 hours (Robertson 2014). Greg Jarboe (2014) makes that number meaningful: 300 hours equals 18,000 minutes, so in each minute of that year, 18,000 minutes were uploaded. That's 18,000 hours per hour, or 18,000 days of video per day. It would take 49 years of non-stop, binge viewing to see just one single day's worth of uploads to YouTube! Clearly, YouTube is not just an ideal place to reach students; it also shapes popular perceptions of teens and youth, while simultaneously shaping their perceptions of the world around them.

Furthermore, YouTube is a powerful platform that encourages certain types of interaction between video producers and viewers around the globe (Wesch 2008a, 2009). Consider MadV.

On November 16, 2006, the illusionist MadV (2006a) posts to YouTube a simple 40-second video consisting of the background music "Með Blóðnasir" by Sigur Rós and a sequence of statements in white text against a black background. Following the first sequence—1) "This is an invitation," 2) "to make a stand," 3) "to make a statement," 4) "to make a difference"—MadV, wearing his characteristic Guy Fawkes mask, holds up to his webcam "ONE WORLD" written across his palm. A second sequence of white text on black follows—1) "Join in," 2) "Be part of something," 3) "Post your response now." The video ends with "4/12/06" written in black, cursive numbers on a white background, indicating the closing date for all contributions. At the time, "One World" is YouTube's most watched upload.

On December 22, 2006, MadV (2006b) posts "The Message," a video slightly over four minutes long, showing people writing on their palms and then holding them to their webcams; "Kids Will Be Skeletons" by Mogwai plays in the background. Wikitubia (2015) describes the video as "an emotional sequence of messages collected from YouTube users with the common theme of love and understanding for the whole human race."

MadV's simple, 40-second "invitation" did more than simply "go viral"—it was "YouTube's most responded [to] video of all time" (Wikitubia 2015). "One World" and "The Message" show the power of YouTube, in particular, and the Internet, in general, to bring together individuals from around the world so that they can engage with each other and share, discuss, and debate ideas, producing new forms of information and knowledge.

Despite the positive potentials, the interactive capacities of the Internet and YouTube and the technological innovations of the digital age pose significant challenges to contemporary education. **Michael Wesch**, the Coffman Chair for Distinguished Teaching Scholars at Kansas State University, is one educator who embraces these challenges and tries to use new communicative technologies to engage with his students.

In 2007, "in collaboration with 200 other students" in his immensely popular Introduction to Cultural Anthropology course, Wesch (2007a) created and posted to YouTube "A Vision of Students Today," which reflects on university students in 2007 and their relationship to postsecondary education. Since then, Wesch (2011a) has taken the "Visions" project further by posting the video "'a few ideas …' (Visions of Students Today)" on YouTube with a hyperlink to an HTML5 interactive video collage of the full project (see Wesch 2001d, 2011e, 2011f). The YouTube video, the associated collage, and Wesch's final "remix" create an elaborate vision of students today, one that parallels the profiles of the Millennials and Gen Zers presented above. The original video and the new project merit closer scrutiny.

The 2007 video begins with the door opening into a large lecture theatre; the camera enters, and a 1967 quotation from one of the first media studies scholars, Marshall McLuhan from the University of Toronto, appears overlaying a series of camera shots, taken from different locations, of the seats in the lecture hall.

The viewer has 16 seconds to read the 32 words—about the rate at which a grade four student reads (Tindal, Hasbrouck, and Jones 2005).

> Today's child is bewildered when he enters the 19th century environment that still characterizes the educational establishment where information is scarce but ordered and structured by fragmented classified patterns, subjects, and schedules. (Quoted in Wesch 2007a; see also McLuhan and Fiore 1967:18)

The video's main point is the apparent disjunction that exists between the way information is treated by the educational establishment and the expectations of twenty-first-century students. It is not clear if Wesch uses the quotation because McLuhan was so perceptive or if Wesch is trying to indicate that a problem in existence almost 50 years ago remains not only relevant today but is even more pressing because the media have changed—as have the messages—in the new cyber-world context. Wesch probably intends both. This video and its complement, "Information R/evolution," clearly establish the different information realities that exist in two cultures—the print-based and often regionally specific culture of the Boomers and the hyper-real, digitally based, cyber-world culture of the Millennials and now the Zers (Wesch 2007b).

The bulk of "A Vision of Students Today" is a self-assessment of the Millennials' main characteristics and their relationship to postsecondary education (see Wesch 2008a, 2009, 2010). From notes presented on various media—pieces of paper, notebook pages, text on laptop screens, multiple-choice exam answer cards—the viewer learns that classes are large and students tend to remain anonymous to their professors; students complete only half their course readings and feel that "only 26% are relevant to ... life."[7] Students buy expensive, never-opened texts and some pay hefty tuition for classes they seldom attend. A student in 2007 reads only 8 books a year but consumes 2,300 web pages and almost 1,300 Facebook profiles; in 2007, she or he produces 42 pages for class papers and assignments but generates over 500 pages of email.

Time matters—although it is also clear where students place their priorities. Spending 7 hours sleeping, 1.5 watching television, 3.5 online, 2.5 listening to music, 2 on a cell phone, 3 in class, 2 working in a part-time job, 3 studying, and 2 eating—for a total of 26.5 hours per day—one student writes "I am a multi-tasker" and then flips the notebook page to reveal the words "(I have to be)."

---

7 It is interesting to note that smartphones are completely absent from the 2007 video—a circumstance that certainly contrasts with the videos in the 2011 project.

The students recognize their privilege but also the uncertainty of a potentially problem-laden future. Holding up a multiple-choice response card with 19 wrong out of 50, a student writes, "filling this out won't help me get there" and then indicates, with arrows pointing to other signs, "or deal with" more than a dozen global problems, which different students identify by holding up signs that read "war" and "poverty" and "inequality," for example. "I did not create the problems," a different student emphasizes, "but they are *my* problems."

"Some have suggested that technology can save us," the text on the video continues. For emphasis, this statement is repeated in modified form: "Some have suggested that technology alone can save us." But the ensuing images challenge those claims. "I Facebook through most of my classes," and "I bring my laptop to class, but I'm not working on class stuff." The video ends with Wesch demonstrating the limitations of the erasable chalkboard as an educational tool in an implicit comparison with today's digital media.

The main video in "Visions of Students Today" is Wesch's "a few ideas …"— a remix of various videos that his students and others have contributed to the 2011 "Visions" project (see Wesch 2011a, 2011b, 2011c, 2011e).[8] Unlike the 2007 video in which there is no dialogue or vocal narration—an original, distinctive music track by Try^d plays throughout—and there is one video image with, from time to time, text superimposed over it, "Visions of Students Today" is a far more complex audiovisual construction.

The main 2011 remix video features a large square in the centre where several simultaneous video images play along with multiple audio tracks. The area around the audiovisual centre fills, throughout the remix, with numerous digital images that serve as hyperlinks to videos posted to VOST2011. A complex collage of audio, video, and digital images develops over the almost six-minute remix. Occasionally, the centre square contains a single video image, often overlaid with different modes of text, and one voice or music track, and then the multiple audio-video activity returns to the centre (see Wesch 2011d). The overall presentation captures contemporary students' multi-tasking, information-laden, digitally complex life-world.

Two selections from Blake Hallinan's contribution to the project, "Cracks and Fissures," capture the dominant theme that emerges from the remix. The first, about halfway through the video, features Hallinan speaking what she had written across her t-shirt while in high school—"Standardized testing equals standardized students." The second occurs in the final section of the video—an edited, audio section of Hallinan at a poetry slam extolling the diversity of individuals, learning styles, and approaches to education,

---

8 The project now features more than 150 different videos comprised of various drafts of Wesch's students' videos, their final submissions, and posts other students and instructors have made following Wesch's invitation to submit to VOST2011 on YouTube (see Wesch 2011f).

which Wesch mixes with video from several other student submissions.[9] The video ends with Hallinan's conclusion to this poetry slam, an ending that also inspires the title of the remix:

> Mr. Fulkerson [Hallinan's high school history teacher], when you asked me what I was going to do about the problems of standardization, I didn't know what to say [pause]. Now [pause] I've got a few ideas [pause]. Hope you like them. (Hallinan 2011a)

That main theme—how the existing, standardized, mass education system, trapped in a nineteenth-century mindset, creates standardized students—is pervasive in the videos making up the entire collage. Nate Bozarth (2011), Hallinan (2011a, 2011b), Lindsey Iman (2011a, 2011b, 2011c), Joseph Savage (2011a, 2011b, 2011d, 2011e), and others, in their early drafts and final submissions, thoroughly undermine the idea of student uniformity as they detail the complexity of today's students and their life-worlds (see also ddavies315 2011). Others, for example, Steven Kelly (2011a, 2011b, 2011c), Rebecca Norman (2011a, 2011b, 2011c, 2011d), Caitlin Reynolds (2011a, 2011b), and Derek Schneweis (2011) critically examine the structure and culture of contemporary higher education, emphasizing how it fails to meet students' needs in the digital age.

In structuring his remix, Wesch threads in his own educational philosophy and the overriding reason for his two projects. Instructors, Wesch emphasizes in his public lectures and in his two projects envisioning today's student, can and should use digital media and technology. And they should encourage digital natives to use the continually and rapidly developing technology of the digital world to create more collaborative, interactive, student-centred educational experiences. True to his philosophy, Wesch leads by example.

In the main remix, Wesch (2011d) quickly introduces the project and then splices in clips from students' videos highlighting how deeply embedded their lives are in digital media as well as their own sense that they are distracted and "academically adrift." This introduction quickly leads into the other main theme as Wesch, using other edited selections and inclusions, reorders short audio clips from Schneweis's (2011) video:

> The student is taught that discovering knowledge is beyond the power of the student and is, in any case, none of their business.... Recall is actually the highest form of intellectual achievement and the collection of

---

9 According to David Silverberg, artistic director of Toronto Poetry Slam (torontopoetryslam. ca), "slams are to poetry readings what lightning is to static cling" (Harris 2007). Poets perform their poetry without "props, costumes, or musical instruments," competing before judges randomly selected from the audience.

unrelated facts is the goal of education.... We are taught that one's own ideas and those of one's classmates are inconsequential.

Text inserted from Iman's (2011b) "Generation Me" video indicates, in rapid succession, that students are "confident," "independent," "free," "assertive," but also "more miserable [pause] than ever before."

As student voices and images continue to underscore the importance of self-exploration and how the education system denies that opportunity, Wesch integrates an edited audio clip from an early draft of Savage's final submission (see Savage 2011c) with video images contained in "Visions of Minecrafters Today" (see popopopopo159 2011). The video image is a "first-person" perspective. Walking through the game world of Minecrafters, one encounters signs noting, "It's sometimes difficult to make the best decision" and "I mean, it's hard to study chemistry" and then "When I could be here building this"—the video then pans across the artificial world of Minecrafters.[10] The audio from Savage emphasizes how students avoid a genuine engagement with their schoolwork by treating it with irony.

> We don't learn the material because that isn't what the simulationists ask us to do. The artificial environment steers us to meet artificial requirements and bureaucratic regulations so we "read" and "do homework." We couldn't get rid of the words, so we put them in scare quotes scaring away all the meaning with irony. Students mediated and inauthentic and numb and vulnerable put course requirements in scare quotes and laugh a hollow laugh of an impossible Pyrrhic victory, not as a joke but as a lifestyle.[11]

Following a short pause in the action, Hallinan (2011a) asserts, "Standardized testing equals standardized students," and Marceau tells us, "Traditional education needs to die; it needs to go away" (see also Marceau 2011).

Wesch follows the comments with an audio segment from Kelly's final submission, "The Old Future of Ed Reform," emphasizing that "these revolutionary ideas are not so new" (Kelly 2011c). Images of **Neil Postman** and

---

10 The main point of "Visions of Minecrafters Today" is the distracted lives that contemporary students live and the difficulties or challenges they face in focusing on their studies or even on one specific task at a time.

11 There are two parts of Savage's message about students' relationships with their instructors and the education system that Wesch omits in his editing but are relevant to Savage's main point. Following the comment about the artificial environment steering students, Savage (2011c) continues: "It isn't an option to read or do homework but we always *have options* that's how we understand the world around us, so we 'read' and 'do homework.'" At the end of the segment, he adds, "Technology doesn't change the classroom as much as it changes students." As his other drafts show, students use technology to avoid genuine engagement with course material, undermining the real potential of education.

Charles Weingartner's (1969) *Teaching as a Subversive Activity*, Paulo Freire's ([1968] 1970) *Pedagogy of the Oppressed*, and Ivan Illich's (1971) *Deschooling Society* appear in sequence. A clip of John Dewey, one of America's greatest educators, found in the very creative "RE:Birth of Education," submitted by Reynolds (2011a), confirms the point: "Going to college is not the same thing as getting an education, though the two are often confused."

Over a copy of *A New Culture of Learning: Cultivating the Imagination for a World of Constant Change*, a student asks, "Are you going to be a passive recipient of education or are you going to be an active, owner of your own education." The video image then zeroes in on text within the book: "The goal is for each of us to take the world in and make it part of ourselves. In doing so, it turns out we can re-create it" (see Thomas and Brown 2011:38).

"We need new media literacy": These words are typed across a Google search box, and the link to a PDF copy of the report by Henry Jenkins (2009), *Confronting the Challenges of Participatory Culture: Media Education for the 21st Century*, comes into focus. "Changes in the media environment are altering our understanding of literacy and requiring new habits of mind": This quotation appears next, as an audio excerpt from a 1967 interview of McLuhan on CBC television plays in the background. That excerpt is featured in the student submission "RE:Birth of Education" (Reynolds 2011a; see also McLuhan 1967). Responding to this question—"What do you think Marshall McLuhan should be doing if he wants to be taken more seriously in the world today?"—McLuhan replies, "Marshall McLuhan is taken far too seriously." This clip leads into the final segment of the remix—a short selection of Hallinan's slam poem showing Mr. Fulkerson "a few ideas" about how to address standardization:

> … with tools stolen from hands of gods …
> With blogs, words written daily by people like you, like me, that have no other choice but to share what they know with someone, anyone, everyone
> To complain of over-determination gives power to walls that did not exist before we believed in them.
> Why should we submit to a theory that denies agency?
> Let's look around and see ways to make things work, to subvert imposed expectations. (Wesch 2011d)

At one level, there is no doubt that the entire project is engaging, impressive, and innovative, both technologically and pedagogically. But stepping back from all the complex imagery, one has to ask—does the Visions project give me deeper insight into today's students than the profiles of the Millennials and Generation Z sketched earlier in this chapter? Or, like those profiles, does one simply have an assemblage of information? Most important, is collecting information and assembling a profile enough—or do students want to be able to do more? Should postsecondary education expect them to be able to do more and prepare them to do more?

Ironically, perhaps, the answer begins with Wesch and the inspiration he draws from Postman, particularly that scholar's *The End of Education*.[12] Outlining his teaching philosophy, Wesch (2008a) emphasizes that learning begins with "a grand narrative to provide relevance and context for learning." One must also "create a learning environment that values and leverages the learners themselves (addresses personal meaning)." Finally, one does "both in a way that realizes and leverages the existing media environment (allowing students to realize and leverage the existing media environment)."

The "grand narrative" required at the outset is fundamentally important to postsecondary education today. It is a grand narrative that will provide "ever wider perspectives," which, according to the Beloit Mindset List, are critical for students to assess and profitably employ "the burgeoning mass of information that will be heading their way" in their studies and beyond (Beloit College 2015g). Finally, as the profile of Gen Zers indicates, although they can easily leverage the existing media environment to gain information, they do not possess a sufficiently adequate grand narrative upon which they can move from passive information consumers to active knowledge producers—the fundamental end of a transcendent and personally expanding educational experience. If we want to find that grand narrative, there is no better place to begin than with sociology and what C. Wright Mills calls "the sociological imagination."

Key Terms and Names

Beloit College Mindset List
Generation X
Generation Y
Millennials
Generation Z
Michael Wesch
Neil Postman

---

12 The title *The End of Education* exploits the double meaning of "end," which can denote either "purpose" or "finish." If education cannot achieve a "transcendent and honorable purpose," Postman maintains that "schooling must reach its finish, and the sooner we are done with it, the better" (Postman 1995:x). But with an honourable end, or purpose, schooling can inspire the young to educate themselves continually throughout their lives. This is "the end of education" Postman seeks to inspire.

Questions for Review and Further Reflection

1. On the basis of just the Beloit College Mindset List, what characteristics do you think professors should note about students entering postsecondary education today?

2. On a sheet of paper divided into three columns, list the main characteristics for Generation X, the Millennials, and Generation Z. What are the most important differences between Generation Z and the other two cohorts?

3. What are the main features of students that Wesch and his students convey in the 2007 video "A Vision of Students Today?" How many of those features still apply to students entering postsecondary education now?

4. What are the main features of students that Wesch, his students, and outside collaborators convey in the 2011 "Visions of Students Today" project? How many of those features apply to students in your first year class?

5. What aspects of these profiles do you find the most unsettling? Which aspects do you find the most reassuring?

GENERATION Z AND THE PROMISE OF SOCIOLOGY

Main Objectives

This chapter will

1. Draw attention to how students normally think about the world around them, introduce Alfred Schutz's terms "natural attitude" and "everyday stocks of knowledge at hand," and consider the significance of these terms for thinking sociologically.

2. Describe C. Wright Mills's conception of "the sociological imagination" and the terms "personal troubles of milieu" and "public issues of social structure."

3. Discuss Manuel Castells's ideas about the information age and Marshall McLuhan's analysis of the nature of information predominant within the typographic and mechanical era and the electric age, in order to examine Mills's first and second sets of questions essential to the sociological imagination—the structure of society as a whole and where it stands in human history.

4. Explain McLuhan's terms a "hot medium" and a "cool medium" and their significance for employing his aphorism "the medium is the message" to examine critically the types, nature, and impact of the information sources Generation Z uses on a regular basis.

5. Build sociological vocabulary by introducing further key terms in sociology.

The Millennials and Generation Z are not alone in needing to acquire a grand narrative within which they can locate themselves and the problems and issues they must face going forward—it is a circumstance that every individual in every generation faces.

In their daily activities, individuals operate on the basis of what Schutz ([1932] 1967:80–81) identifies as "the **natural attitude**." That is, people "naturally"—automatically, unreflectively, by not thinking about it—see themselves and their situations from their own personal, individual perspectives. This perspective leads them to "naturally"—that is, in a taken-for-granted manner—draw upon their "**everyday stocks of knowledge at hand**," upon the personal knowledge they have accumulated throughout their lifetime as they engage with the world from their own egocentric perspective. Through the natural attitude, individuals know how to act appropriately and then follow conventional expectations or deviate from them (Schutz [1932] 1967:78). This has three consequences of particular note.

First, because individuals develop extensive stocks of knowledge at hand throughout their lifetime, all people are very sophisticated human agents who can quickly and unreflectively navigate through a vast array of social situations without any problems at all. It is when individuals find themselves in situations where they do not feel they have the appropriate "**recipe knowledge**" to know how to proceed "naturally" that they have to abandon the natural attitude and reflect upon their circumstances, consciously survey the situation, and look for clues as to how to act or behave appropriately (Schutz [1932] 1967:81). Those instances remind individuals of how socially constructed their knowledge of the social world actually is.

Second, because those situations are infrequent and most people can routinely carry out their day as sophisticated social agents, many think that a discipline like sociology is either irrelevant or almost intuitive. One knows what is appropriate in social interaction, so what does sociology offer? To some extent, a sociological frame of reference is not essential to most of an individual's everyday activities. However, to go beyond the routine, to engage successfully with and solve some of the larger issues of life, the stocks of knowledge at hand within the natural attitude are far from sufficient. Nevertheless, many students, on the basis of their successful experiences in most social situations think that sociology will be easy—a bird course—because "I know how the world works."

This thinking leads to the third consequence. Because both the natural attitude and each person's unique stock of knowledge at hand are so deeply rooted in everyday life, it is actually quite difficult to move beyond an ego-centric understanding of the world to one that encompasses the larger social processes that enable and constrain everyday activities. One of the major challenges that instructors and students face in an introductory sociology course is finding a way to make the transition from this "natural," egocentric perspective on the world, with its reliance on everyday stocks of knowledge at hand, to a questioning, "sociological" frame of mind that will allow critical reflection. One of the most successful attempts to introduce students to a sociological frame of reference is found in the opening chapter of *The Sociological Imagination*.

Like Schutz, **C. Wright Mills** is fully aware that individuals tend to view and understand the world from their own personal, limited perspective. "What ordinary men are directly aware of," Mills (1959) writes, "[and] what they try to do are bounded by the private orbits in which they live; their visions and their powers are limited to the close-up scenes of job, family, neighbourhood" (p. 3).[13] Individuals see their successes, in particular, resulting from their own personal initiative and abilities. "The well-being they enjoy," Mills (1959) indicates, is not usually "imput[ed] to the big ups and downs of the societies in which they live" (p. 3).

Unfortunately, life is not always trouble free, and Mills (1959) notes that "men often feel that their private lives are a series of traps. They sense that within their everyday worlds, they cannot overcome their troubles, and in this feeling, they are often quite correct" (p. 3). To escape those traps and overcome different troubles and problems requires moving beyond the natural attitude: "Seldom aware of the intricate connection between the patterns of their own lives and the course of world history," Mills points out, "ordinary men do not usually know what this connection means for the kinds of men they are becoming and for the kinds of history making in which they might take part" (pp. 3–4). To make those important connections requires a specific "quality of mind"—a quality of mind that gives Mills's book its title—it requires "**the sociological imagination**."

> "The sociological imagination enables us to grasp history and biography and the relations between the two within society." This is sociology's "task and its promise." (P. 6)

> The first fruit of this imagination—and the first lesson of the social science that embodies it—is the idea that the individual can understand his own experience and gauge his own fate only by locating himself within his period, that he can know his own chances in life only by becoming aware of those individuals in his circumstances. (P. 5)

Mills (1959) establishes the interrelationship of personal biography, history, and social structure by exploring the troubles and problems that individuals face from two perspectives: "personal troubles of milieu" and "public issues of social structure" (p. 8). At first, those perspectives appear to be separate and distinct from each other but their connection and the

---

13 Writing in 1959, Mills used the noun "man" and masculine pronouns to refer to both men and women, as was customary at that time. To retain the historical accuracy of the document and because introducing more inclusive language in square brackets can be very distracting, quotations from Mills have not been altered to reflect the current, more gender-inclusive practices. The same holds for other early texts. When a new translation is supplied, gender-inclusive language is employed.

importance for grasping the sociological frame of reference becomes apparent as Mills discusses each.

Almost everyone is familiar with **personal troubles of milieu**. Personal troubles, Mills (1959) writes, "occur within the character of the individual and within the range of his immediate relations with others; they have to do with his self and with those limited areas of social life of which he is directly and personally aware" (p. 8). Many of the troubles that first year students face as they enter postsecondary education are personal troubles: adjusting to faster-paced instruction, higher expectations for assignments, making new friends, managing time on their own. The list can be quite long.

Because these are troubles related to the individual student and his or her immediate circumstances, Mills would classify them within an individual's power to address. As he writes, "the statement and the resolution of troubles properly lie within the individual as a biographical entity and within the scope of his immediate milieu—the social setting that is directly open to his personal experience and to some extent his wilful activity" (p. 8). Working on course readings regularly and attending all lectures or viewing online material on schedule; putting more effort into assignments; joining in different campus activities; and setting up daily, weekly, and monthly schedules with automatic reminders are ways that students, with their own resources, are able to solve the personal troubles of milieu associated with the transition from high school to postsecondary education.

However, not all of the troubles that first year students face are purely personal, so not all can be solved within a student's immediate life-world through his or her own wilful activity. Those larger troubles are often linked to **public issues of social structure**. These troubles concern matters extending beyond the local environments of the individual and his or her inner life:

> Public issues have to do with the organization of many milieu into the institutions of an historical society as a whole, with the ways in which various milieu overlap and interpenetrate to form the larger structure of social and historical life. An issue is a public matter: some value cherished by publics is felt to be threatened. Often there is a debate about what that value really is and about what it is that really threatens it. (Mills 1959:8)

The material on the Millennials and Gen Z presented earlier in this book indicates several issues first year students face that extend beyond their own private orbits—the impact of digital technology on their educational experiences is one example.

The Beloit College Mindset List (2015g) notes that the class of 2019 will find "high technology an increasing factor in how and even what they learn."

Wesch's projects that envision today's students focus on the tensions between the legacy of nineteenth-century approaches to knowledge and the nature of information in the twenty-first century. The profiles of the Millennials and Gen Zers emphasize the impact of digital media on students' writing skills, attention spans, and orientation to information, as well as on the pace with which they conduct all aspects of their lives. So although the transition to higher education is, at one level, a personal trouble of milieu, at another level, it is a public issue of social structure involving the many institutionalized arrangements that constitute higher education, in general, and the university sector in particular.

As a public issue, the transition to postsecondary education involves the intersection of higher education and universities with dominant forms of media, the Internet, the economy, different levels of government, the dynamics of the family, and various forms of leisure activity and entertainment, to list just a few of the most important overlapping structures and circumstances. As a public issue, the question of whether today's students are adequately prepared for university level study is hotly debated due to the importance many business, community, and political leaders place on an advanced education in an information-based society. That debate is heightened by disagreements over what that education should entail and how it should be presented to today's students. An adequate analysis of the difficulties facing the typical first year student, then, is both sociological and personal, requiring application of the "sociological imagination."

In a single, memorable sentence, Mills (1959) captures perfectly the compelling importance of the sociological imagination for the analysis of public issues of social structure: "No social study that does not come back to the problems of biography, of history, and of their intersections within society has completed its intellectual journey" (p. 6).

As profound at that sentence is, it leaves a pressing question unanswered: how does one examine the intersection of personal biography, history, and social structure to sociologically analyse a public issue of social structure? Fortunately, Mills provides excellent direction concerning how one can employ the sociological imagination successfully.

Three Sets of Questions

Those who use the sociological imagination fruitfully, Mills (1959:6–7) points out, ask three types of questions, each of which is drawn from the classical tradition in sociology.

Mills's first set of questions concerns what is often termed the structure of society: "What is the structure of this particular society as a whole?"

Mills (1959) asks.[14] "What are its essential components, and how are they related to one another? How does it differ from other varieties of social order?" One also needs to inquire about "the meaning of any particular feature for its continuance and for its change" (p. 6).

Mills's (1959) second set of questions moves the sociologist and sociological analysis away from the potential reification of social relationships—away from an image of a fixed, static, permanent social structure—toward a critical awareness of the historical and changing dynamic of social relationships. At the most general level, a sociologist must ask these questions:

> Where does this society stand in human history? What are the mechanics by which it is changing? What is its place within and its meaning for the development of humanity as a whole? (P. 7)

Using this second set of questions, sociologists should also look closely at the social relationships within particular societies:

> How does any particular feature we are examining affect, and how is it affected by, the historical period in which it moves? And this period— what are its essential features? How does it differ from other periods? (Mills 1959:7)

Finally, sociologists must integrate into their analyses wilful human action or what sociologists term "human agency." A third set of questions facilitates this integration: "What varieties of men and women now prevail in this society and in this period? And what varieties are coming to prevail?" Mills (1959) emphasizes that sociologists must consider how social agents are "formed, liberated and repressed, made sensitive and blunted" within their particular social relations and relationships:

> What kinds of "human nature" are revealed in the conduct and character we observe in this society in this period? And what is the meaning for "human nature" of each and every feature of the society we are examining? (P. 7)

These three sets of questions bring together social structure, history, and human agency (that is, personal biography and action) into an ensemble in

---

14 Although the term "structure" is a somewhat misleading concept because it conveys the idea that social relationships have a structural permanence to them, like the girders of a building, the term does successfully capture the relatively enduring nature of the key elements that constitute a society. As a result, the term is still widely used by sociologists.

which the sociologist must simultaneously consider all three and how they interact with each other.

Today's World: The Information Age

Manuel Castells (1999, 2000, 2010), one of contemporary sociology's most perceptive and influential analysts of today's globalized world, provides some excellent insight into how one might begin to answer Mills's first set of questions—how to analyse the structure of contemporary society as a whole, identify its essential components, and understand how they differ from those of other social orders and constitute a particular social formation. Castells's major work, now in an updated, second edition, is a trilogy entitled *The Information Age: Economy, Society and Culture*.[15] Before addressing the specific characteristics of the "information age," Castells (2000) establishes some basic premises that are consistent with Mills's three sets of questions.

> Human societies are made from the conflictive interaction between humans organized in and around a given social structure. This social structure is formed by the interplay between relationships of production/consumption; relationships of experience; and relationships of power. Meaning is constantly produced and reproduced through symbolic interaction between actors framed by this social structure, and, at the same time, acting to change it or to reproduce it. (P. 7; see also Castells 2010:15–16)

Further, there is no single aspect that dominates the others—they are "all layers of social structure and social causation, folded into each other, distinguishable only in analytical terms" (Castells 2000:7). Because individuals act on the basis of their understanding of the world around them, meaning is of particular importance. Meaning, Castells notes,

> is not produced in the cultural realm: it is the cultural realm that is produced by the consolidation of meaning. Meaning results from symbolic interaction between brains which are socially and ecologically constrained, and, at the same time, biologically and culturally able of innovation. Meaning is produced, reproduced, and fought over in all layers of social structure, in production as in consumption, in experience as in power. (P. 7)

There is one more "layer" that interacts with production and consumption, experience, power, and culture, and that is technology. Technology,

---

15 Castells is not the first sociologist to analyse the "information age" or "information society"; see also Kranzberg (1985), Webster (1995), and footnote 2 in Castells (2010:28).

Castells (2010:28–29) emphasizes, is not just things or objects; it involves the use of scientific knowledge to carry out actions and activities in a continuous, reproducible manner. Technology arises through socially conditioned relationships and knowledge; it is not an autonomous, non-human product. Furthermore, although technology is most often associated with the production processes of the economy, it is also involved in consumption, and it plays an essential role in individuals' experiences and in the shaping of meaning. In addition, technology is a decisive aspect in the configuration and use of power. Conceptualized in this way, technology is an essential element in the structure and structuring of society and social life.

Although production, consumption, culture, experience, power, and technology constitute the basic elements of any society, their specific characteristics will differ in history and in different parts of the world during the same period. It is the actual features or characteristics of these basic elements of social structure, in a particular location, during a precise period of history, that give rise to specific societies or social formations.

The fundamental elements of social structure in Canada, the United States, western Europe, and other nations in the Global North in the twenty-first century constitute a particular social formation. Castells (2000, 2010) calls each a "network society." The structural elements in the network societies of today, it is important to note, differ significantly—even fundamentally—from the structures of the societies that immediately preceded them. That is, they are different from the social structures found in early industrial capitalist society, as well as from those of the ensuing modified or restructured social formations sociologists identify as late capitalism, industrial society, and post-industrial society (see Mandel [1972] 1975; Dahrendorf 1959; Aron 1961, 1962; and Bell 1973, respectively).

Castells (2010) argues that the latter third of the twentieth century initiates "one of those rare intervals in history" when "a new technological paradigm organized around information technologies" transformed social structures around the globe (p. 28). The dramatic transformation of information technology in the contemporary period is "at least as major an historical event as was the eighteenth-century industrial revolution, inducing a pattern of discontinuity in the material basis of economy, society, and culture" (p. 29). The "*core* of the transformation," Castells specifies, pertains to "*technologies of information processing and communication*" (p. 30).

The revolution that created the social formation of the early twenty-first century—the **information age**—rests on the rapid developments and increasingly widespread use, from 1970 onwards, of micro-electronics, computers, telecommunications, and the Internet. For Castells, because of their significance for contemporary production and consumption, human experience, relationships of power, and the shaping of meaning and culture, the technologies of information processing and communication provide the answer to Mills's first set of questions. These technologies are "essential components" of contemporary society and comprise that "particular feature" significant for its "continuance and for its change" (Mills 1959:6).

As he identifies the key structures of the information age, Castells moves from the first to the second set of Mills's questions. These questions consider how a society's essential features determine its place in human history, how it compares to other societies of the past and present, and how it shapes the lives of its members.

About contemporary society, Castells (2010) makes a profound claim: "I contend that around the end of the second millennium of the common era a number of major social, technological, economic, and cultural transformations came together to give rise to a new form of society" (p. xvii). The world in which today's students live, Castells maintains, is a new social formation that differs from those in existence in the Global North throughout most of the twentieth century and is vastly different from all social formations prior to that time. As mentioned, the core features distinguishing social life in the new millennium are technologies of information processing and communication.

Before moving on to Mills's third set of questions and the insight they provide into the current period, the significance of the answers to these first two sets merits some elaboration.

FROM THE GUTENBERG TO THE INTERNET GALAXY

Castells is not the first scholar to suggest that, during various periods, humankind has created and worked itself through some major transformative juncture in social life and the structures of society.[16] Nor is he the only one to single out the dramatic impact that the communication of ideas and the means of communication themselves have on the structuring or restructuring of a social formation.[17] Finally, he is not alone in suggesting that changes in certain core features of Western societies during the twentieth century had a dramatic, revolutionary impact upon production, consumption, experience, power, culture, and technology.[18]

---

16 See, for example Maxine Berg (1986), John Bury (1920), Phyllis Deane (1979), E.J. Dijksterhuis ([1959] 1986), Michel Foucault ([1966] 1970, 2008), Arnold Gehlen ([1957] 1980), Elie Halévey ([1928] 1972), Christopher Hill (1961, 1972), Eric Hobsbawm (1962, 1969), H. Stuart Hughes (1958), Thomas Kuhn (1957, 1962), Arthur Lovejoy (1936, 1948), Karl Polanyi (1944), and Richard Tawney (1926).

17 The list of such scholars is actually very long and would include those in the previous note. Some additional sources include Daniel Bell (1973), Elizabeth Eisenstein (1979), McLuhan (1962), Edward Thompson (1970), and Alexis de Tocqueville [1856] 1955).

18 See, for example, Raymond Aron (1961, 1962), Bell (1960a, 1973, 1976), Ralf Dahrendorf (1959), Neal Gabler (1998), John Goldthorp (1968, 1969), Jürgen Habermas ([1968] 1971, 1976, [1981] 1984), Herbert Marcuse (1964), Neil Postman (1985, 1992).

In *The Gutenberg Galaxy: The Making of Typographic Man*, **Marshall McLuhan** (1962), whose work Castells draws upon, identifies fundamental differences in Western societies—clearly evident by the second half of the twentieth century—between what he identifies as the outgoing "typographic and mechanical era" and the new "electric age." McLuhan (1962:3) argues that the electric age exhibits "new shapes and structures of human inter-dependence and of expression" that differ significantly from those of the **typographic and mechanical era**.

McLuhan's argument stems from humans' creative capacities to build objects, tools, technologies, and media that extend and intensify humankind's various senses, sensibilities, capacities, and powers. The manner in which humans extend and intensify their senses has profound implications.

A stick or rock used to dig in the ground is a tool, technology, or medium that extends an individual's muscular strength and endurance. In the course of human history in many parts of the world, people replaced that medium with an iron digging tool. A spade, a hoe, an animal-drawn plough, and a motorized tractor and plough follow, over time, to extend humankind's ability to till the soil, plant, and reap crops.

Similarly, moving from the naked eye to the use of an intermediary medium between the observer and the observed, such as a handmade magnifying glass, intensifies sight. From the sixteenth century through to the present, inventors extended that medium by placing two handmade lenses inside a moveable cylinder to create a microscope or a telescope with vastly increased powers of magnification. When one replaces the handmade lenses with precision-machined ones, vision is extended, intensified, and sharpened further. Today, electronic telescopes and microscopes have given way to satellite-based telescopes and electron microscopes, intensifying humankind's visual sense, extending it deeper or further into previously unseen worlds.

For McLuhan, the most significant extension of humankind's senses relates to communication. In *The Gutenberg Galaxy*, he focuses on the impact and consequences of the extension and intensification of communication that occurred after the invention of the printing press. Specifically, he looks at the social transformations associated with the transition from oral cultures, rooted in the spoken word, to the particular print culture that arose with Johannes Gutenberg's integration of moveable type and the screw press. The ultimate domination of print over oral communication is so important because it extends and elevates a particular type of visual information over oral and auditory communication. This "distortion" or unbalancing of sensory information, McLuhan maintains, has significant outcomes because the more open, heterogeneous nature of oral cultures and their natural, mythical worldviews are replaced by the closed, homogenizing forces of print culture and its associated mechanized worldview (see also Rose 2013; McLuhan 1964:77–88, 170–79, 258–64).

The extension and transformation of the spoken word begins around 8000 BCE with clay tokens, inscribed with different symbols, serving as a counting and accounting medium (Eisenstein 1979). Around 3500 BCE, the tokens are replaced by the symbols themselves, which are imprinted on clay tablets. That medium is extended; symbols become more standardized and develop into cuneiform and hieroglyphic systems. After enlargement and even more standardization, these systems become more closed, and the first phonetic alphabets emerge, which scribes employ in writing continuous lines of words across a page without spaces—*scriptura continua*. The separation of words and the addition of punctuation standardizes, extends, and homogenizes written language further as all literate individuals begin to establish and follow the same rules of grammar, allowing authors to make their meanings clearer and more precise (see Carr 2011; Eisenstein 1979).

The truly transformative period in the emergence of print culture begins with Gutenberg's printing press. The screw press with moveable type does more than simply extend the availability of manuscripts beyond a small, privileged and empowered literate elite to what ultimately becomes mass consumers (see Febvre and Martin [1958] 1976; McLuhan 1962). The press and the posters, broadsheets, newspapers, pamphlets, and books to which it gives rise, on an expanding scale, change the "structures of human interdependence and of expression" and initiate the changing perceptions of the world that spawn the Renaissance, the Reformation, the Enlightenment, and the rise of humanism. Most specifically, McLuhan emphasizes throughout *The Gutenberg Galaxy* that, as a particular extension of the visual, Gutenberg's technology and the emergent print culture initiate and encourage a linear, analytic, reflective, individualist approach to the world that is consistent with the mechanistic and scientific worldview of the Enlightenment period and that remains dominant throughout what McLuhan terms the "typographic and mechanical era" (see also Cassirer 1951; McLuhan 1964:145–56, 179–87, 188–202, 217–25; Riesman 1960; Rose 2013; Sohn-Rethel [1971] 1978).

McLuhan details the transition from oral culture to the typographic and mechanical era because periods of major transformation can illuminate the key constituents of change and their implications. McLuhan's main interest, however, is not the typographic and mechanical era but the **electric age** and its distinctive nature:

> Our private senses are not closed systems but are endlessly translated into each other in that experience which we call consciousness. Our extended senses, tools, technologies, through the ages, have been closed systems incapable of interplay or collective awareness. Now, in the electric age, the very instantaneous nature of co-existence among our technological instruments has created a crisis quite new in human history. Our extended faculties and senses now constitute a single field of experience

which demands that they become collectively conscious. Our technologies, like our private senses, now demand an interplay and ratio that
makes *rational* co-existence possible. (McLuhan 1962:5)

McLuhan foresees a transition that would far surpass the accomplishments of the shift from oral to typographic culture because the unique
technologies of the electric age contain the potential for human coexistence
based on reason.

The Gutenberg Galaxy concentrates on "only the mechanical technology
emergent from our alphabet and the printing press" to understand "the new
configurations of mechanisms and of literacy" in the electric age. McLuhan
uses the book to set the stage for a separate study that examines how particular media extend human senses, sensibility, and knowledge of the world.

In his next major work, *Understanding Media: The Extensions of Man*,
McLuhan (1964) demonstrates how various media that extend human senses,
such as the spoken and printed word, clocks, cars, the telegraph, typewriter,
telephone, radio, television, and movies, have significant effects upon social
relations. McLuhan succinctly captures his main point in one of his most
widely cited aphorisms: "**the medium is the message**" (p. 7). As perplexing
as the statement seems, unravelling its meaning is critical to understanding
how the electric age—or Castells's network society—differs from the typographic and mechanical era. More to the point here, identifying the main
features of the network society is central to recognizing the challenges that
today's students face in their experiences of the contemporary postsecondary
education system.

Humans extend their senses by creating a new medium that improves
upon and incorporates an existing one. A "persistent theme" in *Understanding
Media* is that "all technologies are extensions of our physical and nervous
systems to increase power and speed" (McLuhan 1964:89). A new medium
extends and incorporates the older medium. As a result, the content of
any medium is another medium. "The content of writing is speech, just
as the written word is the content of print, and print is the content of the
telegraph" (McLuhan 1964:8). Each medium, as it is developed and implemented, extends humankind's senses, intensifying people's experiences of
the worlds they inhabit and explore. "[T]he 'message' of any medium or
technology is the change of scale or pace or pattern that it introduces into
human affairs" (McLuhan 1964:8).

The railway did not initiate transportation. However, as the incorporation and extension of the medium of horse-drawn wagons, the steam-
powered locomotive—with a horsepower in the hundreds and able to pull
dozens of heavily laden freight cars along smooth, even rail beds stretching
across a nation, and at speeds no thoroughbred could ever match—altered
the physical and social landscape of the industrializing world. Steam-powered

rail transport changed the rural and urban landscape completely, reshaped work and leisure, and necessitated faster means of communication across greater and greater distances (see, for example, Hobsbawm 1969). "The airplane, on the other hand, by accelerating the rate of transportation, tends to dissolve the railway form of city, politics, and association, quite independently of what the airplane is used for" (McLuhan 1964:8). The medium is the message "because it is the medium that shapes and controls the scale and form of human association and action" (p. 9).

For McLuhan, those who are studying technology and media miss the most important point—they focus solely on the most obvious content of a medium; they examine "the message" in its conventional sense. McLuhan, on the contrary, insists that the real message in media that extends humans' senses is not the superficial, conventional message decoded by a recipient. The real message is the impact that the extension and intensification of a medium has on human interdependence and expression. Technologists and communications theorists should be studying not a message's content but "the scale and form of human association and action"—this is the real message.

Using what may seem a curious example, McLuhan makes his point in a slightly different manner. The electric light bulb is "illuminating," McLuhan puns. "The electric light is pure information. It is a medium without a message, as it were, unless it is used to spell out some verbal ad or name" (McLuhan 1964:8). But when that light bulb is used in a surgeon's operating theatre or to illuminate a baseball game at night, those activities become the "content" of the light bulb, as neither could take place without it. Turning on the light bulb allows—or turns on—the surgery or ball game (hence McLuhan's notion that surgery or the night game are "contained" within the light bulb because they could not take place without it—they are the medium's message). The medium is the message because "any new technology gradually creates a totally new human environment" (McLuhan 1964:vi). The message in electric lighting is the extension of human activities well beyond the limited hours of daylight or into closed, windowless spaces such as the sterile operating room, bunkers, ships, and mines where sunlight never shines.

Due to their specific nature, the media extending human senses in the typographic and mechanical era created closed systems of communication and human understanding. But it is not imperative that a medium produces a closed system. To make his point, McLuhan (1964) distinguishes between "hot" and "cool" media.

A **hot medium** extends one's senses in "high definition" (McLuhan 1964:22). It provides rich sensory detail and does most things for the receiver. Every facet is given; there is not much, for example, that a viewer has to fill in when watching a movie. With so much sensory detail immediately present, a hot medium is more or less passively received. A photograph is a hot medium when compared to an editorial cartoon. In the former, all the colour and detail are there to see and study; nothing needs to be added. In contrast, an editorial cartoon requires the observer to fill in information mentally in order to grasp the character or point that the cartoonist is creating. Finally, one may analyse a hot medium in a precise, logical, quantifiable manner, which means that one can read into or discover within a hot medium a linear framework that is uncovered in the precise, sequential approach to its analysis.

A **cool medium** is low in definition; it requires active participation from the receiver, who must fill in missing details and detect the overall pattern (see McLuhan 1964:308–37). Unlike a hot medium, which offers a linear, sequential, and clear ordering of its particulars, a cool medium presents its information more abstractly, requiring the receiver to grasp its elements synthetically and simultaneously. McLuhan (1967) borrows the term "cool" from the 1950s beatnik culture and its slang expressions: "That's cool.... Can you dig it?" Digging it—working to understand or appreciate something in the moment—is exactly what is required of someone confronted by a cool medium. The recipient must figure out what is significant in something that is deemed cool. Jazz and all its spontaneous improvisation is cool while a symphony and its structured orchestration is hot. A seminar is a cool medium requiring far more from a student than attending and taking notes in a lecture. Oral speech is cool when compared to the printed word, which would be hot. And what about comparing an aphorism to a textbook? The aphorism or saying is cool; the book is hot.

A central argument in both *The Gutenberg Galaxy* and *Understanding Media* is that although the extension of human senses through different media or technologies is a natural, historical process, the overextension of one sense, disrupting the normal ratio of human senses and sensibilities, has significant consequences for human association and interaction. The technology that Gutenberg develops in the fifteenth century is a particular case in point.

First, the printing press marks the dividing line between medieval and modern technology (see Usher 1929). Unlike the manuscript as a medium, which has limited reach, a text printed with movable type is easily replicated and has the power and intensity to create mass reading publics on a national scale. Print can unify a culture, a belief system, and a nation (McLuhan 1964:170–78).

Second, the reader of print stands in a totally different relationship to a text than does someone listening to the reading of a manuscript (McLuhan 1964:81–88; Rose 2013). A manuscript, being rare, was often read aloud to more than one listener, with the reader controlling the pace and the listeners only able to pause the reading to reflect or retrace a sentence or section by interrupting the reader. Gutenberg's press allowed multiple individuals to own copies of a printed book, so each owner could read the text, pause, reflect, and mark the book as he or she wished. Typography, McLuhan (1962) maintains, is experienced much like the cinema: "the reading of print puts the reader in the role of the movie projector. The reader moves the series of imprinted letters before him at a speed consistent with apprehending the motions of the author's mind" (pp. 124–25). The creation of books with movable type not only makes the production of a book uniform, linear, and repeatable but the frame of mind developed in reading a book is equally linear, constrained, and one-sided, as it emphasizes a fixed point of view from which the book is read and understood (see also Postman 1985, 1988; Riesman 1960; Rose 2013).

The fixed point of view established through typography is carried over into the world of art in the fifteenth century as painters introduce perspective by portraying the diminishing size of objects as the increased distance between the observer standing before the painting and these objects. The perspective is set from the point at which the viewer sees the painting. This intense extension of the visual modality through print creates a closure of human perceptions into a linear, uniform, mechanistic worldview, which profoundly shapes and constrains the form, scale, and pace of human communication, association, and social interaction.

The electric age, McLuhan (1962) maintains, is dramatically different. It involves "new shapes and structures of human interdependence and of expression which are 'oral' in form even when the components of the situation may be non-verbal" (p. 3). To make his point, McLuhan turns to the Victorian art critic John Ruskin's analysis of Gothic symbolism as an art form that breaks out of the unified, single-vision realism that the typographic and mechanical era solidifies in art and literature. In *Modern Painters*, Ruskin (1885) writes that landscape painters and architects have not truly mastered their craft until their works are shaped by an "understanding of the wilder beauty of nature" (p. 92). The grotesque, Ruskin maintains, displays that quality in "its fullest development" because it captures the "healthful but irrational play of the imagination in times of rest," and "the confusion of the imagination by truths which it cannot fully grasp" (p. 92). Ruskin's emphasis upon the grotesque and the qualities it embodies in painting and architecture provides the perspective that McLuhan (1962) feels will represent the new galaxy of perception that opens with the electric age.

> A fine grotesque is the expression, in a moment, by a series of symbols thrown together in bold and fearless connection, of truths which it would have taken a long time to express in any verbal way, and of which the connection is left for the beholder to work out for himself; the gaps, left or overleaped by the haste of the imagination, forming the grotesque character. (Cited by McLuhan 1962:266; see Ruskin 1885:93–94)

McLuhan may have been ahead of his time in seeing the impact of the electric age in the 1960s, but there is little doubt that the ensuing development of micro-electronic technologies, computers, and the Internet, as extensions of human senses and sensibilities, has dramatically reshaped the scale, pace, and patterns of human perception, interaction, and association.

In his controversial study, *The Shallows: What the Internet Is Doing to Our Brains*, Carr (2011) points out that the arrival and widespread adoption of the Internet, as the source of so many aspects in people's everyday lives and perceptions of the world, means that "[w]e seem to have arrived, as McLuhan said we would, at an important juncture in our intellectual and cultural history, a moment of transition between two very different modes of thinking" (Carr 2011:10). For Carr, however, the move from the typographic and mechanical era to the electric age is not quite as McLuhan envisions it; Carr argues that it is a transition from the linear, contemplative, literary mind of print culture to the distracted, multi-tasking, fragmented mind of the Internet (see also Rose 2013). This observation leads directly to Mills's third set of questions.

WHAT MEN AND WOMEN PREVAIL? WHAT MEN AND WOMEN ARE COMING TO PREVAIL?

Mills is critically aware that particular societies and their social structures, located at specific points in human history, are created by human agents through their meaningful human actions. Moreover, Mills recognizes that although the prevailing social structures may constrain meaningful social action in particular ways, they also enable human actions that lead to continual social change, ranging from shifts in minor details to major social transformations depending on social circumstances as a whole. Mills's third set of questions emphasizes the same point that Castells (2000) phrases so succinctly: "Human societies are made from the conflictive interaction between humans organized in and around a given social structure" (p. 7).

With regard to today's students' postsecondary educational experiences, Mills's third set of questions turns one's attention to what men and women currently prevail in higher education and what men and women may come to prevail. Beginning to answer those questions requires identifying the pertinent conflicts within contemporary society, in general, and within the institutions of postsecondary education, in particular. What are the tensions and dynamics that might allow some men and women to begin prevailing who are quite different from those leading and taking part in higher education at the present?

As the profiles of the Millennials and Gen Zers clearly demonstrate, first year students' lives unrelentingly revolve around micro-electronics, computers, telecommunications, the Internet, and, most significantly, smartphones,

Google, and social media. These students have grown up totally immersed within what one might call "e-culture," and their approach to information, work, and leisure is very different from that of their parents; it is also quite distinct from the orientation to information, knowledge, and work held by those who lead, structure, and deliver higher education today.

Despite all the adjustments and changes that postsecondary instructors and institutions are making to the growth of information technology and to the manner in which information is transmitted, filtered, stored, and utilized, postsecondary education still remains intimately tied to what one might term "print culture." Higher education remains firmly within "the Gutenberg galaxy." The resulting structurally based tension between those who prevail in postsecondary education and those entering into it has significant outcomes.

On the one hand, consistent with the print culture orientation of contemporary postsecondary education, students now have direct contact with more scholarly information than ever before, and they can reach almost all of it from the comfort of their own residence or dorm rooms. Gaining access to scholarly texts has never been easier or required less time. The digitization of text—books, scholarly journals, magazines, newspapers—has revolutionized how students today may access the "printed" word.

In a brief but highly informative overview of the digitization of printed works, Karen Coyle (2006) notes that its history extends back into the late 1960s, involving different forms and levels of digitization, undertaken for varying and sometimes conflicting motives by individuals, corporations, and other institutions, such as libraries, universities, and various archives. Everyone involved in the digitizing of hard copy text has a prior stake and interest in the printed word, which, in turn, influences the goals and outcomes of the digitization process.

The digitization of existing print texts genuinely becomes a public issue of social structure, to use Mills's terminology, with Google's announcement of its Books Library Project in 2006—the first of many mass **digitization projects** (see Coyle 2006; Google n.d.). Prior to that time, after creating the first e-book platform, Michael Hart had launched Project Gutenberg with the relatively modest objective of "encourag[ing] the creation and distribution of e-books" (see Coyle 2006; Project Gutenberg n.d.). Coyle (2006) describes Project Gutenberg as a non-mass digitization project utilizing a "cottage industry approach" and relying upon volunteers to convert and submit e-books (p. 642). In its early years, Project Gutenberg produced fewer than 500 books per year, but that number rose steadily so that, in its 44-year history, the project has converted more than 50,000 books to a digital format and made them freely available as e-books for anyone's use, subject to national copyright laws (Project Gutenberg n.d.). Prior to Google's mass digitization of texts, Project Gutenberg offered the largest single collection of e-books.

In addition to creating greater access to books, in general, via the Internet, the other main goals of non-mass digitization projects are preserving deteriorating texts and increasing the availability of rare books or collections. Gutenberg's bible, a high resolution, interactive copy of which is available from the Harry Ransom Center of the University of Texas, stands as the perfect example of such a goal realized. Coyle (2006) identifies the University of Virginia's "Etext" project and "the beautifully rendered Octavo Editions of rare and precious books" as instances of the preservation of rare books and expanded access to them (p. 642).

Large-scale digitization projects are more focused than those involved in mass digitization. JSTOR, "a not-for-profit digital library of academic journals, books, and primary sources," is designed to "help people discover, use, and build upon a wide range of content through a powerful research and teaching platform," and to preserve "this content for future generations" (JSTOR n.d.). It has produced more than 25,000 e-books and has digitized a comprehensive collection of academic journals extending back into the nineteenth century.

Mass digitization, on the other hand, involves "the conversion of materials on an industrial scale," and it began with the Google Books Library Project (Coyle 2006:641; see also Google n.d.). In 2010, Leonid Taycher, a Google software engineer, publicized Google's plans to digitize all of the 129,864,880 different books that were estimated to be in existence at that time (Jackson 2010). The dream was that by 2016, the Google Books Library Project would be complete (Toobin 2007). To date, Google has scanned over 30 million books in about 480 different languages (Wu 2015; Jackson 2010).

According to Google (n.d.), the project's aim "is simple": to make it easier for people "to find relevant books—specifically, books they wouldn't find any other way such as those that are out of print—while carefully respecting authors' and publishers' copyrights." Google is careful to write that it is working with publishers and libraries to "create a comprehensive, searchable, virtual card catalog of all books in all languages that helps users discover new books and publishers discover new readers." Google works with more than 40 libraries around the world, including those at Columbia, Cornell, Harvard, Oxford, Princeton, and Stanford Universities, the New York Public Library, the Austrian National Library, Ghent University Library in Belgium, Keio University Library in Japan, and the Bavarian State Library in Germany, to collect, scan, and catalogue its digitized books.

In 2007, Amazon also entered the book digitization business through its subsidiary BookSurge, which partnered with Kirtas Technologies in a project to digitize and archive hard-to-find books (C. McCarthy 2007). BookSurge has now become CreateSpace, so as to offer a single platform to help creators publish and distribute books, DVDs, CDs, and video downloads. More recently, Amazon has introduced "Kindle Convert," which is a software program enabling individuals to scan their own print books and documents and convert them to a digital format. After conversion, these Kindle titles can be stored in Amazon's cloud. Even print books are now being stored and read on electronic devices, so the current first year student experiences "print" in a very different way than his or her predecessors.

Along with having unprecedented, direct access to so much information, today's students can produce research papers using sophisticated software packages that check spelling and grammar, offer hundreds of font types and sizes, and allow students to customize their formatting and layout. Desktop publishing is easier than baking a cake. Statistics packages give students discriminatory and analytical powers that continually grow in sophistication and ease of use with each passing semester. Finally, although presentation packages such as PowerPoint (first launched in 1990) and Keynote (first made publically available in 2003) dominate academic and corporate presentations, an increasing array of alternatives are now available, for example, Prezi, PowToon, SlideRocket, Beamer, and Impress. The digital world of information gathering and processing is always present for today's students—on their desktops, laptops, tablets, and smartphones.

The significance and impact of the digital revolution, which has opened access to digitized texts and created numerous platforms to analyse, arrange, and present information, extends far beyond the widespread and instant access to books, journals, magazines, newspapers, and various software packages. The digitization of information directly affects how students actually engage with not only the "digitized word" but also the "digitized world." There is an enormous divide between the e-cultural experiences, skills, and expectations of students and the print culture perspective of their professors. The lived experiences, background, wants, and desires of students who are coming to prevail in colleges and universities differ significantly from those of the instructors who currently prevail in postsecondary education.

THE WORLD OF CONTINUOUS—PARTIAL—ATTENTION

Screen life—indeed, multi-screen life—dominates the lives of the Millennials and Generation Z (Gardner and Davis 2014). Today's students will average more than eight hours a day before one type of screen or another as they move from their laptop and tablet to their smartphone and back, with several screens open and different conversations, tasks, and forms of entertainment all in progress (Roberts, Yaya, and Manolis 2014). Equally important, most of those activities occur through the Internet. Furthermore, the e-culture that the Internet has spawned and currently supports and extends is vastly different than print culture.

The most significant difference is that the Internet is "bidirectional." That is, the Internet is a medium of instantaneous connectivity that allows one to interact with multiple contacts who can be in different locations, almost anywhere in the world. The Internet seems to have the potential to create the global interaction networks that McLuhan envisioned when he speculated that the electric age would usher in "the global village."

Through a variety of bidirectional platforms (e.g., texting) or social media (e.g., Snapchat, Twitter, Pinterest, and Instagram), Millennials and Gen Zers can engage in numerous continuing conversations by simply shifting from one to another. Some technology enables instantaneous and continuous bidirectional communication (e.g., Skype or FaceTime), other media, such as Facebook, LinkedIn, Tumblr, Instagram, Meetup, and Tinder, facilitate bidirectional communication that is less immediate but equally interactive. Both sorts are casually managed by today's students with their multi-tasking approach to information.

The constant use of these interactive technologies requires, fosters, and helps develop an approach to information that is identified as "**continuous partial attention**" or "**hyper attention**" (Rose 2013:87). More important, continuous partial attention is not confined to interactions in the digital world; this kind of orientation carries over into other areas of students' lives (see Bunz 2014; Carr 2011; Gardner and Davis 2014; Rose 2013). As Rose (2013) points out, the implications are far reaching:

> We are only beginning to explore what the emergent cognitive style of short and constantly shifting attention means for teaching and learning. Yet the consequences are bound to be significant because teaching as we know it is essentially the business of capturing and holding attention. It is based upon the premise that learners will be able to perform one task at a time without distraction before moving on to another, which is why many learning difficulties are attributed to short attention spans or attention deficits. (P. 89)

The continual shifting from one communication platform to another is not the full extent of the problem. Continuous partial attention is also fostered by many of the digital texts that the Millennials and Gen Zers read. Online texts with imbedded hyperlinks continually distract individuals as they read the page. Each hyperlink invites readers to move to a new and different page. Often in the middle of a sentence, readers are enticed to redirect their attention to somewhere else.

One of the more ironic examples of how hyperlinks create and reinforce a distracted hyper attention is Jonathon Gatehouse's (2014) recent *Maclean's* magazine article "Why We Need to Clear Our Cluttered Minds." The article has this enticing lead: "A new book probes the problem with multitasking, and how to cope with decision fatigue."

As one reads this article online, however, hyperlinks in red font not only break the flow of the piece, and concentration, but also entice one to click and follow those links. Like it or not, the reader is forced to make a number of decisions while reading an article about how multi-tasking and the constant demand for decision making in the digital world can reduce individuals' abilities to perform at their optimal level.

The first embedded link in this article occurs in the title of the book it reviews; this link is to Amazon to purchase John Levitin's (2014) *The Organized Mind: Thinking Straight in an Age of Information Overload*. The next links are to a 2011 study on memory and a Norwegian examination of the differences in emotional impact when someone reads online as opposed to from text in hard copy (see Mangen, Walgermo, and Brønnick 2013). Then a link to Brian Levine at the University of Toronto precedes a hyperlink to a study of the passengers aboard a 2001 Air Transat flight that ran out of fuel and nearly crashed (see McKinnon et al. 2014). The final link is to a survey of students at Baylor University in Texas, which documents that female students spend an average of 10 hours a day interacting with others and various media through their smartphones while males spend 8 hours. The Baylor researchers warn that this "cell-phone addiction" leaves little time for academic work (see Roberts, Yaya, and Manolis 2014). In a relatively short book review (1,950 words), the reader's attention is distracted six times, to say nothing about all the links at the top, down the side, and at the bottom of the page as one scrolls through the article.

The issue facing the Millennials, Generation Z, and their instructors is something deeper than the time spent on smartphones. The main issue centres on attention, concentration, and the ability to reflect.

The Internet and its hyperlinked structure prompts, encourages, and reinforces humans' natural tendency to shift attention continually from one activity to another. The regular use of the Internet teaches students that reading does not involve a deep and personal understanding of a text or argument. Quite the opposite. Reading now is a series of ongoing choices leading to the rapid switch from one bit of information to another to yet another by simply clicking on embedded hyperlinks. The Internet is "moving us from the depths of thought to the shallows of distraction" (Bunz 2014:32).

There is more to the challenge that e-culture presents to students as they adjust to the demands of postsecondary education. Despite the flexibility they offer to today's students, digital media are very time consuming and instil a rather passive relationship between the medium and the student.

Gen Zers, as the profiles earlier in Chapter 1 indicate, are "the ultimate consumers of 'snack media'" (Sparks & Honey 2014:29). A good deal of their information comes through YouTube, TED Talks, MOOCs (massive open online course), and other Internet audiovisual presentations. While entertaining and informative, those forms of digital information are time consuming and difficult to control with any precision. For example, a viewer cannot easily slow the flow down when the information becomes complex; one cannot quickly go back to a particular point and compare the information there with what is presented earlier or further on. It is also more difficult to gain an overall perspective of the information as a whole in audiovisual, online presentations. Furthermore, as hot media, in McLuhan's terms, they instil a more passive relationship between the viewer and the medium than exists between a reader and a printed text. The details of an argument are often missed or unreflectively glossed over.

In Wesch's (2007a) "A Vision of Students Today," for example, one wonders how many viewers noticed that he put up two different statements about technology three-quarters of the way through the video—"Some have suggested that technology can save us" appears at 3 minutes and 32 seconds and lasts 4 seconds before the background fades and the words are replaced by "Some have suggested that technology alone can save us," which remains visible for 5 seconds. In a written text, such as this, one can instantly glance back over those two sentences to note the additional word in the second—a small but extremely significant addition. One can read the sentence or sentences slowly and simultaneously reflect on what they mean without worrying about the stream of information getting ahead of one's thoughts—the reader controls the pace completely. Reading a text is exactly as McLuhan (1962) describes it—the "reader moves the series of imprinted letters before him at a speed consistent with apprehending the motions of the author's mind" (pp. 124–25). One can read through what is familiar quite quickly and easily, skip over the unimportant, and then slow down for new or complex material.

For today's students, the practice of slowing down the flow of information, stopping and going back over a point, does not come naturally. Part of the reason is the structural nature of the hot media they rely upon so heavily for their information. The information sources in the lives of the Millennials and Gen Zers compel them to keep up—the medium sets the pace and it is passively consumed. As in much of their lives, control is external, and students simply comply and adjust or fall behind, tune it out, and move on to other media and messages.

Another part of the reason for the disjunction between today's students and their professors is the abundance of information these students have learned to consume and multi-task through at any given point in time. As a consequence, each input receives a quick scan, but few, if any, are accorded undivided attention for any length of time. Through a lifetime of multiple, almost simultaneous information scanning strategies, the Millennials and Gen Zers have developed particular learning expectations and techniques appropriate to their e-culture needs, but these are not necessarily conducive to success in the print-culture world of the postsecondary education system.

It is instructive to hone in on the forms that information takes today as it is processed for and through the Internet. In two other YouTube videos,

"Information R/evolution" and "The Machine Is Us/ing Us (Final Version)," Wesch (2007b, 2007c) shows how flexible, fluid, unstable, and ubiquitous information is in the cyber world. Digital information has infinite recombinant capacities. In McLuhan's terms, digital information in the electric age is very cool (in every sense of the term). Digital information is "immaterial." It has almost no material constraints; digital information can be changed instantly and manipulated almost endlessly by anyone who receives it. Electronic information gives enormous potential to the receiver to be highly interpretive, constructive, and even interactive in grasping its "content" and meanings. The recipients and users of digital information can do more than simply fill in certain features; they can actively revise and even reconstruct the text, image, or video to create something vastly different from the original.

At the same time, however, due to digital information's tremendous flexibility and the ease with which various software programs enable it to be carefully scripted and packaged and distributed via the Internet, digital information is potentially very hot. One sees this potential of digital media to engage attention and require minimum participation of the audience in presentations such as the ads introducing iPhone 6s or the Surface. These carefully choreographed blends of rapidly moving images, sound, and narration provide all of the information, persuasively packaged for the consumer, at a pace that is so quick that one cannot stop and reflect upon the sales pitch (Apple 2015a, 2015b; Microsoft 2014, 2015). While more basic, low-technology productions, such as the RSA Animate illustrated lectures available on TED Talks, do not overwhelm the viewer quite as much, the clever, rapidly presented animation and carefully timed narration provide a fully developed, persuasive argument (for example, Harvey 2014; Robinson 2010).

Because digital information has the potential to be hot or cool, the social context within which it is consumed and used is what is most significant. It is here, in the duelling contexts of academia and a young adult's life-world, that one can see the dilemmas facing today's students and their postsecondary instructors most clearly.

The Millennials and Gen Zers grew up with *Sesame Street* (1969–70, 1970–present). Throughout their lives, they have enjoyed information that entertains, is cleverly scripted, and is absorbed through constant repetition rather than focused concentration. There is little to fill in and, as a result, very early in their lives, today's students become accustomed to passively absorbing information delivered in small, repetitive, animated doses coming from different angles and perspectives. Their multi-tasking—chatting online, texting another friend, monitoring a video download, Googling for information, and watching YouTube while listening to iTunes on their computer—has significantly shaped how they process information. The Millennials and Generation Z control the range of information coming in, but they can only process parts of it at one time and thus do so far more passively than actively.

On the positive side, the Millennials and Generation Z are completely at ease with the recombinant capacities of digital information. Among their most highly developed stocks of knowledge at hand is their "Internet first" approach to problem solving. In the natural attitude, they know digital information intimately. They appreciate its tremendous creative potential and how active interaction with—even participation within—a digital information environment offers a route to solutions that those stuck in a print culture world may never recognize. Indeed, many scholars and culture critics suggest the existence of an **information revolution**.

In "Information R/evolution," Wesch (2007b) underlines how digital information breaks out of all the conventions associated with print culture. "Digital information takes different forms," he types using a word processor. He quickly highlights a portion of text and changes the last words: "Digital information has no material form." Then he adds "fixed"—"Digital information has no fixed material form." This demonstration allows one to think about information beyond its material constraints. Algorithms that search the Internet for information replace categories, catalogues, and hierarchies of information; hyperlinks on the Internet can move one, in an instant, from one information source to another. A link can "store" information in several "places" at once, eliminating the restrictions of fixed, closed, limiting categories. "We no longer just find information," Wesch (2007b) indicates, "it can find us." He changes the sentence: "We can make it find us." And then he edits it further: "Together, we can make it find us." The flexibilities of digital information "are not just cool tricks," Wesch (2007b) argues, "they change the rules of order." As liberating as the cool side of digital information may be, that too has its downside for today's students. First, digital technology itself has progressed considerably since 2007 and one of the most dramatic changes is the introduction of the desktop or mobile "application" or "app." Apps are direct shortcuts to specific operating systems that a user can run alongside several other open apps. Based on their extensive research on the Millennials and Gen Z, Gardner and Davis (2014) argue that they represent an "App Generation," which has developed a particular "app mentality."

> The app mentality evokes the on-demand nature of apps and the way they are used to perform discrete tasks, such as locating a restaurant, shopping for an item of clothing, or talking with a friend. The app mentality may be considered an algorithmic way of thinking: any question or desire one has should be satisfied immediately and definitively. There is little room for ambiguity or sitting for a time with uncertainty before arriving at a decision or insight. And inasmuch as the most widely used apps are characterized by striking icons or brands (the Amazon shopping cart, the Twitter bird), the app mentality looks for, expects, or creates such powerful identifying features. (P. xi)

Gardner and Davis also introduce the terms "**app-enabled**" and "**app-dependent**" to indicate that not all Millennials or Gen Zers display the negative consequences of the app mentality. In many ways, digital media, the Internet, and the thousands of apps available are extremely enabling—particularly in the execution of routine tasks. The danger arises when today's students become app-dependent, and they look to their apps and associated technology first rather than looking within themselves to solve a problem on their own or reach out directly to a friend. App-dependence, Gardner and Davis detail at length, impacts students' identity, their feelings and expressions of intimacy, and how they develop and express their imagination.

The app metaphor allows Gardner and Davis (2014) to capture how students today develop their personal identities. For the app-dependent, those identities are "increasingly externalized, packaged selves; a growing anxiety and aversion to risk-taking," while among the app-enabled, apps serve as "as portals to the world" and can broaden young people's awareness of and access to experiences and identities beyond their immediate environment (p. 91).

> As visual icons that are selected to personalize one's phone, apps reflect young people's emphasis on external appearances and individualism. Apps also function as safety nets, removing many of the daily risks we previously took for granted, such as confronting a person's unfiltered reaction to a sensitive topic or finding one's way in an unfamiliar locale. These connections between the identities of today's youth and the qualities of apps illustrate our central argument. New media technologies can open up new opportunities for self-expression. But yoking one's identity too closely to certain characteristics of these technologies—and lacking the time, opportunity, or inclination to explore life and lives offline—may result in an impoverished sense of self. (Gardner and Davis 2014:91)

Second, the volume of information the Millennials and Gen Z have become accustomed to consuming, its apparently infinite recombinant potential, and the speed with which it passes its "best before date" can be anxiety inducing—especially for students who are not accustomed to setting their own priorities and controlling their lives fully. In the fast-paced, competitive world of contemporary higher education, where the Millennials and Gen Zers now find themselves, infinitely recombinant information discourages them from pursuing the practices and activities that Gardner and Davis see as essential for the healthy development of self in the twenty-first century. Today's students struggle to slow down, ponder, reflect, and make broader connections to the real world in which they live. Most important, although experienced scholars such as Wesch, Gardner, Davis, and others can see unlimited potential in the changing rules of how information is ordered and accessed, for students with personal biographies still in flux and limited resources and experiences to draw upon, seeing the overall forest for all the virtual, ever-changing digital trees is difficult to say the least.

SCHOLARSHIP: TIME, LABOUR, AND DETAIL

What separates universities from other institutions in society is their ongoing commitment to scholarship and, to a great but not exclusive extent, print culture. Both of these commitments conflict with the media and information that the Millennials and Generation Z have used most of their lives, have always relied upon, and with which they are comfortable. To succeed fully in higher education—to genuinely benefit from all that postsecondary education has to offer—students entering universities and colleges must adjust to the demands and expectations of print culture. And for those who are willing to engage genuinely with that culture, the rewards are significant because it will provide the foundation and stability that will enable those students to take full advantage of e-culture and the changing rules of order with respect to information.

"A new medium is never an addition to an old one," McLuhan (1964) writes, "nor does it leave the old one in peace. It never ceases to oppress the older media until it finds new shapes and positions for them" (p. 174). Here, McLuhan captures the dilemma facing today's students and their instructors. Digital media and the Internet have reshaped the way the Millennials and Gen Zers approach information, but the institutions of higher learning have, for sound reasons, resisted those new approaches and information forms.

The print culture of university professors rests on the labour-intensive, time-consuming study of texts and data. True scholars build knowledge over decades of long hours devoted to studying things, concepts, events, and ideas. Scholars and researchers labour to make precise connections, to apprehend and grasp complex wholes. Their work demands an ongoing, close, careful, and critical commitment to detail because, often, a tiny difference is of monumental significance.

A small example from Wesch's (2007a) "A Vision of Students Today" illustrates the point. Wesch (2007a) misquotes Josiah F. Bumstead, who argued that whoever invented the chalkboard (blackboard) deserved considerable credit. Wesch writes, "The inventor of the system" instead of "The inventor or introducer of the chalkboard system." That might seem a trivial error, but, upon close examination, it proves otherwise.

Bumstead, in his 1841 essay, had *one very specific system* in mind—the erasable chalkboard as a new means or system of communication within education. Wesch's error—"the system"—moves the mind instantly to notions of a far larger and perhaps even ominous and oppressive system, such as "the education system" or, worse, the dystopian sounding invention of "*the* system" that one finds in George Orwell's (1949) *Nineteen Eighty-Four* or

Eugene Zamiatin's ([1924] 1952) *We*. Perhaps that is how Wesch actually feels—at least about "the education system"—but it is not what Bumstead had in mind (Wesch 2008b).

Many might respond that few, if any, will notice Wesch's error, and it will probably turn out to be irrelevant to anyone watching the video. But, although the first point might be correct, the second one certainly is not.

Wesch's videos are all about digital information and the social and political responsibilities that go along with it. He is painstaking in putting them together—they are original productions of images, music, sound, and text. Wesch's error is almost Freudian because, if people do not understand "*the* system"—the system of digitally based information and hypertexts—then everyone is in danger of being dominated by it because people would no longer consciously control their own creations.

Wesch is a scholar; his work is precise; his videos pay close attention to detail in the lives of his students and to the information world that surrounds them. He studies both with care. Drawing the Millennials and Gen Z into the information age of the twenty-first century as careful, critical scholars, focused on detail while keeping the "bigger picture" in front of them is clearly his goal. It is also the task he sets for all students in postsecondary education today. Without identifying it as such, Wesch is pinpointing an important element in the intersection "of man and society, of biography and society, of self and world" for the Millennials, Generation Z, their instructors, and everyone living in Canada, the United States, and other technologically enhanced societies today (Mills 1959:5).

OLD SCHOOL—NEW SCHOOL: RE-SCHOOLING BOTH

E-culture and **print culture** exist together. Each has its advocates and detractors, but institutions of postsecondary education have to adjust to both. To draw upon the strengths of each means that students and professors must adapt to the structural realities of education in the twenty-first century.

Thus, although "old school" professors may lament what students lose by ignoring the print culture that Johannes Gutenberg helped introduce in the mid-fifteenth century, they have to recognize the extent to which digital media have made it easier and faster for increasingly larger numbers around the globe to access the written word. Digital technology makes print culture more widely available.

Contemporary postsecondary instructors must also recognize that today's students live in a world of continuously changing texts and images, which they download and upload from the Internet with a mouse click or a tap on a tablet or smartphone. The videos on YouTube might be authentic or cleverly constructed fictions and hoaxes; in either case, they are short audiovisual entertainment-information packages that are a standard part of students' everyday stocks of knowledge at hand, conversation, and insight into the world in which they live.

The "new technologies" are also new systems of communication that have to be evaluated in much the same way that Bumstead assessed the erasable chalkboard. The chalkboard allowed an instructor to provide visual illustrations to different points and ideas and, "in real time," alter those images. Digital technology allows an instructor to tap into students' senses and sensibilities in ways that can create a powerfully emotional atmosphere to underline certain material appropriately. Learning can be enhanced significantly as clear, cold, logical reasoning is supplemented by dynamic images and emotionally stirring audiovisual essays. Indeed, as a frequently quoted McLuhan (n.d.) aphorism notes, "Anyone who tries to make a distinction between education and entertainment doesn't know the first thing about either." In addition, as McLuhan (1962) emphasizes by quoting Ruskin, the media of the electric age allow instructors to present images to students that provide insight that would take "a long time to express in any verbal way," leaving students to make connections themselves as the interpretive and creative mind fills in the gaps in a manner that linear thought cannot (p. 93).

Instructors and professors must recognize that the life experiences of Millennials and Gen Zers, including their experiences within the formal education system, have led them, for the most part, to treat the printed text—the most stable source of knowledge for 500 years—as simply one ancillary form of information, and one that competes with the symbolically rich, active, high-resolution, audiovisual vignettes, stories, and statements that they can find, produce, quickly edit, save, play, pause, replay, and relay across the globe in seconds or store on their smartphones for future reference. Cyberspace is a reality that old-school professors must understand and use more extensively.

If old-school instructors need educating, "new-school" students need some schooling too. The students of the twenty-first century have to recognize that there are approaches to information and knowledge that offer deeper, more enriching forms of learning than those with which they are so familiar. Although today's students have not had the same relationship that their Boomer or Generation X parents have had with texts and textual material in hard copy, they must learn that there is much to be gained by devoting time to an enduring, static printed page. "Calm, focused, undistracted, the linear mind [of print culture]," Carr (2011) reminds his readers, "as supple as it is subtle, ... [is] the imaginative mind of the Renaissance, the rational mind of the Enlightenment, the inventive mind of the Industrial Revolution, even the subversive mind of Modernism" (p. 10). The power of print culture and the literary mind is a proven resource of enormous consequence.

Slowing down to reread a paragraph and decide if it really is worth labouring over is not easy for students whose educational past has continually emphasized moving forward almost relentlessly. Giving time—devoting large blocks of undisturbed, active, concentrated time and attention—to an unchanging, discipline-demanding medium such as a printed text is a difficult task for the current generation of students to embrace, but it is vital to their education.

The cooler the medium, the greater the onus is on the receiver to construct the message. If the medium is the message, the most critically important meaning in a cool medium is the active engagement it demands and enables. After years of conducting their lives at high speed, those entering university need to slow down, stop, retrace a path—a few pages, a single page, a paragraph, sentence, or specific word. This is an approach to reading and information gathering that many first year students must learn and develop throughout their undergraduate studies. Attending to detail and engaging in critical reflection are truly liberating experiences—and both are essential to higher education—but this is a freedom one must struggle to achieve.

Thus, the Millennials and Generation Z need to discover the awe and inspiration of running a finger over the volumes—old and new—on the library shelves. Browsing the stacks is an invitation into a world of contemplative pleasure and mystery that connects generations and eras of knowledge. Most important, it is a vital step toward changing the world as an informed citizen drawing upon a set of developing, fully self-conscious values and commitments.

The work world into which today's first year students will graduate is fully global; trade barriers have fallen, and the competition for work is no longer local, provincial, or even national. Governments strive to attract businesses that will bring jobs, and their success is tied to the global capitalism of the late twentieth century (Castells 1999, 2010; Ferguson 2001; Frieden 2006; Harvey 2005; Hobsbawm 1994; Kocka 2016). When one country or one region of a country can offer low-cost labour, other countries or regions, if they are to remain competitive, must do the same. There are inescapable global pressures on every aspect of the labour market to provide either low-cost labour or absolutely unique, highly sought after skilled workers. Although the first year sociology student might be thinking of a secure, high-paying job upon graduation, the labour market is currently creating more short-term, poorly paid, low-skill jobs than long-term, highly paid managerial ones.

No student should read these comments with despair; she or he should, however, read them with an acute sense of the intersection of self and world. More important, each student should see the present situation as an invitation to learn more, so they can better assess their present and future and build the full skill set that will prepare them best to succeed as they move into that future.

There is no better place to begin such an analysis than in university. And even though the task and promise of undergraduate study has changed over the last few decades, if old-school professors are able to embrace digital information and its interactive capacities more fully while their students develop the demanding skills of deep reading and reflective contemplation that have characterized print culture since Gutenberg, then both will prevail in creating and refining a postsecondary educational experience appropriate for the twenty-first century.

Key Terms and Names

natural attitude
everyday stocks of knowledge at hand
recipe knowledge
C. Wright Mills
the sociological imagination
personal troubles of milieu
public issues of social structure
Manuel Castells
information age
Marshall McLuhan
typographic and mechanical era
electric age
the medium is the message
hot medium
cool medium
digitization projects
continuous partial attention / hyper attention
information revolution
app-enabled
app-dependent
e-culture
print culture

Questions for Review and Further Reflection

1. What is meant by the terms "natural attitude" and "everyday stocks of knowledge at hand"? Why might the natural attitude and one's everyday stock of knowledge at hand make it difficult to think sociologically?
2. What are the three key elements in Mills's "sociological imagination?"
3. What are the characteristics of "personal troubles of milieu" and "public issues of social structure?" What is the relationship between the two for Mills? Is one more important for sociologists than the other?

4. Describe and characterize in your own words the three main sets of questions that Mills sets out to guide sociological analyses.

5. Create a mind map of Mills's main ideas. In a short paragraph, note how Mills's ideas take one beyond "the natural attitude" and into a sociological frame of reference.

6. As Castells states,

> Human societies are made from the conflictive interaction between humans organized in and around a given social structure. This social structure is formed by the interplay between relationships of production/consumption; relationships of experience; and relationships of power. Meaning is constantly produced and reproduced through symbolic interaction between actors framed by this social structure, and, at the same time, acting to change it or to reproduce it.

Using Canada or the United States as your reference point, provide some specific examples or instances that will make a case for the accuracy of Castells's insight.

7. McLuhan argues that humans build objects, tools, technologies, and media that extend and intensify humankind's various senses, sensibilities, capacities, and powers. Write out one example from the text that demonstrates what McLuhan means by the statement. Now try to write out a second example based on your own understanding of what he means, an example not discussed in the text.

8. What does McLuhan mean by his aphorism "the medium is the message?"

9. What are the respective characteristics of a "hot medium" and a "cool medium?" Provide examples of each, and describe the relationship between hot and cool media.

10. What is meant by the terms "continuous partial attention" and "hyper attention?" Why do some scholars think that today's students may exhibit these types of attention? What challenges would they pose for students and for instructors?

11. What do Gardner and Davis mean by the terms "app-dependent" and "app-enabling?"

12. In view of all the information presented in this chapter, think of your own personal biography and its intersection with history, social structure, and the existing digital media. Briefly sketch out a short analysis of how well prepared you are for postsecondary education as well as what your limitations might be.

3

THE LIGHT OF REASON: HIGHER EDUCATION'S CHALLENGES

Main Objectives

This chapter will

1. Encourage students to reflect critically upon the nature of higher education, their own goals for postsecondary study, and the strengths and limitations that will influence their success.
2. Introduce three different views of "the university": the "English" conception stemming from John Henry Cardinal Newman's *The Idea of a University Defined and Illustrated*, the "Prussian" conception established by Wilhelm von Humboldt, and the American idea of the "multiversity" developed by Clark Kerr.
3. Describe some of the large social forces that have shaped the structure and nature of universities in the contemporary period.
4. Introduce the term "neoliberalism" and outline how, as a social, economic, and political philosophy, it is influencing the postsecondary student experience.
5. Consider the idea of "craftsmanship," in general; describe C. Wright Mills's particular conception of "intellectual craftsmanship"; and indicate how those conceptions, put into practice, can positively influence students' success within the postsecondary education system and beyond.

In his overview of the history of universities, George Fallis (2007), the former Dean of the Faculty of Arts at Canada's third largest university—York University in Toronto—indicates that "[r]egardless of its type, the central task of a university has always been undergraduate education" (p. 18). Nevertheless, as other demands from within and outside the university have arisen to compete with this central task, today's students and instructors face a growing number of constraints, tensions, and seemingly irresolvable problems as they try to make the undergraduate experience the best it can be.

Based on their own extensive review of the scholarly literature on student experiences in higher education and their intensive interviews with students themselves, Charity Johansson and Peter Felten (2014) find that most college and university students today expect to become "more of the person they already are, not someone new" (p. 10). Few expect the postsecondary experience to transform them significantly. But, Johannson and Felten maintain, whether students or universities like it or not, the undergraduate experience is one of significant personal transformation, and this change should be a critical focal point for students, instructors and university administrators.

> When students first arrive on campus, they carry backpacks heavy with habits, beliefs, expectations, and relationships that will shape their experiences in college. Some of these enable students to experience exciting growth and change. Others constrain, leading them to be cautious about or even fearful of what's ahead. Whatever the nature and balance of the things they are carrying, all first-year students, whether they realize it or not, stand on the threshold of transformation. (P. 10)

"To fulfill the promise of undergraduate education," Johansson and Felten emphasize, colleges and universities must provide students with an appropriately broad overall educational experience that facilitates a full and positive personal, intellectual, and social transformation. However, their concern that higher education is failing to provide students with the opportunities for such personal growth is certainly not new.

The best known account is *The Closing of the American Mind: How Higher Education Has Failed Democracy and Impoverished the Souls of Today's Students*, by **Allan Bloom** (1987). Bloom's book is one of the most scathing, controversial, and intellectually rigorous critiques of higher education as it stood at the end of the twentieth century. It generated and continues to spark a debate that goes well beyond the ivy-clad walls of universities. When it was published, Bloom's book sold over a million copies and spent 10 weeks on the *New York Times* bestseller list (Smith and Bender 2008). More recently, Dinesh D'Souza's (1992) *Illiberal Education*, Peter Emberley and Waller Newell's (1994) *Bankrupt Education*, Bill Readings's (1996) *The University in Ruins*, Annette Kolodny's (1998) *Failing the Future: A Dean Looks at Higher Education in the Twenty-First Century*, and Côté and Allahar's (2007) *Ivory Tower Blues* also express concerns that are similar to Bloom's.

In *The Closing of the American Mind*, Bloom (1987) emphasizes that professors in higher education "must constantly try to look toward the goal of human completeness and back at the natures of [their] students here and now, ever seeking to understand the former and to assess the capacities of the latter to approach it" (p. 19). Emberley and Newell (1994) make a similar point writing that it is "the duty of the teacher to impart and cultivate those talents and excellences which would prepare a student to bear the obligations of citizenship and to begin the exploration of the intellectual and spiritual life" (p. 3).

Johansson and Felten's (2014) *Transforming Students: Fulfilling the Promise of Higher Education* demonstrates that, in a time of economic crises, ever-changing social expectations, continuous technological innovation, and chronic uncertainty, it is more important than ever for the undergraduate years to prepare students to successfully negotiate the future. Providing students with the knowledge and skills needed to develop and transform themselves into mature, informed, critically aware, well-rounded adults is the "fundamental purpose of higher education" (p. 1). Johansson and Felten (2014) quote from author and social activist Wendell Berry's (1987) essay "The Loss of the University" to emphasize their point:

> The thing being made in a university is humanity ... not just trained workers or knowledgeable citizens but responsible heirs and members of human culture. If the proper work of the university is only to equip people to fulfill private ambitions, then how do we justify public support? If it is only to prepare citizens to fulfill public responsibilities, then how do we justify the teaching of arts and sciences? The common denominator has to be larger than either career preparation or preparation for citizenship. Underlying the idea of university—the bringing together, the combining into one, of all of the disciplines—is the idea that good work and good citizenship are the inevitable by-products of the making of a good—that is, a fully developed—human being. This, as I understand it, is the definition of the name *university*. (P. 77)[19]

As clear and adamant as Berry or Johansson and Felten are about the nature of a university and its mission, their positions are more contested than most students might realize.

What Is a University?

Berry, Bloom, Côté and Allahar, D'Souza, Emberley and Newell, Kolodny, and Johansson and Felten, directly or indirectly, all draw their inspiration and many of their arguments from a very long and stalwart tradition in English higher education. The principles of this vision are most clearly set out in two classic works. The first, which Fallis (2007:19) identifies as

---

19 This is a more complete quotation than the abbreviated citation in Johansson and Felten (2014:1).

"the most influential book ever written in the English language on universities" is by **John Henry Cardinal Newman** ([1852] 1886), *The Idea of a University Defined and Illustrated.* The second is Matthew Arnold's ([1868] 1932) *Culture and Anarchy.*[20] Newman and Arnold are both writing as British institutions are adjusting to the economic and social realities of an expanding industrial society. Both want to ensure that the education system prevents individuals in a market-driven, industrial world from living an intellectually impoverished existence. To make their case, Newman and Arnold draw upon conceptions of education found in classical Greek philosophy and upon the early conceptions of the university as these developed in medieval Europe.

In a series of inaugural lectures and essays that Newman ([1852] 1886) writes after establishing the Catholic University of Ireland, he is clear about the idea of a university:

> The view taken of a University in these Discourses is the following:— That it is a place of *teaching* and universal *knowledge.* This implies that its object is, on the one hand, intellectual, not moral; and, on the other, that it is the diffusion and extension of knowledge rather than the advancement. If its object were scientific and philosophical discovery, I do not see why a University should have students; if religious training, I do not see how it can be the seat of literature and science. (P. ix)

In *Culture and Anarchy*, **Matthew Arnold** ([1868] 1932) advises that the well-educated, cultured individual should know, "on all the matters which most concern us, the best which has been thought and said in the world" (p. 6). He emphasizes that culture, "which is the study of perfection," leads individuals "to conceive of true human perfection as a harmonious perfection, developing all sides of our humanity; and as a general perfection, developing all parts of our society" (p. 11). The cultured, well-educated individual develops a spirit and character that unites "the two noblest of things, sweetness and light," Arnold emphasizes ([1868] 1932:54). He sets lofty goals and aspirations for the experience of higher education.

Today's undergraduate students face at least one barrier that might prevent them from transforming themselves as much as they potentially could

---

20 Matthew Arnold is the son of Thomas Arnold who had a profound and lasting impact upon the British public school system. Appointed Rugby's headmaster in 1828, Thomas Arnold fundamentally reshaped the school. He introduced modern history, modern languages (in addition to Greek and Latin), mathematics, and the prefect system in which students maintained order themselves. Arnold also emphasized the role of athletics in developing character and moral fibre. Along with Canon Kingsley, Arnold is seen as one of the founders of "muscular Christianity"—a movement that influenced everything from religion and education to Baron Pierre de Coubertin's image of the Olympic Games (Beamish and Ritchie 2006:11–30; Fitch 1898). The Rugby experience is captured in detail in Thomas Hughes's (1857) classic *Tom Brown's Schooldays.*

and from realizing the full promise of higher education, as put forward by Newman and Arnold. That barrier stems from their longstanding involvement with the Internet and digital information. As Chapter 1 details, the everyday stocks of knowledge at hand and the approaches to learning and expression that the Millennials and Gen Zers developed because of their early and continuous immersion in e-culture do not prepare them fully for the print-culture world of higher education. Students end up expending a considerable amount of energy and time throughout their studies just developing the disciplined, linear, literary frame of mind that will enable them to maximize their postsecondary experience. But that is not the only reason many students fail to realize the full promise of higher education; it is not even the most important one.

More significant than the personal or collective biographies of contemporary students is how their biographies intersect with particular aspects of social structure and history. In *Academic Transformation*, Ian Clark, Greg Moran, Michael Skolnik, and David Trick (2009) document how the constraints placed upon institutions of higher learning in the twenty-first century make the genuine, positive, and expanding transformation of today's students quite difficult (see also Kolodny 1998; Readings 1996). These modern limitations and tensions actually begin in the early nineteenth century and were the consequence of a different vision of higher education than the English model of Newman and Arnold.

A few years after Napoleon's defeat of Prussia in 1806, King Friedrich Wilhelm III assigned **Wilhelm von Humboldt** the task of establishing the University of Berlin as the first step in creating a modern nation. Humboldt had been appointed director of education at the Prussian Ministry of the Interior in 1809. Drawing upon Germany's greatest Enlightenment thinker, Immanuel Kant, and his idea that real knowledge (*Wissenschaft*) only arises through scientific inquiry (*wissenschaftliche Forschung*) and critique, Humboldt made research a central aspect of the Prussian university system (see Fallis 2007; Sigurdson 2013). This decisive departure from Newman's idea of a university had four particular outcomes.

First, German professors did not remain generalists with expertise across the full range of subject matter. They became specialists in narrow fields of knowledge. The German research university of the nineteenth century, then, laid the groundwork for the growth of a number of specific, separate, specialized areas of knowledge and stimulated the formation of the numerous departments found in higher education today.

Second, the idea arose that the real goal of research is to continually test existing knowledge with the power of human reason. This means that universities become the site of a constant tension among tradition, existing knowledge, and the ongoing critical, rational inquiry of the research community.

Third, for knowledge to advance continually, professors must have the freedom to follow their research wherever it leads them—they must be guaranteed academic freedom (*Lehrfreiheit*). Being freed from the constraints of tradition and political or religious interference, academic freedom also ensures that researchers do not have to consider or worry about the utility of their work. Research is guided exclusively by a passion for knowledge, the pursuit of truth, and the honest commitment to following the results of critical inquiry no matter where the logic and evidence leads.

Finally, because critical reason is so central to academic inquiry, as Humboldt defined and established it at the University of Berlin in 1810, the liberal arts with their emphases on rational critique become the most prestigious fields of knowledge. The arts rank above applied faculties such as law, medicine, or theology. In a university dominated by reason, critique, and academic freedom, philosophy—not professional schools or concerns— dominates (Fallis 2007; Humboldt 1963).

Throughout most of the modern period, these two visions of higher learning coexist: the university as the guardian and disseminator of universal knowledge and the university as the generator of specialized research, knowledge, and critical inquiry. The faculty and administrators of the universities in this era believe they are combining the best of both worlds. And it seems that way to most. Within the intimacy of small classes, colleges provide the fundamentals of a liberal education that Newman, Arnold, and many others would consider the ideal undergraduate experience. Larger research-intensive universities provide a less intimate experience, but students in those institutions benefit from the expertise of research-oriented professors who use their cutting-edge knowledge of a discipline to inform their undergraduate instruction. In both cases, universities maintain an existence as separate as possible from commercial pressures and purely utilitarian goals.

By the 1930s, as Abraham Flexner ([1930] 1994) documents, universities begin to transform dramatically.[21] More and more departments have come into existence; institutes now exist within universities; there are vast research libraries; medicine is put into the hands of research scientists rather than doctors. The modern university, Flexner ([1930] 1994) writes, is "an institution consciously devoted to the pursuit of knowledge, the solution of problems,

---

21 Marking a significant break from traditional education, after a 10-year debate over curriculum reform, Yale drops Latin and Greek as required courses for undergraduate students in 1931. Esteemed visiting political studies professor Harold Laski, from the University of London, decries the decision: "Your academic system destroys intellectual initiative. The first thing I would abolish would be compulsory lectures and after that the term and lesser examinations." A Princeton professor emeritus, Henry van Dyke, is equally opposed because "[n]o other studies, with the possible exception of mathematics, have proved as valuable for the training of the mind in clear thought and accurate expression." In the midst of a 15-year debate, Harvard was considering similar changes (see *New York Times* 1931:18).

the critical appreciation of achievement and the training of men at a really high level" (p. 42). "The heart of a [modern] university is a graduate school of arts and sciences, the solidly professional schools (mainly, in America, medicine and law) and certain research institutes" (p. 179).

From the University to the Multiversity

Although tensions exist and universities do not meet all of their students' goals and expectations during the first half of the twentieth century, the real contradictions between the ideal images of higher education and what colleges and universities can actually deliver become apparent amidst the optimism of the post–World War II period. As North American economies expand and governments play an increasingly active role in preparing the Baby Boom generation for the coming of post-industrial society, the debate over the **idea of the university** is rekindled.

To accommodate the postwar baby boom, elementary schools, followed by high schools, are built to accommodate the population bulge as it moves through the education system. By the mid-1960s, North America experiences a rapid growth in university and college enrolment as the Boomers, because of their sheer numbers and their growing rate of participation in postsecondary education, demand more places in institutions of higher learning (Best 2011; Pryor, Hurtado et al. 2007). However, even though the expansion of postsecondary education enables more students to transform and broaden their horizons, the changes made to accommodate the Boomers initiate several conditions—both immediate and long term—that ultimately constrain the mission of colleges and universities (Levitt 1984; Owram 1996; Palmer 2009).

In a very early intervention in what he sees as the emerging crisis in education, Bloom ([1966] 1990) argues that the decline in postsecondary education begins with two major events—the Soviet Union's successful launch of Sputnik on October 4, 1957, and the student movement's demonstrations at several major American universities throughout 1965.

The Sputnik launch shakes American self-confidence to the core. Unjustified as the fear is, the United States becomes concerned that the Soviet Union's early success in the space race means that it possesses superior scientific capabilities. The US response to this fear dramatically changes the focus of higher education across North America and ultimately western Europe.

To close the "science gap," American politicians and university administrators direct more resources toward the natural sciences and into applied research projects (Best 2011:5–6). The funding made available for applied research projects triggers the growth of research-intensive universities and cooperation among the universities, government, and the private sector. With more money, political, and social attention, the sciences and scientific knowledge rise in prestige; philosophy loses its perch at the top of the knowledge hierarchy (Bourdieu [1984] 1988).

To meet the growing need for research scientists, the education system begins to recruit the best and the brightest students to science programs. This active recruitment makes university entrance, particularly into the science streams, more competitive. To ensure that students with the best aptitudes for advanced learning are admitted to the growing number of research-intensive universities, standardized tests such as the Scholastic Aptitude Test are introduced.

Over time, both the competition for students and the specialization of programs spread from the sciences to social science and humanities programs, and universities increasingly become centres for training specialized experts. The intense specialization in all disciplines reduces communication across them. The *uni*versity that brings together diverse forms of knowledge into one place becomes, according to **Clark Kerr** (1963), the *multi*versity (Bloom [1966] 1990).

Kerr, the architect of the state of California's public higher education system, is an unabashed advocate for the multiversity system. The multiversity is the result of a long process of historical development, which Kerr outlines in his prestigious Godkin Lecture at Harvard. Newman's idea of the university, Kerr (1963) reminds his audience, is "a single community—a community of masters and students" animated by a single soul or "central animating principle" (p. 1). But even as Newman articulated his ideas, Kerr continues, the German system was becoming ascendant, and Newman's "beautiful world was being shattered forever as it was being so beautifully portrayed" (p. 3). Kerr turns next to Flexner, showing that his description of the university was out of date even as Flexner was articulating it. As early as 1930, most American universities were "a whole series of communities and activities held together by a common name, a common governing board, and related purposes" (p. 1). By the 1960s, Kerr emphasizes, the traditional image of the university is confined to history; it is the multiversity that has come to prevail in the contemporary period.

The **multiversity**, according to Kerr (1963), is "a complex and an inconsistent institution":

> It is not one community but several—the community of the undergraduate and the community of the graduate; the community of the humanist, the community of the social scientist, and the community of the scientist; the communities of professional schools; the community of all the non-academic personnel; the community of the administrators. Its edges are fuzzy—it reaches out to alumni, legislators, farmers, businessmen, who

are all related to one or more of these internal communities. As an institution, it looks far into the past and far into the future, and is often at
odds with the present. It serves society almost slavishly—a society it also
criticizes, sometimes unmercifully. Devoted to equality of opportunity, it
is itself a class society. A community, like the medieval communities of
masters and students, should have common interests; in the multiversity,
they are quite varied, even conflicting. A community should have a soul,
a single animating principle; the multiversity has several—some of them
quite good, although there is much debate on which souls really deserve
salvation. (Pp. 18–19)

Bloom ([1966] 1990) concurs with Kerr's description of the multiversity
as the reality of higher education by the mid-1960s—with two additions.

First, Bloom argues that the prestige of science and its increasingly
applied and utilitarian focus has a profound impact on the paradigms of
"truth" and "knowledge" in the contemporary period. The successful use of
science and the experimental method to solve particular, applied problems
within the context of the multiversity supports an increasingly atheoreti-
cal, empiricist approach to knowledge and research (see also Gulbenkian
Commission 1996). Also, the rising prestige of the natural sciences and the
declining status of the humanities foster the widespread adoption of a natural science-like approach to knowledge within the social sciences (see also
Bourdieu [1984] 1988).

Bloom's second addition is that within the multiversity, the pursuit of
the "bigger," enduring, unanswerable questions of human existence is marginalized or abandoned. University education becomes more focused and
career outcomes guide students' course selection and their programs of study.

By the mid-1960s, Bloom ([1966] 1990) argues, universities are no longer "preserves for the quiet contemplation of the permanent questions [of
humanity]" (p. 349). The multiversity does not provide the opportunity for
serious students to explore questions like the nature of justice or solutions
to social inequality. Education is now technical and practical.

The narrower, careerist focus of the emerging postsecondary education
system may not be an issue for the majority of students in the 1960s and
beyond; however, Bloom ([1966] 1990) maintains, "for that most interesting
few who can become leaders, pathfinders, and revolutionaries this is a great
source of dissatisfaction" (p. 349). Bloom ventures that the student movement and the campus unrest of the 1960s resulted because universities failed
to meet the needs of their best students.

Although Bloom understands the source of student dissatisfaction in
the 1960s, he does not support the positions or actions that student leaders
took in opposing the multiversity system. On the contrary, Bloom thinks
that, although the student movement represented certain lofty sentiments,

its leaders and supporters did not, and could not, base their claims on an intellectual and knowledge foundation sufficient for determining what was truly significant. Why? The student movement's participants did not have an adequate knowledge base because their life experiences had not challenged them deeply enough—they were, as Cyril Levitt (1984) observes, "children of privilege." Here is the description Bloom ([1966] 1990) gives of the students of the sixties:

> [I]t would be hard to imagine a generation with so little in the way of roots or real education. Their tastes have been given no formation at all, and the learning that has been poured into them gives them competencies but fails to move them. The students' interpretations of the world come from the newspapers and from what is in the air, and neither church, home, nor school add much to that. They know mathematics, for example, but it is taken as a skill and does not inspire them to the theoretical life; nor do they conceive of it as a tool with which to understand nature and hence themselves. (P. 351)

The university experience, Bloom (1987) posits, should allow students to wrestle with the permanent concerns of humanity. It should encourage students to try to obey the Delphic oracle's command: "Know thyself." Higher education should make students aware that, when it comes to the critical question both of education and of life—What is humankind?—"the answer is neither obvious nor simply unavailable" (p. 21). Students should learn that for truly serious individuals, the question arising from the oracle's command remains a continuous issue. In a world of chronic uncertainty, one should continually examine and think about the alternative answers that go as far back as classical Greek philosophy and beyond. The most important result of such an educational experience, Bloom insists, is a student who "is able to resist the easy and preferred answers, not because he is obstinate but because he knows others worthy of consideration" (p. 21).

Bloom's fundamental concern is that the structural changes made throughout the 1960s now prevent higher education from fulfilling its true mandate—stimulating personal growth and broad intellectual development:

> What image does a first-rank college or university present today to a teen-ager leaving home for the first time, off to the adventure of a liberal education? He has four years of freedom to discover himself—a space between the intellectual wasteland he has left behind and the inevitable dreary professional training that awaits him after the baccalaureate. In this short time he must learn that there is a great world beyond the little one he knows, experience the exhilaration of it and digest enough of it to sustain himself in the intellectual deserts he is destined to traverse.

He must do this, that is, if he is to have any hope of a higher life. These are charmed years when he can, if he so chooses, become anything he wishes and when he has the opportunity to survey his alternatives, not merely those current in his time or provided by careers, but those available to him as a human being. The importance of these years for an American [or Canadian] cannot be overestimated. They are civilization's only chance to get him. (Bloom 1987:336)

Two points arise from Bloom's analysis and commentary. The first is the despair that some students and professors might feel both because of his scathing critique of higher education, which seems to offer few prospects for change, and because of how little things have *actually* changed in the ensuing quarter century. But as Mills (2000) emphasizes in one of several letters written to "Tovarich," an imaginary Soviet colleague, "it is possible to live in an overdeveloped society but not be an underdeveloped person" (p. 278).[22] It depends on how one handles the "unpleasant features of oneself and one's condition." And truly handling one's condition means more than making personal commitments; Mills, like Bloom, sought real social change through informed social action.

While acknowledging and respecting the inertia of social structure and history, Mills also recognizes the significance and power of human agency; change occurs because people choose to act, resist, and advocate for their informed positions. Making the best of one's condition—treating it as a personal trouble of milieu and using one's wilful actions to create change—while knowing it is also a public issue of social structure—and drawing upon the support of others—is how human agents make their own history and create their own future. In his essay "On Intellectual Craftsmanship," written to inspire students and guide their studies, Mills (1959) addresses the task cogently.

Do not allow public issues as they are officially formulated, or troubles as they are privately felt, to determine the problems that you take up for study.... Know that many personal troubles cannot be solved merely as troubles, but must be understood in terms of public issues—and in

---

22 Between 1956 and 1960, Mills writes a number of letters to Tovarich hoping to publish them, perhaps with a Soviet colleague writing responses from a Soviet perspective, under the tentative title *Contacting the Enemy: Tovarich*. Mills does not find a publisher for the project before his death. The Russian word товарищ (usually tovarishch, tovarish, or tovarisch when written in the Roman or Latin alphabet) means "comrade" and denotes a particularly close friendship rather than a casual one. "Tovarich" was not an error in the collection Mills's daughters published; to maintain the authenticity of his thought and work, they consciously chose to use Mills's own transliteration in their edited collection of Mills's letters and autobiographical writings (see Mills 2000:xiii).

terms of the problems of history-making. Know that the human meaning of public issues must be revealed by relating them to personal troubles—and to the problems of the individual life. Know that the problems of social science, when adequately formulated, must include both troubles and issues, both biography and history, and the range of their intricate relations. Within that range the life of the individual and the making of societies occur; and within that range the sociological imagination has its chance to make a difference in the quality of human life in our time. (P. 226)

Although Bloom may not have read or drawn directly from *The Sociological Imagination*, his critique of higher education involves the intersection of biography, social structure, and history, and his goal is to spur students and faculty to struggle for change. Therefore, even though Bloom's analysis might cause initial despair, it also provides hope for and the possibility of change. Mills's understanding of how social change occurs means that the nature of the postsecondary experience still significantly rests in students' own hands. In making the very best of their condition, they can be important authors in reshaping higher education throughout the twenty-first century.

The second point is less positive. The concerns Bloom expressed in 1987 are more acute today as postsecondary education in Canada and the United States faces higher student enrolments, as a result of population increases and the highest participation rates in either nation's history (Best 2011:10–16, 33–34). As positive as the increasing democratization of higher education may be, that increase occurred as governments were withdrawing funding and their neoliberal policies made colleges and universities increasingly dependent upon market forces for financial support. It is the new neoliberal context that makes the situation facing universities and students today different than that of the 1960s.

"There has everywhere been an emphatic turn towards neoliberalism in political-economic practices and thinking since the 1970s," writes David Harvey (2005:2). **Neoliberalism** became deeply embedded in political practice and within the public consciousness during Margaret Thatcher's term as Britain's prime minister (1979–90), Republican Ronald Reagan's two-term presidency (1981–89), Helmut Kohl's chancellorship in Germany (1982–98), and Brian Mulroney's term as Canada's prime minister (1984–93).

The primary tenet of neoliberalism is the ordering and productive power of the "unseen hand" of the market. As a result, neoliberals believe that social well-being is best attained when individual entrepreneurial interests and skills are encouraged through the presence of private property rights, a laissez-faire market, and free trade. The role of government is minimized as much as possible. Government ensures that a vibrant market exists primarily through the legal system but also the police and military if necessary. In social undertakings that might not be able to operate for profit in the marketplace, such as education, health care, social security, or environmental protection, for example, government may play a role, but its involvement should be supportive rather than central. A fundamental premise of neoliberal theory is that a market-based economy is too complex for any single institution, such as the federal government, to have sufficient information to second-guess the regulating, unseen hand of the market. Neoliberals also believe that democratic governments are easily swayed by powerful groups with particular vested interests, which results in distorted investment practices whenever the government becomes heavily involved in the economy as a whole (see Harvey 2005:2).

The implementation of neoliberal governance creates a self-sustaining cycle. The change begins with public concerns about government debt and conservative political parties successfully persuading the electorate that the market itself can solve the problem. As those parties come to power and implement neoliberal policy, they use their positions of power to foster a broadening of public support for less government involvement in various areas of social life. As that sentiment gains strength, individuals increasingly support the idea that each person should solve his or her own problems through personal initiative and hard work. Social and economic problems that people had regarded as public issues of social structure are now defined as personal troubles of milieu related to one's personal experience and solved through an individual's own wilful activity. Neoliberalism seems to propose "common sense" solutions to the problems of government debt—the market will support what is needed and the institutions that cannot survive must not be that vital after all.

For many students maturing when neoliberal values and practices dominated social, economic, and political life, the goal of education came to be increasingly defined by the demands of the market: what degree will secure a financially successful career? Thus, the students who begin to prevail in universities and colleges had a particular and instrumental approach to their postsecondary education, and definite ideas about where it should lead. This frame of mind—in concert with the changes in the nature of universities and colleges outlined by Kerr (1963), Bloom ([1966] 1990, 1987), Fallis (2007), Clark et al. (2009), and others—is another reason that higher education today fails to challenge or encourage students to broaden themselves as individuals. No matter how one views neoliberalism and its impact upon universities today, it is clear that the current intersections of biography, history, and the structure of higher education lead students to approach their studies instrumentally—merely as a means to a job rather than as an opportunity for personal growth and transformation.

Many disagree with different aspects of Bloom's argument about why universities allegedly fail to provide a genuine liberal education, and others disagree with his proposed solutions, but even Bloom's sharpest critics agree that the four years a student spends in university are a golden opportunity that is too often wasted. Bloom's notion that those years represent a critical "space between the intellectual wasteland" the student has just left and "the inevitable dreary professional training that awaits" may overstate (or understate) the "before" and "after," but his phrasing certainly captures the unique opportunity that higher education offers—or should offer—all those who are privileged enough to partake in it.

In *The Closing of the American Mind*, Bloom's analysis and solutions turn on the importance of philosophy as a way of both knowing the world and exploring the permanent questions of humankind. In arguing for philosophy's significance, Bloom reflects his own personal, professional, and intellectual interests and strengths. But as Mills (1959) notes in a footnote about disciplines and interests, "every cobbler thinks leather is the only thing" (p. 19). So while Bloom can make a strong case for philosophy serving as the foundation of a truly transformative educational experience, the arguments he presents in his 1966 essay point to the need for a more encompassing solution.

In his early essay, Bloom ([1966] 1990) echoes Arnold's premise that the best way to open students' horizons is to help them "see the world as it was seen in the most thoughtful perspectives" (p. 359). But more than having students read, as Arnold ([1868] 1932:6) phrases it, "the best that has been thought and said in the world," professors should provide students with works "in the great tradition" that address issues of universality in a serious manner and raise questions relevant to life as a whole, according to Bloom ([1966] 1990). In addition, professors should encourage students to engage with the issues examined in those enduring texts "as they were understood by their authors, not fitting them into a pre-existing framework" (p. 359). Students should learn to see the world and its problems being systematically studied through the eyes of the great minds that first wrestled with these problems.

Bloom also acknowledges the benefits that the specialized expertise of professors within the multiversity can bring to the student experience. Rather than asking professors to teach outside their areas of research and study, the university, Bloom ([1966] 1990) maintains, should have them teach from within their areas of specialization but in a framework that enables them to relate their expertise to issues that will stimulate student growth. Professors should seek to persuade students of the importance of the material being covered and encourage them to see how it contributes to their growth and to their understanding of themselves and the world in which they live.

Bloom is writing before the Internet and e-culture begin to dominate students' habits and approaches to information and knowledge. In addition, the current need for students to find emotional security and career trajectories in a precarious world was not as urgent in the 1960s or even in the 1980s as it is today. Nevertheless, Bloom's proposals for improving the quality of the undergraduate experience by giving students the opportunity and tools to transform themselves dramatically through their involvement with higher education, while also developing specialized skills and knowledge, remain as vital for today's students as they were for those Bloom taught throughout his career.

Students learning about sociology are particularly fortunate because the best that has been thought and said in the discipline are studies that tackle the issues Bloom identifies as critical to a transformative undergraduate experience. Studying classic and contemporary works in sociology, as each author examines the intersection of personal biography, history, and social structure, takes students on an intellectual journey that challenges them to broaden their horizons and hone their academic skills. This study also prepares them for a wide array of occupational opportunities following their undergraduate studies.

There is, however, an important element missing from Bloom's proposals for improving the undergraduate experience. The process of knowledge production that occurs within universities is never a short-term commitment. It involves a significant investment of time and self to develop the background and research skills required by a discipline like sociology. The undergraduate years should be seen as an apprenticeship period during which students learn the craft of scholarship. Fortunately, Mills provides students with an excellent guide to learning this craft.

C. Wright Mills and Intellectual Craftsmanship

Mills's conception of the sociological imagination and his respect for the classical tradition in sociology stemmed largely from his intimate knowledge of the work of Marx, Durkheim, and Weber—three thinkers who are frequently referred to as the "founding fathers of sociology." Before learning about these three thinkers in the next few chapters and appreciating why the classical tradition influenced Mills's sociology so much and retains its relevance today, one should consider some questions that students often ask about Mills. What was he like? How did he die so young? Most important, what did sociology and the sociological imagination really mean to him?

While watching a production of *Medea* at Oberlin College on March 20, 1962, Mills's eldest daughter, Pamela, is called to the phone and learns that her father has died, at the age of 45, from a second myocardial infarction—a heart attack—at his home in West Nyack near New York City. "In the decades since then," she writes, "the ghost of my father has made many appearances, often provoked by gratifying references to his work" (P. Mills 2000:xxi). "Large and vibrant," she notes, the images have ranged from canoeing in Lake Temagami, where Mills built, from the ground up, a summer home, to the cadence of his voice as he read *David Copperfield* to her aloud or to sitting behind her father, feeling the throbbing power of the BMW motorcycle that Mills loved to race along an open road. But among all the memories, the image "that most impressed me," Pamela Mills (2000) indicates, "is that of a muscular figure of energy and determination, overflowing with ambitious plans for the future, envisioning books that would cut through official distortions to produce uncompromising versions of truth as his logical mind perceived it" (p. xxiii).

Mills's second daughter, Kathryn—"the only child in ... nursery school whose father delivered her there on his motorcycle and also let her honk the horn"—remembers being afraid of the dark and the way her father attempted to cure the fear (K. Mills 2000:xvii). "He took me on a daytime tour of our house," she writes, "armed with a flashlight, which he used to light up the far corners of every single closet, every single dark storage place—showing me that there was nothing frightening hiding in the darkness" (K. Mills 2000:xviii).

She continues,

> In my mind's eye, I can still see my father standing by the closet door shining his flashlight into the darkness. Yes, it was possible to light up the far corners. No, we should not be afraid to confront what we find there. I believe that my father's lesson for me was also his message to the world. His was the light of reason, humane purpose, and moral passion, and he struggled to dispel the darkness of apathy, confusion, and irresponsibility. (K. Mills 2000:xx)

Born in Waco, Texas, on August 28, 1916, Mills was a robust, strongly independent iconoclast who thought of himself as largely self-made:

> There is a certain type of man who spends his life finding and refining what is within him, and I suppose I am of that type.... [T]here is nothing I need that can be given to me by others. In the end, a man must go to bat alone. (Mills 2000:40)

Elsewhere, Mills notes that he did well at bat in spite of the circumstances into which he was born, that he did not owe much to his cultural or economic background. In one of his unfinished letters to Tovarich, Mills (2000) writes that his upbringing "contained no intellectual or cultural benefits." He informs his fictitious Soviet friend that he grew up in "houses that had no books and no music in them." Mills heard his first piece of classical music in his second year of university. "Thus intellectually and culturally I am as 'self-made' as it is possible to be" (pp. 28–29). The decision to pursue a postgraduate degree in sociology meant "a further cutting off of self from my family background and the social setting at large as well." Even as he first entered university, Mills (2000) felt set apart: "I think no one I had previously known, including family members, really counted for me as a point of reference. I was cut off and alone, and I felt it at the time" (p. 29).

Nevertheless, as independent and critical of his background as he was, Mills (2000) recognized that he owed a great debt to his parents. He credits his mother with nurturing his sensibilities and his sensitivity to the world around him, enabling Mills to tap into the "tang and feel" of any social situation (p. 41). From his father, a white-collar representative for an insurance company, Mills (2000) "absorbed the gospel and character of work, determination with both eyes always ahead":[23]

> That is part of the America he knows, and it is part of him too. There was a time when I thought he did not possess a feeling for craftsmanship. But I was wrong. It is merely that his line of effort is one I did not understand. Looking back, I see he always did a good job, that he never quit until it was finished. (P. 41)

Mills (2000) ends this letter to his parents, which he wrote in 1939, with these words: "So from both of you I have gotten a living craftsmanship" (p. 41). And it is this concept of craftsmanship and what it entails that rests at the centre of Mills's conception of the sociological imagination.

One of Mills's most important essays is directed explicitly at beginning students in sociology; it deals at length with what he calls "Intellectual Craftsmanship" (Mills 1959:195–226). "To the individual social scientist who feels himself a part of the classic tradition," Mills (1959) emphasizes, "social science is the practice of a craft" (p. 195).

Craftsmanship is a central, recurring theme in Mills's writing and in his approach to sociology. His discussion of intellectual craftsmanship stems from his analysis of the personal and social consequences resulting from the growing domination of white-collar work and the declining opportunities for craftsmanship in the work world of the twentieth century. The theme retains its relevance even today. Richard Sennett (2008) writes *The Craftsman* to explore the idea of craftwork in extensive and intensive detail. A craft worker, Sennett explains, is dedicated to good work for its own sake, and although it is possible "to get by in life without dedication," craftsmanship entails the "special human condition of being *engaged*" (p. 20). Craftwork

---

23 Another of Pamela's recollections reflects this same spirit in Mills: "I am no older than seven, and I see his hazel eyes behind horned-rimmed glasses intently focused on my face, teaching me to always look people straight in the eye when I talk to them. He wants me to be like he is—self-confident, straightforward, no-nonsense" (P. Mills, 2000:xxii).

represents skills developed to a high degree—ten thousand hours of experience is the commonly used measure for achieving sufficient expertise so that individuals can "feel fully and think deeply what they are doing once they do it well" (Sennett 2008:20). Craftsmanship extends far beyond even excellent technique; it involves the development of deeply imbedded tacit knowledge, "unspoken and uncodified in words." This knowledge becomes "a matter of habit, the thousand little everyday moves that add up in sum to a practice" (p. 77). True craftwork involves a level of skill and knowledge that lies beyond the capacity of language to explain (Sennett 2008:88–98).

To convey the essential character of craftsmanship, Sennett quotes Mills who, in turn, draws upon Marx:

> The laborer with a sense of craft becomes engaged in the work in and for itself; the satisfactions of working are their own reward; the details of daily labor are connected in the worker's mind to the end product; the worker can control his or her own actions at work; skill develops within the work process; work is connected to the freedom to experiment; finally, family, community, and politics are measured by the standards of inner satisfaction, coherence, and experiment in craft labor. (Quoted in Sennett 2008:27)

The ideal of craftsmanship, Mills points out, involves six major features. "There is no ulterior motive in work other than the product being made and the processes of its creation," Mills begins.

> The hope in good work, William Morris remarked, is hope of product and hope of pleasure in the work itself; the supreme concern, the whole attention, is with the quality of the product and the skill of its making. There is an inner relation between the craftsman and the thing he makes, from the image he first forms of it through its completion, which goes beyond the mere legal relations of property and makes the craftsman's will-to-work spontaneous and exuberant. (Mills 1951:220)

Second, because of the craft workers' spontaneous and exuberant "will-to-work," which makes the quality of both the product and the skills going into it central, the details of work become significant and are not seen as separate from the work process itself. Craft workers derive their main rewards intrinsically, as they successfully struggle to overcome any and all difficulties in the labour process. The satisfaction craft workers have in the finished product "infuses the means of achieving it"; and even difficulties encountered in the work experience can enhance this satisfaction because workers feel "finally victorious over that which at first obstinately resists [their] will" (Mills 1951:221).

Third, craft workers devise and follow their own plans; they can modify them and change the projected outcome. Control and responsibility for the end product gives added value and satisfaction in the planning and creative process leading to the completion of a project.

Thus, through their work, craft workers develop their skills and themselves as individuals. Self-development is not a goal but "the cumulative result obtained by devotion to and practice of [their] skills." Living in and through their work, craft workers "confess and reveal [themselves] to the world" (p. 222)—this self-revelatory potential is craftsmanship's fourth feature.

Fifth, there is no separation between work and play (see also Sennett 2008:269–74). True play occupies one happily, and if work occupies one happily then there is no distinction between the two. "[A]ctive craftsmanship, which is both play and work, is the medium of culture; and for the craftsman there is no split between the worlds of culture and work" (Mills 1951:223).

Finally, the "craftsman's work is the mainspring of the only life he knows; he does not flee from work into a separate sphere of leisure; he brings to his non-working hours the values and qualities developed and employed in his working time" (p. 223). But because creativity lies at the centre of craftsmanship, for work to be continually creative, there must be processes for rejuvenation; the sensitivities of renewal found in leisure must also be integrated in the craft worker's labour process.

On the basis of this idealized depiction of craftwork, Mills turns his attention in *The Sociological Imagination* to the precise features of the scholarly craft, or intellectual craftsmanship. Mills (1959:224–26) develops eight points in his full argument but five constitute the core of his conception.

Beginning with his final two points on craftsmanship, Mills maintains that the best scholars "do not split their work from their lives." They take both seriously and strive to use each to enrich the other and in the process develop and enrich themselves.

> Scholarship is a choice of how to live as well as a choice of career; whether he knows it or not, the intellectual workman forms his own self as he works toward the perfection of his craft; to realize his own potentialities, and any opportunities that come his way, he constructs a character which has as its core the qualities of the good workman. (Mills 1959:196)

In other words, the integration of life and work allows the scholar to use individual life experiences to reflect critically upon intellectual work while that work helps the scholar realize her or his own personal potential.

Mills (1959) also stresses a second dimension of integration—the integration of biography and social structure, the constant shifting from one perspective to the other that, in the process, develops "an adequate view of a total society and of its components" (p. 211). It is this nimbleness of

mind—imagination—that separates the craft worker from the mere techni-
cian. Mills emphasizes that playfulness of mind, backed by a fierce drive to
make sense of the world, is central to intellectual craftsmanship. Notice here
the unity of play and work that is critical to all forms of craftwork. Moreover,
the mental dexterity of scholarship is not an innate quality—it is a skill that
one develops and perfects through constant practice over time. One is not
born a scholar; one becomes one through work, imaginative creativity, and
commitment.

If the ability to integrate is the first element in intellectual craftsmanship—one that enables the craft worker to develop his or her character
and skills through hours too numerous to count of concentrated, exhaust-
ing, yet also playful, creative mental labour—the second is an active, ongoing commitment to learning. Mills's long-time friend, Ralph Miliband
(1968), emphasizes that every working day—"and every day was a working
day"—Mills was engaged in silent debate with authors across the political
and intellectual spectrum as he read books, journal articles, essays, and newspapers. "I have never seen anyone read as creatively as Mills did," Miliband
(1968) writes. "He couldn't even read a detective story without pencil in
hand" (p. 6).

The third building block in intellectual craftsmanship is the concerted,
difficult balancing act of applying critical reason to an empirically informed
analysis. Gaining enlightenment from a world where insight is obscured by
ideology, prejudice, and misrepresentation is fundamental to the craft of
sociological analysis, according to Mills. "All social scientists," Mills emphasizes, "are involved in the struggle between enlightenment and obscurantism"
(quoted in Miliband 1968:6).

Gathering empirical information is also critical to good sociology, as
Mills maintains and demonstrates in his own work, but the main purpose of
empirical inquiry "is to settle disagreements and doubts about facts" giving
arguments a substantive rather than a speculative basis (Mills 1959:205). But,
Mills continues, although "facts discipline reason," "reason is the advance
guard in any field of learning." A critical mind—one committed to intellectual craftsmanship and all that it entails—employing the sociological
imagination is the fundamental requirement of good sociology.

The fourth component to intellectual craftsmanship is the dissemination of one's research, which entails a commitment to public scrutiny and
criticism. For Mills, however, it is more than just making an argument publically available; the craft worker presents the best-honed argument possible.
In craftwork, product, process of production, and personal development are
all intertwined. That is the hope—the potential—in good craftwork. It is
what makes the will-to-work exuberant.

Mills laboured over the act of writing—it never came easily to him,
and he was rarely satisfied with the final result. No project was ever the

masterpiece he wanted it to be. In 1949, labouring over the manuscript of the book many regard as his best, Mills (2000) writes candidly to his close friend William Miller. The reflection merits quotation at length:

> I am disillusioned about *White Collar* again. I can't write it right. I can't get what I want to say about America in it. What I want to say is what you say to intimate friends when you are discouraged about how it all is. All of it at once: to create a little spotlight focus where the alienation, and apathy and dry rot and immensity and razzle dazzle and bullshit and wonderfulness and how lonesome it is, really, how terribly lonesome and rich and vulgar and god I don't know. Maybe that mood, which I take now to be reality for me, is merely confusion which of course might be so and still worthwhile if one could only articulate it properly.
>
> I can write an ordered statement of this and that; I can go lyric for a paragraph or two, I can moan well and feel sad sometimes without showing sentiment too cornily; but I cannot get them all into each sentence or even each chapter. I think, I really do, that my medium is not studies of *White Collar* people etc. but that I ought to launch out in some new medium that is not so restricting, but I don't have the guts to do that because my skill, my tested talent, is in handling the facts and contour according to my own brand of "social science." It is all too god damn much to try to do. The problem is the old problem of creation. How many minutes in a lifetime do we ever get that are creative in any sense? (P. 136)

Even an intellectual giant like Mills, struggling to organize and present his thoughts on paper, feels the same crushing doubts that every first year student will experience a number of times over while working on various writing assignments in the course of his or her undergraduate studies.

Creating an argument—presenting it clearly and with compelling force—is an intimidating task each and every time one must prepare something for public consumption and scrutiny. However, as daunting as the task may be, it is an unavoidable requirement of an intellectual's craft. Successful novelist and accomplished American essayist Harvey Swados deeply admired Mills for his "unending and humble desire to learn how to commit to paper with precision and fluency all that he believed" (quoted in Wakefield 2000:8). Writing with skill, precision, and fluency is a central component of intellectual craftsmanship. This accurate and creative presentation of information and ideas is also one of the final steps that will turn the sociological imagination from mere potential into an actual, active force in the world.

Even though writing is difficult, it is heartening to know that there are times when the words flow smoothly and the scholar or student can feel the joy of expressing ideas clearly and effortlessly. Writing to a friend in 1957,

Mills (2000) shares such a moment: "I must tell you, the world in which I live has again turned upside down: I am about to complete one book, and I am halfway through a second one." "I mean this literally," he continues. "Never have I written so continuously (yesterday I wrote for 15 hours) and, I do believe, turned out such [a] well written first draft" (p. 230).

The final aspect of intellectual craftsmanship that Mills (1959:198–204) emphasizes is keeping files and a journal. Mills is not alone in this practice. McLuhan also kept a dozen or more files as he developed his ideas for an essay, journal article, or book manuscript (McLuhan and McLuhan 1988).

In a pre-digital age, Mills and McLuhan kept paper files. McLuhan's son Eric describes the process his father followed:

> When he decided to start on a book, my father began by setting up some file folders—a dozen or two—and popping notes into them as fast as observations or discoveries, large or small, occurred to him. Often the notes would be on the backs of envelopes, or on scraps of paper and in his own special shorthand, sometimes a written or dictated paragraph or two, sometimes an advertisement or press clipping, sometimes just a passage, photocopied from a book, with notes in the margin, or even a copy of a letter just sent off to someone, for he would frequently use the letter as a conversational opportunity to develop or "talk out" an idea in the hope that his correspondent would fire back some further ideas or criticism. (McLuhan and McLuhan 1988:vii)

When the McLuhans were working on a new edition of *Understanding Media*, they kept 30 or 40 folders active, one for each chapter of the book, and they added files to sort material about the new technologies they encountered during research, "such as computers, video recorders, and cable TV" (p. vii). Like McLuhan's, Mills's files are the physical embodiment of how his life and work coalesced—a comment overheard or an apparently random flyer often went into his files along with extensive notes taken from the work of other scholars. Keeping files, Mills maintains, helps develop one's self-reflective habits and keeps one's "inner world awake."

According to Mills (1959), taking notes is critical to the intellectual craft. The mere taking of a note, he instructs, "is often a prod to reflection" (p. 199). Mills kept two sorts of notes. The first type captured the structure of an author's argument and noted important details. One could refer back to these notes for substantive information or to confirm the form and content of an argument. The second type—one that becomes more predominant as Mills gains experience—does not reflect the original author's argument but takes his or her ideas and recasts them within Mills's own developing position. The entries in McLuhan's files, as his son indicates, are of a very similar nature.

The files begin as almost random collections, but over time they coalesce into identifiable interests and projects. But the files are more than repositories of information. Simply keeping a file and updating it involves an active engagement with ideas—it is intellectual production. At the same time, a scholar's files can stimulate his or her sociological imagination and provide new questions or angles of inquiry. By simply resorting and rearranging a file, Mills notes, one may stumble upon different connections not seen previously or discover a hole in the information assembled, thus stimulating a new search for sources.

Perhaps the most profound comment Mills makes on his files is one that brings together the physical dimensions of scholarly activity—the collecting and sorting of information—with the demanding, creative task of assimilating and presenting that information in a clear, cohesive, precise argument. "Books," Mills (1959) writes, "are simply organized releases from the continuous work that goes into them" (pp. 200–1). McLuhan's gathering of information for his file long after *Understanding Media* had been published shows the same commitment to engaging continually with a research project when others might think all was said and done. For the true craft worker, no project is ever perfect, so publications are all steps along the road to that unattainable goal, which she or he never ceases striving to reach.

In his tribute to Mills, Miliband (1968) writes what stands as a fitting conclusion to the idea of intellectual craftsmanship.

> C. Wright Mills cannot be neatly labelled and catalogued. He never belonged to any party or faction; he did not think of himself as a "Marxist"; he had the most profound contempt for orthodox Social Democrats and for closed minds in the Communist world. He detested smug liberals and the kind of radical whose response to urgent and uncomfortable choices is hand wringing. He was a man on his own, with both the strength and also the weakness which go with that solitude. He was on the Left, but not of the Left, a deliberately lone guerrilla, not a regular soldier. He was highly organized, but unwilling to *be* organized, with self-discipline the only discipline he could tolerate…. In a trapped and inhumane world, he taught what it means to be a free and humane intellect. "Get on with it," he used to say. "Work." So, in his spirit, let us. (P. 11)

The work that lies immediately ahead is to become familiar with the scholarship of three thinkers whose contributions rank among "the best that has been thought and said" in sociology. Understanding the issues that Marx, Durkheim, and Weber address, from their particular perspectives, is the first step in discovering the roots of sociological inquiry and the source for Mills's passion for the sociological imagination. Equally as important, learning about Marx, Durkheim, and Weber is an opportunity for students to broaden their intellectual horizons and develop the tools of intellectual craftsmanship with which they can guide their own personal transformation within the undergraduate experience.

Key Terms and Names

> Allan Bloom
> John Henry Cardinal Newman
> Matthew Arnold
> Wilhelm von Humboldt
> the idea of the university
> Clark Kerr
> the multiversity
> neoliberalism
> craftsmanship
> intellectual craftsmanship

Questions for Review and Further Reflection

1. Write down the goals that you have for your university experience; what do you hope to experience and achieve over the next four years?
2. Two different images of "the university" are presented in this chapter. What are the characteristics of each? A third image is introduced by Kerr; what did he mean by "the multiversity?" Which of those three images is closest to what you thought university would be like? Which best describes the university or college at which you are studying?
3. Outline Bloom's argument about why universities have declined. What are the additional impacts of neoliberal policies on the nature of the university experience for today's students?
4. Mills argues that there are six major features to craftsmanship. List each of them, and in a sentence or two explain what they are. Are there aspects of craftsmanship that you think Mills has missed? If so, what are they?
5. In "On Intellectual Craftsmanship," Mills identifies eight different points, five of which are covered in the text. List the five along with a sentence or two to capture the essence of each. Do you think that this list needs to be updated to take into account the contemporary realities of e-culture and the Internet? If so, what needs to be changed and how? Imagine yourself developing these particular attributes, and describe what obstacles, both personal and societal, you would have to surmount to become an intellectual craftsperson?

PART TWO

The Classical Tradition

4

MARX AND THE DIALECTIC OF DYNAMIC, UNSTABLE SOCIAL FORMATIONS

Main Objectives

This chapter will

1. Introduce students to the Enlightenment and the role it played in the development of sociology as a discipline.
2. Provide a detailed examination of the work of Karl Marx—the "founder" of one of the dominant macrosociological frameworks used by sociologists.
3. Present the relationship between German idealist philosophy and political economy as it is developed in Marx's work.
4. Pinpoint key aspects in the intersection of Marx's personal biography, history, and social structure so as to build an appreciation for how his ideas developed and the magnitude and complexity of his project.
5. Detail three progressively more comprehensive understandings of the "base" and "superstructure" framework Marx presents in the 1859 preface to *Towards the Critique of Political Economy*.

Sociology is a child of **the Enlightenment** although certain elements extend back to Francis Bacon's *The Advancement of Learning* of 1604 and *Novum organum scientiarum* of 1620, René Descartes's 1637 *Discourse on the Method of Rightly Conducting One's Reason and Seeking Truth in the Sciences* and his 1641 *Meditations on First Philosophy*, as well as Isaac Newton's three-volume *Philosophiæ Naturalis Principia Mathematica* of 1687.[24] But it is the Enlightenment—usually dated from the rise of the French *philosophes'* works in 1740 through to the French Revolution of 1789—that is critical in shaping sociological thought and its overall ethos.

---

24 See Bacon (1864), Descartes (1911), and Newton (1953) for modern translations or reprints of these texts.

One can capture the spirit of the Enlightenment in three words—freedom, mastery, and progress. Enlightenment thinkers sought to escape the darkness of ignorance; the cruel, unknown vicissitudes of nature; the arbitrary constraints of religious dogma and mysticism; and the shackles of tradition. Knowledge obtained through the powers of human reason—enlightenment—would allow humankind to understand, control, and master the natural and social worlds. Enlightenment would also enable "the people" to control their lives and events rather than leaving them the passive, powerless objects of nature, the monarch, and the pope in Rome. Progress would be measured by the advancement of knowledge, personal control over individuals' lives, and the spread of freedom to more and more members of society. These three elements—freedom, mastery, and progress—intertwined to form a revolutionary force in western Europe during the eighteenth century.

Some of the key works of this period, which capture the spirit of freedom, mastery, and progress, include David Hume's *A Treatise of Human Nature* (published anonymously in 1739) and his 1748 *Enquiry Concerning Human Understanding*, which laid the foundation for British empiricism (Hume [1739–40] 1941, [1748] 1966). By focusing on "the nature of things themselves," Charles-Louis de Secondat, baron de La Brède et de Montesquieu—almost always referred to simply as Montesquieu—wrote, in 1748, one of the first real studies in sociology, *The Spirit of the Laws* (see Montesquieu [1748] 1989). In 1762, Jean-Jacques Rousseau ([1762] 1963) published *The Social Contract, or Principles of Political Right* to address questions of freedom, order, and governance in a manner that fundamentally challenged Hobbes's ([1651] 1968) *Leviathan* of 1651. Finally, *An Essay on the History of Civil Society*, by **Adam Ferguson** ([1767] 1971), and *An Inquiry into the Nature and Causes of the Wealth of Nations*, by **Adam Smith** ([1776] 1976), also addressed fundamental questions of freedom, social organization, and social progress.

Despite having a common spirit, at least three different intellectual traditions emerged from the Enlightenment and shaped sociology from its birth as a discipline. A largely Gallic tradition—the dominant one in North America up to the late 1950s—extends from Descartes and Montesquieu through Rousseau to Claude Henri de Rouvroy, comte de Saint-Simon and Auguste Comte and, ultimately, to Émile Durkheim (see Chapters 6 and 7). This tradition, which tends to be quantitative and somewhat ahistorical, opposes (or complements, depending on one's willingness to draw together opposites) a largely German tradition that emphasizes the importance of interpretive meaning in understanding social life.

The interpretive tradition is closely associated with Wilhelm Dilthey, Heinrich Rickert, Georg Simmel, and Max Weber (see Chapters 8 and 9). Interpretive sociology also tends to be more historical than the more natural, science-like, positivist tradition of Saint-Simon, Comte, and Durkheim (Aron 1964).

Finally, even though the ideas of **Karl Marx** and later Marxists circulated outside of sociology and, in many ways, opposed it as a "bourgeois science," various social events and a number of debates in the 1960s lead to a serious examination of the sociological aspects of Marx's work (Giddens 1971; Gouldner 1970; Marcuse [1941] 1954). From the late 1960s onward, Marx's ideas exert a profound effect on the discipline, and his thought constitutes a third tradition extending from the Enlightenment into contemporary sociology. This chapter and the next focus on Marx's work in some detail.

For many students, Marx's name is associated with the former Soviet Union. As a result, he is a controversial figure, at best, and often a demonized one, given Soviet history. To others, however, Marx is just a classical political economist whose work is long, pedantic, and dry.

Socialist scholar Isaac Deutscher (1971) recounts his early attitude to reading Marx:

> His exposition seemed to me too slow and leisurely for someone like myself, who was impatient to understand the world and to change it quickly. I was relieved to hear that Ignacy Daszynski, our famous member of parliament, a pioneer of socialism, ... admitted that he too found *Das Kapital* too hard a nut. "I have not read it," he almost boasted, "but Karl Kautsky has read it and has written a popular summary of it.[25] I have not read Kautsky either; but Kelles-Krauz, our party theorist, has read him and he summarized Kautsky's book. I have not read Kelles-Krauz either, but ... Herman Diamand, our financial expert, has read Kelles Krauz, and has told me all about it." (P. 257)

There are many people who have not read Marx or any summaries of his work and rely, instead, on others' opinions to come to firm conclusions about how good or evil, intelligent or foolish Marx and Marxism were or are. That is unfortunate because Marx is a gifted thinker, writing at a vital point in time, when a wide array of ideas and perspectives competed for attention and adherents.

Most of Marx's work is complex and sophisticated; his analyses are multilayered, and the reader needs to take time to understand them, although some of his writing is clear and didactic. Easy to understand or not, Marx

---

25 Ignacy Daszynski was the founder of the Polish Socialist Party and played a significant role in founding the briefly lived "Polish People's Republic" (1918–39). Kazimierz Kelles-Krauz was a member of the Polish Socialist Party who corresponded with Kautsky and entered into a number of Marxist debates on the nature of "historical materialism," the Hegelian basis of Marx's work, and the impact of nationalist interests on the prospects for socialism (Kautsky 1898–1903; Snyder 1997). For the summaries of Marx discussed in this quotation, see Kautsky ([1887] 1925).

is, nevertheless, a key figure in the development of contemporary sociology, and no student today should skip over his work too quickly.

To present Marx's ideas, this chapter will review some background material to contextualize Marx fully and then examine, in some detail, the preface to Marx's 1859 *Towards the Critique of Political Economy* (Marx [1859] 1980:99–103; Marx [1859] 2005). The preface is chosen for specific reasons.

The "1859 preface," as it is often called, represents one apparently clear, didactic introduction to the "guiding thread" of Marx's analyses of the political economy of different social formations (Marx [1859] 2005:61). But the preface is more complex than first meets the eye; it is a multilayered analysis, and the discussion of the preface allows one to see the complexity and sophistication of Marx's ideas in a very short, seemingly straightforward text (see also Ryazanov 1930).

Before discussing the 1859 preface, the chapter will focus on the intersection of Marx's biography with the structure of social thought during his lifetime to show what aspects of his ideas prevailed at the time and what aspects came to prevail in later readings and interpretations of his work. Marx may have thought of himself as a social revolutionary, but the Marx who came to prevail was very much a critical sociologist whose work shaped scholars' understandings of the world in a fundamental manner.

From Poetry and German Idealism to Political Economy and the Proletariat

Marx was born in 1818 in Germany's oldest city, Trier, which is located in the Rhineland not far from the French border. Closer to Paris than Berlin, Trier was, during Marx's youth, a liberalized, progressive city that was saturated with the spirit of the Enlightenment and the French Revolution and with republican political views.

Marx was the eldest son in a comfortable middle-class family of nine children (four of whom lived to adulthood). Marx's father Heinrich was a lawyer, and his mother Henrietta a stay-at-home mom. A bright fellow who was home schooled to the age of 12, Marx underachieved in high school, but his parents still hoped he would become a lawyer like his father.

In 1835, his first year of study at the University of Bonn, Marx becomes actively involved in student life. He spends a night in jail with friends for "disturbing the peace of the night with drunken noise" and is wounded in a duel (McLellan 1973:17). In his first year at university, Marx devotes himself to writing romantic poetry for his sweetheart back home, Jenny von Westphalen; reading the works of **Georg Hegel**, Germany's leading philosopher at the time; and debating political issues with like-minded, liberally oriented students (Adoratsky 1934:2–4). Believing his son is too focused on romance and frivolity, Heinrich transfers Marx to the University of Berlin, but there Marx finds more reasons to avoid study, focusing instead on debates with other students about Hegel's political philosophy.

Hegel, by the end of his teaching career in Berlin, had developed a large following of radically oriented students who filled his lectures. Following Hegel's death, however, the Prussian king, Friedrich Wilhelm III, appoints Schelling as Hegel's successor, and Schelling's conservative philosophy prompts the growth of a group known as the "Left Hegelians." This group emphasized the radical elements in Hegel's thought in opposition to Schelling and conservative interpreters of Hegel.

Marx, finding the debate swirling around Hegel and the Left Hegelians quite intoxicating, joins a group of academically oriented Left-Hegelian students and faculty members; attends lectures by liberal, left-leaning Hegelian professors; and writes extensively on philosophy and the philosophy of law. Because of his experiences in the Doctors' Club, as the group was popularly known, Marx aspires to becoming a professor. He eventually completes a doctoral degree at the University of Jena in 1841 (Marx [1841] 1968). However, Marx's dreams of a professorship end when Bruno Bauer, a close friend and potential academic sponsor, loses his position at the University of Bonn for publishing a piece portraying Hegel as an atheist and Antichrist.[26]

With an academic career blocked, Marx ([1859] 2005:60–61) works as a journalist for the liberal-oriented *Rheinische Zeitung* (*Rhineland Gazette*). Away from the academic world of ideas and philosophical disputes, Marx begins to examine the real issues and problems that were affecting people's lives. For example, he covers debates on the peasantry's right to fallen wood in the forests—a longstanding right the nobility was in the process of rescinding—and the ensuing deteriorating living conditions of the Mosel peasantry. Throughout this period, Marx argues from a progressive, liberal, industry-oriented perspective that opposes the Prussian monarchy and favours a republican governing structure.

As the editor of the *Rheinische Zeitung*, Marx becomes increasingly disenchanted with his former Left-Hegelian friends and their continuous proposals that if Hegel's ideas were realized, a perfectly harmonious communist society would result. Determined to address the "communist musings" of the Left Hegelians, Marx studies the writings of the French socialists—Charles Fourier, Étienne Cabet, Louis Auguste Blanqui, Pierre-Joseph Proudhon, Armand Barbès, and others.

Marx's pro-industry and pro-republican articles, published in the *Rheinische*, and his critical editorials provide an excuse for Wilhelm to close

---

26 It is not certain whether Marx collaborated with Bauer on the piece, but it was widely speculated that the two had co-authored *The Trump of the Last Judgement on Hegel the Atheist and
   Anti-Christ* (McLellan 1973:42).

the paper in 1843. Forced out of work, Marx moves to Paris and engages fully in animated debates with French socialists and communists. He experiences first hand the living and working conditions of the German immigrant workers in Paris, and he is deeply impressed by the spirit of solidarity that characterizes their associations and meetings.

In addition to Moses Hess's essay "The Essence of Money," Marx is also strongly influenced by Friedrich Engels's ([1844] 1975) "Outlines of a Critique of Political Economy." Both pieces reinforce Marx's belief that, to bring about social change, one must focus upon workers' real social experiences and the material-economic questions that Marx had first confronted at the *Rheinische Zeitung*.

Through a detailed critique of Hegel's *Rechtsphilosophie* [*Philosophy of Law*], Marx ([1843] 1927, [1844] 1975) identifies the **proletariat** as the key to significant social transformation. In his analysis of the fundamental exploitation of people under nineteenth-century capitalism in Germany, Marx asks and answers this question:

> Where then is the *positive* possibility of German emancipation? *Answer:* In the formation of a **class** with *radical chains*, a class of bourgeois society which is no class of bourgeois society, an estate which is the dissolution of all estates, a sphere which possesses a universal character by its universal suffering and claims no *particular* right because no *particular wrong* but *wrong generally* is perpetrated against it; which can no longer invoke an *historical* but only a *human* title; which does not stand in any one-sided opposition to the consequences but in an all-round opposition to the premises of the essence of the German state; a sphere, finally, which cannot emancipate itself without emancipating itself from all other spheres of society thereby emancipating all the other spheres of society, which, in a word, is the *total sacrifice* of mankind, thus which can gain for itself only through the *full recovery of mankind*. This dissolution of society as a particular estate is the *proletariat*. (Marx [1843] 1927:619–20)

From this point on, Marx immerses himself in the study of **political economy**—developing his ideas concerning the nature of class-divided societies, investigating the central importance of the economy in shaping society, and discovering the conflict and the dynamic that he believes will create social change.

Political Economy and German Idealism

Classical political economy did more than shape Marx's work; it was one of the traditions of social analysis that influenced sociology as it was coming into existence. The roots of political economy lie in the work of Hume and extend into Adam Ferguson, Adam Smith, and Dugald Stewart (1968)—members of the "Scottish Enlightenment." Each of these thinkers emphasizes how social context influences people's behaviour.

Hume's *Treatise on Human Nature* suggests that there is a common and consistent "nature" to humanity; Ferguson ([1767] 1971) accepts that assumption although his conception of human nature differs from Hume's. Ferguson strongly opposes Hobbes and Rousseau's notions that a "state of nature" preceded the existence of civil society. For Ferguson, civil society is an "historical-natural constant ... beyond which there is nothing to be found" (Foucault 2008:298). Ferguson's ([1767] 1971) baseline premises in *An Essay on the History of Civil Society* involve the following:

> Man, in the perfection of his natural faculties, is quick and delicate in his sensibility; extensive and various in his imaginations and reflections; attentive, penetrating, and subtile, in what relates to his fellow creatures; firm and ardent in his purposes; devoted to friendship or to enmity; jealous of his independence and his honour, which he will not relinquish for safety or for profit: under all his corruptions or improvements, he retains his natural sensibility, if not his force; and his commerce is a blessing or a curse, according to the direction his mind has received. (P. 171)

There is a lot packed into that description. In the perfection of "natural faculties," humankind is quick and delicate in sensibility, imaginative, attentive to others, and firm and ardent in purpose. Humankind would not give up independence or honour for safety or profit, and this natural sensibility remains under all social conditions. All of these elements, Ferguson ([1767] 1971:23–29) establishes in his essay, favour the spontaneous synthesis of individuals. One does not need an explicit social contract, a renunciation of rights, or the delegation of natural rights to a sovereign to create an integrated civil society. However, the natural social bonds of civil society can be jeopardized by a social formation's economic foundation—"commerce is a blessing or a curse, according to the direction his mind has received." This is Ferguson's chief concern in the essay, so he focuses on the social impact resulting from the increasing dominance of industrial production, the growth of the division of labour, and the continual simplification of work tasks in the manufacturing industries.

Ferguson ([1767] 1971) fears that the increasing division of labour will have significant deleterious consequences for people in capitalist societies:

> Many mechanical arts ... require no [mental] capacity; they succeed best under a total suppression of sentiment and reason; and ignorance is the mother of industry as well as of superstition. Reflection and fancy are subject

to err; but a habit of moving the hand, or the foot, is independent of either. Manufacturers, accordingly, prosper most where the mind is least consulted, and where the workshop may, without any great effort of imagination, be considered as an engine, the parts of which are men. (P. 280)

Modern industry, according to Ferguson, will affect the development of workers' intellectual capacities and their "natural faculties." Ferguson sees a tension—a contradiction—between civil society's natural, integrative features that promote humanity's natural faculties and the suppression of those faculties within an increasingly divisive and competitive market economy.

"From the tendency of these reflections," Ferguson ([1767] 1971) explains at the end of his essay, "it should appear, that a national spirit is frequently transient, not on account of any incurable distemper in the nature of mankind, but on account of their voluntary neglects and corruptions" (p. 343). As Ferguson's history indicates, humankind, through its political leaders, could promote and stimulate the national spirit, but it could also let that spirit decline, and the nation would then decay and come to ruin. The key contradiction for Ferguson lies in the tension between capitalist commerce and humankind's natural faculties, which were being distorted by the growing dominance of a market-based economy.

Smith and Stewart are not particularly concerned with a nation's spirit, but they do find Ferguson's attention to the fundamental bases of social organization quite significant. Smith and Stewart examine the impact of the economy and its political consequences on the social whole (hence the term "political economy" and why it would rival the term "sociology").[27] Smith ([1776] 1976), for example, notes three particular points related to human nature, the economy, and society at the outset of his much celebrated *An Enquiry into the Nature and Causes of the Wealth of Nations*. First, he observes that humanity has a "natural propensity to truck, barter, and exchange one thing for another" (Smith [1776] 1976:25). Bringing goods to the market, haggling over their value, and trading them, all these economic activities are simply part of human nature.

---

27 The term political economy first appeared in 1615 in *Traicté de l'economie politique* (Treatise on Political Economy) by Antoine de Montchréstien ([1615] 1889). The term was first used in English in Sir James Stewart's ([1770] 1776) *An Inquiry into the Principles of Political Economy*. James Mill ([1821] 1844) noted that "Political Economy is to the State, what domestic economy is to the family. The family consumes; and, in order to consume, it must supply. Domestic economy has, therefore, two grand objects; the consumption and supply of the family. The consumption being a quantity always indefinite, for there is no end to the desire of enjoyment, the grand concern is, to increase the supply.... The same is the case with Political Economy. It also has two grand objects, the Consumption of the Community, and that Supply upon which the consumption depends." These are the central issues of political economy from Ferguson, Smith, Simonde de Sismondi ([1815] 1966), and David Ricardo ([1817] 1891) right through to the work of Marx.

Second, Smith ([1776] 1976:26–30) argues that, by nature, each person pursues his or her own self-interest, but this does not lead to a war of all against all, as Hobbes ([1651] 1968) had argued; it actually integrates people. In view of the first propensity of humans to barter and trade, the pursuit of individual interest furthers the collective interests of all because what one person enjoys doing—and others might not—is shared through barter and exchange in the market. Each person pursuing his or her own self-interest, then, yields a number of different products that can be exchanged to meet all of the community's various needs and wants.

Finally, Smith ([1776] 1976) uses his famous pin-making example to show that the key to the wealth of a nation is the division of labour. "The greatest improvements in the productive powers of labour," he writes, "and the greater part of the skill, dexterity, and judgement with which it is any where directed, or applied, seem to have been the effects of the division of labour" (p. 13). Smith argues that when each worker in a group of workers performs just one task in succession—straightening the wire, cutting it, sharpening the point, or putting on the head—production is far higher than when each worker makes the entire pin individually.

On the basis of his socio-economic analysis, then, Smith maintains that the wealth of nations depends on the propensity to truck, barter, and exchange; on the pursuit of individual interest; and on the added productive capacity arising from the systematic division of labour in production. Smith shows, in effect, that a free and open market is the most conducive social arrangement for meeting everyone's needs. But Smith also recognizes that the growing division of labour in market-based societies has limitations that citizens and governments should not ignore.

In the little-read section on education in Chapter 1 of Book 5 of *The Wealth of Nations*, Smith ([1776] 1976:758–87) recognizes that market forces will not support the appropriate development of the institutions needed to ensure the education of everyone in a free-market or laissez-faire society. Smith agrees with Ferguson that a completely unrestricted division of labour will diminish the intellectual capacities of workers, which is not in the common interest.

There are two choices: restrict the extent to which industries refine the division of labour and simplify work tasks—a solution Smith does not favour because it is contrary to the natural propensities that most stimulate the wealth of nations—or ensure that workers are able to develop themselves outside of the workplace. This is the solution Smith favours.

As a result, Smith, the champion of laissez-faire capitalism, demonstrates the need for some state involvement in the society as a whole. Through tax revenue, the state is best placed to provide formal educational opportunities for workers who would otherwise be completely dulled by the division of labour.

The key point to note is that Ferguson, Smith, and Stewart, followed by other British political economists such as Thomas Malthus (1827), David Ricardo ([1817] 1891), James Mill ([1821] 1844), Robert Owen ([1814] 1927), and John Stuart Mill (1848), all develop their analyses of society on the basis of the economy.

A second rival to sociology as the science of society began with Immanuel Kant, whom Hume "interrupted from his dogmatic slumber," giving his "investigations in the field of speculative philosophy a completely new direction" (Kant [1783] 1968:118). Kant's influence and concerns extend to Johann Gottlieb Fichte, Friedrich Wilhelm Joseph von Schelling, and Georg Wilhelm Friedrich Hegel—the central figures in German idealism.

Unlike Plato and Descartes, Hume ([1748] 1966) maintains that the only true and certain knowledge humankind has arrives through its senses. In response, Kant proceeds to explore the limits and possibilities of human reason. Kant's *The Critique of Pure Reason* sets out the relationship that exists between the external world and humankind's possible knowledge of that world. The external world, Kant ultimately argues, is never directly known—humanity wrestles with perceptions of that world that are shaped by pre-existing categories of the mind. Because the categories filter or shape how the external world is perceived, it is impossible, according to Kant, to actually know the external world "in and of itself." In other words, human reason can never attain absolutely certain knowledge of the external world.

Fichte, Schelling, and Hegel each explore the same problem. Is Kant correct or can the human mind overcome the apparent gap between the external world and humanity's conceptions of that world? The goal of scholarship, they argue, is to refine these mental images or ideas so that they reflect, as fully as possible, the objective world they represent and use that knowledge to guide social and political decisions and conduct. The role of the human mind and the development of human consciousness, then, are the central concerns of idealist philosophy.

This tradition emphasizes the active side of humanity in the creation and interpretation of the social world. Kant, Fichte, Schelling, and Hegel did not philosophize for the intrinsic joy of developing their own minds; they wanted to provide humans with the best knowledge and the best tools to shape and improve the societies in which they lived. The German idealists were socially engaged and, in that sense, they share the same ultimate objectives as any other social thinker who seeks to understand the world in order to change it. In this sense, German idealism was very much a motive force for and a product of the Enlightenment. Hegel, in particular, emphasizes human freedom, which, he argues, can be attained through the progressive development of philosophical knowledge until it allows human beings to comprehend fully—or master—the world in which they live. The advance of philosophy, the mastery of "Absolute Reason," and the increased freedom this provides to human action equate with positive development, and, indeed, Hegel sees history as the march of human progress.

Marx's Work: A Dynamic, Unstable, Dialectical Whole

Marx's particular approach to social analysis begins with German idealism; it is soon influenced by British and French political economy, and he later incorporates insights from French revolutionary thought and some elements of German romanticism. At no point in his life, however, does Marx ever think of himself as a sociologist. In fact, Marx, his close friend and collaborator **Friedrich Engels**, as well as many of the early Marxists, such as Wilhelm Liebknecht, August Bebel, Franz Mehring, Eduard Bernstein, Karl Kautsky, Laura Marx Lafargue (one of Marx's daughters), Paul Lafargue (Laura's husband), and Eleanor Marx (Marx's other daughter), would be offended that sociologists would one day claim Marx as one of their own.

On the basis of all the material that scholars may now easily access (although a good portion of Marx's handwritten manuscripts still lie in the former Institute for Marxism-Leninism in Moscow and in the Institute for Social History in Amsterdam), there is no doubt that Marx is an extremely gifted, synthetic thinker who draws together a number of different perspectives (Rojahn 1998).[28] However, Marx never develops a clear statement of his principles or a thematic account around which Marxists could rally.[29] Rather than producing a single, clear, finalized theory—as some contend— Marx's work can be described as an unfinished, dynamic, unstable whole. Some view the unresolved tensions in a positive light, as confirming that Marx's writings are extremely complex and stimulate considerable thought and debate. But the unfinished and unstable character of Marx's work can

---

28 The following gives some perspective on the volume of material that Marx left unpublished at his death. The German texts for volumes two and three of *Capital* (Marx and Engels 1963, 1964) are 518 and 919 pages in length, the *Theories of Surplus Value* (Marx and Engels 1965, 1967, 1968) total 1,514 pages, the *Grundrisse* (Marx [1857–58] 1953) is 1,102 pages, the *German Ideology* (Marx and Engels [1845] 1932) is 528 pages of text, the Paris manuscripts of 1844 a mere 121 pages (Marx [1844] 1932), and Marx's 1843 critique of Hegel is 148 pages (Marx [1843] 1927)—totalling over 4,700 pages of text. In the newest *Gesamtausgabe* (*Complete Works*), Part IV—Marx and Engels's study notebooks and various draft manuscripts—is projected to be 32 volumes. To date, seven volumes comprising almost 7,000 pages (Marx and Engels 1976–91) and three more of about 3,300 pages (Marx and Engels 1992–2015) have been published.

29 Aside from his writings as a journalist in 1842–43; *The Poverty of Philosophy* ([1847] 1950); the *Manifesto* of 1848 (with Engels); his 1849 serial publication of *Wage-Labour and Capital* ([1849] 1933); his historical essays *The Class Struggles in France* ([1850] 1935), also published serially in 1850; *The Eighteenth Brumaire of Louis Napoleon* ([1852] 1937); *Towards the Critique of Political Economy* ([1859] 1980); and three editions of volume one of *Capital* ([1867] 1983, [1872] 1987, [1875] 1989), Marx publishes very little from the vast corpus of his lifetime's work.

be viewed negatively because it is impossible to know *What Marx Really Meant* (to borrow G.D.H. Cole's 1934 book title). One wonders, what is most important? Where does one begin to understand the full complexity of his ideas?

Because of the complex nature of Marx's ideas, there are more books claiming to state or clarify his position than there are for any other social theorist.[30] Each author feels she or he is presenting the "real Marx" even though each "Marx" is quite different and one is often the complete opposite of another.[31] Although a few authors distort or misrepresent Marx's ideas for political reasons, most of them simply try to present Marx's ideas as a clear, meaningful (and often consistent) whole. To accomplish this task, the author often places her or his emphasis on specific aspects of Marx's work and brings the other parts, which are not necessarily fully consistent with the aspects selected as central, into line. The result is a more consistent whole but one that masks the tensions, revisions, and rethinking that lie within Marx's unfinished project and, in the end, misrepresents Marx's *oeuvre*.

Part of the difficulty of grasping Marx's ideas fully is due simply to the complexity and dynamic nature of the social formation he wants to comprehend and change—industrial capitalism. There are times over the course of his adult life when Marx feels that he has discovered the key (or keys) to understanding and explaining capitalist society, but most of the time he knows he is struggling with that very task.[32] Although Marx wrestles with

---

30 Attempts to clarify Marx have taken many forms, including two comic books in the Pantheon Documentary Comic Book series: *Marx for Beginners* (Rius 1976) and *Marx's Kapital for Beginners* (Smith and Evans 1982). One may also purchase the Coles Notes (Lichtman 1979), SparkNotes (SparkNotes Editors 2007), or Cliff Notes on Marx. Limited as these are, they are far superior to the overwhelming majority of Soviet-produced summaries of Marx.

31 There are numerous examples one could use to demonstrate this point, and some are discussed later in this chapter. For example, there is the "revolutionary Marx" of the Social Democratic Party that Karl Kautsky presents (Kautsky 1927a, 1927b) versus Eduard Bernstein's ([1899] 1909) "revisionist Marx" of evolutionary socialism (see also Haupt 1982; Jones 1982; Labriola 1904). There is the "young Marx" versus the "old Marx" (Althusser 1977a, 1977b; Bell 1960b; Schmidt 1972) and the "Marx of continuity" (Fetscher 1985; Mészáros 1975:217–26) bridging the young and old. One can point to Kautsky's revolutionary Marx versus Lenin's (1943) assessment in "The Proletarian Revolution and the Renegade Kautsky." One could note that the view of Marx and Marxism in Lenin's (1972) *Philosophical Notebooks*, which emphasizes the significance of Hegel's dialectic in Marx's thought, differs from that in Lenin's (1927) *Materialism and Empirio-Criticism*, which subordinates the evolution of society to the laws of nature as conceived by Darwin and rejects idealist elements completely (Lichtheim 1965:244–58, 325–51). Finally—in this note, which is not comprehensive—one should mention *The Postmodern Marx* of Carver (1998), Derrida's (1994) *Specters of Marx*, and Bensaïd's (2002) *Marx for Our Times*.

32 When drafting the *Grundrisse* in 1857–58, Marx sketched out five different plans for the project. He discussed several more with Engels and others in his correspondence (Beamish 1992:161–68, 181; Rubel 1981a, 1981b).

how best to examine, explain, and criticize capitalism, he is, nonetheless, very certain about how *not* to proceed with these projects, and he never hesitates to produce scathing critiques of those who have different perspectives.[33] Two points result.

First, reading some of Marx's criticisms of others often provides critical insight into what Marx rejects as well as aspects of what Marx would propose instead.

Second, when one reads something by Marx or cites from his work, it is always critical to identify the work, when it was written, and where it stands within the whole corpus of his project. Marx's ideas shift over time, and it is possible to cite statements that appear to completely contradict each other, but, once these ideas are seen in their full context, the contradiction usually disappears, although a tension between the two statements will remain. *When* Marx wrote something and *the context* in which it was written are as important as *what he wrote*. This is true of many sociologists, but it is especially true of Marx, who left his life's work—the critique of political economy—unfinished when he died.

There is, however, another reason that Marx's work is so complex. Marx's perspective—the very approach he uses to grasp the whole of capitalism—relies very heavily on Hegel's (1841) dialectical logic (Marcuse [1941] 1954). As a result, although Marx's work may be described as unfinished, dynamic, and unstable, it is *best* described as "a dynamic, unstable, 'dialectical whole.'" All dialectical wholes are unstable and thus dynamic, but Marx's position is more so than others.

Marx's analyses are less stable than Hegel's *Phenomenology of Spirit* ([1807] 1977), the *Lectures on the History of Philosophy* (1840, 1844), or the *Encyclopaedia of Philosophical Knowledge* ([1830] 1983), for example, because Marx tries to grasp the totality of an actual social formation and not simply construct a conceptual map of the history of social thought. This point merits some elaboration.

In *Capital*, Marx ([1890] 1976:103) notes that Hegel was the first to present the dialectical aspects of history in their "general forms of motion in a comprehensive and conscious manner," but, with Hegel, the dialectic "is standing on its head." Hegel's dialectic deals simply with the development of ideas. The dialectic, Marx continues, "must be inverted, in order

---

33 One might note Marx's *The Holy Family, or Critique of Critical Criticism: Against Bruno Bauer and Consorts* (Marx and Engels [1845] 1975), which is a rejection of his former Left-Hegelian comrades who were writing for the Berlin-based newspaper the *Allgemeine Literatur-Zeitung* (*General Literature Gazette*); his critique of Ludwig Feuerbach, Bauer, Max Stirner, and others in 1845 (Marx and Engels [1845] 1932); his 1847 polemic against Joseph-Pierre Proudhon (Marx [1847] 1950) and against *Herr Vogt* in 1860 (Marx [1860] 1982); and his critique of Adolf Wagner's *General or Theoretical Political Economy* (Marx [1881] 1975).

to discover the rational kernel within the mystical shell." The dialectic must be used to grasp the material world in which real people walk, labour, and act. So Marx attempts to accomplish that task—to develop a comprehensive analysis of capitalism as a real social formation that takes into account its dialectical dynamic. This sounds extremely complex, but it is not as mystifying as it might first appear—the key is to remember what "dialectic" means and where it comes from.

Hegel's conception of the **dialectic** is indebted to classical Greek philosophy and the work of Socrates. In the **Socratic method**, through the dialectical back and forth of dialogue, one continually probes knowledge to find its limitations. As continuous questioning uncovers limitations or errors in thought and understanding, one revises ideas to develop more complete (or comprehensive) knowledge than before. Hegel maintains, then, that by incorporating new insights with corrected, previously existing knowledge, basic human understanding (*Verstand*) develops into something more powerful and complete; it becomes reason (*Vernunft*). This development occurs through two processes.

The first process is one of negation—through the critique of existing, imperfect knowledge (the very point of Socratic questioning). The second is a process of transcendence; new knowledge is incorporated into what was previously known creating a new, more nuanced, and complete form of knowledge. Hegel argues that the processes of negation and transcendence, through the dialectic (or through the mind's own disciplined, introspection and dialogue), allow humanity to advance its knowledge from simple forms of understanding to an ultimate, all-encompassing form of absolute reason. Absolute reason would fully grasp all of reality's complexity. Hegel also maintains that this advancement to absolute reason is naturally inherent in the way humans develop their conscious awareness of the world. Over the course of history, humanity elevates its knowledge from naïve understanding to comprehensive, absolute reason through the natural, dialectical dynamic of thought and mind (Hegel 1840, 1844).

Marx, however, does not believe that conceptual awareness is the real basis for the advancement of human societies. For Marx, the real processes of negation and transcendence—the real dialectic of change—occur within social relationships themselves rather than in the realm of ideas. To distinguish his position from that of Hegel and other idealists, Marx calls it "materialist."[34]

---

34 Materialist is a word with different meanings. In common usage today, "materialist" means interested in the acquisition of material things. Second, materialism, or physicalism, is also a philosophical position that views all things, including the human mind, as dependent upon physical processes. Marx did not intend either of these two meanings.

The term "materialist" also draws attention to the ultimate focus of Marx's analyses—the real, practical, everyday lives of those exploited under capitalism. At the same time, the term emphasizes Marx's primary goal—to create change in those real, palpable conditions of life. Real change, according to Marx, only occurs when social relationships in the real, material world of existence are transformed.

Marx argues that pre-communist social formations are characterized by their own dialectic of social relations of production, their own internal tensions and contradictions, which are irresolvable within those formations. Through a process of negation and transcendence, human history moves through a series of newer, more advanced social formations. Marx maintains that the processes driving change are internal to each of the pre-communist social formations in their entirety.

One can now begin to appreciate why Marx's work might seem so complicated and be so multifaceted. One of his greatest challenges—once he thought he had sorted out the convolutions of capitalist society—was to determine how to present his ideas so people could grasp them. That proved to be very problematic, so Marx and then Engels, followed by later Marxists, have struggled to find the best way to convey Marx's ideas to a popular audience without compromising them too much. The search for a way to present Marx's ideas has some significant political and intellectual consequences, including when and how Marx entered the pantheon of sociology.

The Critique of Political Economy

In the graveside eulogy for his closest comrade, Engels ([1883] 1958) portrays Marx's work, and thus the essence of **Marxism**, in the following way:

> Just as [**Charles**] **Darwin** discovered the law of development of organic nature, so Marx discovered the law of development of human history: the simple fact, hitherto concealed by an overgrowth of ideology, that mankind must first of all eat, drink, have shelter and clothing, before it can pursue politics, science, art, religion, etc.; that therefore the production of the immediate material means of subsistence and consequently the degree of economic development attained by a given people or during a given epoch form the foundation upon which the state institutions, the legal conceptions, art, and even the ideas on religion, of the people concerned have been evolved, and in the light of which they must, therefore, be explained, instead of vice versa, as had hitherto been the case.
>
> But that is not all. Marx also discovered the special law of motion governing the present-day capitalist mode of production and the bourgeois

society that this mode of production has created. The discovery of surplus value[35] suddenly threw light on the problem, which all previous investigations of both bourgeois economists and socialist critics, had been groping in the dark looking for the solution. (P. 167)

Engels drew all these ideas directly from the most concise statement Marx had published about his overall approach to the systematic study of capitalist society—his preface to *Towards the Critique of Political Economy.*[36]

The 1859 preface became the specific reference point within Marx's own writings that Engels and the early orthodox Marxists would use in their consolidation and popularization of a doctrine of Marxism.[37] The revolutionary movement Marx had spent much of his life building and

---

35 The concept of surplus value (*Mehrwert* or "more value" in German) is actually rather simple. A capitalist must purchase raw material and machinery and hire workers to produce a commodity that will be sold in the market. The capitalist must calculate the cost of the raw material, machinery, and labour that is present in each commodity. The capitalist calculates the portion of value that is transferred from the machinery, the raw material used, and the wage costs of the workers. The production process is designed so that it will generate more than just cost recovery; it must also generate a profit or "more value" than the value that goes into the production of the commodity. Surplus value (*Mehrwert*) is the source of profit for the capitalist, and Marx's contribution is his analysis showing that *the worker* is the real source of this extra value that the capitalist can collect for his or her own—not the division of labour, as Smith argues, or differential rent, as Ricardo maintains, or the abundance of nature, as the French Physiocrats claim (Marx [1849] 1933).

36 The link Engels makes between Charles Darwin and Marx is interesting for three reasons. First, by coincidence, Marx's *Critique* and Darwin's *Origin of the Species* both appear in 1859. Second, Engels wants to capitalize on that coincidence by connecting the two names in an attempt to lend greater scientific credibility to Marx's work and Marxism in view of the parallels that appeared to exist between some aspects of Marx's preface and Darwin's notion of evolution, development, and the survival of different species. Finally, consistent with the spirit of the time and, in many ways, sharing the same ambitions as Comte and other social scientists, Engels also wants to create a theory of dialectical change that applies to both the natural and social worlds. Engels hopes to one day establish a new science of historical materialism that will replace its non-dialectical bourgeois rivals (Engels 1940). This objective had numerous negative consequences and significantly impeded a real understanding of Marx's theory of social change (see Korsch [1923] 1970, 1971).

37 The term "orthodox Marxism" emerged from a struggle over the political platform of the German Social Democratic Party at the turn of the twentieth century. In *Evolutionary Socialism*, Bernstein ([1899] 1909) argued that the party should forsake its longstanding commitment to revolution and pursue social reform through parliamentary legislation. Those opposed, who wanted to maintain the party's commitment to revolution, proudly referred to themselves as orthodox Marxists, calling Bernstein's supporters "revisionists." But the revisionists saw things differently. Exploiting the religious connotation of the term "orthodox"—orthodox believers usually follow a very narrow, strict reading of religious texts—the revisionists suggested that "orthodox Marxist" revolutionaries in the party were slaves to certain Marxist texts and to Marxist orthodoxy; the revisionists, who were willing to revise their understanding of capitalism based on an analysis of social change, were Marx's true heirs, they claimed.

leading would, it turned out, find its predominant textual inspiration in the just over 500-word preface to one of Marx's least read, most obscure books. Marxism, at the end of the nineteenth and turn of the twentieth century, constituted itself as a self-contained system of thought that offered a Darwinist-like scientific understanding of social history.[38] It was presented in opposition to a number of other socialist and anarchist positions, as well as to bourgeois social and political theory, including the emerging discipline of sociology.

Unfortunately, the context Engels provides to the reading of Marx's 1859 preface does a serious injustice to the complexity of Marx's pursuit of a comprehensive critique of capitalist society. Over the course of his intellectual life, Marx will struggle for almost 40 years over how to grasp and then present the complex, dynamic nature of capitalist society. In 1859, under considerable pressure from his publisher, Engels, and others in the socialist movement to make his insights public, Marx writes *Towards the Critique of Political Economy*, but this work is a far cry from the comprehensive plans that Marx has for his entire project (Beamish 1992:54–59; Rubel 1968:lxxvi–cxxi). The book has only one chapter on the commodity and another on money; Marx does not even begin to address the nature of capital (that is, money invested in raw materials, machinery, and employees to produce commodities that are sold for profit in the economic market).

To confirm that his analysis is founded on a detailed understanding of the dynamics of capitalist society and that more is forthcoming, Marx writes the preface to provide a straightforward outline of his dialectical understanding of the dynamic, unstable nature of pre-communist social formations. Although the preface is intended as a mere outline of Marx's studies, because it seems so clear and didactic, many readers miss its underlying complexity and Marx's dialectical approach. As simple as the preface appears, by unravelling its hidden complexities, one can gain significant insight into how Marx understood the complex processes involved in social change and why sociologists see his work as so instructive for understanding the complex world of today.

THE ECONOMIC INFRASTRUCTURE, THE IDEOLOGICAL SUPERSTRUCTURE

In the 1859 preface, Marx ([1859] 2005:60–61) provides an overview of his intellectual labours between 1843 and 1859 and of the ideas he developed over

---

38 It was long believed that Marx had asked Darwin if he could dedicate *Capital* to him. It turns out that the letter upon which the claim was made was actually from Eleanor Marx's partner, Eduard Aveling—a great fan of Darwin's—to Darwin about a book Aveling was writing (Avineri 1967; Fay 1978).

that decade and a half. He notes that the "guiding thread" that emerged for his analysis of society and social change was quite straightforward (Marx [1859] 2005:61).

In the social production of their lives, humankind, independently of its will, enters determinate, necessary relations, relations of production (*Produktionsverhältnisse*) that are appropriate to a determinate stage of development of their material forces of production (*materiellen Produktivkräfte*).

Marx argues that people, whether they like it or not, are born into or enter into a particular set of social relations that predates them. In making this statement, Marx is claiming two things. First, as Marx and Engels ([1845] 1932) indicate in a manuscript drafted in 1845, *The German Ideology*, "The premises from which we begin are not arbitrary ones, not dogmas, but real premises ... real individuals, their activity and the material conditions under which they live" (p. 10). One can distinguish humankind from animals "by consciousness, by religion, by whatever else one wants," they argue. But "humans distinguish themselves from animals as soon as they begin to *produce* their means of subsistence.... Insofar as humans produce their means of subsistence, they indirectly produce their material life itself" (Marx and Engels [1845] 1932:10).

Production, Marx and Engels maintain, is fundamental to social life; it is an ontological condition of humankind. But, they also note that the form of production changes with time. Although social relations of production, in general, are one of the universal conditions of humankind, the actual social relations of production will vary with time and place. Marx ([1859] 2005) makes the same point in the 1859 preface.

In the social production of their lives, Marx ([1859] 2005) argues, people will enter into "determinate, necessary relations, relations of production that are appropriate to a determinate [or specific] stage of the development of their material forces of production" (p. 61). This means, as he makes clear a few sentences later, that history and change are also fundamental (or ontological) to the human condition.

Having established that humankind enters into certain, historically created, social relations of production, Marx makes his next important claim. He argues that the "totality of these relations of production shape the economic structure of society" (Marx [1859] 2005:61). More important, the economic structure of society is "the real basis upon which a legal and political superstructure rises and to which determinate social forms of consciousness are appropriate" (p. 61).

These statements present the famous "**base** and **superstructure**" or "**infrastructure** and superstructure" conception that characterizes orthodox Marxism. There is an economic base (or infrastructure) that determines or shapes the superstructure: "The mode of production of material

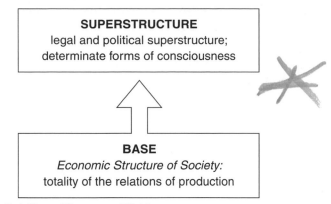

FIGURE 1: *The Basic "Base and Superstructure" Model*

life conditions the social, political, and intellectual processes of life overall"
(Marx [1859] 2005:61).

Although it might seem unnecessary to provide a diagrammatic representation of the "base and superstructure" model at this time, because the model becomes more complex, a basic diagram is helpful. Figure 1 shows the components of the superstructure and the economic base, as well as the direction of determination or conditioning that Marx identified.

Next, Marx introduces the term "the **mode of production**" in place of the broad, encompassing term "base." He then specifies further that the mode of production is comprised of two basic elements: the **social relations of production** and the **material forces of production**. The social relations of production—"or property relations"—encompass the ownership and control of the forces of production (see Figure 2).

In slave societies, for example, the patrician class owns and controls the forces of production, and slaves are used to produce the basic goods and services needed for the society to exist. In feudal societies, the king or queen and feudal lords own and control the forces of production. Serfs are given access to the land as well as certain rights and privileges in exchange for an allocation of their production. In capitalist societies, industrial capitalists own the factories, purchase and own machinery and raw material, and, by paying wages, hire workers who make the products (or commodities) the owner will sell in the market. Master and slave, lord and serf, owner and employee characterize three different "relations of production" or "property relations."

The "material forces of production" encompass the material elements that are involved in production. In slave societies, the material elements are slaves using their labour to convert raw materials into goods for consumption.

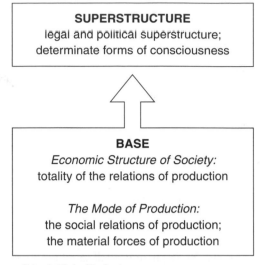

FIGURE 2: *Conceptualizing the Mode of Production*

In capitalist societies, the material forces of production include the factories, the machinery, the raw material, and the physical workers, which all combine to produce commodities that are sold in the market.

Up to this point in the 1859 preface, Marx's premises and propositions lead to two provisional conclusions. First, the mode of production is the key to understanding all social relations, including the "social, political, and intellectual processes of life overall" that constitute the superstructure. The second conclusion is a corollary of the first. It is not consciousness or ideas that determine or shape social life; on the contrary, social life (living within a society) determines consciousness.

Figure 3 presents the essential relations that Marx seems to have had in mind while writing the preface. Although Marx begins with conceptions of the state and judiciary as the superstructure ("the legal and political super-structure"), he also includes "determinate social forms of consciousness" appropriate to the relations of production in the base. He then suggests the more inclusive idea that "the mode of production of material life conditions the social, political, and intellectual process of life overall." This general conception is the most inclusive of all his formulations.

If the relations of production as a whole constitute the basic infrastructure of society, they are also central to the social dynamism and change that characterize society and social history. On the basis of his studies, Marx ([1859] 2005) argues that, at "a certain stage of their development, the material productive forces of society come into contradiction with the existing relations of production.... From forms of development of the productive forces, these relations [of production] transform into their fetters. It gives

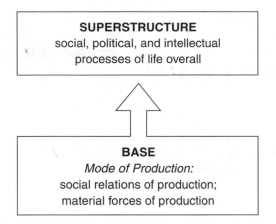

FIGURE 3: *The Social, Political, and Intellectual Processes Overall; Contradiction and Revolutionary Change*

rise to an era of social revolution" (pp. 61–62). With change in the economic foundation, "the whole immense superstructure sooner or later revolutionizes itself" (Marx [1859] 2005:62).

Before examining the specific dynamic that Marx sees in social history, it is important to re-emphasize the sources of his conceptions.

The idea that there is an internal dynamic to social change was inspired by Marx's reading of Hegel. Hegel argues that historical change results from the development of ideas. Marx, however, rejects the notion that new theories, bodies of ideas, or changes in the legal and political superstructure are the driving forces of history that can produce significant revolutionary change.

From the mid-1840s onward, Marx develops the position that the genuine, far-reaching transformation of society can only result from change within its material infrastructure. Moreover, his analyses convince him that it is the dynamic, contradictory nature of the economic infrastructure—the internal dynamic of the mode of production—that generates the social contradictions that lead to revolutionary social change.

Three important conclusions arise from this overview of Hegel and Marx's assertion of the primacy of the economic infrastructure. First, on the basis of his own life experiences, his study of political economy, and the changes he saw in the world around him, Marx, along with political economists such as Malthus, Ricardo, Jean-Baptiste Say (1817), and Smith, firmly believed that social analysis has to begin with the economic infrastructure of society. This idea was a common theme in political economy at that time.

Second, Marx wanted to create social change and was opposed to capitalism (a social system that he felt squandered the full potential of humankind). To create revolutionary social change, Marx urges revolutionaries to focus upon the most important features of society that must be transformed.

The dominant tradition of the humanities in Germany led most reformers, including socialists such as Bruno Bauer, his brother Edgar, and Hess and Wilhelm Weitling, to focus upon the realm of ideas rather than the real material relations of society.[39] So, in breaking from Hegel and proposing his critique of capitalist society through political economy, Marx advocates a form of social analysis that he believes will create genuine, meaningful—indeed, revolutionary—social change.

Third, and most important, in asserting his own particular position, Marx, it seems, rules out the notion that ideas or changes in the superstructure can be sources for fundamental social change. Is this because Marx thought that the superstructure is of little consequence, or is it that he wants to make his position most emphatically? For the orthodox Marxists, the answer is clear: the superstructure is simply a reflection of the infrastructure. Revolutionary change can come only from the contradictions in the economic infrastructure. The superstructure is determined by the infrastructure. As a result, the superstructure, as a mirror reflection of the infrastructure, is not of much importance.

Even though these points comprise what becomes a widely accepted interpretation of Marx's 1859 preface, this interpretation arises from a rather simplified, narrow understanding of Marx's specific terms and of his argument as a whole. Marx fully recognized the unstable, dialectical nature of the social whole, and he wanted to convey the full interrelated texture of social life, but one cannot present such complexity all at once. As a result, Marx begins with the infrastructure, enumerates its key elements, and then proceeds, in his more complete works such as the *Grundrisse*, to create a more integrated, comprehensive presentation of the full complexity of social life. This intricacy is one of the primary reasons that Marx's project kept expanding in size and that he continually revised his plans for presenting his entire critique of political economy. The simple "base determines superstructure" model is only one step in a presentation that is more complex and sophisticated than many orthodox Marxists recognized.

Still, the 1859 preface does present the idea that the motor of historical change is the tendency of the material productive forces to grow and come into conflict with the social relations of production, ushering in an age of social revolution. What is the basis of this dynamic? Why does Marx think that the forces of production will continually develop and come into conflict with the social relations of production? The dynamic of production is easy enough to understand: one need only think of a factory and its long assembly lines to conceptualize the dynamic of production. But how does the everyday

---

39 Marx had addressed this tendency in German socialism critically in his sardonic critique of
    some of his former associates, for example, the Bauers, in *The Holy Family* (Marx and Engels
    1957:3–224) and in the last section of the *Manifesto* under the heading "German or 'True'
    Socialism" (Marx and Engels [1848] 1934:31–34).

dynamic of production create contradictory forces that lead to the existing relations of production serving as a fetter on their further development, and how does that lead to revolutionary change?

TECHNOLOGICAL DETERMINISM

The dynamic tension that Marx sees within capitalist society and presents in his brief 1859 preface is more complex and layered than first meets the eye. One can progress through three different levels of analysis within Marx's preface statement. By beginning with the most basic reading and proceeding to more nuanced readings, one gains helpful insight into how, as noted earlier, Marx's conception of capitalist society is best described as a dynamic, unstable, dialectical whole; one can see the way Marx layers the elements of dynamic tension that he perceived within capitalist economies.

The first reading of the dynamic tension between the forces of production and the social relations of production is quite straightforward. The social relations of production in capitalist society facilitate, encourage, and, in fact, require production for profit. A capitalist factory owner employs workers to turn raw material, through the use of various machines, into commodities that the capitalist will sell for a profit in the marketplace. To increase profits, the factory owner is always looking for ways to improve and speed the production processes. The key focus in this reading of the conditions that create revolutionary change is the role of machinery.

"At a certain stage of their development, *the material productive forces of society* come into contradiction with the existing relations of production [my emphasis]" (Marx [1859] 2005:61–62). Machinery is obviously the key, the material productive force that permits capitalists to increase productivity and thereby increase profits. As a result, it seems apparent and logical that Marx has machinery and technology in mind when he notes the conditions that would create revolutionary change.

The idea that machinery is the key to social change is found in many writers' works, and it is often termed **"technological determinism."** Technology, in this type of argument, determines the course of social change and development. And a number of statements throughout Marx's work, when taken out of context, appear to be quite technologically deterministic. The statement most often used to claim that Marx is a technological determinist is found in *The Poverty of Philosophy*: "the hand-mill gives you society with the feudal lord; the steam-mill, society with the industrial capitalist" (Marx [1847] 1950:127). The statement reads like a causal relationship—a lower form of technology ("the hand-mill") allows for a feudal society to exist while a more developed form of technology ("the steam-mill") creates the more complex society of industrial capitalism.

Certainly, one of the major forces of change in nineteenth-century capitalism was technological development. And such development took place extremely rapidly and on a massive scale. So people reading Marx's preface in 1859 have good historical reasons for thinking that Marx has machinery in mind. Such a reading equates "the motor of history," appropriately enough, with technological development. As technology advances, society progresses.

As familiar as Marx was with technologically deterministic arguments, his conception of change is not that narrow, although he certainly sees technology as one of the major sources of change (Marx [1845] 1982, [1851] 1981). By reading the preface very narrowly, however, generations of orthodox Marxists, critics of orthodox Marxism, and commentators on Marx's texts have argued that Marx is a technological determinist, and the proof, they all maintain, is in this section of the 1859 preface. As one element in Marx's understanding of the dialectical tensions within the material relations of production, technology is important—but it is not the only element.

ECONOMIC DETERMINISM

A technologically determinist reading of the 1859 preface places the emphasis upon how the development of "the material productive forces of society" creates the contradictions that lead to revolutionary social change. However, if one shifts the emphasis to the latter half of the sentence concerning how change will occur, one may develop a different aspect of the dynamic of change that Marx outlines in this work. "At a certain stage of their develop-ment, the material productive forces of society come into contradiction with *the existing relations of production* or, what is only a legal expression for it, *with the property relations within which they have operated to that point in time* [my emphasis]" (Marx [1859] 2005:61–62). This reading will produce an argument that is identified as **"economic determinism."** This position was also taken up and explored by orthodox Marxists, their critics, and commentators on Marx.

In an economically deterministic argument it is not machinery or tech-nology that drives history and social change but the economy as a whole. The economy determines or shapes the types of contradictions that will emerge and create, animate, or drive revolutionary change. This reading is also some-times referred to as "economic reductionism" because the course of history—the source of the major tensions that create social change—is "reduced to" the economy. As in the case of technological determinism, sound historical reasons exist for thinking that Marx subscribes to economic reductionism, but those interpretations ignore the dialectical aspects of Marx's presenta-tion and insights.

In the course of his own lifetime, Marx lived through several economic crises. In the *Manifesto*, his essay *Wage-Labour and Capital*, and at some length in the draft manuscript for the third volume of *Capital*, Marx outlines a theory of what he calls "overproduction." Marx argues that, in the regular dynamic of the capitalist economy, the drive for profit puts pressure on capitalists to continually increase their productive advantage over others. That drive leads to technological innovation and more efficient production, but better technology and increased productive efficiency often lead to the replacement of workers by more efficient machines. The surplus workers are then relegated to what Marx terms "the reserve army of the unemployed," which creates a dilemma for capitalists pursuing profit. The reserve army of the unemployed is too poor to purchase goods in the market, so, as more and more workers are replaced by machines, the number of potential consumers for the growing bounty of commodities falls. That is one problem, but the situation gets worse.

The unemployed workers compete with the employed for jobs and are willing to work for less money just to secure employment, which puts a dampening effect on workers' wages, often causing them to fall. Thus, a second major problem arises. Through capitalist competition for increased profits, even the workers with jobs find themselves facing economic insecurity or economically worsening situations. This employment instability also leads to decreased consumer demand and falling sales. Consequently, in the pursuit of profits, capitalists inevitably run the risk of unleashing one of the many periodic crises of overproduction that characterized late nineteenth- and early twentieth-century capitalist societies. The system itself, then, seems to generate its own contradictions and potential downfall.

Before writing the 1859 preface, Marx had already described this situation graphically in the *Manifesto of the Communist Party*:

> Modern bourgeois society with its relations of production, of exchange and of property, a society that has conjured up such gigantic means of production and of exchange, is like the sorcerer who is no longer able to control the powers of the nether world whom he has called up by his spells. (Marx and Engels [1848] 1934:14–15)

In the *Manifesto*, Marx notes the numerous economic crises during which "modern productive forces" revolted "against modern conditions of production," with each crisis more threatening than the last.

> In these crises, there breaks out an epidemic that, in all earlier epochs, would have seemed an absurdity—the epidemic of over-production. Society suddenly finds itself put back into a state of momentary barbarism; it appears as if a famine, a universal war of devastation, had cut off the supply of every means of subsistence; industry and commerce seem to be destroyed. (Marx and Engels [1848] 1934:15)

Marx ominously argues that history was showing through these crises that the "productive forces at the disposal of society no longer tend to further the development of the conditions of bourgeois property; on the contrary, they have become too powerful for these conditions, by which they are fettered, and as soon as they overcome these fetters, they bring disorder into the whole of bourgeois society, endangering the existence of bourgeois property" (Marx and Engels [1848] 1934:15).

The tendency for the **rate of profit** to fall is a different dimension of the same problem that the pursuit of profit creates. Marx argues that workers, through the sale of their ability to do work—or their **labour-power**—are the sole source of value and surplus value, which are actualized into profit. Although details of the theory of value and surplus value are not important here, the argument that Marx makes in *Wage-Labour and Capital* (Marx [1849] 1933) and presents in greater detail in the draft manuscript for volume two of *Capital* (Marx and Engels 1963:101–52) shows that the tendency for the increased mechanization of production sets in motion a tendency for the rate of profit to fall. Each worker a capitalist employs generates a continually shrinking rate of profit, as more technology is introduced into production. The only way to offset the loss in profits inherent in this tendency is to find a technological advantage that will increase the rate of profit over less technologically advanced competitors, to increase the speed with which products are produced and sold, or to find new markets.

The first solution is only a stopgap measure and part of the vicious cycle inherent in the tendency for the rate of profit to fall. Every advance in technology might bring brief respite, but it exacerbates the situation in the long run because more workers will have been replaced by the new technology. More machinery means fewer workers and a decreased rate of profit.

Speeding the rate of commodity turnover requires technological innovation, so it too contributes to the same vicious cycle that pushes the rate of profit downwards.

The last solution is only effective as long as new markets can be found. It buys time, perhaps, but, inevitably, the crisis will emerge as all the markets become saturated. Worse yet, as Marx notes in the *Manifesto*, "the conquest of new markets" and "the more thorough exploitation of the old ones" simply "pav[es] the way for more extensive and more destructive crises" and diminishes "the means whereby crises are prevented" (Marx and Engels [1848] 1934:15).[40]

The final dimension of the economically determinist reading of the 1859 preface concerns the contradiction that exists between the planned efficiency that characterizes capitalist production and the free-flowing competition of

---

40 There was a lively debate between Marxists and mainstream economists over the various "breakdown theses" that exist in Marx's work. See, in particular, Grossmann (1929), who started the debate by demonstrating the tendencies were correctly predicted, Böhm-Bawerk ([1896] 1949), who responded, Hilferding's ([1904] 1949) response to Böhm-Bawerk, and Luxemburg's (1951) argument that capitalism would only expand so far until it would break down under its own contradictions.

the capitalist market. Marx was not the only person who recognized that the private ownership of the means of production—one of the centrally defining features of capitalist society—would create problems over the supply of commodities that were produced and put onto the market. Before Marx, Ferguson ([1767] 1971), Smith ([1776] 1976), Sismondi ([1815] 1966), and James Mill ([1821] 1844), for example, all noted the potential problems associated with overproduction.[41] This is one aspect of the problems that Marx had in mind as he wrote that "the material productive forces of society come into contradiction with the existing ... property relations."

All of the economic crises Marx identifies ultimately stem from the drive to increase or maintain levels of profit through increased efficiency in production. But the outcome is overproduction, a tendency for the rate of profit to fall, and the creation of an impoverished reserve army of the unemployed. One solution—a solution that a number of socialists put forward with different emphases—is to coordinate the economy as a whole—to introduce the same rational, calculated planning within the total economy that each capitalist uses in his or her particular enterprise. Centralized planning, of course, conflicts with the tenets of a free market. It conflicts, in other words, with the existing property relations.

All of these "economically deterministic" readings of the 1859 preface were supported by the history of capitalist society as it existed in the late nineteenth and early twentieth century. As a result, they would all have assisted Marx in seeing the internally generated, dialectical dynamism of capitalist society as it stemmed from within its economic infrastructure. Marx's preface, then, reflects each of these different layers of the contradictory nature of capitalist production.

LABOUR-POWER, CONSCIOUSNESS, POLITICAL ACTION

There is a third level of argument within the preface. This one includes the first two but is more comprehensive and thus goes beyond them. Although it includes the first two levels of analysis, the third one brings into play the significance of **class consciousness** within the proletariat and political action.

---

41 Modern economists also recognize the problems associated with the regulation of supply and demand. The most significant struggle in economic thought and public policy is between those who argue that the economy needs regulation versus those who want it completely unregulated. This debate pits the work of John Maynard Keynes (1936) and the Cambridge school against that of Friedrich von Hayek (1931, 1934), Ludwig von Mises (1934), and the Austrian school. The debate still exists; "embedded liberalism," which supports state regulation of market processes and corporate activity, is in the defensive position as neoliberalism and the absence of regulatory action dominate the public agenda (see Harvey 2005).

In the *Manifesto*, Marx focuses upon the central role of class struggle in history. According to some, his description of the means by which technology, crises of overproduction, and the falling rate of profit create crises seems to imply that social transformation is a more or less automatic, almost mechanistic, process—that one need only wait for the conditions of revolution to emerge and then erupt, leading to the revolutionary transformation of capitalist society. Many orthodox Marxists insisted that this was, indeed, Marx's position. But, as one reads the preface more closely, it is also apparent that Marx has made room for the "revolutionary subject"—the proletariat— to become conscious of its situation and begin to push for change.

Drawing upon his background in analytical philosophy and Marxism, Gerald Cohen (1978) intensively dissected the key concepts in the 1859 preface. He argues that the means of production within the mode of production are more complex than most commentators have noted. What are the material forces of production in Marx's work, Cohen asks. What are they in any capitalist enterprise? The material forces of production break down into three basic elements: the means of production, which are comprised of the raw material and machinery that are used to produce commodities; the spaces where production takes place (factories in the case of industrial production); and the human labour-power that is required to carry out productive work.

The technological explanations for social change are encompassed in the dimensions that are relevant to the means of production narrowly understood. Economic determinist explanations still all apply because the same contradictions between the property relations and the relations of production will continue to be in effect. The new elements are the acknowledged presence of labour-power and its congregation in factories.

On the one hand, it is surprising that the central importance of labour-power in Marx's 1859 preface could have been overlooked for so many years. Workers and their labour-power are a key element in Marx's analysis of capitalist production. Labour-power, according to Marx, is the sole source of surplus value. The proletariat is the revolutionary force that Marx thinks will change the world. And the conditions under which workers live and work are central to all of Engels and Marx's major analyses of capitalist society. Figure 4 presents this expanded model of the key elements in Marx's 1859 preface.

As was the case earlier, this layer of analysis in the preface incorporates technological determinism and economic determinism. The key differences within this deeper, more comprehensive understanding of the dynamic that Marx points to are the identification of labour-power as a factor in social change, the role that ideas will play, and the unique environment within which they will germinate and grow.

The social relations of production under capitalism centre on the generation of profit. Value and surplus value, the bases for profit, are created

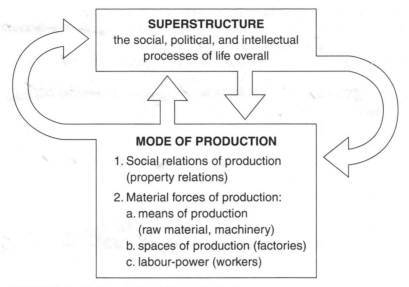

FIGURE 4: *Breaking Down the Material Forces of Production*

in the production process when workers animate machinery to turn raw material into finished products that are sold on the market. Over the course of the nineteenth century and into the twentieth, employers consolidated production into larger and larger mechanized factories to gain the efficiencies of a growth in productive scale, improved mechanization, and increased control over the workers (Smith [1776] 1976). Marx notes this trend in the *Manifesto* (Marx and Engels [1848] 1934:16–17). In the technologically determinist and economically determinist levels of analysis in the preface, workers are seen as mere factors of production. They are much like other raw materials and treated as an expense. But labour-power is more than simply a factor in production. Labour-power is irrevocably tied to a human being. This connection is critically important for four specific reasons.

First, humans are conceptual beings. Humans reflexively monitor their actions; they conceptualize the tasks they are asked to perform; they consciously engage with the world around them (see Marx [1872] 1987:192–93; Schutz [1932] 1967). As a result, one key factor within the material forces of production that constitute part of the mode of production (which constitutes the economic infrastructure) is the group consisting of *conscious human workers*.

Ideas and consciousness are not located solely in the superstructure. The very presence of labour-power, of humans, among the material forces of production indicates that one of the processes Marx explicitly locates in the superstructure—"intellectual processes of life"—is also present in the infrastructure. Marx's model must be thought of as much more integrated than the distinct, two-tiered conception that most people derive from the 1859 preface. Marx's conceptual understanding of capitalist society is heavily indebted to Hegel, and all of Hegel's analyses—his work on the phenomenology of mind, the history of philosophy, the encyclopaedia of knowledge, or the philosophy of law, for example—are synthetic wholes. Marx may argue that Hegel looked in the wrong place in his efforts to understand the dynamic of history, but Marx is never critical of Hegel's overall conceptual framework.[42] Marx, too, sought to grasp and present capitalist society as a dialectically unstable, synthetic whole; he did not want it understood as a hierarchical, stratified layer cake.

Second, while workers are conscious producers and use their minds as much as necessary to fulfil their work tasks, their consciousness expands beyond the specific tasks they must carry out in the production process. Reflexively monitoring their work experiences will encompass more than recognizing when they need to carry out a specific production task.

As a result, workers take in and assess the conditions under which they work. They inevitably develop a political consciousness of their role in the production process and of their place in the factory, as well as perceptions concerning their treatment by employers. Workers develop political consciousness in the work process. This fact, too, brings another explicitly defined aspect of the superstructure into the infrastructure—political consciousness.

Third, because workers reflexively monitor their conditions of work and industrial production brings together an increasing mass of workers, a growing political force is created. This force was becoming evident in industrial Britain during the second half of the nineteenth century. Even though capitalist owners controlled the majority of resources and could establish most of the rules that would structure the workplace, the power that those rules and resources generated was not all in the hands of the employer. The emergence of trade unions and the impact that workers in Britain had on parliamentary legislation to curb the length of the working day and introduce some basic worker protections demonstrated that the workers were politically conscious and active (Lichtheim 1965). The workers of the late nineteenth and early twentieth century were becoming an increasingly powerful political

---

42 Marx ([1890] 1976) argues that "For Hegel, the process of thinking, which he even transforms into an independent subject, under the name of 'the Idea,' is the creator of the real world, and the real world is only the external appearance of the idea. With me the reverse is true: the ideal is nothing but the material world reflected in the mind of man, and translated into forms of thought" (p. 102).

force. Marx also emphasizes this trend in the *Manifesto* (Marx and Engels [1848] 1934:17–18).

Finally, when Marx reviews his early intellectual labours in the preface, he notes that his critique of Hegel had "led to the conclusion that legal relations and forms of state cannot be comprehended by themselves or on the basis of the so-called general development of the human mind or spirit" (Marx [1859] 2005:61). Instead, he maintains, "they are rooted in the material relations of life whose totality Hegel, following the lead of the English and French in the eighteenth century, brought together under the name 'civil society.'" And, he continues, "the anatomy of civil society is to be sought in political economy" (p. 61).

To clearly distinguish himself from Hegel and many other socialists and to emphasize what he believed was his most important contribution to the understanding of societies and their dynamics, Marx used the term "materialist" to identify his position. However, there was a tendency among orthodox Marxists to inflate the notion of materialism in Marx's work and to regard ideas as purely side effects or by-products of the "material relations of society." But Marx was never a crude materialist. The statements cited previously demonstrate what he meant, and the preface provides a more elaborate explanation of his position.

This expanded or more nuanced interpretation of the preface begins with Marx's comments on Hegel and then moves to the importance of labour-power to bring out the full meaning of Marx's position in 1859.

The vast majority of social analysts, from Socrates, Plato, and Aristotle in antiquity through to classical political theorists such as Hobbes, John Locke, Montesquieu, Rousseau, Saint Simon, Comte, and John Stuart Mill, are concerned with issues of power. They tend to see power solely in terms of the state—hence Hobbes's ([1651] 1968) *Leviathan*, Locke's ([1694] 1967) *Two Treatises on Government*, Rousseau's ([1762] 1963) *Social Contract*, Montesquieu's ([1748] 1989) *Spirit of the Laws*, Saint-Simon's (1975) *The Industrial System* (published in 1821), and Comte's (1974) *Plan of Scientific Studies Necessary for the Reorganization of Society* (published in 1822).

Marx argues that this view of power is wrong. While the state holds tremendous power, that power can only be understood by examining "the material relations of life," which Hegel and Rousseau discuss under the label "civil society." Marx goes a step further: the "anatomy of civil society"—the anatomy of the material relations of civil society—"is to be sought in political economy."

For Marx, materialism represents the observable realities of everyday life in civil society, and, to begin to analyse civil society, one should begin with its anatomy—political economy. None of this excludes the importance of ideas, per se, in either civil society or in political economy; they are just not the place where one should begin the study of power and social dynamics.

Through this more inclusive, nuanced understanding of Marx's preface, one can more fully appreciate Mills's notion of the intersection of personal biography, history, and social structure. Mills emphasizes this intersection because of his appreciation of Marx's work. By recognizing the role that conscious human labour-power plays in the production process and the awareness that develops, one can see that intersection very clearly and, most important for Marx, within a strategic area of social life. One can also see how that dynamic—working under the demanding and exploitative conditions of unregulated, nineteenth-century capitalism— would lead to particular forms of conscious resistance to the system and to a new type of worker beginning to prevail. The intersection of workers' biographies (their personal histories of keeping pace with automated production running at full speed) and the structural demands of profit production within capitalist social relations of production shaped worker consciousness and resistance in very specific ways during Marx's era and beyond (see Hobsbawm 1964, 1999; Thompson 1970). One is now in a position to grasp the full dialectical whole that Marx sketches in his 1859 preface.

In setting out an apparently two-tiered conception of base and super-structure, Marx uses terms that position the economic base opposite the "legal and political superstructure." He then establishes the key elements within "the totality of the relations of production"—the social relations of production and the material forces of production. He then sets these oppo-site a broader conception of the superstructure, which he identifies as the "social, political, and intellectual process of life overall." When one breaks down the material forces of production into their key elements—material means of production, spaces for production, and labour-power—it becomes clear that what was originally presented as a two-tiered conception is actually fully integrated (see Figure 5). Social, political, and intellectual processes may be found within labour-power in Marx's analytical point of departure—the base—as well as within the larger social institutions such as the family, edu-cation, the church, and the state, which constitute "the social, political, and intellectual processes of life overall."

The social whole has a number of tensions and contradictions. To begin to enumerate those contradictions, Marx maintains, one has to begin with the base and work from there, keeping in mind that, intellectually, one is grasping an unstable, dynamic, contradictory whole. This is the conceptual framework Marx sought to sketch out in his 1859 preface.

When one then breaks down the material forces of production into the means, spaces, and animate components of the production process, labour-power must serve the double function of being part of the production process

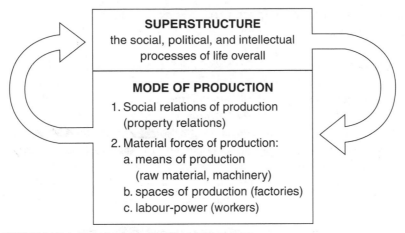

SUPERSTRUCTURE
the social, political, and intellectual
processes of life overall

MODE OF PRODUCTION

1. Social relations of production
   (property relations)

2. Material forces of production:
   a. means of production
      (raw material, machinery)
   b. spaces of production (factories)
   c. labour-power (workers)

FIGURE 5: *Moving Toward an Integration of Base and Superstructure*

and part of the "social, political, and intellectual processes of life overall."
Figure 6 captures this more integrated model.

The arrows are important; Marx argues that to understand the social
whole, one must start with the anatomy of society as a whole (which is to
be sought in the economic infrastructure). After critically grasping the social
relations and material forces of production and their relationship, as the
arrow on the left indicates, one may proceed to considering the elements of
the superstructure. Based on one's knowledge of the economic infrastructure,
one can now more fully grasp how the material practices in the economic
infrastructure shape (or determine) the elements contained in the superstructure. Once one has grasped how the social, political, and intellectual
processes of life are shaped by the infrastructure, one can then, as the arrow
on the right indicates, return to the social relations and material forces of
production and consider them more fully in light of one's knowledge of the
superstructure. Analysis now becomes a recurring cycle in which one gains
a deeper, more complex and synthetic understanding of the social whole.

Social, political, and intellectual
processes of life overall

Social relations of production and
material relations of production
(raw material, machinery, spaces of
production, living labour-power)

FIGURE 6: *Marx's Model as a Conceptual Totality*

MARX'S 1859 PREFACE, THE ENLIGHTENMENT LEGACY, AND SOCIOLOGY

If the Enlightenment's legacy to sociology can be captured in the words "freedom," "mastery," and "progress," it is clear that Marx's contribution to sociology draws upon these same themes as they are developed within his 1859 preface to *Towards the Critique of Political Economy*. Marx's fundamental concerns in this preface are freedom from exploitation, greater equality in the sharing of social resources, and the full expression of human potential. Each of these, in Marx's view, requires some fundamental change in the structure of society, and the key to understanding what will bring about that change lies in the anatomy of civil society—in its political economy.

Marx believed that the intellectual critique of political economy—his analysis of the mode of production—followed by the requisite changes to the social relations and material forces of production would allow humanity to master its material conditions of existence. He was convinced that the knowledge and practices such mastery sets in motion would bring to fruition the Enlightenment dream of greater human freedom and progress toward a more advanced social formation.

Conflict, power, tension, struggle, and revolutionary transformation are also all part of Marx's analysis of capitalist society. One of the main reasons his work was drawn into sociology is the attention his perspective brings to questions of power and to the political processes that occur within the texture of everyday life. In Marx's analysis, civil society may be characterized by exploitation and inequality, but that is due to a specific set of property relations. Those relations, in turn, are constituted and reconstituted in the everyday activities of workers in their workplaces. In that process of constitution and reconstitution, however, the rules and resources that structure the production process and the sale of goods in the marketplace are continually in flux. Through the flow and reflexive monitoring of everyday activities, workers and citizens gain new levels of awareness and political insight and seek change.

Marx ends the preface with an ominous challenge. Quoting from Dante's *Divine Comedy*, he notes that "the same challenge must be made at the entrance to science as at the entrance to hell: 'Here must all distrust be left; All Cowardice must here be dead'" (Marx [1859] 2005:64). Marx's sociology challenges sociologists to examine the world around them critically, irrespective of what they will find. One must trust one's findings, no matter how painful, if they have been obtained through a careful, unbiased analysis of the social world. These dimensions of Marx's work, along with the questions he posed and the framework he employed, drew Marx into the pantheon of early sociologists.

Although Marx wrote in the late nineteenth century, his work remains alive today because the intersection of his personal and intellectual biography with the history and social structures of his time placed him at a particularly propitious vantage point. From this perspective, he could capture the dynamics of modern society as it was being consolidated and anticipate the impact of industrial capitalism as it expanded across Europe. The next chapter focuses upon the *Manifesto of the Communist Party* not because it is the *communist* manifesto but because it is also a manifesto of *modernity* (Berman 1988). The *Manifesto* presents, in vivid imagery, the dynamic vitality of the modern world as it was unfolding in the 1840s and as it continued to develop, with greater speed and deeper impact, over the next century and a half. Reading the *Manifesto* in this light brings Marx directly into the most pressing debates in sociology today.

Key Terms and Names

the Enlightenment
Adam Ferguson
Adam Smith
Karl Marx
Georg Hegel
proletariat
class
political economy
Friedrich Engels
dialectic
Socratic method
materialist
Marxism
Charles Darwin
base
superstructure
infrastructure
mode of production
social relations of production
material forces of production
technological determinism
economic determinism
rate of profit
labour-power
class consciousness

Questions for Review and Further Reflection

1. Before you read this chapter, what was your impression of Karl Marx and his theories? Describe at least two ways in which reading this chapter has changed this impression. Outline what surprised you about Marx's biography.

2. How do you see Marx's personal biography intersecting with history and social structure to shape his scholarly work? What are the main social, political, and intellectual influences that shaped his ideas?

3. Although a technological deterministic reading oversimplifies Marx's theory, he does believe technology plays an important role in shaping society. How have recent technological developments shaped the contemporary work world? How have they shaped people's everyday lives?

4. Using Marx's model as a guide, describe the dominant mode of production in Canada or the United States today (including social relations and material forces).

5. In what ways has this mode of production influenced the social, political, and intellectual processes of life overall in Canada or the United States?

6. How would Marx explain the recent financial crises of 2008 and 2016?

5

MARX, THE *COMMUNIST MANIFESTO,* AND MODERNITY

Main Objectives

This chapter will

1. Present the *Manifesto of the Communist Party* as a contested document and not as "a sacred text."
2. Examine the *Manifesto* as a document reflecting key aspects of modernity (or the modern era).
3. Identify the key themes in the *Manifesto of the Communist Party.*

The anonymous 23-page *Manifest der Kommunistischen Partei* that rolled off the presses located in the office of the Bildungs-Gesellschaft für Arbeiter (Educational Society for Workers), 46 Liverpool Street, London, in February 1848 had little impact upon the revolutionary insurrections that took place in Berlin, Cologne, Königsberg, and other parts of Prussia that March.[43] Part of the reason was due to the Prussian government's diligence in intercepting and confiscating large numbers of the pamphlet, but its late arrival and the **Communist League**'s low profile among revolutionaries also undermined its impact. Nevertheless, the *Manifesto* was circulated among and read by many bourgeois and working class revolutionaries in 1848.

---

43 The anonymous, first edition of the *Manifesto* went through four printings, with the first printing appearing in serial instalments in the *Deutsche Londoner Zeitung* (German London Gazette) from March 3 to July 28, 1848. The second edition, a 30-page anonymous pamphlet, was most likely published in April or May 1848 and, along with an 1866 edition, served as the basis for all future editions of the *Manifesto*. Although the preamble to the *Manifesto* states that it would appear in English, French, German, Italian, Flemish, and Danish, with the exception of a Swedish translation in 1849, only the German text appeared in 1848–49 (Andréas 1963:15). The *Manifesto* now appears in more than 35 languages; 544 editions were printed between 1848 and the beginning of the Russian Revolution in 1917.

Despite its rather undistinguished beginning, the **Communist Manifesto** (as its title became after the 1872 Leipzig edition) gained a much higher profile following the Paris Commune of 1871 (Andréas 1963; Beamish 1998). Under changed social and political circumstances and after almost 20 years of underground discussion, the *Manifesto* had attained a growing reputation for its cogency, power, and insight, and it became, in the second half of the nineteenth century, the principle statement of how and why the revolutionary workers' movement in western Europe would succeed in transforming society into a more egalitarian social formation. In addition, Marx, the pamphlet's principal author, enjoyed a significantly higher political profile in 1871 than he had held as an exiled German émigré living and writing in Brussels in 1848 (Lichtheim 1965).

By 1871, Marx had been living in London, the centre of British political radicalism and the home of other socialist and communist refugees, for 22 years. By then, Marx had published *Towards a Critique of Political Economy*, which presented the preliminary arguments for his critique of bourgeois political economy and a powerful summary, in the preface, regarding how societies changed and the apparent inevitability of a communist society in the future. Also, Marx had assumed a leading role in the International Working Men's Association, founded in 1864, and he had published the first volume of his magnum opus *Das Kapital* ([1867] 1983).[44]

From 1871 onwards, the *Communist Manifesto* has been recognized as one of the most important social documents of the modern era. Correctly or not, disadvantaged, repressed, exploited groups in widely differing parts of the world have viewed the *Manifesto* as an inspiration, and sometimes as a blueprint, for social change. Different communist states have claimed it justifies various policies and decisions as well as a particular interpretation of history. Finally, critics of social democracy, socialism, or communism have claimed that the *Manifesto* is an example of all that is wrong and evil in those movements.

Written during a key period in European history, the *Manifesto* captures the dynamics of market societies as they were becoming dominant across western Europe. England, by this time, had undergone almost a century of industrial development, France was becoming increasingly industrialized, and

---

44 The first International Working Men's Association (the "First International") was founded in 1864 in St. Martin's Hall, London. It held its first congress in Geneva in 1866 and held together until 1876. Marx was a member of the General Council throughout the First International's existence although he was in constant conflict with the leaders of the various strands of socialism that the organization brought together. Marx fought with the German workers who followed Ferdinand Lassalle, the Italians supporting Giuseppe Mazzini's republican nationalist leanings, the French mutualists who backed Proudhon's particular anarchist program, the Owenites who promoted Owen's socialist ideas, and the workers who followed Mikhail Bakunin's anti-state anarchism (Cole 1954:88–133).

Germany was then undergoing industrialization as a weak middle class began to struggle for power against well-established landed and military interests. Although similar documents were written at that time, the *Manifesto* has endured because of its vivid imagery and the way it expresses the essential dynamic of modern industrial capitalist society as its prodigious potential was just beginning to become fully apparent.

The *Manifesto* was also a significant accomplishment in Marx's quest for recognition as a scholar, social critic, and revolutionary leader. It represents one of the high-water marks in Marx's life for three particular reasons.

First, by 1848, Marx had arrived at fundamental solutions to the major theoretical and philosophical issues with which he had been struggling since he switched to the University of Berlin in 1836. In 1848, Marx believed he had identified the key factors that would provide genuine insight into societies and their dynamics—aspects of the material world, which he felt revolutionaries could use to create the social change they all thought was necessary to improve the human condition.

Second, the *Manifesto* represents the victory of Marx's intellectual vision in the political arena. Following two different international conferences organized by the League of the Just and held in London, Marx was entrusted with presenting the league's new position on socialism and on the transition to a communist society. Drafting the *Manifesto* moved Marx from the obscurity of his writing desk at his home in Brussels to the public stage of the European socialist movement. At the same time, it allowed Marx to draw together all the work he had been slaving over to arrive at his particular sociological understanding of capitalist society (as barebones as that analysis might have been at the time).

Finally, in writing the *Manifesto*, Marx is able to demonstrate his skill and craft as a revolutionary writer—the rhetoric and imagery he uses emphasizes the importance he places upon the development of a revolutionary consciousness within the working class. Class struggle requires a clear, unambiguous class consciousness, and the *Manifesto* sought to provide workers with a moving and motivating understanding of their reality and their role in history so they would be inspired to take action. This dimension of the *Manifesto* has proven to be one of its most enduring qualities for today—if one wants to capture the imagery of modernity, the anonymous 1848 pamphlet does it extremely well.

Even though Marx is the pamphlet's author and the work represents the League of the Just's acceptance of his particular analysis of capitalist society, it was not then, and is not now, a set of uncontested, scriptural truths. The *Communist Manifesto* emerged as the result of a complex process in which personal biographies (those of Marx, Engels, Hess, Karl Schapper, and Joseph Moll, in particular); the history of social structure (of Britain, France, and Germany, mostly); and the types of men, women, and political associations (such as the League of the Just, which became the Communist League) prevailing at that time all played important roles.

Rather than representing a single, monolithic position—one that puts forward the uncontested, universal views of the Communist League—the *Manifesto* is the product of debate, struggle, negotiation, concession, and Marx's own particular style of presentation and argument. The *Manifesto* represents an extremely interesting compromise of the intensely competing views that gave the Communist League unity and a vision, but this was a historically located and temporally bound unity and perspective—one that would, and needed to be, adjusted, debated, and contested as the social world around the socialist movement changed (Beamish 1998). It was also a tremendously compelling and historically significant vision of bourgeois society and of the future of the industrial world.

The *Manifesto* and Modernity's Dynamism

Marx begins the *Manifesto* powerfully and ominously: "*Ein Gespenst geht um in Europa—das Gespenst des Kommunismus* [A spectre moves about Europe— the spectre of communism]" (Marx and Engels 1848:3).[45] He continues,

> All the powers of old Europe have entered into a holy alliance to exorcise this spectre: Pope and Tsar, Metternich and Guizot, French Radicals and German police-spies.[46] Where is the party in opposition that has not been decried as communistic by its opponents in power? (Marx and Engels [1848] 1934:9)

Two points arise from these facts—first it is clear that all European powers acknowledge communism to be a powerful force. Second—and

---

45 The first English translation of the *Manifesto*—produced by Helen Macfarlane and serialized in Julian Harney's *The Red Republican* throughout November 1850—lost some of Marx's dramatic imagery: "A frightful hobgoblin stalks throughout Europe. We are haunted by a ghost, the ghost of Communism" (Beamish 1998:239, note 63).

46 Marx is taking some literary licence here by collapsing two events into one. The 1815 Congress of Vienna, which proclaimed a loose alliance of European powers called the "Holy Alliance," was spearheaded by Klemens von Metternich, an Austrian prince who was a staunch reactionary opposed to any ideas of liberalism. In this 1815 alliance of Russia, Austria, Prussia, and England, Metternich sought the return of conservative, absolute monarchies. A smaller "holy alliance" was forged by Metternich between the Russian Tsar Alexander I and Prussia's Frederick Wilhelm III. The pope, though sympathetic to the forces of reaction, was never part of either alliance, and Guizot, who expelled Marx from Paris, was never important enough to represent France in any of these alliances. Finally, both alliances were conservative insofar as their main targets were liberal reformers—not the communist or workers' movements (which they would most certainly have also opposed). Socialists used "proletariat" to convey graphically how exploited and downtrodden the working class was in the nineteenth century.

here Marx negates or inverts the ominous opening—it is high time that "Communists should ... meet this nursery tale of the spectre of Communism with a manifesto of the party itself." The opening section, then, takes one from a frightening spectre to a down-to-earth dismissal of such fictions and the presentation of the international communist movement's position on the dynamics of social change.

Part I of the *Manifesto* returns to vivid imagery to present its dominant theme:

> The history of all hitherto existing societies is the history of class struggles.
>
> Free man and slave, patrician and plebeian, lord and serf, guild-master and journeyman, in a word, oppressor and oppressed, stood in constant opposition to one another, carried on an uninterrupted, now hidden, now open fight, a fight that each time ended, either in a revolutionary reconstitution of society at large, or in the common ruin of the contending classes. (Marx and Engels [1848] 1934:10)

Through the use of a carefully crafted history, Marx proceeds to sketch out the two great titans that would soon confront each other—the **bourgeoisie** and the proletariat.[47] As Marx argues, "Our epoch, the epoch of the bourgeoisie ... has simplified class antagonisms," so modern society "is more and more splitting up into two great hostile camps, into two great classes directly facing each other—bourgeoisie and proletariat" (Marx and Engels [1848] 1934:10).

In broad, powerful strokes, Marx sketches out the rise of the bourgeoisie as a class and the implications this has for life in the emerging modern world:

> [T]he modern bourgeoisie is itself the product of a long course of development, of a series of revolutions in the modes of production and of exchange.
>
> Each step in the development of the bourgeoisie was accompanied by a corresponding political advance in that class. An oppressed class under the sway of the feudal nobility, an armed and self-governing association in the medieval commune: here independent urban republic (as in Italy and Germany); there taxable "third estate" of the monarchy (as in France); afterward, in the period of manufacturing proper, serving either the semi-feudal or the absolute monarchy as a counterpoise against the nobility, and, in fact, cornerstone of the great monarchies in general—the bourgeoisie has at last, since the establishment of Modern Industry and of the world market, conquered for itself, in the modern representative state,

---

47 The noun "proletariat" is derived from the Latin noun "*proles*" meaning "offspring." The *proles* were an impoverished, subordinate class in ancient Rome. Each member of that class was a proletarian, and, collectively, they were the proletariat. The only economic assets proletarians had were their sons—their offspring (hence the *proles* had nothing to offer other than their offspring).

exclusive political sway. The executive of the modern state is but a committee for managing the common affairs of the whole bourgeoisie. (Marx and Engels [1848] 1934:11–12)

The bourgeoisie, Marx argues, was a revolutionary class that radically transformed society as it rose to dominance from within the feudal order. Some of those changes centred on the social relations among people; for example, market society fundamentally changed the basis of human interaction, the nature of work, and the reality of every occupation:

The bourgeoisie, wherever it has got the upper hand, has put an end to all feudal, patriarchal, idyllic relations. It has pitilessly torn asunder the motley feudal ties that bound man to his "natural superiors," and has left no other nexus between man and man than naked self-interest, than callous "cash payment".... It has resolved personal worth into exchange value, and in place of the numberless indefeasible chartered freedoms, has set up that single, unconscionable freedom—Free Trade. In one word, for exploitation, veiled by religious and political illusions, it has substituted naked, shameless, direct, brutal exploitation.

The bourgeoisie has stripped of its halo every occupation hitherto honoured and looked up to with reverent awe. It has converted the physician, the lawyer, the priest, the poet, the man of science, into its paid wage labourers. (Marx and Engels [1848] 1934:12)

As a consequence, Marx continues, the modern era is unlike any before it—tradition, the mystification of magic or religion, and "natural rights" no longer structure social relationships. The cash nexus and the ethos of unrestricted trade dominate production, interpersonal relations, and the social structure as a whole.

While replacing a veiled form of exploitation with a naked, direct form that leaves factory workers toiling long hours for meagre wages, the bourgeoisie demonstrates the power of industrial, market-based production. The accomplishments of the bourgeoisie are breathtaking; it has produced "wonders far surpassing Egyptian pyramids, Roman aqueducts, and Gothic cathedrals" (Marx and Engels [1848] 1934:12).

According to Marx, the most important revolutionary change that the bourgeoisie accomplished in the transformation of feudal society into a market-based one was the constant revolutionary change of the "instruments of production, and thereby the relations of production, and with them the whole relations of society":

Conservation of the old modes of production in unaltered form was ... the first condition of existence for all earlier industrial classes. Constant revolutionizing of production, uninterrupted disturbance of all social conditions, everlasting uncertainty and agitation distinguish the bourgeois epoch from all earlier ones. All fixed, fast-frozen relations, with their train of ancient and venerable prejudices and opinions, are swept away, all new-formed ones become antiquated before they can ossify. All that is solid melts into air, all that is holy is profaned, and man is at last compelled to face with sober senses his real condition of life and his relations with his kind. (Marx and Engels [1848] 1934:12–13)

Marx's imagery is powerful, and it remains fresh when one thinks of the contemporary world in which the drive to shorten time and shrink distances now dominates people's lives. In the globalized world, the sun never sets and information circles the globe constantly and almost instantaneously, so "all that is solid" really does melt "into air," and people recognize that they have few choices outside of meeting the demands of tighter schedules, as time and space shrink within an increasingly ruthless and fiercely competitive global marketplace (see Castells 2010).

Over the next six paragraphs, Marx illustrates graphically the tremendous change that modernity had already brought to the face of the globe by the middle of the nineteenth century, as markets expanded, production improved, and modernity revolutionized the world in its own image. Concentration, centralization, and increasingly rationalized production characterized this modern era. The bourgeoisie, Marx's argument confirms, was rapidly becoming a new Promethean force in the history of humanity:

The bourgeoisie, during its rule of scarce one hundred years, has created more massive and more colossal productive forces than have all preceding generations together. Subjection of nature's forces to man, machinery, application of chemistry to industry and agriculture, steam navigation, railways, electric telegraphs, clearing of whole continents for cultivation, canalization of rivers, whole populations conjured out of the ground— what earlier century had even a presentiment that such productive forces slumbered in the lap of social labour? (Marx and Engels [1848] 1934:14)

To this point in the text, the bourgeoisie seems all powerful—omnipotent. But, Marx continues, there are two forces that will undermine the power of the bourgeoisie and take modernity in a different direction.

The first force is rooted in the economic relations of market-based society itself—contradictions within the mode of production. The bourgeoisie initially arose within feudal society as the means of production and exchange began to change and feudal production was replaced by capitalist production. As the bourgeois order began to establish itself, feudal production, Marx argues, was "no longer compatible with the already developed productive forces" (Marx and Engels [1848] 1934:14). Feudal production became restrictive—an anachronism, "so many fetters":

> They had to be burst asunder; they were burst asunder.
>   Into their place stepped free competition, accompanied by a social and political constitution adapted in it, and the economic and political sway of the bourgeois class. (Marx and Engels [1848] 1934:14)

The essential features of feudal production were kings, lords, and aristocrats holding title to large tracts of land and the landless serfs or peasants who were tied to the land, working it in return for traditional protections and rights. The church guided and restricted behaviour, emphasizing the acceptance of toil in this life for the everlasting rewards in an afterlife. Wealth was accumulated in goods through plunder and war; the manor's production met immediate needs alone. The key features of feudal production were its heavy reliance on tradition and its enduring stability.

Capitalist production was completely different—it centred on "wage-labour," and its goal was the pursuit of unlimited financial wealth. The pursuit of (potentially) unrestricted wealth introduced a totally new dynamic—one that would require continual improvements in the speed of production and the sale of goods, with capital augmenting itself through turnover during every cycle.

Peasants who had left the manor and found refuge in the emerging cities were freed from their feudal obligations, but, to survive, they had to sell the one good they had to exchange on the market—their ability to do work (their labour-power). Capitalists with sufficient resources to own implements of production (tools and, eventually, machines) and to purchase raw materials could also hire wage workers to produce goods for the market. So an entirely new mode of production—a new economic foundation to society—emerged in which the pursuit of monetary profit centred on the sale and purchase of "free wage labour." This labour was free in that it had severed its permanent ties to the feudal manor and was thus free to sell itself in the market in exchange for wages. Wealth was created by the profit—or surplus value—workers produced as they laboured in factories, and the accumulation of money became the central motive force within the economy (Dobb 1947; Marx [1890] 1976:270–80, 873–95). Although this new mode of production created wonders, it too, according to Marx's analysis, had its own dynamic and set of contradictions:

> Modern bourgeois society, with its relations of production, of exchange and of property, a society that has conjured up such gigantic means of production and of exchange, is like the sorcerer who is no longer able to control the powers of the nether world whom he has called up by his spells.

For many a decade past, the history of industry and commerce is but the history of the revolt of modern productive forces against modern conditions of production, against the property relations that are the conditions for the existence of the bourgeoisie and of its rule. It is enough to mention the commercial crises that, by their periodical return, put the existence of the entire bourgeois society on trial, each time more threateningly. In these crises, a great part not only of the existing products, but also of the previously created productive forces, is periodically destroyed. In these crises, there breaks out an epidemic that, in all earlier epochs, would have seemed an absurdity—the epidemic of over-production. Society suddenly finds itself put back into a state of momentary barbarism; it appears as if a famine, a universal war of devastation, had cut off the supply of every means of subsistence; industry and commerce seem to be destroyed. And why? Because there is too much civilisation, too much means of subsistence, too much industry, too much commerce. The productive forces at the disposal of society no longer tend to further the development of the conditions of bourgeois property; on the contrary, they have become too powerful for these conditions, by which they are fettered, and so soon as they overcome these fetters, they bring disorder into the whole of bourgeois society, endanger the existence of bourgeois property. The conditions of bourgeois society are too narrow to comprise the wealth created by them. And how does the bourgeoisie get over these crises? On the one hand, by enforced destruction of a mass of productive forces; on the other, by the conquest of new markets, and by the more thorough exploitation of the old ones. That is to say, by paving the way for more extensive and more destructive crises, and by diminishing the means whereby crises are prevented.

The weapons with which the bourgeoisie felled feudalism to the ground are now turned against the bourgeoisie itself. (Marx and Engels [1848] 1934:14–15)

There are few more accurate, graphic descriptions of the dynamic, ever-expanding nature of modernity: growing production that results in overproduction, increasing productive power that escapes from the sorcerer and pulls everything helplessly along into its swirling orbit, the conquest of new markets creating a brief respite before giving way to even greater crises.

In the *Manifesto* of 1848, Marx argues that, already, the dynamic of modernity has created more than its own, internally generated crises—it has also "forged the weapons that bring death to itself; it has also called into existence the men who are to wield those weapons—the modern working class—the proletarians" (p. 15).

Over the next five paragraphs, Marx sketches the dynamic of modernity and indicates how it produced the force that will oppose the bourgeoisie. Wage workers must find work, and, as modern industry develops, they are brought together in increasingly larger factories where they are reduced to mere appendages of the machines that run endlessly; "as the use of machinery and division of labour increases, in the same proportion the burden of toil also increases" through longer working hours and the increased speed of the machinery. By building the factory system, modern industry "has converted the little workshop of the patriarchal master into the great factory of the industrial capitalist," Marx writes:

> Masses of labourers, crowded into the factory, are organised like soldiers. As privates of the industrial army, they are placed under the command of a perfect hierarchy of officers and sergeants. Not only are they slaves of the bourgeois class, and of the bourgeois state; they are daily and hourly enslaved by the machine, by the over-looker, and, above all, by the individual bourgeois manufacturer himself. The more openly this despotism proclaims gain to be its end and aim, the more petty, the more hateful and the more embittering it is. (Marx and Engels [1848] 1934:16)

Marx uses the next section of the *Manifesto* (10 paragraphs) to indicate the dynamics within the capitalist mode of production that turned the workers, who initially struggled against capital as individuals, into a unified, powerful class that grew in size and in political power as its grievances mounted (Marx and Engels [1848] 1934:16–17). With the development of industry, Marx argues,

> the proletariat not only increases in number; it becomes concentrated in greater masses, its strength grows, and it feels that strength more. The various interests and conditions of life within the ranks of the proletariat are more and more equalised, in proportion as machinery obliterates all distinctions of labour, and nearly everywhere reduces wages to the same low level. The growing competition among the bourgeois, and the resulting commercial crises, make the wages of the workers ever more fluctuating. The increasing improvement of machinery, ever more rapidly developing, makes their livelihood more and more precarious; the collisions between individual workmen and individual bourgeois take more and more the character of collisions between two classes. Thereupon, the workers begin to form combinations (trade unions) against the bourgeois; they club together in order to keep up the rate of wages; they found permanent associations in order to make provision beforehand for these occasional revolts. Here and there, the contest breaks out into riots. (Marx and Engels [1848] 1934:17)

Marx has now set the stage for the two titans of the modern world to face one another, and, although dynamics can obscure this conflict, he suggests that the overall relationship between capital and wage labour is one of growing antagonism and polarization and that time will see the increasing consolidation of power within the working class. At this point, Marx argues, not only will the proletariat grow in strength, but the forces of right and justice will grow along with it:

> All previous historical movements were movements of minorities, or in the interest of minorities. The proletarian movement is the self-conscious, independent movement of the immense majority, in the interest of the immense majority. The proletariat, the lowest stratum of our present society, cannot stir, cannot raise itself up, without the whole superincumbent strata of official society being sprung into the air. (Marx and Engels [1848] 1934:19)

Even though its mandate is the universal emancipation of humankind from class rule, the revolutionary struggles of the working class, according to Marx, will begin in national struggles—"The proletariat of each country must, of course, first of all settle matters with its own bourgeoisie" (Marx and Engels [1848] 1934:20). Ironically, in the pursuit of its own narrow economic interests, in following the imperatives of market-based society, the bourgeoisie had produced the class that would, on the basis of those same dynamics, grow to not only oppose it but also ultimately overthrow it.

> The essential conditions for the existence and for the sway of the bourgeois class is the formation and augmentation of capital; the condition for capital is wage-labour. Wage-labour rests exclusively on competition between the labourers. The advance of industry, whose involuntary promoter is the bourgeoisie, replaces the isolation of the labourers, due to competition, by the revolutionary combination, due to association. The development of Modern Industry, therefore, cuts from under its feet the very foundation on which the bourgeoisie produces and appropriates products. What the bourgeoisie therefore produces, above all, are its own grave-diggers. Its fall and the victory of the proletariat are equally inevitable. (Marx and Engels [1848] 1934:20)

THE *MANIFESTO* AND SOCIOLOGY

As a sociological analysis, the *Manifesto* is a groundbreaking text for four reasons. First, the *Manifesto* presents a version of one of Marx's most important contributions to sociology—the argument that social formations and social history can be best understood by carefully examining their real, material social relations. Focusing upon, gathering information about, and studying social processes is now so central to sociology that it is hard to believe that this approach once had to be asserted, but in the mid-nineteenth century, there were still a number of competing and very different approaches to the study of societies.

The power of speculative philosophy had to be challenged, and social theorists such as Marx did so, arguing that ideas did not create social formations, nor were societies the actualization of ideas as they came into being. Instead, every social formation was the product of real human activity. Societies were the larger product of the interaction patterns of individuals that constituted and reconstituted social relationships of a relatively enduring nature.

Second, Marx goes further in the *Manifesto* than simply saying that one must focus on the material conditions of a social formation to study it properly. He presents an argument that he will later outline in his 1859 preface to *Towards a Critique of Political Economy*—it is the economic infrastructure of society upon which one should most carefully focus. The significant emphasis Marx places upon the determining role of the economic infrastructure has led to extensive debate in the social sciences. Irrespective of where sociologists finally fall in this debate—whether they think Marx overly emphasizes the centrality of the economy in shaping the power relationships that tend to constitute social relationships and social formations more generally—it was within the Communist League's congresses and in writing the *Manifesto* that Marx first successfully established this position in a public forum.

Third, consistent with his focus upon the economic infrastructure, Marx identifies class struggle as one of the major motive forces of history. Marx was not the first to emphasize the class nature of bourgeois society, nor was he the only one to see class struggle as an inherent dynamic in social relationships, social formations, and social history. But the idea that major social change occurs through class struggle is firmly associated with his name, his theoretical position, and his approach to social analysis. The main reason for that association is the *Communist Manifesto*. When questioned in March 1852 about his major contributions to the working class movement, Marx replied,

> [N]o credit is due to me for discovering the existence of classes in society or the struggle between them. Long before me bourgeois historians had described the historical development of this class struggle and bourgeois economists, the economic nature of the classes. What I did that was new was to prove:
>
> (1) that the *existence of classes* is only bound up with *particular historical phases in the development of production*,
> (2) that the class struggle necessarily leads to the dictatorship of the proletariat,

(3) that this dictatorship itself only constitutes the transition to the *abolition of all classes* and to a *classless society*.[48] (Marx and Engels 1955:69)

The final contribution that Marx makes to sociology in the *Manifesto* is a somewhat contradictory yet vitally important one. Marx identifies two forces that will overturn bourgeois society—the internal contradictions of the economic infrastructure (Marx and Engels [1848] 1934:14–15) and the "men who are to wield those weapons [that will bring about the death of the bourgeoisie]—the modern working class—the proletarians" (p. 15). Many commentators on Marx have focused on the economic contradictions of bourgeois society as the major source of social change, but, in the *Manifesto* and elsewhere, Marx also emphasizes the "subjective" side of social change—the development of class consciousness and the desire on the part of classes to make change.

For Marx, the capitalist mode of production had its contradictions and internal dynamic, but change would not occur without real men and women acting and creating it. Yes, capitalist production brought workers together in unprecedented numbers within single factories, often located in large cities; it created working conditions that led to numerous grievances; it provided the opportunity for workers to develop their own understandings and interpretations of the world; and it provided the opportunity for them to press for social change. Still, although it is often overlooked, the interpretive role of human agents, who collectively pursue the goals they see as important within the context of their particular historical and social location, is central to Marx's sociological perspective.

Marx fully expected a revolutionary transformation of European society in the 1840s—he believed it would happen because the material conditions of existence for workers were such that they would want to rebel; they would want to change society in radical ways to their benefit. Marx also believed, based on his own lived experiences, that workers would develop a revolutionary consciousness, and this consciousness, coupled with a desire for change created from within their everyday lives, would lead them to action. The role of human understanding—how people grasp the world around them—*is*

---

48 In that same letter, Marx writes the following: "Finally, if I were you, I should tell the democratic gents *en général* that they would do better to acquaint themselves with bourgeois literature before they venture to yap at its opponents. For instance they should study the historical works of [Augustin] Thierry, [François] Guizot, John Wade and so forth, in order to enlighten themselves as to the past 'history of the classes.' They should acquaint themselves with the fundamentals of political economy before attempting to criticise the critique of political economy. For example, one need only open Ricardo's *magnum opus* to find, on the first page, the words with which he begins his preface: 'The produce of the earth—all that is derived from its surface by the united application of labour, machinery, and capital, is divided among *three classes* of the community; namely the proprietor of the land, the owner of the stock or capital necessary for its cultivation, and the labourers by whose industry it is cultivated'" (Marx and Engels 1955:68).

part of Marx's sociological insight, although he does not spend much time developing this aspect of his sociological understanding of industrial capitalist society (Lichtheim 1965).

Thus, the *Manifesto* also reflects the core ethos of the Enlightenment, as Marx carries it forward in his work—the themes of freedom, mastery, and progress reverberate throughout the document. History, as Marx presents it, is a continuous dialectic of progress, until freedom from exploitation and class division is gained through the ongoing struggle. As soon as the bourgeoisie established its mastery over the remnants of the feudal aristocracy, it began to create the conditions from which it would be challenged by a class that represents the universal interests of humanity rather than partial, class interests. The material conditions of capitalism, Marx argues, create the circumstances under which the proletariat will gain the political will and material means to transform society and move it forward to a higher level of universal development. In the *Manifesto*, then, Marx brings freedom, mastery, and progress together with the French Revolution's themes of liberty, equality, and fraternity to form a striking and inspiring synthesis.

On the basis of this discussion of Marx's work, it is clear how much Mills's conception of the sociological imagination draws from Marx, although there are important differences in emphasis. To begin with, Mills (1959) argues that the sociological imagination involves the intersection of biography with history and social structure. Marx's position is very similar, although it would be more accurate to state that, for Marx, the intersection of the history of the social structure with the biography of *social classes* is the critical aspect. In both cases, however, the objective dimensions of society (the social relationships that are constituted and reconstituted), the subjective dimensions of society (the human agents who constitute social relationships and seek to maintain or change them), and their intersection within a specific socio-historical context must all be taken into account for a sociological study to meet its task and promise. Both Marx and Mills can be described as holistic thinkers who were extremely aware of the dynamic tensions and contradictions that existed in the social formations they studied and criticized.

Second, both Marx and Mills wrote from the vantage point of the societies in which they lived and concentrated on the social formations they wanted to examine. Consequently, Marx focused on the early industrializing period of capitalist society in western Europe. His work emphasizes the dramatic changes that occurred in the nature of the political economy in England, France, and Germany as industrial capitalism swept aside the remnants of feudal power, privilege, tradition, and governance. Marx wrote when a variety of social critics—socialists, anarchists, and liberal reformers, for example, as well as reactionary, conservative traditionalists and Christian reformers—were intensely engaged in exposing the problems inherent in market-based society and proposing a variety of solutions that would alter civil society fundamentally. Chief among those proposals was the redistribution of property or an alternative form of ownership and control of the productive forces in society and the results of social production.

The point in time and, as a result, the nature of the social formation about which Mills wrote were different in key ways, even though some of the fundamental aspects of capitalist society still prevailed in North America and western Europe during the mid-twentieth century. The social product of 1950's Canada, the United States, and western Europe was far greater than it had been in 1848. The absolute standard of living of wage workers and the conditions under which they laboured were far better in the world Mills inhabited in 1955 than the one Engels ([1845] 1975) described in 1845. Most important, the composition of the labour force had changed by the mid-twentieth century, the perceived routes that workers had for ameliorating their working conditions and life chances were different, and their commitment to political change had altered as the strata of white-collar workers grew absolutely and proportionately in North America and western Europe. Three of Mills's most important studies—*New Men of Power: America's Labor Leaders* (1948), *White Collar* (1951), and *The Power Elite* (1956)—all addressed these changes (see also Mills 1963).

The most significant difference between Marx's socio-political world and the one Mills addressed, however, was the threat of thermonuclear war, the "immediate causes" of which lay "in the fearful symmetry of the cold warriors on either side: an act of one aggravates the other; the other reacts, in turn aggravating the one" (Mills 1958:9). Behind those apparent immediate causes were intermediate causes although the "ultimate causes" were, according to Mills, "part of the very shaping of world history in the 20th century." But despite this enormous change in the global power structure—indeed partly because of it—Mills championed the classical tradition and its particular sociological imagination as the way to understand events in order to change them. Furthermore, as Mills (1962) maintains in *The Marxists*, the sociological imagination is heavily indebted to Marx—his empirical work and his conceptual grasp of capitalist society.

Consequently, Marx cannot be ignored if one wants to deepen one's grasp of the sociological imagination and of the classical tradition in sociology, Mills (1962) argues: "Many of those who reject (or more accurately, ignore) Marxist ways of thinking about human affairs are actually rejecting the classic traditions of their own disciplines" (p. 10). At the same time, Mills (1962) maintains that there is no longer any "'marxist social science' of any intellectual consequence" either:

> There is just—social science: without the work of Marx and other marxists, it would not be what it is today; with their work alone, it would not be nearly as good as it happens to be. No one who does not come to grips with the ideas of marxism can be an adequate social scientist;

no one who believes that marxism contains the last word can be one either. Is there any doubt about this after Max Weber, Thorstein Veblen, Karl Mannheim—to mention only three? We do now have ways—better than Marx's alone—of studying and understanding man, society, and history, but the work of these three is quite unimaginable without his work. (P. 11)

In addition to Weber, Veblen, and Mannheim, Mills could have mentioned Émile Durkheim—although Mills was highly critical of the path that many sociologists had taken on the basis of the positivist dimensions of Durkheim's work. Durkheim's contributions will be the focus of the next chapter, but, before turning to Durkheim, let us reflect on one of Mills's suggestions in the *Images of Man: The Classic Tradition in Sociological Thinking*—the sociological frame of reference can begin with "the acquisition of a vocabulary that is adequate for clear social reflection," a vocabulary that involves only 20 or so pivotal terms (Mills 1960:17). With regard to Marx, what might be his most pivotal contribution to that vocabulary?

Marx and a Vocabulary for Clear Social Reflection

On the basis of the material presented in Chapters 4 and 5, one can identify several pivotal terms from Marx that enable "clear social reflection": "economic infrastructure," "proletariat," "revolution," or "materialism" are all excellent candidates. As one reads more of Marx's work, the terms "alienation," "the labour process," "the labour theory of value," and "the fetishism of the commodity" present themselves as possible contenders. But, if one has to choose only a single concept at this moment, the best one might be *Klassenkampf* (class struggle), and several reasons recommend it as a key Marxian contribution to sociological vocabulary.

First, the term *Klassenkampf* (class struggle) is widely associated with Marx and with his most celebrated revolutionary pamphlet—the *Communist Manifesto*. "The history of all hitherto existing societies is the history of class struggles," Marx provocatively writes in the first section of his rallying cry to the proletariat (Marx and Engels [1848] 1934:10).

As a term that is popularly associated with Marx, "class struggle" serves to remind one that the popular, often superficial familiarity with Marx's work is frequently very uninformed and misleading. Therefore, it is not just the term but also the term and its full meaning that should be kept in mind. To do this, one must think of class struggle within the full context of Marx's work (after all, Marx took no credit "for discovering the existence of classes in society or the struggle between them" [Marx and Engels 1955:69]). Properly understood, class struggle suggests at least seven aspects to Marx's work that are both critical to his sociology and important contributions to the classical tradition.

First, the notion of class clearly indicates that social change centres on the actions of many people—not individuals. Second, the notion of class struggle also emphasizes that groups pushing for social change are located in particular, objective locations within the social whole. The working class exists as a class of wage workers that will struggle for change due to the particular way in which the means of social production are distributed and controlled. Third, class struggle simultaneously reminds us that there is a subjective element to social change—a particular class consciousness within human agents must develop before they will push for change (revolutionary change or reform). Fourth, the notion of struggle and class struggle bring to the fore Marx's belief that social formations are dynamic, unstable, contradictory, dialectical wholes. At the same time, that realization reminds us that Marx's work, although powerful and insightful, was never completed to his satisfaction; Marx did not finish his project, and, as Mills (1962:11) emphasizes, Marx's work is neither the definitive word in sociological analysis nor the definitive contribution to the classical tradition.

The term itself—especially in its German original, *Klassenkampf*—appears, initially at least, as precise and provocative, but it is really suggestive of several forms of conflict. *Kampf* is clearly "struggle," but the notion of struggle (particularly in German) carries a range of meaning that stretches from combat to strife and even to a simple encounter. This potential ambiguity is important within the overall context of Marx's work as a sociologist because it reminds us that he was fully aware of the different forms that class struggle could take at varying points in time under changing social conditions with differing objective outcomes in view (see Lichtheim 1965). That is the fifth point: *Klassenkampf* is provocative but also nuanced, which is how Marx's work should be understood.

Sixth, class struggle, as an objectively based aspect of social change, takes the sociologist directly into the economic infrastructure of society, which is, according to Marx, the correct departure point for a critique of political economy and the basis for a truly critical social analysis. The economic infrastructure is more than simply the relationship between the physical means of production and the social relations of production (the property relations or class relations); the economic infrastructure involves real and living working men and women as one component of the means of production, the conditions under which they work, and their growing consciousness of those conditions in association with the social relations of production. It is the subtle ways in which class consciousness develops and is directed within the context of specific relations of property ownership that is fundamental to Marx's overall analysis of capitalist society and to his conception of class struggle.

Finally—although this list could be extended much further—*Klassenkampf* reminds us of the impact that the Enlightenment had upon Marx's work. According to Marx, freedom—freedom from exploitation—increases as the working class recognizes and masters the circumstances in which it is located and then engages in the political struggle to overcome them. Progress toward greater freedom, equality, and human fulfilment were Marx's major objectives, and *Klassenkampf* encapsulates the Enlightenment aspect of Marx's project so well.

Although other terms from Marx contribute to our understanding of social relations and processes, "class struggle" is an important one to incorporate into a vocabulary "adequate for clear social reflection"; it enhances intellectual craftsmanship and helps stimulate the sociological imagination.

Key Terms and Names

Communist League
Communist Manifesto
bourgeoisie
class struggle
modernity

Questions for Review and Further Reflection

1. Think about Marx's description of the bourgeoisie and the proletariat. To what extent does this capture the reality of class relations in Canada or the United States at the present time? Identify two other countries with which you are familiar—does the *Manifesto* capture the dynamic of class relations there?

2. This chapter refers to the *Manifesto* as a manifesto for modernity. What are the features of modernity that Marx captures in the *Manifesto*? Are those features still relevant to today's social world? Are there other features that one would have to include to update the *Manifesto* as a manifesto of modernity?

3. Create a mind map of the most significant elements in Marx's theoretical position. Compare it to the mind map you made earlier of Mills's idea of the sociological imagination. Where do those mind maps overlap? Where are they different? What is important about the differences?

4. If you were to choose five key terms (rather than one) for understanding Marx's theory, what would they be and why? Define each in your own words. Describe how they interrelate.

6

FROM DESCARTES TO DURKHEIM: TOWARD A SCIENCE OF SOCIETY

Main Objectives

This chapter will

1. Introduce the work of Émile Durkheim—the "founder" of one of the dominant macrosociological frameworks used by sociologists.
2. Describe the overall intellectual context within which Durkheim's sociology arose.
3. Present the key aspects of the work of Descartes, Montesquieu, Saint-Simon, and Comte and indicate their contributions to the development of sociology, in general, and Durkheim's work in particular.
4. Identify Durkheim's major contributions to sociology.
5. Describe the development of Durkheim's thought within his work *The Division of Labor in Society*.
6. Discuss five key terms and their interrelationship within *The Division of Labor in Society*: conscience collective, mechanical solidarity, organic solidarity, repressive law, and restitutive law.

The second key figure within the classical tradition is **Émile Durkheim**. Although Comte named the discipline "sociology," Durkheim is justifiably considered the principal founder of sociology as a specific area of study. Durkheim secured sociology's first foothold in higher education by establishing the Department of Sociology at the University of Bordeaux in 1895 and beginning, a year later, the publication of the first sociology journal—*L'Année sociologique*. He also dedicated his career to demonstrating the unique nature and strengths of the empirically based, systematic study of society. *The Rules of Sociological Method*, which Durkheim publishes in 1895, charts a new, formal path for the study of the social world—not one without controversy, to be sure, but Durkheim's work is clearly central to the future directions of sociology as a discipline.

Born in Épinal, France, in 1858, Durkheim had a life and academic career far more tumultuous, contested, and controversial than most commentators acknowledge. For example, some speak or write dismissively of the "dead, white, European males" (the DWEMs) who founded sociology (the usual reference is to Marx, Weber, and Durkheim, but it could include others). They write as though the DWEMs all lived similar lives, as if they were all privileged patriarchs, securely established in the dominant class, maintaining and reproducing the system that gave them their advantages. Durkheim would have had great difficulty reconciling his personal or academic life with that characterization (Peyre 1960).

Far from being a member of the ruling elite, Durkheim was marginalized as a member of the Jewish minority within a country and educational system that the Roman Catholic Church dominated. Throughout his life, Durkheim experienced anti-Semitism in a number of overt and subtle ways, and his social standing was frequently fragile and uncertain.

Durkheim had one particularly painful period in his life. His son André, once a student under Durkheim at the Sorbonne and on his way to becoming his father's intellectual collaborator, was conscripted into the army and killed in action on the Bulgarian front during World War I in the spring of 1915 (Lukes 1973:555). A very short while later, due to Durkheim's religious affiliation, his residency in France was challenged and the ensuing senate debate was covered in the daily newspapers. In January 1916, *Libre parole* slanders him as a Jew collaborating with the Germans although, in truth, Durkheim strongly supported the French war effort (Lukes 1973:557).

But Durkheim was resilient, and, as Lukes's (1973:99–102) extensive biography indicates, he pursued his intellectual labours within a caring, supportive extended family environment. Durkheim was not an exclusionary, dominating patriarch. Along with his wife Louise (née Dreyfus), his son André, his daughter Marie, various nephews (the most famous of whom was the anthropologist Marcel Mauss), and other friends and colleagues, Durkheim worked collaboratively on the advancement of sociology, as they edited, proofed, and kept *L'Année sociologique* going in its early years. The deaths in World War I of several friends and supporters who had worked in the Durkheim household were felt as deep personal losses and had a devastating impact upon French sociology because the household's work had become such a shared undertaking.[49]

Jeffrey Alexander (1986) emphasizes that Durkheim came into maturity "in the crucible of the formation of the Third Republic in France" (p. 94). That experience helped Durkheim crystallize some particular concerns and

---

49 The impact of war on French sociology extended into World War II when the Nazis invaded Paris, forcing Marie to flee and leave behind all of Durkheim's books and manuscripts, which the occupying forces destroyed (Meštrović 1988).

issues that he explored throughout his career as a sociologist. Durkheim recognized that French society had to change if it were to become more stable; he believed that stability would only come with greater social justice (particularly in the distribution of economic product). He also believed that the state had to be restructured to ensure greater justice but that this restructuring should not occur at the expense of individual freedom. "Durkheim," Alexander (1986) notes, "described these goals as socialism, but he insisted, to use contemporary terms, that this be socialism with a voluntaristic or human face" (p. 94).

Similarly, Durkheim's intellectual struggles are largely overlooked in most of the standard accounts of his work as a sociologist. Part of the reason is the extremely influential presentation and interpretation of Durkheim's work in the magnum opus of Talcott Parsons (1949)—*The Structure of Social Action*. In critiquing utilitarian theory and individualist accounts of social action—one of the main objectives of *The Structure of Social Action* and a perspective Parsons shares with Durkheim—Parsons (1949:352–55) emphasizes the holistic, functionalist, organic, and positivist dimensions of Durkheim's work at the expense of the more historically and empirically based accounts of the dynamic tensions in social life, accounts that Durkheim addressed from his first review essays in 1885 through to *The Elementary Forms of the Religious Life* of 1912.[50]

Parsons's interpretation was so dominant partly because of the stature Parsons and his work held in the post–World War II period but also owing to the limited range of Durkheim's work available in English translation. Additionally, although Durkheim's key studies—*The Division of Labour in Society* ([1893] 1933), *The Rules of Sociological Method* ([1895] 1982), *Suicide* ([1897] 1951), and *The Elementary Forms of the Religious Life* ([1912] 1915)— were all published during his lifetime, a number of additional works appeared posthumously, which further constrained sociologists' exposure to his ideas. *Sociology and Philosophy* ([1924] 1953), *Moral Education* ([1925] 1973), *Socialism and Saint-Simon* ([1928] 1958), *The Evolution of Educational Thought in France* ([1938] 1977), *Leçons de sociologie: physique des moeurs et du droit* (*Sociology Lessons: The Physics of Morals and the Law*; 1950), *Pragmatism and Sociology* ([1955] 1983), and *Durkheim's Philosophy Lectures* (2004) were not available until much later in the twentieth century or early in the twenty-first, and none of them was translated until after Parsons's book had already become one of the most influential studies in North American sociology.

These additions to Durkheim's published work are critical because they allow scholars to appreciate the development of Durkheim's ideas more fully

---

50 For more on the nature and impact of early North American interpretations of Durkheim, see Alexander (1986:91–93) and Giddens (1972:38–48). Compare with Parsons (1949:301–450, 1968).

and to understand some of the important struggles—as well as the reasons for them—that he deals with in sharpening his conception of sociology. Far from following a simple, internally driven developmental progression, Durkheim's work evolves through its author's active engagement with his social and intellectual environment.

Although French thought from Descartes through Montesquieu and Rousseau to Saint-Simon and Comte is the primary influence in Durkheim's work, he also draws critically from other traditions and perspectives. One such focal point is the individualist theory of the English utilitarians and their instrumental, rationalist explanations for the emergence of collective order. The social and the individual, Durkheim ([1892] 1960:137) maintains throughout his career, are dissimilar, and sociology must focus on the way and extent to which the social creates a socialized individual rather than beginning with fictitious, isolated individuals and explaining society as the unintended or unseen consequence of their individual actions or their individual, rational calculation. Providing an alternative explanation for the basis of social interaction and of the emergence of society leads Durkheim to his position that society is a *sui generis* (self-generating) entity into which individuals are born and through which they are socialized (or made into social beings). Society, he will argue, is a separate entity that can only be understood from a unique perspective—a sociological one. Sociology must develop as a discrete social science that deals exclusively with social relationships and social facts.

In a similar manner, Durkheim criticizes the materialist reductionism of the orthodox Marxists. The social whole cannot, Durkheim maintained in opposition to the growing influence of various Marxist positions in France, be reduced to the instrumental rationality of economic actors. Nor is the superstructure simply a direct, automatic reflection of the economic infrastructure (see Durkheim [1897] 1982). Durkheim placed far more emphasis on the role of ideas and what he terms collective consciousness and collective representations than did the orthodox Marxists of his day.

Finally, as explanations of how societies are held together, Durkheim rejects the ahistorical and metaphysically based arguments of the idealist holists, such as Hegel, or of those proposing a universal moral imperative, such as Kant. Rather than following the philosophers' attempts to discover a single, absolute criterion of morality—Hegel's absolute reason or Kant's categorical imperative, for example—and using it as a measuring rod for different societies in history, Durkheim argues that one must start with the complex moral rules that actually exist within a society and determine how these arose from particular social arrangements. Morality, cohesiveness, and solidarity are all, in Durkheim's view, created by and within a social whole. Social phenomena must be understood inductively and not deductively. Thus, rather than starting with a specific premise or set of premises and then deducing a set of philosophically based social laws, Durkheim argues that sociologists must start with observable "social facts" as they exist. The sociologist sees how these seemingly separate facts link together and builds them into a more complex, cohesive explanation of the society as a whole. The ultimate goal is to establish some specific sociological laws (see Durkheim [1909] 1982).

Two interwoven threads run through Durkheim's debates with various intellectual traditions. One focuses on the conundrum of the modern world. How can modern societies continue to thrive? Durkheim sees that social cohesion requires "collective ideals which surpass the experience and activities of the individual," yet "in the course of social development, traditional values seem to become increasingly dissolved" in modern societies, creating greater individuation and allowing each individual greater and greater freedom (Giddens 1972:2).

The other thread is his commitment to a realist conception of knowledge. That is, there is a real basis to society as a self-generating entity—society is an empirical reality. To understand that reality, however, one must develop concepts that are not "an idea of the mind" but are revealed through the study of phenomena that are observable and lead to concepts which, though "less apparent are doubtless more essential" (Durkheim [1895] 1982:75). Sociologists must pursue the study of the underlying laws of society in the same manner as "physicists, chemists and physiologists when they venture into an as yet unexplored area of their scientific field" (p. 37).

Before focusing directly on Durkheim, this chapter will highlight some of the key elements within French social thought that influenced Durkheim's particular approach to sociology. What becomes most apparent in such an overview is the extent to which Durkheim accepted some aspects of earlier French social thinkers while also sharply rejecting others—forcing him to clarify exactly what an empirical social science involves.

Descartes and Montesquieu

René Descartes is a pivotal thinker in the early development of the empirical, observationally based social science that Durkheim advocates. Descartes wrote his *Discourse on the Method of Rightly Conducting Reason and Seeking Truth in the Sciences* in 1637 to establish firmly the basis for certain knowledge. His system of methodological scepticism begins by doubting anything that is not clearly true (Descartes 1911:92). In order for problems to be resolved properly and adequately, Descartes then argues, they should be divided into as many parts as necessary, and the analysis must begin with those elements that are the simplest and easiest to understand. Progressing to the more complex, the analysis must ensure that no possible explanations are overlooked or left out of consideration.

This *Discourse* was groundbreaking in the seventeenth century for four reasons. First, in opposition to the classical tradition in philosophy (the scholastic theology and church doctrine that had dominated the intellectual world since medieval times), Descartes shifts the focal point for the pursuit of true knowledge from metaphysical premises or religious doctrines to a method involving rigorous contemplation of the world. The foundation for certainty starts with rigorous deductive practices, according to Descartes, but those deductions must then be tested through observation and the careful consideration of those observations. This standard for empirically based knowledge becomes central to Durkheim's aspirations for sociology as a scientific undertaking (see Durkheim [1895] 1982:40–43, 72–74).

Second, Descartes's conception of method and his radical doubt cast all previous knowledge into question; unless knowledge is derived from rigorous deduction and observation, it cannot make any claim to certainty or truth. So all previously accepted truths about the natural or social world can no longer be accepted automatically simply because they existed or were supported by tradition or traditional beliefs. Descartes's method, then, undercuts tradition as the justification for existing ways of doing things and existing social and political relationships.

Third, Descartes's method firmly supported the then-emerging inductive methodologies of the natural sciences and maintained that the scientific method should apply to all forms of human knowledge in order for that knowledge to be reliable, unbiased, and certain.

Finally, Descartes's method positions critique as central to the scientific method—all claims must be open to scrutiny, criticism, and confirmation before they can be accepted as true.

Although other philosophers would refine Descartes's rules of method over the next two centuries, his philosophy was central in fundamentally changing the way scientists—natural and social—approached the gathering, synthesizing, and testing of knowledge from the mid-seventeenth century onwards. Descartes's method is also the thin edge of the wedge that ultimately divides philosophical thought from scientific thought. Because of Descartes's method, some social scientists began to believe that philosophy produces largely speculative knowledge that might serve as a source for hypotheses while science empirically tests hypotheses to develop positive knowledge that is highly, if not completely, certain. This distinction led some sociologists to argue that sociology could only develop further if it broke away from philosophy completely and pursued the systematic collection of "social facts" or empirical information (see Durkheim [1909] 1982).

Montesquieu is often identified as the first, genuine precursor of sociology—and for good reason. Although Montesquieu, like Hobbes before him and Rousseau who follows, is mainly concerned with forms of government, his approach to understanding the state and the social order is highly sociological—more sociological, in fact, than that of almost any other scholar of his day who attempted a systematic analysis of political or social issues. In fact, Durkheim ([1892] 1960) argues that, although it is a mistake to link the birth of a science to a particular thinker—"since every science is the product of an unbroken chain of contributions and it is hard to say exactly when it came into existence"—it is Montesquieu "who first laid down the fundamental principles of social science" (p. 61).

Montesquieu came from a privileged background and was genuinely interested in the realm of ideas, the world of letters, and the various salons of eighteenth-century France. Montesquieu read widely, kept detailed notes from his readings, and genuinely sought to advance knowledge. Finally, he travelled extensively and used those opportunities to meet other scientists and scholars (Cohler 1989:xii–xviii).

Montesquieu's works include the *Persian Letters* ([1721] 1972) and *Considerations on the Causes of the Greatness of the Romans and Their Decline* ([1734] 1968), but it is *The Spirit of the Laws* ([1748] 1989) that represents the culmination of his life's work (Montesquieu [1748] 1989:xliii).[51] *The Spirit of the Laws* draws upon over 300 sources and contains 3,000 references and 2,000 notes. Although rich in insight, the text is poorly organized, lacks a coherent argument, and ranges over almost every domain of human behaviour and into questions of philosophical judgement, even though it claims to be a treatise on law. Despite those weaknesses, it is groundbreaking in several important respects.

First, *The Spirit of the Laws* is one of the most empirical works in social thought produced in the mid-eighteenth century. On the basis of his own observations or those found in the historical record, Montesquieu develops several basic principles about how societies are governed. From these simple principles, he argues, one can virtually predict the histories of the nations under study. Laying this groundwork for an empirical approach to the study of social and political life, then, was Montesquieu's major contribution to sociology (Durkheim [1892] 1960:3–24).

In *The Spirit of the Laws*, Montesquieu classifies societies on the basis of how they are governed, and he identifies three types—despotic governments, monarchies, and republics (which can take an aristocratic or a democratic form). Each form of government is characterized by a "nature" and a "principle."

---

51 In a letter written in the same year that *The Spirit of the Laws* was published, Montesquieu notes, "I can say that I have worked on it my whole life: I was given some law books when I left my *collège*; I sought their spirit, I worked, but I did nothing worthwhile. I discovered my principles twenty years ago: they are quite simple; anyone else working as hard as I did would have done better. But I swear this book nearly killed me; I am going to rest now; I shall work no more" (quoted by Cohler 1989:xi; see also Montesquieu [1748] 1989:xlv). *The Spirit of the Laws* was his last book.

"He derives these three types not from any a priori principle [as Aristotle did]," Durkheim ([1892] 1960) observes, "but from a comparison of the societies known to him from his study of history, from travellers' accounts, and from his own travels" (p. 25).

The "nature" of government refers to who (or what group) holds sovereign power—a despot, a king, or a legislative body—while the "principle" refers to the passion or spirit that animates those who govern. Fear is the principle of despotism; honour the principle of monarchy; and virtue the principle of a republic. Good governments, Montesquieu concludes after more than two decades of research, have a nature and principle that are consistent with the dominant spirit of the people who make up the society as a whole. This idea of a collective spirit determining the nature of acceptable governance is of considerable significance for Durkheim's understanding of both society as a *sui generis* entity and how society shapes individuals' behaviour.

Although many of his arguments are difficult to accept today, Montesquieu's work has sociological import because it breaks down the entire social system into its component parts and then examines how they work together to produce a whole that is greater than the simple sum of its parts. To comprehend the laws of a society fully, he maintains, one has to see them as part of a larger system within which they serve a particular purpose. In order to do that, one has to understand the different parts of a social system as they and the system itself develop over time. This, in turn, means that one has to examine the system's underlying causes—both physical and moral.

Durkheim agrees with both of these ideas. In *The Rules of Sociological Method*, he uses biology to establish his own claim that society—the domain of sociology—is more than the sum of the individuals comprising it. A living cell, Durkheim ([1895] 1982) argues, is comprised of molecules of "crude matter." But those molecules are in association with one another, "and it is this association which is the cause of the new phenomena which characterise life, even the germ of which it is impossible to find in a single one of these associated elements" (p. 128). In *The Division of Labor in Society*, Durkheim compares the moral order—the *conscience collective* (collective conscience and consciousness)—of traditional and modern societies to understand their differing forms of social integration and cohesion.

According to Montesquieu's *The Spirit of the Laws*, physical causes—for example, the climate, terrain, and population density—play a role in a social system's development, but moral causes are of much greater importance because they shape a society's spirit. Building his argument on the basis of historical material drawn from Roman, Chinese, and European history, Montesquieu argues that this spirit grows out of a society's dominant religion, its laws, maxims, mores, customs, styles of thought, and the atmosphere in a nation's capital or court (Montesquieu [1748] 1989:308–33, especially p. 310). Law, in Montesquieu's analysis, is only one way of controlling people's conduct—which makes Montesquieu among the first to focus upon mechanisms of social control other than a centralized state or government.

Four aspects of Montesquieu's approach were influential in Durkheim's conception of sociology. First, Montesquieu places a heavy emphasis on the importance of empirical observation in the study of societies. Although contemporary sociologists might think he overstates the claim that he develops his principles from "the nature of things themselves," there is a far greater empirical basis to his work than one finds in that of other social and political thinkers of this period. In conjunction with the work of Saint-Simon and Comte, this would become a central feature of Durkheim's sociology.

Second, Montesquieu bases his holistic approach to the study of forms of government and the laws regulating human action on a unique analysis of more basic social processes—customs, mores, and styles of thought. Durkheim also adopts a holistic approach to understanding social phenomena, drawing in a similar manner upon customs, mores, and styles of thought to serve as the key indicators of a social formation (see Durkheim [1895] 1982:39–43).

Third, Montesquieu's notion of the spirit of a society resonates strongly with Durkheim's concept of the *conscience collective*. Both Montesquieu and Durkheim see this spirit or consciousness developing within the social whole and also changing as the social formation and the relationships among individuals change.

Finally, in *The Division of Labor in Society*, Durkheim ([1893] 1933) focuses upon two different types of law—repressive and restitutive—to serve as indicators of which form of social solidarity, mechanical or organic, dominates within a social formation. Montesquieu created the basis for that undertaking by linking the nature of laws within a society to the spirit of the society as a whole. Durkheim did not fully agree with Montesquieu's analysis, but he certainly profited from Montesquieu's approach.

Saint-Simon and *The Industrial System*

Claude Henri de Rouvroy, comte de **Saint-Simon** is one of the more interesting and tragic figures in sociology.[52] Saint-Simon lived through the French Revolution and its turbulent aftermath. As a result, he experienced and felt, at first hand, the powerful optimism of the French *philosophes'* Enlightenment rationalism, he believed in progress, and he shared the hope that the French monarchy's demise and the fall of French feudalism would

---

52 The material on Saint-Simon's biography presented here is based on Markham (1964) and Taylor (1975), but see also Durkheim ([1928] 1958:82–89).

usher in a new era of human freedom. But the Reign of Terror (September 1793 to July 1794) left Saint-Simon deeply concerned with the problem of social order in the post-feudal era.[53]

Saint-Simon's works parallel, to a large extent, his personal and intellectual fortunes and misfortunes. These works include *Letters from an Inhabitant of Geneva*, first published in 1802; *Memoir on the Science of Humankind* and *A Work on Universal Gravitation*, two manuscripts from 1813; *The Reorganization of European Society*, a booklet written with Augustin Thierry in 1814; his contributions to the periodicals *L'industrie* between 1816 and 1818, *L'Organisateur* between 1819 and 1820, *The Industrial System* between 1821 and 1822, and *The Catechism of Industry* between 1823 and 1824; and, finally, his book *Social Organization, the Science of Man* ([1825] 1964) and his unfinished *The New Christianity*. Saint-Simon's writings are extremely broad in scope, and, although he left no genuinely enduring work, his legacy is one of intriguing insights that led later thinkers in many directions. Saint-Simon is best regarded as a catalyst for those who came afterwards.

From 1800 to 1813, Saint-Simon was primarily concerned with the unity of knowledge based on Newton's law of gravitation—the clearest example of scientific thought in Saint-Simon's estimation. In 1814, Saint-Simon turned to issues of social organization, and his work *The Reorganization of European Society* drew considerable, positive attention. From 1816 to 1825, Saint-Simon considered the coming of industrial society, what its structure would be like and the implications it had for the future of humanity. This period culminated in *On Social Organization*. Finally, Saint-Simon's unfinished *New Christianity* aimed to establish a new sense of religiosity, one appropriate to an industrial society and able to constitute the cohesive force that religions had provided throughout human history.

Saint-Simon's contributions to the development of sociology are numerous, and they are important for Durkheim. First and foremost, Saint-Simon champions the development of an empirically based science of society (Durkheim [1928] 1958:90–109). Following Montesquieu, Saint-Simon's work, and that of his successors, reinforced the break from metaphysical and speculative social thought and affirmed the use of an empirical, scientifically inspired approach to the study of society. Although he never developed the idea systematically, Saint-Simon tried to establish a "social physics" that would eventually lay out the laws of social development. These laws were complemented by his "social physiology," which focused on the scientific

---

53 *La Terreur* (The Reign of Terror) was a period of brutal repression that followed the Jacobins' seizure of power in June 1793. (The Jacobins constituted a powerful political force in the French Revolution.) The Jacobin-controlled Convention passed "the Law of Suspects," which permitted arrest for any "crime against liberty." The Jacobins terrorized their domestic enemies using the guillotine to display publicly the revolutionary government's power.

study of human interaction. Both of these concepts are catalysts in the development of what emerged as a sociology that sought to employ the same methodology as the natural sciences.

Second, Saint-Simon's emerging sociology was heavily influenced by conservative thinkers such as the Marquis de Condorcet and Louis de Bonald. In his *Letters from an Inhabitant of Geneva*, Saint-Simon uses the structure of medieval society as his enduring reference point. According to Saint-Simon, medieval society was comprised of different orders, which were arranged in an important, functional hierarchy that eliminated all class conflict. At the base, there were the producers (the feudal serfs) who were coordinated by a ruling, or temporal, elite (the nobility), and the entire society was integrated by the spiritual elite—the Roman Catholic Church.

These three orders—the spiritual elite, the governing elite (or temporal elite), and the productive classes—became the template for Saint-Simon's conception of both social structure and the evolutionary development of societies through history (Saint-Simon 1975:70–77). This conception of society as an integrated, functional, evolving entity is the third point of importance in his work.

Although Saint-Simon views society in holistic and functional terms, he also sees it as an evolutionary, developmental entity. According to Saint-Simon—although Comte would later articulate this point more clearly as "the law of three stages"—human history moves through an identifiable progression of stable, organic civilizations. Western history began with classical Greece and Rome, societies that had a polytheistic ideology, a slave economy, and a monolithic state. By the eighth century, this polytheistic and slave-based social formation had given way to medieval society, which was characterized by Roman Catholic theology, a feudal economy, and a ruling nobility. The benefits of medieval society were a more humane means of production (indentured versus slave labour), a more systematic theology, and the separation of temporal and spiritual power within the state.

In the fifteenth century, Saint-Simon argues, as craftwork grew and independent workshops became increasingly important in social production, one sees the beginning of the emerging industrial society within medieval Europe. Craft, guild, and eventually industrial production meant that more and more serfs and peasants found work in the cities as wage earners freed from the life-long obligations of serfdom. Enlightenment rationality and science became the new spiritual system (or theology), and the state, in Saint-Simon's view, would be increasingly controlled by industrialists and scientists to ensure the maximum technological and industrial development. In *The Industrial System*, Saint-Simon praises the virtues of this emerging industrial society.

Industrial societies, Saint-Simon maintains, will eliminate war and poverty through the tremendous productivity that large-scale, scientifically planned industrial production can deliver. There will be work for all, assigned on the basis of ability and merit, and all will have the opportunity for advancement in an open, classless, knowledge-based society. Continuous development will be ensured by the central role of science in the spiritual realm, and the state will change from one of government characterized by class power and national rivalries to one of social welfare or administration that is scientifically managed by skilled technocrats. In this emerging industrialized society, Saint-Simon sees the scientists, artists, and men of letters as constituting the spiritual elite, the industrialists the temporal elite, and the workers the highly valued, direct economic producers.

Saint-Simon synthesized many diverse influences into his various writings, and his work inspired a variety of very different intellectual and political projects. Read by many and recorded at an important time in European history, Saint-Simon's ideas—his call for a "science of society"; his holistic, organic conception of society comprised of functionally interdependent orders (or institutions); and his stage theory of history—were provocative and generated considerable interest. But although his ideas were intriguing, they were not well integrated. The task of systematizing and developing Saint-Simon's scattered ideas fell to his former secretary, **Auguste Comte**, whose primary ambition was to found the new science of society.

Comte and Sociology as a Positive Science

From 1817 to 1824, Comte served as Saint-Simon's recording secretary, and it is clear from Comte's subsequent work that the elder Saint-Simon had a tremendous impact on his thought. At the same time, Comte was a strong, independent thinker in his own right who ultimately broke from Saint-Simon and set out his own grandiose goals. In 1822, Comte published his *Plan of Scientific Studies Necessary for the Reorganization of Society*—the blueprint for his ambition to change the moral, intellectual, and social landscape of Europe.

Viewed in total, Comte's work involves five key elements. First is the idea that human societies and human knowledge had progressed through three stages (this idea came to be known as "the **law of three stages**"). As Comte boldly notes at the outset of his six-volume *Course in Positive Philosophy: A Discourse on the Positivist Spirit*,

> Studying the total development of the human intelligence in its various spheres of activity, from its first trial flights up to our own day, I believe I have discovered a fundamental law to which it is subjected from an invariable necessity.... This law is that each of our principal conceptions, each branch of our knowledge, passes successively through three different

theoretical states: the theological or fictitious, the metaphysical or abstract, and the scientific or positive.... Hence there are three mutually exclusive kinds of philosophy, or conception systems regarding the totality of phenomena: the first is the necessary starting point of human intelligence; the third its fixed and final state; the second is only a means of transition. (Comte 1974:19–20)

Comte also notes that, due to the varying complexity of the different sciences, the least complex develops first and the most complex at the end. As a result, the scientific or positive stage first developed in astronomy and physics and then in chemistry and physiology before finally shaping social physics (or sociology).[54] Comte's first goal, as outlined in his *Plan of Scientific Studies Necessary for the Reorganization of Society*, is to establish the positivist form in all branches of knowledge, including the study of societies.

The second key element of Comte's thought is his notion of **positivism**. He views positivism as a system of knowledge based exclusively on the methodology of the natural sciences. "Positivism," Comte (1974) argues, "is first of all characterised by that necessary and permanent subordination of imagination to observation which constitutes the scientific spirit, as opposed to the theological or metaphysical spirit" (p. 139). Comte's goal was to treat social phenomena in exactly the same way that natural phenomena were treated in the natural sciences. The main emphasis in social thought, according to him, should be centred fully and squarely on the collection and examination of empirical, observationally based knowledge.

Comte's real concern, however, is understanding social stability and social change the third element of importance in his work. "Order and progress," Comte (1974) writes, "which antiquity regarded as irreconcilable, constitute, from the nature of modern civilization, two equally necessary conditions whose combination is at once the principal difficulty and the principal strength of every political system" (pp. 126–27). "No order," he continues, "can now be established, and above all can now endure, if it is

---

54 Comte first designated the positivist study of society as "social physics" but abandoned the term in 1838 in favour of his newly minted term "sociology." He derived the word from the Latin word *socius* ("companion," "associate") and the Greek term *lógos* (which has various meanings including "word," "speech," "logic," and "thought"). Thus sociology would deal with thought regarding association or the logic of association. The first book with sociology in its title was Herbert Spencer's 1873 *The Study of Sociology*. Part of the reason Comte abandoned social physics was the publication of Belgian statistician Adolphe Quetelet's book *Physique sociale* in 1835, but the deeper reason was a shift in Comte's own thought. Up to 1838, Comte had regarded mathematics as the methodological basis of all the sciences, including his social physics. However, as he progressed further and further into the *Course of Positive Philosophy*, he began to give greater emphasis to the importance of history. His use of the Latin and Greek terms suggests that Comte came to view sociology as being focused on the logic of, or thought about, human association.

not fully compatible with progress; and no great progress can be effected, unless it tends to consolidate order" (Comte 1974:127).

To emphasize his position, Comte contrasts the existing situation in France with his notions of order and progress. He depicts the period following the French Revolution and continuing up to the writing of his *Course in Positive Philosophy* as one of revolution, an ensuing reaction, and a return to an ongoing revolutionary struggle—a period, in other words, of tremendous social instability. The former defenders of Louis XVI's *ancien régime* reacted to the revolutionary changes of 1789 by trying to re-establish the monarchy and the feudal order. Comte understands this as an attempt by the aristocracy and clergy to turn back the clock—to return to the lower theological stage of development.

Those who tried to resist the gains of the revolution, in Comte's view, were motivated by irrational desires and lacked a coherent plan. "In the half century during which the revolutionary crisis of modern societies has been developing," he contends, "one cannot disguise the fact that all the great efforts in favour of order have been guided by a retrograde spirit, and the principal efforts for progress by radically anarchical doctrines" (Comte 1974:127).

Comte (1974) maintains, then, that "the development and the propagation of science, industry, and even the fine arts" result from the rise of the positivist spirit as society moves into its highest stage of development. "It is the ascendancy of the scientific spirit which preserves us today" (p. 131). Because of this belief, he works fervently to establish positivism in general and sociology—the positivist study of societies—in particular.

Comte also presents the principles of social physics at great length in the *Course in Positive Philosophy*—in far too much detail to discuss here. There are, however, three key aspects worth noting, and these demonstrate his conception of a scientific sociology. It is Comte's conception of sociology as a science that represents the fourth key element of his thought.

Positive philosophy, according to Comte, ensures that observation, "which constitutes the scientific spirit," replaces "imagination" as the basis for knowledge. Referring to his elaboration of the fundamental sciences, which he presents in three earlier volumes, Comte (1974) notes that positive philosophy

> restricts its activity to discovering or perfecting either the exact coordination of the facts as they stand, or the means of undertaking new investigations. It is this habitual tendency to subordinate scientific conceptions to the facts—it being the sole function of these conceptions to demonstrate the interconnection of the facts—that must be introduced into social studies, where vague and ill-defined observation still offers no sufficient foundation for truly scientific reasoning, and is continually being modified by imagination under the stimulus of very lively passions. (P. 139)

What Hobbes, Montesquieu, and Saint-Simon suggested, Comte fully and formally asserts—observable facts are the groundwork of science, both natural and social.

Second, positive philosophy rejects the notion of absolute truths—all of its findings and observations are relative—that is related to a particular situation. If we consider "the actual scientific conceptions in positive philosophy," Comte (1974) writes, "we see that in contradistinction to theologico-metaphysical philosophy it has a constant tendency to make all those notions relative which had been considered absolute" (p. 140). "From the purely scientific point of view," he continues, "it seems to me we may regard the contrast between the relative and the absolute as expressing the antipathy between modern and ancient philosophy":

> Every study of the inner nature of beings, of their primary and final causes, etc. must obviously be absolute, while every investigation of the laws of phenomena is eminently relative, since it presupposes that the progress of thought is dependent on the gradual improvement of observation, exact reality being never, in any subject, perfectly disclosed: so that the relative nature of scientific conceptions is inseparable from the true notion of natural laws, just as the chimerical attachment to absolute knowledge accompanies the use of theological fictions or metaphysical entities. (Comte 1974:140)

In other words, because of the absolute spirit inherent in political studies under the theological and metaphysical forms of thought, the only means by which people can propose solutions to social and political problems is through the search for conclusive and unqualified truth. And these solutions are inevitably cast in all or nothing terms: some men are born free while some are born slaves in Plato's *Republic*, only the Leviathan can prevent the war of all against all in Hobbes, humankind needs to return to its former state of nature to escape the problems of the current social contract, according to Rousseau. Gradual reform can find no genuine place in these absolutist metaphysical systems; however, gradualism, progressively better understandings, and reform are all consistent with the new scientific worldview of positivism.

Finally, Comte (1974) argues that positive sociology allows for one other important advantage for social reform—the capacity for rational prediction. "The very idea therefore of rational prediction presupposes that the human mind has definitely quitted the region of metaphysical idealities in politics, in order to take its stand on the firm ground of observed realities through a systematic and constant subordination of imagination to observation" (p. 145).

This dimension of positive sociology has tremendous political implications—social systems and social problems can be observed carefully and systematically, leading to relative insight appropriate to that time and the given knowledge of a society. This analysis would suggest reforms, which, once in place, would allow for further careful observation and a prediction of outcomes if nothing more were done or if other changes were made. This leads to the fifth and final key idea in Comte's thought—positive sociology as a science of **social statics** and **social dynamics** (Comte 1974:147–50).

Positive sociology focuses on societies as they are at given moments in time—the science of social statics. On the basis of that science, reforms can be implemented that lead to an evolutionary development of the society—Comte's social dynamics. Comte draws upon biology for an analogy to make his point clear—social statics deals with the anatomy of a society and social dynamics with its physiology. With this example, Comte brings the metaphoric similarity of societies and biological organisms into the centre of his positive sociology, and that organic analogy will be adopted by ensuing sociologists to their great profit and loss. For Comte, the notions of social statics and social dynamics link to his conceptions of order and progress. Comte considers social change to be the evolutionary development of science and all social formations.

To summarize, Comte's key contributions to the emergence of sociology are the following. Comte, for better or for worse, names the positive study of societies "sociology." Comte insists that knowledge passes through three stages—the theological, the metaphysical, and the positive. The positive stage, according to him, emphasizes the central importance of observation and rejects the theological and metaphysical conceptions of absolutes. On the basis of positivist knowledge, scientifically based knowledge can inform social reform and thereby remove the threat of reaction or revolution, so there will be a stable relationship between order and progress. Reform also allows for progressive change—scientifically planned and monitored progress.

Comte associates his idea of order and progress with his conceptions of social statics and social dynamics, and all these concepts lend support to his use of an organic analogy for the study of societies—the anatomy and physiology of society. Finally, the law of the three stages and the triumph of positive science as well as the conceptions of order and progress, social statics and dynamics, and social anatomy and physiology are all consistent with Comte's idea that all realms of knowledge can be known on the basis of the same rational, observationally based, positive science. Comte was one of the most passionate advocates for what is often called the unity of the sciences—the belief that there is one true scientific method and that it can be applied to both natural and social phenomena.

Forms of Social Solidarity and *La Conscience Collective*

Durkheim's major contributions to the development of sociology really stem from his 1893 study *The Division of Labor in Society*. His other key contributions—*The Rules of Sociological Method* ([1895] 1982), *Suicide* ([1897] 1951), and *The Elementary Forms of the Religious Life* ([1912] 1915)—consider in greater detail specific aspects of some of the central issues Durkheim addresses in *The Division of Labor*. Despite the apparent specificity of *The Division of Labor*, it constitutes the departure point for almost all that followed in Durkheim's career—including his work on methodology, his debate with French Marxists, and his conception of socialism. In *The Division of Labor*, Durkheim introduces a key concept in the development of his sociological perspective—*la conscience collective*—and expresses his commitment to a particular conception of "positive sociology" (Durkheim [1893] 1933:79, 32).[55]

In view of the strategic importance of *The Division of Labor* in Durkheim's work, it is worth noting how it provided the impetus behind the encompassing sense of sociology that emerges from his research and writing. The quick overview to follow will highlight the relationship between Durkheim's first systematic, sociological study and the key dimensions of his sociology.

Faced with the emerging tensions of modernity that Durkheim experienced firsthand in the Third Republic, the growth of class conflict that culminated in the massive Decazeville strike of 1886, and the cleavages that led to and were fostered by the growing challenge of European socialism, French intellectuals at the end of the nineteenth century felt an immediate and urgent need to know whether an industrializing society could ever become stable. Durkheim was no exception. In the preface to the first edition of *The Division of Labor*, he acknowledges that this work "had its origins in the question of the relations of the individual to social solidarity" (Durkheim [1893] 1933:37; Gouldner 1958:xxiv–xxv).[56] The nature of social cohesiveness—social solidarity—remains a central element in all of Durkheim's sociology. But, it should be emphasized, it is the *nature of social solidarity within specific social contexts* that Durkheim makes the focus of his work—he was not engaged in the pursuit of some abstract question of social order or some universal explanation for social order or social solidarity.

Because the demise of feudalism across western Europe was associated with so much social strife, dislocation, and conflict, the transition from agrarian to modern society became the focal point of a growing body of academic analysis. The theme is addressed to some extent in Montesquieu's

---

55 The French noun *conscience* contains two meanings—consciousness as well as conscience. Both are important because, according to Durkheim, the dominant social consciousness also serves as a guide to behaviour—as a conscience of what is appropriate and what is not. Parsons (1949) argues that, because the way the term is translated may result in "an interpretive bias, ... [i]t seems best here [in *The Division of Labor*] to leave it untranslated" (p. 309, note 3; see also the translator's comments in Durkheim [1893] 1933:ix).

56 The subtitle of the first edition of *The Division of Labor* is *A Study of the Organization of the Advanced Societies*.

and Rousseau's works, and it is certainly central to the work of Saint-Simon and Comte who, according to Durkheim ([1928] 1958), viewed it very differently (Gouldner 1958:x–xv). The theme also resonates with work in Germany undertaken by sociologists such as Ferdinand Tönnies ([1887] 1957), Albert Schäffle (1896), and Paul von Lilienfeld (1873).

Although *The Division of Labor* concentrates almost exclusively on the substantive problem of social solidarity, Durkheim also uses it to introduce another of his major contributions to sociology: sociology's methodology.

In *The Division of Labor*, Durkheim first presents his case—elaborated more fully in *The Rules of Sociological Method* and in *Suicide* and also central to his discussion of *Socialism and Saint-Simon*—for sociology as a positive science (Durkheim 1972:117–20, 121–22). "This book," the opening sentence of the preface to *The Division of Labor* reads, "is pre-eminently an attempt to treat the facts of the moral life according to the method of the positive sciences" (Durkheim [1893] 1933:32). In making this decision, Durkheim criticizes the approach others used to explain social solidarity while presenting the key elements of his own, empirically inspired approach to sociology's methodology (Durkheim [1893] 1933:44–46).

The question of stability in the modern world concerns the relationship between the individual and the social whole. In many respects, Durkheim's entire sociology stems from how he presents this relationship within both *The Division of Labor* and some of his subsequent studies. As a result, Durkheim's key concepts—society as a *sui generis* phenomenon that pre-exists individuals and the internalization of an externally existing collective consciousness—developed out of his analysis of the changing form of solidarity within what he calls "the advanced societies."[57]

In *The Division of Labor*, Durkheim ([1893] 1933) poses two specific questions:

> Why does the individual, while becoming more autonomous, depend more upon society? How can he be at once more individual and more solidary? Certainly, these two movements contradictory as they appear, develop in parallel fashion. This is the problem we are raising. (P. 37)

His answer involves the social effects of the division of labour. "It appeared to us," he writes at the end of his first preface, "that what resolves

---

57 Perhaps the most controversial aspect of Durkheim's sociology is his use of language and his apparent reification of (or giving reality to) entities that do not have a real, palpable existence. But Durkheim is very careful to emphasize that these references are analogies—ways to help conceptualize social phenomena—and not reifications. Thus, for example, when he writes in *The Rules* that "social facts" can be treated "like things," he is constructing a simile and not a statement of identity. This issue is addressed at greater length in Chapter 7.

this apparent antinomy is a transformation of social solidarity due to the steadily growing development of the division of labor. That is how we have been led to make this the object of our study" (Durkheim [1893] 1933:37–38).

Consequently, it is the general question of social cohesion and stability, examined within the context—an increasingly controversial context—of advanced societies that leads Durkheim to focus on the division of labour. This specific focus would draw him to more general insights and to claims that he would pursue in detail within the context of other specific, empirical social situations, such as rates of suicide or forms of religion. As a result, from a very specific social issue—the relationship of individuals within a social whole—Durkheim begins a study that ultimately evolves into his particular approach to understanding the intersection of personal biography with history and social structure.

THE DIVISION OF LABOUR IN SOCIETY

The central argument in *The Division of Labor* distinguishes Durkheim from almost all other commentators on and analysts of either the division of labour—for example Smith, Say, and Sismondi—or the differing natures of traditional and modern societies—for example, Saint-Simon, Comte, Tönnies, Schäffle, and Lilienfeld. The work also draws together those two seemingly disparate topics into one integrated analysis that features Durkheim's key contributions to sociology. It is a fascinating study and presentation.

At the outset, Durkheim ([1893] 1933:49–56) demonstrates that the division of labour is much more than an economic phenomenon and that to view it solely in economic terms misses its most important social function. The key aspect of the division of labour, for Durkheim, rests in its fundamental role as the basis for social cohesion.

Acknowledging that "everybody knows that we like those who resemble us, those who think and feel as we do," Durkheim ([1893] 1933) notes that "the opposite is no less true":

> It very often happens that we feel kindly towards those who do not resemble us, precisely because of this lack of resemblance. These facts are apparently so contradictory that moralists have always vacillated concerning the true nature of friendship and have derived it sometimes from the former, sometimes from the latter. (P. 54)

Quoting Aristotle and Heraclitus, Durkheim shows that both positions extend back to classical philosophy and to ancient Greek conceptions of morality. "These opposing doctrines," Durkheim ([1893] 1933) maintains, "prove that both types are necessary to natural friendship. Difference, as likeness, can be a cause of mutual attraction" (p. 55). But not all differences can serve as the basis of friendship—only those differences that "instead of opposing and excluding, complement each other" constitute the basis for friendship:

> As richly endowed as we may be, we always lack something, and the best of us realize our own insufficiency. That is why we seek in our friends the qualities we lack, since in joining with them, we participate in some measure in their nature and thus feel less incomplete. So it is that small friendly associations are formed wherein each one plays a role conformable to his character, where there is a true exchange of services. One urges, another consoles; this one advises, that one follows advice, and it is this apportionment of functions, or to use the usual expression, this division of labor, which determines the relations of friendship. (Durkheim [1893] 1933:55–56)

Durkheim then moves from the personal to the social in his investigation of the division of labour. This shift is the first step in Durkheim's study of the relationship between the division of labour in a society and that society's form of social solidarity:

> We are thus led to consider the division of labor in a new light. In this instance, the economic services that it can render are picayune compared to the moral effect that it produces, and its true function is to create in two or more persons a feeling of solidarity. In whatever manner the result is obtained, its aim is to cause coherence among friends and to stamp them with its seal. (Durkheim [1893] 1933:56)

To open the way for his argument that the division of labour serves as the basis for "the integration of the social body to assure unity," Durkheim uses Comte's notion that the division of labour is "the most essential condition of social life, provided that one conceives it 'in all its rational extent; that is to say, that one applies it to the totality of all our diverse operations of whatever kind, instead of attributing it, as is ordinarily done, to simple material usages'" (Durkheim [1893] 1933:62–63).

The empirical study of social solidarity presents one fundamental problem: social solidarity "is a completely moral phenomenon which, taken by itself, does not lend itself to exact observation nor indeed measurement" (Durkheim [1893] 1933:64). One needs an empirical indicator of social solidarity that one can observe, study, and measure—the indicator that Durkheim ([1893] 1933:64–68) selects is the law.

This decision is critical for two reasons in particular. First, it moves the analysis of social solidarity—the basis for a moral order—away from abstract philosophy directly into the concerns of sociology. Sociology, it turns out, can develop an empirically based understanding of the moral order within a society. Also, Durkheim suggests, to inform social policy, social solidarity can and should be studied through an empirically based sociology rather than through the well-worn paths of abstract philosophical argument.

Second, the examination of law as an indicator of social solidarity requires (and allows) Durkheim to introduce his central conception—*la conscience collective*—which is the social substratum of the legal system. Different types of law are indicative of different types of social conscience or consciousness and different types of social solidarity.[58] This concept is an excellent example of Durkheim's scientific realism. The scientist or sociologist starts with an observable entity—in this case the law. In studying the law, breaking it down into its constituent elements and understanding their relationships, one discovers an underlying reality that cannot be otherwise seen—the real basis for a society's moral order and cohesion, that is, the precise nature of *la conscience collective* in the society under study.

Before focusing on the two types of law that Durkheim discusses, one should examine his notion of the *conscience collective*. Because the term is so critical to his sociology and also to the way he links law to forms of solidarity, it is worth citing Durkheim's presentation at length.

> The totality of beliefs and sentiments common to average citizens of the same society forms a determinate system which has its own life; one may call it the *collective* or *common conscience*. No doubt, it has not a specific organ as a substratum; it is, by definition, diffuse in every reach of society. Nevertheless, it has specific characteristics which make it a distinct reality. It is, in effect, independent of the particular conditions in which individuals are placed; they pass on and it remains. It is the same in the North and in the South, in great cities and in small, in different professions. Moreover, it does not change with each generation, but, on the contrary, it connects successive generations with one another. It is, thus, an entirely different thing from particular consciences, although it can be realized only through them. It is the psychical type of society, a type which has its properties, its conditions of existence, its mode of development, just as individual types, although in a different way. Thus understood,

---

58 The study of law in *The Division of Labor* also provides insight into another relationship that Durkheim presents in some of his later work—the connection between different levels of social integration and the extent to which an individual follows or deviates from the expected course (or norms) of behaviour, a relationship that represents or allows for changes in the existing collective conscience/consciousness. According to Durkheim, deviance plays an important function in determining the limits of what is accepted by the overall collective conscience in society (see Durkheim [1895] 1982:97–104).

it has the right to be denoted by a special word. The one which we have just employed [*conscience*] is not, it is true, without ambiguity ... [and even though it might be preferable] to create a [new] technical expression especially to designate the totality of social similitudes ... the use of a new word, when not absolutely necessary, is not without inconvenience.... [Therefore] we shall employ the well-worn expression, collective or common conscience, but we shall always mean the strict sense in which we have taken it. (Durkheim [1893] 1933:79–80)

Durkheim packs a lot into that lengthy paragraph.

The *conscience collective* is not a palpable thing—it cannot be seen directly, touched, smelled, or tasted—and yet it exists. It is there before the individuals constituting a society are born so it exists separately from the conscience or consciousness of each individual—it is virtually external to them. Nevertheless, the *conscience collective* is learned and internalized by each individual and comes into existence during individuals' lives through their thinking, judging, and acting. As a result, it is also a product of their existence, but it is not set in stone—the collective conscience or consciousness may change over time, even though it demonstrates a relatively enduring content. The *conscience collective* will endure after the individuals in a society are gone. Finally, the collective conscience/consciousness is enormously encompassing, even though few people can enumerate all of its aspects with any precision. It is captured quite well in the very simple, yet deeply profound phrase, "that's just the way it's done," which suggests operational instructions about how to do things as well as a moral assessment of what one ought to do.

The term *conscience collective* is ambiguous in some ways, but it can be examined and elaborated upon. Most important, it can and must be examined and elaborated upon through a discussion of different indicators drawn from real social life. It is through the *conscience collective* that the individual and society are actually brought together in social action.

With this pivotal term in place, the remainder of Durkheim's argument in *The Division of Labor* centres on the extent to which one of the two basic types of law—repressive or restitutive—serves as an indicator for a particular form of **social solidarity** and the implications that this has for life in the modern world.

Durkheim ([1893] 1933:102–5) argues that **repressive law** is a highly intense response by the members of societies in which it is found to anyone who has transgressed the ideals embodied in the *conscience collective*. It is, Giddens (1972) explains, "an expression of anger on the part of the community, the avenging of an outrage to morality" (p. 6; see also Foucault [1975] 1995:3–32). Repressive law, Durkheim ([1893] 1933:70–110) details at length, is consistent with traditional, face-to-face societies—societies characterized by what he terms "mechanical solidarity" (pp. 105–9).

Durkheim ([1893] 1933:129) uses the term **mechanical solidarity** to emphasize that the individual is bound almost directly to the society through a *conscience collective* that provides a single, powerful, total belief system. The term also conveys an analogy that links this form of organization with that of a simple organism, one having a mechanical unity insofar as each cell is wholly compatible with every other and necessary for the survival of the whole—if any part of the organism fails, the organism would die.

On the other hand, **restitutive law** corresponds to a social solidarity "of a totally different kind" (Durkheim [1893] 1933:111). Restitutive law does not involve the suffering of the transgressing individual but simply "*the return of things as they were*, in the reestablishment of troubled relations to their normal state" (Durkheim [1893] 1933:69).[59] Restitutive law, Durkheim ([1893] 1933:111–29) documents, is only possible in societies in which individuals are increasingly dependent upon other individuals carrying out specialized social functions—in other words, in societies with an advanced division of labour.

This second type of solidarity—**organic solidarity**—represents a solidarity in which each individual "depends on society, because he depends upon the parts of which it is composed": it is "a system of different, special functions which definite relations unite" (Durkheim [1893] 1933:129).

According to Durkheim, mechanical solidarity dominates "only if the ideas and tendencies common to all members of the society are greater in number and intensity than those which pertain personally to each member." He continues, "Solidarity which comes from likenesses is at its maximum when the collective conscience completely envelops our whole conscience and coincides in all points with it" (Durkheim [1893] 1933:129–30).

Organic solidarity, on the other hand, presumes people are different. Under the conditions of mechanical solidarity, "the individual personality is absorbed under the collective personality"; whereas organic solidarity is "only possible if each one has a sphere of action which is peculiar to him":

> It is necessary that the collective conscience leave open a part of the individual conscience in order that special functions may be established there, functions it cannot regulate. The more this region is extended, the stronger is the cohesion which results from this [organic] solidarity. In effect,

---

59 "What distinguishes [restitutive] sanction," Durkheim ([1893] 1933) writes, "is that it is not expiatory, but consists of a simple *return in state*. Sufferance proportionate to the misdeed is not inflicted on the one who has violated the law or who disregards it; he is simply sentenced to comply with it. If certain things were done, the judge reinstates them as they would have been. He speaks of law; he says nothing of punishment. Damage-interests have no penal character; they are only a means of reviewing the past in order to reinstate it, as far as possible, to its normal form" (p. 111).

on the one hand, each one depends as much more strictly on society as labor is more divided; and, on the other, the activity of each is as much more personal as it is more specialized.... Here, then, the individuality of all grows at the same time as that of its parts. Society becomes more capable of collective movement, at the same time that each of its elements has more freedom of movement. This solidarity resembles that which we observe among the higher animals. Each organ, in effect, has its special physiognomy, its autonomy. And, moreover, the unity of the organism is as great as the individuation of the parts is more marked. Because of this analogy, we propose to call the solidarity which is due to the division of labor, organic. (Durkheim [1893] 1933:131)

Durkheim uses the remainder of *The Division of Labor* to examine the dynamic that leads from mechanical to organic solidarity.

In summarizing the main arguments of his book, Durkheim ([1893] 1933) maintains that, even though advanced society has become increasingly dependent upon an advancing division of labour, "it does not become a jumble of juxtaposed atoms." Instead, its "members are united by ties which extend deeper and far beyond the short moments during which exchange is made" (p. 227).

Men cannot live together without acknowledging, and consequently, making mutual sacrifices, without tying themselves to one another with strong, durable bonds. Every society is a moral society. In certain respects, this character is even more pronounced in organized societies. Because the individual is not sufficient unto himself, it is from society that he receives everything necessary to him, as it is for society that he works. Thus is formed a very strong sentiment of the state of dependence in which he finds himself. He becomes accustomed to estimating it at its just value, that is to say, in regarding himself as part of a whole, the organ of an organism. Such sentiments naturally inspire not only mundane sacrifices which assure the regular development of daily social life, but even, on occasion, acts of complete self-renunciation and wholesale abnegation. On its side, society learns to regard its members no longer as things over which it has rights, but as co-operators whom it cannot neglect and towards whom it owes duties. Thus, it is wrong to oppose a society which comes from a community of beliefs to one which has a cooperative basis, according only to the first a moral character, and seeing in the latter only an economic grouping. In reality, co-operation also has its intrinsic morality. There is, however, reason to believe, as we shall see later, that in contemporary societies this morality has not yet reached the high development which would now seem necessary to it. (Durkheim [1893] 1933:228)

In this summary, Durkheim presents the empirical insights that he had gained from his study of the growing division of labour in advanced societies and the changing form of social solidarity upon which it was based. At the same time, however, he imparts his own optimistic, normative view of what the future should hold—a future in which the *conscience collective* will accord greater justice for all members of society and in which everyone shares a moral position that safeguards the social whole and the individuated individual at the same time. On the basis of this summary statement at the end of *The Division of Labor*, one gains a glimmer of insight into Durkheim's notion of what lay ahead in the future and into his conception of what a truly socialist society would be like.

Key Terms and Names

Émile Durkheim
René Descartes
Montesquieu
Saint-Simon
Auguste Comte
law of three stages
positivism/positive philosophy
social statics and social dynamics
conscience collective (collective conscience/consciousness)
social solidarity—mechanical and organic
repressive law
restitutive law

Questions for Review and Further Reflection

1. Compare and contrast the biographies of Marx and Durkheim. Why do you think the brief biographies of each thinker are included before examining their theories?
2. Divide a sheet of paper into four columns. In each column, list the main ideas associated with Descartes, Montesquieu, Saint-Simon, and Comte presented in this chapter. What are the similarities or themes common to the four? What are the differences among the four?
3. To what extent does the movement from Descartes to Comte represent a linear progression in theory?
4. What is meant by the term *conscience collective*? Why does Durkheim feel that he has to find an "empirical indicator" for the *conscience*

collective? What is the indicator that he settles upon, and why is it a good choice? Is there a better indicator?

5. What are the main characteristics of mechanical solidarity? What are the main characteristics of organic solidarity?

6. How would you describe the *conscience collective* among Canadians or Americans today? Are there other countries or regions of the world that exhibit a very different *conscience collective*? Pick one such place and describe the differences between its people's *conscience collective* and that of Canadians or Americans.

7

DURKHEIM AND THE SYSTEMATIC STUDY OF SOCIAL FACTS

Main Objectives

This chapter will

1. Trace the development of Durkheim's thought from *The Division of Labor in Society* through *The Rules of Sociological Method* to *Suicide*.
2. Introduce four key elements in Durkheim's *Rules of Sociological Method*—society as a *sui generis* reality, social facts, collective representations, and sociology as the science of institutions.
3. Outline Durkheim's study *Suicide*, and demonstrate its importance for the development of sociology as an empirical science.
4. Compare some of Durkheim's concepts to similar concepts in Marx's work, and discuss how they complement each other.
5. Describe how Durkheim's key concepts have been extended by later sociologists drawing upon Durkheim's perspective.

Although the central concern in *The Division of Labor* is the question of social order or social solidarity, this study also triggered Durkheim's concerns about establishing sociology as an independent, scientific discipline. As a result, in the preface to the first edition of *The Division of Labor*, drawing upon Descartes, Durkheim ([1893] 1933) argues that science "presupposed a complete freedom of mind" and that "we must rigorously submit ourselves to the discipline of methodical doubt" (p. 36). The arguments he presents in the study, Durkheim maintains, rest on authentic proofs given with "the greatest possible exactness." "To subject an order of facts to science," Durkheim ([1893] 1933) continues, "it is not sufficient to observe them carefully, to describe and classify them, but what is a great deal more difficult, we must also find, in the words of Descartes, *the way in which they are scientific*, that is to say, to discover in them some objective element that allows an exact determination, and if possible, measurement" (p. 36–37). The latter part of this sentence is the challenge Durkheim takes up in his next major publication, *The Rules of Sociological Method*—a text that has fundamentally shaped the methodology many sociologists have employed for more than a century in their study of the social world, as well as how they conceptualized the world they have systematically examined.

In the preface to *The Rules*, Durkheim ([1895] 1982) writes that his primary goal "is to extend the scope of scientific rationalism to cover human behaviour" and demonstrate relations of cause and effect in social action that would then allow sociologists to predict future actions (p. 33). *The Rules of Sociological Method*, Lukes (1982) emphasizes, is intended "as a manifesto on behalf of 'the cause of a sociology that is objective, specific and methodical'" (p. 2; see Durkheim [1895] 1982:35).

To accomplish this task, however, Durkheim has to answer the question he poses in *The Division of Labor*; he has to discover some "objective element" that sociologists can focus upon and that allows for "an exact determination, and if possible, measurement." The first chapter of *The Rules* addresses that question: Is there such an objective element in sociology, can it be determined exactly, and can it be measured? In other words, what is a social fact? What is the subject matter of sociology as a science?

"SOCIAL FACTS" AND THE SYSTEMATIC STUDY OF SOCIETIES

"Before beginning the search for the method appropriate to the study of social facts," Durkheim ([1895] 1982) writes in *The Rules*' opening paragraph, "it is important to know which facts are termed 'social'" (p. 50). There are many facts one might gather and learn about people, Durkheim points out: "Every individual drinks, sleeps, eats, or employs his reason and society has every interest in seeing that these functions are regularly exercised" (p. 50). But if these are **social facts**, "sociology would possess no subject matter peculiarly its own, and its domain would be confused with that of biology and psychology" (p. 50). But sociology is unique because in every society there are distinct phenomena that are different from those studied in the other sciences. Before this chapter examines how Durkheim identifies and defines those phenomena, it is worth noting why Durkheim feels compelled to distinguish sociology from biology and psychology.

Durkheim wants to separate sociology from biology because—of all the basic, natural sciences—biology is the one that deals with living beings, which is also the case for sociology. He demarcates the two by noting that sociology deals with shared ideas and patterns of conscious action as well as with social institutions and structures. Although social structures and processes might be *analogous* to biological structures and their functions, they are distinct enough to distinguish easily the subject matter of sociology from that of biology.

The distinction between sociology and psychology is less obvious and, for that reason, a more crucial one to make. More important than the need to make the distinction, however, is that the *way* Durkheim differentiates the two determines, fundamentally, his conception of sociology as the study of "society" as a macro-entity. In *The Rules*, Durkheim specifies that sociology's domain is the study of a pre-existing, self-generating entity, comprised of identifiable, institutionalized patterns of action into which individuals are born. Those individuals become social beings—they are socialized—and become members of a society as they internalize the existing ways of thinking, feeling, and acting—that is, the norms of the society.

To distinguish sociology from psychology, Durkheim notes that although both deal with consciousness and thought processes, psychology is concerned with the thought processes that are internal to the individual. Sociology, Durkheim ([1895] 1982) contends, is very different. Sociology deals with "ways of acting, thinking and feeling which possess the remarkable property of existing outside the consciousness of the individual ... [and] are endued with a compelling and coercive power" that imposes itself upon individuals (p. 51).[60] This is the subject matter of sociology, and it defines the types of facts that sociologists should study.

Although Durkheim's designation of sociology's field of study may appear contrived—thereby allowing him to distinguish sociology from psychology— his elaboration of what he intends clarifies the claim considerably.

> When I perform my duties as a brother, husband or a citizen and carry out the commitments I have entered into, I fulfil obligations which are defined in law and custom and which are external to myself and my actions. Even when they conform to my own sentiments and when I feel their reality within me, that reality does not cease to be objective, for it is not I who have prescribed these duties; I have received them through education.... Similarly the believer has discovered from birth, ready fashioned, the beliefs and practices of his religious life; if they existed before he did, it follows that they exist outside him. The system of signs that I employ to express my thoughts, the monetary system I use to pay my debts, the credit instruments I utilise in my commercial relationships, the practices I follow in my profession, etc., all function independently of the use I make of them. Considering in turn each member of society, the foregoing remarks can be repeated for each single one of them. (Pp. 50–51)

---

60 Further on in *The Rules*, Durkheim ([1895] 1982) returns to the distinction between sociology and psychology, stating that because social facts are external to the individual and exercise a coercive power, they cannot be derived from the individual. As a result, "sociology is not a corollary of psychology"—it is a separate discipline (p. 127).

One sees here that, for Durkheim, the ways an individual acts, thinks, and what she or he believes predates the individual and exist "outside" her or him. Further, as those ways of acting, thinking, and believing are internalized by each member of the society, they become social forces that constrain and enable each individual's particular actions. Durkheim ([1895] 1982) reinforces the point by referring to how children are raised.

Within the family and the education system, there is a continuous effort "to impose upon the child ways of seeing, thinking and acting which he himself would not have arrived at spontaneously" (p. 53). For example, children are taught table manners, what and when to eat, personal hygiene, etiquette, particular customs and conventions, respect for authority, punctuality, how to work cooperatively and independently, and so on.

These examples concern well-established practices, but not all social facts have reached such a "crystallised form," although they exercise the same external objectivity and coercive power over the individual. Durkheim ([1895] 1982) identifies these as "social 'currents'" (p. 52). In a public gathering, for example, individuals can be swept along in "the great waves of enthusiasm, indignation and pity that are produced [and] have their seat in no one individual consciousness" (pp. 52–53).

"We have" Durkheim ([1895] 1982) maintains,

> succeeded in delineating for ourselves the exact field of sociology. It embraces one single, well defined group of phenomena. A social fact is identifiable through the power of external coercion which it exerts or is capable of exerting upon individuals. The presence of this power is in turn recognisable because of the existence of some pre-determined sanction, or through the resistance that the fact opposes to any individual action that may threaten it. (Pp. 56–57)

With sociology's domain established and social facts defined, Durkheim ([1895] 1982) proceeds to specify how social facts must be studied: "The first and most basic rule is *to consider social facts as things*" (p. 60). Here Durkheim views the development of sociology as a science that is like any other science. Social phenomena are things insofar as a thing is the sole datum scientists study.[61] The careful observation of social facts and their relationships is the only way sociology can establish itself as an independent science and generate true, objectively based knowledge about social life.

In the preface to the second edition of *The Rules*, Durkheim remarks that this basic proposition created the greatest opposition to his rules of method.

---

61 "To treat phenomena as things is to treat them as *data*, and this constitutes the starting point for science" (Durkheim [1895] 1982:69).

How could Durkheim reduce social existence to the mere material world, his critics asked. But that was neither Durkheim's ([1901] 1982) claim nor his intent: "Indeed, we do not say that social facts are material things, but that they are things just as are material things, although in a different way" (p. 35). Durkheim elaborates:

> What indeed is a thing? The thing stands in opposition to the idea, just as what is known from the outside stands in opposition to what is known from the inside. A thing is any object of knowledge which is not naturally penetrable by the understanding. It is all that which we cannot conceptualise adequately as an idea by the simple process of intellectual analysis. It is all that which the mind cannot understand without going outside itself, proceeding progressively by way of observation and experimentation from those features which are the most external and the most immediately accessible to those which are the least visible and the most profound. To treat facts of a certain order as things is therefore not to place them in this or that category of reality; it is to observe towards them a certain attitude of mind. It is to embark upon the study of them by adopting the principle that one is entirely ignorant of what they are, that their characteristic properties, like the unknown causes upon which they depend, cannot be discovered by even the most careful form of introspection. (Pp. 35–36)

Treating **social facts as things** is Durkheim's foundational rule for the scientific study of social phenomena. From this rule, he proceeds to establish three "principal rules for this discipline, all of which are corollaries of the previous rule" (Durkheim [1895] 1982:72).

Durkheim ([1895] 1982) turns directly to Descartes to formulate the first corollary. "*One must systematically discard all preconceptions*"—this, he emphasizes, is the foundation of all scientific methodology (p. 72).

Second, Durkheim ([1895] 1982) maintains that science requires the precise definition of its subject matter. "To be objective," he continues, "the definition clearly must express the phenomena as a function, not of an idea of the mind, but of their inherent properties. It must characterise them according to some integrating element in their nature and not according to whether they conform to some more or less ideal notion" (p. 75). To clarify the point, Durkheim indicates that any actions taken by a member of a society that result in a response involving formal, legal punishment should be defined as crimes. Thus, the definition for a crime becomes acts that result in formal, legal punishment—a clear, objective definition that allows the sociologist to categorize all acts that meet that specific definition as criminal acts. There is no subjectivity involved; the classification of acts as criminal comes directly from the observed actions fitting the precise definition of criminal action.

Durkheim uses this point to lead into his third corollary on the **objectivity** of sociological knowledge. Objective knowledge stems from the actual properties of the object under study, not from one's idea of what that object might be like. As a result, all definitions in sociology must characterize the phenomena under study on the basis of their fundamental elements and not through some "ideal notion" of what they are like. This leads to the following rule:

> *The subject matter of research must only include a group of phenomena defined beforehand by certain common external characteristics and all phenomena which correspond to this definition must be so included.* (P. 75, Durkheim's emphasis)

Durkheim uses several examples to illustrate his point—examples related to crime, kinship, monogamy, and morality. On the last issue, in the language of his time, Durkheim ([1895] 1982) writes that "certain observers deny to savages any kind of morality." He sees this denial as a methodological error based on the existing European prejudices of what constitutes moral action (p. 79). Rather than beginning with the fundamental, distinguishing elements of the actions they are studying, many sociologists begin with a preconceived idea of morality and use that "ideal conception" to stand as their definition of moral action.

> To decide whether a precept is a moral one or not we must investigate whether it presents the external mark of morality. This mark consists of a widespread, repressive sanction, that is to say a condemnation by public opinion which consists of avenging any violation of the precept. Whenever we are confronted with a fact that presents this characteristic we have no right to deny its moral character, for this is proof that it is of the same nature as other moral facts. (Pp. 79–80)

Durkheim ([1895] 1982) links the importance of the clear and rigorous definition of terms back to his third corollary on objectivity. He emphasizes that the data sociologists use must be free from any taint of subjectivity. Just like natural scientists, sociologists must "discard observable data which may be too personal to the observer, retaining exclusively those data which present a sufficient degree of objectivity" (p. 81).

Objectivity, Durkheim notes, is dependent upon the clarity of the definitions of each social fact and the stability of that social fact. The example he uses comes from *The Division of Labor in Society*. The legal code is a stable collective representation of a society's attitude toward criminal behaviour. It is an objective social fact that imposes itself on the ways of thinking and acting in a particular society. The law is the law, so there is not, Durkheim claims, any subjectivity involved in using it as a useful, objective indicator of how the members of the society view themselves and their relationship to one another—it is a strong indicator of the type of social solidarity found in a particular society.

Aside from his description of social facts and how they should be analysed, four further points in *The Rules* merit elaboration. The first concerns the idea that "society" is a ***sui generis*** (self-generating) reality. The idea stems primarily from Durkheim's desire to establish sociology as a unique discipline. To do so, he must distinguish it from psychology, which is the discipline closest in subject matter. Indeed, Durkheim grants that both deal with forms of consciousness: psychology deals with individual consciousness while sociology deals with collective consciousness. But, Durkheim insists, collective consciousness is of a different order than individual consciousness: each is unique.

This claim arises from Durkheim's holistic philosophy: the whole is greater than the sum of its parts. The strength of bronze, Durkheim ([1901] 1982:39) indicates in the preface to the second edition, does not lie in the malleable properties of the copper, tin, or lead that make it up; it stems from their combination into one metal. The same is true of a living cell. Life does not exist inside atoms of hydrogen, oxygen, carbon, and nitrogen. "For how could living movements arise from amidst non-living elements?" Durkheim ([1901] 1982:39) asks rhetorically. "It is in the whole and not in the parts. It is not the non-living particles of the cell which feed themselves and reproduce—in a word, which live; it is the cell itself and it alone." And this is true of every type of synthesis, Durkheim affirms.

This principle applies to social life as well. A collective consciousness is not the same as an individual consciousness, nor is it equal to a number of them added together—according to the law of synthesis, it is something more. It is a unique phenomenon that is the subject matter solely of sociology. A collective consciousness exists: it is outside the individual members of a society, it is an ongoing entity, and it produces the consciousnesses of the society's individual members. The collective consciousness is a separate, self-generating entity.

> Social facts differ not only in quality from psychical facts; they have a different substratum, they do not evolve in the same environment or depend on the same conditions. This does not mean that they are not in some sense psychical, since they all consist of ways of thinking and acting. But the states of the collective consciousness are of a different nature from the states of the individual consciousness; they are representations of another kind. The mentality of groups is not that of individuals: it has its own laws. The two sciences are therefore as sharply distinct as two sciences can be, whatever relationships may otherwise exist between them. (Durkheim [1901] 1982:40)

In elaborating the distinction between sociology and psychology and defining the nature of social facts, Durkheim is inevitably led to the idea that society, in the form of collective representations, exists in and of itself. It predates its members and determines each individual's consciousness; and, in that manner, it is a self-generating entity.

The second point of note is Durkheim's attitude to history. In response to a question posed in 1908 on the method of sociology, Durkheim ([1908] 1982) responded that "it must be historical and objective" (p. 245). Because his particular conception of society emphasized its institutional structure and the collective representations that give it substance, Durkheim, like Mills, believes that good sociology involves the intersection of history and social structure.

"The purpose of sociology," Durkheim ([1908] 1982) writes, "is to enable us to understand present-day social institutions so that we may have some perception of what they are destined to become and what we should want them to become" (p. 245). But those institutions are complex entities that have developed over time in a piecemeal manner. History, Durkheim maintains, is "analogous to the microscope in the order of physical realities" (p. 245). That is, it provides detailed information about how particular institutions and ways of thinking and acting took shape. History provides insight into how collective representations arise, are consolidated, and change. The sociologist, Durkheim insists, cannot explain contemporary social life without examining how it comes into being.

The third issue of note concerns a change in terminology that Durkheim introduces in *The Rules*: a switch from the term *conscience collective* to "collective representations." He introduces the new term in his discussion of social facts. The impetus for the change appears to stem from "a watershed moment" Durkheim ([1907] 1982:261) experienced in the same year he published *The Rules*, 1895. That year, during a lecture course he delivered, Durkheim had a clear view of the profound importance played by religion in social life and how he could tackle religion sociologically. After this course, he started to focus on cultural or symbolic representations of the *conscience collective*, which he then began calling "collective representations." **Collective representations** express "the way in which [a] group thinks of itself in its relationships with the objects which affect it," Durkheim ([1895] 1982:40) writes in *The Rules*. Collective representations are the symbols a group or society uses to think of and visualize itself.

The advantage of studying collective representations over *conscience collective* stems from Durkheim's desire to establish an empirically based, scientific method for sociology and for the way he defines social facts and how to study them. *Conscience collective* sounds too philosophical, something that has been rationally deduced. Collective representations in the form of symbols, flags, dress, customs, mythologies, and totems, for example, form a far more concrete concept. In addition, the concept "collective representations" connects directly with numerous identifiable and empirical referents that a sociologist can study and relate to the "ways of acting, thinking and feeling which possess the remarkable property of existing outside the consciousness of the individual ... [and] are endued with a compelling and coercive power" that imposes itself upon individuals (Durkheim [1895] 1982:51).

In his debate with Marxism two years after writing *The Rules*, Durkheim ([1897] 1982) insists that social life and its causes "must be sought mainly in the way in which individuals associating together are formed in groups" (p. 171). A key element in how individuals form cohesive groups and create stability and coherence centres on how they represent themselves to themselves—that is, through their collective representations.

The final issue of note concerns the idea of institutions. In the preface to the second edition of *The Rules*, Durkheim ([1901] 1982) recognizes that his account of how social facts and collective representations come into existence is incomplete. He acknowledges that individuals play a role in the creation of social facts but insists that it must be several members interacting together that do this. This still means that the synthesis occurs outside those interacting members; the process involves "the crystallising" or "instituting outside [of themselves], certain modes of action and certain ways of judging which are independent of the particular individual will considered separately" (p. 45). It is the idea of "being instituted" that Durkheim now adds to his technical vocabulary. "In fact," Durkheim ([1901] 1982) writes, "without doing violence to the meaning of the word, one may term an institution all the beliefs and modes of behaviour instituted by the collectivity." And now, rather than defining sociology as the study of social facts, Durkheim defines it "as the science of institutions, their genesis and their functioning" (p. 45).

Durkheim and the Study of Suicide

Establishing sociology as a discipline was one of Durkheim's major objectives. *The Division of Labor in Society* and *The Rules of Sociological Method* were crucial steps toward that objective, but it is in his third major work, his study of **suicide**, that Durkheim ([1897] 1951) demonstrates the importance and power of sociological analysis. Here, Durkheim undertakes what seems to be an impossible challenge—a sociological explanation of what appears to be the most decisive, individual decision a person can make—deliberately self-inflicted death. Durkheim successfully demonstrates that a number of social factors predispose some and protect others from making that very critical decision.

Suicide is a sociological classic for three reasons. First, it successfully employed the methodology that Durkheim outlined in *The Rules*—the collection and analysis of particular social facts. Second, by showing how much sociology could contribute to a problem that seemed so far outside its area of analysis, *Suicide* demonstrated the power of sociological analysis. Finally, the study had a long-lasting impact upon one of the most interesting areas of sociological study—the sociology of deviant behaviour.

In general, Durkheim identifies three major categories of suicide—egoistic, altruistic, and anomic—and one minor type of "little contemporary importance," which he tentatively terms **fatalistic**.[62] Durkheim relates each to the way that different individuals, through the particular collective representations with which they identify, view the world around them and their lives within it.

With respect to **egoistic suicide**, Durkheim's analysis demonstrates that Protestants are more likely to commit suicide than Roman Catholics. Catholicism and Protestantism, which are based on fundamentally different collective representations of how the individual relates to the scriptures and therefore to God, leave believers differently vulnerable to egoistic suicide. In the Catholic Church, the pope is clearly and decisively God's messenger; the pope and his cardinals hold full authority in the interpretation of the Holy Scriptures. Church liturgy reinforces the pope's authority; the church is thoroughly hierarchical with the roles and responsibilities of pope, cardinals, priests, and parishioners well-defined. The Catholic credo is also highly unified and has a long, consistent history.

The collective representation of the proper relationship between the layperson and God is dramatically different within Protestantism. The dominant difference is the direct link between parishioner and God—although Church authorities aid in the interpretation of the scriptures, it ultimately falls to the parishioner to find his or her own meaning within the holy texts. The very structure of the Protestant Church and the reasons for its emergence form a very different social basis for the collective representations of religious meaning, religious affiliation, and religious obligation. These different collective representations lead Protestants and Catholics to see and understand the world in fundamentally different ways, according to Durkheim.

In the absence of a strong, centrally controlled religious credo, the spiritual bonds giving support and comfort to Protestants are much less encompassing and cohesive than those in the Catholic Church. When Catholics

---

62 The reference to fatalistic suicide occurs in a footnote on the last page of his discussion of anomic suicide. Durkheim ([1897] 1951) writes that one type of suicide, the "opposite" of anomic suicide, results from "excessive regulation" (p. 276). It is found among those whose "futures [are] pitilessly blocked and passions violently choked by oppressive discipline." It is the suicide, he notes, of the very young husband or a childless married woman, as well as of slaves in the historical past. "But," Durkheim indicates, "it has so little contemporary importance and examples are so hard to find aside from the cases just mentioned that it seems useless to dwell upon it."

have problems, they can rely on the church establishment for unfailing guidance and on the aid of the parish priest; in short, they find that they are not alone in facing difficult situations.

Protestants, on the other hand, have a less authoritarian religious belief system to draw from; they have to commune directly with God when in search of solutions to deeply perplexing problems. Protestant parishioners are left much more to their own devices than are Roman Catholics. The greater degree of individualism permitted by the Protestant faith, Durkheim argues, leaves Protestant parishioners more vulnerable to egoistic suicide.

If religion is one source of specific and powerful collective representations that influence people's decisions regarding suicide, there could well be others, and Durkheim's study of the data on suicides shows that this is indeed the case. Durkheim ([1897] 1951:171–216) found that the social facts pertaining to marriage had a different impact on men and women. Although marital status had no impact on women's decisions about suicide, married men were less apt to commit suicide than single men. Also, for both married men and women, the larger the family unit, the less likely they were to take their own lives.

In sum, according to Durkheim's research, the more others depend on an individual's social actions within a social situation the less likely it is that the individual will pursue his or her own goals exclusively (including, in some cases, suicide). Marital status (for men) and family size (for married men and women) create the social conditions in which people see themselves as part of a larger social unit, and this perspective, in turn, tempers feelings of excessive individualism or egoism and directly affects the likelihood of a person committing egoistic suicide. The internalized collective representations of family life shift one's focus from the self to the family unit as a whole.

The notion of collective representation also applies to tightly organized, highly integrated social situations (Durkheim [1897] 1951:217–40). The data that Durkheim studied showed that, in smaller, closed societies, several forms of suicide arose because the collective representations of those groups or societies placed the social whole well above the individual. As a result, individuals in those social situations were much more willing to sacrifice themselves for the greater collective good than to preserve their own individual lives. Durkheim concludes that, when collective representations value the individual less than the social whole, one finds a higher incidence of **altruistic suicide**.

Durkheim's example of altruistic suicide is also connected to a religious belief system. He notes that in India at that time, "the Hindu was already inclined to self-destruction under Brahminic influence" (Durkheim [1897] 1951:223–24). According to Durkheim, that tradition stipulates that once a man attains a certain age and has at least one son, he has fulfilled his life on earth and is free to "have nothing more to do with life." Durkheim ([1897] 1951) quotes from *The Laws of the Manu*: "The Brahmin who has freed himself from his body by one of the methods employed by the great saints, freed from grief and fear, is honourably received in the abode of Brahma" (p. 223). However, Durkheim ([1897] 1951) spends considerably more time examining altruistic suicide in the military, arguing that "the profession of a soldier develops a moral constitution powerfully predisposing man to make away with himself" (p. 239).

The third condition conducive to suicide, according to Durkheim, is one in which the normal, dominant collective representations of society are broken or significantly changed, leaving the individual with no guidelines to follow—people feel directionless and insecure (Durkheim [1897] 1951:241–76). Durkheim argues that, as religion loses its influence and as the distribution of goods, services, and wealth falls more and more to the growing capitalist market, individuals feel that there are fewer and fewer certainties in their lives. This loss of normality or "normlessness" leaves people in a state of **anomie**.[63]

"In one sphere of social life," Durkheim ([1897] 1951) argues, "the sphere of trade and industry, [anomie] is actually in a chronic state":

> For a whole century, economic progress has mainly consisted in freeing industrial relations from all regulation. Until very recently [1897], it was the function of a whole system of moral forces to exert this discipline. First, the influence of religion was felt alike by workers and masters, the poor and the rich. It consoled the former and taught them contentment with their lot by informing them of the providential nature of the social order, that the share of each class was assigned by God himself, and by holding out the hope for just compensation in a world to come in return for the inequalities of this world. It governed the latter, recalling that worldly interests are not man's entire lot, that they must be subordinate to other higher interests, and that they should therefore not be pursued without rule or measure. (Pp. 255–56)

But, Durkheim continues, "religion has lost most of its power. And government, instead of regulating economic life, has become its tool and servant" (p. 256). In the absence of regulation, Durkheim notes, people employed

---

63 The term "anomie" has its English equivalent—anomy—in seventeenth-century theology where it represents a state of lawlessness or a disregard of divine laws. The *Oxford English Dictionary* (OED) cites its first use in 1591 by William Lambarde in *Archion; or a commentary upon the High Courts of Justice in England*: "That were to set an Anomy, and to bring disorder, doubt, and incertaintie over all." Durkheim's use of the word stems from this meaning and is recognized by the OED as establishing a new definition for the term: "Also commonly in French form anomie. [F. (Durkheim *Suicide*, 1897).] Absence of accepted social standards or values; the state or condition of an individual or society lacking such standards."

in industrial or commercial occupations are more likely to commit **anomic suicide** than those who find their livelihoods in more stable environments.

The emerging dominance of the market economy posed a significant challenge to Europe during Durkheim's era because trade and industry were rapidly becoming the central social institutions in people's lives. As a result, Durkheim's study of suicide had far-reaching implications because, in view of the declining moral and guiding force of religion, a new institution was needed to integrate members of industrial capitalist society together to prevent deviant, asocial, or destructive behaviours from becoming more and more widespread and entrenched in people's lives. A healthy society requires strong collective representations that fully integrate individuals into the society.

At the end of *Suicide*, Durkheim ([1897] 1951:361–78) examines some potential forms of social integration. He argues, tentatively and with several important qualifications, that the *syndicates*—occupational organizations— have the potential to constitute the social groupings that will be able to generate the type of collective representations that can integrate people into an industrializing French society and prevent suicide or a growing sense of social isolation (Durkheim [1897] 1951:386–92).

Durkheim's study of suicide has four important implications for sociology. First, it demonstrates the power of sociology as a positive science to explain and predict social behaviour—even behaviour that seems to be completely personal and individually controlled.

Second, it exemplifies and confirms the strengths of Durkheim's rules of sociological method. It does so in three ways. Durkheim defines his social facts (or variables) objectively on the basis of how they exist in the real social world—Roman Catholicism, Protestantism, marital status, family size, and gender, for example. Next, he examines their interrelationships to discover some specific patterns of action that arise from the particular combinations of the social facts under study. Finally, Durkheim's use of a large body of data to examine the relationship between an independent variable (for example, religious affiliation) and a dependent variable (suicide) on the basis of a number of intervening variables—age, marital status, family size, or economic condition—shows that sociology can establish the same types of causal relationships and predictive capacities that are found in other sciences.

The third important implication of Durkheim's study of suicide is that it confirms the idea of society being greater than the sum of its parts and having an existence independent of the individuals who comprise it.

Finally, *Suicide* shows that through the generation of particular collective representations, which arise from specific social circumstances and change as those circumstances change, people internalize ways of seeing the world. Those representations then guide and control people's behaviour—including the apparently individual decision to commit suicide.

Durkheim's analysis of suicide indicates its author's perception that people are ultimately controlled by the social worlds in which they live. Following from Durkheim, Berger (1963:73–78) suggests that people are located at the centre of a set of concentric circles, each one representing a set of particular social facts. The mechanism by which external social facts are internalized is the social generation of particular collective representations of the world. As one lives within a world that is represented in particular ways, one's actions are then contoured by those understandings and images. Those who live in largely religious situations interpret all their actions according to the dominant collective representations of religion; those who live in abject poverty see the world in a very different way, and the collective representations stemming from genuine survival-of-the-fittest life experiences shape how these individuals think about the world and act within it.

Durkheim and Sociology as a Science

Durkheim is one of the founders of sociology partly because he played a major role in establishing Europe's first department of sociology and then launched and edited sociology's first academic journal—*L'Année sociologique*. As significant as those endeavours were, Durkheim's real importance centres on three specific accomplishments.

First, Durkheim is a pivotal figure in the development of an empirical approach to the study of society, an approach that looks toward the natural sciences. The general orientation to an empirically based science began with Francis Bacon (1864), Galileo Galilei (1967), and Descartes, all of whom contributed to the development of the scientific method during the seventeenth century. It was extended to the study of society by Montesquieu, Saint-Simon, and Comte. In the work of Durkheim, an empirically based scientific approach is consolidated and presented in a manner that leads to its further development by ensuing generations of sociologists. Less polemical, more measured, and far more methodical than Comte's writings, Durkheim's research and publications systematically build the foundation for a macro-oriented, empirical, and realist understanding of society.

Durkheim's *Rules of Sociological Method* proposes a methodology for sociology that later sociologists adopt and develop. *Suicide* sets the early standard for the empirical collection and analysis of objective social facts. Later sociologists will improve upon Durkheim's treatment of quantitative data, but Durkheim's work establishes the basic principles and methodology. In addition, Durkheim's empirical orientation to sociology is consistent with that of scholars who later maintain that the natural and social sciences are part of a unified, single approach to understanding the world. As one considers Durkheim's methodology, it is apparent why it is so central for sociologists who are committed to the unity of the sciences.

Those who support an empiricist or positivist approach to science argue that true scientific knowledge is built up from a number of axioms or propositions; these begin with basic, simple propositions that are logically coherent and form the basis for more complex propositions and conclusions. Positivists maintain that one must be able to test at least some, or all, of these statements to see if they might be falsified by empirical observations. Empiricists also argue that scientific knowledge is cumulative. As data are gathered and propositions are tested, new, more complex relationships and propositions can be formulated and tested, leading, ultimately, to a comprehensive theory. Finally, those who support a positivist approach to science believe in the integration of all the sciences—natural and social. Durkheim's work is consistent with this particular perspective and important in both establishing it and spreading its acceptance and influence among other sociologists.

Durkheim's second major contribution to sociology stems from his desire to establish sociology as an independent field of study with its own methodology. This meant he had to distinguish sociology from biology and psychology. In making the latter distinction, Durkheim defines social facts and demonstrates that "society" consists of a collective consciousness, which exists outside the individuals constituting this society and which shapes and controls their individual behaviours. Durkheim recognized that people are born into societies—or particular locations in societies. A society surrounds people in its symbols, customs, and **norms**—in short, in its collective representations. As a result, people are, to draw upon Berger's (1963:73–78) image, located at the centre of a number of concentric circles that shape each individual's behaviour.

The question of social order had haunted the classical thinkers from Plato and Aristotle through Hobbes and Montesquieu to Rousseau. Durkheim's work brings the question of social order directly and explicitly into the realm of sociology and connects it with an understanding of how societies are created and function. More important, his ideas about social control are much more far reaching than those of early philosophers and political theorists.

For political theorists, the solution to the problem of order rests with the state. A strong state or a just state is responsible for maintaining social order. For Durkheim, order is based on the collective representations that give a society its stability and coherence. Durkheim argues that every society, located within its own particular history, develops specific collective representations that are appropriate to its specific social makeup and made evident through a variety of different mythologies, traditions, and ways of thinking, for example. Through the **socialization** process, individuals internalize the dominant, socially accepted behaviours, attitudes, and beliefs. It is through this internalization process that the relationship of the individual and society—personal biography, history, and social structure—remains dynamic and changing.

In the event that the dominant ways of acting are not internalized, or only partially accepted, social order is still maintained because there are a number of mechanisms of social control that ensure some measure of compliance by all individuals in a society. The mechanisms of control include physical violence; political, legal, and economic regulation and sanction; and group pressures such as persuasion, ridicule, gossip, or ostracism. Indeed, these informal mechanisms of control that operate in daily life, such as mockery and isolation, are the most important for the ongoing functioning of a society in an orderly fashion.

Finally, although Durkheim is not recognized very often for his political activities, his work carried forward the ideas and aspirations of Saint-Simon and Comte for the orderly development of social change. Living within the cauldron of the Third Republic, Durkheim knew how important social change would be for the future of France, and, like Saint-Simon, he was sceptical about revolutionary transformation. Consequently, Durkheim's empirical sociology studies the key forces involved in social change so as to enable the development of social policy that would ensure an orderly progress toward an increasingly cohesive and just society.

Durkheim and a Vocabulary for Clear Social Reflection

On the basis of the material covered in this chapter, there are two key terms that Durkheim could add to the vocabulary one needs for "clear social reflection"—social facts and collective representations—although social facts alone might be sufficient.

The term "social facts" emphasizes several significant aspects of Durkheim's work and delineates his contributions to the classical tradition. First, it underscores his efforts to establish sociology as an empirically based science—efforts that grew out of a strongly positivist strand of French thought. For better or for worse, Durkheim wanted to establish sociology as a positive science by drawing heavily upon the work of Saint-Simon and Comte and upon their efforts to use the methodology of the natural sciences for the study of society. Saint-Simon, Comte, and Durkheim, more than any other sociologists in the eighteenth or nineteenth centuries, believed in the unity of the sciences.

Because social facts are external to an individual, the term "social facts" also reminds one that sociology has a distinct subject matter that focuses on the manner in which an individual is incorporated within or socialized into a pre-existing society comprised of other individuals who interact with one another on an ongoing basis. The internalization of social facts—the process of socialization—creates the important social bond that is central to Durkheim's sociology, and his conception of internalization leads directly to the notion of different forms of social solidarity.

The idea of social solidarity is critical to Durkheim for two reasons. First, the bonds of social solidarity—mechanical or organic—indicate that society predates the individual, is greater than the mere sum of its parts, and will continue to exist long after the individual is gone. Second, the fundamental factors determining and sustaining social solidarity, according to Durkheim, are 1) the collective consciousness that characterizes a society and 2) the collective representations its members create to identify themselves as a group.

It is through collective consciousness and collective representations that the individual and social are brought together—they are central concepts in Durkheim's conception of society as a whole, the source for tension and dynamism, and the focal point of almost all his work.

The notions of collective consciousness and collective representations have parallels to Marx's concept of the dominant ideology and Weber's concern with the enduring "frames of mind" that are critical to his sociology. As a result, collective consciousness and collective representations are useful focal points for comparing and contrasting the main ideas in Marx, Durkheim, and Weber while also serving as critical concepts in one's "vocabulary for clear social reflection."

Key Terms and Names

social facts
social facts as things
objectivity
sui generis
collective representations
suicide—altruistic, anomic, egoistic, and fatalistic
anomie
norms
socialization

Questions for Review and Further Reflection

1. Why does Durkheim feel that it is so important for him to establish the nature of "social facts?" What is a social fact according to Durkheim?
2. How does Durkheim try to clarify his idea that social facts exist "external to the individual?" What does he mean by saying that social facts have a "coercive power" over individuals?

3. What does Durkheim mean when he says that social facts should be treated as "things?" How does this relate to his idea that sociologists should treat social facts with "objectivity"? Why are these points so important to Durkheim's conception of sociology?

4. What does Durkheim mean by the term "collective representations"? Explain his idea that collective representations are "crystallizations" of how people act and that these representations become "instituted" or "institutionalized."

5. Think about Canada or the United States today. Using Durkheim's sociological explanation for suicide, discuss which types of suicide might be most prominent in view of the existing structural conditions and current collective representations of one of these societies.

6. Reflect on a social problem, such as unemployment. Basing your answer on Durkheim's differentiation between sociology, biology, and psychology, describe how a sociologist, biologist, and psychologist would go about understanding and addressing this issue differently.

7. How successful do you think Durkheim is in specifying why sociology is a unique discipline that has its own particular subject matter?

8. You have already created a mind map of the most significant elements in the theoretical positions of Mills and Marx. Now draw one for Durkheim. Where does the Durkheim mind map overlap with the other two? Where is it different? What is important about the differences? Which one do you think is most useful for studying the contemporary world?

8

WEBER AND THE INTERPRETIVE UNDERSTANDING OF SOCIAL ACTION

Main Objectives

This chapter will

1. Familiarize students with the work of Max Weber who, like Mills, advocates an approach to sociology that links micro action and meaning with macro social frameworks.
2. Present some of the key concepts in Weber's work: the pure or ideal type; *verstehen* (or understanding); and traditional, affective, value-rational, and goal-rational action.
3. Position Weber's contributions to the discussion of how sociology should be approached, understood, and developed through an outline of his work on the methodology of the social sciences.
4. Familiarize students with Weber's particular position on methodology in the social sciences and indicate its importance for sociology.
5. Present Weber's discussions about the limits and possibilities of science as the basis for a moral order.

Max Weber is regarded by most sociologists as the third major figure in the classical tradition of sociology. Born in Erfurt on April 21, 1864, Weber spent most of his childhood in Berlin, where his father, a prominent attorney, served as a member of the national parliament from 1872 to 1884. As a result, the Weber household was the site of numerous political discussions and debates as professors, parliamentarians, and other politically engaged figures came and went on a regular basis. In addition to these influences, Weber's mother, a devout Protestant, played an important role in shaping her son's outlook on the world. As a result, Weber was an extremely disciplined, principled, politically engaged scholar with a highly developed work ethic and a deep commitment to scholarship of the highest standard.

Although Weber was a full-time lecturer in Roman, German, and commercial law at the University of Berlin after 1892, his academic career really began when, in 1894, he became a full professor of economics at the University of Freiburg. In 1896, he moved to the University of Heidelberg, where he assumed the chair in political economy previously held by Karl Knies, one of Weber's former teachers and an economist of significant stature within Germany at the time. Weber's tenure as a professor was short-lived, however; he suffered from a debilitating emotional breakdown in 1897 and was unable to return to teaching, although he did not withdraw from scholarly work completely. In 1903, Weber became the lead editor of the prestigious *Archiv für Sozialwissenschaft und Sozialpolitik* (*Archive for Social Science and Social Policy*), which placed him at the centre of the most important methodological and substantive debates in the social sciences and humanities within turn-of-the-century Germany. In fact, it was as the editor for the *Archiv* that Weber first began to advocate for the approach to the social sciences that he pursued for the remainder of his active, academic life. Like Durkheim, Weber had a very specific notion of how social research must be conducted if it were to make a genuine contribution to social and political life.

Wanting to shape the social sciences did not mean that Weber wrote in a popular, accessible manner. On the contrary, Weber's formidable body of scholarly work is characterized by its painstaking research and thorough documentation. Weber is renowned—and sometimes vilified—for his attention to detail and nuance. Weber's work is often difficult to read because of the lengthy, complex sentences he constructs in order to carefully qualify each thought and present his arguments with the greatest possible precision. A reader must labour over Weber's texts to extricate all of his meaning and profound insight, but the rewards for taking the time to sift carefully through the density of Weber's arguments are enormous.

The vast corpus of Weber's work can be grouped under four headings—his studies in methodology (Weber [1903, 1905, 1906] 1975, [1905] 1949, [1907] 1977, 1949, 1968b, 2012); his more or less empirical studies (for example, of the relations of production in the ancient world or of economic history; Weber [1891] 1976, [1923] 1927); his studies of religion (Weber 1922, 1923a, 1923b, [1920] 2002); and his general treatise on sociology entitled *Economy and Society*, which was left incomplete at his death in 1920 (Weber 1956, 1968a). The discussion of Weber in this chapter will focus upon selected essays on methodology and his discussion of the basic principles and concepts of an interpretive sociology, which constitute the opening chapters of *Economy and Society*. Chapter 9 will examine one of Weber's most celebrated works—*The Protestant Ethic and the Spirit of Capitalism*—which brings together all four areas of Weber's work and can serve as the basis for useful comparisons with the work of Marx and Durkheim; that chapter will also examine Weber as a bridging figure between the modernist approach of classical sociology and the postmodernist perspectives one finds in a good deal of sociology today.

In many ways, Mills's conception of the sociological imagination is most heavily indebted to Weber's legacy. For Weber, sociology involves the development of a comprehensive understanding of social action. According to Weber, social life is the product of meaningful social action, and sociologists must strive to develop an interpretive understanding of the social world from the perspective of the human agents involved in it and then locate that meaningful action within the broader social framework within which it developed. Meaning, interpretive understanding, social action, and social context are key concepts for Weber, as they are for Mills.

How did Weber arrive at this particular conception of social action and the task of sociology? This chapter focuses primarily on the manner in which Weber's involvement in a critical debate on methodology in the social sciences and humanities (*Geisteswissenschaften*) led to his emphasis upon sociology as the systematic, interpretive study of social action. The chapter then examines Weber's commitment to scholarly activity, his understanding of what is entailed in science and scholarship as forms of social action, and the implications this understanding has for the role of science and sociology in determining the fundamental principles upon which a society should be ordered and governed.

The Historical School, Orthodox Marxism, and Interpretive Sociology

Writing in Germany at the end of the nineteenth and the beginning of the twentieth century, Weber was faced with two competing and mutually exclusive approaches to method within the social sciences and humanities in Germany. On the one hand, there is the longstanding, extremely influential approach of the historical school and, on the other, the emergence of **historical materialism**, popularly referred to as **orthodox Marxism**.

The position of the **historical school** was quite straightforward and very well established. Proponents of the methodology of the historical school maintained that the work of historians, economists, and other social analysts involved the collection of facts pertinent to any and all events in social life. The goal was to produce as complete and exhaustive an account as possible— one that was fully based on the facts and emphasized the unique nature of each social event. The only legitimate approach to the study of human social life, in their view, was an ideographic one, in which the scholar concentrated on the unique nature of each event.

Any attempt, the supporters of the historical school maintained, to see regularities in social life or social history was completely misguided.

They vehemently opposed any argument claiming that there were nomothetic or law-like tendencies in social life. The suggestion that one might try to establish generalizations from the unique events of everyday life, members of the historical school maintained, was completely inappropriate for any undertaking within the humanities or social sciences.

Eduard Meyer's (1902) *On Theory and Methods in History* is one of the main statements from the conservative historical school. R.G. Collingwood (1962) captures succinctly the essence of Meyer's position (and that of the historical school):

> Against all this [generalization in history], Meyer contends that the proper object of historical thought is historical fact in its individuality, and that chance and free will are determining causes that cannot be banished from history without destroying its very essence. Not only is the historian as such uninterested in the so-called laws of this pseudo-science, but there are no historical laws. (P. 178; see also Weber [1905] 1949)

This unqualified emphasis on the ideographic nature of social life and its attendant focus on the collection of the primary facts of any social situation would remain the dominant practice among many scholars in the social sciences and was certainly true of the vast majority of historians well into the middle of the twentieth century. Historians only began to abandon their strident emphasis on the empirical and the unique with the rise of social history in the 1960s (see Carr 1961; Thompson 1970).

At the other end of both the political and methodological spectrum, historical materialism, as it was being developed by Engels and the first generation of Marxists, was emerging. Engels initiated the process of presenting all of Marx's varied works in the form of a system. The two most influential pieces that Engels writes are *Socialism: Utopian and Scientific* ([1886] 1935)—a relatively concise summary of the main principles of and approach to "scientific socialism," which Engels produced in pamphlet form in 1880—and the larger 1878 text, *Anti-Dühring: Herr Eugen Dühring's Revolution in Science* ([1878] 1939) from which the pamphlet is drawn.

Another contributor to Marxist social theory was Karl Kautsky. Just before Marx's death (in 1883), Kautsky founded what quickly became one of Marxism's most influential journals—*Die Neue Zeit* (*New Times*). Under Kautsky's editorship, the journal published portions of Marx's literary estate and engaged in commentary and analysis of current social issues from a Marxist perspective.

Indeed, following Engels's death in 1895, the development and elaboration of Marx's historical materialism fell primarily on the shoulders of Kautsky, with August Bebel and Eduard Bernstein playing a less central role (see Kautsky 1935).[64] With the 1887 publication *The Economic Doctrines of Karl Marx*, Kautsky became Marxism's main theoretician and the chief architect of the Marxian system (Kautsky [1887] 1925).

The historical materialist position that Kautsky and other orthodox Marxists developed in *Die Neue Zeit* drew criticism from traditional historians in Germany, German legal scholars, a growing body of German sociologists, as well as certain revisionist Marxists, Austro-Marxists, and Hegelian Marxists. These different criticisms of the orthodox Marxist approach to historical materialism are important insofar as they situate Weber's writings on methodology.[65]

Members of the historical school launched the most strident attack on historical materialism. Scholarship from this perspective emphasized the specific facts of unique historical events. Consequently, Eduard Meyer, Rudolf Stammler, Wilhelm Roscher, Karl Knies, and others within the school presented a position in diametrical opposition to the orthodox Marxist's claim that there are dialectical laws of social life that explain and lead to a succession of modes of production and that this succession, in turn, leads to communism. In short, the historical school disputed the historical processes that Marx had identified in his 1859 preface to *Towards the Critique of Political Economy* and in the *Communist Manifesto*.

The Hegelian-Marxist critique, presented by Karl Korsch (1922, [1923] 1970, 1929), Georg Lukács ([1923] 1970), and Antonio Labriola (1904), supports the argument that history can unfold in a particular direction due to the internal contradictions of different modes of production but holds that those contradictions, in and of themselves, are not sufficient to create change or to guide it toward a higher stage of history. Drawing upon the Hegelian heritage in Marx's work, Korsch, Lukács, and Labriola argue that consciousness is a key factor in the historical process—one that orthodox Marxists discount far too much. Maintaining that Marx's historical materialism focuses on the material factors of history, Korsch, Lukács, and Labriola argue that

---

64 Kautsky was actively recruited for the preparation and wider dissemination of Marx's major economic works. Engels entrusted Kautsky with the responsibility of transcribing, editing, and publishing the manuscripts for Marx's so-called fourth volume of *Capital—The Theories of Surplus Value* (Marx [1861–63] 1921a, [1861–63] 1921b, [1861–63] 1921c, [1861–63] 1921d). Kautsky also painstakingly checked all Marx's references in the three volumes of *Capital* (Marx was far from meticulous in his referencing), added a complete bibliography, and translated all foreign citations and terms into German to produce a *Volksausgabe* or popular edition of *Capital*. Kautsky produced the first volume on his own; his son Benedikt assisted him with the second and then assumed the primary editorial role with his father assisting on the two parts that constituted volume three (Marx [1872] 1914, [1885] 1926, [1894] 1929a, [1894] 1929b).

65 The growing impact of orthodox Marxism in methodological questions is indicated by Durkheim's critique of the orthodox Marxist position to defend his own position in *The Rules of Sociological Method* (Durkheim ([1897] 1982).

consciousness and ideology are, in fact, one of the material constituents of social history and that one has to examine the ways in which consciousness and ideology facilitate and constrain the material practices of humankind within different social formations. This view of the role of consciousness in social processes became important for Weber and informs his contributions to the debate between the historical school and the proponents of historical materialism.

When this debate was lively, Weber was at the University of Heidelberg. He had attracted a small but active group of like-minded thinkers there, and they constituted an informal Weber circle. Weber and this circle of academics played a dominant role in the development of German sociology. The circle included a number of people who attained significant stature in their respective disciplines. Heinrich Rickert, one of the more influential philosophers in the systematic demarcation and separation of the humanities and social sciences (*Geisteswissenschaften*) from the natural sciences (*Naturwissenschaften*), was a close friend of Weber's. Lukács, who was deeply interested in the sociological study of literature and aesthetics, was a student of Weber's (and of Simmel's). Georg Simmel was also Weber's friend and collaborator, and he became an influential figure in the development of German sociology, although with a lower profile than Weber.

This circle of academics weighed in on the issue of historical materialism. Interestingly, the critique from the Weber circle is not directed primarily at Kautsky and the orthodox Marxists. Instead, Weber and his colleagues mainly target the historical school—especially its unyielding emphasis on the idiosyncrasies of social life and its refusal to develop any conception of generalization. In making the critique, Weber and his colleagues accept certain aspects of the historical materialist position, but they are also critical of historical materialism's shortcomings, as they see them. Not surprisingly, Weber argues that consciousness and the formation of human understanding in the social world cannot be reduced solely to the economic base, as the orthodox Marxists maintained.

WEBER AND THE METHODOLOGY OF THE SOCIAL SCIENCES

Methodology in the social sciences mattered a great deal to Weber—between 1903 and 1920, he composed more than 500 pages of text on methodological issues. Weber first enters the dispute over the method appropriate to the humanities and social sciences with a searing rebuttal of Stammler's ([1894] 1924) *Economy and Law According to the Materialist Conception of History: A Socio-Philosophical Investigation*—an attack on historical materialism by one of the historical school's leading thinkers. Weber ([1907] 1977) constructs a four-part response entitled "R. Stammler's 'Refutation' of the Materialist Conception of History." It was one of eight essays on methodological questions and issues that Weber wrote between 1903 and 1918.[66]

Weber's critique of Stammler establishes three main points. First, Weber argues that Stammler completely misrepresents many key aspects of historical materialism and then proceeds to attack a caricature of the orthodox Marxist position. This aspect of Weber's critique takes up most of the essay, but its next two points are most significant for this discussion.

Weber's second main point focuses on how complex questions of method are and on the need to explore them with great care and precision. One must clearly establish one's fundamental premises and demonstrate how the arguments that follow build from those premises.

Finally, Weber claims that "something like a methodological pestilence" was beginning to prevail in the social sciences (quoted in Weber [1907] 1977:11). One essay on methodology would lead to a refutation, followed by an answer to the refutation, followed by yet another restatement of the original refutation. The result, according to Weber: a pestilence or plague of inward looking and self-referential essays that contributed little to the real advancement of sociological knowledge. The main problems of methodology, Weber argues, can only be resolved on the basis of the actual analysis of the empirical social world—on the basis of genuine lived experience.

In a critique of Meyer, which establishes the same point regarding Stammler, Weber ([1905] 1949) insists that purely epistemological reflections do little to genuinely advance methodology in the social sciences. Progress only comes by tackling substantive empirical questions.

Consistent with the emphasis upon meaning and understanding found within the German *Geisteswissenschaften*, Weber's sociology is built upon the role that meaning plays in all forms of social action. He elaborates this foundation in an unfinished draft of his systematic treatise on interpretive sociology:

> Sociology (in the sense in which this highly ambiguous word is used here) is a science [*Wissenschaft*] concerning itself with the interpretive understanding [*deutend verstehen*] of social action [*soziales Handeln*] and thereby with a causal explanation of its course and consequences. "Action" signifies human conduct (whether overtly or covertly, by omission or acquiescence) that is associated with subjective *meaning*. But an action is "social" action ["*soziales*"

---

66 Weber published four parts of his Stammler critique, promising a fifth that he did not publish in his lifetime. Weber ([1903, 1905, 1906] 1975, [1905] 1949) wrote equally critical review essays against Roscher, Knies, and Meyer, although his critique of Roscher and Knies and of their approach to the historical study of economics also remained incomplete. Weber's widow, Marianne, republished some essays on this topic along with several draft manuscripts that Weber had left unfinished at his death. The collection was later updated and expanded slightly by Johannes Winckelmann, who succeeded Marianne Weber as the executor of her husband's literary estate (Weber 1968b; see also Weber 2012).

Handeln] when its intended meaning takes account of the behaviour of *others* and is thereby oriented in its unfolding [*Ablauf*]. (Weber 1956:1, 1968a:3)

The importance Weber places on the ***deutend verstehen***, or **interpretive understanding**, of human social action has five implications for his work.

First, it means that Weber approaches sociology as "a comprehensive science of *social action*"—with the emphasis upon social action. Weber wants to understand "social action"—the *specific categories of human action which*, throughout the course of the action, *take into account the behaviour of others and the meaning they and the initiator of the action attach to it*.

Second, Weber views sociology as "a *comprehensive science* of social action"—with the emphasis upon comprehensive science this time. Sociologists have *to interpret and understand* social actions and produce *comprehensive accounts of social action*. To understand or grasp the meaning of social action, Weber argues, sociologists must assume an interpretive position—a *verstehende Ansatz*—rather than simply collect quantitative data based on a variety of external social facts. An interpretive position involves either trying to understand the meaning the person carrying out the action might be intending or what meaning a person's actions might convey to others—sometimes it involves both. The key is to try to understand interpretively "the intended meaning" a human agent associates with an action as it is conducted.

A comprehensive account has to go beyond simply describing an action—it has to place the action into as full a socio-historical context as possible, and it has to explore the meaning different agents ascribe to that action. A comprehensive science explores all the information that it can find, and, in the humanities and social sciences (the *Geisteswissenschaften*), meaning is of critical importance.

Third, Weber notes that, in all cases, "'understanding' [*Verstehen*] involves the interpretive grasp [*deutende Erfassung*] of the meaning present in one of the following contexts":

> (a) the actually intended meaning for the specific action (as in the historical approach); or (b) the average of, or an approximation to, the actually intended meaning (as in cases of sociological mass observation); or (c) the meaning appropriate to a *pure* type [*reinen Typus*] (an ideal type) of a common phenomenon. (Weber 1956:4, 1968a:9)

Although recognizing the three respective levels of understanding, Weber views only one of those levels of understanding as the ultimate objective for sociology as a form of systematic inquiry—as a comprehensive science of social action:

> Sociology constitutes—as we have frequently assumed as self-evident—*type*-concepts and seeks *general* rules of events. This is in contradistinction to

history, which seeks causal analyses and explanation of *individual, culturally significant* actions, structures, and personalities. (Weber 1956:9, 1968a:19)

Sociology, in contrast to history, then, should move away from the specific and unique to establish more generalized knowledge and theories of social action. Sociology involves a process of **abstraction**—the process of moving from the specific to the more general and, ultimately, to broadly inclusive analyses of social behaviour.

IDEAL TYPES OR PURE TYPES

It is important to explore this point further because it is critical to understanding Weber's work as a sociologist and his aspirations for sociology as a comprehensive science of social action. On the one hand, Weber's quest to produce empirically based, generalized understandings of social action is completely consistent with the objectives of other sciences. In this respect, Weber, Marx, Durkheim, and even Bacon, Galileo, and Hume share a common objective—to develop generalized knowledge that begins with careful, detailed observations of the empirical world and proceeds, through the process of abstraction, to the identification of generalized trends, which might ultimately become universal laws or comprehensive theories. The main objective of scholarship (science or *Wissenschaft*) is the development of the most widely applicable knowledge possible. (In the natural sciences the goal is often universally applicable knowledge while, in the social sciences, although some may aspire to discover universal laws, most would argue that economists, political scientists, and sociologists can only achieve knowledge that one may generalize to specified locations, circumstances, and periods of time.)

On the other hand, Weber differs from Marx, Durkheim, Bacon, and Galileo in two important respects. First, unlike Bacon and Galileo, Weber was not trying to develop universal laws. Weber did not believe that sociology could ever aspire to uncovering the universal laws of human behaviour, although he did believe, as did Durkheim and Marx, that sociologists could develop different concepts and generalized interpretations of social action, ones that they could use to understand social action under any conditions—past or present or anticipated in the future.[67]

---

67 Weber was very aware that the social world changed, as did sociologists' understanding of it. As a result, the concepts adequate for understanding western European societies in the early twentieth century were not necessarily the ones that would still be in use at the end of the century or those needed to examine life in the twenty-first century. Thus, although Weber believed that sociologists should strive for and could often develop concepts enabling the examination of social life in the past, present, and, potentially, into the future, he also knew that changes in society might require the development of new concepts and the rejection of some that had been used previously.

Second, Weber differs from Durkheim, Galileo, and Bacon with respect to the type of knowledge sociology should be pursuing. Knowledge must begin with the direct observation and study of the empirically existing world—all agree on that point. But, rather than simply collecting directly observable facts or social facts in the form of variables that can be related causally to one another, Weber argues, sociologists must offer sociological explanations and generalizations. Sociologists have to develop an *interpretive understanding* of social action. The process of abstraction and the attention to meaning that Weber has in mind when he discusses this interpretive understanding is apparent in one of his major contributions to sociology—Weber's fourfold typology of social action.

On the basis of all the different and varied types of social action that he encountered in his research, Weber maintains that it is possible to categorize all meaningful **social action** into one of four distinct pure types: **goal-rational**, **value-rational**, **affective**, and **traditional** action:

> *Goal-rational* action (*zweckrationales Handeln*) is *rational action*—mentally calculated action—*that is aimed at achieving a particular goal.*
>
> *Value-rational* action (*wertrationales Handeln*) is *rational action guided by a particular value or belief.*
>
> *Affective* or emotional action is action *guided by desires or emotions* (fear, anger, hate, vengeance, lust, or love, for example).
>
> *Traditional* action is action *guided by the dictates of tradition.*[68]

Each type of action describes the external nature of the action and the subjective meaning the action holds for the person carrying it out; each also takes into account the behaviour of others and the anticipated meanings they might associate with the action.

For Weber, this conceptualization of action—this process of abstracting from the immediately observable activities one finds in everyday life—leads to the development of concepts or, as Weber prefers, "ideal types" or "pure types." (Weber uses these terms interchangeably.) In other words, the generalizations that sociologists develop from observation establish a general framework, based on generalized concepts, which can then be used as a reference point or the basis for comparison with actual events and meaningful actions in the reality of everyday life or in the recorded history of other

---

68 On the basis of this typology of social action, Weber (1956) also develops his typology of what he calls "the three *pure* types of legitimate domination [*drei reine Typen legitimer Herrschaft*]" that one finds in societies throughout history. Weber argues that there are three pure types of legitimate domination—traditional, charismatic, and rational (or legal-rational). See Weber (1956:122–76, 1968a:941–1374).

periods. Weber explains both the advantages and disadvantages of these generalized concepts:

> As is the case of every generalizing science the abstract character of the concepts of sociology is responsible for the fact that, compared with actual historical reality, they are relatively lacking in fullness of concrete content. To compensate for this disadvantage, sociological analysis can offer a greater precision of concepts. This precision is obtained by striving for the highest possible degree of adequacy on the level of meaning. (Weber 1968a:20)

In essence, Weber takes what could be considered a weakness—sociology must abstract from (or move away from) the real world of lived experience and thereby lose the fullness of concrete content—and regards it as a strength. The concepts that sociologists develop can incorporate all aspects of meaning (for example, the impact of mystical, prophetic, and affective or emotional dimensions of action along with the rational and calculated dimensions) to produce an enriched concept that one can then use as a reference point for analyses.[69]

As a result, Weber views an **ideal type** (or **pure type**) as a deliberate conceptualization that sociologists produce on the basis of their comprehensive understanding of social action in people's everyday lives. The sociologist constructs the ideal type so that it sharply and precisely identifies the key characteristics that are pertinent to the action under study (for example, goal-rational action). The ideal type brings to conscious awareness aspects of action that are often only partially conscious or that are subconscious, thereby enriching the analysis the sociologist can undertake.

The tendency to produce ideal types operates, consciously or not, in all systematic discussions of cultural or social behaviour. Whenever people discuss or write about religion, power, crime, or even bureaucracy, they stylize, simplify, and accentuate certain aspects so the analysis can focus on the most important features of the issue at hand.

Economists, for example, develop specific concepts (supply, demand, monopoly, or monopsony) so that they can make the economy intelligible.[70]

---

69 Weber's pure type analysis is employed in the study of culture in Chapter 10 and in the assessment, in Chapters 11 and 12, of whether or not popular culture can meet the standards of "high" culture.

70 Monopoly and monopsony are distinct concepts differentiating the conditions of the market in precise and important ways. A monopoly is a one-seller market; a monopsony is a one-buyer market. In a monopoly, the seller has the advantage and may drive prices accordingly; in a monopsony, the purchaser has greater influence over the prices in the market. The best situation for a business is a monopoly in the market in which it sells products—so it can keep sale prices and profits high—and a monopsony in the market in which it purchases raw materials and labour—so it can keep costs to a minimum.

They do not discuss the economy in all of its concrete detail and daily flux. Economists approach the economy conceptually (that is, theoretically).

The same is true of sociology—sociologists can discuss capitalism, for example, intelligently when they begin with the main concepts or features that comprise capitalism as a pure case (or pure type or ideal type).[71] On the basis of that pure type, they can then examine Canada as a capitalist society and compare it to the United States, Russia, or the United Arab Emirates, for example.

In the construction of ideal types that are consciously created as abstractions derived from the complexity of reality, sociologists sacrifice one thing to gain another. They sacrifice the detail and flux of the phantasmagoria of everyday life, but they gain the enriched insight ideal types can generate by accentuating particular, key features while also including aspects of meaning that are missed or lost in the immediate context of the life-world. The pure type approach that Weber advocates for the humanities and social sciences allows him to maintain the central significance of meaning to social action while also contributing to a science of society that produces meaningful generalizations about social action and social life.

This leads to the final implication that Weber's emphasis upon sociology as a comprehensive science of social action has for his sociology in general and for his work on the methodology of the social sciences in particular. Weber uses his approach to sociology to examine the degree to which sociology, in particular, or science, in general, can serve as the ultimate guide to human action. Can science—especially social science—serve as the ethical guide to human action? Put in different terms, are there limits to scientific knowledge?

Science and Ethics: The Limits of Goal-Rational Action

Weber lived through the turmoil in Europe that led to World War 1; he lived through the war and long enough to experience all the political tensions and personal anxieties that Germans, in particular, and others in Europe experienced after the war.

Besides the economic and political insecurities that caused and followed World War 1, Weber's generation often experienced spiritual and ethical uncertainty, as faith and religion seemed to be giving way to doubt and to

---

71 Werner Sombart (1991), who shares Weber's approach to understanding in the social sciences, argues that the key constituent elements of a capitalist society are (1) the spirit or outlook (characterized by acquisition, competition, and rationality), (2) the form (or institutional order), and (3) technology.

various and relative worldviews. As early as 1882, Nietzsche's "The Parable of the Madman" had announced God's demise:

> God is dead. God remains dead. And we have killed Him.... Led out [of churches] and called to account, ... [the madman] is said always to have replied nothing but: "What after all are these churches now if they are not the tombs and sepulchres of God?" (Nietzsche [1882] 1974:181–82)

Although the philosophy behind the parable is complex, Nietzsche is not using it to mourn the death of God; he advocates humankind taking charge of its own affairs rather than passively accepting the dictates of the church. Whether Nietzsche's contemporaries agreed with him, his parable struck a chord at the turn of the twentieth century because many people then were looking for a moral compass that could guide human behaviour. They wanted a firm basis for ethical conduct. If not in traditional religions, could this basis be found in science?

As a scholar committed to the idea that social science should inform people's lives at every level, from the mundane matters of daily life to the formation of national policies, Weber ([1919] 1946b) wrestles with this question—can science be the ultimate source of ethical conduct? Weber's answer is no. In reaching this conclusion, he makes some important contributions concerning both how one should understand scientific inquiry as meaningful human action and how one must understand ethical decision making as a type of meaningful human action.

Weber's answer to the question of whether science can serve as the moral compass of human social action stems directly from his fourfold typology of social action. Looking at science as meaningful social action—action that has meaning to the agent and takes into account the behaviour of others (Weber 1956:1, 1968a:3)—Weber notes that the goal of science is to produce propositions of fact and statements of causality or, in the case of the social sciences, comprehensive interpretations of social action. The social action that characterizes scientific or scholarly action is goal-rational action. Scientists and scholars *use rational means (the specific techniques of their field of science or scholarship) to pursue a specific goal—universally valid truth.*[72]

---

72 The phrase "universally valid truth" can cause some confusion because even though the objectives of natural scientists and social scientists or scholars seem to differ in terms of their interest in universal laws (in the case of the natural sciences) versus empirically based, accurate, generalized understandings or theories (in the case of the social sciences and humanities), they all share the goal of producing knowledge that has *truthful validity that anyone can examine and test.* The goal of modernist scholars is to develop accurate statements (truths) about the natural and/or social worlds that are based on the systematic, theoretically informed scrutiny of the real worlds within which humankind lives.

As the pursuit of universally valid truth, science might seem capable of serving as the moral compass for the modern world. But, Weber argues, scientific action is not simply or exclusively goal-rational action. The action of scholars and scientists is also value-rational action because these truth seekers are committed to a specific value. Scientific action, Weber maintains, is fundamentally committed to *the value of truths demonstrated by universally valid facts or arguments*.

Before a scholar can engage in scientific activity as a goal-rational action, she or he must have already made a commitment to the value of truths demonstrated by universally valid facts or arguments. Any scholar who manipulates data; fails to examine alternative hypotheses (no matter how uncomfortable or unpopular); or in any other way fails to subject her or his findings, arguments, and conclusions to rigorous analysis and critique does not place a high enough value upon the pursuit of truth to be a genuine scholar or scientist. Without this unyielding commitment to the value of scientific truths, scientific action can never serve as the means for the discovery of universally valid truths.

Scientific action, it turns out, is goal-rational and value-rational action. It is within the value-rational dimension of scholarship, Weber's work demonstrates, that the real problem lies for anyone's hope that science might serve as the ultimate moral compass for society or as the basis for a system of absolute ethics. The value-rational dimension of scholarly action poses three limitations to science's potential to act as the definitive moral compass for society or as a determiner of universal ethics.

First, scientific activity is, in and of itself, a value-rational activity. As such, it represents one specific commitment to a particular value—the importance of the pursuit and discovery of universally valid truth. But, as one specific value commitment, it cannot also serve as an unbiased, independent arbiter of various other different, competing values.

On what basis, then, can anyone, even a scientist, argue that the pursuit of the universally valid truths of science is a higher value than the pursuit of truth through the Holy Scriptures, for example, or the traditional ways of the Haudenosaunee (or Iroquois) confederacy. A commitment to a particular value or value system, Weber maintains, is a judgement of value (*Werturteil*, meaning a commitment to value or a value judgement). As such, it cannot be assessed, supported, or undermined by any other judgement of value, including a value commitment to some transcendental position of supreme wisdom.

A judgement of value, a commitment to a value, means precisely this—placing a high value (*Wert*) on a key (*ur*) part (*teil*) or notion or set of notions (*Wert-ur-teil*).

That judgement can be based on reasoned calculation, faith, or emotional attachment, or it might be taken out of fear or because of the charismatic attraction of certain values, but it is not based on any absolute measure and cannot be based on any absolute measure (at least not within the knowledge system to which Weber subscribed). Therefore, Weber argues, science, being a judgement of value, is limited and cannot stand as the definitive moral compass for contemporary society.

The second reason scientific knowledge cannot serve as an absolute reference point, according to Weber, is quite simple. The world (natural and social) is infinitely complex. It can never be fully known.

Science generates abstract theories that give meaning to the world, allows humankind to interact meaningfully with it, and, to a certain extent, controls it. But even the most advanced scientific insights remain incomplete. Science makes the world intelligible—but not fully known and comprehended.

Scientists commit themselves to an impossible task—they commit themselves to a fundamental value judgement that is, ultimately, unrealizable (although commitment to that value ensures that their work unerringly *strives* toward the realization of that value). Scientists seek to discover universally accepted truths that can advance scientific knowledge, but the abstract laws they generate will never achieve an absolute form of knowledge because an infinite, changing world can never be fully known.

That the final aim of science will remain unachieved does not mean that scientific activity is useless, however. Scientists have produced countless accomplishments in the process of trying to reach science's ultimate goal, but attaining *universal truths* for an infinitely complex and continually changing world *is not possible*.

Finally, the ways in which science develops and advances do not and cannot lead to the development of absolute knowledge. Weber argues that scholars assess the world in which they live and work, and, in the process, they discover certain questions, problems, or issues that become important to them. Through a process of relevance—what Weber terms value-relevant action (*Wertbeziehung*—a relationship of value)—scholars choose the issues they will research and study.

Part of the reason a question or issue becomes relevant is internal to a scholar's discipline at a particular point in time. Thus, for example, members of the historical school in the early 1900s chose to examine historical materialism critically because it was rivalling scientific theory, which they thought was seriously flawed.

Another part of the reason was that historical materialism was associated with a rising socialist movement in Germany, and the politically conservative members of the historical school wanted to undermine historical materialism as a scientific basis for German socialism. In this instance, the value relevance of historical materialism for scholars in the historical school was due to factors and events in the broader social environment in which they all lived.

The historical school became relevant to Weber because of his interest in questions of method and his belief that the school's position was influential but also wrong and needed to be addressed.

Based on his own experiences and his interpretive understanding of how issues or questions become relevant to other researchers, Weber acknowledges that the questions scholars address are related to issues that hold **value relevance** for them. The value relevance that motivates a scholar to pursue a particular question may be strictly scholarly, but it may also involve broader extra-scientific concerns.[73] No matter what the source from which a value-relevant question arises, if value relevance is guiding the research process then it will not be systematic and comprehensive enough to yield perfectly comprehensive knowledge.

What about when scholars only pursue questions directly related to the search for universally valid truths? Under those circumstances, they would never be interested in a question because of its political importance or personal relevance; the only relevance a question could have would be exclusively related to the pursuit of universally valid truths (and any political or personal relevance would be coincidental). Will this scholarship result in the inevitable advancement of science toward its value-relevant goal of universally valid truth? Unfortunately—no.

Prior to the time when humankind finally achieves absolute, universal knowledge, the selection of topics and issues would be tied to value-relevant interests and questions stemming from less than perfect knowledge. Consequently, there would be no guarantee that the scientific community would pursue the absolutely necessary value-relevant questions that would lead to absolute universal truth. Having an imperfect comprehension of the world, scientists might ask and pursue the right questions, but, more likely, it would be only by chance that they would choose the correct issues to lead to absolute knowledge. And in a world of infinite complexity, the odds of posing the correct questions time and again as knowledge advances toward an absolute truth are astronomically stacked against science. In fact, the most perplexing problem confronting scientists is that in answering one question they usually open the door to several more unresolved questions. Truth seems to recede the more scientists work to get closer to it. As a result, the way in which problems are chosen is a serious obstacle to the scientific community ever finding the path to absolute knowledge—despite the fact that, once a problem is chosen, scientists follow the value-rational commitment to pursue universal truths.

In summary, Weber's position is that scientific action cannot serve as the basis for a system of universal ethics or as the ultimate moral compass for a

---

73 Once a scientist or scholar chooses a value-relevant question or issue, she or he, as a scientific scholar, is then committed to suspending all personal interest in the question and pursuing that question on the basis of a commitment to the value of scholarship (that is, the value judgement or value commitment to the pursuit of universal truth). Scholars are committed to the pursuit of universally valid truths because that is both the goal of science and the value that determines acceptable from unacceptable behaviour and action as a scientist.

society for three specific reasons. First, as a form of social action, science is a form of value-rational action. It represents one value-based form of action among many. Even though those who live in an increasingly rationalistic age might highly esteem a value commitment to scientific knowledge, there are no absolute grounds upon which that valuation can be proven as the correct one. In an age dominated by Roman Catholicism, for example, the value commitment to Christianity would be higher and scientific action would hold less value. Similarly, if C.S. Lewis's (2001) arguments about God and Christianity are accepted, then, even in this highly secular age, science would not be the route to absolute knowledge. In both cases just mentioned, scientific action and religious action represent value-rational forms of action and none of them, despite what might be felt from within each of those value commitments, can serve as a universal value system other than through faith—a value commitment to be sure.

Second, if it were possible for scientific action to produce absolute, universal truth (or truths), then the case that science could serve as the basis for a system of absolute ethics would be strong. However, according to Weber, science can never really attain the goal it steadfastly pursues. It cannot achieve that goal for three reasons.

First, the real world in which humankind lives is infinitely complex and changing. Infinite complexity is the first challenge, and its changing nature makes the problem even worse.

Second, science sacrifices the fullness of concrete reality for the precision of the concepts it develops. The precision of concepts in science means that the conceptual apparatus of science is never static—it must develop as more is learned about the real worlds in which people live.

Third, even if the infinite complexity of the natural world could be encompassed by the conceptual systems of science, the objective behind establishing an absolute ethical system is not the ethical guidance of natural objects—it is to guide human conduct. A system of absolute ethics would guide people's actions in their personal, social, and political lives; as a result, it is the universally valid truths of *social action* that are most central to the issue of an absolute ethical system. But the world of social action and the meanings that are central to it are *always changing* (see also Giddens 1984). Science could not possibly provide the absolute knowledge needed to guide human action (that is, meaningful social action).

Finally, science cannot serve as the basis for a system of universal ethics because of the way scientists and scholars conduct their work. Researchers select their research topics and agendas based on the questions they find relevant. They base their research on value-relevant issues. Value relevance, however, even when the scholar is committed to the pursuit of universally valid truth, cannot serve as an infallible guide to absolute knowledge because even scientific interests are shaped within a world of imperfect knowledge—an infinitely complex world that is imperfectly understood.

On the basis of all these arguments, Weber draws one of his most significant conclusions. The goals or ends that an individual, a group, a society, or
even all of humanity chooses to pursue can never be determined by an infallible
ethical system based upon science (Weber [1919] 1946a). Scientific knowledge
is limited; it is just one form of knowledge among many, and, as a result, it can
never be an infallible guide to human action. The goals that individuals, groups,
or societies pursue are determined within the realm of political discussion,
debate, and decision making. So what purpose *can* science serve, according to
Weber? Once these goals are chosen, science can serve as an important guide
to reaching those goals. Science can serve as one of the most effective means
of goal-rational action, but it cannot determine any system of absolute ends.

It is here that one can further appreciate Weber's complexity as a
sociologist. On the one hand, Weber outlines the highest standards for
scholarship—especially scholarship in the social sciences. Scholars should
undertake, to the fullest of their ability, the pursuit of absolute truths, even
though Weber knows that this quest is impossible to achieve. In this sense,
Weber holds science and scholarship in the highest regard possible, yet he is
also wary of science—not because scholars might fail to live up to the highest
standards of their calling (although this was a concern for Weber) but because
of the pedestal upon which people in the modern era had placed science
and its pure, goal-rational approach to understanding and controlling the
world. Weber ([1920] 2002:123–24) was acutely aware that, in an increasingly
secular world in which the performance imperatives of industrial capitalism
dominated, goal-rational action had become a pervasive force in all aspects
of social life. In the modern era, goal-rational action was already almost sac-
rosanct, and it would be increasingly regarded as beyond criticism, despite
the fact that it was only one type of social action—and not one that could
establish an infallible set of ethical principles or ensure true human fulfilment.
Weber ([1920] 2002) argues that modernity is trapped in a "steel-hard casing
(***stahlhartes Gehäuse***)" of goal-rational action (p. 123).[74] Weber continues,

> No one any longer knows who will live in this steel-hard casing and
> whether entirely new prophets or a mighty rebirth of ancient ideas and

---

74 The term "*stahlhartes Gehäuse*" has entered English-language sociology almost universally as
   "iron cage" due to the tremendous influence of the first, widely used translation of Weber's *The
   Protestant Ethic and the Spirit of Capitalism* (see Weber [1920] 1958:181). Because of this early
   translation by Talcott Parsons, students will often read about Weber's fear of "the iron cage of
   reason." "Steel-hard casing," or even "steel-hard housing" in view of the role that a "housing"
   plays in the production and operation of machines, or Peter Baher's "shell as hard as steel," are
   superior translation for two reasons. First, iron is an existing metal; steel is an alloy of iron and
   carbon which is far stronger than iron alone—so the shell/casing/housing is harder than iron
   and will be tougher to break out of. Second, as an alloy, steel is a modern product resulting
   from the use of science and goal-rational action to build a stronger metal (see Baher 2001).

ideals will stand at the end of this prodigious development [i.e., the modern industrial world]. *Or*, however, if neither, whether a mechanized ossification, embellished with a sort of rigidly compelled sense of self-importance, will arise. Then, indeed, if ossification appears, the saying might be true for the "last humans"[75] in this long civilizational development: "Narrow specialists without mind, pleasure-seekers without heart; in its conceit, this nothingness imagines it has climbed to a level of humanity never before attained." (Pp. 124; see also pp. 35–37)

The next chapter will examine Weber's understanding of goal-rational action, its rise to a position of domination in the modern world, and why his outlook is so pessimistic. The study of *The Protestant Ethic and the Spirit of Capitalism* in the next chapter will also demonstrate how Weber employed his methodological prescriptions and the manner in which Weber's thought has renewed relevance for contemporary sociology as a bridge from modernist to postmodernist approaches within the discipline.

Key Terms and Names

Max Weber
Geisteswissenschaften
historical materialism
orthodox Marxism
historical school
deutend verstehen (interpretive understanding)
abstraction
social action—affective, goal-rational, traditional, and value-rational
pure type/ideal type
value relevance
stahlhartes Gehäuse (steel-hard casing)

Questions for Review and Further Reflection

1. Think about a major historical event you learned about in high school or more recently. How would a theorist from the historical school study and analyse this event? What about an historical materialist? Try to research the event using each of these methods; what are the strengths and weaknesses of each approach?

---

75 The reference here is to Nietzsche's *letzte Menschen*, often translated as "last man."

2. Make a list of all the things you have done today. How many of these items fit Weber's definition of "social action?" Classify each item on your list within Weber's typology of social action.

3. Now make a list of what you think are the five most important decisions you have made in your life. Beside each, identify which pure type of social action best represents that decision.

4. What does Weber mean when he says that sociology should be "a comprehensive science of social action?" What are the implications of that definition?

5. Weber writes about "pure types" and "ideal types" as interchangeable terms. What is a pure or ideal type? How does Weber justify making them; what is his purpose?

6. On a sheet of paper, list the following terms: bureaucracy, rap song, cult, democracy, "developing" nation, sweatshop, factory farm, and terrorist organization. Beside each, list the main features that should go into an ideal or pure type for each.

7. Refer to Weber's discussion on how research questions are guided by the personal interests and values of scientists. What areas of study interest you the most? How have these been influenced by the intersection of your personal biography with history and social structure?

8. Do you agree with Weber that goal-rational action has become increasingly dominant? What factors might be contributing to this shift? What consequences—positive or negative—might this have for North American society and those living in it?

9

THE SPIRIT OF CAPITALISM, MODERNITY, AND THE POSTMODERN WORLD

Main Objectives

This chapter will

1. Introduce and familiarize students with one of Weber's most important contributions to sociology—*The Protestant Ethic and the Spirit of Capitalism.*
2. Describe Weber's relationship to the Marxism of his time as that relationship is developed in *The Protestant Ethic and the Spirit of Capitalism.*
3. Outline three key terms that are essential to understanding some of the central debates and discussions in contemporary sociology—modernism, modernization, and postmodernism.
4. Indicate the significance of the shift from modernism to postmodernism by many contemporary sociologists.

The discussion on Weber in Chapter 8 focused mainly on his work in methodology and indicated how that led to his particular emphasis upon sociology as the interpretive study of social action. The chapter then examined Weber's notion of pure (or ideal) types and the four pure types of social action he identified—affective, traditional, goal-rational, and value-rational. The final section explored the limitations that Weber's understanding of social action places upon science and scholarship as the means for determining a system of ethical conduct and social governance.

Two aspects of Weber's thought were noted but not addressed at length in the last chapter's discussion of science and social action. The first is Weber's position on the infinite complexity of the social world and how it might situate him as a bridging figure between classical modernist sociology and the postmodernist conceptions of sociology found today. This theme is taken up at length in the second major section of this chapter.

The second is the idea noted at the end of Chapter 8—Weber's fear that the growing domination of goal-rational action in the modern world could leave humanity trapped in the *stahlhartes Gehäuse* of reason. Weber discusses the origins of the control of life by a cold, dispassionate, calculating, and instrumental reason in his most widely cited essay, *The Protestant Ethic and the Spirit of Capitalism*. Originally published in two parts in the *Archive for Social Science and Social Policy* in 1905, Weber published it as a revised and extended monograph in 1920. The study does more than express a concern about the future impact of goal-rational action; the work embodies almost all of Weber's major concerns as a sociologist. It deals with the impact of religion on social action and the manner in which a dominant "frame of mind" arises and leads individuals to interpret and understand the world in a particular manner. The study exemplifies Weber's method and demonstrates his acumen as a historical sociologist. Because of the work's comprehensive nature, the first part of this chapter will explore *The Protestant Ethic and the Spirit of Capitalism* in detail.

ASCETIC PROTESTANTISM AND THE ETHOS OF MODERN LIFE

In his discussion of methodology that critiques Meyer, Weber ([1905] 1968) writes emphatically, "Only through the discovery and solution of *factual* [*sachlicher*] problems are sciences [*Wissenschaften*] founded and their methods developed, not through purely epistemological or methodological delibera-tions" (p. 217). Weber, like Durkheim before him, wants to free sociology from philosophy and metaphysical debates and establish it as an empirically based science—although the nature of Weber's sociology differs from that of Durkheim. *The Protestant Ethic and the Spirit of Capitalism* is an excellent example of Weber doing exactly what he was advocating in his critique of Meyer—examining a concrete historical issue (the spirit of modern capi-talism), while employing and developing his interpretive approach to the understanding of social action as well as his ideal type methodology. Also, in contrast to presenting the ideographic explanations of the historical school, Weber establishes the important insights that a generalizing sociological understanding of the spirit of modern capitalism can yield as it demonstrates the origin and growing dominance of goal-rational action and what such dominance may mean for the future. *The Protestant Ethic* is a majestic, multi-purpose study that has earned its status as a sociological classic.

Weber ([1920] 2002) outlines his main objectives for the study in the middle of Chapter 3 where, under the heading "The Task of the Investigation," he describes exactly what he is trying to achieve and how (p. 47).

> In light of the immense confusion of the reciprocal influences among the material foundations, the forms of social and political organizations, and the various spiritual streams of the Reformation epoch, we can only

proceed in the following manner. *First*, we will investigate whether (and in what ways) specific "elective affinities" (*Wahlverwandtschaften*) between certain forms of religious belief and a vocational ethic (*Berufsethik*) are discernible. Doing so will allow us, whenever possible, to illuminate the type of influence that the religious movement, as a consequence of these elective affinities, had upon the development of economic culture. In addition, the general *direction* of this influence upon economic culture, as a consequence of these elective affinities, can be clarified. Second, *only after* this influence has been satisfactorily established can an attempt be made to estimate to what degree the historical origin of the values and ideas of our modern life can be attributed to religious forces stemming from the Reformation, and to what degree to other forces. (Pp. 49–50)

Weber's main goal is to demonstrate the extent to which religion, after the Reformation of the sixteenth century, was the source of the values and ideas of the modern world. More than that, his focus is on the rise of instrumental reason, or goal-rational action, to the position of dominance that it holds at the turn of the twentieth century and continues to hold today. He will build his argument on the basis of specific "elective affinities" that he will detail between Protestantism and a particular vocational or work ethic and the development of the economic culture of modernity.

All of Weber's work is characterized by the methodical, step-by-step analysis of issues that one finds here. He always invests great care in both the logic of his arguments and the evidence that supports them.

Weber notes that the title of his study contains "a concept that sounds rather intimidating: the *'spirit'* [*Geist*] of capitalism." He then asks, "What should be understood by it?" He answers:

If one can discover at all an object for which the phrase *spirit of capitalism* is meaningful, then it can only be a specific *historical case*. Such a singular entity is nothing more than a complex of relationships in historical reality. We join them together, from the vantage point of their *cultural significance*, into a conceptual unity. (Weber [1920] 2002:13)

In plain language, "the spirit of capitalism" is a culturally significant entity that is comprised of a number of social factors. The act of drawing together and studying the complex unity of several observable factual or material (*sachlich*) factors into a conceptual unity is, of course, a fundamental characteristic of Weber's ideal or pure type methodology. One begins by studying the complexity of reality and then moves back, or abstracts, from that empirical reality into a conceptual one that captures the most essential features—the pure or ideal features—of the material world under study. On the basis of this more precise conceptual unity, one may demonstrate how those different factors combine to create a specific social outcome relevant to a specific point in history. Weber's main interest in this study is to establish the "ancestral lineage" of the spirit of capitalism—how the modern era's dominant form of social action came into existence (see Weber [1920] 2002:37, 49–50, 54–55).

Although capitalism had a relatively long history when Weber began to study it, he writes that he is only interested in the "*modern* capitalism" of the "last few centuries" found in western Europe and America "rather than the 'capitalism' that has appeared in China, India, Babylon, the ancient world, and the Middle Ages" (Weber [1920] 2002: 16). Modern capitalism, according to Weber, is animated by a different frame of mind—a different spirit—than the earlier forms. How did this unique spirit arise? Did it emerge from the internal dynamic of capitalism itself (as orthodox Marxists suggested) or from other sources (as other economic historians asserted)? If there were other sources, what were they exactly?

Weber argues that the type of **economic rationalism** that had begun to dominate western Europe and North America depended on more than the advanced development of technology. The economic rationalism of modern capitalism rested on people's willingness to organize their lives in a controlled and rational manner. This willingness to engage in disciplined goal-rational action—to determine the most efficient means to a particular end—represents the spirit of capitalism that Weber sought to investigate.

Weber opens his discussion about the "*Geist des Kapitalismus* [the spirit, mind, culture, and ethos of capitalism]" with a number of maxims drawn from Benjamin Franklin, words that capture the spirit of modern capitalism in its pure form, freed from any religious connections:

> Remember, that *time* is money. He that can earn ten shillings a day by his labour, and goes abroad, or sits idle, one half of that day, though he spends but sixpence during his diversion or idleness ought not to reckon *that* the only expense; he has really spent, or rather thrown away, five shillings besides....
>
> Remember, that money is of the prolific, generating nature. Money can beget money, and its offspring can beget more, and so on. Five shillings turned is six, turned again it is seven and threepence, and so on, till it becomes a hundred pounds. The more there is of it, the more it produces every turning, so that the profits rise quicker and quicker. He that kills a breeding-sow, destroys all her offspring to the thousandth generation. He that murders a crown, destroys all that it might have produced, even scores of pounds. (Weber [1920] 2002:14)

Franklin's maxims capture the ethos of modern capitalism in a pure form. Before tracing the ancestral lineage of that frame of mind, Weber wants to capture the ethos of modernity as precisely as possible. Weber points to the significance of the connection between money and life. For him, the spirit of modern capitalism speaks in these words, and they form a particular view of the world, an ethic or philosophy. As he writes,

> Indeed, rather than simply a common-sense approach to life, a particular "ethic" is preached here: its violation is treated not simply as foolishness but as a sort of forgetfulness of *duty*. Above all, this distinction stands at the center of the matter. "Business savvy," which is found commonly enough, is here not *alone* taught; rather, an *ethos* is expressed in this maxim. Just *this* quality is of interest to us in this investigation. (Weber [1920] 2002:16)

Weber ([1920] 2002) devotes an entire chapter to differentiating between early capitalist worldviews and the unique "spirit of modern capitalism" captured in Franklin's maxims (pp. 13–37). He concludes that the development of the spirit of modern capitalism is one component "in the larger and overarching development of rationalism as a whole," and it derives from rationalism's involvement with "the ultimate problems of life" (p. 36). Having shown the nature and historical emergence of the spirit of modern capitalism, Weber's next task "is to investigate from whose spiritual child this matter-of-fact form of 'rational' thinking and living grew" (p. 37). The short answer is **ascetic Protestantism**, but it is how Weber demonstrates this point that matters most.

In his analysis, prior to the Reformation, Roman Catholicism served as the divine justification for the feudal order in medieval Europe. Catholic doctrines were a major force in the consolidation of the feudal formation, as well as a key locus of resistance to any changes threatening feudalism's overall hierarchical structure or central dynamics. But the Roman Catholic Church was not omnipotent, and Catholicism's success in bringing order and stability led to its obsolescence as a guiding doctrine for millions of Europeans as the spiritual, political, and economic landscape changed dramatically in the sixteenth century.

The consolidation of feudalism created the social conditions for expanding trade and travel, and the import of exotic goods from afar served as a stimulus for kings and lords to direct more of the productive activity on their estates to the creation of goods that could be exchanged. This shift had disastrous implications for the feudal peasantry: they were slowly squeezed off the land and lost almost all of their feudal rights. As more and more peasants were forced off the land into destitution, the European peasantry became a mass of homeless wanderers eking out their existence wherever and however possible and the Catholic Church's teachings began to lose meaning for people.

The newly emerging and austere social conditions of the displaced population became fertile soil for a religious belief system that gave dignity to poverty and destitution and turned self-denial and sacrifice into a sacred calling. Weber ([1920] 2002) argues that the origin of the ethos of modern capitalism lies in the particular "this-worldly asceticism" found in the ascetic Protestant belief systems of the Calvinists, Pietists, Methodists, Baptists, Mennonites, and Quakers (p. 53–101).

Weber ([1920] 2002) builds his argument by drawing extensively from the specific dogma of these different belief systems. To do this effectively, he examines "the religious ideas as ideal types, namely, as constructed concepts endowed with a degree of consistency seldom found in actual history." Because historical reality does not show the sharp boundaries that he wants to emphasize, the investigation has to focus on "their *most consistent* forms" (p. 55). For Weber, the teachings of **John Calvin** comprise one such form because they constitute the foundation of the beliefs of all these ascetic Protestant groups.

According to Calvin, religion is a highly individual, personal matter. One can and must communicate as directly as possible with God. More important, Calvin believes in the god of the Old Testament, a highly judgemental creator who wants to test people to determine who are the most worthy of heaven. Calvin preaches that God will admit only a tiny fraction of humanity into heaven—everyone else is condemned to eternal damnation.

Although God will not disclose in advance which people will enter heaven (the elect), he has created a life on earth that will test and prepare humanity for his final decision. Life on earth is unjust, demanding, irrational, and burdensome: some in the afterlife will have these burdens removed and rejoice in an eternal life with God in heaven. Others—the vast majority—will not. Suffering is God's way of deciding who merits everlasting life in his kingdom. Earthly hardship and an ascetic lifestyle are God's way of drawing individuals into direct communication with him.

Calvinism presents a rather bleak worldview—no matter what one does, only a tiny minority is predestined to everlasting life. Calvinism, as a religion, accepts the existing world of impoverishment and urges believers to lead a life committed to stoic survival in the hope that they are among the elect. But, like life itself, nothing is certain: one can never know if one is among the elect—one must simply believe in God, trust his judgement, faithfully follow the scriptures, and pray for salvation. The strength of one's belief is the sole basis for comfort and the only indicator that one might be among the elect (see Weber [1920] 2002:55–77).

Weber ([1920] 2002) turns next to analysing Pietism and Methodism and the doctrines of the Baptists, Mennonites, Quakers, and Puritans. These sects all follow Calvin's teachings but add a significant element of far reaching consequence (pp. 77–101). Still believing in predestination, these Protestant believers read the Holy Scriptures to see exactly what God expects from humankind on earth. God, they believe, wants people to rise above their natural condition—to tame and control all of their natural desires and conduct their lives in ways that conform strictly to His commandments and glorify God in heaven. This belief results in a particularly ascetic lifestyle, and because English Puritanism, "which grew out of Calvinism," provides the most consistent foundation for the development of "**this-worldly asceticism**," Weber uses it to demonstrate the nature of ascetic Protestantism and its link to the spirit of modern capitalism (p. 103).

The seventeenth-century Puritans believed that if they could prove themselves capable of mastering their natural desires and of leading righteous, dignified lives, then that would prove to themselves that God had given them the ability to conduct their lives as he wanted, signalling that they were likely among God's elect. The Puritans' religious beliefs represent more than a religious doctrine; they comprise a value system, a frame of mind, and a set of meaningful actions that Puritan believers can use to guide their daily actions and determine whether they are among God's elect. The Puritan religion espouses a highly disciplined, restrained, passionless way of life that completely tames the natural inclinations of humankind. This Protestant asceticism, Weber argues, directs all of its force against the spontaneous enjoyment of life. The crucial link between the "this-worldly asceticism" of the Protestants and the spirit of capitalism, Weber ([1920] 2002) maintains, is the idea of a "**calling**"—"the *task* [one] is given by God" (p. 39; see also p. 19).

In separating themselves from their natural condition, individuals receive from God particular callings through which they can glorify the Lord. A calling gives order and direction to life. A person's calling dispels doubt and anxiety because it is a way of demonstrating commitment to the glorification of God. Also, and most important for Weber's argument, the idea of each person having a calling moves the spirit of ascetic Protestantism directly into the economic sphere. Weber maintains that there is an important **elective affinity** between the ethos of modern capitalism and the spirit of ascetic Protestantism, in general, and the calling, in particular. Weber establishes the link in two different ways: through an analysis of language and an examination of the actual historical relationship between the calling and the behaviours of ascetic Protestants.

With respect to language and meaning, Weber engages in a lengthy discussion of the term "calling" and of the meanings associated with the word, which, in German, is **Beruf**. Part of the discussion is directly within the text of the essay (Weber [1920] 2002:39–47), but he also writes a lengthy note that explores the history of the word and, most important, examines how the terms *Beruf* and "calling" are introduced into Protestant theology through the translation of ancient Hebrew, Greek, and Latin texts into German and English (Weber [1920] 2002, note 3:180–83).

Weber's discussion shows that, when Martin Luther translated the Bible into German, there was already an economic connotation to the term *Beruf*. A *Beruf* is a profession. A *Beruf* is a position to which one is called as a vocation for the non-material rewards it offers through personal fulfilment, but it nonetheless requires commitment and dedication.

On the historical relationship between *Beruf* and the actions of the Puritans, Weber ([1920] 2002) argues that the pursuit of a calling for the glory of God makes the acquisition of capital acceptable within Protestantism, even though the enjoyment of wealth or its pursuit for its own sake is not:

> On the one hand, this-worldly Protestant asceticism fought with fury against the spontaneous *enjoyment* of possessions and constricted *consumption*, especially of luxury goods. On the other hand, it had the psychological effect of *freeing* the *acquisition of goods* from the constraints of the traditional economic ethic. In the process, ascetic Protestantism shattered the bonds restricting all striving for gain—not only legalizing profit but also by perceiving it as desired by God.... The struggle against the desires of the flesh and the attachment to external goods was *not*, as the Puritans explicitly attest (and also the great Quaker apologist, Barclay), a struggle against rational *acquisition*; rather, it challenged the irrational use of possession. (P. 115)

In sum, Weber ([1920] 2002) argues that, "as far as its power extended, the Puritan life outlook promoted under all circumstances the tendency toward a middle-class mode of organization of life." Moreover, he maintains that this outlook was "the most substantial and, above all, only consistent social carrier of this middle-class mode of organizing life. Just this rational organization of life stands at the source of modern 'economic man' (*Wirtschaftsmenschen*)" (p. 118).

With the dynamic of ascetic Protestantism and its integration into economic activity established, Weber turns to the ways in which that ascetic ethos was generalized as well as how it continued to operate in social and economic life even as the importance of religion declined in an increasingly secular Europe.

Weber argues that Franklin's maxims about time and money parallel the ethos of ascetic Protestantism; the idea of work as renunciation and disciplined activity had become widespread by the eighteenth century, when Franklin penned his "Advice to a Young Tradesman." As Puritan asceticism began to

> rule over this-worldly morality, it helped to construct the powerful cosmos of the modern economic order. Tied to the technical and economic conditions at the foundation of mechanical and machine production, this

cosmos today determines the style of life of all individuals born into it—
not only those directly engaged in earning a living. This pulsating mechanism does so with overwhelming force. Perhaps it will continue to do so
until the last ton of fossil fuel has burnt to ashes. (Weber [1920] 2002:123)

The depth to which "the powerful cosmos of the modern economic
order" and its "pulsating mechanism" dominate all of modern life leaves
Weber with his pessimistic conclusion regarding the *stahlhartes Gehäuse* of
goal-rational action. What forces in the present or future could save humanity from the hollow existence of a life dominated by instrumental reason?
That, however, is a different analysis; one that must wait.

"[T]he next *task* is a different one," Weber ([1920] 2002) writes, "to chart
the significance of ascetic rationalism" (p. 124). Although there are suggestions throughout his writing of how Weber might analyse that significance,
his early death prevents him from ever undertaking that project.

THE MARX-WEBER RELATIONSHIP

The Protestant Ethic and the Spirit of Capitalism is an empirical examination
of the impact that different denominations of Protestantism had upon the
development of capitalism. At the same time, however, because of its level
of abstraction and generalization, it is an extended, implicit critique of the
methodology of Stammler, Meyer, Roscher, Knies, and other members of
the historical school, a methodology emphasizing historical specificity and
the gathering of discrete "facts."

However, *The Protestant Ethic* can also be seen as a challenge to historical
materialism. In fact, at the end of the entire essay, Weber acknowledges that
some will see the piece as an attempted refutation of historical materialism
(Weber [1920] 2002:125). The heavy emphasis on the role of ideas in Weber's
account of the Protestant ethic and the rise of modern capitalism seems to
challenge directly the Marxist emphasis on the economy as the main or even
sole driving force in history. To clarify where he stands with respect to that
framework, Weber writes the following in the last paragraph of *The Protestant
Ethic and the Spirit of Capitalism*:

> This study has attempted, of course, merely to trace ascetic Protestant-
> ism's influence, and the particular *nature* of this influence, back to ascetic
> Protestantism's motives in regard to one, however important, point. The
> way in which Protestant asceticism was in turn influenced in its devel-
> opment and characteristic uniqueness by the entirety of societal-cultural
> conditions, and especially *economic* conditions, must also have its day. For
> sure, even with the best will, the modern person seems generally unable to
> imagine *how* large a significance those components of our consciousness

rooted in religious beliefs have actually had upon culture, national character and the organization of life. Nevertheless, it cannot be, of course,
the intention here to set a one-sided spiritualistic analysis of the causes of
culture and history in place of an equally one-sided "materialistic" analysis. *Both are equally possible.* Historical truth, however, is served equally
little if either of these analyses claims to be the conclusion of an investigation rather than its preparatory stage. (Weber [1920] 2002:125)

There are several points of importance in this paragraph.

To begin with the statement "the modern person seems generally unable
to imagine *how* large a significance those components of our consciousness
rooted in religious beliefs have actually had upon culture, national character
and the organization of life" indicates Weber's belief that, in an increasingly
secularized and industrialized Europe, religion's influence on people's lives
was becoming progressively less obvious. Weber seeks to emphasize that,
despite their low profile, religious ideas still have a powerful and important
impact, although not necessarily as religious ideas and dogmas. This point
shows Weber's conclusion that ideas and values from the past penetrate
deeply into the present and extend into the future even though the way they
are understood across time can alter.

Next, Weber's statement that it is not his "intention here to set a one-
sided spiritualistic analysis of the causes of culture and history in place of an
equally one-sided 'materialistic' analysis" carries three important messages.

First, it shows Weber's recognition that, at various points in his analysis,
he aims critical barbs at the materialism of the orthodox Marxists (e.g., Weber
[1920] 2002:19–20, 35–37). Weber knows his argument critiques historical
materialism, but he does not want it to be misconstrued as a substitute for
that perspective.

Second, the statement and Weber's essay as a whole certainly comprise an
implicit dismissal of historical materialism as the orthodox Marxists had been
developing it. The phrase "a one-sided 'materialistic' analysis [of culture and
history]" clarifies Weber's position on historical materialism for his readers.

Third, the statement underlines Weber's rejection of all one-sided or
single-factor explanations of social life. Weber's work always maintains a
delicate balance among various features and forces, which, in his view, shape
social meaning, social action, and, as a result, larger social formations. Weber
is even more explicit about his rejection of single-factor analyses in one of
the essay's notes:

For those whose conscience remains troubled whenever an economic (or
"materialistic" as one, unfortunately, says even today) interpretation is
omitted from discussions on causality, let it be noted here that I find the
influence of economic development on the destiny of the formation of

religious idea very significant. I will later seek to demonstrate how, in our cases, mutually interacting adaptive processes and relationships produced both economic development on the one hand and religious ideas on the other.... Nonetheless, by no means can the content of religious ideas be *deduced* from "economic" forces. These ideas are, and nothing can change this, actually, *for their part*, the most powerful elements shaping "national character"; they carry purely within themselves an autonomous momentum, lawful capacity (*Eigengesetzlichkeit*), and coercive power. Moreover, the *most important differences*—those between Lutheranism and Calvinism—are predominantly, to the extent that non-religious forces play a part, conditioned by *political* forces. (Weber [1920] 2002, note 94:240)

So where does Weber stand vis-à-vis Marx in explanations of culture, society, and economic history? Are their perspectives the same? Are they compatible? Or are they fundamentally different?

The answer to those questions depends partly on how one interprets Marx's position—and, as the discussion in Chapter 4 shows, there are several levels at which one can read Marx's 1859 preface statement outlining his materialist position. But no matter how much importance contemporary Marxists give to the realm of culture and consciousness, there are certain aspects of Weber's work that they cannot accept as compatible with their materialist position. Similarly, Weberians find parts of Marx's work useful and compatible, but, fundamentally, the theoretical differences between Marx and Weber are significant enough that it would be incorrect to argue that the two men share a common theoretical orientation. Two major points of incompatibility between Marx and Weber centre on the direction or outcome of history and the role of meaning.

According to Marx's studies of history and political economy, history is moving toward a particular outcome. Marx, much more than Weber, was influenced by the grand narrative of progress that was a legacy of Enlightenment thought. Weber, however, sees no universal direction to history; his sociology centres on case studies rather than on sweeping analyses and predictions. Marx thought that his study of history, political economy, and the dynamics of industrial capitalist society had discovered forces that would create long-term, sweeping social change and progress. Weber was more cautious—especially on the question of progress.

Although there is debate over the extent to which Marx's analyses actually support the notion that capitalism will give way to socialism, it is impossible to escape the fact that Marx stated a number of times, in a variety of contexts and in various ways, that the dynamics of capitalist society would lead to periods of revolutionary tension and conflict (and possibly revolutionary change). It is also certain that Marx advocated for the revolutionary transformation of capitalism to socialism.

Weber did not believe there was an apparently inevitable course to history. He did not accept Marx's ([1859] 2005) conclusion in the 1859 preface to *Towards the Critique of Political Economy* that "the forces of production developing themselves within the womb of bourgeois society create ... the material conditions for the solution of this antagonism [between the forces and relations of production]" and that, through their dynamic, "the prehistory of human society closes with this social formation" (p. 62). In addition, Weber did not embrace Marx's claim in the *Manifesto* that "the development of modern industry ... cuts from under its feet the very foundation on which the bourgeoisie produces and appropriates products. What the bourgeoisie therefore produces, above all, are its own grave-diggers. Its fall and the victory of the proletariat are equally inevitable" (Marx and Engels [1848] 1934:20).

Weber was far more cautious about making any claims concerning the long-term direction of history although, as noted earlier in this chapter, he did acknowledge that there were certain historical trends, which, if they were not altered, would continue to unfold. In Weber's view, the social, economic, and political trends in Europe, if they continued, would lead to societies that were increasingly bureaucratic, dominated by goal-rational action, and organized on the basis of a legal-rational order (the rule of law).

Goal-rational action and legal-rational authority were trends that would, according to Weber's research, unfold for some time into the future, but he decisively rejected any notion that "laws of society" existed that were comparable to "laws of nature." A sociologist might discover certain trends, but different social forces could arise at any time and redirect the path of social history. On the basis of his own particular methodological perspective, Weber never thought that social history was following a single trajectory. History was far more open ended for Weber than it was for Marx.

Although Labriola, Korsch, and Lukács argued that Marx's materialist analysis took into account issues of consciousness, class consciousness, political struggle, and class struggle, the trajectory of Marx's own work suggests that he firmly believed that the deep, underlying dynamics of capitalist production were of fundamental importance for sociologists and political activists to grasp—more important, that they were crucial to social change. The *Grundrisse* makes clear Marx's profound awareness of the complexity of the capitalist mode of production and of the ways in which its apparent contradictions and weaknesses might be resolved or mitigated. This understanding is likely why he spent so much of his life exploring the political economy of capitalism in progressively greater depth without preparing his full analysis for publication. But despite all of the tendencies and countertendencies that Marx examines in his voluminous study notebooks and drafts, he never seems to move away from the conviction that to discover the secret of capitalist society, one has to begin with an understanding of the labour process within the specific context of the capitalist political economy.

Weber, too, is aware of the importance of economic relations, but his sociology clearly emphasizes the significance of meaning and meaning construction in social life. Weber's emphasis on interpretive understanding places the dominant accent of his sociology in a different place than on the economic factors that comprise Marx's primary focus. The work of each might complement the other, but, in the final analysis, Marx maintains that the economic relations of society have to be changed to produce a better society whereas, for Weber, social action is complex, multifaceted, and inescapably tied to social meaning. Even a radical change in the economic infrastructure, without an equally radical transformation of the dominant ideology within a society and of the meanings people associate with their social actions, will not, according to Weber, produce a fundamentally different society.

Weber, Modernism, and Postmodernism

Weber's emphasis upon sociology as a comprehensive science of social action places him at what can now be seen as an interesting intersection between modernism and postmodernism. The quest for a comprehensive science of social action in which scholars make a value commitment—or judgement of value—to the pursuit of universally valid truth, grounds Weber squarely in the tradition of modernism. Even though he refuses to believe there are any universal laws or grand narratives of human history, Weber still commits to the strictures of scientific procedure and the principle of objectivity (that is, the knowledge gained through scholarly or scientific inquiry accurately captures or reflects the reality of the object under study, and the knowledge produced is not distorted or misrepresented by the values, beliefs, or personal biases of those conducting the analysis). Modernist scholars and scientists want to know the fundamental or essential reality of the empirical world in which they live; they strive to move beyond the everyday experiences of knowing the world as the phantasmagoria of the infinitely complex, concrete, life-worlds in which people live. Modernist researchers focus on what earlier scientists and scholars have identified as the most meaningful aspects of the infinitely complex world and build upon that knowledge base. Modernists produce and develop meaningful concepts or ideal types (pure types) that sacrifice the fullness of real events to gain the advantages of an abstract, stylized, simplified, and even distorted or accentuated understanding of the complex social and natural worlds.

Conceptual ideal types (or pure types) refine researchers' understandings of the phenomena they study. Scholars develop them on the basis of an unwavering value commitment to the pursuit of objectively valid truths. As a result, these pure types are continually open to critical scrutiny by others who are also seeking to grasp the infinite complexity of reality interpretively.

Ideal types serve as the reference point for comparisons with the fullness of concrete events and actions. Type analysis allows researchers to penetrate more deeply into a more systematic and analytical understanding of the worlds they are studying. Ideal types provide the opportunity for scholars to refine their concepts further, and, most important, these types serve as the vehicles through which scientists may make statements about generalized patterns or processes.

A commitment to the unyielding pursuit of universally valid truth does not require one to be committed to the discovery of universal laws in science (natural or social), but it does allow a scholar to determine the consequences that will follow from his or her conceptual analysis and to understand how that may extend into the future (even the very distant future). These generalizations are recognized as provisional, yet, at the same time, they stand as the best understanding, from a scientific perspective, of what the past and present suggest about the future. Charting the past and present to predict and potentially control the future is central to the modernist perspective, and Weber is committed to these aspects of modernism.

But for all of Weber's desire to rein in the fullness of concrete life and grasp it in the form of pure types, his particular conception of sociology as a comprehensive science of social action opens up the possibility for others to emphasize the limitations related to the construction of ideal types and to consider the ways in which ideal types might fundamentally misrepresent the complex natural and social worlds they are designed to grasp abstractly. Weber's premises and arguments take sociology well down the road to the perspective that many now identify as postmodern. In this sense, read from the vantage point of the twenty-first century, Weber's work provides a bridge that leads from modernism to postmodernism.

As a bridging figure, Weber can be seen as a sociologist who anticipates many of the questions and theoretical problems that postmodernists later identify. His emphasis upon the interpretative perspective and his decision to make social action the focus of sociology can be seen as methodological and theoretical interventions addressing the shortcomings of modernism, shortcomings that, at the time, were just beginning to become apparent.

On the other hand, one can argue that Weber's work in methodology allows sociologists in the contemporary world to hold fast to the tenets of the classical tradition. This argument would show that the legacy of the Enlightenment has always been misunderstood—because people put too much faith in the Enlightenment's promise—and that Weber simply reminds us of the limits to thought that were always part of Enlightenment reason. Instead of giving in to postmodernism, Weber's sociology might be regarded as a framework that can re-establish the dominant concepts of modernism and the classical tradition—the pursuit of universally valid truth on the basis of precise, conceptually based observation of the natural and social worlds that is open to critique and unfailingly committed to the value judgement of scientific objectivity.

In either event, because he wrote during the first two decades of the twentieth century and lived in Germany through World War I and into the early interwar years, Weber had to struggle to understand a social world that was in considerable turmoil and transition. As a result of his social location and the intellectual debates with which he engaged, Weber developed an approach to sociology that helps us understand the emerging social reality while still maintaining the analytical, methodological, and scholarly principles and objectives of modernism. The final section of this chapter explores the terms "modernism" and "postmodernism" and investigates how Weber's work can be viewed as a bridge between those two divergent conceptions of the world.

MODERNISM

Since the end of World War II, there have been three different comprehensive encyclopaedias of the social sciences or sociology: the *Encyclopaedia of the Social Sciences* (Seligman and Johnson 1957), the *International Encyclopedia of the Social Sciences* (Sills 1968), and the *Blackwell Encyclopedia of Sociology* (Ritzer 2007). Each of those encyclopaedias was produced under very different social conditions and dominant theoretical understandings of the social and natural worlds. As a result, one finds not only different emphases and foci in the entries that are common to all of them—see, for example, the entries on Durkheim, Marx, and Weber or on feudalism, the family, science, and sociology—but entries in one that are not found in the other two. For the student of contemporary sociology, it is interesting to note that neither "modernity" nor "postmodernism" is an entry in the first two encyclopaedias, despite the fact that the widespread use of these terms in sociology today suggests their longstanding history within the discipline.

In place of "modernity," one can examine other terms in the *Encyclopaedia of the Social Sciences* and the *International Encyclopedia of the Social Sciences* to determine why the term "modernity," per se, was not identified as a key term. One can examine the terms that were used in its place to see what they convey about sociological thought at the time of the two earlier encyclopaedias. Exploring this terminology is useful in understanding how and why the concepts of modernity and postmodernity are so important to contemporary sociologists as well as why neither term was explicitly included in earlier comprehensive compilations of knowledge in the social sciences.

In the *Encyclopaedia of the Social Sciences*, instead of modernity, one finds the term "**modernism**." Horace Kallan (1957) writes that "modernism may be described as that attitude of mind which tends to subordinate the traditional to the novel and to adjust the established and customary to the exigencies of the recent and innovating" (p. 564). Modernism, he continues, places a high value "upon the new as distinguished from the contemporary or the past" (p. 564).[76] Modernism, in this entry, is almost a generic concept describing a general process that encourages innovative change.

For the contemporary reader, the most striking feature of this 1957 entry is the absence of a strong link between modernism and the rise of the scientific worldview during the Enlightenment. To be sure, Kallan locates the ascendance of the modernist worldview within the context of the French Revolution and the *philosophes'* approach to the underlying rationality of reality, but he spends only two sentences on a relationship that sociologists in the latter part of the twentieth century would see as crucially important. "Never regarded as modernist in itself," Kallan (1957) indicates, "science has been the occasion of modernism in everything else—from economics, sex, and politics to religion and art." "Modernism," he continues, "indeed might be described as the endeavour to harmonize the relations between the older institutions of civilization with science" (p. 565).

On the whole, however, Kallan's (1957) conception of modernism is best captured in the following:

> The modernistic attitude, in sum, arises where a fission develops in the social or intellectual order because a new invention or discovery has become powerful enough to impose adjustment to itself upon the resistant environment which it has entered as an interloper. The process of adjustment begins in some individual or small group whose life or work has been dislocated. Automatic at first, it soon gets rationalized into a program which wins adherents from a wider and wider range of personalities and vocations. None who ally themselves with the program are likely in the beginning to have any thought of conflict or rebellion. That comes as their conduct and labours arouse anxieties, the fears, and finally the active antagonism of the masters of the traditional establishment—the princes and nobles of the church, the academicians of the arts, the academics of the schools. Antagonism leads to self-consciousness, formal definition and propaganda. Freely cooperative individuals become a disciplined school. Their program becomes in its turn a dogmatic object of faith and authority now fighting for its life not only against the established order it rejected but also against a fresh innovation which rejects it. (P. 567)

Kallan's presentation of modernism from the perspective of the 1950s is revealing in three particular respects.

---

76 It is worth noting that the 1957 encyclopaedia does not contain an entry on postmodernism or post- anything, for that matter.

First, the process of modernization and the modernistic attitude are directly tied to processes of change and moving forward out of the constraints and confines of tradition through innovation—modernism means updating and progressive change. It is also an ongoing, recurring process. Kallan's discussion of art demonstrates his conception of modernism clearly.

Modern art, Kallan notes, must be distinguished from classicism, on the one hand, and from modernist art, on the other. Following the French Revolution of 1789, the revolutionary government appointed Jacques-Louis David to govern art in the new republic. Schooled in the classical tradition of Rome, David imposed that style on French art. "Rome became the pictorial hieroglyph of the republic of France" (Kallan 1957:566). David's massive six-by-nine-metre painting—the *Consecration of the Emperor Napoleon I and Coronation of the Empress Josephine*—typifies the classical style that reigned supreme during the Napoleonic Empire.

Following the fall of Napoleon and the 1814 restoration of the Bourbon king Louis XVIII, there was a reaction to the Enlightenment rationalism that lay behind the French Revolution. Consistent with the restoration of the Bourbons as well as with the emotional turmoil that spanned the period from the Revolution and the ensuing Reign of Terror through the Napoleonic period, a Romantic style emerged within French art. The new style accentuated colour, passion (rather than reason), and realism (rather than a contrived classicism). Théodore Géricault's 1819 *The Raft of the Medusa* and Eugène Delacroix's 1830 *Liberty Leading the People* epitomize this new form.

Even though romanticism, as a reaction against the overwhelming emphasis and central importance that Enlightenment thinkers placed upon human reason, was grounded in the recent past, the new art form was termed modern because it represented a definitive break from the classical forms that European artists had inherited from ancient Greece and Rome. The realist focus and the use of colour and line to evoke emotion firmly located this new art form in the modern world—hence the adjective "modern" and the term "modern art."

The invention of the camera, which reproduced reality with an accuracy no artist could rival, stimulated the rise of a new modernist approach to painting. Continuing to use colour to create an emotional response in the viewer, painters moved away from the realism of romanticist (modern) art and experimented with different techniques. As a result, artists such as Camille Pissarro, Paul Cézanne, Claude Monet, Pierre-Auguste Renoir, and Armand Guillaumin forged a new modernist style that experimented with colour and brush techniques to express form, atmosphere, depth, and action to generate an internal, emotional experience for the viewer. Monet's *Impression, soleil levant* (*Impression, sunrise*) of 1873 gave the new style its perfect, descriptive identification—impressionism.

The impressionists, in turn, were challenged by other modernists—the post-impressionists, Vorticists, cubists, futurists, and Dadaists. These developments represented a rejection of the romanticists' refusal to engage with science and technology and, instead, tried to reconcile science and machinery with the creativity of art. Art in the impressionist and post-impressionist periods rejected all traditional art forms as well as the mechanical forms of reproduction ushered in by the camera; modernist art attempted to capture the creativity of humanity in an increasingly mechanical, technological world. Science and art, technical and emotional, innovation and tradition were drawn together in the various expressions of modernist art.

Viewed in this fashion, the unfolding history of art shows ongoing innovation that overturned established practices and an existing aesthetic. Although he notes that there is a reconciliation of art, culture, and various aspects of social life with the emerging influence and growing importance of science, Kallan spends little time considering the impact of science and scientific knowledge in his entry. Modernism, in Kallan's 1957 entry, is largely associated with breaking from tradition.

Today, modernism is strongly associated not only with the dismissal or marginalization of tradition but also with an overriding belief in progress and an increasing reliance on the systematic use of human reason and scientific knowledge to create technologies and social arrangements that will permit greater human freedom and more precise control of the social and natural worlds that humankind inhabits. The contrast with Kallan's view of modernism is clear. Kallan suggests that modernism is *relative*; there are no inherent characteristics of a piece of art or scholarship that make it modernist—rather each new innovation represents a break from tradition. The association of Enlightenment reason and science with modernist thought is central to most contemporary discussions of modernity but was marginal to Kallan's 1957 entry in the *Encyclopaedia of the Social Sciences*.

MODERNIZATION

"Modernity" does not appear in the *International Encyclopedia of the Social Sciences* either.[77] The closest entry is Daniel Lerner's (1968:386–95) discussion of modernization. Lerner's entry is significant for two particular reasons. First, in his 1957 discussion of modernism, Kallan had identified the process of modernization, but he described it as a general process of change, progress, and the updating of things. By 1968, the importance of modernism as a concept and its use as the root term associated with modernity—the term of greatest significance and worthy of elaboration—had declined as the conceptualization of the process of modernization gained in importance in

---

77 Like the 1957 encyclopaedia, the *International Encyclopedia* does not contain entries on postmodernism, postmodernity, or any other post- entity.

the social sciences. In about a decade, a subcategory had become the main concept, and "modernism," as a term denoting a general category of social change, had almost disappeared. *Modernization* mattered far more than *modernism* and the general processes it encompassed.

"**Modernization**" became the key term because the social processes that it described had risen to paramount importance politically and conceptually. Modernization as a political objective and modernization theory as a way of understanding social, political, and economic progress in the post–World War II period dominated all discussions of the contemporary, modern world by the late 1960s. The presence of a definition of modernization in the *International Encyclopedia* is, therefore, not at all surprising—it was consistent with the times. Similarly, modernism, as it was presented by Kallan, was pretty much past its "best-by" date.

"Modernization," according to Lerner (1968),

> is the current term for an old process—the process of social change whereby less developed societies acquire characteristics common to more developed societies. The process is activated by international, or inter-societal, communication. As Karl Marx noted over a century ago in the preface to *Das Kapital*: "The country that is more developed industrially only shows, to the less developed, the image of its own future." (P. 386)

Lerner's statements reveal two key aspects about how the term "modernization" was understood and used in the late 1960s. First, it was associated with processes that were clearly identified with development, and development was associated with increased industrialization. The nations that experienced industrialization first, the "First World," represented, in the sixties, what was commonly considered the "most developed, highest" form of social organization. Through modernization, social and political theorists argued, the "underdeveloped" or "developing nations" of the "Third World" could reach the levels of development found in the First World, and this end point was considered desirable.[78]

Second, the citation from Marx indicates two additional features of modernization as Lerner and other social scientists understood it. First is Lerner's obvious main point—the highly industrialized nations represent the future of the less industrialized. There is a strong sense of the inevitability of the progressive industrialized development of all societies around the globe. But Lerner's use of Marx is particularly interesting for a second reason.

---

78 The countries in the socialist bloc, less industrially developed than the First World but ahead of the Third World constituted the "Second World."

Lerner omits the two sentences that precede the one from Marx that he quotes favourably, the two sentences expressing the idea of the inevitability of the "natural laws of capitalist production" and their inherent tendencies "working themselves out with iron necessity" (Marx [1867] 1983:12). The working out with iron necessity fits Lerner's conception of modernization, but the natural laws of capitalist production that Marx was writing about were the contradictory laws of capitalist production that would, ultimately, lead to severe economic crises and the revolutionary transformation of capitalist society into a socialist one. "Modernization," as sociologists used the term in the late 1960s, did not include this notion at all—on the contrary, modernization theory presented an image of progress in which capitalist societies had already moved beyond the potentially volatile phase examined by Marx. Academics of that time, at least those working outside the Marxian tradition, considered capitalist societies to have entered an era of ongoing progress, development, and stable growth (Aron 1961, 1962; Bell 1960a, 1973; Dahrendorf 1959; Goldthorpe 1968, 1969).

Lerner's (1968:386–87) discussion of modernization also notes that social development was once conceptualized in nationalist terms—the anglicization of India, the gallicization of Indochina, for example—and then in regional terms—the Europeanization of parts of the world and, in the post–World War II period, the Americanization of many parts of the globe, including Europe. But soon these terms were viewed as too parochial to describe the pattern of change that social scientists were seeing around the world—it was clear that the "regularly patterned social change" seen so widely throughout the globe "required a global referent." "In response to this need," according to Lerner (1968), "the new term 'modernization' evolved" (p. 387).

Economic development is the central element of modernization, for Lerner (1968), but it is also associated with a number of broader social changes and developments:

> Modernization, therefore, is the process of social change in which development is the economic component. Modernization produces the societal environment in which rising output per head is effectively incorporated. For effective incorporation, the heads that produce (and consume) rising output must understand and accept the new rules of the game deeply enough to improve their own productive behaviour and to diffuse it throughout their society. As Harold D. Lasswell (1965) has forcefully reminded us, this transformation in perceiving and achieving wealth-oriented behaviour entails nothing less than the ultimate reshaping and resharing of all social values, such as power, respect, rectitude, affection, well-being, skill, and enlightenment. This view of continuous and increasing interaction between economic and non-economic factors in development produced a second step forward, namely, systematic efforts to conceptualize modernization as

the contemporary mode of social change that is both general in validity and global in scope. (P. 387)

In short, Lerner (1968) believes that the convergence of different disciplinary ways of thinking—he identifies economics, sociology, political science, and psychology—upon "a general model of modernization" has established the idea that change is "the distinctive component of virtually every social system" (p. 389). Few traditional societies remain; change, development, and modernization are found everywhere; and the pace of change is accelerating.

The modernization process, Lerner (1968) argues, brings all modernizing societies around the globe closer to realizing the same main features of modernity, and he identifies these "salient characteristics of modernity" as

(1) a degree of self-sustaining growth in the economy—or at least growth sufficient to increase both production and consumption regularly; (2) a measure of public participation in the polity—or at least democratic representation in defining and choosing policy alternatives; (3) a diffusion of secular-rational norms in the culture—understood approximately in Weberian-Parsonian terms; (4) an increment of mobility in the society—understood as personal freedom of physical, social, and psychic movement; and (5) a corresponding transformation in the modal personality that equips individuals to function effectively in a social order that operates according to the foregoing characteristics—the personality transformation involving as a minimum an increment of self-things seeking, termed "striving" by Cantril (1966) and "need achievement" by McClelland (1961), and an increment of self-others seeking, termed "other-direction" by Riesman (1950) and "empathy" by Lerner (1958). (P. 387)

There are four important points to note about Lerner's discussion of modernization. First, the term has grown out of a general concept—modernism—and now accentuates the industrialization of economies around the world and the associated social impacts that such economic development has on societies throughout the globe.

Second, there is a very strong emphasis upon the "Global North" leading the way for the rest of the world. Modernization describes the process through which less developed parts of the world will come to be more similar, if not identical, to the industrialized nations of western Europe and North America.

Third, the process of modernization involves the functional development and integration of a wide variety of institutions in modernizing societies. One is reminded of Saint-Simon's or Comte's notions concerning the three stages of human history—with industrial societies representing the pinnacle of human development.

Finally, modernization, as it was understood in the late 1960s, was a global process in which certain essential features of the "advanced societies" of the world would work themselves out—that is, become manifest—in other parts of the globe. Modernization was a project that was unfolding toward an ultimate telos or higher goal.

POSTMODERNISM

The *Blackwell Encyclopedia of Sociology* is the most recent attempt to draw together a comprehensive presentation of sociology and of the sociological understanding of the past and present.[79] Although there are still very strong modernist elements, entries, and discussions in the encyclopaedia, it is heavily influenced by postmodernist approaches to sociology. It contains entries on modernity, modernization, postmodernism, postmodern culture, and postmodern theory.[80] The entry that is most relevant here is the one on postmodernism by Julie Albright (2007).

Although modernism and modernist approaches dominated sociology in the post–World War II period, by the late 1970s, a growing number of social thinkers were arguing that modernism, as a frame of mind, prevented many sociologists from recognizing the full complexity of the societies in which they lived and that they studied. Modernism, as a metanarrative—as a particular underlying framework or discourse—filtered and shaped how people understood the world. More attention, this group maintained, had to be directed at contemporary social formations from the perspective of various critical theories or from a completely different intellectual vantage point.

In one very succinct formulation, Gary Woller (1997) notes that modernism is the frame of mind that represents the "trinity of the Enlightenment—reason, nature, and progress" (p. 9). **Postmodernism** is the frame of mind that seeks to depose that trinity. Jean-François Lyotard (1984:3), in one of the most influential examinations of the postmodern condition, also argues that knowledge has changed, in terms of its status and nature. Knowledge

---

79 The forthcoming second edition of the encyclopaedia—as the *Wiley-Blackwell Encyclopedia of Sociology*, still edited by Ritzer—was not available when this edition of *The Promise of Sociology* went to press. How much the new edition of the encyclopaedia will differ from the first is unknown.

80 The entry on modernization emphasizes many of the same themes that Lerner (1968) notes although Ronald Inglehart and Christian Welzel (2007) also review the key debates around the notion of modernization that took place from the 1970s to the present. In essence, Inglehart and Welzel (2007) write, "Modernization is an encompassing process of massive social changes that, once set in motion, tends to penetrate all domains of social life, from economic activities to social life to political institutions, in a self-reinforcing process. Modernization brings an intense awareness of change and innovation, linked with the idea that human societies are progressing."

has changed in three fundamental ways. First, knowledge—all knowledge, including science—is, according to Lyotard, a form of discourse. Second, in the digital age, knowledge, more than ever, is power. Finally, "by concerning itself with such things as undecidables, the limits of precise control, conflicts characterized by incomplete information, '*fracta*,' catastrophes, and pragmatic paradoxes," postmodern science has changed the meaning of knowledge: "It is producing not the known, but the unknown" (Lyotard 1984:60).

> The postmodern ... [is] that which, in the modern, puts forward the unpresentable in presentation itself; ... that which searches for new presentations, not in order to enjoy them but in order to impart a stronger sense of the unpresentable. A postmodern artist or writer is in the position of a philosopher: the text he writes, the work he produces are not in principle governed by preestablished rules, and they cannot be judged according to a determining judgement, by applying familiar categories to the text or to the work. Those rules and categories are what the work of art itself is looking for. The artist and the writer, then, are working without rules in order to formulate the rules of what *will have been done*. (Lyotard 1984:60)

In the postmodern period, science—the formerly dominant almost unchallenged form of knowledge and certainty—now faces rivals that are rewriting the rules of how one can best interpret and understand the world.

In her *Blackwell Encyclopedia* entry, Albright (2007) writes that postmodernism embodies a shift in sensibility, particularly evidenced in the arts, music, and architecture. Changes include a shift from concern with form to a concern with skill and craftsmanship, from structure to surface, from purity to pastiche (the incorporation of different styles or parts drawn from a variety of sources), and from substance to image or simulation. The shift from modernism to postmodernism is best exemplified by two quotations. The first is from the definitive modernist architect Ludwig Mies van der Rohe: "Less is more." This encompasses the modernist sensibility in architecture—form follows function, all is stripped to essences, and there is simplification and a lack of ornamentation. The second quotation, from postmodern architect Robert Venturi, is "Less is a bore." It captures the spirit of postmodern architecture and, indeed, of postmodernism itself—a spirit that revels in playfulness, irony, and ornamentation and produces a pastiche of styles.

Modernism, rooted in the razor of Enlightenment reason, strips away everything that is extraneous to get to the essence of things. Modernism emphasizes function over form. Postmodernity "problematizes" or puts into question these modernist assumptions.

Like modernism, postmodernism is also an attitude of mind. It is one that calls into question, on the basis of the people's life experiences in the contemporary period, the fundamental assumptions and outlook of modernism. Postmodernism, as it has developed within modernity, focuses on three particular outcomes.

First, postmodernists seek to make people aware that the basic assumptions, goals, and principles of the modern era are the result of one particular metanarrative (or intellectual framework)—the Enlightenment worldview. The quest for scientific truths, postmodernists maintain, is not a quest for eternal truths or for a set of underlying natural laws but merely an aspiration that arose from the particular social conditions existing in Europe during the Age of Reason and the Enlightenment.

Second, to establish the argument that human history is shaped by grand narratives or specific metanarratives, postmodernists focus on how events in the contemporary period have apparently exhausted the dominant Enlightenment perspective. Rather than moving toward more precise knowledge and enduring truths about nature or the social worlds in which people live, postmodernists point to the way in which the polarities that Enlightenment thought identified as mutually exclusive now exist simultaneously in the contemporary period. Postmodernists argue that relationships that should be, according to mainstream social thought, totally incompatible with one another have now collapsed into one another—apparently opposing conditions exist simultaneously, in proximity to each other. For example, postmodernists argue that colonialism, in the traditional sense, has declined, yet there is increased globalization and greater exploitation of the Global South by the Global North. The modern world established and was then centred on secular values, material interests, and consumerist practices, but one now sees a resurgence of religious beliefs and a dramatic growth in religious fundamentalism. As evangelists of various types preach about the evils of carnal pleasure to larger and larger live television and Internet audiences around the globe, sexual liberation continues to grow and a variety of sexualities flourish.

Instantaneous global communication through the Internet and digital technologies has ushered in a new information age that seems to promise to expand the exchange of ideas and to increase social freedom. At the same time, postmodernists note, there is greater surveillance, increased suspicion, and the suspension of basic human rights through legislation such as the American Patriot Act of 2001. The fall of the Berlin Wall and the breakup of the Union of Soviet Socialist Republics resulted in the end of the Cold War and the creation of a number of new, independent states. But there are new global power blocs, a growing fear of the proliferation of nuclear weapons, and the return to a siege mentality among some of the world's most powerful nations.

Finally, the presence of these collapsed polarities, postmodernists maintain, indicates that the dominant canon of Western thought is no longer adequate; it can no longer help us understand or explain this increasingly complex world.[81] Arguing that many cultures have achieved sophisticated accomplishments in art, literature, and social and political theory, as well as knowledge of the natural world, postmodernists maintain that the Western canon comprised of the great works of Western societies—a body of writing that includes, for example, Plato, Aristotle, Jane Austen, Francis Bacon, Honoré de Balzac, Geoffrey Chaucer, Descartes, Goethe, Elizabeth Gaskell, Niccolò Machiavelli, Newton, Rousseau, Shakespeare, Mary Wollstonecraft Shelley, Adam Smith, Henry David Thoreau, Leonardo da Vinci, and Voltaire (Bloom 1987:243–312)—is too restrictive and limiting.[82] By focusing critically on the way in which Enlightenment metanarratives shaped how people in the modern era have interpreted the world and then demonstrating the weaknesses of that discourse, postmodernists seek to establish the view that all of human history has been shaped by particular metanarratives (worldviews or discourses).

As much as humans might wish for a discoverable underlying order in the natural and social worlds, this promise of the Enlightenment, most postmodernists argue, will always remain unfulfilled. Postmodernists maintain that people must still attempt to understand the world around them, but they do not believe that it is possible or even desirable for people to seek grand, overarching theories about the natural or social world. Instead, people need to examine nature or social life in much more specific terms. The world is infinitely complex, postmodernists argue, and the best that researchers can do is develop conceptual "theorizations" that enlighten people about the complexity. These understandings, however, will not and cannot produce universally applicable theories of the social or natural worlds. Every theory—every theorization—is simply a conceptual understanding of the world—a social construction that is based on a set of specific assumptions. If one rejects an assumption, then the understanding is no longer valid; postmodernists argue that the way people now understand the world shows that the basic assumptions in science are open to question.

FROM MODERNISM TO POSTMODERNISM

The modern world, which began to emerge with the challenge to feudal society, gave rise to the hypothetico-deductive approach to understanding

---

81 Canon has two meanings and both are implied in the phrase "canon of Western thought." A canon is a standard, a norm, or a principle. A canon is also a catalogue or a list. The canon of Western thought suggests there is a list of great works and great thinkers whose contributions to Western culture represent the highest standards of cultural and intellectual achievement. The canon of Western thought is the list of works demonstrating the standards of excellence and the insights that thinkers in Western societies have achieved.

82 Former Harvard President Charles Elliot's 51-volume *Harvard Classics* is a useful guide to what many people consider the Western canon.

the natural and social worlds. This emergent scientific perspective seemed to represent the fundamental key to understanding the underlying laws of nature; it was considered the source of all that humanity needed to comprehend nature fully, so humankind could control nature and human interactions with it rationally. The success and power of the scientific worldview held out the promise that the social world could also be understood, controlled, and shaped in a similar manner.

A belief in the power of science to enable humankind to act upon nature and create changes advancing the interests of humanity became a central feature of modernism—the frame of mind that progressively spread from the Renaissance to the Enlightenment and on into the nineteenth century. By the mid-nineteenth century, the industrializing societies of western Europe were characterized by increasingly rapid change, as modernity, in all of its complexity, began to come fully into being. During the next 100 years, the scope and pace of social change widened and accelerated; transportation expanded, and people, goods, and ideas moved around the globe with increased speed and deeper penetration into all areas of the world. These changes, in turn, made people aware of the vast cultural diversity existing in a wide variety of different social formations. As well, they came to appreciate the productive power of market societies, the technologies they produce, and the extent to which Western rationalism can revolutionize the way people carry out all aspects of their daily lives.

By the last quarter of the twentieth century, the heightened pace of change, the increasing use of ever-evolving information technologies, the shrinking of space and time, and the increasingly dense interconnections of the global economy all suggested that the promise of modernity was turning into reality. At the same time, however, the negative impacts of each of modernity's so-called advances, the legacy of two world wars, and an increasing sense that instrumental reason was enslaving humanity rather than liberating it brought modernism, as a frame of mind, and scientific reason, as the only way of achieving "true" knowledge, under closer and closer scrutiny.

Modernity, the actual experience of social and economic modernization in which "all that is solid melts into air," provided the impetus for some sociologists and cultural critics to question whether modernism was the only frame of mind for grasping the social and natural worlds. Enlightenment rationality was a powerful way for organizing one's understanding, but did it really represent the only way, the best way, or the single best way for understanding, or was it simply one possible way, one particular discourse?

As soon as scholars stepped outside the scientific worldview, other possibilities became apparent, and postmodernism, as a new attitude of mind, enabled them to focus upon the different metanarratives humans used to organize their daily activities, their understanding of nature, and their interaction with the natural and social world. And, according to postmodern thinkers, the variety of these metanarratives poses a challenge to modernist claims about objective and scientific knowledge. The condition of knowledge among the most developed societies of the world, Lyotard (1984) argues, demonstrates how much human understandings are shaped historically by metanarratives and why no single metanarrative can have greater absolute truth or value than another. Postmodernism, then, opens up a totally different way of thinking about the unity of science, the nature of the natural world, and the way knowledge or power channels people's understandings and actions within a relatively narrow set of options.

Yet despite the swirling world of change, the growing impact of cyber reality, and the increasing sense of humanity's limited knowledge, is it wise for sociologists to abandon the classical tradition? Sensitivity to a more artistic, a more craft-like approach to knowledge (to use Mills's imagery) is certainly required, but the task and promise of sociology will still remain essentially the same no matter how it is dressed up in different metanarratives. The best sociology will continue to explore critically the intersection of personal biography with history and social structure, which means that Weber's sociology will remain relevant—indeed, critical—to understanding the postmodern world.

Weber and a Vocabulary for Clear Social Reflection

What key concept or term can Weber's work add to the vocabulary required for clear social reflection? Although there are several possibilities, if one were restricted to a single term, then it would be "interpretive understanding." Interpretive understanding is a good choice for several reasons.

First, Weber, like Durkheim, argues that sociology has to be an observationally based undertaking, but his commitment to the empirical foundation of sociological investigation differs significantly from that made by Durkheim. Weber wants sociology to become a comprehensive science of social action. By this phrase, he means two things. By comprehensive, he means that sociology should be an all-encompassing undertaking; sociology should deal with the full extent of social life and social action. In addition, sociology should be comprehensive in the sense that the sociologist should interpret, grasp, or *comprehend* the meaning of social action.

Second, the term "interpretive understanding" also reminds us that Weber's conception of social action is directly tied to meaning—action is social "when its intended meaning takes account of the behaviour of *others* and is thereby oriented in its unfolding," he maintains (Weber 1956:1, 1968a:3). As a result, the interpretive perspective—the *verstehende Ansatz*—is critical to Weber's work.

Third, Weber's major substantive contributions to sociology address frames of mind and the role that ideas—particularly religious ideas and value systems—play in shaping social life. His essay *The Protestant Ethic and the Spirit of Capitalism* is just one example of Weber's goal to integrate the impact of particular frames of mind with the economic structure of society and the dominant forms of social action within a particular social formation. Through interpretive understanding, Weber attempts to establish general levels of understanding while also focusing on the specific aspects of each social formation he analyses.

Fourth, the general trends that Weber's work tracks—the rise of goal-rational action, the growth of bureaucracy, the structure of social power, and forms of domination—all centre on how particular forms of meaningful action shape and contour the way people understand, or *interpret*, the world in which they live. As some interpretive frameworks become dominant, others recede or disappear, leaving the range of human action limited because "other ways of doing things" do not come to mind.

Finally, **interpretive sociology**—*verstehende Soziologie*—is a critical term that differentiates Weber's conception of sociology from that of Durkheim or Marx. With respect to Durkheim, although collective consciousness and collective representations are central concepts in Durkheim's work and emphasize how people view and think about the world around them, his treatment of them as "social facts," as "things," despite his explanation of what he means, leaves virtually unexamined the questions of how they are internalized and how they control individual action. In striving so hard to distinguish sociology from psychology and to establish sociology as a positive science, Durkheim established a methodology that cannot address the micro processes of learning the norms of society.

Weber's emphasis on the interpretive position, on the other hand, draws a stark line between the methods of the natural sciences and those of the humanities and social "sciences." The objects of study in sociology are, for Weber, radically different than the objects of study in the natural world; meaning is critically important in the human sciences or *Geisteswissenschaften* (translated literally, the sciences of the mind/spirit); as a result, the methodological approach has to be different. And the term "interpretive understanding" encapsulates the methodology Weber recommends and reminds us how different Weber and Durkheim are in their particular approach to the systematic study of social life.

The term "interpretive understanding" also captures the fundamental division between Marx and Weber, and it does so in two ways. First, Marx's materialist position begins with the central importance of labour (or the process of production), and, even though Marx sees labour as a creative, mediating process through which humankind externalizes its ideas, plans, and objectives, his approach identifies the social relations of production that emerge over the course of history as the fundamental departure point for analysis.

Weber's sociology is closely associated with Marx's image of social history; Weber's concerns over the growing dominance of goal-rational action and legal-rational authority along with his deep engagement with various aspects of economic history show shared concerns and focal points of investigation. In the final analysis, however, it is meaningful action and an unwavering emphasis upon interpretive understanding that characterize Weber's sociology and separate him from even the most Hegelianized Marx. The term "interpretive understanding" brings to mind not only the similarities that Durkheim and Weber, on the one hand, and Marx and Weber, on the other, share in their work as sociologists but also the fundamental differences between Weber's sociology and that of either Durkheim or Marx.

Key Terms and Names

Geist
economic rationalism
ascetic Protestantism
John Calvin
this-worldly asceticism
calling (*Beruf*)
elective affinity
modernism
modernization
postmodernism
(interpretive sociology) *verstehende Soziologie*

Questions for Review and Further Reflection

1. Refer to Weber's discussion of "economic rationalism" and "the Protestant ethic." What does he mean by "economic rationalism?" What does he see as the major features of "the Protestant ethic?" In your own experiences (with education, part-time jobs, and daily life), what examples of economic rationalism have you encountered? To what extent is the disciplined, ascetic lifestyle described by Weber valued in today's society?

2. In your own words, describe or define Weber's notion of "elective affinity." How is it important in his study *The Protestant Ethic and the Spirit of Capitalism*? Can you think of examples of this phenomenon that would help you remember what Weber has in mind with this conception?

3. What is Weber's main argument about the relationship between capi-
    talism and the Protestant ethic? Does this explanation seem viable?
    Describe ways in which this explanation is not comprehensive. What
    has he missed? (Or, if you think the explanation is comprehensive,
    support this view.)

4. How does Weber's analysis in *The Protestant Ethic and the Spirit of
    Capitalism* challenge the methodological positions of both the histori-
    cal school and historical materialism?

5. Compare and contrast how Marx and Weber approach their research
    on capitalism. What are the strengths and weaknesses of each approach?

6. How has historical context affected the definition of modernism and
    modernization over time? Are there problems with the term "modern-
    ism" and its definition? How about modernization?

7. What is meant by postmodernism? How does postmodernism challenge
    the perspective of modernism? On a sheet of paper write "modernism"
    in one column and "postmodernism" in the other. List the main features
    of each. Which of the two do you feel best represents the world in which
    you live today?

8. You have already created mind maps of the most significant elements
    in the theoretical positions of Mills, Marx, and Durkheim. Now
    draw one for Weber. Where does the Weber mind map overlap with
    the other three? Where is it different? What is important about the
    differences? Which of these theoretical positions do you think is most
    useful for studying the contemporary world? Now draw a theoretical
    mind map that you feel represents the best ideas found in the work of
    Marx, Durkheim, Weber, and Mills.

PART THREE

Sociology and Contemporary Popular Culture

10

CULTURE AND CRITIQUE

Main Objectives

This chapter will

1. Through the work of Raymond Williams, analyse the term "culture," and indicate why it is a complex, often contested concept.
2. Review how Marx, Durkheim, and Weber, respectively, understood the production of ideas and thus the production of culture.
3. Describe the debates over the term culture put forward by different sociologists throughout the twentieth and early twenty-first century.
4. Build a pure or ideal type construct of "culture" that can serve as the basis for studying different types of popular culture in the contemporary period.

This book begins with profiles of the Millennials and Generation Z and a particular focus on how their everyday life-worlds contribute—positively and negatively—to their experiences in higher education. The discussion in Chapter 1 ends with Wesch's (2008a) emphasis that learning in colleges and universities requires "a grand narrative to provide relevance and context." Mills's "sociological imagination," introduced in Chapter 2, is the type of narrative Wesch is advocating. It enables one to understand sociologically and analytically how the everyday life experiences of the Millennials and Gen Zers are shaped within the information age.

In Chapter 2, the questions that are integral to the sociological imagination uncover the main features of contemporary social life. The analysis utilizes Castells's *The Information Age* and McLuhan's *The Gutenberg Galaxy* and *Understanding Media* to provide some of the broader social and historical context that explains why and how today's students are so deeply engaged with digital media and the Internet and what that entails. Complementing

Mills's position, Castells (1999) demonstrates that "societies are organized around human processes structured by historically determined relationships of *production, experience,* and *power*" (pp. 14–15). Arising from those processes, Castells emphasizes, symbolic communication between humans generates "*cultures* and *collective identities*" (p. 15).

McLuhan's (1962) work documents how communication and the resulting culture in the electric age "differ significantly from those of the typographic and mechanical era" (p. 3). Through an elaboration of his aphorism, "the medium is the message," McLuhan (1964) details how, from the mid-twentieth century onwards, the media of the electric age "shape and control the scale and form of human association and action" creating a profoundly different social world (p. 9).

Part I of this text introduces the concept of the sociological imagination and investigates how this concept enables us to study the impact of digital media on the university experiences of Millennials and Generation Zers. However, there is far more to the scale and form of human association in the contemporary period than online communication. One can broaden the scope and examine how other types of symbolic communication shape and produce particular cultures and collective identities. That is the task in Part III, and it brings the text full circle—back to the study of selected issues in the everyday life-world. This time, because of the theories elaborated in Part II, the analysis can use a far richer set of interpretive tools and a firmer grasp of the sociological imagination.

Through two case studies, the next two chapters address some specific themes concerning popular culture. The first case is folk music, in general, and the early work of Bob Dylan in particular. The second examines what begins as rock and roll and subsequently "morphs" into a wide range of popular music forms, which, despite their differences, are tied to the original roots of rock and roll. The analysis of each case is based on work that is deeply indebted to the ideas of the classical social theorists studied in Part II. Before this chapter considers what is meant by "culture," by examining the concerns expressed about popular culture by a host of social thinkers and public intellectuals, a summary of the relevant material in Part II will be helpful.

In Marx's ([1859] 2005) most concise statement of how to understand the social world, he writes that in the social production of their lives, individuals enter social relations of production that are determined by the material forces of production. Marx emphasizes that the totality of the relations of production—the mode of production—constitutes the real basis of society and "conditions the social, political, and intellectual processes of life overall" (pp. 61–62). For Marx, the dynamic, unstable, dialectical processes of social production are the departure point for analysing the dominant ideas within a society and how individuals understand the world they create.

Marx is drawing upon the insight that he and Engels developed when they first set down their basic premises for understanding and changing the social world. "The production of ideas, of conceptions, of consciousness, is above all, immediately interwoven with material activity and the material interaction of men—the language of real life" (Marx and Engels [1845] 1932:15). Within class societies, the shaping of consciousness by the mode of production has a particular impact on how individuals understand the social world in which they live. The class that "is the dominating *material* force [*Macht*] in society is at the same time its dominating *intellectual* force [*geistige Macht*]." Possessing the "means of material production" gives that class control "over the means of intellectual [*geistigen*] production" (Marx and Engels [1845] 1932:35). Critically detailing the origin of the "intellectual processes of life overall" and how some worldviews become the "dominating intellectual force" in a society is a central endeavour in Marx's work.

In *The Rules of Sociological Method*, Durkheim ([1895] 1982:40) introduces collective representations as a fundamental analytical concept. These are the symbols, myths, customs, and other social facts that a group or society uses to identify, conceptualize, and represent itself. Although individuals within groups are the basis for the creation of collective representations, the representations result from "the crystallising" or "instituting" of "certain modes of action and certain ways of judging" that take on an "existence" outside and independently of the individuals themselves (p. 45). Collective representations are institutions—institutionalized practices—that have crystalized out of all the beliefs and modes of action found within the collectivity. Thus, sociology becomes "the science of institutions, their genesis and their functioning" (p. 45). The study of institutionalized collective representations is the central focal point of Durkheim's sociology.

A dominant theme throughout Weber's work is the impact that frames of mind (or ideas)—particularly institutionalized frames of mind such as religion—have in shaping people's perceptions of the world and their social action. Weber (1922, 1923a, 1923b) is acutely aware of the elective affinity existing between certain religious belief systems and the dominant forms of social action found in societies where those religions are practised. Pursuing this theme in his study of the spirit of modern capitalist society, Weber ([1920] 2002:123) maintains that "the powerful cosmos of the modern economic order" and its "pulsating mechanism" dominate all of modern life. This particular dominant type of social action, he argues, stems from the influence of ascetic Protestantism, and it has left the modern world trapped within the *stahlhartes Gehäuse* of goal-rational action. Weber's entire sociology, from his substantive studies of different religions to the methodological importance he places on the interpretive understanding of social action, centres on how the prevailing frame of mind shapes a social formation.

Clearly, in each case, Marx, Durkheim, and Weber recognize the significance of how the social world is conceptualized—class consciousness for Marx, collective representations for Durkheim, and frames of mind for

Weber. A second point of similarity is that each attributes the form and content of that consciousness to particular aspects of the social formation that give rise to the predominant worldview. In addition, each has a complex, synthetic theorization of how societies are constituted, how they should be analysed and comprehended, and how they give rise to a dominant form of consciousness. Third, each of the classical thinkers is aware of the impact of power in shaping the dominant forms of consciousness, and each is critical of the contemporary world that he is studying. Finally, each believes that how individuals and groups understand the social world is crucial—it is why they engage in their detailed studies of social life, publish their findings, and engage with others in striving to create progressive change.

Neither Marx nor Durkheim or Weber use the term "culture" to designate the body of ideas found in a society. Marx uses ideology and the adjective "*geistig*" (mental, intellectual, spiritual) with different, appropriate nouns; Weber tends to use *Geist, geistig*, and frame of mind; and Durkheim uses *conscience collective* and collective representations. Nevertheless, "culture" *is* the term that contemporary sociologists use to designate the aspects of social life that each of these classical theorists is addressing through their own appropriate vocabularies. In fact, the term culture does not take on the general meaning and usage that it has today until after Marx, Durkheim, and Weber have made their analyses of how worldviews are generated and then shape further conceptions of the world and social formations as a whole. Before turning to the significance of culture—particularly its importance for contemporary social life—the history of the concept requires consideration.

Culture and Society

"Culture," **Raymond Williams** (1983) argues, "is one of the two or three most complicated words in the English language" (p. 87). His work *Culture and Society, 1780–1950* was instrumental in reshaping how sociologists and other scholars thought about the word and the phenomenon (actually phenomena) designated by the complex term.

"In the last decades of the eighteenth century, and in the first half of the nineteenth century," Williams (1961) observes, "a number of words, which are now of capital importance, came for the first time into common English use, or, where they had already been generally used in the language, acquired new and important meanings" (p. 13).[83] He argues that the general pattern of

---

83 Williams (1961) notes that because *Culture and Society* cannot include "any detailed accounts of the changes in [these] words and meanings," he will publish the "supporting evidence, later, in a specialist paper on *Changes in English during the Industrial Revolution*" (p. 11). Williams did even better, producing an extensive account in *Keywords: A Vocabulary of Culture and Society* (Williams 1983).

change in those words serves as "a special kind of map" that makes it possible to examine the "wider changes in life and thought to which the changes in language evidently refer" (p. 13).

Williams identifies five key words for the map—industry, democracy, class, art, and culture. Although **culture** had previously meant "the 'tending of natural growth,' and then, by analogy, a process of human training," in the eighteenth and early nineteenth centuries, Williams (1961) contends, its meaning changed "to *culture* as such, a thing in itself":[84]

> [Culture] came to mean, first, "a general state or habit of the mind," having close relations with the idea of human perfection. Second, it came to mean "the general state of intellectual development, in a society as a whole." Third, it came to mean "the general body of the arts." Fourth, later in the century, it came to mean "a whole way of life, material, intellectual, and spiritual." It came also, as we know, to be a word which often provoked either hostility or embarrassment. (P. 16)

This shift in meaning, which began in the eighteenth century, took "culture" from its basic, material, and agricultural roots to its emerging and then dominant connotations—it first signified intellectual development, then the arts, and finally "a whole way of life." In this transformation, "culture" came to be recognized as a major force in constituting social relations, and remains so in the present.

One begins to see the basis for Williams's argument by remembering that his focus is the period of "the great transformation" (see Durkheim [1893] 1933; Hobsbawm 1999; Marx [1867] 1983; Polanyi 1944; Tönnies [1887] 1957). It is during the industrialization of Europe that "culture" becomes "a thing in itself." It is a process in which class, industry, and culture are intertwined.

The growth of industry dramatically changes the social and material forces of production. The formation of large factories, the introduction of steam-powered machinery, and the relentless pursuit of profit through the unbridled use of goal-rational action create dangerous, exploitative conditions for workers (see Engels [1845] 1975; Hobsbawm 1999). To resist such exploitation, workers and social reformers require a reference point in which they can ground their opposition to the treatment of workers under industrialized working conditions. The demanding and dangerous conditions themselves

---

84 In *Keywords*, Williams adds the word "nature" into his "record of an inquiry into a *vocabulary*"—a collection of words that are "virtually forced ... on ... [one's] attention" because their meanings are inextricably bound to key debates and issues (Williams 1983:15). Nature, Williams (1983) notes, "is perhaps the most complicated word" (p. 219). "Any full sense of nature" he writes, "would be a history of a large part of human thought," and then he directs readers to consult Lovejoy's *Essays in the History of Ideas* (p. 220).

and the low rates of pay, while obvious enough at one level to support their claim, cannot serve as the necessary reference point for two reasons.

First, although the conditions appear unfair and exploitative, the question remains: *why* are they exploitative? On what basis are they exploitative? Why should the circumstances be different? In relative terms, one might argue, industrial workers are treated better than slaves or serfs had been in earlier periods of European history. Reformers have to provide a distinct reference point outside the working conditions themselves to justify why those conditions, in particular, are exploitative and unjust.

Second, reformers cannot appeal to the basic principles of the economy because utilitarian philosophy and the domination of goal-rational action justify the practices found within industrialized production. Business owners can defend large factories, low wages, long hours of work, and the use of machinery on the basis of the science of political economy. Political economists had overwhelmingly championed the competitive nature of the laissez-faire market, the idea that the pursuit of individual interests served the interests of all, and the legitimacy of production techniques that were the most efficient means of building the wealth of the nation (see, for example, Mill [1821] 1844; Ricardo [1817] 1891; Sismondi [1815] 1966; Smith [1776] 1976).

Neither can an appeal to the former feudal relations of production serve as the reference point partly because those conditions were, themselves, highly exploitative. In addition, they tied individuals permanently to the feudal manor restricting their freedom. Breaking the ties of feudalism to create individual freedom was viewed by everyone as progress despite its attendant price tag. Finally, and most important, the new industrial economy was creating greater wealth and more material goods than the old regime. It was in perfect harmony with the dominant philosophy (or ideology) of the time—it was consistent with the "legitimate form of authority [*Herrschaft*]," to use Weber's (1968a) term.

Religious values might be a possible point of resistance—but with religion's declining influence, such an appeal offered little chance of success. Moreover, as Weber ([1920] 2002) documents, the areas of Europe that were industrializing most rapidly did so on the basis of religious values. The ascetic Protestant belief systems legitimated and even sustained the harsh working conditions of early industrialization.

Although an appeal to feudalism did not seem effective or legitimate, a legacy from that period concerning peasants' "natural rights" did. Reformers and workers—with the support of the landed gentry, which had a particular class interest in curtailing the growth of industrial production and the power of the emerging capitalist class—developed a "rights-based" reference point to challenge the exploitative conditions of labour. This argument based in basic human rights was consistent with Enlightenment values and represented an educated, elevated, "cultured" response to the industrialists' lowly material interests in money and profits.

Consequently, the differing class interests of the landed gentry and industrial capital were partly defined by their attitude toward the conditions of the working class. For the gentry, ethical issues should temper or prevent the severe exploitation of the working class. By fostering this informed, educated, and cultured position regarding workers and economic processes overall, the landed gentry, as it lost economic power, distinguished itself from, and asserted superiority over, the new capitalist class. For industrial capital, on the other hand, the ethical systems of greatest consequence were the laws of the market and the pursuit of profit through goal-rational action. In this way, "culture," as a measure of "the general state of intellectual development, in a society as a whole," provided a moral reference point that workers, reformers, the gentry, and others used to oppose the ethos of unfettered, goal-rational, industrial production; the dynamics of the capitalist market; and the domination of the cash nexus (Williams 1983:16; see also 87–93).

Even in this brief overview, one sees why Williams emphasizes the importance of the changing meaning of culture and why its change must be understood within the context of other central terms, such as industry and class, in the period of the great transformation. There are three major points to keep in mind.

First, the word "culture" has taken on different meanings at different points in time. Because it has changed under different social circumstances, the meaning of culture can be studied sociologically. One can use the socio-logical imagination to grasp the term more fully and meaningfully. Second, each of the four meanings Williams identifies as dominant in the late twenti-eth century continues to prevail. The term "culture" still represents a state of mind and the cultivation of the intellect. It implies or inspires the continual expansion of human knowledge. Finally, "culture" refers to the level of intel-lectual development within a society as a whole. Used in this way, the term encourages one to rank societies or civilizations on the basis of their culture or cultural achievements.

The level of culture attained by a society or its cultural status is closely associated with the third meaning—"culture" as "the arts." Societies with cul-tures judged to be "advanced" or "high" demonstrate their development and achievement through abstract, intellectual pursuits that show the sophistica-tion of the society's leading minds. The arts—literature, painting, sculpture, drama, dance, music, and other art forms—embody and project a society's cultured creativity, imagination, development, and achievements.

"Culture" also refers to a way of life—one can think of Canadian culture in contrast to American or British; one can differentiate between French Canadian and English Canadian culture or between Texan and New England culture. When using the word "culture" in this sense, people often think of one dominant culture and of other subcultures competing for influence or status or simply coexisting within this overarching and predominant culture. The idea of "the American melting pot," where immigrants leave their old cultures and melt into the predominant culture of America is consistent with this sense of culture as a way of life. Although Canada's multiculturalism suggests that Canada remains a vibrant mosaic of different cultures, the power and dominance of American cultural institutions results in, despite local variations across Canada, the heavy Americanization of culture among English-speaking Canadians.

The final major point is the most important. Williams demonstrates that, to grasp culture, one must link the term's meaning to the social activities from which it has arisen. The idea of culture was originally associated with "the tending *of* something, basically crops or animals" (Williams 1983:87). It had a very direct, material, physical, and active basis and point of origin—it involved physical work. The word "culture" comes from production—"to cultivate" is the transitive verb from which the noun arises. The labour of cultivation produces the agricultural—or cultured—products.

As the meaning of culture expanded to involve cultivating minds, the material and labour-related basis of cultural production began to fade, as did the idea that culture is linked to social and economic relations. The relationship between people within a set of social relationships producing agricultural products is obviously connected to their material situation. However, the cultivation of the mind, the cultivation of ideas, does not seem to be tied as closely to people's social circumstances. But it is, as Williams demonstrates. The manner in which Williams documents and develops this connection is his fundamental contribution to the study of culture and is central to the material presented in Chapters 11 and 12. Culture—even intellectual culture—is produced by people living in specific social circumstances who actively cultivate things, people, and ideas. As Marx and Engels ([1845] 1932) maintained, culture is the result of the "production of ideas, of conceptions, of consciousness" that is "immediately interwoven with material activity and the material interaction of men" (p. 15). As a result, culture is a *social* product and can be studied sociologically.

THE PRODUCTION OF CULTURE

Williams draws some of his insight and much of his approach to the study of culture from Marx although, as noted earlier, Durkheim and Weber also emphasize the creation of culture through material production and social action and make important contributions in their own right. Nevertheless, because Williams builds primarily upon Marx and because Williams's approach to the study of culture influences so many sociologists today, the Marxian roots of Williams's framework merit some elaboration.

Marx's position on "intellectual production"—its creation and impact on social life—presented in the opening section of this chapter and in more detail in Chapters 4 and 5, relies on work leading up to his magnum opus, *Das Kapital*. In *Capital*, Marx provides some unique insight into how the "production of ideas, of conceptions, of consciousness" is interwoven with the specific dominant forms of material activity and production found within commodity-based societies (Marx and Engels [1845] 1932:15).[85]

"The wealth of societies in which the capitalist mode of production rules [*herrscht*]," Marx ([1872] 1987) begins *Capital*'s opening chapter, "appears like an 'immense collection of commodities,' the single commodity as its elementary form" (p. 69). Following 32 pages of careful analysis of the commodity's intricacies, Marx concludes that although, "at first sight," the **commodity** appears as "an easily understood, trivial thing," its analysis shows it is "a very tricky thing, full of metaphysical craftiness [*Spitzfindigkeit*] and theological peculiarities [*Mucken*]" (p. 102).[86]

Among those crafty subtleties is the appearance that "the social character of [the commodity producers'] own labour reflects back [*zurückspiegelt*] to them as the objective [*gegenständliche*] character of the products of labour themselves, as the socio-natural properties of these things." That is, commodities and commodity production appear to exist and function in a world of their own—a world determined by the objective properties of the commodities themselves. These commodities are part of "the economy," which possesses its own natural properties and laws based on the nature of commodities and the capitalist mode of production. As a result, the objects and social relations that the workers produce—that exist only because workers have made them—*appear* to exist outside and independently from the real productive activities that created them. "The determinant social relationship of men and women themselves assumes the illusionary [*phantasmagorische*] form of a relationship of objects [*Gegenständen*]" (p. 103). To find an equivalent circumstance, Marx points out, one must go to the "misty world of religion" where "the products of the human mind are endowed with life and appear as independent figures [*Gestalten*] entering into relationships with one another and humankind" (p. 103).

---

85 When Marx wrote, the only commodity-based societies in existence were capitalist. Since then, the command economies of different state-socialist societies, such as the former Soviet Union and China, have created commodity-based economies different than those Marx studied. The discussion of Marx's ideas here will continue to use Marx's terminology although these other commodity-based economies should be kept in mind as well.

86 *Spitzfindigkeit* is an interesting term for Marx to choose; *metaphysischer Spitzfindigkeit* can range in meaning from metaphysical subtlety through to metaphysical craftiness and metaphysical sophistry (something that is intentionally deceptive). In other words, far from a simple thing, the commodity hides an enormous amount of its full, comprehensive reality, the details of which Marx will examine in the three volumes of *Capital*.

In short, for Marx, the capitalist mode of production and all its social and material relations, as well as how it is perceived, is akin to the world of religion. Rather than recognizing that the social relations and material forces of production are the products of real individuals interacting with one another and the material world within a particular historical context, the economy seems to be a world unto itself with its own hierarchal structure, particular regularities, and universal, timeless laws, which individuals must accept and obey so that society as a whole, and all the individuals within it, will prosper. "The production of ideas, of conceptions, of consciousness" is not understood as "immediately interwoven with material activity and the material interaction of men" (Marx and Engels [1845] 1932:15)—it is mystified (Marx [1872] 1987:103).

In place of a genuine understanding of how the capitalist mode of production arose and is constituted, there is a body of ideas—an ideology—that serves as "the dominating *intellectual* force" in capitalist society. Possessing the "means of material production" gives the bourgeoisie control "over the means of intellectual production" and with that power, it establishes an overall culture that maintains the illusion of an economy with its own objective laws, which all members of society must follow (Marx and Engels [1845] 1932:35). This ideology soon expands beyond just the economy and begins to establish a culture in the sense of "a whole way of life."

While Marx was intent on emphasizing the material, or social, basis for culture, Weber's work in *The Protestant Ethic* reminds sociologists that cultural products themselves, such as religion, also influence the dominant culture of a society (see also Korsch [1923] 1970; Lukács [1923] 1970). Weber ([1920] 2002), like Marx and Durkheim, understood that these cultural products were the institutionalized result of the conceptual understandings that groups of individuals develop through their social circumstances and practices, and he did not advocate for "a one-sided spiritualistic analysis of the causes of culture and history in place of an equally one-sided 'materialistic' analysis." However, it was his clear intent to emphasize the important role that culture plays in the shaping of the everyday life-world (p. 12).

These analyses of the economic and societal foundations of culture are essential to the critical study of how culture shapes everyday life. Before this text turns to that question, however, it traces attitudes toward culture in the modern period, and the contemporary economic and intellectual developments that led people to fear a cultural decline. This fear brings into striking detail the interaction of culture and material and social production.

Culture and Fears of Cultural Decline

As "the general state of intellectual development in a society as a whole" and, at the end of the nineteenth century, in its association with "the arts," culture had come to represent the highest creative achievements of a society. But as commodity production became increasingly widespread and extended well beyond the creation of material goods into intellectual and artistic products, a wide variety of educators, public intellectuals, educated laypersons, and scholars began to lament the "**commodification**" of culture and its decline. Culture came to be seen as something sold in the mass market to mass consumers. Social commentators as diverse as F.R. Leavis and Denys Thompson (1933), Theodor Adorno and Max Horkheimer ([1944] 1972), Richard Hoggart (1958, 1970), Williams (1961), Herbert Marcuse (1964), Walter Benjamin (1968), Stuart Hall (1964), Herbert Schiller (1973, 1989), Neil Postman (1985, 1988), John Fiske (1989), and Neal Gabler (1998) have expressed different concerns about the state of culture, its meaning, its nature, and, most significantly, its impact upon social life.

Today, one rarely sees "culture" as an unmodified noun—the term is almost always qualified with one of its many modifiers: classical culture, modern culture, high culture, mass culture, popular culture, middlebrow culture, lowbrow culture, plastic culture, authentic culture, or e-culture, for example. But, to commentators at the end of the nineteenth century, culture did not require a modifier; it stood on its own. For Arnold ([1868] 1932), culture was "the pursuit of [humanity's] total perfection by means of getting to know, on all matters which most concern us, the best which has been thought and said in the world" (p. 6). Through this knowledge, humanity could turn "a stream of fresh and free thought upon our stock notions and habits," allowing people to escape entrenched, narrowing thoughts, ideas, and actions. "Culture, which is the study of perfection," according to Arnold ([1868] 1932), will lead humankind "to conceive true human perfection as a *harmonious* perfection, developing all sides of our humanity" and "as a *general* perfection, developing all parts of our society" (p. 11).

As culture is turned into a commodity and sold for profit in the twentieth century, commentators began to lament its decline. **F.R. Leavis and Denys Thompson** (1933) are concerned with the demise of English literary culture, arguing that it was being overwhelmed by a growing number of simple and simplifying forms of entertainment and information such as films, newspapers, advertising, "indeed the whole world outside the classroom" (p. 1).[87] They felt

---

87 Leavis and Thompson were involved in adult education. They wrote *Culture and Environment* to help teachers develop students' critical awareness: "This book, though designed for school use, was not designed for that alone. Its range of application is wide and varied and its methods flexible. The earlier the age at which the kind of work it deals with is begun the better; but all its topics are capable of subtlety and a depth of development demanding the maturest approach. It invites an unlimited number of applications at the university level. And in particular the need for teachers of some training on these lines will appeal to directors of Teachers' Training Colleges. Those interested in adult education, too, may recognize here something that will help to solve some of their most difficult problems. Indeed one of the incitements to writing this book was experience of work under the W.E.A. [Workers' Educational Association]" (Leavis and Thompson 1933:vii).

that the organic community that sustains a living, thriving culture was being lost. According to them, works such as *Pilgrim's Progress*—"the supreme expression of the old English people"—*Change in the Village*, or *The Wheelwright's Shop* remain as testaments that "the English people did once have a culture (so nearly forgotten now that the educated often find it hard to grasp what the assertion means)"; however, as the rural and agricultural world was supplanted by the urban and industrial one, English culture was cut adrift from its roots (Leavis and Thompson 1933:2–3). They argue that the modern world has replaced an authentic, centuries-long tie to the natural rhythms of agricultural life with mechanization and industrialization that responds only to the superficial needs of the market economy:

> The great agent of change, and, from our point of view, destruction, has of course been the machine—applied power. The machine has brought us many advantages, but it has destroyed the old ways of life, the old forms, and by reason of the continual rapid change it involves, prevented the growth of new. Moreover, the advantage it brings us in mass-production has turned out to involve standardization and levelling-down outside the realm of mere material goods. Those who in school are offered (perhaps) the beginnings of education in taste are exposed, out of school, to the competing exploitation of the cheapest emotional responses; films, newspapers, publicity [advertising] in all its forms, commercially-catered fiction—all offer satisfaction at the lowest level, and inculcate the choosing of the most immediate pleasures, got with the least effort. (Leavis and Thompson 1933:3)

Here one sees the split between "popular culture" and "high culture," as some might label these two concepts, tied to industrialization, urbanization, and the expansion of the market into the sale of simplified, "dumbed down" cultural products. Other scholars and commentators echo these concerns.

Hoggart's (1958) *The Uses of Literacy: Aspects of Working-Class Life with Special Reference to Publications and Entertainment* builds directly on the Leavis and Thompson work while also confronting it critically. **Richard Hoggart** (1958:3–14) quickly sketches a tentative profile of "the working class" to examine more meaningfully the impact of print and mass circulation publications on the lives of working class individuals and on their understanding of the world in which they lived. To tell the story, he uses the experiences of his family and ancestors.

Hoggart's grandparents and the working people of their generation lived a rural existence, but the generation of his parents, aunts, and uncles, who were also from the working class, only retained a few rural habits, largely out of nostalgia. Hoggart (1958) and his generation were urbanites, fully at home with mass transit, chain stores, and the pace and feel of city life;

the country or seaside had become merely places one might visit. The deep personal connection of earlier generations to the natural world was gone.

In the wake of this separation from the land, working class youth engaged with the "modern mass media of communication"; for example, young people went to "the picture-palaces," which were "optical fairylands," often housed in grand buildings with spacious foyers and balconies placing patrons inside an arcade of mesmerising images and sounds. However, according to *The Uses of Literacy*, the second or third generation of the working class in England did not passively internalize a bland, commercialized culture. Hoggart presents a more nuanced examination of the effects of industrialization and the commodification of culture than do Leavis and Thompson. Nevertheless, despite the working class resistance to being subsumed by a banal, commercial culture—a resistance Hoggart describes with such respect and care—he is left with some serious reservations and concerns.

Hoggart (1958:286) recognizes that many are familiar with the rise of mass culture and its potential consequences, but he feels that, although they "know all the arguments," they do not really understand how profoundly mass culture penetrates into people's everyday lives, limits their horizons, and seduces them into accepting banal entertainment. It is possible "to live in a sort of clever man's paradise" without really recognizing the assault of mass culture on human sensibility, he argues.

Hoggart fears that, without a conscious intervention into the commercial dynamic that is increasingly dominating and shaping culture, the substantial freedom provided by a complex, varied culture will be lost in the levelling down of the market as it appeals to the greatest mass of consumers. When that freedom is lost, Hoggart (1958) concludes, "the great new class would be unlikely to know it: its members would still regard themselves as free and be told that they were free" (p. 287).[88]

Hoggart addresses the problem of culture and literature from a different perspective a few years later in order to make the same points regarding the decline of both in the post–World War II era. First, he describes the benefits of what he terms "**live literature**":

> I value literature because of the way—the peculiar way—in which it explores, re-creates and seeks for the meanings in human experience; because it explores the diversity, complexity and strangeness of that experience (of individual men or of men in groups or of men in relation to the natural world); because it re-creates the texture of that experience; and because it pursues its explorations with a disinterested passion (not wooing nor apologizing nor bullying). I value literature because in it men

---

88 Note that a Huxleyan theme runs through a number of these critiques of mass culture (Huxley 1932). For more on Huxley, see the discussion that follows in this chapter.

look at life with all the vulnerability, honesty and penetration they can command ... and dramatize their insights by means of a unique relationship with language and form. (Hoggart 1970:11)

But this is literature at its best—literature as a cultural rather than a commercial production. Not all writing has this impact.

Conventional literature merely reinforces the existing way of seeing the world while live literature, properly read, may disturb us, lead us to reflect, and even "subvert our view of life" (Hoggart 1970:12). Echoing Leavis and Thompson, Hoggart (1970) maintains that live literature seeks "to articulate something of the 'mass and majesty' of experience" (p. 16). But most people tend to narrow their focus; they "ignore embarrassing qualifications and complexities" so that the world remains comfortable. Live literature prevents us from slipping into complacency as it "bring us up short," and stops "the moulds from setting firm." It "habitually seeks to break the two-dimensional frame of fixed 'being' which we just as habitually try to put round others; it keeps us responsive and alert, extending our humanity and understanding of the world" (p. 16). Hoggart, like Leavis and Thompson, juxtaposes two cultural categories: one that is creative, exploratory, and complex and another that reinforces convention, ignores complexity, and seeks to comfort, entertain, and give instant and easy pleasure. Hoggart continues his argument by noting that what is true of individuals applies to societies as a whole. A society in which literature is becoming increasingly conventional through commercialization loses its capacity to inspire people to consider and explore the full potential of human life. "Things can never be quite the same," Hoggart (1970) concludes, "after we have read—really read—a good book" (p. 18).

Hoggart, like Leavis and Thompson, fears the outcome of the growing impact of the market economy on literature (or culture) and the declining standards that result in increasingly simplified entertainment being sold to more and more consumers in the emerging mass society. Mass culture reinforces the dominant, mystified conceptions of the social world. Because it is so simplified, popular culture cannot comprehend and critique the existing social relations of production and the life-world that sustains them.

Although their backgrounds differ significantly from those of Arnold, Leavis, Thompson, and Hoggart, members of the Frankfurt school—Adorno, Horkheimer, and Marcuse—express similar concerns over the growth of what they term "the totally administered society," which they associate with the increasing power of the market and goal-rational action over social life. This power, they argue, led to the rise and predominance of "one-dimensional man" (Marcuse's term) and to a modern world in which cultural forms are being continually levelled down by what they identify as "the culture industries." **Theodor Adorno and Max Horkheimer**, whose work is deeply rooted in the traditions of great classical music, art, and literature, were heavily influenced by Marx's critique of capitalist society, Weber's analyses of the growth of legal-rational domination in the increasingly bureaucratic world of the early twentieth century, and the rise of Fascism in Germany. According to them, the Enlightenment (and the process of becoming "enlightened" in the modern era), the growth of science, and the spread of technical, instrumental reason had significant negative consequences that remained insufficiently explored (Habermas 1970; Horkheimer 1974).[89]

In their 1944 essay "The Culture Industry: Enlightenment as Mass Deception," Horkheimer and Adorno ([1944] 1972:120) argue that the culture industries—films, radio, and magazines—impress the same stamp on everything. Every aspect of modern society is dominated by technical efficiency, mass production techniques, and standardization—automobiles, bombs, and movies are subjugated to the same system of instrumental rationality (the most effective means of producing a mass product that is sold to mass publics). Culture is subordinated completely to capital.

Horkheimer and Adorno draw attention to the manner in which industries that might appear at first sight to be separate and independent—radio, the banks, the film industry, and utilities producers—are all tightly interwoven economically. Indeed, they argue, the integration is so complete that one can actually ignore any features that might demarcate different firms or branches of industry. They then focus their attention on "the **culture industry**" in a manner that is even more pessimistic than the perspectives of Leavis, Thompson, or Hoggart. The gap between high and mass culture is replaced, in the outline provided by Horkheimer and Adorno, by the careful, calculated differentiation of consumers and their tastes, and "the culture industry" then churns out mass produced goods to suit consumer groups, but these are "mechanically differentiated products" that "prove to be all alike in the end" (Horkheimer and Adorno [1944] 1972:123).

Horkheimer and Adorno's assessment of entertainment and culture in mass society is scathing and relentless. All cultural products—music, film, art, literature—are reduced to standardized formulae wherein every consumer can predict, from the outset, what will come next and anticipate the conclusion. Mass culture comforts and even flatters the consumer even though its banality is so obvious. The "dialectic of enlightenment" turns out to be the

---

89 Horkheimer and Adorno took advantage of the ambiguity of the German language to convey a double meaning with respect to the word "enlightenment." In German, nouns are always preceded by an article, and they are always capitalized; as a result, *die Aufklärung* can mean "the Enlightenment" or simply "enlightenment." A central focus of Horkheimer and Adorno's critique of modern society centres on the rise of science and the associated domination of technical, instrumental rationality, which took place during the Enlightenment and has become the basis for what is perceived of as real knowledge—or true enlightenment; the dual meaning of *die Aufklärung*, then, allows them to develop their critique at several levels simultaneously.

negation of learning and of expanding one's horizons, as the producers of mass culture lower the intellectual depth of art, music, film, and literature to meet the manufactured wants of mass market consumers.

The most troubling theme within "The Culture Industry" is the extent to which Horkheimer and Adorno see the entertainment industry as the vehicle for what ultimately amounts to mass deception. "The fusion of culture and entertainment that is taking place today leads not only to a depravation of culture, but inevitably to an intellectualization of amusement" (Horkheimer and Adorno [1944] 1972:143). The intellectual energies of those working in the production of mass culture are focused on perfecting the techniques that will entertain and amuse rather than challenge and stop people short. The formula for success revolves around the production and reproduction of easily and then passively consumed entertainment. "The less the culture industry has to promise, the less it can offer a meaningful explanation of life, and the emptier is the ideology it disseminates" (Horkheimer and Adorno [1944] 1972:147).

It is within this context that Horkheimer and Adorno begin to draw parallels between the culture industry of North America and the Fascists' control of the media and their calculated manipulation of the masses in Hitler's Germany. The culture industry and advertising merge since the assembly-line nature of the culture industry and the indistinguishable hollow products it offers are perfectly suited to the world of advertising. And advertising is barely a short step away from propaganda, as it offers half-truths and illusions to a public looking for simple solutions to its media constructed wants. The freedom to choose, they note, turns out to be simply the freedom to choose from what is always the same.

Building on Horkheimer and Adorno's *Dialectic of Enlightenment* and the concept of the administered society, Marcuse's *One-Dimensional Man: Studies in the Ideology of Advanced Industrial Society* is an extended examination of "the paralysis of criticism" in the postwar Western world—a paralysis that created a "society without opposition."[90] Echoing central themes from

---

90 Marcuse (1958) was equally critical of the Soviet Union: "No matter how high the level of technological progress and material culture, of labor productivity and efficiency, the change from socialist necessity to socialist freedom can only be the result of conscious effort and decision. The maintenance of repressive production relations, enables the Soviet state, with the instrumentalities of universal control, to regiment the consciousness of the underlying population.... Left without a conceptual level for the 'determinate negation' of the established system, for comprehending and realizing its arrested potentialities, the ruled tend not only to submit to the rulers but also to reproduce themselves in their subordination. Again, this process is not specific to Soviet society" (Marcuse 1958:190). *One-Dimensional Man* takes up these themes, focusing particularly on repression through production relations and on the need for "determinate negation" of the established system, which Marcuse begins to call the "great refusal" of forms of modern domination.

George Orwell's (1949) *Nineteen Eighty-Four*, **Herbert Marcuse** (1964) begins his study provocatively: "Does not the threat of an atomic catastrophe which could wipe out the human race also serve to protect the very forces which perpetuate this danger?" (p. ix). Due to the potentially apocalyptic conse quences of an East-West confrontation in the Cold War era, the public is almost immobilized by fear, Marcuse argues, and fails to search for ways that such a catastrophe could be prevented or the threat of it eliminated. More important, if people did begin to search for solutions to the postwar geopolitical situation, they would soon see that the dangerous state of affairs in which they find themselves actually benefits some very powerful vested interests in advanced industrial societies. Echoing Horkheimer and Adorno, Marcuse (1964) notes that the media have no problem in presenting these particular vested interests as "those of all sensible men," and, as a result, the apparent needs of society as a whole are accepted as individual needs and aspirations, the satisfaction of which is for the common good and seems to be completely rational (p. 12).

Yet the entire structure of the administered society, Marcuse (1964) maintains, is irrational: its productivity is destructive of the free and full development of human needs and creative capacities, peace is maintained by the constant threat of war, and growth depends upon the repression of the real possibilities for pacifying the struggle for existence. Most problematic of all, the "productive apparatus and the goods and services which it produces 'sell' or impose the social system as a whole" (pp. 11–12).

> If the individuals are satisfied to the point of happiness with the goods and services handed down to them by the administration, why should they insist on different institutions for a different production of different goods and services? And if the individuals are pre-conditioned so that the satisfying goods also include thoughts, feelings, aspirations, why should they wish to think, feel, and imagine for themselves? True, the material and mental commodities offered may be bad, wasteful, rubbish—but *Geist* and knowledge are no telling arguments against the satisfaction of needs. (Marcuse 1964:50)

Like Horkheimer and Adorno, Marcuse (1964) focuses on the commodification of all that humans produce, even thoughts, feelings, and cultural works. He describes how "mass communications blend together harmoniously, and often unnoticeably, art, politics, religion, and philosophy with commercials, they bring these realms of culture to their common denominator—the commodity form" (p. 57). High culture becomes material culture and, in that transformation, loses its critical tension and impetus to challenge the status quo. "The spectre that has haunted artistic consciousness since Mallarmé—the impossibility of speaking a non-reified language—has ceased to be a spectre" Marcuse (1964:68) laments.[91] That is, creative artists, rather than finding a mode of communication that breaks away from conventional expression, are trapped in conventional forms of representation, and their art becomes just one of many commodities for sale in the market.

The expression of concerns about the decline of culture from the 1930s through to the 1970s did not abate in the latter part of the twentieth century. Postman, for example, shifted the focus from print culture to television. In *Amusing Ourselves to Death: Public Discourse in the Age of Show Business*, he writes,

> To say it, then, as plainly as I can, this book is an inquiry into and lamentation about the most significant American cultural fact of the second half of the twentieth century: the decline of the Age of Typography and the ascendancy of the Age of Television. This change-over has dramatically and irreversibly shifted the content and meaning of public discourse, since two media so vastly different cannot accommodate the same ideas. (Postman 1985:8)

Postman's position flips McLuhan's (1962) optimism for the electric age versus the typographic and mechanical era on its head. Postman (1985:30–63) extols the cultural power and possibilities of typography as a medium and the mindset "the Age of Exposition" facilitates:

> Exposition is a mode of thought, a method of learning, and a means of expression. Almost all of the characteristics we associate with mature discourse were amplified by typography, which has the strongest possible bias toward exposition: a sophisticated ability to think conceptually, deductively, and sequentially; a high valuation of reason and order; an abhorrence of contradiction; a large capacity for detachment and objectivity; and a tolerance for delayed response. (Postman 1985:63)

Although typography and exposition dominated Canadian and American culture throughout the eighteenth and nineteenth centuries, their impact began to decline with the rise of what Postman (1985) calls "the Age of Show Business" (pp. 64–98). In this age, history, politics, religion, and education are reduced to forms of entertainment, and Canadians and

---

91 Stéphane Mallarmé (1842–98) was a French symbolist poet who used the sound of the spoken word to bring different levels of meaning to his poetry. He believed that poetry was independent of the world and should be read with a focus on the music of its words rather than on referential meaning. The Tuesday night salons Mallarmé hosted were at the centre of the Parisian avant-garde's intellectual life in the 1890s.

Americans become less able to cope with complexity, nuance, ambiguity, and uncertainty (see Postman 1985, 1988, 1995). If Irving Berlin had changed one word in his great Broadway hit, Postman (1985) muses, he would have been prophetic—today, "There's No Business *But* Show Business" (p. 98).

One illustration demonstrates Postman's concerns regarding the dominance of the entertainment culture and the way in which this culture has subverted meaning, cohesive thought, and analysis—the nightly news (the source of most people's information about the world).[92] News, Postman (1985) argues, has become reduced to "Now ... this":

> "Now ... this" is commonly used on radio and television newscasts to indicate that what one has just heard or seen has no relevance to what one is about to hear or see, or possibly to anything one is ever likely to hear or see. The phrase is a means of acknowledging the fact that the world as mapped by the speeded-up electronic media has no order or meaning and is not to be taken seriously. There is no murder so brutal, no earthquake so devastating, no political blunder so costly—for that matter, no ball score so tantalizing or weather report so threatening—that it cannot be erased from our minds by a newscaster saying, "Now ... this." The news-caster means that you have thought long enough on the previous matter (approximately forty-five seconds), that you must not be morbidly pre-occupied with it (let us say, for ninety seconds), and that you must now give your attention to another fragment of news or a commercial. (P. 99)

In the age of show business, then, events and circumstances are presented as disconnected, almost random events in which one is equally as important as the next. The "Now ... this" format obliterates history, ignores social context, and keeps the viewer watching through the constant flow of images, stories, and superficial information, which is paced to permit only passive attention; there is never the time or depth of coverage that would stimulate real reflection. The news captures and entertains viewers enough to keep them staying tuned from one set of commercials to the next.

In the conclusion of *Amusing Ourselves to Death*, Postman (1985) argues that there are two ways in which "the spirit of a culture may be shrivelled" (p. 155). The first is Orwellian—culture becomes a prison. The citizens of Oceania in Orwell's (1949) *Nineteen Eighty-Four* are imprisoned in a world where the Ministry of Truth controls culture through "prolefeed," which consists of newspapers reporting almost nothing but crime, sport, and astrology; sensational novelettes; overly sexed films; and sentimental songs mechanically

---

92 Postman (1985:114–54) also describes the impact of the electronic media, particularly television, and show business culture on religion, politics, and education.

produced by the "versificator." Thought is limited and distorted as Oldspeak is replaced by the ever-shrinking vocabulary of Newspeak and "doublethink." And there is the ever-present threat of the pain that the Ministry of Love inflicts on dissidents.

The second way culture dies is Huxleyan—the state controls through pleasure and entertainment. In Aldous Huxley's (1932) *Brave New World*, citizens are conditioned to consume, everything from the ubiquitous drug soma, which offers hangover-free "holidays" and eliminates the need for religion by replicating religious experiences, to recreational sex.[93] In this world, what matters is "happiness rather than truth and beauty." No doubt Postman would argue that we now live in a world in which life is replicating art.

Neal Gabler (1998), in his more recent analysis of the extent to which entertainment has conquered reality, echoes many of Postman's concerns. "While an entertainment-driven, celebrity-oriented society is not necessarily one that destroys all moral value," Gabler (1998) writes, "it *is* one in which the standard of value is whether or not something can grab and then hold the public's attention" (p. 8). Serious ideas, serious literature, "serious anything" is marginalized. In such a society, Gabler notes, "*Homo sapiens* ['man' the thinker] is rapidly becoming *Homo scaenicus*—man the entertainer" (p. 8).

Gabler's position differs from Postman's insofar as Postman placed a heavier burden on television for the decline in culture and the blunting of sensitivity; Gabler (1998) argues that, although television may well be what Postman calls "the command center of the new epistemology [basis for knowledge]," entertainment "was the cosmology that had governed American life with increasing vigour since at least the turn of the century" (p. 56). Today, the argument goes, entertainment has become the universe—the cosmos—within which television, radio, print media, the Internet, smartphones, and e-culture orbit, operate, and exert their influence.

By the end of the twentieth century, according to Gabler, the great cultural debate had shifted from considering the differences between high culture and mass culture to one in which the key tension was between a culture of reality versus one of entertainment. (Note that Gabler uses the same *Brave New World* imagery as Postman.) The debate became one between "the realists who believed that a clear-eyed appreciation of the human condition was necessary to *be* human and the postrealists who believed that glossing reality and

---

93 Huxley wrote *Brave New World* following a trip to the United States during which he was repulsed by American youth culture, sexual promiscuity, and what he perceived as an artificial, commercially driven cheeriness in American interaction. The sex-hormone chewing gum was a parody of the ubiquitous chewing gum of US teens. But the book is more than a critique of American culture and is based on more than a fear of the Americanization of Europe—it was also a critical response to the utopian literature that came after H.G. Wells's *The World Set Free: A Story of Mankind* (1914) and *Men Like Gods: A Novel* (1923) and George Bernard Shaw's (1889, 1912) various pieces supporting socialism.

even transforming it into a movie were perfectly acceptable strategies if these made us happier" (Gabler 1998:243). "Is reality," Gabler asks rhetorically, "as it was traditionally construed, morally, aesthetically and epistemologically preferable to postreality?" In other words, is life, "as traditionally construed, preferable to the movie version of life?"

Do the concerns about culture's decline extend into the twenty-first century? The short answer is "yes." If the medium is the message, as McLuhan insists, then the work of **Nicholas Carr** (2011), Rose (2013), and Gardner and Davis (2014), discussed at length in Chapter 2, indicate that the media through which popular culture is now most widely consumed undermine the ability of individuals to develop a sustained, nuanced, critical understanding of their life-worlds. Carr (2011) echoes and updates Postman's (1985) concerns about the loss of the linear, contemplative, literary mind of print culture, as it turns into the distracted, multi-tasking, fragmented mind of the Internet. Rose (2013:87) expresses a similar concern, arguing that the increasingly extensive use of multiple, immediate, and bidirectional communication platforms fosters the development of "continuous partial attention" or "hyper attention" and of individuals who constantly jump from one information source to another and lose the capacity for a sustained, integrative approach to comprehending the complex world in which they live. Similarly, Gardner and Davis (2014:91) state that extensive reliance on the digital world for information and entertainment creates an "app-dependent" relationship to the world. Individuals turn to various apps and assorted technologies to solve their personal troubles of milieu rather than to their own critical abilities and resources. They no longer assess their life-worlds and place personal troubles within the larger context of public issues of social structure.

Assessing Popular Culture Today through Weber's "Pure Type" Method

The foregoing discussion demonstrates important continuity along with significant change in critics' reactions to the commodification of culture in the modern period. The material is important because it documents concerns about the demise of culture as it became a commodity sold to mass consumers. Equally important, the various responses to culture's commodification identify what essential aspects of culture are lost in its reduction to a mass-market commodity. This identification is significant because, taken together, these critical assessments provide an image of culture in its purest or ideal form. One can use the debate about culture's decline to engage in an assessment of popular culture using Weber's pure (or ideal) type method.

Each of the analysts, from Arnold to Gardiner and Davis, identifies one or more of the qualities a cultural product must have to capture, "the conflictive interaction between humans organized in and around a given social structure" (Castells 2000:7). To be comprehensive, a cultural product should demonstrate, ideally, the interplay of production, experience, and power (Castells 2010:15). The cultural artefact should enable its consumer to recognize both that meaning "is constantly produced and reproduced through symbolic interaction between actors framed by [the existing] social structure" and that their actions simultaneously reproduce and change this structure (Castells 2000:7). Finally, a cultural product must demonstrate that the cultural realm is "produced by the consolidation of meaning" and that "meaning is produced, reproduced, and fought over in all layers of social structure, in production as in consumption, in experience as in power" (p. 7). Building upon this conception of culture, located within a dynamic, unstable, contradictory social whole, the "pure" or "ideal" cultural product contains the following essential elements.

First, according to Arnold ([1868] 1932), culture, as a pure type, will address "matters that most concern humanity" and bring forward "the best that has been thought and said in the world" (p. 6). Culture will turn "a stream of fresh and free thought" upon individuals' everyday stocks of knowledge, helping them "escape entrenched, narrowing thoughts, ideas, and actions" (p. 6). The ideal cultural product will portray human perfection as "a *harmonious* perfection, developing all sides of our humanity" and "all aspects of society" (p. 11).

A second aspect, which Leavis and Thompson (1933) emphasize, is that culture, as a pure type, must have roots in a genuine community of individuals and express the careful reflections of its most artistic and creative members. Culture must be protected from the "standardization and levelling-down" that mechanization and commodification have caused even "outside the realm of mere material goods" (p. 3).

Third, Hoggart (1970) maintains, as did Arnold, that a pure type of cultural production will induce members of a society to break out of their conventional understandings by providing "peculiar" explorations, re-creations, and alternative meanings to human experiences (pp. 16, 11). Cultural products should explore "the diversity, complexity, [texture,] and strangeness of that experience (of individual men or of men in groups or of men in relation to the natural world)" (p. 11). The best cultural products encourage individuals to "look at life with all the vulnerability, honesty and penetration they can command" (p. 11); the ideal cultural product disturbs the consumer, subverts his or her view of life, attends to the complexity of the everyday life-world, and brings that consumer "up short," preventing the moulds of habit and familiarity from becoming set and finalized (p. 16). The pure type should also "articulate something of the 'mass and majesty' of [human] experience" (p. 16).

Hoggart (1958) also addresses class-based issues in culture, arguing that even though the working class is the most susceptible to consuming the lowest forms of cultural production, its location within the social structure provides its members with a "privileged" position to experience directly and thus articulate the deepest injustices, inequalities, and contradictions existing in the contemporary world (p. 286). As a result, although the ideal cultural product expresses the universalizing themes of human perfection that Arnold ([1868] 1932:11) emphasizes, for Hoggart, the idea of "a *harmonious* perfection" is best felt and expressed by members of the class that suffer most from the imperfections of contemporary social life. For Hoggart (1958), consequently, ideal cultural products are imperative because without them, all members of class-divided societies will have their freedoms slowly eroded and constrained without ever knowing they have disappeared (p. 287). A fourth characteristic of a pure type of cultural production, then, is that it provides critical insight into the complex nature and impact of class division on all members of a class-based society.

Horkheimer, Adorno, and Marcuse focus on the commodification of culture in association with Weber's ([1920] 2002) insight into the legitimate domination of goal-rational action in the modern era and humanity's entrapment in the *stahlhartes Gehäuse* of goal-rationality. The goal-rational pursuit of profit turns culture into a commodity that is standardized to appeal to the lowest of tastes. The formulaic nature of mass culture can lead, they fear from their experiences in Nazi Germany, to the rising power of propaganda, mass deception on a growing scale, and an ensuing loss of freedom. For Horkheimer, Adorno, and Marcuse, the ideal cultural forms must resist the power of "the culture industries" and return cultural production to the same classical standards Arnold identifies.

Postman and Gabler offer definitions of an ideal cultural product that echo many of the themes noted above. Two unique additions, however, concern the form of culture. In what he identifies as the transition from the Age of Exposition to the Age of Show Business, Postman (1985) maintains that contemporary society loses exposition as a mode of thought. For him, the best cultural products still contain a mode of thought that is sophisticated, values reason and order, is detached and objective, recognizes history and social context, and allows time for critical reflection. Gabler's (1998) main addition to the delineation of culture as a pure type is that this ideal culture must resist the "post-realists" who simplify reality and present it like a movie to entertain. The best cultural productions stem from the premise that "a clear-eyed appreciation of the human condition [is] necessary to *be* human" (p. 243).

Finally, Carr, Rose, and Gardner and Davis recognize that the ideal cultural form will not exist or have much impact unless the everyday life-world is freed from its current "app-dependence" and individuals create the material and social conditions whereby they habitually access information from a variety of sources other than the Internet. The ideal cultural products must stimulate the transition back from the distracted, multi-tasking, fragmented mind of the Internet to the calm, focused, undistracted, linear mind of print culture. "[A]s supple as it is subtle," Carr (2011) reminds his readers, the linear mind is "the imaginative mind of the Renaissance, the rational mind of the Enlightenment, the inventive mind of the Industrial Revolution, even the subversive mind of Modernism" (p. 10). This mode of thought, all four analysts of the contemporary life-world contend, is fundamental to both the creation and productive consumption of the ideal cultural forms.

Taken together, the standard for a pure or ideal type of cultural product is extremely demanding. No cultural creation will meet all of its criteria, but different cultural products can be assessed against the pure type presented in this chapter. In concise terms, the pure type reference point for the study of different cultural products is one in which a well-reasoned, fresh, and critical awareness of the mass and majesty of human existence is presented to an audience or readership. Culture, in its ideal form, is rooted in the experiences of a community, and cultural products explore the complexity and diversity of social life often in ways that are disturbing and undermine conventional understandings of the everyday life-world. Cultural products, in their pure form, demand a focused, sustained attention to their nuanced expositions of life, which frequently address injustices of different types. These products stop one short and inspire the struggle for social change and progress. In the next two chapters, two genres of popular music will be compared to the ideal standard developed here; this comparison will assess whether these genres measure up to culture as a pure type.

Key Terms and Names

Raymond Williams
culture
commodity
commodification
F.R. Leavis and Denys Thompson
Richard Hoggart
live literature
Theodor Adorno and Max Horkheimer
culture industry
Herbert Marcuse
Neal Gabler
Nicholas Carr

Questions for Review and Further Reflection

1. Before reading this chapter, how would you have defined "culture"? In your own words, define it now.

2. Divide a sheet of paper into four columns. In the first column, write down the key points concerning how ideas are created in society according to Marx. In the next two columns, do the same for Durkheim and Weber, respectively. In the last column, identify what you see as common elements. Below that, write out the key points that you think best describe how ideas are created and perpetuated within a society.

3. What points do Leavis and Thompson make about English culture? Think of some contemporary examples of culture that support their argument, and some that refute it.

4. Think of your all-time favourite books; explain how they fit or do not fit Hoggart's description of "live literature."

5. What are the key concepts developed by members of the Frankfurt school? Explain how Marx influenced their arguments. And how does Weber influence them?

6. According to Postman, what are the two ways in which a culture can become shrivelled? Which (if either) do you think poses the greatest danger today? Why? Explain your answer.

7. Imagine you were having a debate with the cultural critics discussed in this chapter over the impact of media today. What counter-arguments would you make to indicate that culture, even popular culture, is strong and vibrant today?

8. Make a chart displaying each of the theorists mentioned in this chapter and the elements they identify as necessary for an "ideal cultural product." What similarities can you identify? Can you think of any real cultural products that would meet all or at least most of these criteria? If so, what are they, and, if not, are there any products that come close?

11

THE DIALECTICS OF POPULAR CULTURE

Main Objectives

This chapter will

1. Illustrate how changes in the recording industry, radio, and television influenced the emergence of different forms of music within popular culture.
2. Introduce and familiarize students with the roots of contemporary popular music in folk, blues, rhythm and blues, jazz, and country.
3. Use Bob Dylan's early career (including his first four albums) and a pure type construct of "culture" as a case study examining the nature of popular culture and its complexity.

The explosion of music as popular culture in the latter half of the twentieth century did not occur in a vacuum—it began in the sparse soil of hardship, in the period between 1910 and 1939, when folk, jazz, and different blues sounds gave expression to the heavy sighs of individuals and families eking out their existence (see, for example, Agee and Evans 1941; Dos Passos 1932, 1936, 1937; Steinbeck 1937, 1939, 1952). Those sounds blended with the optimistic flights of hope and the bright tapestry of cultural experience that waves of European immigrants brought to Canada and the United States as they sought to forge new lives and lay the foundation for the next generation's prosperity.

World War I, the Great Depression, Franklin Delano Roosevelt's New Deal, William Lyon Mackenzie King's programs in industrial reconstruction in Canada, and World War II mixed sombre tones with the unyielding belief that rewards would come to those who committed themselves to an unselfish, collective effort against foes that would be overcome. Long before Barack Obama campaigned on "Yes we can!" or Justin Trudeau promised "*real* change," Canadians and Americans believed that, through national mobilization, they could overcome economic depression and war. And, as each crisis was met and endured, Canadians and Americans reaffirmed their belief in the promise of social renewal through steadfast faith and commitment to the cause. Regular people found themselves involved in extraordinary struggles, and they rose to the challenge. Common people displayed heroic achievement in ways that demanded celebration and cultural recognition. There was a fundamental democratization of hardship, but also leadership, commitment, recognition, and reward; significant cultural transformation was underway.

When Fascism was finally pushed back into Hitler's bunker beneath the Reich Chancellery, the sounds of war gave way to those of reconstruction, and North Americans soon found themselves in the midst of what Lizabeth Cohen (2003) terms "the landscape of mass consumption." This landscape was soon to include the Trans-Canada Highway, begun in 1950, and the American Interstate Highway System, authorized in 1956. Along these routes "suburban settlements sprouted on what had been fields of corn, celery, spinach, and cabbage." Shopping centres "became the new centers of community life, providing a place to spend a Saturday, to attend an evening concert, [and] to take the children to visit Santa Claus" (Cohen 2003:6). Cohen and the rest of the Baby Boomers were born into a dramatically different and changing world—an urban world of asphalt, concrete, construction, burgeoning commerce, mass production, mass advertising, and mass consumption (see also Owram 1996). In many ways, if the transition from rural, agrarian (even feudal) society to urban, industrializing, capitalist society represents the first great transformation, then the dramatic shifts that began in the mid-twentieth century constitute a second great transformation in the life experiences and life chances of people in Canada, the United States, and western Europe.

Although, during the war years, Canadian and American families had saved, lived on rations, and bought war bonds to support the war effort, at the end of World War II, businesses lost little time in telling people what to do with those savings. "WHAT THIS WAR IS ALL ABOUT," a Royal typewriter ad of the time reads, is the right to "once more walk into any store in the land and buy anything you want" (Cohen 2003:73). As the end of war approached, Cohen (2003) writes, "the return to normalcy increasingly referred to a lifestyle that purchaser consumers would soon be able to buy" (p. 73). After "total war," Canadians and Americans looked forward to "**total living**."

Mass consumption in postwar North America was not regarded as an indulgence; it was viewed as a civic responsibility that would ensure full employment, the expansion of the economy, and a thriving society that would contrast with, confront, and quash Soviet aspirations to spread communism around the globe. Film, the popular press, business leaders, and academics drew links between the benefits of mass production, mass consumption, an expanding economy, the *embourgeoisement* of blue-collar workers through their increased purchasing power, and the strengthening of democratic nations with the same shared values (Aron 1961, 1962; Bell 1960a, 1973; Dahrendorf 1959, 1967; Goldthorpe 1968, 1969).

What Cohen (2003) terms "the Consumers' Republic" was the foundation for the proliferation of popular cultural forms that would far surpass the greatest fears of Arnold or Leavis and Thompson (p. 127). Moreover, although the vast array of popular culture forms suggested a growing diversity in tastes and cultural products to consume, much of popular culture was drawn toward homogeneity irrespective of the cultural medium (music, art, literature, drama, television, or movies). The tension between diversity and homogeneity and between creativity and copycat replication is best understood by analysing how the "production of ideas, of conceptions, of consciousness"—that is, cultural forms—is "interwoven with material activity and the material interaction of men—the language of real life" (Marx and Engels [1845] 1932:15). In other words, one needs to examine the intersection of the history of social structure with the development of cultural forms and their production.

FROM 78s TO 45s AND LPS: THE GROWTH OF CULTURAL DIVERSITY

The **consumers' republic** provided the overall framework and context for the rise to dominance of mass cultural forms, an eventuality to which Hoggart, Marcuse, Postman, Gabler, and others responded. However, by going inside that republic, one begins to appreciate that far from being utterly homogenous and banal, popular culture was and remains far more complex, dynamic, and unstable than its critics were, or continue to be, willing to acknowledge. The history of popular music and the record industry provide some insight into this development.

"Why 1955?" Richard Peterson (1990) asks. In the brief span between 1954 and 1956, he maintains, there was a major aesthetic revolution as rock and roll replaced the big bands, jazz, and what was referred to as the "Tin Pan Alley" sound of "the crooners."[94] "Frank Sinatra, Tommy Dorsey, Patty Page, Perry Como, Nat King Cole, Tony Bennett, Kay Starr, Les Paul, Eddie Fisher, Jo Stafford, Frankie Lane, Johnnie Ray and Doris Day," Peterson (1990) writes, "gave way to Elvis Presley, Chuck Berry, The Platters, Bill Haley, Buddy Holly, Little Richard, Carl Perkins and the growing legion of rockers" (p. 97; see also Palmer 2008; Sagolla 2011). The reasons for the

---

94 Tin Pan Alley referred to the type of popular music (e.g., ballads, dance music, and vaudeville) that songwriters and publishers working on West 28th Street between Fifth and Sixth Avenue in Manhattan were producing.

change were complex and involved far more than the birth of the Baby Boomers (the oldest of whom would have been only nine in 1955).

Peterson's argument focuses on copyright law, patent law, the regulatory practices of the Federal Communications Commission in the United States, technological development, changes in the broadcast and record industry, and changes in the organizational structure of radio stations, phonograph record producing firms, and television studios. Peterson also considers the way careers changed in the recording industry and on radio, as well as the segmentation of the consumer market in the wake of all the changes taking place (see also Sagolla 2011). In short, tensions and contradictions within the material forces of production and between those forces and the social relations of production, as well as the wielding of economic and social power, created brief periods of artistic struggle, innovation, and change followed by periods of consolidation and stability, as new forms of collective representations were created and subsequently institutionalized.

The 1909 changes in American copyright law that protected musical compositions allowed sheet music writers and publishers to invest in the development and promotion of new songs because others could not legally reproduce their work without paying royalties. Although the law gave writers and publishers the right to royalties, collecting them was not easy (Garofalo and Chapple 1978). As a result, a number of writers, composers, and publishers banded together in 1914 to form the **American Society of Composers, Authors, and Publishers (ASCAP)**.

By the 1930s, ASCAP was not only collecting royalties on behalf of its membership and delivering music to musicians, radio stations, musical theatre, and the film industry, for example, it was also promoting its members' interests by influencing what music was played. "It did this," Peterson (1990) writes, "by, in effect, mandating that only ASCAP licensed music could be played in Broadway musicals, performed on the radio, and incorporated into movies" (p. 99). As late as 1950, an oligopoly of only 18 publishers controlled the music that the public heard (Ryan 1985). Tin Pan Alley songs such as "Tea for Two," "Stardust," and "Always" are representative of the music the group favoured—well-crafted, sentimental love themes with smooth melodies and muted jazz rhythms and harmonies. "The work of black musicians in the blues, jazz, r&b [rhythm and blues], and what later came to be called soul genres was systematically excluded, as were the songs in the developing Latin and country music traditions" (Peterson 1990:99–100).

The copyright law modification and the establishment of ASCAP are significant because they represent the forces leading to the homogenization of the music industry in the pre–World War II period, a uniformity that encouraged the increasingly banal, levelled-down cultural production that Leavis and Thompson, Hoggart, and Adorno and Horkheimer criticized so heavily (Sagolla 2011).

In response to the oligopoly control that ASCAP exercised over the production and performance of music, a number of radio networks formed a rival licensing agency in 1939—**Broadcast Music Incorporated (BMI).** BMI signed its own stable of music publishers and songwriters including those whom ASCAP had excluded (Ryan 1985; Sagolla 2011). The BMI challenge to ASCAP's control of the music industry began to broaden the type of music that reached the public and created new taste publics for previously excluded musical forms. But this alone did not open the door to rock—it would take much more than a shift in who wrote the music and an increase in the venues from which it could be played.

The second step toward the birth of rock and roll involved the broadcast industry itself. During the 1930s, the **Federal Communications Commission (FCC)** had restricted the number of stations across the United States. Each market had only three to five stations—NBC, CBS, and MBS (Mutual Broadcasting System) were always present, which left room for one or two independents. Leading up to World War II, a number of groups, in the public interest, applied for radio broadcast licences, but, due to pressures from the three major broadcasters, the FCC held off on its decisions until after 1945. By then, the advent of television reduced the major networks' opposition because they saw television, and not radio, as the wave of the future.

Peterson's (1990:103–8) analysis of the rise of rock music presents a useful contrast between the 1948 and the 1958 radio and recording industries, and how television's advent contributed to the changing nature of popular culture. Prior to television, radio was the dominant form of home entertainment, and the three major networks competed for an increased slice of the listening public. Because of the comparable strength and market positions of these major networks, each was risk averse, so, rather than introduce radically different programming, they produced daily and weekly schedules that were virtually identical. Here is Peterson's description of the evening radio schedule in 1948:

> On weekend evenings, each of the radio networks featured the major dance bands of the era broadcast *live* from one of the many large dance halls or elegant hotels around the country. The popular hits of the day were also played on the air by studio orchestras as part of the mix of the comedy and variety shows hosted by the likes of Bob Hope and Jack Benny. There was a programme called "Your Hit Parade" that featured the top ten selling records of the week. But the *records* were not played! Rather, the studio band and its male or female singer, as appropriate, performed each of the songs in turn. Since the hit songs of 1948 were written, arranged and recorded by professionals to fit widely understood swing era conventions, it was easy for the studio band to faithfully reproduce the sound of the record. (Peterson 1990:103)

The major networks did not play records on their national programs in the 1940s, but, Peterson (1990:104) notes, several local affiliates did— although the format was telling. Martin Block's *Make Believe Ballroom*, first broadcast over New York's WNEW, virtually duplicated, through his introductions, the sequencing of songs, and the pseudo-interviews with band leaders, the live broadcasts of the majors.

NBC, CBS, and MBS's decision to invest heavily in television and withdraw their opposition to the spread of radio licenses had three major implications. First, the growth of local radio networks ended the near **monopoly** control of radio by the majors, and the emerging stations had to compete fiercely for a particular niche in the market if they were to survive. Finding those niche markets really meant creating them. So radio became a leading force in broadening musical tastes and supporting innovation; radio took different sounds of music to audiences that would never have otherwise heard them. At the same time, however, it was still middle-class, white America that the stations had to reach in order for them to attract sufficient advertising revenue to remain solvent. Thus, although the expansion of radio stations added to musical diversity, the economics of the market put certain limits on the musical tastes that would be fostered.

Second, as the major networks shifted their attention and resources to television, the national networks slashed their radio budgets. As those funds disappeared, the size of production crews decreased, and greater programming responsibility fell on the shoulders of fewer and fewer people. Live entertainment was quickly abandoned, and records became an integral part of the radio industry.

During the **oligopoly** years of the 1930s and 1940s, songwriters worked in "the tune factory" to produce "well-crafted songs much like those that were hits at the time or were tailored to satisfy the demands of the person commissioning the song" (Peterson 1990:110). Music was written to formulae. With the spread of radio, each small station's search for a unique sound and identity, and the turn to records, the scope of music began to extend well beyond the standardized Tin Pan Alley sound. By the mid-1950s, Chuck Berry, Bo Diddley, Buddy Holly, Little Richard, Richie Valens, and Elvis Presley were recording brand new sounds—for radio at least—that created and kept feeding a new taste culture in music.

Third, the new sounds needed "salesmen." Disk Jockeys (DJs) quickly acquired greater latitude in the music they played, and became, themselves, the focal point for their increasingly specialized audiences. Dewey Phillips of WHBQ in Memphis is a particular case in point.

Phillips began his career as the DJ on *Red, Hot, and Blue*—a mere 15-minute slot where he played popular music. Possessing what Sam Phillips— the founder of Sun Records who launched the careers of Presley, Johnny Cash, Carl Perkins, Roy Orbison, and Jerry Lee Lewis—called "a platinum ear,"

"Daddy-O-Dewey," as he soon became known, found himself hosting a full three-hour slot and playing blues, rhythm and blues, boogie-woogie, country, and jazz (Halberstam 1993:459–61). In July 1954, Daddy-O-Dewey was the DJ who introduced radio audiences to Presley's first record: "That's All Right," a blues tune on the A-side, and "Blue Moon of Kentucky," a bluegrass song on the other. True to his own "free form" style, Dewey just kept flipping the record over and over as the switchboard lit up with calls for more (Halberstam 1993).

Alan Freed is another pivotally important celebrity DJ. Hosting a late night classical music show, Leo Mintz, the owner of Cleveland's largest record store, Record Rendezvous, told Freed that white teens were buying so many blues and R & B records that they were flying off the shelves. It was all about the beat, Mintz claimed, which was so strong "anyone could dance to it even without a lesson" (Halberstam 1993:465). At Mintz's urging, Freed began *The Moondog Show* in the summer of 1951. Beating his hands on a phone book in time to the music, Freed played what he called "rock and roll" because of the surging sound of the beat (and the phrase's connection to sex). As a 50,000-watt, clear channel station, WJW carried Freed's program to the northeastern United States, into the vast Midwest, and across the Great Lakes to Ontario and Quebec.

Freed also organized the first rock concert. The "Moondog Coronation Ball," featuring the Dominoes, Paul Williams and his Hucklebuckers, Tiny Grimes and his Rocking Highlanders, Danny Cobb, and Varetta Dillard, was held on March 21, 1952, at the Cleveland Arena. As the venue could hold about 10,000 and the concert attracted more than 20,000 fans, it was clear that a sea change was occurring in teen culture.

Other celebrity DJs included Wolfman Jack (Robert Weston Smith) of XERF-AM and later XERB in the Tijuana area, Cousin Brucie (Bruce Morrow) of 770 WABC in New York, and Al Boliska of 1050 CHUM in Toronto. Each was a vital force in capturing audiences, promoting specific styles of music, and generating revenue for themselves, their stations, the record companies, and the artists whose music they played.

The expansion of radio licences, a decline in operating budgets, and the rise of celebrity DJs meant that the record became the second essential ingredient in the creation of new tastes in music and the raising of subterranean music cultures into the mainstream of post–World War II popular culture.

In the same way that radio came to be controlled by the big three networks before World War II, the record industry experienced a concentration of control during the 1930s and 1940s. By 1948, RCA, Columbia (CBS), Capitol, and American Decca (MCA) released 80 per cent of the songs that reached the top ten hit list, and eight firms released 95 per cent of all the hits (Halberstam 1993; Peterson and Berger 1975). The major record companies ensured their dominance by signing the best creative people to long-term contracts and investing in the promotion of their work. The majors also enjoyed near monopoly control over the distribution of their music to radio stations, and they kept in close contact with the national networks to ensure that their music played (while other music did not). They were equally successful, Peterson (1990) notes, "in controlling the songs that reached the public ear via Broadway musicals and movies" (p. 104).

Throughout the pre-war period, the 10-inch, 78 revolutions per minute (rpm) shellac disk was the standard record in the industry. These 78s had their limitations; the quality of sound reproduction was not particularly high—the constant low-level scratching sound in the background associated with 1930s and 1940s records was due to the poor reproductive quality of the 78—and they were quite fragile.

To enhance its profits in the emerging consumers' republic, CBS was motivated to produce a high-fidelity record that could hold more music than the standard 78. In 1948, CBS released a stunning technological breakthrough— the 12-inch, 33⅓-rpm, long-playing record (the LP). CBS offered to share the technology with its larger arch-rival RCA to establish a common industry standard, but RCA refused the offer. RCA brought out its own alternative to the 78—the 7-inch, 45-rpm vinyl record with the large hole in the middle (the 45). By 1952, the 78 had almost disappeared, the 12-inch LP was the predominant medium for classical music, and 45 singles dominated popular music and were played on the radio and in jukeboxes and stores.[95] The 45 was crucial to the development of popular music forms aimed at young consumers for three reasons.

First, like free access to music videos on YouTube today, jukeboxes became a platform that a wide variety of musicians could use to get needed exposure. With respect to rock, in particular, jukeboxes put this new music form into the soda shops, restaurants, and hangouts where young consumers could play and replay and replay a record at minimal cost. Jukebox 45s helped build the taste culture for an emerging style of music.

Second, compared to the brittle 78s, the vinyl 45s were almost unbreakable. This durability allowed major record companies to send 45s to radio stations and wholesale distributors through the mail, rather than being dependent on the expensive private distribution systems required for the fragile 78s. At the same time, the inexpensive, durable 45 meant that small record companies could also distribute their songs at an affordable cost and compete head to head with the big corporations.

Third, with smaller companies now able to make, sell, and ship records, the recording industry was opened up to a far broader range of artists and

---

95 The reason for the large hole in the centre of the 45 was the primitive technology of the jukebox. The mechanism that selected the record and then placed it on the turntable was not precise enough to always line the pin in the turntable with the standard, smaller hole of a 78; the larger hole allowed for greater error in the system and ensured that the automated system worked time after time after time.

music, as the small record companies claimed their own niche within the market. In 1949, in response to the growing scope of recorded music, the industry's leading trade magazine, *Billboard*, renamed "hillbilly music" as "country and western" and "race music" as "rhythm and blues" (Sagolla 2011:1–2). The new names gave legitimacy to both styles, making it easier for small companies to record and sell both sounds.

In the case of R & B, the 45 brought the music out of the nightclubs, onto the radio, and into people's homes. Most significantly, this technology made R & B readily available to young white consumers looking for a new and vibrant sound. The R & B of the early 1950s—immortalized in "the Chicago blues" sound of Muddy Waters, Howlin' Wolf, Elmore James, Sonny Boy Williamson, Jimmy Reed, and others—involved small bands comprised of a piano, bass, drums, electric guitars, and horns. The sound emerged from what is often termed "jump blues"—an up-tempo music played by bands larger than a standard jazz band but smaller than any of the big bands. R & B also drew from the more raucous blues shouters who belted out their lyrics at full volume, with no amplification and little regard for their vocal dynamics. The shouters exuded an energy and frenzy that brought audiences to their feet, feeling the music and responding to it viscerally. Loud, fast, and ragged, the blues shouters were the extreme opposite of the polite white crooners of the day. The lyrics were very different too; blues artists sang sexually explicit and often misogynistic songs like "Work with Me, Annie," "The Girl Can't Help It," "Sixty Minute Man," or Little Richard's original "Tutti Frutti" (Cohn 1969; Sagolla 2011; White 1984).[96] Doo-wop, another blues strand, had a smoother sound and featured close harmonies rooted in Southern black gospel music. While jump blues and the blues shouters captured the moving, driving, exciting side of teenage sexuality, doo-wop provided a means for teens to explore their anxieties around love, social acceptance, and the uncertainty of their own independence (Sagolla 2011).

As radio stations looked for and created niche markets and the costs of producing and shipping 45s across the United States decreased, small record companies sprang up almost everywhere, and a lot of them tapped into the R & B sound. Lew Chudd, for example, established Imperial Records and featured R & B legends such as Fats Domino and Frankie Ford. Ahmet Ertegun, the son of the first Turkish ambassador to the United States, and Herb Abramson founded Atlantic Records—named after the ocean Ertegun had crossed to arrive in the United States, and over which he wanted to send the sound of America to build an international consumer market.

---

96 Written while Little Richard was a dishwasher at a Greyhound bus terminal, "Tutti Frutti" had its original lyrics revised in 1955, to make them publically acceptable. Dorothy La Bostrie replaced the chorus lyrics "Tutti Frutti, good booty / If it don't fit, don't force it / You can grease it, make it easy" with "Tutti Frutti, oh rutti" (White 1984:55).

Atlantic promoted a wide variety of sounds but mainly R & B and jazz. In 1952, Atlantic signed Ray Charles (Jones, Meyrowitz, and Salzman 1995).

Looking back on his success, Ertegun regarded his "outsider status" as an advantage. He was not confined by the dominant codes and prejudices of American culture; he could enjoy R & B and doo-wop for their intrinsic sound, and he believed he could bring that music into the mainstream.

> I felt that I knew what black life was in America, and I knew what black music was in America, and I knew what black roots were or what black gospel music and black blues—from the [Mississippi] Delta that went on to Chicago and the Texas blues that went on to the West Coast—I knew what they were, and I knew all about that and I loved all of that. So in loving America, I thought I loved something more than the average American knew about. (Jones, Meyrowitz, and Salzman 1995)

The 45 allowed the Chess brothers to found Chess Records and record Bo Diddley—one of the claimants to "inventing" rock and roll. Sam Phillips set up Sun Records and distributed the sounds emanating from his Memphis recording studio (Memphis Recording Services) across the country, launching Elvis Presley and then Carl Perkins and Jerry Lee Lewis—a who's who of early rock and roll (Jones, Meyrowitz, and Salzman 1995). Breaking the oligopolistic control of the major networks and recording studios opened the way for an explosion in popular culture.

Television and the vinyl record may have been the most visible technological changes that encouraged and facilitated the proliferation of radio stations and thus increased demand for music of varying types, but the tiny transistor that replaced large and cumbersome vacuum tubes was the third revolutionary innovation that changed the form and content of music as popular culture. Lightweight, pocketbook-sized, and relatively inexpensive made-in-Japan transistor radios, complete with an earphone, became almost as ubiquitous among teenagers in the late 1950s as the smartphone is today. The transistor radio made music more than portable, however—it also allowed it to be personal.

Prior to the transistor radio, most homes had one large cabinet radio-record player in the household. The cabinet housed the radio and record player and provided storage space for 78s, LPs, and 45s—it was a standard piece of household furniture, and, depending on its quality and appearance, it conferred status on the family. Because the cabinet was located centrally in the house, parents controlled the selection of radio stations and records. The inexpensive transistor radio allowed households to have more radios and loosened parental control over what was heard (Halberstam 1993). For teenagers, the portable transistor and the quickly popular portable record player gave unprecedented freedom of choice when it came to music.

By the mid-1950s, then, rock and roll—"[a]n electrifying cultural force ... launched with supersonic speed and brawn"—was changing the face of popular music in North America (Sagolla 2011:1). From 1954 to 1959, the forces of homogeneity were in retreat. A growing number of independent radio stations and record producers were drawing in an increasingly diversified talent pool of DJs, writers, and performers—all of whom created a broader range of taste cultures and an expanding audience. And, by the end of the 1950s, the Baby Boomers were entering their teens as full-fledged members of the consumers' republic, eager to be a part of the growing *American Bandstand.*[97]

If one considers the history of rock and roll as an exposition of the dialectics of popular culture, an interesting set of somewhat contradictory forces created or enabled significant change while others resisted or constrained that change. As the major broadcast corporations shifted their interest and resources from radio to television, the risk-averse practices that had kept music production and the shaping of popular taste within fairly narrow parameters were removed. With fewer resources, radio stations had to restructure themselves, and this restructuring had two significant outcomes. First, stations began to compete for niche markets that they could maintain on relatively low budget operations. Second, as the cost of launching an independent radio station fell, the number of stations, also looking for niche markets, grew. This expansion meant that each station, wanting to reach a particular target audience, had to provide content that would appeal. Taken as a whole, these factors resulted in a major diversification of styles and sounds on radio. At the same time, those changes took place within an economic market dominated by white consumers and a very white middle-class value system.

To examine popular music as a cultural product, one must ask additional questions about this dialectical process. How did the forces pushing for diversity and renewal balance those resisting change? Did these diverse musical forms make significant contributions to culture, to the way humans understood themselves and the social world? Did they have aesthetic and intrinsic value, or did they provide only a broader range of "bread and circus" entertainment for the indiscriminating masses? To answer these questions, one must look more closely at the music traditions out of which some of these new styles developed and at the substance of post-1950s' music as it reached wider audiences over the next few decades—and compare popular music to the pure type reference point developed at the end of Chapter 10. Consequently, the focus will move to two case studies to illustrate what Weber's methodology offers and to present critical insight into the nature and potential of popular culture as an institutionalized collective representation that is internalized at a critical point in individuals' lives.

---

97 This TV show, featuring teens dancing to "Top 40" songs, aired in various versions between 1952 and 1989.

From Robert Zimmerman to the Dialectical Dylan

There are a number of figures one could use to determine how well pop music measures up against the qualities of an ideal cultural form. Few, however, are more appropriate than Bob Dylan. In Dylan's work, the layers of artistry seem to be endless, and each one leads to a renewed perspective and a deeper level of appreciation. Probing Dylan's work also explodes some cherished myths and sometimes shatters illusions. Dylan, the artist, to say nothing of Dylan the person, is a genuinely tension-filled, dialectically unstable, dynamic totality. But Dylan—the artist, person, cultural icon, or, most important, producer of popular culture—cannot be appreciated fully without examining the intersection of his personal biography with history and social structure.

Born Robert Zimmerman in Duluth, Minnesota, on May 24, 1941, Bob Dylan (1962a), along with his family, soon moved to Hibbing, Minnesota, as his 1963 poem "My Life in a Stolen Moment" indicates. Dylan describes Hibbing as quintessentially small town America with a store-lined main drag that teens cruised in their hot rods. As a teen, Dylan tuned his transistor radio to the budding blues and country radio stations broadcasting from Shreveport, Louisiana, and later to early rock and roll stations, where he found inspiration and a sound with which he could identify in the music of Chuck Berry, Elvis Presley, and Buddy Holly (Dylan 2006:433). As rock became bland during the 1950s, Dylan was drawn to folk by the sound of the Kingston Trio and later Odetta,[98] Lead Belly,[99] and then Woody Guthrie.

In 1959, Zimmerman enrolled at the University of Minnesota, but he rarely went to class (Dylan 1962a). Instead, his main interest was folk music—all he needed was a guitar and a repertoire of songs to perform (Dylan 2006:56). Dylan played at the Ten O'clock Scholar, a coffee house near campus, and became involved in the folk music circuit of Dinkytown, an area within the Marcy Holmes neighbourhood of Minneapolis that had restaurants, diners, cafés, coffee shops, bars, and student housing (Dylan 2004:234–44). It was then that he began to introduce himself as Bob Dylan.

At the end of his freshman year, Dylan dropped out of university, and in January 1961—at the age of 20, not 18 as he often claimed—he headed for New York City (Dylan 2006:20–22). During his first brushes with the music industry, Dylan presented himself as a mystery whose true depth had to be plumbed. He began the obfuscation by telling many different versions of how he landed in New York. Dylan was never a "carnie" running the Ferris

---

98 Odetta Holmes, known as Odetta, sang folk, blues, jazz, and spirituals; she is frequently called "the voice of the civil rights movement."

99 Huddie William Ledbetter (1888–1949) was a virtuoso on the 12-string guitar; his vocals, too, had a clear, forceful blues and folk sound. Ledbetter adopted the stage name "Lead Belly," and, although some of his recordings list him as "Leadbelly," he always spelled it "Lead Belly."

wheel or a drifter who had worked dozens of different jobs, and he was not estranged from his family, riding the rails in search of his fortune (see Dylan 2004:8, 230–304; Dylan 2006:3–4, 8–9, 24–25; Scorsese 2005). Like so many before and after him, Dylan (2004) hitchhiked across the Midwest, arriving in midwinter in a city he describes as "too intricate to understand," and he certainly was not going to try (pp. 8–9).

Dylan went to New York to find singers such as Dave Van Ronk, Peggy Seeger, Ed McCurdy, Brownie McGhee and Sonny Terry, Josh White, the New Lost City Ramblers, and Reverend Gary Davis, but he went there "most of all to find Woody Guthrie" (Dylan 2004:9). Why them and why Guthrie in particular? Before exploring Dylan's frenetic first few months in Greenwich Village in 1961, this chapter will take a step back into the larger context within which Dylan planned to immerse himself. Like the products of every artist who makes a mark in the realm of culture, even popular culture, Dylan's work had its roots within a genuine community. This community was of a particular type that had its initial roots thousands of miles from New York. But by the time Dylan arrived, its centre had been transplanted to America's most populous urban landscape.

WOODY GUTHRIE, PETE SEEGER, AND THE FOLK MOVEMENT

Although New York City seems an odd place for the centre of the folk movement, especially since folk's roots are deeply rural, this music thrived in Washington Square Park and Greenwich Village, in the clubs and coffee houses around the intersection of Bleecker Street and Macdougal during the 1940s, fifties, and early sixties.[100] Folk music flourished as singers and instrumentalists played for the intrinsic rewards of sharing their music with others; they consequently became part of a long-standing tradition—carrying a message and tying into the temper of the times through sound and lyric. Folk was non-commercial—it came from the heart, spoke to the soul, and nourished a spiritual community. Folk singers, songwriters, Beat poets, and street philosophers along Macdougal and Bleecker streets created their own subculture and community amid the concrete, glass, skyscrapers, and grey flannel suits of mainstream urban life.

Folk originated, however, "in the backwoods of Appalachia, where families would gather to sing in their homes, in their fields, on their porches, and in their churches," according to Richie Unterberger (2002:22). The music endured, "despite severe poverty and repression, among the descendants of African slaves in the deep South, where the form known as blues began to

---

100 New York was not the only place where folk was vibrant—Toronto's Yorkdale was the bohemian centre of folk life in the 1950s and 1960s. There were similar satellite communities in Cambridge (Massachusetts), Berkeley, Los Angeles, Chicago, and Vancouver.

prosper," he continues (Unterberger 2002:22). But folk music also includes cowboys' ballads and lamentations, as well as music with the rhythms, melodies, and lyrics that new immigrants brought from Europe. By the 1920s, folk found its way on to records, although sales were small and fell with the Great Depression.

The Depression and "the dirty thirties" revitalized folk and guided its themes toward contemporary political and social circumstances. This new thematic focus can be seen clearly in the works of Woody Guthrie as they arose from the intersection of his personal biography with the contemporary public issues of social structure. Born and raised in the Oklahoma wheat belt, which became known as the "Dust Bowl" in the 1930s, Guthrie travelled by boxcar, thumb, and on foot across the United States listening to, remembering, writing down, adding to, and recording the music of the people, especially of the marginalized and the dispossessed. Guthrie captures the spirit of his quest and his legacy in the opening paragraphs of his autobiography:

> I could see men of all colors bouncing along in the boxcar. We stood up. We laid down. We piled around on each other. We used each other for pillows. I could smell the sour and bitter sweat soaking through my own khaki shirt and britches, and the work clothes, overhauls and saggy, dirty suits of the other guys.... [Amidst] the raving and cussing and the roar of the car ... ten or fifteen of us guys was singing:
>
>> This train don't carry no gamblers,
>> Liars, thieves and big-shot ramblers;
>> This train is bound for glory,
>> This train! (Guthrie 1943:19)

"Like Scotland's Robert Burns and the Ukraine's Taras Shevchenko," Pete Seeger (1971) writes, "Woody was a national folk poet" (p. viii). His talent ultimately brought him to New York City, where he was "lionized by the literati ... from whom he declared his independence and remained his own profane, radical, ornery self" (Seeger 1971:viii). Guthrie's folk, just as Hoggart expected, reflected the cultural perspective of a class siding with labour and working for social justice. As Seeger (1971), himself a victim of the McCarthy blacklist, remarks, it may surprise some to learn "that the author of *This Land Is Your Land* was in 1940 a columnist for the small newspaper he euphemistically called *The Sabbath Employee*"—*The Sunday Worker*, the weekend edition of the Communist *Daily Worker* (p. viii).

Although Guthrie and Seeger were instrumental in popularizing folk music because they tapped deeply into its roots and kept them alive, it was the recording industry that made the folk archive permanent and allowed its sound to spread into the cities and reach audiences it would otherwise never have touched. During the 1930s, for example, one of America's most influential blues artists, Robert Johnson, recorded all his works, which helped preserve the blues and spread its influence well beyond the stingy soil in which it first found life (Marcus 1997). Similarly, Bill Monroe, one of the key originators of bluegrass, cut his first record in 1936. The Delmore Brothers' tight harmonies laid the groundwork for rockabilly and set the table for the Everly Brothers' music in the 1950s and 1960s, and Bob Wills mixed swing jazz, blues, country, and pop into a unique western swing sound (Unterberger 2002). Records not only brought the otherwise invisible music of folk culture to centre stage but also spread folk's reach and brought innovative collaboration into the mix.

Part of that collaboration took place in New York City, where urban intellectuals and political activists absorbed the folk culture and soon became some of folk music's most important producers. New York had long been a centre of intellectual ferment. In the postwar period, the city had at least 20 institutions of higher learning, spanning the spectrum from Ivy League universities such as Columbia to City College, which began as the Free Academy of the City of New York and became a hotbed of left-wing radicalism from the 1930s through to the 1950s (Hook 1987; Wald 1987). Lee Hays of the Weavers; Sis Cunningham and Gordon Friesen, who later founded the folk magazine *Broadside*; and Guthrie all lived in Greenwich Village in the 1940s, as did folk song collector John Lomax (Cohen 2002).[101] Lomax and his son brought blues and folk legend Lead Belly from a Louisiana prison to New York and the new folk scene.

Seeger, who dropped out of Harvard in 1938 when his political activism began to hurt his grades, was instrumental in cementing an enduring link between folk and progressive politics. Seeger formed the Almanac Singers, featuring himself, Hays, Guthrie, Burl Ives, and others, to promote union causes, racial integration, and religious freedom. The group, Unterberger (2002) writes, "[used] the best of folk traditions, while crafting rousing lyrics pertinent to burning social issues of the day" (p. 24). In 1942, after the United States entered World War II, the Almanac's anti-draft stance forced the group to lie low for a time. But its members resurfaced in 1945 as Seeger launched the People's Songs, an organization committed to reviving the folk tradition and carrying it forward.

In January 1946, writing in *The Daily Worker*, Mike Gold reported that "a group of Almanac Singers, plus others concerned with labor music, started

---

101 *Broadside* took its name from the tradition extending back to the sixteenth century of printing, on a single sheet of cheap paper, music, rhymes, or news so this material could be circulated quickly and widely among the people. Balladeers would often sell broadsides at fairs or have them distributed ahead of performances to attract audiences. Seeger, the folk traditionalist, named *Broadside* in honour of that tradition because he intended the periodical to spread modern folk music more broadly.

to organize something again the day before New Year. Songs, songs of, by, and for the people." He continues, "The spirit has not died, it has only been unemployed" (quoted in Cohen 2002:43). The first issue of the *People's Songs* newsletter exuded a new, postwar optimism:

> The people are on the march and must have songs to sing. Now, in 1946, the truth must reassert itself in many singing voices.... It is clear that there must be an organization to make and send songs of labor and the American people through the land. (Cohen 2002:43)

All of the above coalesces in the following points about Dylan and popular culture. First, the music and styles of Lead Belly, Guthrie, Seeger, Hays, Ives, and others constitute an informal standard by which all music claiming to be folk can be measured. The essential elements in the "folk sound" are acoustic instrumentation and well-crafted lyrics focused on issues of conscience and social relevance; both are supported by harmonies of care, hope, and the struggle for change.

Second, during the Great Depression and World War II, the folk tradition began to shift from its early roots. Although folk has always been socially conscious and has reflected the realities of America's poor, it began to lean more explicitly to the left during the 1930s and 1940s, as singers and their ballads were tied ever closer to the labour movement and linked directly and indirectly to socialist and communist political groups and to issues such as religious freedom and racial integration. Folk was no longer simply, to paraphrase Marx ([1844] 1975), "the sigh of the oppressed creature, the heart of a heartless world" (p. 175); it was becoming an increasingly politicized sound and movement that not only "interpreted the world in various ways" but also sought "to change it" (Marx and Engels [1845] 1932:535).[102]

Third, despite folk's rural roots, the growth of New York City as the centre of the first folk revival meant that this music would become urbanized and modernized. Part of that change centres on the spread of folk through radio and record sales. Folk changed from something people shared among friends and sang on their porches or in churches to something people listened to on the radio or by playing phonographs in the privacy of their own homes or heard live at small clubs, coffee houses, or college hootenannies. By the 1960s, folk had become "cool"—it had become, in fact, an urban cool:

> Those raised in subsequent generations of sensory overload may find it hard to comprehend that quiet acoustic folk, which sounds so tame to many

---

102 Many themes of the music of the 1960s have their roots in the songs that Seeger, Guthrie, and others wrote in the 1930s and 1940s. The idea of "A Better World A-Comin'"—a dominant refrain in the 1960s—comes directly from the title of a Guthrie composition of the 1940s.

twenty-first century listeners, was once considered *the* counter-cultural music. In part that was because, beneath the layer of the Kingston Trio and the like, folk was still fairly underground, and in-the-making bohemians are always attracted to movements in which the mere discovery of obscure records and books helps set one apart from the mainstream. In part it was also because of its lingering associations with egalitarian activism, which was implicit (and sometimes explicit) in the humane concerns voiced by many of the songs, whether traditional or newly penned. (Unterberger 2002:32)

This background serves as the primer for the raw canvas upon which the popular cultural artistry of Dylan will begin to take shape. The base coat to the unfinished work is Guthrie—with sketching, colour, texture, and continual refining and experimentation to follow.

DYLAN, GUTHRIE, AND FOLK

Dylan's relationship to Guthrie provides one set of insights into Dylan's work as a cultural producer. In Hibbing and on the Dinkytown folk circuit in Minneapolis, Dylan wanted to be a folk singer. Flo Castner, a friend from a coffee house, introduced Dylan to Guthrie's sound and power. Picking up a set of 12 double-sided Guthrie 78s, Dylan (2004) recalls, "When the needle dropped, I was stunned—didn't know if I was stoned or straight.... It was like the land parted"— it was an epiphany (pp. 243–44).[103]

Studs Terkel, famous for his unique poetic revelations of the most intimate thoughts of the common men and women of America in works such as *Division Street: America* (1967), *Hard Times: An Oral History of the Great Depression* (1970), and *Working* (1974), asked Dylan in 1963 about Guthrie's influence. Guthrie was "a big factor," Dylan (2006:5) replied. Dylan was a boy when he first heard the legendary folk singer, and one fact stuck in Dylan's mind: "he was Woody, and everybody else I could see around me was everybody else" (p. 6).

A year after talking to Terkel, Dylan (2006) said that Guthrie was the main reason he "came East." "He was an idol to me," Dylan continued (p. 25). In his autobiography, Dylan (2004) writes that the song that brought him to the attention of Leeds Music's John Hammond in the first place was "an homage in lyric and melody to the man who'd pointed out the starting place for my identity and destiny—the great Woody Guthrie" (p. 229). Dylan admired how Guthrie had dedicated himself to building the genealogy of

---

103 Some of the reverence and tender care Dylan had for Guthrie comes across in Dylan's account of his visits with Woody at the Greystone Hospital in Morristown, New Jersey, where Guthrie was hospitalized as his Huntington's disease advanced (Dylan 2004:98–100).

American folk music; and then the younger singer added his own unique voice to the tradition. One aspect of Guthrie's music that Dylan appreciated was that it captured the wide-ranging experience of living in America.

> Woody's songs were about everything at the same time. They were about rich and poor, black and white, the highs and lows of life, contradictions between what they were teaching in school and what was really happening. He was saying everything in his songs that I felt but didn't know how to. (Dylan 2006:430)

In his "Song to Woody," written in the early 1960s, Dylan (2004) pays homage to Guthrie and his inclusive perspective—to his travels over vast geographic distances and the broad spectrum of humanity that he embraced. Dylan captures Guthrie's own perceptions of a world that is tired and torn, filled with the hungry and sick, and, some would lament, coming to an end. However, for Guthrie, this world is only at the beginning—with the future of a newborn child lying ahead.[104]

Upon arriving in New York for the first time, Dylan explored the coffeehouse scene and hung around Café Wha?, but he soon began frequenting the Folklore Center (Dylan 2004:18). Located on Macdougal between Bleecker and Third, up one flight of stairs, "it was like an ancient chapel, like a shoebox sized institute" run by Izzy Young, a long-time folk aficionado who was as much a fixture and character as the archive of folk treasures that he collected, sold, and cherished (Dylan 2004:18–19).

In the back room, by the potbellied stove, Young had a treasure trove of old records, sheet music, and scrolls. Dylan sat back there playing Young's disks on the record player, ignoring the modern world and all its complications, and reflecting on John Henry driving steel, the sinking of the Titanic, the Galveston flood, or "the desperate John Hardy shooting a man on the West Virginia line" (Dylan 2004:20). Young introduced the neophyte singer-songwriter to the history of folk and began Dylan's journey forward by taking him back into the lore of folk and its genuine roots.

In his early club and coffeehouse days, Dylan sang so much from Guthrie's repertoire that he was dubbed a "Woody Guthrie jukebox." When he discovered that Ramblin' Jack Elliott was doing exactly the same thing, Dylan changed his approach immediately. He quickly realized that what set

---

104 See also Dylan's (1963c) "Last Thoughts on Woody Guthrie," a Whitman-like, free flowing poem that Dylan read on April 12, 1963, at the end of a concert at the New York Town Hall. After capturing in Guthriesque images all the ways people feel uncertain about life, Dylan indicates that it's possible to solve these problems by going to church or making your way to the Brooklyn State Hospital. In one, you will find God, and, in the other, you will find Woody Guthrie—a poignant lament for a great humanitarian who would soon be lost to Huntington's.

him apart was his ability to write songs. Writing songs and explaining how one writes them are, however, two very different things. The first came easily to Dylan; the latter he has always presented as something of a mystery.

Becoming a songwriter, Dylan (2004) maintains, happens by degrees. It might begin when a singer wants to do something a little different, turning "something that exists into something that didn't yet":

> Sometimes you just want to do things your way, want to see for yourself what lies behind a misty curtain. It's not like you see songs approaching and invite them in. It's not that easy. You want to write songs that are bigger than life. You want to say things about strange things that have happened to you, strange things you've seen. You have to know and understand something and then go past the vernacular. The chilling precision that these old-timers used in coming up with their songs was no small thing. Sometimes you could hear a song and your mind jumps ahead. You see similar patterns in the ways you were thinking about things. (Dylan 2004:51–52)

Dylan often uses the notion of turning something upside down or inside out. The best songs unveil a side of people that they never knew was there (Dylan 2004:54).

Writing is a craft that Dylan began to learn about and fully appreciate in the musty archives of the Folklore Center. "You can't just copy somebody," however, Dylan (2006) emphasizes: "If you like someone's work, the important thing is to be exposed to everything that person has been exposed to" (p. 429). One has to listen to as much folk music as possible and study its form and structure right back to its origins 100 years ago. "I go back to Stephen Foster," Dylan offers.[105]

Steeped in the history and craft of folk music and in the folk tales of the misty past, Dylan finds the process of writing songs a bit mysterious. There is artistry and mystery in writing a song, he claims, especially a multilayered one such as "Like a Rolling Stone." "I'm not thinking about what I want to say," he tells Robert Hilburn in an interview. "I'm just thinking 'Is this OK for the meter?'" But the result is so much more: "It's like a ghost is writing a song like that. It gives you the song, and it goes away, it goes away. You don't know what it means. Except the ghost picked me to write the song" (Dylan 2006:432). Hilburn points out that some critics complain about Dylan's songs being too ambiguous. Most acknowledge, however, that

---

105 Stephen Foster (1826–64) is frequently referred to as "the father of American music." His songs "Oh! Susanna," "Old Black Joe," "My Old Kentucky Home," "Old Dog Tray," and "Beautiful Dreamer" are learned and sung generation after generation. Foster's music combines the intricacies of classical music, the politeness of parlour music, and the spirited freedom of minstrel songs and carnival entertainment.

the competing images responsible for this ambiguity constitute his greatest strength—they are, to use Hoggart's (1970) words, what "bring us up short," prevent "the moulds from setting firm," and articulate the mass and majesty of the human experience (p. 16). Dylan's work certainly breaks out of the *stahlhartes Gehäuse* of goal-rational thought.

Does the music or do the words come first? Dylan (2006) claims that, for him, the music is already there (p. 437). He is not a melodist; his music springs from old Protestant hymns, Carter Family songs, or variations of the blues. Dylan says that he starts with some song playing in his head—meditating on it—until he reaches the point at which the words begin to change and a new song emerges (Dylan 2006:438, 2004:228–29). He wrote "Blowin' in the Wind" in 10 minutes by putting new words to the old spiritual "No More Auction Block," which he probably learned from listening to Odetta. "The Times They Are A-Changin'" has its inspiration in Irish and Scottish folk songs, Dylan once admitted (Crowe 1985).

Dylan's songs and their impact stem from his unique blend of folk music and its traditions; his compressed, high-speed apprenticeship in New York City, which was conducted in coffee houses, jam sessions, and conversations with Young, Guthrie, Seeger, and others; his distinct and changing vocal sound; and his unique talent with words. "Dylan's admirers have come to accept and even delight in the harshness [of his voice]," Nat Hentoff writes in 1964, "because of the vitality and wit at its core. And they point out that in intimate ballads he is capable of a fragile lyricism that does not slip into bathos" (quoted in Dylan 2006:22).

> It's Dylan's work as a composer, however, that has won him a wider audience than his singing alone might have. Whether concerned with cosmic spectres or personal conundrums, Dylan's lyrics are pungently idiomatic. He has a superb ear for speech rhythms, a generally astute sense of selective detail, and a natural storyteller's command of narrative pacing. His songs sound as if they were being created out of oral street history rather than carefully written in tranquillity. On a stage, Dylan performs his songs as if he had an urgent story to tell. In his work there is little of the polished grace of such carefully trained contemporary minstrels as Richard Dyer-Bennet. Nor, on the other hand, do Dylan's performances reflect the calculated showmanship of Harry Belafonte or of Peter, Paul and Mary. Dylan off the stage is very much the same as Dylan the performer—restless, insatiably hungry for experience, idealistic, but sceptical of neatly defined causes. (Quoted in Dylan 2006:22–23)

Throughout a career that now spans more than half a century, a career that has taken some different turns and is still unfolding, Dylan has remained restless and curious. Dylan's artistry with words, however, has been constant. Dylan's lyrics uniquely capture the complexity and diversity of human existence; they are what draw people to his work and hold them as they try to unravel the many layers of meaning he has crafted.

DYLAN AND THE AVANT-GARDE OF POPULAR CULTURE

Like a rolling stone, Dylan has not stayed in any one place in his music and artistry, so there are many "Dylans" one could choose from to explore the avant-garde nature of the popular culture he produces. Despite the abundance of choice, perhaps the best way to appreciate Dylan as an artist producing complex popular culture is to focus on his first four frenetic years in New York City and on his first four LPs (Lerner 2007).

Dylan's first album, *Bob Dylan*, released in March 1962, was a quickly produced collection derived from Dylan's performances in various coffee houses. At that time, his repertoire consisted mainly of traditional folk and blues tunes interspersed with some of his own material. Even the two original songs on the album—"Talkin' New York" and "Song to Woody"—directly reflect Guthrie's impact on Dylan as he began to emerge as a singer-songwriter, as well as Dylan's roots in folk and blues (Dylan 1962b, 1962c).

Dylan has claimed that, at the time, he did not want to reveal too much of himself, but that claim is highly misleading on two counts. First, in 1962, Dylan was still an insecure fledgling artist who, despite undergoing a rapid maturation process within the New York coffeehouse scene, was still looking to find his own footing.

Second, at this time, Dylan was a great imitator, a sponge, a living jukebox, a receiver, a collector and an amalgam of all that he had been hearing, encountering, and absorbing since his immersion in the New York world of folk music and Beat poetry. His version of "The House of the Rising Sun" is a good example. The song was an old folk standard—Lead Belly had sung it; Lead Belly, Guthrie, and Seeger had performed it together; and Odetta had her own searching and disturbing interpretation. However, the version Dylan cut on *Bob Dylan* features the chording that he had heard Dave Van Ronk use in New York. Without thinking to ask, Dylan cut that version—one that the Animals would later duplicate but express, to greater acclaim, electrically rather than acoustically—to bring new life to the song.[106] Despite the LP, Dylan was still apprenticing to become an artist.

---

106 Van Ronk would laugh years later when recounting the story (Scorsese 2005). After Dylan cut "The House," whenever Van Ronk played it people said "Hey that's Dylan's song." However, once the Animals released a version—essentially Van Ronk's chording used by Dylan and then the Animals—whenever Dylan sang the song people responded with "Oh yeah, that's the Animals' song." So Dylan too, like Van Ronk before him, dropped it from his repertoire. Revitalized by Van Ronk, Dylan, and the Animals, "The House of the Rising Sun" became a blues standard in the 1960s and was sung by the Beatles, Hendrix, the Stones, the Doors, and Led Zeppelin, to name just a few.

The Freewheelin' Bob Dylan appeared in May 1963 and coincided with Dylan's involvement with the civil rights movement, in particular, and with "the protest movement" more broadly. The link between Dylan and the civil rights movement is intimately tied, in several ways, to his lyrics for "Blowin' in the Wind"—the first cut on the album.

Dylan first published the lyrics in May 1962 in *Broadside*, a magazine devoted to topical songs. The melody was taken from "No More Auction Block," which originated in Canada among former slaves who had fled the United States for the British colony after England abolished slavery in 1833. That is the first strand connecting Dylan, "Blowin' in the Wind," and the civil rights movement.[107]

Dylan's manager at the time, Albert Grossman, also managed Peter, Paul, and Mary, and they were the first to record "Blowin' in the Wind." In the first week of its release, it sold 300,000 copies—an unheard of sale for a folk song at that time—and reached number two on *Billboard* magazine's pop chart (which ranked songs on a composite statistic based on air play and sales and was the gold standard ranking for the industry). The fine harmony of Peter, Paul, and Mary and, later, the sweet inspirational power of Joan Baez's voice quickly turned "Blowin' in the Wind" into one of the anthems of the civil rights movement.

In Scorsese's *No Direction Home* (2005), blues and gospel singer Mavis Staples recounts that, upon hearing "Blowin' in the Wind," she experienced initial incredulity that a white man could write something to capture the spirit and frustrations of blacks. However, she quickly recognized the enduring power of the lyrics and melody.

Dylan's link to the civil rights movement and the centrality of "Blowin' in the Wind" to that movement were cemented further with the 1963 march on Washington, the occasion of Martin Luther King Jr.'s "I Have a Dream" speech. Baez and Dylan sang the song in front of the thousands gathered by the Washington Monument, galvanizing the crowd and connecting Dylan and the song to social protest.

Finally, "Blowin' in the Wind," as music critic Andy Gill (1998:23) observes, represents a crucial shift in emphasis in Dylan's work. His focus moved from the particular—see his earlier songs "Talkin' Bear Mountain," "Rambling, Gambling Willie," or "Who Killed Davey Moore"—to the more abstract and general; Dylan's musical poetry took on a more timeless, universal quality.

Freewheelin' also included some surrealist, talking blues pieces—"Masters of War" and "Talkin' World War III Blues"—which would soon link Dylan's

---

107 Bauldie (1991) notes that Dylan may have heard the song on Odetta's 1960 Carnegie Hall concert LP. And he performed the song live at New York's Gaslight Cafe in October 1962, forging a second link to traditional folk and the civil rights movement.

music to the anti–Vietnam War movement in the mid-1960s. Those pieces stood alongside some finely crafted, bittersweet love songs, such as "Don't Think Twice, It's Alright," and "Girl of the North Country."

However, the most complex and compelling song on *Freewheelin'* was "A Hard Rain's A-Gonna Fall," which Hilburn describes as an "apocalyptic tale of a society being torn apart on many levels" with lyrics "rich and poetic enough to defy age" (Dylan 2006:436; see Dylan 1963a). Dylan wrote the song during the most threatening confrontation between the United States and the Soviet Union—the Cuban missile crisis of October 1962 (Dylan 2006:6).

In response to the Soviets building missile-launching sites in Cuba, President John F. Kennedy, addressing an international television audience, stated bluntly that any nuclear missile launched from Cuba against any nation in the western hemisphere would result in a full retaliatory response against the Soviet Union. Kennedy also established "a strict quarantine"— avoiding the term "blockade," which is a term of war—of all offensive military equipment destined for Cuba. Up to the moment Soviet Premier Nikita Khrushchev finally blinked and ordered his ships to turn back to the USSR, the media and public discourse were filled with fears of nuclear attack, the ensuing nuclear fallout, nuclear rain, and nuclear winter. But Dylan always insisted that "Hard Rain" had nothing to do with the Cuban crisis.

In one interview, Terkel comments that "Hard Rain" will become a classic even though it is about atomic rain. Dylan (2006) responds emphatically: "No, no, it wasn't atomic rain. Somebody else thought that too. It's not atomic rain, it's just a hard rain. It's not the fallout rain, it isn't that at all" (p. 7).

Terkel continues the conversation describing "Hard Rain" as a great tapestry. Dylan (2006) agrees, explaining why:

> Every line ... could be used as a whole song.... I wrote that when I didn't know how many other songs I could write.... I wanted to get the most down that I knew about into one song. It was during the Cuba trouble ... I was a little worried, maybe that's the word. (P. 7)

The song opens like so many folk tunes with a simple question for a rambling son—Where has he been?—but the lyrics quickly shift to a mesmerising avalanche of places, images, and metaphors that follow one after the other: from mountains and highways to forests, oceans, and graveyards (Dylan 1963a). The next three verses explore, in the same imagery and style, questions about what the boy had seen and heard and whom he had met on his travels—before the song asks about what will come next. The answer is desperate but defiant: the son will return to the depths of the forest—an apparently desolate place where people are hungry, water is poisoned, there are prisons and executioners, and souls perish alone and neglected—a bleak, black, empty world. But the boy will capture the harsh truth of it all and, like a hard rain that everyone feels as it falls from the mountain, this truth will create at least the potential for rebirth and growth as he struggles against drowning in the sea of sorrow surrounding him. In one of the more profound images, Dylan notes that the boy's experiences will mean he knows his song well before he starts singing—the words, images, and cadence will emerge from lived experience and a commitment to lay the truth bare.

At the same time, however, *Freewheelin'* expresses Dylan's irreverence and symbolizes his refusal to be what others think he is or should become. The final cut is entitled "I Shall Be Free," and, within the context of the times and the album itself, this title suggests that the track is a "protest song." In reality, this song speaks for nobody but Dylan. "I Shall Be Free" is an extended, surrealist, and personal commentary on the consumers' republic (Dylan 1963b). Far from the world of high culture, the song explores the way that a drunk eases his mind and escapes in fantasies that really leave him trapped in the past and present—anything but free.

Dylan's (1964g) third album—*The Times They Are A-Changin'*—hit the record stores eight months after the release of *The Freewheelin' Bob Dylan*. Dylan intentionally wrote the album's lead song, "The Times They Are A-Changin'," to be an anthem for the times. It was, in his words, a song with a purpose, influenced by Irish and Scottish ballads such as "Come All Ye Bold Highway Men" and "Come All Ye Tender Hearted Maidens," tunes that he had absorbed listening to the Clancy Brothers. "I wanted to write a big song," Dylan discloses, "with short concise verses that piled up on each other in a hypnotic way," and "The Times" certainly met that objective (Crowe 1985).

The song opens with some of Dylan's (1964h) most familiar lyrics, but it is their cadence that is most remarkable, striking, and engrossing. "The Times They Are A-Changin'" begins by invoking classical and biblical imagery—the people gather around a prophet as the swelling flood waters of change grow and what feels like an impending doom looms. This first verse provides a timeless background for the next three verses, which focus on the immediate and contemporary. Writers and critics, congressmen and senators, and mothers and fathers across the land are faced with a world they do not understand—a world that is rapidly changing. They are told to get out of the way if they cannot lend a hand. Dylan returns, however, to timeless imagery to close the song and bring it full circle. Echoing the Sermon on the Mount and the eight beatitudes, Dylan notes that the slow will be fast, the first shall be last, and the old order is fading as generational change pushes forward.

The album, as a whole, remains classic Dylan insofar as he combines his anthem for the times with some cynical, bleak, tormenting, and melancholy material. The opening cut is followed by a number of pieces that challenge the anthem—material that accentuates the tensions and contradictions inherent in change: that change is a necessary and inevitable natural occurrence, that change is resisted by established powers and legal structures, and that struggles, won and lost, create change. Rather than a collection of individual songs, *The Times They Are A-Changin'* is a complete symphony comprised of different movements and can only be appreciated fully as a synthetic whole greater than the sum of its individual parts.

For many, *The Times* represents a politicized Dylan, but the reality is that it denotes a Dylan grounded in the events of his time, capturing and chronicling them but in a manner that presents those events in the upside-down, inside-out, distorted manner Dylan was perfecting—a style that stops the listener short and, to use Hoggart's (1970:16) expression, keeps the moulds from setting. Nothing in *The Times* is cliché. There is no hint of a levelling-down formula of interchangeable parts in these songs. They are probing and disturbing, and the more one reflects upon the lyrics and locates the potential sources for their inspiration, the more complex each song and the album as a whole becomes. After one listens to *The Times*, really listens to it, things can never be quite the same—to place Hoggart's (1970:18) point in a different context.

The second song on the album describes an extremely troubling murder-suicide that leaves a wife, five children, and a destitute South Dakota farmer dead—the "Ballad of Hollis Brown" (Dylan 1964b). "With God on Our Side" follows—a song of cynicism and change (Dylan 1964i). With God on its side, the education system teaches people what to believe, even as those lessons change with time and circumstance. Death and destruction and hatred—whether pursued in the expropriation of First Nations' lands or during the Spanish-American War, the American Civil War, the world wars, or the Cold War—can be justified, with God on one's side. In the last verse, Dylan raises his level of cynicism further by noting that, despite their recognition of how education and popular prejudice shape people's knowledge and beliefs, even those who begin to see through the distortions cannot break away fully—God remains as the best hope for preventing more war.

"Only a Pawn in Their Game"—the sixth song on the LP—puts Dylan's comments at the Tom Paine Award dinner into an interesting perspective. The award dinner was in December 1963, and, although *The Times* was released in February 1964, it was produced in August 1963, so "Only a Pawn in Their Game" was not inspired by the events at the dinner, which occurred after the song was written. Nevertheless, Dylan's comments at the dinner and the perspective taken in "Only a Pawn" do overlap and, more significantly, capture perfectly his upside-down, inside-out approach to thinking about the complex world of everyday life. Both also provide insight regarding Dylan as a cultural producer.

Following some fundraising work that Dylan and Baez had done for the Emergency Civil Liberties Committee, the group decided to award Dylan with the Tom Paine Award (Spitz 1989:240).[108] The award presentation was the centrepiece of the committee's main fundraising endeavour—a dinner held in the grand ballroom of the American Hotel in New York. As Dylan looked around the room that evening, he could not see anyone his age, connected with his politics, or sharing his particular worldview. The room was filled with members of the Old Left, who were now supporting civil rights drives (Dylan 2006:26). Despite what others may have expected, Dylan felt no connection to them. He began to leave but was told he had to stay to receive the award. Dylan complied, although his speech was not like anything the group expected.

During the dinner, people around Dylan had been talking about Kennedy's assassination, the deaths of Bill Moore and civil rights leader Medgar Evers, and Buddhist monks setting themselves aflame to protest the war in Vietnam.[109] In his acceptance speech, Dylan could not get his focus off Kennedy's alleged assassin—Lee Harvey Oswald. Dylan told the audience that he had read a lot about Oswald, about how uptight he was, and Dylan said that he had experienced those feelings too. "I saw a lot of myself in Oswald, I said, and I saw in him a lot of the time we're all living in" (Dylan 2006:26–27). Members of the audience thought Dylan saw something positive in Oswald killing Kennedy, "that's how far out they were":

> I was talking about Oswald. And then I started talking about friends of mine in Harlem—some of them junkies, all of them poor. And I said they need freedom as much as anybody else, and what's anybody doing for them? ... Now, what I was supposed to be was a nice cat. I was supposed to say "I appreciate your award ... and I'll support your cause." But I didn't, and so I wasn't accepted that night. That's the cause of a lot of those chains I was talking about—people wanting to be accepted, people not wanting to be alone. But, after all, what is it to be alone? I've been alone sometimes in front of three thousand people. I was alone that night. (Dylan 2006:27)[110]

---

108 The Tom Paine Award, named for the radical author and intellectual Thomas Paine (1737–1809), was given to honour a nonconformist who cried out for justice (Spitz 1989:240).

109 William Lewis Moore (1927–63) was a postal carrier and member of the Congress on Racial Equality. Moore staged one man protests against segregation by walking to key capital cities and hand delivering letters of protest to civic leaders. He was murdered on April 23, 1963, as he walked toward Jackson, Mississippi, carrying a letter and wearing a sandwich board declaring "Equal Rights for All" on one side and "Mississippi or Bust" on the other. Medgar Evers was a civil rights activist who was denied acceptance to law school at the University of Mississippi, leading to the National Association for the Advancement of Colored People's campaign to desegregate the school. Evers was assassinated in the driveway of his home in June 1963.

110 In 2004, Dylan once again discussed his orientation to politics: "I never set out to write politics. I didn't want to be a political moralist. There were people who just did that. Phil Ochs focused on political things, but there are many sides to us, and I wanted to follow them all. We can feel very generous one day and very selfish the next hour" (Dylan 2006:435).

"Only a Pawn" also reflects on an assassination—that of civil rights activist Medgar Evers—but like Dylan's ruminations on Oswald, it does so from the perspective of the poor white man who shot Evers. It is the quintessential inside-out, upside-down perspective as Dylan (1964e) constructs the event from the assassin's perspective. Equally important, the drawn out, throbbing cadence of the beat and the lyrics and imagery capture the way in which beliefs and prejudices are driven, through constant and ongoing repetition, deep into one's mind where they shape and motivate one's actions. "Only a Pawn" challenges the opening anthem to the LP. Time may pass but are the times really changing?

In the final cut, "Restless Farewell," Dylan (1964f) returns to his Guthrie roots to symbolically bid adieu to the civil rights movement and to the constraining expectations that were growing up around him as a "folkie." The sound is deeply wistful and melancholy, but it reflects the realization that he cannot stay. Ironically, perhaps, there is an overriding sense of inevitability that seems to contradict the opening anthem of the album. Or perhaps Dylan places one element of the dialectic of freedom and determination at either end of the album and the dynamic tensions involved in the human struggle for meaning in the cuts in between.

Dylan's (1964a) fourth album—released just three months later—is aptly entitled *Another Side of Bob Dylan*, and one does encounter a very different Dylan here. "All I Really Want to Do" sets the dominant tone for the album. "Spanish Harlem Incident," "To Ramona," "Ballad in Plain D," and "I Don't Believe You" show a sensitive, deeply emotional side of the songwriter—one responding to love and love lost. Dylan's flippant surrealism is still there in "I Shall Be Free #10" and "Motorpsycho Nightmare," but the two critical songs in terms of Dylan's artistic development are "The Chimes of Freedom," with, as Ginsberg enthuses, its "chains of flashing images," and "My Back Pages" (Dylan 1964c, 1964d; Scorsese 2005). Both of these cuts are deeply metaphorical, conjuring powerful images; they evince the new maturity that enters Dylan's work from this point on—a maturity that is captured in the ironic refrain of "My Back Pages," which speaks of his escape from age and tradition into a "younger" and freer self: "Ah, but I was so much older then, / I'm younger than that now" (Dylan 1964d).

Culture as a "Pure Type" and Dylan's Popular Culture

Very few artists from the 1960s can rival the commercial success that Dylan has enjoyed—he is one of the enduring icons of mass culture consumed by a mass audience. And that is part of Dylan's dialectic; he is as critical of mass culture as he is a master at using it to present his audiences with some of the twentieth century's most probing analyses of the modern world and the human condition. Thus, although Dylan's early work took shape within the world of Marcuse's (1964) *One-Dimensional Man*—in a "society without opposition" characterized by "the paralysis of criticism"—Dylan's sound and lyrics directly challenge the claim that the "productive apparatus and the goods and services which it produces 'sell' or impose the social system as a whole" (pp. ix, 11–12). This section will document how well Dylan's work measures up to the pure type construct of culture developed in Chapter 10.

First, Dylan's work began in the type of deeply rooted culture that Leavis and Thompson (1933) identify as so crucial to genuine cultural production. Odetta, Lead Belly, and Guthrie provided the first hook enticing Dylan into the folk sound and its original traditions. Drawn to New York in search of Guthrie, Seeger, Young, and the Folklore Center, Dylan was taken deeper into Guthrie's world and folk's rural roots. However, in line with Hoggart's (1958) emphasis that the roots of culture do not have to remain in the agrarian world and will thrive and adapt to the urban landscape, the New York coffeehouse scene, Beat poets, and the character of urban existence brought out a new blend of folk music that remained true to the folk tradition of using what is handed down and adapting it to new circumstances. Dylan's unique lyrics and sound epitomized an extremely creative blending of the folk tradition with the trends of the contemporary urban world, which allowed him to grow musically over the course of his first four albums and beyond.

In addition, those roots shaped his work in the early sixties in ways that were unexpected. Rather than generating a simple, easy-to-grasp, easy-to-assimilate, and easy-to-duplicate product for popular culture, the early folk sounds, blended with the depth of Dylan's urban folk experience, became the foundation for the complex artistry found in his first LPs.

Second, much of Dylan's early work addresses themes that "matter most to humanity ... turning a stream of fresh and free thought upon our stock notions and habits" (Arnold [1868] 1932:6). Some of Dylan's lyrics stem from "the best that has been thought and said in the world," and his songs inspire listeners to think about the potential for the "harmonious perfection" of the human condition (p. 11). Beat poet Allan Ginsberg emphasizes how Dylan meets Arnold's standards for cultural production.

Commenting on the impact that "A Hard Rain's A-Gonna Fall" had on him, Ginsberg says that he was knocked out by its eloquence—"particularly 'I'll know my song well before I start singin' and the images of biblical prophecy the song conveyed" (Scorsese 2005). Dylan's power, according to Ginsberg, stems from the imagery Dylan creates with words and from the unusual combinations of words and angles of observation he presents—there is a powerful, eloquent grandeur to Dylan's work.

At the same time, Ginsberg explains, Dylan's words "are empowered and make your hair stand on end," and his descriptions turn something into a subjective truth that also has an "objective reality to it because somebody has realized it" (Scorsese 2005). The words come first, and, as Ginsberg notes, words that achieve those ends are later called poetry.

Third, for Hoggart (1970), culture in its ideal form "explores the diversity, complexity and strangeness of [human] experience," inducing people to break out of their conventional understandings of the world in which they live (p. 11). A pure cultural form "re-creates the texture of that experience" and encourages people to "look at life with all the vulnerability, honesty and penetration they can command" (p. 11).

Beginning with his ballads, such as "Talkin' New York," "Song to Woody," "Iron Ore Blues," "Ballad of Hollis Brown," "Only a Pawn in Their Game," or "The Lonesome Death of Hattie Carroll," Dylan gives his listeners the full range of human experience. He presents a sensitive and tender touch in "Girl from the North Country," "Spanish Harlem Incident," and "To Ramona" and expresses bitter resentment in "Ballad in Plain D" following his breakup with Suzie Rotolo in 1964. The pathos of "Man of Constant Sorrow" and the layers of mystery wrapped in the lyrics and images of "It's All Over Now, Baby Blue" show his more introspective side. Yet whether in the playful "I Don't Believe You (She Acts Like We Never Have Met)," the timeless "Blowin' in the Wind," the anthem "The Times They Are A-Changin'," the poetic "Chimes of Freedom," or the deeply personal "My Back Pages," Dylan piles a multitude of images and perspectives on top of each other. His portrayals are rich in texture, honest, and vulnerable. They examine life at different levels ranging from the immediate details of a single incident to universal problems with which humankind must continually struggle. Dylan's imagery and sound bring one "up short" and prevent "the moulds of habit and familiarity from becoming set and finalized" (p. 16). Certainly his anthems capture the "mass and majesty" of human experience, while his ballads portray injustices, inequalities, and the contradictory nature of contemporary life (p. 16).

Far from the Huxleyan-Marcusean world of simplified satisfactions and one-dimensionality, Dylan's cultural production is disturbing, layered, and challenging. As Dylan (2006:7) explained to Terkel, every line of "A Hard Rain's A-Gonna Fall" could be the basis for a whole song. The same, Ginsberg emphasized, is true of "The Chimes of Freedom," with its "chains of flashing images" (Scorsese 2005). Dylan's restlessness dominates his work, and no listener can "chill" to his sound and its accompanying imagery—sometimes impressionist, sometimes surrealist or Dadaist—with all of its dialectical contradictions and dynamism.

Dylan's work undermines not only the idea that the products of popular culture will be one dimensional but also the fear, expressed by Horkheimer and Adorno ([1944] 1972), that mass culture, reduced to mere formulae, would create a culture ripe for mass deception and an ensuing loss of freedom. Dylan tends toward complex lyrics that unmask the simple fictions societies perpetrate. Assessing "A Hard Rain's A-Gonna Fall," Hilburn describes the song as an "apocalyptic tale of a society being torn apart on many levels" and its lyrics as "rich and poetic enough to defy age" (Dylan 2006:436). At the time, Dylan's imagery and wordsmithery were being influenced by many artists, from blues musician Robert Johnson to French symbolist poet Arthur Rimbaud. After reading Rimbaud's "I is somebody else," Dylan (2004) recalled that he could "hear the bells going off everywhere"—suddenly everything was in transition, and his view of the world, and *how* to view the world, changed dramatically (p. 288).

Although Dylan's lyrics are arguably complex, poetic, and thought provoking, do they require the kind of supple, subtle, and attentive mind that Carr (2011), like Postman (1985), associates with the age of typography? As explained previously, the "sophisticated ability to think conceptually, deductively, and sequentially" and to do so calmly, with focus, and without distraction are, according to some, prerequisites for both the creation and appreciation of cultural products as pure types (Postman 1985:63; see also Carr 2011:10) This is also the frame of mind that is required for one to appreciate complex songs such as "Iron Ore Blues," "With God on Our Side," "Masters of War," or "Talkin' World War III Blues." Just try to understand any of these storytelling songs without starting at the beginning and listening attentively to capture the ironies, juxtapositions, pain, and struggle Dylan wraps into his lyrics.

Consider "Iron Ore Blues," for example. The song begins by calling on friends to gather around, but the tale that follows is anything but happy. It is a first-person account that recalls the time when the mines were thriving. But it is the wife of a miner telling the tale, not the miner as expected. He is dead. As she speaks about the times of plenty, she also reflects on the tragedies that are among the everyday realities of mining communities— sorrows that are woven into her life story as a whole. Set during the postwar American economic boom, the story told by the miner's widow reminds the listener of the harsh reality of impersonal capital and its interests—despite the American mines' productivity, ore is cheaper in South America where miners work for almost nothing. The globalized economy, built on the backs of the American workers, creates wealth for some but leaves others impoverished in one of the wealthiest nations in the world. And most Americans, striving after their own "American Dream" are oblivious to miners' plight and how closely connected they are to those left abandoned in a globalized economy. The story runs deeper still as the widow turns to reflect on her children who will soon be leaving her and a town that holds no future. Listening to the song again, one knows it is not just about mining.

Postman may be correct that television represents a different epistemology than typography, but the age of exposition did not necessarily die with the age of show business. Dylan has taken Berlin's "There's no business like show business" and turned it inside out and upside down by using show business to persuade audiences to reflect on themselves as they may never have before—to take his listeners from entertainment back to the realities they have missed or ignored. Postman is correct: one can shrivel the spirit of a culture through Orwellian or Huxleyan techniques, but one can also expand the spirit of a culture by capturing the popular imagination and taking it on rides it has never previously experienced.

Carr's and Postman's positions and Dylan's success as an entertainer point to an important dialectic in assessing the impact of culture—particularly popular culture—on a society's institutionalized collective representations and the frames of mind they develop. McLuhan (1964) maintained that the medium is the message because it "shapes and controls the scale and form of human association and action" (p. 9). He believed that the electric age would transcend the limitations of the typographic and mechanical era by introducing "cool media," which could free the mind from the uniform, linear, and repeatable frame of mind developed in the Guttenberg galaxy. To illustrate his point, McLuhan (1962) referred to Gothic symbolism and Ruskin's work with the grotesque to emphasize how "a series of symbols [are] thrown together in bold and fearless connection" to reveal truths that would be difficult to express verbally (p. 266).

Dylan's work exemplifies both Carr's and Postman's positions and McLuhan's contradictory one. Dylan's songs are cool media, in McLuhan's terms—they contain symbols and images that are boldly and fearlessly thrown together leaving much for the listener to probe, untangle, and interpret. To do that successfully, however, requires the calm, focused, and undistracted mind of print culture along with its imaginative, inventive, and subversive capacities, which Carr and Postman emphasize.

Dylan's work might not surpass Beethoven's Fifth Symphony but, taken as a whole, his songs are popular cultural productions that aspire to the heights of Beethoven's genius. To ignore "The Times They Are A-Changin'" or consider it a simple anthem of the 1960s misses the mark. One must recognize that it is the opening prelude to an entire symphony that runs through "The Ballad of Hollis Brown," "With God on Our Side," "Only a Pawn in Their Game," "The Lonesome Death of Hattie Carroll," "Restless Farewell," and "Boots of Spanish Leather"—a symphony that both provokes thought and provides soothing balm to counteract the harsh realities of the modern world.

Dylan is an artist of enormous talent, but the substance of his artistry, as this chapter has documented at some length, comes from the intersection of his own personal biography with history and social structure. Moreover, Dylan's artistry is sophisticated, multilayered, and critically insightful because it explores that intersection from a number of different perspectives and vantage points. His lyrics capture the malaise of the times and force the listener to think beyond the moment into the roots of anomie, alienation, and social dissatisfaction. Dylan's work compares favourably with all the criteria by which one might judge culture as a "pure type." Additionally, by using Weber's ideal type method, one can gain a far deeper appreciation of why Dylan's work is so probing, powerful, disturbing, and fulfilling. Regardless of whether Dylan ever read Mills or Mills ever listened to Dylan, they both tapped into some of the deepest issues in people's lives during the latter half of the twentieth century, and their work continues to stimulate critical reflection on social life today.

Key Terms and Names

total living
consumers' republic
American Society of Composers, Authors, and Publishers (ASCAP)
Broadcast Music Incorporated (BMI)
Federal Communications Commission (FCC)
monopoly
oligopoly

Questions for Review and Further Reflection

1. Describe the transition from "total war" to "total living" and its relation to cultural production in America.
2. Why might the notion of the "consumers' republic" be problematic? Which groups benefit—and which lose out or suffer—from the idea of "total living" in a "consumers' republic," do you think?
3. Divide a sheet of paper into four columns. In the first column, list the points that Marx would emphasize to answer Richard Peterson's question, "Why 1955?" In the subsequent columns, use Durkheim, Weber, and Mills to answer this question. What are the common themes across the columns, and what themes are unique to just one?
4. As Ginsberg explains, Dylan's words "are empowered and make your hair stand on end," and his descriptions turn something into a subjective truth that also has an "objective reality to it because somebody has realized it." What do you think Ginsberg means by this? Can you think of a song that had this effect on you? How did it accomplish this?
5. How exactly do Dylan's sound and lyrics directly challenge the claim that the "productive apparatus and the goods and services which it produces 'sell' or impose the social system as a whole"? Use specific examples from his first four LPs. Are there any contemporary artists whose work accomplishes this task (write down some examples and why you chose them)?
6. In what ways does this chapter illustrate the strengths of using Mills's sociological imagination (understanding the intersection of biography, history, and social structure) to study contemporary forms of cultural production?

12

ROCK 'N' ROLL AS COMPLEX CULTURE

Main Objectives

This chapter will

1. Present some of the history of rock and roll and study its complex nature through the development of a pure type construct examining three fundamental aspects of the genre.
2. Introduce and familiarize students with some of the key figures, events, and controversies in the history of rock and roll as a form of popular culture.
3. Use the pure type construct of "rock and roll" in a case study of the genre and provide another example of how sociologists can investigate "culture" as a complex social form.

On the surface, rock and roll seems to be such a simple thing—it is the music of "The King," Elvis Presley. It dies in the February 3, 1959, plane crash that kills 22-year-old Buddy Holly, 17-year-old Ritchie Valens, and "The Big Bopper," 28-year-old J.P. Richardson.

Rock is the music that the Beatles, the Rolling Stones, the Animals, the Who, the Kinks, and the rest of the "British Invasion" bring back to life in the mid-1960s. And rock comes back in a different form in the California sound of the Beach Boys, Jan and Dean, and the Mamas and the Papas. At the same time, the Motown sound of the Supremes (after 1967 Diana Ross and the Supremes), the Jackson 5, the Four Tops, Stevie Wonder, Marvin Gaye, and the Temptations give it a different rebirth (see Ford 1971). And rock is the contemporary sounds of the Arctic Monkeys, Billy Talent, Foo Fighters, Green Day, Nirvana, Pearl Jam, Red Hot Chili Peppers, The Black Keys, Weezer, and more. If, as Neal Gabler (1998) claims, life has become a movie, rock is the soundtrack for many an individual's youth, playing as it does in

American Graffiti, *Grease*, *Dirty Dancing*, *Forrest Gump*, or *Boyhood*—not in the background but surrounding and shaping the whole story. Everyone knows rock and roll—what it is, who makes it, what it sounds like, and why it matters—simple as that. But is rock and roll really so simple?

After 30 ceremonies, the Rock and Roll Hall of Fame (2016) has 312 inductees, of which 113 are groups, totalling 749 individuals. It would take a multi-volume production to cover all the artists and sounds that have constituted and now comprise "rock 'n' roll." Greil Marcus (2014) provides interesting insight into what that project would entail. From "the first class" of rock and roll, he lists "the performers Chuck Berry, James Brown, Ray Charles, Sam Cooke, Fats Domino, the Everly Brothers, Buddy Holly, Jerry Lee Lewis, Little Richard, and Elvis Presley," along with the "non-performers" of the 1950s: DJ Alan Freed and record producers Sam Phillips and John Hammond. Also mentioned are the 1930s "early influences": Robert Johnson, Jimmie Rodgers, and Harmonica Frank. Moving forward in time—Marcus offers six pages of name after name after name of rock's greats—the dizzying list finally reaches potential inductees such as Tupac Shakur, Pearl Jam, Radiohead, Green Day, Beyoncé, Eminem, and Jay Z (pp. 3–8). One has to pause: all those artists, all their styles and sounds, in just a 60 or so year history. And then one Googles "rock and roll" only to discover that, with 222 subgenres, rock has almost as many styles as it has inductees to its hall of fame (*Wikipedia* 2016).

Now rock and roll no longer looks like such a simple thing—it starts to look more like "the commodity" that Marx ([1872] 1987) analysed: "a very tricky thing, full of metaphysical craftiness and theological peculiarities" (p. 102). Part of the reason is, of course, that rock and roll *is* a commodity, but its complexity is due far more to *what* it is and how one tries to conceptualize that "what." What is rock and roll? What are its fundamental characteristics? How is it distinguished from other forms of music? Thinking about those questions makes Marx's complex commodity, in comparison to rock and roll, seem like an "easily understood, trivial thing."

Perhaps one could define rock by separating it from other musical forms, focusing, for example, on the instruments used to play it and its general character. "Classic rock" features an electric lead and an electric rhythm guitar, a string bass (replaced in the mid-1950s by an electric bass guitar), and a drum kit. Some of the early groups included a piano to drive the beat. Later, a keyboard replaced the piano, and its function changed; it played more in the background before leaping forward during some of the bridges. As for the music itself, the main beat is a blues rhythm, and there is a strong backbeat. But this definition is too narrow. Focusing on artists whose work conforms to those parameters would certainly simplify matters, but it would omit too many pivotal artists and, most important, the really essential ingredients that constitute rock and roll's social significance.

Recognizing that every "pure type" is a construction and that others might construct their pure type differently, this chapter will employ a pure type construct comprised of three elements. These elements, not in order of importance, are the physicality of the rock sound; the continual crossing over, blending, merging, amalgamation, and divergence in the sounds; and the dialectical tension between simplicity, joy, and freedom, on the one hand, and loss, resignation, brooding fear, and oppression, on the other. Looking at each of these takes one through much of the history of rock and roll while creating a framework to compare rock and roll to the characteristics of culture as a pure type developed in Chapter 11.

"ONE, TWO, THREE O'CLOCK, FOUR O'CLOCK, ROCK ...": FEELING THE BEAT OF ROCK 'N' ROLL

One characteristic of rock and roll is its physicality, the visceral and sexualized energy of the music. Jimmy Rogers Snow, the son of country star Hank Snow, understands that quality well—the sensual feel of rock as it crosses over from R & B to a new sound of freedom and liberation. Snow, who knew Presley, Holly, and other early rock stars, was in Memphis at the very beginning of the genre ("Jimmie Rogers Snow" 2014). However, he left his promising career as a singer with RCA, joined the ministry, and began actively preaching against the evils of rock:

> I believe with all of my heart that it is a contributing factor to our juvenile delinquency of today.... Why I believe that is because I know how it feels when you sing it. I know what it does to you. I know the evil feeling that you feel when you sing it. I know the lost position that you get into in the beat. If you talk to the average teenager of today and you ask them what it is about rock 'n' roll music that they like, and the first thing that they'll say, is the beat, the beat, *the beat*. (Snow [1958] 2009)

Snow is far from alone in emphasizing the visceral power of rock and how far it might take white, middle-class youth into emotional territory that would destroy the calm, peaceful, *"Father Knows Best* world" that parents in post–World War II Canada and the United States thought they were creating (Halberstam 1993; Medovoi 2005). The *New York Herald Tribune* recognized the threat and called Presley "vulgar," joining religious organizations in protesting against the implied sexual nature of his movements after a June 5, 1956, performance during which he gyrated his hips in time to "Hound Dog" (Anderson 2011).

Indeed, using a vivid analogy, U2's Bono claims that "Elvis Presley is like the 'big bang' of rock and roll." He continues, "It all comes from there. You had two cultures colliding there. The rhythm of black music and the melody and chord progression of white music—and it all came together in that kind of spastic dance of his" (Jones, Meyrowitz, and Salzman 1995). Bono's description is true in many ways but also misleading. Presley's deep, alluring voice; his black hair, greased back in a ducktail style; the sexual physicality of his performance; the high tempo and driving music and lyrics; and the fomented frenzy he created in an audience—all of these provide the first mass consumer image of what constituted "rock and roll." In fact, however, rock and roll begins with "a one-eyed, twenty-nine-year-old yodeling champ with a heavy jaw and a spit curl that couldn't hide his receding hairline" (Dawson 2005:4). Bill Haley and the Comets[111] are the first rock and rollers, as it is with their music that black R & B and jump blues cross the racial divide and are carried forward by white bands to a growing mass consumer market. Mixing his metaphors, Jim Dawson (2005) writes, "If Elvis Presley was the King, Bill Haley was John the Baptist" (p. 6).

In June 1951, Bill Haley and the Saddlemen covered "Rocket 88," a tune by Jackie Brenston and His Delta Cats, several months after Sam Phillips had produced the original and licensed it to Chess Records (Guralnick 1994). The original "Rocket 88," a salute to the Oldsmobile Rocket 88, has a prominent R & B sound with boogie-woogie piano coming up around Brenston's ragged vocals and Ike Turner's saxophone wailing through the bridge (Brenston and His Delta Cats [1951] 2016). The Haley cover has smoother vocals, tones down the piano and saxophone, and carries hints of the rockabilly for which the group was known (Haley and the Saddlemen [1951] 2009b).

Haley and the Saddlemen's ([1951] 2009a) next release was a cover of "Rock the Joint," by Jimmy Preston and His Prestonians ([1949] 2016). In the original, the piano keeps the backbeat moving, the vocals are unrefined, and the saxophone soars as the band rocks the club for the whirling hucklebuck and jitterbug dancers on the floor. Keeping a strong R & B sound, Haley and the Saddlemen ([1951] 2009a) let Marshall Lytle's "slap bass" carry the beat and turn Danny Cedrone loose on his electric guitar in the first bridge, setting a standard that lead guitarists would struggle to achieve from that point onwards. The group's country roots stay alive; the dances mentioned in the lyrics are no longer the hucklebuck and the jitterbug but the Sugarfoot Rag and Virginia Reel (Dawson 2005). The fusion of R & B and country to produce the visceral Memphis sound is almost complete.

With "Crazy Man, Crazy," recorded in April 1953 by Bill Haley with Haley's Comets ([1953] 2012), the group sheds its country and western image for good. The title and most of the lyrics of this original song are composed

---

111 This group changed its name frequently. General references to it will use "Bill Haley and the Comets"; all citations of songs by the group will use the group's name at the time but will be under Haley, ignoring the "Bill."

from the "lingo" Haley hears at concerts and dances—"Crazy man, crazy / Man that music's gone, gone.... Go, go, go everybody" (*Bill Haley Tapes* 1995). Reaching number 12 on the *Billboard* chart in 1953, the song is generally seen as the first rock and roll hit (Whitburn 2004). In addition to its *Billboard* success, "Crazy Man, Crazy" is included in the soundtrack of an episode of the CBS series *Omnibus*, making it the first rock number to play on national television in the United States. This episode, "Glory in the Flower," featured the then unknown James Dean. Dancing to the beat of "Crazy Man, Crazy," Dean and his teenage friends establish the unmistakeable sexuality of the music and provide an indelible image of exactly what white, middle-class parents fear; the rebellious nature of teenagers, juvenile delinquency, and rock and roll are all rolled together into a single package (see "James Dean" [1953] 2015).

Dawson (2005) notes that "Rock Around the Clock," the next song from Bill Haley and the Comets, was a very unlikely hit: "It began as a patchwork of Jewish folk melody, minstrelsy, 1920s blues, and a TV theme song for late-night movies, and ended as an amalgam of nearly every popular American musical strain of the first half of the twentieth century" (p. 6). As the B-side of "Thirteen Women (And Only One Man in Town)"—a song about life after a nuclear holocaust—"(We're Gonna) Rock Around the Clock," released by Decca on May 10, 1954, had no impact on the music scene (Haley with His Comets [1954] 2012a, [1954] 2012b). But the release of the MGM movie *Blackboard Jungle* in March 1955 changed everything (Brooks 1955).

Based on Evan Hunter's (1954) novel of the same title, *Blackboard Jungle* opens with text scrolling to the beat of a single drum playing a march. The words express concern over the growing problem of juvenile delinquency in American schools. The march changes into the driving rhythm of "Rock Around the Clock" when the words end and the title of the movie appears on a chalkboard. As the opening credits finish, the song continues, but the scene cuts to a schoolyard where students jitterbug, boys wolf whistle at a young woman as she walks past, and Richard Dadier (Glen Ford), a new, idealistic teacher enters the inner-city, racially and ethnically diverse, all-male North Manual High School. An instrumental version of "Rock Around the Clock" also plays through the scene where Dadier and another teacher are beaten by teens in an alleyway, and it plays again over the closing credits (Brooks 1955).

Playing "Rock Around the Clock" through a movie theatre's big speaker system made the opening minute and a half of *Blackboard Jungle* sound like a rock concert, and Cedrone's guitar riff even brought kids into the aisles jiving and rocking as the movie began. As a result, the movie created controversy from its first showing (Medovoi 2005). School authorities in the small city of New Brunswick, New Jersey, forced theatres to run a disclaimer at the end stating the movie did not represent school conditions in that city. The city of Pasadena did the same. Delegates to the National Education Association denounced the film as a "Hollywood gangster story in a school setting" (cited in Golub 2009:26). The school where Hunter had briefly taught, Bronx Vocational High School, which had served as the basis for his novel, was quickly exonerated in two different reports. Both affirmed that students there were not at all like those in the film (Golub 2009). *Blackboard Jungle* was banned in Atlanta, as white authorities found it offensive that some of the students portrayed in the film as "leering" at white women were black (K. McCarthy 2007:325), and a Boston theatre muted the sound until "Rock Around the Clock" was over to prevent pandemonium during the movie's opening (Golub 2009).

The movie was quickly criticized for inciting delinquent behaviour (United States Senate 1955). In Rochester, reports claimed that "young hoodlums cheered the beatings and methods of terror inflicted upon a teacher by a gang of boys pictured in the film" (cited in Medovoi 2005:138). Reminding city hall of the "great applause" that had occurred in the theatre when "a 'tough guy' pupil told a teacher to 'go to hell' and then drew a knife and stabbed the teacher," a Toronto alderman maintained that "Hollywood has succeeded, as usual, in glorifying in the minds of teenagers just the things it claims to attack"; he vowed to have the film banned (cited in Medovoi 2005:138). Canada's National Film Board rejected a similar request by a Toronto women's group. In Memphis, a group of girls, who easily snuck in despite the movie's "adults only" restrictions, later burned down a barn because they "wanted to be like those tough kids in that picture" (cited in Medovoi 2005:138). Claire Boothe Luce, the American Ambassador to Italy at the time, blocked the film's screening at the Venice Film Festival, claiming it would give "ammunition to Italian Communist and anti-U.S. propaganda" (Golub 2009).

Nevertheless, as Metro-Goldwyn-Mayer's (MGM) top hit, grossing seven million dollars, *Blackboard Jungle* was too successful for public opinion to suppress it.

Three interrelated social forces are evident in the 1955 controversy occasioned by "Rock Around the Clock" and its use in *Blackboard Jungle*. First, fears of juvenile delinquency were taking hold of the nation; second, television networks were engaged in a fierce competition for audiences and were searching for formats that attracted a broad spectrum of viewers; and third, postwar prosperity was creating a new youth culture that commercial interests wanted to exploit but middle-class parents wanted to curtail or eliminate. All three pull and push rock and roll in different ways; all three, along with the social impact of rock and roll, play a significant role in shaping the 1950s as a whole (Halberstam 1993).

The contrasting images of life in the post–World War II period could not be stronger than in the mid-1950s. On the one hand, as David Halberstam

(1993) writes, no matter what the reality was, "[b]y the mid-fifties television portrayed a wonderfully antiseptic world of idealized homes in an idealized, unflawed America" (p. 508). Shows such as *Father Knows Best* (1954–60), *Leave It to Beaver* (1957–58, 1958–63), and *The Adventures of Ozzie and Harriet* (1952–66) presented a world where parents are optimistic and upbeat and never raise their voices, money is not a problem, being normal and average is seen as better than having fame and fortune, there are no drugs, children follow their parents' wisdom, siblings support each other, and everyone lives in a suburb with green lawns and an always-shining sun (see also Owram 1996). On the other hand, as James Gilbert (1986) emphasizes, "[d]uring the 1950s and particularly from 1954 to 1956, Americans [and Canadians] worried deeply about the rise in juvenile delinquency" (p. 63).

A subcommittee of the United States Senate Committee on the Judiciary had already investigated the link between comic books and juvenile delinquency prior to *Blackboard Jungle*'s release (United States Senate 1954). Shortly afterwards, this Subcommittee to Investigate Juvenile Delinquency turned to the impact of television and movies. William Mooring, a movie and television editor, identified "*Blackboard Jungle, The Wild One, Big House U.S.A., Kiss Me Deadly, Black Tuesday, Cell 2455,* [and] *Death Row,* [as being] among many films having a potentially harmful influence on behavior patterns, particularly those of young men and women at a high pitch of sexual curiosity and imitativeness" (United States Senate 1955:76). The message from police chiefs and other civic and educational authorities was identical.

To defend the economic interests of the film industry, Dore Schary, MGM's vice-president for production, emphasized in his testimony before the subcommittee the educational value of *Blackboard Jungle*. Because of the reception given to the book, he explained, MGM knew the film might be controversial, but the studio felt that "it would make a very good report on a very serious problem of juvenile delinquency" (United States Senate 1955:110). He proceeded to tell the subcommittee that movies do not lead public opinion, they reflect it: "In connection with *Blackboard Jungle,* I believe that what we have done is make a picture that again reflects a rise in public tide against the menace of delinquency that has gone too long unchecked" (United States Senate 1955:111–12).

Not to be outdone, the president of the Screen Actors Guild, Ronald Reagan, claimed that no other communications industry—not publishing, records, radio, or television—"has the same self-restraint as does the motion picture industry" (United States Senate 1955:94). With respect to *Blackboard Jungle*, Reagan emphasized that it is the end of the story that juveniles will remember: "a feeling of disgust for the boys who were on the wrong side of the fence" and a "feeling of triumph when the one boy was won over and became a leader for the right" (United States Senate 1955:94). Reagan also maintained that the movie "was a great tribute for a very much maligned and misunderstood and abused segment of American humanity, the school-teacher" (United States Senate 1955:94).

Although in 1955 their parents might have been following the subcommittee's hearings closely, teens turned "Rock Around the Clock" into the first rock and roll song to top the *Billboard* charts; it remained number one for eight solid weeks beginning that July. If the growing sales of R & B records among white teens had not already made the point, "Rock Around the Clock's" sales made teen entertainment and musical preferences crystal clear—prompting an intense competition for their purchasing power.

Whether the subcommittee liked it or not, by the mid-1950s, television, the emerging "teen culture," and commercial interests could not be controlled by legislation; nor could their interrelationship be predicted. The major networks, feeling their way in the new medium of TV, began their television programming by migrating their popular variety shows over from radio. Ed Sullivan and Milton Berle, for example, both had hosted variety shows on the radio in the 1940s. By 1955, although Ed Sullivan commanded the highest ratings of any of the televised variety shows, Jackie Gleason, Milton Berle, and Steve Allen still represented dangerous competition. Sullivan, to deepen his success, decided to broaden his audience and capitalize on the growing consumer power of suburban white teens. Consequently, in August 1955, with "Rock Around the Clock" topping the charts, he brought Haley and the Comets to *The Toast of the Town*, as Sullivan's show was then named. Haley, in his plaid jacket and bowtie, and his band members, who wore matching suits, looked and sounded like an energetic group of mainstream entertainers and fitted in perfectly with the family entertainment image that Sullivan and TV executives wanted to project at the time. It is simply upbeat, wholesome fun.

Just a few months later, on November 20, 1955, Sullivan also unintentionally featured the song that launched the rock and roll beat: "Bo Diddley." The performance set him against rock and roll forever—or so he said at the time. Because of the growing popularity of R & B, the success of the Haley appearance, and "the newsreel shots of thousands of people jamming the streets around Frank Shipman's [sic] Apollo Theater, all trying to get in to see Dr. Jives' Rhythm and ... Blues show," Sullivan decided to bring the young black DJ from WWRL to his stage to introduce middle-class Canadians and Americans to this new music ("Elvis Presley Dokumentation Karriere 1956" 2010). Dr. Jives introduced *the singer* Bo Diddley, who was supposed to play Tennessee Ernie Ford's "Sixteen Tons," but the audience got *the song* "Bo Diddley" instead. The playlist called for "Bo Diddley, Sixteen Tons," so thinking he was supposed to open with his recently written and released tune that he had named for himself, Bo Diddley and the band played a true rock song that roused Sullivan's usually sedate audience. Sullivan, incensed by the music, vowed to never feature it again.

Meanwhile, Presley, who had adopted aspects of Bo Diddley's musical style, was achieving fame in Memphis and streaking toward the national spotlight. Playing Presley's "That's All Right" and "Blue Moon of Kentucky" over and over in July 1954 on WHBQ, Daddy-O-Dewey had successfully kick-started the rock and roll revolution. Within months, Presley ([1954] 2014) was driving audiences into a frenzy with performances on the *Louisiana Hayride*, a broadcast that was second only to the *Grand Ole Opry* for showcasing white country talent. In early 1955, Presley began travelling with a show headlined by Jimmy Snow's father, country's great Hank Snow—but Presley quickly became the main attraction ("Jimmie Rogers Snow" 2014). Colonel Tom Parker, Snow's agent, immediately saw Presley's potential and, with the support of friends at RCA, outbid Mitch Miller at Columbia and Ertegun at Atlantic to purchase Presley's contract from Sam Phillips at Sun Records, for the then astronomical sum of $30,000.00 (Halberstam 1993).

Parker knew that television was the medium for building stars in the "electric age" (McLuhan 1962:3). Soon, he began trying to arrange Presley's first national TV appearances. Contrary to what many think, Presley did not make his national television debut on *The Ed Sullivan Show*. Indeed, it was because he had played on other variety shows first that Sullivan had little choice but to book him. Capitalizing on the publicity generated by *Blackboard Jungle* and the success of "Rock Around the Clock," Parker booked Presley on Tommy and Jimmy Dorsey's *Stage Show*, which was produced by Jackie Gleason for CBS and preceded his own program, *The Honeymooners*. In signing a talent that would upstage Sullivan's ratings, Gleason, as Gerald Nachman (2009) notes, "had no qualms about unleashing the guitar-strumming sex machine's hips and legs" (p. 281). The medium, as McLuhan maintained, is the message, and Presley's image drew millions of viewers and paid enormous dividends for the network and the performer. The television wars and the shaping of rock's image, sound, and feel were underway.

Presley's first performance on CBS's *Stage Show* was broadcast January 28, 1956. He sang a rousing set: "Shake Rattle and Roll / Flip Flop and Fly" and "I Got A Woman" (Presley [1956a] 2012). A week later he was back, singing "Baby, Let's Play House" and covering Little Richard's "Tutti Frutti" (Presley [1956b] 2012). Presley made a third appearance on February 11, when he featured a rock version of "Blue Suede Shoes" and, backed by the Dorsey brothers' full band, sang "Heartbreak Hotel" with a trumpet solo wailing through the bridge to give the number a jazz sound (Presley [1956c] 2012).

On February 18, Presley made a fourth appearance on the show. He had been "causing quite a sensation," according to Tommy Dorsey's introduction of that date. Presley reprised "Tutti Frutti" from two weeks earlier, dancing without restraint through Scotty Moore's guitar riffs during the bridge.

With doo-wop vocal accompaniment, Presley closed with a deep and sultry version of "I Was the One" (Presley [1956d] 2012).

Before Presley's fifth appearance, Tommy Dorsey introduced the singer as "an entertainer whose provocative style has kicked up a storm all around the country ... the singing star of the *Louisiana Hayride* ... the one and only, Elvis Presley" (Presley [1956e] 2012). Presley opened his set with "Blue Suede Shoes" and, without Dorsey's orchestra, launched into a full rock version of "Heartbreak Hotel." In his final appearance on the Dorsey brothers' *Stage Show*, Presley covered the R &B song "Money Honey" but performed it in a full rock and roll style, gyrating in Moore's guitar solo through the bridge. The band finished the set with the increasingly popular "Heartbreak Hotel" (Presley [1956f] 2012).

Although, for the most part, the camera shots in all six appearances closed in tightly to Presley's head and upper torso, taking advantage of the personal intimacy that television offers, the producers shifted to the overhead camera through the bridges as Presley rocked with his "spastic dance," to use Bono's description, and Presley certainly cut loose in his closing number of the final show.

Just over two months later, Presley made what Halberstam (1993:478) describes as "a rather sedate appearance" on Milton Berle's show, broadcast by NBC, but when he was invited back two months later, he sang a moving version of "I Want You, I Need You, I Love You" and followed it with a raucous "Hound Dog" (see Presley [1956g] 2011, [1956h] 2009). After these performances, there was a huge media outcry at "Elvis the Pelvis's" vulgarity, and "suddenly the American home was a house divided" (Halberstam 1993:478). Sullivan, the self-appointed guardian of family entertainment, vowed that Presley would never appear on his show.

Following the success of Presley on Berle's Tuesday evening show, NBC's Steve Allen, Sullivan's closest rival in the Sunday evening time slot, seized the opportunity to boost his ratings by featuring Presley on July 1, 1956. Conscious of the tastes of his family-oriented show, Allen put Presley in a tuxedo to sing a very constrained version of "Hound Dog." Although Presley teased the audience with sudden jerks and twitches, he never followed through with any of his already famous "gyrations." Presley, to his credit, managed to find some humour in his ridiculous serenade of the hound dog that Allen had brought on stage (see Presley [1956i] 2015). Allen did outdraw Sullivan on that day, but the fans who tuned in hated the show.[112]

---

112 Presley also took part in a ridiculous, slapstick comedy skit "Range Roundup," playing "Tumbleweed Presley." At Dewey Phillips's urging, Elvis returned immediately to Memphis, and at a concert in Phillips's honour, "cut loose a pure rock-a-billy performance"—pure, uncensored Presley—reassuring his fans "I just want to tell y'all not to worry—them people in New York and Hollywood are not going to change me none" (Halberstram 1993:478).

Sullivan recognized the threat Presley and others posed to his success. "It was one thing to guard public morals for the good of the nation and the good of your career," Halberstam (1993) wryly notes, "it was another thing to guard public morals at the cost of your career" (p. 479). Rock and roll—Presley's brand of rock and roll—was welcomed with open arms into the Sunday evening living rooms of Canadians and Americans on September 9, 1956. Or so it seemed. Although Sullivan backtracked considerably by bringing Presley to *The Ed Sullivan Show* for economic reasons, he did everything he could to maintain his "family entertainment" image by blunting the Presley brand of rock and roll. For his part, to gain the legitimacy that appearing on Sullivan's show would bring, Presley mostly complied with the strictures Sullivan imposed.

The show's opening announcer named the headliners—The Vagabonds and Dorothy Sarnoff—and continued with "and starring Elvis Presley," but Sullivan, who was absent recovering from a near fatal car accident, had the substitute host, British actor Charles Laughton, make Presley as invisible as possible (Marcus 2006; see also "Elvis Presley Dokumentation Karriere 1956" 2010; Raymond and Raymond [1987] 2000). Rather than opening the show, as the star headliner always did, Presley, televised from a sound stage in Los Angeles where he was shooting his first film, *Love Me Tender*, was the sixth act to appear. Singing "Don't Be Cruel" and "Love Me Tender," he gave a subdued performance. However, when he came back as the last act on the show, Presley ripped it up with "Ready Teddy" and "Hound Dog," but all of the camera angles were carefully controlled: close-ups of Presley's head and shoulders when he really moved and long shots only when it was safe to show his full figure. What the television audience saw was considerably less animated than the live audience's experience (Marcus 2006; Raymond and Raymond [1987] 2000).

Presley was booked for two more performances on *The Ed Sullivan Show*, and he commanded the price of $50,000 for the three appearances, an unprecedented amount for that time. For his second appearance, broadcast on October 28, 1956, Elvis sang a set of "Don't Be Cruel" and "Love Me Tender," which was followed by "Love Me" in a second set. In the final set, Presley did belt out "Hound Dog." However, in a shirt and tie and a buttoned jacket and slacks, he gave an understated performance in comparison to others he had given live that year. A live show in Tupelo in September had Elvis wearing black from head to toe, his shirt wide open at the top, his hips swirling, and his hair falling across his forehead, shaken back every so often with a toss of his head (see Raymond and Raymond [1987] 2000).

During Presley's final appearance on Sullivan's show, January 6, 1957, the cameramen were ordered to shoot the singer only from the waist up. The first set was a medley of "Hound Dog," "Love Me Tender," "Heartbreak Hotel," and "Don't Be Cruel." Sullivan controlled the pace by slowing down the second set, which featured just Presley and the Jordanaires singing "Too Much" and "When My Blue Moon Turns to Gold Again," although Presley used the bridge of the first song to excite the live audience. The last set was chosen to meet Sullivan's ultimate goal—to put the rock and roll genie back into the bottle. After Presley finished a solemn version of the gospel song "Peace in the Valley," Sullivan walked over to a rather uncomfortable Presley, shook his hand, and made this announcement: "I want to say to Elvis Presley and the country that this is a real decent, fine boy.... You're thoroughly alright, so now, let's have a tremendous hand for a very nice person" (see Presley [1957] 2015; Raymond and Raymond [1987] 2000). It was Sullivan's final attempt to sanitize Presley and thereby rock and roll, to eliminate the visceral sexuality and rebel image that was making rock such a hit among white, middle-class teens.

The partnership between television and rock and roll was cemented. In his six appearances on the Dorsey brothers' *Stage Show*, Presley drew six million viewers per night. For Berle, the number rose to about 20 million, and Presley's appearance on NBC's *The Steve Allen Show* was watched by 42 million. Elvis broke records on *The Ed Sullivan Show* too. On a typical Sunday evening, Sullivan had about 14 million viewers, but for the three Presley shows he had 62 million, 55 million, and 42 million, respectively. The only other time Sullivan reached those numbers was when the Beatles appeared on his eight o'clock, Sunday evening show (Marcus 1997). Television and Sullivan, despite his best efforts to control the emerging teen culture and rock and roll, made Elvis Presley "The King," placing him at the centre of the national spotlight. Presley moved on after gaining the "Ed Sullivan seal of approval" to perform any way he chose.

At a Seattle concert in 1957, as the crowd settled down following his entrance on stage, Presley exercised his newly established position of power: "I alluz like to begin mah concerts with the national anthem.... Will y'all please rise." As the crowd stood, "Elvis picked up his guitar, twitched once more, took a breath, and groaned: 'You ain't nothing but a hound dog....'" Stunned for a moment, the crowd "erupted into a frenzy that dwarfed the one a few minutes earlier" (cited in Marcus 1997:264–65). By 1957, nation's teens had their own national anthem and the feeling that went with its visceral sound.

Marcus (1997) maintains that Presley's television appearances redefine, to use Jimmy Snow's words, "how [rock and roll] feels" and "what it does to you."

A single look at *This is Elvis* or *Elvis '56* makes it plain why Elvis's early TV performances caused so much trouble: Elvis, clearly and consciously perceiving the limits of what Americans had learned to accept as shared culture, set out to shatter them. He turns toward the camera, and suggests a body in freedom, a kind of freedom for which, at the time, there was no acceptable language; he turns away, and suggests that he is only kidding; then he moves in a manner so outrageous memory cannot hold the image. (Pp. 263–64)

The medium is the message.

By the end of 1957, Sullivan thought he had found the perfect band for the new genre he wanted to shape—the clean-cut and bespectacled Buddy Holly and the Crickets. On December 1, Holly's band provided the free, fun, wholesome sound of "parentally approved" rock and roll as they played "That'll Be the Day" and "Peggy Sue" on Sullivan's show. There is almost no trace of R & B in Holly's rock sound, and despite the patriarchal, misogynistic theme of "That'll Be the Day," Sullivan's audience only noticed the fresh energy and good-times feeling that Holly projected through his Stratocaster guitar, youthful smile, and "this could be any nice boy" image.

For the band's second appearance, Sullivan tried to get Holly to play something other than "Oh, Boy!" because the raw energy in the song's bridge threatened to take the sound back into rebellious territory. Holly refused, and Sullivan cut the set to one song: "Oh, Boy!" That song became a rousing success, so Sullivan had no choice but to invite Holly back. A headstrong Holly replied that no amount of money would bring him and the Crickets back to Sullivan's show again. A little over a year after Holly's second performance on the *The Ed Sullivan Show*, he was killed in a plane crash.

Despite the constraints that television put on the rock and roll performances in the 1950s, radio, the recording industry, and live concerts needed the full energy and passion of this music to continue to draw listeners. Presley performed without constraints at live shows while Jerry Lee Lewis pounded and stomped on his piano with abandon at other performances (Palmer 2008; Jones, Meyrowitz, and Salzman 1995). Throughout the period, Little Richard's "Tutti Frutti," "Long Tall Sally," "Heeby Jeebies," "Bama Lama, Bama Loo," "Hound Dog," "Rip It Up," and "A Whole Lotta Shakin' Goin' On" upped the tempo of rock and brought back some of the raw R & B feel that most white rock stars either could not or would not project (Medovoi 2005; White 1984). Chuck Berry tore up the stage with guitar riffs and antics that raised the bar well above Danny Cedrone's, and more black R & B singers began to migrate over to the emerging genre (Palmer 2008). It is at this point that the sound of rock becomes complicated.

By 1957, as Leerom Modovoi (2005) maintains, there are three major styles of rock: R & B rock, country rock, and pop rock. Pop rock "combined musical and lyrical elements from R & B and country with Tin Pan Alley sounds, especially for its favorite genre, the love ballad" (p. 115). The "teenage idols"—Paul Anka, Pat Boone, Tab Hunter, Ricky Nelson, Cliff Richards, Bobby Rydell, Neil Sedaka, Bobby Vee, and Bobby Vinton, as well as their female counterparts, Marcie Blane, Teresa Brewer, Sandra Dee,

Shelley Fabares, Connie Francis, Annette Funicello, Lesley Gore, Brenda Lee, Little Peggy March, Linda Scott, Connie Stevens, and Natalie Wood—blended a smooth sound and lyrics that searched through feelings that teens of the era could relate to directly. This style required a softer, more flowing melody and lyric than did up-tempo rock and roll. Yet both types of rock distinguish teens from adults. Consider "Puppy Love," a pop rock song written and recorded by Paul Anka for his girlfriend Annette Funicello in 1960. It marks a different part of the generation gap between teens and their parents, who could never understand the desperate passion of the young singer: "How can I, oh how can I tell them? / This is not a puppy love!" (Anka [1960] 2012). Similarly, songs such as Dion and the Belmonts' "I Wonder Why," the Drifters' "There Goes My Baby," Danny and the Juniors' "Daydreamer," the Chantels' "Maybe," or the Diamonds' "Why Do Fools Fall in Love?" used a predominantly doo-wop sound to express teenage angst. Although the pop rock sound was a far cry from the harder rock of Presley, Berry, Lewis, Little Richard, or even Holly or Valens, it also distinguished the teen world from the adult one.

The "classic" backbeat sounds of "Bo Diddley," "Rock Around the Clock," or "Hound Dog"; the softer, smoother hits of the teenage idols, such as "Put Your Head on My Shoulder," "Poor Little Fool," "I've Told Every Little Star," or "I'm Sorry"; and the doo-wop tunes such as "Runaround Sue," "My Girl," or "Will You Still Love Me Tomorrow?"—all have at least one thing in common. This rock and roll music reaches the soul because of the way it makes listeners feel when they hear it. At the same time, the music, the market, and the audience that rock and roll "revealed and created," as Marcus (2014:17) explains, challenged the status quo. Because of a growing sense that "the world in which their parents had come of age had changed or in some deeper, inexpressible manner disappeared," teens wanted music that let them feel the authenticity of their new and different world, even if the feeling only lasted a minute and a half. And so it remains today—artists try to find the sounds that will resonate with teenagers searching for something that separates them from their parents, expresses their lives, and moves their bodies and souls. Alarmist views aside, Snow did understand why the teens of his day were drawn to the beat of rock and roll music.

A RIVER OF MANY STREAMS

Rock and roll's exuberant, youthful physicality and its rebel image combine to form one of the fundamental aspects of this genre as a pure type construct, but a second is equally as important. Rock and roll emerged from the blending of several musical genres, and there is a constant return to rock's roots as artists put their own personalized twist on the sound to entertain and comment on particular public issues of social structure. Freed, the celebrity DJ credited with giving the musical style its name, noted that rock is "a river of music which has absorbed many streams—rhythm and blues, jazz, ragtime, cowboy songs, country songs, folk songs—all have contributed greatly to the big beat" (Rosenberg and Subotsky 1956). Cyndi Lauper emphasizes the opportunity that the many streams making up rock and roll open up for contemporary artists. Like others, Lauper draws from rock's roots and blends them with more contemporary work to continually create an innovative, developing sound. Lauper (2014) puts "a lot of things together" in her songs, "a bit of Elvis Presley, a bit of Billie Holiday, a bit of Big Maybelle, a bit of Frankie Lymon, Joni Mitchell, everything that I hear." She borrows from the Police, the Clash, and R & B:

> If it was a rock song I thought hell yeah let's take all of the pieces of things that I absolutely love and put them together. We were all listening to this music anyway and we loved it. It was just incorporating bits of it, just little bits of it to have the flavour of something new and build on that. (Lauper 2014)

Rock, then, is an amalgam of different musical styles that artists throughout rock's short history have creatively drawn upon and blended with contemporary influences—musical, social, and political—to produce a cultural form that remains fresh, innovative, and often edgy and rebellious.

Aimed primarily at teens, rock and roll has to be current and move with the trends and issues of the day. To achieve that end, singer-songwriters frequently return to rock's roots, transporting some of those early styles into the present and mixing them to produce a continually evolving, contemporary sound that resonates in a new and creative way with each new generation on the brink of the adult world. Four artists who are not normally considered together—Etta James, Beyoncé, Christina Aguilera, and Adele—can serve as examples of how work from the past is woven into the present to produce those different, innovative twists that keep rock and popular music vibrant and relevant for teens.

Etta James, who died in 2012, was a gritty pioneer of rock music. She has been described as having a "rage to survive"; soothed by drugs and alcohol, she kept herself alive with her music (James and Ritz 1995). James's artistry spans blues, R & B, soul, rock and roll, jazz, and gospel. It has placed her in four different halls of fame: Rock and Roll, Blues, Rockabilly, and Grammy. James began in blues and R & B in the 1950s, achieving her best R & B successes between 1960 and 1965. In the 1970s, she ventured into rock and roll. She played alongside rock greats such as Chuck Berry, Eric Clapton, Alice Cooper, Bo Diddley, Jimi Hendrix, the Rolling Stones, and Tina Turner, to name a few. James returned to her jazz and R & B roots in the 1990s (James and Ritz 1995). Her rock style, one that keeps the R & B elements alive but with a stronger backbeat, comes through forcefully in songs such as "Money (That's What I Want)." It was her version of the song that launched Motown and has been covered since by the Beatles, the Rolling Stones, Freddie and the Dreamers, the Doors, the Kingsmen, the Flying Lizards, and many more artists.

James's music exemplifies rock as the "river" Freed describes; it draws from so many sources and then becomes a source in its own right. James's style and emotional range span from the deep bluesy emptiness of inescapable abandonment in "I'd Rather Go Blind" through to the strident confidence of her own style of rock and roll in "Tell Mama."

Beyoncé, the "Queen Bey" of popular music today, is a striking contrast to James. In 2009, Beyoncé performed at Barack Obama's first presidential inaugural ball. Four years later, she closed Obama's second inauguration ceremonies with an effortlessly regal rendering of "The Star Spangled Banner." Raising her left arm, as well as the pitch, during the final phrase—"home of the brave"—Beyoncé repeated *"the braaaave"* in her powerful, melismatic style to triumphantly finish with her left arm outstretched and her head high, as if she were celebrating her own inauguration rather than Obama's. She then basked briefly in the grandeur of the moment, allowed Obama a quick kiss on her cheek, and strolled away elegantly to the resounding applause of the crowd and the president (ABC News 2013). Two weeks later, Beyoncé dominated the largest stage in the United States—the Super Bowl XLVII halftime show (Knowles 2013). James never experienced such formal recognition or public esteem of this magnificence or magnitude.

It is not a surprise that upon learning Beyoncé would play her in the 2008 film, *Cadillac Records*, James was sceptical: "She's going to have a hill to climb, because Etta James ain't been no angel" (cited in Marcus 2014:87). Could Beyoncé identify enough with James to genuinely capture the sound she had blended together from the social, political, and musical forces that had made her a fighter, survivor, and innovator? To the surprise of many, Beyoncé's masterful performance of "All I Could Do Was Cry" was a resounding tribute to James and the music she had crafted over the years (Martin 2008).

Buoyed by such respect from a contemporary artist, James was soon deeply embittered when, a year after the release of *Cadillac Records*, Obama chose Beyoncé to sing James's heart-touching "At Last" at his first presidential inaugural ball (Marcus 2014). Missing from Beyoncé's interpretation that night were the years of pain and anguish that made James's "At Last"—and the dream the song says she has finally found—so emotionally powerful. Beyoncé's drawn out opening was smooth and clear but it lacked James's deeply embodied, emancipatory triumph. Perhaps James's craggy vocals would have been too emotional for the inaugural ball of the first black president—but after all her struggles through the Jim Crow era, James deserved the opportunity to serenade that particular dream coming alive ... at last.

Beyoncé has never identified James as a major influence. Given the opportunity, Beyoncé went deep into the roots of James's diverse repertoire and brought one specific, deeply emotional song to life in 2008, but she sang it much as it had been sung in the mid-twentieth century. At Obama's inaugural ball, Beyoncé used tradition differently, giving "At Last" the elegance she felt appropriate for the occasion. It was the interpretation of a wealthy, secure, image-conscious, pop-music icon; it was not the original sound of the poor, black, female singer—struggling for survival, recognition, and love—who first gave the song life. Others have approached James's work differently.

Aguilera, like James, works in a variety of styles—R & B, blues, soul, jazz, and rock. She acknowledges that James is her major source of inspiration, although Aguilera's range, melismatic style, and vocal clarity make her a completely different singer (Aguilera 2012). Like James, however, Aguilera's work has emphasized themes of independence and self-determination. Although her 1999 debut album, *Christina Aguilera*, is primarily a market-driven, "teen pop" collection, it contains an interesting twist. Aguilera's songs focus on explicit feminine sexuality and even female sexual dominance. Other artists had previously expressed themes of female independence and power: Cyndi Lauper in "Girls Just Want to Have Fun" (1983), Madonna in "Material Girl" (1985) and "Express Yourself" (1987), No Doubt's "I'm Just a Girl" (1995), and the Spice Girls in "Wannabe" (1996). But Aguilera's approach is different. The muted R & B sound provides the background for a return to the sexually explicit lyrics characteristic of many black R & B songs of the 1940s—though with a gender reversal regarding who is in control. In "What a Girl Wants," "Genie in a Bottle," or "Come on Over Baby (All I Want is You)," the focus is on what a woman desires and needs, which is often a man who gives her sexual pleasure. Moreover, these needs are described without euphemisms or substitutions such as "oh rutti," showing how far commercial interests, in a "24/7" YouTube world, can resist the pressures that have historically pulled the sound and lyrics of rock and roll back toward mainstream respectability. Now, even teen pop is explicit.

Aguilera's fourth studio album, *Stripped*, shows a far more overt "Jamesian" independence. "Can't Hold Us Down," featuring Lil' Kim, is an R & B, hip hop mix of female defiance and sexual independence that conveys the overall theme of the album—respect—though in very different terms than Aretha Franklin's version in 1967. "Fighter's" strong rock sound makes the connection between Aguilera and James, in a contemporary context, much more evident. Refusing to be defeated by others' abuse, nothing is forgotten, and the remembering makes the singer become stronger, work harder, and grow into wisdom—it makes her a fighter. "Dirrrty" and "Get Mine,

Get Yours" are powerful extensions to "Can't Hold Us Down"—there is no question that the fighter now controls her own destiny, even in the intimate world of sexuality. Aguilera is inspired by James's rebellious independence as much as she is by her movement among the different styles that flow within the rock and roll river. Aguilera channels James to address issues that resonate with today's teens, pushing them to see beyond the sexual stereotypes that still hold young women down at the turn of the twenty-first century.

Adele contrasts significantly with Aguilera and James, although Adele (2009) acknowledges that James is her favourite singer. In fact, James's rendition of "Fool That I Am" is the song that inspired her to become a singer-songwriter. Adele has a far greater vocal range than James ever did, but even though Adele writes from her own experiences and conveys them with tremendous emotion, her covers of James's "I Just Wanna Make Love to You" and "Fool That I Am" do not have the same deep resonance that James managed to deliver—the two women's lives have been too different, and although James is a source of inspiration for Adele, other streams that have flowed into Adele's sound take her music to another part of the river.

Like James and Aguilera, Adele is extremely versatile, drawing from blues, R & B, and some rock. Adele has the same ability as James to bring her audience into her inner emotional world, sharing her pain, regret, love, or hope. Whether she is singing "Rolling in the Deep" in front of a classic rock band (lead, rhythm, bass guitars, drum kit, and two backup singers) or an acoustic version of "Daydreamer," Adele's voice carries one along an emotional journey that easily rivals the music and feeling that ultimately blended into the rock and roll sound.

All music reaches into the emotions—each genre in its own way—and rock is no exception. Classic rock brought a driving beat to an electrified blend of blues, R & B, jump blues, gospel, country, and elements of jazz. The combination produced a sound with, as Alice Cooper expresses it, "a certain amount of outlaw" to it (Jones, Meyrowitz, and Salzman 1995). To remain relevant to each new generation of teens, artists frequently return to the musical streams that first blended into the rock sound and, to use Lauper's (2014) words, incorporate "just little bits of it to have the flavour of something new." James lived through the first coming together of the river, and she travelled along with it as it pulled in more streams and was contoured by the social landscape. Aguilera, throughout her musical career, has drunk deeply from James's sound and inspiration, but she turned pop's current in a direction that encouraged and challenged girls, women, and female artists to express themselves with greater freedom and creativity. Beyoncé, called by *Forbes* magazine the most powerful female musician of 2015, has used her blend of R & B, pop, and rock to become an astounding commercial success. And Adele, whose career began with an Internet posting, has revisited the traditional roots of R & B and created a haunting blues sound with her uniquely clear and powerful voice, which, at its best, lets the listener explore the darkest depths of loss. Crossing and merging genres, and returning to its roots to renew itself, rock is a river made up of, and breaking into, many streams.

TWO SIDES OF THE COIN: THE DIALECTIC OF EMOTIONS

The third element of rock and roll as a pure type is the dialectic between simplicity, joy, and freedom, on the one hand, and loss, resignation, a brooding fear that sometimes becomes terror, and oppression, on the other. That tension often exists within the different sounds of a specific artist or group and occurs throughout the history of rock.

When Sullivan brought Buddy Holly and the Crickets to his show, he wanted the audience to hear the simple joy, innocence, and wholesome yearning of "Peggy Sue"—and to identify these emotions with rock and roll. That same "rock-is-fun" attitude comes through in "Rave On," "Everyday," "Well … Alright," "It's So Easy," and "Oh Boy!"—and it shaped the memorable, buoyant sound of Holly and the Crickets. What made Holly unique was his use of guitar to play a "rhythm lead"—that is, Holly played all six strings on his guitar when he played a lead, accentuating the sound by continuously using the down stroke (Spence [1991] 2004).

Holly also explored the yearning side of teen life in "True Love Ways"—a very mellow, searching song for Holly—or in one of his earliest records, "Blue Days, Black Nights." On an Amex tape recorder he purchased in December 1958, just over a month before his death, Holly left some rough takes of several personal songs that he was writing. In these songs one hears Holly's trademark vocals, the rhythm line carried on an acoustic guitar, and some upbeat riffs in the bridges, especially in "Crying, Waiting, Hoping" and "Peggy Sue Got Married," for example. These qualities maintained an optimistic tenor, even when his songs were about what seemed to be or had been lost (Holly [1958] 2009). Despite conveying pain, Holly's expressions of sorrow are overshadowed by his own personal confidence and the optimism of the times.

The Beatles, too, had many light-hearted, optimistic hits, especially early on. Indeed, there is a connection between the Fab Four and Buddy Holly and the Crickets in that the Beatles came to have this name partly because the group's early repertoire, as the Quarry Men, included several of Holly's songs, for example, "That'll Be the Day." The group decided to play up the association between crickets and beetles—as well as between the homonyms "beetles," the bugs, and "Beatles," as in the "beat music" of rock and roll (Persails 1996). Like Holly, the Beatles were on the "light" side of the joy-sorrow tension. Just consider the clear joy, simplicity, and energy in so many of the group's hits—"I Want to Hold Your Hand,"

"It Won't Be Long," "I Saw Her Standing There," "Love Me Do," "Please, Please Me," and "Paperback Writer."

In numbers such as "Yesterday" and "Hey Jude," the Beatles also stay on the lighter side of loss and sorrow. Like Holly, the Beatles never explored the full depths of the fearful, brooding, and oppressive side of the dialectic. "Let It Be" and "Nowhere Man" express both sides of the tension, as the prayed for or the lost are given words of solace—Mother Mary's words of wisdom or "don't worry / take your time / don't hurry" because someone will lend a hand. Can religion or patience, waiting for inspiration really be the answer? But both songs are in C major, which prevent them from falling into the abyss of resignation.

The music of another British rock band, the Libertines, shows how time, place, sound, and lyrics can give expression to both sides of the dialectic.[113] "Time for Heroes" is a complex song that blends dark lyrics with, as Julian Lee notes, "loud, jangly guitars being played through Vox amplifiers, harkening back to the sounds of the British Invasion period in music history."[114] So the music of a simpler time presents scenes of Wombles being beaten with truncheons, youths coughing up blood, people being trapped all their lives in the same class, the Americanization of British culture, and something so obscene only *Treasure Island*'s drunk, Bill Bones, could understand it. In addition, the Libertines temper these images by using particular chord progressions: "use of a major V chord and then the minor V chord is a progression utilised prolifically by the Beatles. This creates a sense of romance musically."[115]

Written in the aftermath of the 2001 May Day riots in London in which Libertine Pete Doherty was an active participant, "Time for Heroes" was an attempt to emancipate and motivate the listener to take action against the grim reality depicted in the lyrics (see Left, Jeffery, and Perrone 2001; Whaite and Doherty 2004). In the mayhem of May Day 2001, Doherty saw the potential for change through unified action directed toward identifiable goals:

> [Y]ou've got this unrest, this general feeling that things are wrong. But you call it anti-capitalism—and you can pick that apart bit by bit, and show where that's wrong and doesn't make sense—but basically you've got a heading for it, and you can channel it there. It's a direction, and it's the right direction, and people notice—anti-capitalism, pro-society, pro-equality, anti-inequality. That's the way I see it. (Whaite and Doherty 2004)

---

113 My thanks to Julian Lee, in particular, and to his Jack the Lads bandmates, Paddy Beirne and Will Macquarrie, for the suggestion to include the Libertines and also for the insight and analysis they gave me on this group's music.

114 Email message to author, February 3, 2016.

115 Email message to author, February 3, 2016.

Green Day's "American Idiot," is the obverse of "Time for Heroes."[116] The instrumentation is driving, straightforward, upbeat, and contagious. As Lee emphasizes, the song utilizes only three major chords—"a staple in fun, energetic, rock and roll"—to produce "the harmonic qualities that the modern music listener instinctively associates with happiness." The sonic aesthetics "include loud, distorted guitars; heavy drums in standard rock and roll, 4/4 time; and a simple driving bass line—all of which culminate in an incredibly joyful listening experience."[117] Unlike Doherty and the Libertines, however, Green Day wanted the lyrics to sink into the listener. The music is upbeat and captivating, but because listeners focus on and enjoy its beat, the lyrics, in an almost subliminal manner, bring the harsh realities of America in the post–9/11 world into their conscious minds. Do you want to be an American idiot? Are you part of the redneck agenda, controlled by the media, accepting the propaganda, paranoia, and hysteria? Or do you feel the tension running through the nation's alienation, calling out to "idiot America" that we are not meant to follow because everything is not okay? The song sets up the entire album, which presents songs about struggling against apathy, resignation, and oppression. These idiocies can be overcome, according to Green Day, although the odds against success are tremendous (Green Day 2004a).

Other songs on this album offer music that focuses on the anomie and alienation that Green Day felt was paralysing Americans and preventing them from actively taking control of their lives. In the "Boulevard of Broken Dreams," Green Day (2004b) uses heavy instrumentation and minor chords to pound away at a futility the band wants to shake out of its listeners. The images in this song's official video are desolate and disturbing—a chrome hood ornament of a hand holding a grenade, devastated fields, and abandoned homes, gas pumps, mailboxes, and streets. These create a brooding fear that, as band members walk past and see fleeting glimpses of historical injustices, no one will act to create change. Green Day builds an ominous sense of anxiety and possible terror. Walking alone will leave those dreams broken and life barren.

"Wake Me Up When September Ends" may be the most moving song on the *American Idiot* album because Billie Joe Armstrong wrote the song about his father's death. In the video, however, the song takes on several layers of meaning—all of them haunting. A young man and woman want the love they feel to never end; they promise to stay together forever. Keeping those moments of youthful love alive forever seems so simple, initially, and the images the video presents are joyful and free. But the young man joins

---

116 I am again indebted to Julian Lee and Jack the Lads for this particular recommendation from Green Day's works.

117 Email message to author, February 3, 2016.

the military, leaves for combat, and shatters the couple's moment forever. The promise is broken. The young man who has the courage to take up what he believes is the country's cause—a young man not much different from the Dixie Chicks' 18-year-old "Traveling Soldier" who dies in Vietnam—is taken in another war. And like the girl "with a bow in her hair" that the Dixie Chicks sing about, another young woman is left to endure and ask the same unanswerable questions. Who pays the cost, why, and what would happen if he or she refused to go?

Pink's "Dear Mr. President," released in 2006, takes up many of Green Day's themes but in a straightforward manner with the lyrics matching the instrumentation.[118] While Green Day sees an America blinded by the media and propaganda, Pink's citizens are painfully aware of the realities of poverty, homelessness, mothers losing children without the chance to say goodbye, and the ostracism faced by the LGBT community. She tells the president what hard work is—rebuilding a house blown away by bombs, struggling on minimum-wage pay to support a family, and making do and improvising with anything one can scrounge. Pink is correct: no world leader would want to take that walk with her.

As low as she takes us with "Dear Mr. President," Pink turns those issues on their head in "Raise Your Glass"—a fully upbeat, energy-filled, "Don't be fancy, just get dancy" set of lyrics, vocals, and sound. Images of Norman Rockwell's "Rosie the Riveter," high school nerds, skaters, "gangsta" spoofers, and university graduates flash by in the official video version. Just as she does in "Stupid Girls," Pink uses the upbeat energy of a light, driving rock sound to shatter stereotypes; some of these are trivial, but others related to gender, sexuality, and social marginalization are significant. Pink's refrain—"So raise your glass if you are wrong / In all the right ways, all my underdogs / We will never be, never be anything but loud"—gives voice to those who are silenced by oppressive high-school norms, for example.

As powerful and probing as the music, lyrics, and videos of The Libertines, Green Day, and Pink may be, even as they mix optimistic themes in their work, other artists have created combinations of image and sound that epitomize how rock music can embody the dialectic of hope and fear, joy and sorrow, freedom and oppression, and contentment and resignation. Rihanna's official video version of "American Oxygen" is one such work.[119] The song begins with a deep, sombre piano playing, as, in the video, the person who walks up and sits on the steps of city hall is soon obscured by the shadows of people marching in front. This is the first conflicting image to decode. Are these the protesters of another police shooting, civil

---

118 My thanks to Nicole Hills for reminding me of Pink's "Dear Mr. President" and her further suggestion to explore "Raise Your Glass."

119 I am indebted to Nicole Hills for suggesting that I examine Rihanna's "American Oxygen."

rights marchers from the 1960s, or immigrants hoping to find prosperity in the United States? Rihanna first appears walking—the stripes of the American flag in the background—a black female immigrant climbing the steps to city hall to become a citizen. A close-up of Obama taking his oath as president briefly appears. The video cuts back to Rihanna, with the flag still in the background, and she starts singing the very simple chorus that Sam Harris crafted with his co-writers Rihanna and Alex Da Kid (Stutz 2015)—"Breathe out, breathe in / American oxygen." The simplicity of the chorus and Rihanna's clear voice give the song emotional power right at the outset. Such perfection did not come easily: "It took three or four months, going back and forth, back and forth" while Kid revised the sound track to create that impact, Harris points out (cited in Stutz 2015). The song itself took almost a year to write.

Rihanna and Kid, Harris notes, were the ones who suggested that the song should be framed from the perspective of an immigrant coming to the United States and breathing in the air of America. Forty-five seconds into the video, a homemade cardboard sign appears showing a vote for "A. Nation of Immigrants" rather than "B. Nation of Ignorance" (Rihanna 2015). This theme returns several times in different guises throughout the video— immigrants wave the flag after their citizenship ceremony, illegal immigrants steal across the border, and police patrol the border wall.

While writing the lyrics, Harris listened to a lot of Bruce Springsteen, particularly "Born in the U.S.A." As Harris acknowledges,

> [Springsteen] gets that there's pride to living here in this country. This country is great and has the potential to be something really, really incredible, but there are a lot of problems that we don't acknowledge, and it's important to shed light on both those things. (Quoted in Stutz 2015)

That is precisely what "American Oxygen" does so well, although not in the traditional manner. Harris's lyrics are sparse and simple; they complement and at appropriate moments accentuate complex visual footage displaying contradictory images of the American Dream.

The video "American Oxygen" presents a kaleidoscope of images that evoke fear, hope, terror, pride, horror, and despair. Dark tragic events are depicted: the mushroom clouds of the first atomic bomb tests, the twin towers of the World Trade Center aflame, the assassinations of President Kennedy and Martin Luther King Jr., Americans fighting in Vietnam and Iraq, the Klan burning a cross. Images of homelessness, poverty, and racism are juxtaposed with ones of victory and pride: Marines raising the flag at Iwo Jima, Don Larsen's perfect game in the World Series, fireworks over the Statue of Liberty, astronauts heading into space, the lunar landing, firefighters and others working in the rubble of 9/11. Video clips are taken from various decades. All portray the struggle for the American Dream and for justice. There are shots of the Occupy Wall Street movement, of the unemployment lines during the Great Depression, of people perched on the top of freight cars searching for work during the Dust Bowl, of protesters with Molotov cocktails, and of oil production and car manufacturing in the 1950s and 2000s. Many images depict the heroic but brutal struggle for racial integration.

Amid it all, Rihanna keeps returning to the new America, and an optimism in the lyrics challenges the deep, sombre music in the background. In contrast to the images of a boy hustling drugs on the street, for example, the lyrics say, "But he can be anything at all." The dualism is also presented in the reverse: the solemn music is juxtaposed with images of young children, their faces full of faith in the future, breathing in American oxygen. They are "the new America."

Though few can rival Rihanna's ability to capitalize on the purely commercial side of rock music, which she does in songs such as "Don't Stop the Music" or the provocative "Only Girl in the World" or "Rude Boy," her "American Oxygen" is completely different. Here Rihanna performs a complex work of art that confronts the viewer with numerous juxtaposed images, a sombre musical score, and lyrics that convey the complexity of the American Dream while remaining optimistic about the future. This song is an excellent example of the way in which popular music can carry and convey a duality of emotion.

In addition to this characteristic of expressing emotion (and sometimes emotional duality), three things have been consistent across the 60-year history of rock and roll. First, it has met resistance in every one of its phases, and, on each occasion, rock and roll has adapted to the times while also forcing the times to accept its changing sound. Second, to keep rock and roll's creative edge alive, singers, songwriters, and musicians have continually drawn from the original roots of this music and built on classic and contemporary artists' work to keep the beat going. Finally, rock and roll succeeds because the music speaks to teenage audiences through lyrics, sound, and, more recently, images. Rock is successful because of "how it feels … what it does to you."

Culture as a "Pure Type" and Rock and Roll as Culture

Those who feared the demise of culture in the modern era found much to worry about when rock and roll started to become a mainstream entertainment form. Similar concerns run throughout rock's 60-year history because rock and roll is a commodity, and it cannot escape the levelling down pressures of the economic market, as entrepreneurs try to create and then meet mass-market tastes with mass-produced commodities. Despite their enormous creative artistry, Presley, Holly, the Beatles, the Rolling Stones, the Beach Boys, the Mamas and Papas, the Chantels, the Ronettes, the Supremes, Michael Jackson, Pink Floyd, the Doors, Hendrix, Nirvana, Pearl Jam, Metallica, Green Day, and the Red Hot Chili Peppers—really, all successful rock bands and performers—have found a style and sound that they turn into a formula to stay on top. Rock and roll is, above all else, a business, and successful businesses find what sells and then, with small adjustments to spur further demand, keep producing what has proven to be successful. Rock and roll is no more immune than any other type of cultural entertainment to the pressures of the "culture industry" that Horkheimer and Adorno ([1944] 1972) identify. The formula for success revolves around the production and reproduction of easily created and then passively consumed entertainment. "The less the culture industry has to promise, the less it can offer a meaningful explanation of life, and the emptier is the ideology it disseminates" (p. 147).

However, despite the pressures of the market, as the examples used in the foregoing discussion show, rock, throughout its history, has met all the criteria that one would find in a pure type construct of high culture.

Leavis and Thompson (1933) identify the importance of culture's roots extending deeply within a community. Rock and roll does this in two significant ways. First, the streams that converge to create the river of rock and roll have a long lineage in the North American experience. Blues, R & B, jump blues, soul, ragtime, folk, and country, blended in different ways by various artists, make rock and roll as much the music of the people as any one of those forms alone. Second, rock and roll is also firmly rooted in the community of teens and youths. It may be that one's tastes in popular music are formed and consolidated in the teen years and that each new generation of teens identifies with a remade and different rock trend, but as each cohort ages, it takes its music along for the duration.

Arnold ([1868] 1932) wants culture to address the issues that "matter most to humanity." It should turn "a stream of fresh and free thought upon our stock notions and habits" (p. 6). The songs of Bill Haley and the Comets, Little Richard, Presley, Berry, and Holly may not have turned a fresh stream of thought on the nation's stock notions and habits, but their music and actions, and the reactions of teens and the public to both, certainly drew attention to some of the issues that do matter most to humanity—issues of racial integration, freedom of expression, and family relationships, to name only three. Later rock stars such as the Beatles, Hendrix, and Crosby, Stills, Nash and Young address issues of peace and war, as do Green Day and Pink within a different social context. Springsteen, the Libertines, Pink, and even Rihanna force their listeners (or viewers, as rock becomes a multimedia experience) to rethink stock notions and habits, to examine their everyday lives and the decisions they do and do not make.

All of the artists discussed in this chapter explore "the diversity, complexity and strangeness of [human] experience" (Hoggart 1970:11). Adele's smooth vocals and tremendous range take her listeners deeply within themselves while James achieves the same result with her own harsh, raw, searching sound. Sometimes the message is carried by a simple melody and profound lyrics, as in Pink's "Dear Mr. President"; at other times, multimedia creations like "Wake Me Up When September Ends" and "Time for Heroes" challenge those experiencing them to break out of their conventional understandings of the world in which they live.

A pure cultural form, Hoggart (1970) argues, "re-creates the texture of [lived] experience" and encourages people to "look at life with all the vulnerability, honesty and penetration they can command" (p. 11). Holly's Amex tape recording, in all of its unfinished purity, embodies a genuine vulnerability in not just the lyrics and sound but also the timing and symbolic nature of the tapes left in his apartment.

Far from the Huxleyan-Marcusean world of simplified satisfactions and one-dimensionality, Aguilera's "Stripped Intro," "Can't Hold Us Down," and "Fighter" turn the world upside down and inside out. Each song, building from one to the next, strips away conventional wisdom and stereotypes to produce images of female pride, self-confidence, independence, and respect.

Postman (1985), Gabler (1998), Carr (2011), Rose (2013), and Gardner and Davis (2014) all express reservations about the impact of digital culture and the Internet on contemporary culture and how and what one may learn. Although the appeal of rock and roll is largely in how the beat makes the music "crazy man, crazy," the success of Dick Clark's *American Bandstand* and the furor over Presley's various television appearances show that, even early on, rock and roll was popular because it was highly visual. As the music video replaced the single as the most consumed musical medium, the message came to be carried in the juxtaposition of the music and powerful imagery. "Boulevard of Broken Dreams" and "American Oxygen" are two examples. The medium is the message for McLuhan (1964) because the medium "shapes and controls the scale and form of human association and action" (p. 9). Because of the manner in which today's music videos are crafted, they remain largely "cool media" that free the mind from the linear confines of print culture. The images, lyrics, and sound all require interpretation. Sometimes, as in "Time for Heroes," the chording and instrumentation are meant to override the apparent message in the lyrics. At other times, in "Boulevard of Broken Dreams," for example, the lyrics, images, and sound coalesce to create a single, cohesive message—not necessarily one the artists want their fans to accept, but a coherent message to which the audience can respond.

"Fighter" is another example of how music videos, disseminated around the globe through the Internet, are the challenging, opening, and thought-expanding cool media that McLuhan values. The sound, lyrics, and imagery in "Fighter" create the grotesque that Ruskin marvels about and McLuhan enthuses over. "A fine grotesque," Ruskin (1885) writes, "is the expression, in a moment, by a series of symbols thrown together in bold and fearless connection, of truths which it would have taken a long time to express in any verbal way, and of which the connection is left for the beholder to work out for himself" (p. 93). That is what contemporary rock videos provide.

Rock and roll has embraced the Internet and its multimedia possibilities, just as it has encompassed other aspects of culture and various streams of music throughout its history. Indeed, rock and roll's ability to recreate itself in response to each new generation is responsible for its longevity. It did not die with the plane crash that killed Buddy Holly, as suggested by the famous lines in Don McLean's "American Pie." In response to that song and to the numerous inaccuracies in *The Buddy Holly Story*, Sonny Curtis—who had played rhythm guitar in Holly and the Two Tones before Holly formed the Crickets—sang his own "Buddy Holly Story." It ends with a truth that all teenagers who have heard the music know, even if they have never heard of Holly—"The levy ain't dry and the music didn't die / Because Buddy Holly lives every time we play rock and roll" (Spence [1991] 2004).

Questions for Review and Further Reflection

1. When you think of rock and roll, which artists come to mind? What makes their music "rock?"
2. This chapter notes that "rock is the soundtrack for many an individual's youth." Do you feel this is true for yourself? What genres or songs have shaped your youth so far?
3. This chapter identifies the movies *American Graffiti*, *Grease*, *Dirty Dancing*, *Forrest Gump*, and *Boyhood* as examples of how rock and roll does more than play in the background; it shapes the movie as a whole. How does music shape the story in these films? List a few other films in which the soundtrack shapes the story, and detail how and in what way this shaping occurs.
4. Describe the main issues involved in the interplay between social context and the development of rock and roll in the 1950s.
5. Dore Schary argues that "movies do not lead public opinion, they reflect it." Think about contemporary films: to what extent do you agree with Schary's claim?
6. Think about your favourite contemporary rock artist. How can this artist's music be seen as an amalgamation, influenced by previous artists and other genres?
7. How does this chapter illustrate the strengths of pure type analysis? Are there weaknesses to pure type analysis that become evident in this

discussion of rock and roll? Think of another musical genre—how would you go about defining this genre as a pure type?

8. Do you agree with the statement that rock and roll is rooted in the community of teens and youth in particular? If so, what implications does this have for rock and roll as a cultural form, and if not, how would you answer that same question?

9. Arnold argues that culture should address the issues that "matter most to humanity." In today's world, what do you think these issues are? Which songs or artists do you believe meet this standard?

10. If you were to provide a third case study for the pure type analysis of culture, what cultural form would you choose? Why would you choose that form of cultural production, and what aspects of the cultural form would you focus on when developing your pure type?

THE PROMISE OF SOCIOLOGY

This text has introduced students to sociology by focusing on its classical tradition, on three of sociology's most significant thinkers, and on the manner in which C. Wright Mills draws the tradition's key elements together in his concept "the sociological imagination." In the final analysis, Mills (1959) argues, sociologists working in the classical tradition examine "history and biography and the relations between the two within society" (p. 6). This, Mills maintains, constitutes sociology's task and promise.

Mills's (1959) neat formulation and the three sets of questions that he proposed to guide a sociologist's work are necessary for any study "to complete its intellectual journey" (p. 6). They also bring a helpful unity to what is, in fact, a complex and internally divided tradition. Although this unifying formulation is helpful, it is also important to understand where the differences, tensions, and divisions lie so that one can use the classical tradition critically and perceptively—fully aware of many of the classical tradition's strengths, limitations, contradictions, and prospects for further development. To this end, this book has overviewed the work and thought of three key founders of sociology—Karl Marx, Émile Durkheim, and Max Weber—and indicated how their work arose from within earlier currents of thought and contributed to the formation of the classical tradition in sociology.

The classical tradition has two different interrelated yet also somewhat antagonistic strands running through it. Both strands were shaped by the social and intellectual currents of Renaissance and Enlightenment Europe; both share a fundamental belief in the power of human reason and the idea that there is an underlying order or rationality to the natural and social worlds.

The strand running from Bacon, Galileo, and Descartes to Montesquieu, Saint-Simon, and Comte emphasizes the central importance of observation and observationally based knowledge in the quest for knowing the underlying, law-like order of the natural and social worlds. This strand is tightly tied to the growing significance of the systematic observation of the empirical world that developed within the natural sciences, and its proponents sought to distance their analyses from the metaphysical debates and premises of classical philosophy and medieval theology. The ultimate reference point for this strand is the controlled methodology of experimental science. Although the human mind would, on the basis of precisely directed observation, seek to explain the law-like interconnections of the disparate parts of the natural or social worlds, for thinkers within this strand, the role of the mind was secondary to the status of empirical facts gained by dispassionate, objective observation and the interrelationships that could be observed and that others could replicate and verify.

Thinkers within the second strand that shaped the classical tradition include Descartes, Hume, Kant, Schelling, and Hegel. Before they would commit to trying to understand the empirical world, they wrestled with the fundamental question of metaphysics—what could the human mind really know? According to proponents of this strand, the mind plays a significant role in interpreting—in moving knowledge from a superficial understanding to one that grasps the natural and social worlds as a complex, integrated totality. Their view is that knowledge must be based upon fully developed reason. Below the level of appearance (reality), which one can observe, they argue, lies a deeper actuality or essence that the mind has to construct interpretively. The thorough theorization of the world, then, is centrally important because it is only through theory that one can know what to observe, what those observations mean, and how they fit together into the totality and full actuality of the natural or social world.

The first strand directly influenced Durkheim's image of sociology as a positive science and his approach to sociology, although he was also swayed by the German intellectual tradition. One of Durkheim's most important contributions to sociology—the concept of collective representation—is a theoretical construction. This construct arose from an empirically based understanding of how societies are held together, and it served as a guide for which social facts Durkheim would focus upon in later studies. However, the construct is also deeply tied to a theoretical, systematic conception of society as a *sui generis* entity. Nevertheless, despite the fundamental infusion of theory within his sociology, Durkheim advocated openly and passionately for the empirical nature of sociology. For him, collective representations were existing social facts for which there were various observable indicators, and one could know them indirectly through those indicators. Durkheim considered the *collective representations as real, existing social facts* (with each word emphasized separately and together as a whole). In the end, although Durkheim was fully aware of the role that theory plays in guiding observation, he believed that, in the last instance, sociology had to be—and should strive to become—an empirical, observationally based, positive science.

Marx began his intellectual development thoroughly immersed in the German idealist tradition—particularly in the work of Hegel—but he ultimately tried to move beyond idealism into an empirically informed analysis and understanding of different social formations. Marx's materialism centres on the intellectual construction of a holistic grasp of the dialectical complexity of capitalist society. Marx's critique of capitalism, however, stems from observation and the systematic study of the social world. Still, this examination took place within—and added to—a rationally constructed, theoretical comprehension of the underlying actuality of the social world. Drawing upon Saint-Simon and political economy, Marx turns Hegel's focus on the active mind into one that emphasizes the full creative capacities of human labour, and he uses this new conception of the dialectics of labour as the ontological foundation for understanding the complex totality of the social world and for changing it.

Weber's sociology rejects the first strand of the classical tradition; he does not seek to understand the social world using an approach rooted in the natural sciences. Instead, heavily influenced by Kant, Rickert, and Dilthey, Weber draws a sharp distinction between the methodology and objectives of the natural sciences (*Naturwissenschaften*) and the humanities and social sciences (*Geisteswissenschaften*). For Weber, sociology is the comprehensive study of social action and rests upon an interpretive approach to social life. Like Durkheim, Weber recognizes and emphasizes the importance of dominant frames of mind in the ordering and structuring of different social formations. Weber differs from Durkheim, however, regarding how one can best grasp the dominant frame of mind, as well as in his concern over the prospects for the future given the rise of goal-rational action to such prominence in modernity.

Nevertheless, although Weber rejects any notion of the unity of the sciences, he shares Durkheim's fundamental concerns about developing sociology as an observationally based undertaking that requires a complete commitment to the canons of science—the highest standards of dispassionate observation. Both agree—as does Marx—that one can only change the world when it has been correctly grasped, although all three have different standards concerning what is involved in fully comprehending the world.

In addition to presenting the key aspects of the classical tradition, this text explores the complex concept of culture—once in the context of the Millennials and Generation Z and their heavy reliance upon e-culture and the Internet and later in two case studies of how one might apply the sociological imagination to particular social phenomena.

Culture is, as Williams notes, one of the most complex words in the English language. Part of the analysis in the introduction and in Chapter 10 underscores why culture is such a complex concept. At the same time, the analysis of culture—particularly in Chapter 10—indicates that, despite its complexity, one can critically assess culture and evaluate how it contributes to the quality of social life.

Culture arises from human interaction with the material world within which human agents live. It is tied to the social relationships that shape people's indirect, mediated relationship with the natural world. At the same time, culture serves as a filter through which people view the social and natural worlds, and it influences their understandings and actions in their daily lives. It is for these reasons that thinkers as diverse as Marx, Durkheim, Weber, Arnold, Nietzsche, Leavis, Thompson, Adorno, Horkheimer, Marcuse, Hoggart, Williams, Postman, Gabler, Carr, Rose, and Gardner and Davis have all expressed different concerns about the social determination of culture. If culture becomes increasingly one dimensional, to use Marcuse's term, then people begin to lose the capacity to assess critically the society in which they live—they may be left with a sense of malaise and discontent, but they remain unsure of how to take those feelings further or of how to act upon and change their social circumstances.

Drawing its inspiration from the classical tradition in sociology, the sociological imagination helps people recognize that their personal troubles of milieu are tied to broader, public issues of social structure. The sociological perspective that develops from the intersection of personal biography, history, and social structure provides a more encompassing vantage point to assess the way forward critically.

The discussion of culture is tied to one more theme discussed in this text—the social world today that many term postmodern. The postmodern world and its associated postmodernist perspectives are, on the one hand, very different from modernity and the modernist perspective represented by the classical tradition. There are some who would reject all traces of modernist social thought in favour of thoroughly postmodernist approaches. This decision may ultimately prove correct, but it is not one that a sociologist should make without first fully exploring the critical and analytical power of sociology's centuries-old classical tradition. Understood properly, especially within the context of the public issues that exist in an increasingly globalized world, the classical tradition still offers penetrating insight into social concerns and social relationships. It is also the foundation upon which postmodernist theories developed, so those recent theories assume a detailed understanding of the various strands of social thought that are woven into sociology's classical tradition.

There is one more point to note about this text. In *Images of Man: The Classic Tradition in Sociological Thinking*—the companion volume to *The Sociological Imagination* (Mills 2000:136)—Mills (1960) notes that the sociological frame of reference can begin with "the acquisition of a vocabulary that is adequate for clear social reflection" (p. 17). Such a vocabulary requires "only some twenty or so pivotal terms" (Mills 1960:17). In reading

The Promise of Sociology, students have had the opportunity to start to build that vocabulary. Five terms that one might include in such a vocabulary are "the sociological imagination" and "intellectual craftsmanship" (from Mills), "class struggle" (from Marx), "collective representations" (from Durkheim), and "interpretive understanding" (from Weber).

Each of these terms is a shorthand—or rich symbol—for some of the central concerns of each thinker. Each term becomes useful as one draws upon the complex ideas that surround it and make it so central to the work of Mills, Marx, Durkheim, or Weber.

Students who have completed this book are now ready to take these terms and use them to explore some of sociology's main areas of concern— work, social inequality, deviant behaviour, war, and social movements, for example. Drawing upon an emerging language for critical reflection and the power of the sociological imagination, students can expand their vocabularies further while learning more about the social world in which they live. That is the promise of sociology now lying ahead.

GLOSSARY OF KEY TERMS AND NAMES

Abstraction: Abstraction is the mental process through which ideas or conceptions are formed by considering diverse objects, events, or thoughts and determining their essential features rather than their particular concrete properties. Weber's pure or ideal types are abstractions; they are created by abstracting from the infinite complexity of the real world to produce mental constructs (or conceptions) that isolate particular properties or characteristics of the phenomenon under study.

Adorno, Theodor (1903–69) and Max Horkheimer (1895–1973): German philosophers and sociologists, Adorno and Horkheimer were among the founding members of the Frankfurt school and the initiators of its particular form of critical theory. Their *Dialectic of Enlightenment* (1944) was a scathing analysis of what they called "the culture industries." They argued that culture and advertising have merged because the assembly-line nature of the culture industry and the indistinguishable hollow products it offers are perfectly

suited to the world of advertising. And advertising is like propaganda, offering half-truths and illusions to a public looking for simple solutions to its media-constructed wants. The freedom to choose, they note, turns out to be simply the freedom to choose from what is always the same.

Affective action: See *social action*.

Altruistic suicide: See *suicide*.

American Society of Composers, Authors, and Publishers (ASCAP): Established in 1914, ASCAP was an association of music writers, composers, and publishers who banded together to ensure they would receive the royalty payments due to them when their works were used by others.

Anomic suicide: See *suicide*.

Anomie: Often described as a state of normlessness, anomie exists when the normally accepted social standards or values are no longer understood or accepted and new ones have not developed. It usually occurs in periods of rapid social change.

App-dependent: Gardner and Davis (2014) use this term to describe those who attempt to solve problems first by turning to apps or associated technologies rather than looking within themselves or reaching out directly to a friend. App-dependent individuals have identities that are "increasingly externalized, packaged selves," and they exhibit "a growing anxiety and aversion to risk-taking" (p. 91).

App-enabled: Gardner and Davis (2014) use this term to describe the ways digital media, the Internet, and the thousands of apps available to individuals are extremely enabling—particularly in the execution of routine tasks. For the app-enabled, apps serve "as portals to the world," which can broaden young people's awareness of and access to experiences and identities beyond their immediate environment (p. 91).

Arnold, Matthew (1822–88): The son of Thomas Arnold, the famous headmaster at Rugby School, Matthew was an English poet, school inspector, and cultural critic whose *Culture and Anarchy* remains a classic defence of not only "high culture" but also a university education system that puts emphasis "on all the matters which most concern us, the best which has been thought and said in the world." Arnold ([1868] 1932) maintains that culture and higher education should involve the study of perfection, leading individuals "to conceive of true human perfection as a harmonious perfection, developing all sides of our humanity; and as a general perfection, developing all parts of our society" (p. 11).

Ascetic Protestantism: Weber classified certain Protestant sects such as the Calvinists, Pietists, Methodists, Baptists, Mennonites, Quakers, and Puritans as ascetic Protestants, whose beliefs led them to adopt a "this-worldly asceticism" by rejecting the spontaneous enjoyment of life. This asceticism was "the spiritual child of this matter-of-fact form of 'rational' thinking and living," and ultimately created the predominant, goal-rational orientation to action that became the ethos or spirit of modern capitalism.

Base: In the preface to *Towards the Critique of Political Economy*, Marx ([1859] 2005) notes that in the social production of their lives, independently of their will, individuals are born into specific relations of production that are appropriate for the development of the existing material forces of production. The "totality of these relations of production constitute the economic structure of society, the real basis on which a legal and political superstructure rises and to which determinate social forms of consciousness are appropriate" (p. 61). This creates the basic "base-superstructure" model used to represent Marxian materialism and Marx's theory of history. The complexity of this analogy is rarely fully recognized, however, and it is often turned into a simplistic, monocausal model of social change. See also *mode of production*.

Beloit College Mindset List: Beginning in 1998, Tom McBride and Ron

Nief, joined by Charles Westerberg in 2015, have released the annual "Beloit College Mindset List," which provides a capsule summary and a list of the cultural touchstones that have shaped the lives of students entering higher education each year. It is a useful reminder to instructors of the similarities and differences that exist between themselves and their students.

Beruf: See Calling (Beruf).

Bloom, Allan (1930–92): An American philosopher specializing in classical Greek, continental, and political philosophy, Bloom is best known for his bestselling, controversial book *The Closing of the American Mind: How Higher Education Has Failed Democracy and Impoverished the Souls of Today's Students*, which delivered a scathing critique of university education in the late twentieth century. Bloom ([1966] 1990) believed that universities should be "preserves for the quiet contemplation of the permanent questions [of humanity]" (p. 349).

Bourgeoisie: A sixteenth-century French term originally referring to the class of freemen living in cities, the word "bourgeoisie" is usually associated today with Marx's social and political theory. In the *Communist Manifesto*, Marx uses the term to refer to the capitalist class that owns the means of production. Marx outlines the bourgeoisie's massive achievements in revolutionizing industry and modernizing society: "The bourgeoisie, during its rule of scarce one hundred years, has created more massive and more colossal productive forces than have all preceding generations together" (Marx and Engels [1848] 1934:14). However, in expanding production the bourgeoisie creates its own "grave-diggers": "[T]he proletariat not only increases in number; it becomes concentrated in greater masses, its strength grows, and it feels that strength more" (p. 17).

Broadcast Music Incorporated (BMI): Formed in 1939 in response to the American Society of Composers, Authors, and Publishers' near monopolistic or oligopolistic control of the production and performance of music, BMI initially included a number of radio networks that then signed up its own music publishers and songwriters—including some whom ASCAP had excluded. BMI's challenge to ASCAP's control of the music industry broadened the type of music that reached the public and created new taste publics for previously excluded musical forms. It is now the largest music rights organization in the United States.

Calling (Beruf): In separating themselves from their natural condition, ascetic Protestants believed that individuals are given particular "callings" through which they can glorify God. A calling gives order and direction to life. The German word, *Beruf,* makes a link between the idea of a calling and economic activity. Weber ([1920] 2002) argued that "calling"—"the *task* [one] is given by God" (p. 39)—is the crucial link between the "this-worldly asceticism" of the ascetic Protestants and the spirit of modern capitalism.

Calvin, John (1509–64): An influential French theologian during the Protestant Reformation, Calvin saw religion as a highly individual, personal matter. He believed in the highly judgemental God of the Old Testament who tested people to determine their worthiness for heaven. Calvin believed that only a tiny fraction of humanity—the elect—would enter heaven. Calvinism urged believers to lead a committed, stoic life to demonstrate their devotion to God. This philosophy led to the "this-worldly asceticism" Weber attributed to the spirit of modern capitalism.

Carr, Nicholas (b. 1959): An American writer who focuses on technology and culture, Carr examines the consequences of society's growing dependency on computers, devices, and apps. His most important book to date is *The Shallows: What the Internet Is Doing to Our Brains* (2011), in which he argues that the present moment represents "an important juncture in our intellectual and cultural history ... [the] transition between two very different modes of thinking"—from the linear, contemplative, literary mind of print culture to the distracted, multi-tasking, fragmented mind of the Internet. Though he recognizes the strengths of the Internet and digital information, Carr is also highly critical of how heavy reliance on digital media affects patterns of thought, expression, and critical insight.

Castells, Manuel (b. 1942): A highly influential Spanish sociologist whose work features the study of information, communication, and globalization, Castells is the author of more than 20 books. His trilogy entitled *The Information Age: Economy, Society and Culture* may be his most influential. In it he argues that the social structure and activities in contemporary society are intimately tied to micro-electronic information technologies and networks. Moreover, those networks create a logic or way of thinking about the world that shapes economic, political, and social practices as a whole.

Class: The discovery or first use of the term class is almost always associated with Marx although he pointed out that political economists such as Ferguson, Smith, James Mill, Ricardo, and others had used it long before he did. For Marx, class had three particularly important features. First, class is an objective category that is determined by one's position in the social relations of production—those in the landed gentry owned land, which they farmed or rented for income; the capitalist class owned the dominant means of production; and members of the proletariat had only their labour-power to sell in order to live. Marx referred to this concept of class as "class in itself." Class also has a subjective dimension. Members of a class must also become conscious of their class position and what that means—they must attain class consciousness. Marx termed this consciousness as "class for itself"—that is, conscious of their class position, members of a class would begin to act for their own interests. Finally, Marx believed that a class such as the proletariat would, over time and based on economic circumstance, become "in and for itself"—that is, it would develop a revolutionary consciousness that would lead to significant political change.

Class consciousness: A central concept in Marx's theory of social change, class consciousness is the self-understanding of members of a social class, a developed awareness of their position in the productive processes and of their common interests. Class consciousness coalesces around the hardships members of a class face and a recognition of the true origin of these hardships; class consciousness is consolidated in a plan to struggle for significant social change. Marx believed that the class consciousness of the proletariat would result in political change so far reaching that it would catalyse social changes ultimately resulting in the elimination of class divisions within a future communist society.

Class struggle: The term is most closely associated with Marx and the opening sentence in Part 1 of the *Communist Manifesto*: "The history of all hitherto existing societies is the history of class struggles" (Marx and Engels [1848] 1934:10). Marx did note, however, that others had delineated both class struggles and the nature of classes: "Long before me bourgeois historians had described the historical development of this class struggle and bourgeois economists, the economic nature of the classes" (Marx and Engels

1955:69). His contribution was to maintain that classes existed only in particular periods of history and that a proletarian revolution would abolish all classes, creating a classless society.

Collective conscience / consciousness: See *conscience collective*.

Collective representations: Durkheim ([1895] 1982) introduces this term in *The Rules of Sociological Method* to replace *conscience collective*. Collective representations express "the way in which [a] group thinks of itself in its relationships with the objects which affect it" (p. 40). They exist in the form of flags, dress, customs, mythologies, totems, and other symbols. The term connects directly with numerous identifiable and empirical referents that Durkheim associates with social facts—that is, the "ways of acting, thinking and feeling which possess the remarkable property of existing outside the consciousness of the individual ... [and] are endued with a compelling and coercive power" that imposes itself upon individuals (p. 51).

Commodification: Commodification describes the process that stems from the inherent tendency in capitalist societies to turn more and more of the products of human creation into goods (commodities) sold in the market for profit. In the pursuit of profit, entrepreneurs continually strive to create new wants that can be met by the sale of particular products, leading to the continual expansion of economic production into all realms of human creation. The result is that even artistic and other types of esoteric activities are turned into commodities although, when sold as commodities, they are often standardized and simplified, so they will appeal and sell to a broad range of consumers and thereby generate more profit.

Commodity: A commodity is something sold in the market; Marx ([1872] 1987) argues that it is the "elementary form" of capitalist production and that, although it may seem simple or trivial, a commodity is in fact "a very tricky thing, full of metaphysical craftiness and theological peculiarities" (p. 102). Commodities and commodity production appear to exist in a world of their own governed by the objective properties of commodities themselves. As a result, the social character of production is mystified or misunderstood because the specific social relations of production appear to be based on the properties of the objects or things involved in the production process. They are not seen as social relationships that people have created and could create in a different manner.

Communist League: This league was officially formed in 1846 when the League of the Just amalgamated with the Communist Correspondence Committee of Brussels, to which Marx and Engels belonged. Hosting two international conferences of socialists and communists in 1847, the Communist League commissioned

Marx to write a manifesto of its views, aims, and tendencies in order to challenge misleading allegations about communism. It published the *Manifesto of the Communist Party* in 1848.

Communist Manifesto: Originally titled the *Manifesto of the Communist Party*, this 23-page document, authored by Marx, was published anonymously by the Educational Society for Workers in February 1848 and was the result of debate and compromise during two international conferences sponsored by the Communist League. Representing the League's particular political ambitions at the time, the document is a major accomplishment for Marx because it represents his particular view of history and the revolutionary potential he saw within the class struggle between the bourgeoisie and the proletariat in the mid-nineteenth century. With his authorship confirmed in later editions, the *Communist Manifesto*, as it became known after the Leipzig edition appeared in 1872, conferred recognition for Marx as a scholar, social critic, and revolutionary leader. In dramatic imagery, Marx sketches out the two titans of modernity— the bourgeoisie, which "has created more massive and more colossal productive forces than have all preceding generations together" and the proletariat, which "increases in number" and "becomes concentrated in greater masses" until "its strength grows, and it feels that strength more" (Marx and Engels [1848] 1934:14–17). Then it becomes a revolutionary force confronting the bourgeois class.

Comte, Auguste (1798–1857): Initially Saint-Simon's recording secretary and later a junior peer, Comte became an independent thinker who considered naming the discipline concerned with social phenomena "social physics" because of his strong commitment to a positivist epistemology. Ultimately, he settled on the name "sociology"—a portmanteau of the Latin word *socius* ("companion" and "associate") and the Greek term *lógos* ("logic" and "thought"). Sociology, for Comte, would deal with thought regarding human association or the logic of that association.

Conscience collective (collective conscience / consciousness): This French term means both "collective conscience" and "collective consciousness." It is a central term in Durkheim's study *The Division of Labor in Society*. Durkheim believed that social order emerged from a *conscience collective* that predates individuals, is internalized by them through socialization to govern and control their actions, and exists after their death. The *conscience collective* tends to endure but may change over time. It is replaced in Durkheim's later work by the term "collective representations."

Consumers' republic: Lizabeth Cohen uses this term for the mass production/mass consumer society that developed in Canada and the United States in the post–World War II period. It was associated with families moving to the suburbs to own their own home, the creation of shopping malls, and the modern highway system. Mass consumption was seen almost as a right and responsibility, rather than a privilege. As a Royal typewriter ad noted, the end of war brought the right to "once more walk into any store in the land and buy anything you want" (Cohen 2003:73). See also *total living*.

Continuous partial attention: This emergent cognitive style of short and constantly shifting attention appears to be related to heavy Internet usage, but it carries over to other aspects of individuals' lives.

Cool medium: A cool medium, according to McLuhan (1964), is low in definition; presenting its information abstractly, it requires active participation from the receiver to fill in the lacking details and detect the overall pattern. The receiver must grasp a cool medium's elements synthetically and simultaneously in order to determine what is most significant. A seminar would be a cool medium in comparison to a lecture.

Craftsmanship: Craftsmanship involves the feeling of being engaged with work in and for itself. The crafts worker determines the object of work, controls the work process, is free to experiment, and employs skills so fully developed that all can know when work is done well; craftsmanship involves skill and knowledge that lies beyond the capacity of language to explain. There is no ulterior motive in craftwork; the rewards are intrinsic as one successfully overcomes any difficulties in the labour process. Though not a goal, self-development is a major outcome of this work. Finally, for craftwork to be continually creative, the sensitivities of renewal and rejuvenation found in leisure must be integrated into it: play and work become inseparable. See also *intellectual craftsmanship*.

Culture: Williams (1983) argues that culture "is one of the two or three most complicated words in the English language" (p. 87). It begins as a word for "tending natural growth," extends by analogy to connote "a process of human training," and then comes to mean "a general state or habit of the mind" closely associated with the idea of human perfection. Culture is soon seen as a "thing in itself," first as "the general state of intellectual development, in a society as a whole"; next as "the general body of the arts"; and finally as "a whole way of life, material, intellectual, and spiritual" (Williams 1961:16).

Culture industry: In their 1944 essay "The Culture Industry: Enlightenment as Mass Deception," Horkheimer and Adorno ([1944] 1972:120) argue that the capitalist economy has turned the artistic production of various expressions of culture into mass produced commodities sold to mass audiences. What they term the culture industries—films, radio, and magazines—impress the same stamp on everything. All cultural products—e.g., music, film, art, literature—are reduced to standardized formulae wherein every consumer can predict what will come next and anticipate the conclusion. The "dialectic of enlightenment" includes the negation of expanding one's horizons as the producers of mass culture lower the intellectual depth of art, music, film, and literature to meet the manufactured wants of mass market consumers with the disastrous consequence that "the less the culture industry has to promise, the less it can offer a meaningful explanation of life, and the emptier is the ideology it disseminates" (Horkheimer and Adorno [1944] 1972:147). Horkheimer and Adorno draw parallels between the culture industry of North America and the Fascists' control of the media and their calculated manipulation of the masses in Hitler's Germany. The culture industry and advertising merge since the assembly-line nature of cultural production and the shallow products it offers are perfectly suited to the world of advertising. And advertising is barely a short step away from propaganda, as it offers half-truths and illusions to a public looking for simple solutions to address its media-constructed wants.

Darwin, Charles (1809–82): An English naturalist best known for his book *Origin of the Species* (1859) and its contributions to the theory of evolution in the biological world, Darwin did not believe that the strongest species survive but the species most able to adapt to their changing environment. His idea of evolutionary development spread from biology into social and political thought giving those disciplines an apparent scientific basis. Engels's graveside speech and an inaccurate rumour that Marx wanted to dedicate *Capital* to Darwin suggested, incorrectly, that Marx was a Social Darwinist.

Descartes, René (1596–1650): A French philosopher and mathematician, Descartes is important to sociology because of his method of systematic doubt. His *Discourse on Method* is regarded as the beginning of modern philosophy as it shifts the focal point for the pursuit of true knowledge from metaphysical premises or religious doctrines to a method involving rigorous contemplation of the world. His conception of method and his radical doubt cast all previous knowledge into question; his method supports the emerging inductive methodologies of the natural sciences and maintains that the scientific method should apply to all forms of human knowledge; his discourse positions critique as central to the scientific method.

Deutend verstehen: In advocating a particular methodology for the social sciences and humanities, Weber emphasizes the significance of "*deutend verstehen*" (interpretive understanding). For Weber, the goal of sociology is the interpretive understanding (*deutend verstehen*) of social action through which one can explain its course and consequences. The methodology brings together both macro and micro levels of human action to deeply and fully understand why individuals act as they do in particular situations.

Dialectic: Originally a form of logical argument, the dialectic came to mean a concept of how change was generated by an internal dynamic of contradiction, negation, and transcendence. This meaning of the dialectic emerged first in the Socratic method of continually questioning existing knowledge, which led to the overturning or the gradual refining of previously held ideas. Hegel believed that in overcoming the contradictions found within existing knowledge, philosophy would progress from immediate, partial, one-dimensional forms of understanding to a fully integrated, comprehensive form of "Reason." Rather than in the realm of ideas, Marx locates the dynamic of dialectical change in the actual labour taking place within class-divided societies, where workers produce commodities and an entire social system that confronts and exploits them. This dialectical contradiction of creating a system that opposes its creators produces the dynamic of class struggle.

Digitization projects: The digitization of books, scholarly journals, magazines, newspapers, and other forms of print text has revolutionized access to the written word. The digitization of published works began in the late 1960s and 1970s. Early projects were in the cultural heritage sector: Project Gutenberg (1971) and the Oxford Text Archive (1976). During the 1980s and 1990s, with the expanding use of the Internet, digitization projects proliferated. The size and scope of these projects varied. Some were personal digitization projects facilitated by commercial software such as Kindle Convert; others were volunteer-based yet ambitious projects, such as the Smithsonian's newly launched transcription project. Many undertakings were very comprehensive: University of Virginia's "Etext" project digitized texts for scholars in the humanities, and massive digitization operations have been run by JSTOR and the Google Books Library Project, which has already digitized more than 30 million books in about 480 languages. The motivation for such projects ranges from purely commercial interests to a desire to preserve rare books while at the same time making them widely accessible.

Durkheim, Émile (1858–1917): Born in Épinal, France, Durkheim faced several significant hardships throughout his life. He is justifiably considered the principal founder of sociology as a specific area of study, establishing Europe's first department of sociology at the University of Bordeaux in 1895 and founding the first sociology journal—*L'Année sociologique*. Durkheim dedicated his career to demonstrating the unique nature and strengths of sociology as an empirically based, systematic study of society. His major works are *The Division of Labour in Society* (1893), *The Rules of Sociological Method* (1895), *Suicide* (1897), and *The Elementary Forms of the Religious Life* (1912).

E-culture: E-culture is both a technological and a social phenomenon. It is based on the widespread use of digital technologies and information and incorporates the effects of the Internet on information creation, exchange, and transformation. Significant features include openness for people to both create and access digital cultural forms, virtuality, real distance from subject, absence of strict rules and norms, dominance of visual things over conceptual ones, and a high speed of change. These technologies and information flows affect all aspects of social life, from the everyday life-world to the globalized economy, international political structure, and the distribution of power.

Economic determinism: In describing the dynamics of social change in the preface to *Towards the Critique of Political Economy*, Marx ([1859] 2005) writes, "At a certain stage of their development, the material productive forces of society come into contradiction with *the existing relations of production*, or, what is only a legal expression for it, *with the property relations within which they have operated to that point in time* [emphasis added]" (p. 61–62). These statements suggest an economically deterministic argument that sees the economy, as a whole, determining or shaping the types of contradictions that will emerge and create, animate, or drive revolutionary change. Marx saw these tensions in the tendency of the rate of profit to fall, workers being laid off as they are replaced by technology, falling consumer demand leading to the "overproduction" of commodities that could not be sold, and the economy collapsing into periods of depression.

Economic rationalism: Weber argued that a particular economic rationalism characterized modern capitalism. It rested on individuals' willingness to organize their lives in a controlled, rational manner and engage in disciplined, goal-rational action (using the most efficient means to a particular end).

Egoistic suicide: See *suicide*.

Elective affinity: An important aspect of Weber's methodology, an elective affinity represents an affinity or resonance between two phenomena that reinforce each other or mutually influence each other. For Weber, there was an important elective affinity between the spirit of ascetic Protestantism, in general, and the calling, in particular, and the ethos of modern capitalism and its characteristic disciplined and goal rational action.

Electric age: This term refers to the mid-twentieth-century era that, according to McLuhan (1962), follows the typographic and mechanical era and involves "new shapes and structures of human interdependence and of expression" (p. 3). It is the age during which the extension of human senses will not result in closed systems but, through the coexistence of different technologies, will require a collective awareness of those technologies and the information they create. Television was the key medium of the electric age, and McLuhan thought this medium created serious, realistically minded

individuals who were both more self-reflective and apt to become involved with the social issues of the day.

Engels, Friedrich (1820–95): Describing himself as playing second violin to Marx, Engels was Marx's closest collaborator and supporter, giving Marx critically important advice in the writing of the *Manifesto of the Communist Party* and helpful suggestions to make *Capital*, volume one, more accessible. A scholar in his own right, Engels authored *The Condition of the Working Class in England* (1845); "Outlines of the Critique of Political Economy" (1844), which had a significant impact on Marx's ideas; and more controversial works such as *Anti-Dühring: Herr Eugen Dühring's Revolution in Science* (1877–78) and the posthumously published *Dialectics of Nature* (1925), which implied a more traditional materialist philosophy than Marx's materialist ontology. Engels became the leader of the socialist movement following Marx's death, and he edited and published the unfinished second and third volumes of Marx's *Das Kapital* while supervising Kautsky's publication of the fourth volume—the three books constituting the *Theories of Surplus Value*.

The Enlightenment: Usually dated from the time of the French *philosophes* through to the French Revolution of 1789, the Enlightenment can be described in three words—freedom, mastery, and progress. Enlightenment thinkers wanted to escape the darkness of ignorance; the cruel, unknown vicissitudes of nature; the arbitrary constraints of religious dogma and mysticism; and the shackles of tradition. Enlightenment—that is, knowledge obtained through the powers of human reason—would allow humankind to understand, control, and master the natural and social worlds. "The people" could control their lives and events rather than being the passive, powerless objects of nature, the monarch, and the pope in Rome. Progress would be measured by the advancement of knowledge, personal control over individuals' lives, and freedom's spread to more and more members of society.

Everyday stocks of knowledge at hand: Schutz uses this term to describe the personal knowledge individuals accumulate throughout their lifetime as they engage with the world from their own egocentric perspective using the natural attitude. These stocks of knowledge are the basis for the tacit understandings that individuals use to carry on in the world.

Fatalistic suicide: See *suicide*.

Federal Communications Commission (FCC): The FCC was responsible for radio and television licences. Prior to 1945, under pressure from NBC, CBS, and MBS, the FCC restricted the number of radio stations across the United States. With the advent of television, the major networks reduced their pressure on the FCC over radio licences, which led to the proliferation of radio stations and an ensuing broadening of music played on radio as stations competed for niche markets.

Ferguson, Adam (1723–1816): A Scottish philosopher, historian, and early political economist, Ferguson ranks among the great thinkers of the Enlightenment. His major work, *An Essay on the History of Civil Society* (1767), argued that the increasing division and simplification of labour under industrializing capitalism would undermine workers' intellectual capacities and the spirit of the nation. He warned that political leaders could either reduce the tensions between capital accumulation and workers' needs or face possible decay of the national spirit. Ferguson's work was influential in Marx's considerations of alienated labour.

Gabler, Neil (b. 1950): An American journalist and film and popular culture critic, Gabler investigates what it means to live in today's "celebrity society." In *Life: The Movie—How Entertainment Conquered Reality*, Gabler (1998) notes that the current "entertainment-driven, celebrity-oriented society" reduces what is important to what grabs and holds the public's attention (p. 8). Though television may be "the new epistemology," entertainment is "the cosmology" that governs social life (p. 56). Using Huxley's (1932) *Brave New World* imagery, Gabler maintains that reality has been turned into a movie to entertain rather than presenting "a clear-eyed appreciation of the human condition" and what it means "to *be* human" (p. 243).

Geist: This complex German noun is used by philosophers and social thinkers to mean "mind" but also "spirit" and "intellect"; some exploit all these meanings simultaneously when they use the word's substantive or adjectival form. The term is critical to the work of Hegel, Marx, and Weber, in particular, and is at the root of Weber's methodological writings distinguishing the *Geisteswissenschaften* (human and social sciences) from the *Naturwissenschaften* (natural sciences).

Geisteswissenschaften: Literally, the sciences of the mind or spirit, it is the German word for what is generally referred to as the humanities. The German tradition in sociology tends to make a strong distinction between the natural sciences, on the one hand, and the social sciences and humanities, on the other, arguing that the latter require a specific interpretive methodology rather than the experimental method used in the natural sciences.

Generation X: The generational cohort born between the early 1960s and 1981. This generation follows the large Baby Boom generation, gaining its highest public profile in Canadian novelist Douglas Coupland's 1991 novel *Generation X: Tales for an Accelerated Culture*. It is a generation that began with many obstacles—part of the "baby bust" period when the birth control pill allowed individuals to control family size, Gen Xers experienced the failures of the open classroom, the new math curricula, high rates of parental divorce, and the malaise of Carter-era America. Generation X had the lowest SAT scores since the tests were first implemented and higher crime and drug abuse rates than the Boomer generation. As adults, however, members of Generation X are well educated, have a high employment rate, and find themselves, with the Boomers now in retirement, working in largely satisfying occupations.

Generation Y: See *Millennials*.

Generation Z: The generational cohort born between 1996 and the present, Generation Z differs significantly from the Millennials. Growing up in small families, with less helicopter parenting, its members are more self-directed, confident, and adept at problem solving. Their educational experiences open them to racial, cultural, and physical ability diversity; they are engaged with academic work and have considerable self-confidence, creativity, drive to achieve, and entrepreneurial ambition. The cohort is more immersed in digital technology than the Millennials, relying heavily on social media to communicate; many of its members are "addicted" to their smartphones. Like the Millennials, Gen Zers' extensive use of digital information through the Internet has shaped the neural pathways in their brains, leading to distracted attention spans and habits of multi-tasking. This cohort has also grown up in a world faced with economic, political, and environmental crises, which create significant stresses for its members.

Goal-rational action: See *social action*.

Hegel, Georg (1770–1831): Seeking to overcome the barriers to absolute knowledge proposed by Descartes and Kant, Hegel wrote key works— *Phenomenology of Spirit* (1807), *Science of Logic* (1812–16), and *Encyclopedia of Philosophy* (1817)— that made him Prussia's foremost post-Kantian idealist philosopher. Hegel served as a critical foil to Marx's most important intellectual developments. Marx's critique of Hegel's *Philosophy of Right* (1821) identified the proletariat as the revolutionary subject of bourgeois society, and Hegel's *Phenomenology of Spirit* affected Marx's *Economic and Philosophic Manuscripts* of 1844, wherein Marx first began to envision labour as the key ontological aspect of social life and the history of different social formations.

Historical materialism: This term has been used to describe Marx's theory of society and social change, although Marx never used either "historical materialism" or "dialectical materialism" in any of his work. Historical materialism is closely associated with the principles of Marxism or orthodox Marxism that Engels, Kautsky, Mehring, and others sought to establish after Marx's death. Historical materialism tends to emphasize the economic contradictions of society as the foremost, if not the sole, basis for revolutionary change. It is to this narrow, reductionist reading of Marx's work that Weber critically responds in *The Protestant Ethic and the Spirit of Capitalism*.

Historical school: This school of thought maintained that the study of history should involve the collection and detailed study of the particular empirical facts related to specific events in the past; this view was a well-established methodological tradition in German scholarship by the nineteenth century. Members of the historical school argued that historians, economists, and other social analysts should simply collect the facts pertinent to events in social life in order to produce comprehensive accounts showing the unique nature of each social event. Maintaining that chance and free will are determining causes in social life, their ideographic approach excludes any attempt to find nomothetic or law-like tendencies in social life.

Hoggart, Richard (1918–2014): A British academic whose work centred on literature and popular culture, Hoggart was involved with the launching of cultural studies at the Centre for Contemporary Cultural Studies at the University of Birmingham in 1964. His *The Uses of Literacy* (1958) presents a nuanced examination of the effects of the commodification of culture on the working class. While describing the resistance that an authentic working class culture provides to the banal, levelling down of commercial culture, he also expresses some serious reservations and concerns about the dilution of popular culture.

Horkheimer, Max: See *Adorno, Theodor and Max Horkheimer*.

Hot medium: A hot medium, according to McLuhan (1964), extends at least one sense by conveying material in "high definition" (p. 22). The extension of sensory information through a hot medium provides rich detail, and all interpretation is done for the receiver. With so much sensory detail immediately present, a hot medium is more or less passively received.

Humboldt, Wilhelm von (1767–1835): At the direction of Prussia's King Friedrich Wilhelm III in 1806, Humboldt established the University of Berlin, which opened its doors in 1810. His vision for the university stemmed from Kant's belief that real knowledge only arises through scientific inquiry and critique. Humboldt made research central to the Prussian university system, requiring professors to be specialists in narrow fields and to continually test and expand upon existing knowledge. Professors had the academic freedom to follow research wherever it led, without concern about the practicality of their work. For Humboldt, in a university system dominated by reason, critique, and academic freedom, philosophy—not professional schools or concerns— should dominate.

Hyper attention: See *continuous partial attention*.

The idea of the university: A university is defined by the *Complete Oxford English Dictionary* as "An institution of higher education offering tuition in mainly non-vocational subjects and typically having the power to confer degrees. Also: the members, colleges, buildings, etc., of such an institution collectively." The idea of a university concerns the ongoing debate about what such an institution is actually to be, what its true purpose is, and what it should provide to students, members of the university, and the social whole.

Ideal type: See *pure type*.

Information age: A term used by Castells and others to characterize the most important characteristics of advanced societies in the twenty-first century: the rapid development and increasingly widespread use, from 1970 onwards, of micro-electronics, computers, telecommunications, and the Internet. These information technologies have significant influence over contemporary production/ consumption, human experience, relationships of power, and the shaping of meaning and culture.

Information revolution: In his video "Information R/evolution," Wesch (2007b) plays with the dyad that includes evolution, the long and gradual process of evolving change, and revolution, a dramatic and sudden change of considerable magnitude. He relates this dyad to digital information. The long, slow shift from analogue information, which directly creates or copies, to digital information, which is coded in binary bits (0, 1), results, according to Wesch, in a revolutionary transformation regarding how information can be collected, stored, communicated, and altered. Digital information has infinite recombinant capacities. The recipients and users of digital information can actively revise and even reconstruct the text, image, or video to create something vastly different from the original. The information revolution requires individuals and institutions to rethink completely how information should be treated and how people can best utilize its strengths while minimizing its weaknesses and liabilities.

Infrastructure: See *base.*

Intellectual craftsmanship: Building on his discussion of craftsmanship in *White Collar*, Mills (1951) proposed and described the term "intellectual craftsmanship" in his essay "On Intellectual Craftsmanship." For sociologists who feel they are "part of the classic tradition," Mills (1959) emphasizes, "social science is the practice of a craft" (p. 195). The six most important traits are (1) integrating life and work, or using life experiences to reflect critically upon intellectual work while the work helps develop one's personal potentials; (2) developing the mental dexterity to shift constantly between biography and social structure to gain an adequate view of the social whole; (3) sustaining an active, ongoing commitment to learning; (4) balancing the power of critical reason, "the advance guard in any field of learning," with empirical evidence that can "discipline reason" (p. 205); (5) presenting, for public scrutiny, the best-honed arguments possible; and (6) developing and referring regularly to one's files from which books and articles become "organized releases

from the continuous work that goes into them" (pp. 200–1).

Interpretive understanding: See *deutend verstehen.*

Interpretive sociology: See *verstehende Soziologie.*

Kerr, Clark (1911–2003): A professor of economics, Kerr was an academic administrator at the University of California (UC) between 1952 and 1967. In his book *The Uses of the University* (1963), he describes "the multiversity"— the modern research university of twentieth-century North America. Caught between the student movement of the 1960s, which he was asked to stop but refused to meet with violence, and the newly elected Governor Ronald Reagan's promise to clear the universities of protestors, Kerr was forced out of the UC presidency in 1967. With his characteristic wit, Kerr joked that he left UC as he had joined it—"fired with enthusiasm" (Hechinger 2003).

Labour-power: The ability to do work. This is the commodity that workers sell in the marketplace in exchange for wages. It is, for Marx, the basis for the creation of commodities and the sole source of surplus value, which capitalists need to expand their capital.

Law of three stages: Comte argued that it was a fundamental and invariable law that human knowledge progressed through three stages: the theological or fictitious, the metaphysical or abstract, and the scientific or positive. In addition, the simplest forms of knowledge passed through the three stages sooner than the more complex forms, which meant that sociology, the most complex form of knowledge, would be the last to advance to the positivist stage.

Leavis, F.R. (1895–1978) and Denys Thompson (1907–88): Frank Raymond Leavis and Denys Thompson were influential British literary critics in the mid-twentieth century. Their book *Culture and Environment: The Training of Critical Awareness* (1933) expresses their concern that, although mechanized production has brought the advantages of "mass-production [it] has turned out to involve standardization and levelling-down outside the realm of mere material goods," leading to the demise of English literary culture. This damage is caused in part by a growing number of simple and simplifying forms of entertainment such as films, newspapers, advertising, which "offer satisfaction at the lowest level, and inculcate the choosing of the most immediate pleasures, got with the least effort" (p. 3).

Live literature: Hoggart (1970) contrasts the simplified literature of mass consumer society with what he terms "live literature." Live literature explores and recreates the texture, complexity, and diversity of the human experience (e.g., man against man, woman against herself, humans against nature). It allows one to look at life honestly and deeply and to feel the vulnerability of human existence.

Marcuse, Herbert (1898–1979): A German philosopher and sociologist, Marcuse was a member of the Frankfurt school and one of the architects of its particular form of critical theory. After fleeing Hitler's Germany, Marcuse remained in the United States the rest of his life. A guru for the student movement in the 1960s, Marcuse wrote many important works, including *Reason and Revolution: Hegel and the Rise of Social Theory* ([1941] 1954), *Eros and Civilization* (1955), *Soviet Marxism: A Critical Analysis* (1958), and the book for which he is best known, *One-Dimensional Man: Studies in the Ideology of Advanced Industrial Society* (1964).

Marx, Karl (1818–83): The eldest son in a comfortable middle-class family of nine children, Marx studied at the University of Bonn and the University of Berlin before earning a doctorate from the University of Jena in 1841. Bringing together British political economy, German idealism, and French radical thought, Marx dedicated his life to critiquing capitalist society and theorizing and promoting its transcendence by a classless socialist society. The principal author of *The Manifesto of the Communist Party* and acknowledged in his lifetime to be a leader of the socialist movement, Marx was recognized after his death as the founder of one of the dominant perspectives in sociological thought because of his unfinished four-volume *Das Kapital* and other posthumous publications, such as *The German Ideology, The Economic and Philosophic Manuscripts*, and *Grundrisse*. Marx's work is best described as an unfinished, dynamic, unstable, dialectical whole.

Marxism: Marxism, often thought of in the singular, actually encompasses several variants of positions that begin with Marx's work. It is Engels, following Marx's death, who initially systematized Marx's ideas into a consistent theory. Engels's Marxism focuses on how the inherent contradictions between the social relations of production and the material forces of production will inevitably lead to the revolutionary transformation of capitalist society. Based on the longevity of capitalism, various political changes within Europe, and the posthumous publication of some of Marx's early works, a number of "Marxisms" came into being and claim to be the "true" Marxism: e.g., revisionism, Hegelian Marxism, structural Marxism, and "scientific" Marxism. Each emphasizes different aspects of Marx's political and theoretical legacy. See also *orthodox Marxism*.

Material forces of production: This term refers to one of the two elements making up "the mode of production" or the economic base, as described by Marx in the preface to *Towards the Critique of Political Economy*. The material forces encompass the material elements that are involved in the social production of a society. In capitalist societies, they include the factories, machinery, raw material,

and actual workers, which together produce commodities that are sold in the market. See also *social relations of production*.

Materialist: To distinguish his ideas from Hegel's and those of the predominant idealist philosophical tradition, Marx referred to his position as "materialist." This idea has created problems for some in grasping his fundamental premises. Materialism (or physicalism) is a philosophical position from which all things, including the human mind, are viewed as dependent upon, and stemming from, particular material or physical processes. However, this is not Marx's meaning. Marxian materialism recognizes that real individuals, through their activity within the "real" (or material) world, must produce their means of existence and, in doing so, create the real existing social conditions within which they live.

McLuhan, Marshall (1911–80): A pioneer in the study of media and media theory, McLuhan was a professor of English at the University of Toronto. His major works include *The Gutenberg Galaxy: The Making of Typographic Man*; *Understanding Media: The Extensions of Man*; and *The Global Village: Transformations in World Life and Media in the 21st Century*.

Mechanical solidarity: See *social solidarity*.

The medium is the message: This phrase is one of McLuhan's (1964) most significant aphorisms; it refers to the idea that it is "the medium that shapes and controls the scale and form of human association and action" (p. 9). Consequently, "any new technology gradually creates a totally new human environment" (p. vi). For McLuhan, the "'message' of any medium or technology is the change of scale or pace or pattern that it introduces into human affairs" (p. 8).

Millennials: This generational cohort, born between 1982 and 1995, is often referred to as the "Echo Boomers," the "Boomlet," the "Nexters," the "Nintendo Generation," the "Digital Generation," or the "Net Generation." But members prefer the "Millennials." Members of this cohort come from small, close families; they are optimistic, cooperative team players, who trust and respect authority. They have been closely supervised by "helicopter parents" who hover over them continually. Although that protection has advantages, so much attention and reassurance has left many in the cohort with an exaggerated sense of entitlement that makes it difficult for them to be self-reflective and self-critical and can cause them to be unable to trust their own judgements. Accustomed to instant gratification and frequent rewards, many lack the patience for sustained work and the ability to budget time. This is the first generation growing up completely surrounded by digital media. The first "digital natives" (Prensky's term), they like to receive and treat information quickly; they multi-task, prefer graphic information to text, and like being networked with others. Some scholars argue that the Millennials extensive use of digital information and the Internet has shaped the neural pathways in their brains, which are now different than those of previous generations, leading to compromised attention spans.

Mills, C. Wright (1916–62): One of the leading sociologists in the United States in the 1950s, Mills is the author of several highly influential books, including *New Men of Power: America's Labor Leaders*; *White Collar: The American Middle Classes*; *The Power Elite*; and *The Sociological Imagination*. His daughter Pamela (2000) describes him as a "muscular figure of energy and determination, overflowing with ambitious plans for the future, envisioning books that would cut through official distortions to produce uncompromising versions of truth as his logical mind perceived it" (P. Mills:xxiii).

Mode of production: In the preface to *Towards the Critique of Political Economy*, Marx ([1859] 2005) terms the way material life is produced and reproduced as the "mode of production (*die Produktionsweise*). It is another term for the base; it conditions or determines "the social, political, and intellectual processes of life overall" (p. 61) and is comprised of the social relations of production and the material forces of production.

Modernism: In the *Encyclopaedia of the Social Sciences*, Kallan (1957) writes that "modernism" is an "attitude of mind" that subordinates the traditional to the novel (p. 564); modernism values the new and innovative over the current or the past.

Modernity: *The Communist Manifesto* is also a manifesto of modernity insofar as Marx emphasizes the massive concentration, centralization, and increasingly rationalized and expanded powers of production in the modern era. Marx's description of the transformation to the modern— "All fixed, fast-frozen relations, with their train of ancient and venerable prejudices and opinions, are swept away, all new-formed ones become antiquated before they can ossify. All that is solid melts into air"— captures the essence of modernity and of the ubiquitous, rapid change it brings (Marx and Engels [1848] 1934:12–13).

Modernization: In the *International Encyclopedia of the Social Sciences*, Lerner (1968) identifies modernization as "the current term for an old process—the process of social change whereby less developed societies acquire characteristics common to more developed societies. The process is activated by international, or intersocietal, communication" (p. 386). Modernization became a social and political theory supportive of the idea that the "underdeveloped" or "developing nations" of the "Third World" would, over time, reach the levels of social, political, and economic development of the "First World," making all nations similar.

Monopoly: A monopoly refers to a market with only one seller; under monopoly conditions, there are no other competitors, so a business can set its selling price as high as it believes the market will bear. Prior to the formation of Broadcast Music Incorporated, the American Society of Composers, Authors, and Publishers enjoyed near monopoly conditions in the sale and distribution of music.

Montesquieu (1689–1755): Charles-Louis de Secondat, baron de La Brède et de Montesquieu was a French *philosophe* who may be seen as the first sociologist. His major works include the *Persian Letters* (1721), *Considerations on the Causes of the Greatness of the Romans and Their Decline* (1734), and his most significant study, *The Spirit of the Laws* (1748). *The Spirit of the Laws* is one of the most empirical works in social thought produced in the mid-eighteenth century. Based on his own observations as well as on historical records, Montesquieu classifies societies according to their mode of governance—as despotisms, monarchies, and republics—with each characterized by a particular nature and principle. He maintains that the spirit of a society grows out of its dominant religion, laws, maxims, mores, customs, styles of thought, and the atmosphere in a nation's capital or court. This heavy emphasis on the importance of empirical observation in the study of societies influences Durkheim significantly.

The multiversity: Kerr (1963) used this term to describe universities empirically and positively as they had become by the middle of the twentieth century; he called the university "a complex and an inconsistent institution" (p. 18). The multiversity consists of several communities—undergraduates, graduate students, humanists, social scientists, natural scientists, professional schools, non-academic personnel, and administrators. It engages in teaching and research and scholarship; it engages with alumni, legislators, farmers, and businessmen. The multiversity looks far into the past and well into the future, but is often at odds with the present. Committed to equality of opportunity, the multiversity has a class structure, and its communities have varied and conflicting interests.

Natural attitude: Schutz uses this term to indicate the manner in which individuals normally—that is, automatically, unreflectively, without thinking about it—see themselves and their situations from their own personal and individual perspectives. In the natural attitude, individuals, in a taken-for-granted manner, use their "everyday stocks of knowledge at hand" to manoeuvre themselves within their life-worlds.

Neoliberalism: This theory of political and economic practices maintains that human well-being is best achieved through promoting individual entrepreneurial freedoms and skills within an institutional framework that values and privileges private property rights, free markets, and free trade over communal responsibilities, local economies, and managed trade. The state creates and protects this institutional framework and is minimally involved with the economic market.

Newman, John Henry Cardinal (1801–90): The author of *The Idea of a University Defined and Illustrated*, Newman ([1852] 1886) believed that universities were places of teaching and universal learning. Their object was intellectual and their goal to diffuse and extend existing knowledge rather than to advance new knowledge.

Norms: This term designates behaviour that is the expected or "normal" way of conducting one's social actions. Norms represent the customary ways of acting, thinking, and feeling and are thus shaped by the dominant collective representations of a society. In contrast to formalized rules of action, or laws, norms are the "unwritten" ways of acting that that do not result in any formal punishments when they are broken.

Objectivity: One of the most complex terms in sociology, objectivity is viewed by some as a foundational pillar of scientific knowledge. For Durkheim ([1895] 1982), objectivity involves studying "phenomena as a function, not of an idea of the mind, but of their inherent properties. It must characterise them according to some integrating element in their nature and not according to whether they conform to some more or less ideal notion" (p. 75). Objectivity means discarding data influenced by the observer's subjective impressions; all knowledge should come from the *object* under study.

Oligopoly: An oligopoly is a market in which there are only a few competitors. Prior to the involvement of various foreign auto makers, the automobile industry in the United States was an oligopoly, dominated as it was by the "Big Three": General Motors, Ford, and Chrysler. In an oligopoly, there is less competitive pressure, so prices are generally higher than expected under normal competitive conditions. Prior to the 1950s, the major record firms and the national radio networks consisted of an oligopoly that controlled popular music production and broadcasting in the United States.

Organic solidarity: See *social solidarity*.

Orthodox Marxism: The term "orthodox" suggests a very strict reading of texts. Following Engels's lead in *Socialism: Utopian and Scientific*, the "orthodox Marxists" tried to present and codify Marx's ideas in a clear and consistent manner, emphasizing the significance of some specific texts, such as the *Communist Manifesto*, a deterministic reading of the preface to *Towards the Critique of Political Economy*, and some commentaries on Marx's more complex and ambiguous texts. The modern meaning of the term, however, emerged from a struggle over the political platform of the German Social Democratic Party at the turn of the twentieth century. In *Evolutionary Socialism*, Bernstein ([1899] 1909) argued that the party should forsake its longstanding commitment to revolution and pursue social reform

through parliamentary legislation. Those opposed, who wanted to maintain the party's commitment to revolution, proudly referred to themselves as orthodox Marxists, calling Bernstein's supporters "revisionists." Exploiting the religious connotation of the term "orthodox"—orthodox believers usually interpret religious texts in a literal and narrow manner— the revisionists suggested that "orthodox Marxist" revolutionaries in the party were slaves to certain Marxist texts and to an excessively rigid Marxist doctrine. On the other hand, the revisionists, who willingly revised their understanding of capitalism based on an analysis of social change, were Marx's true heirs, they claimed.

Personal troubles of milieu: Mills (1959) developed this term to describe personal problems that occur "within the character of the individual and within the range of his immediate relations with others; they have to do with his self and with those limited areas of social life of which he is directly and personally aware." Their resolution lies "within the individual as a biographical entity and within the scope of his immediate milieu" (p. 8).

Political economy: The term first appears in Antoine de Montchréstien's ([1615] 1889) *Traicté de l'economie politique*. James Mill ([1821] 1844) notes that "Political Economy is to the State, what domestic economy is to the family"; it addresses issues of supply and demand within a society and the connections between the political processes governing the economy and distribution of wealth. Smith emphasizes that the economy should provide sufficient revenue and resources for the population as a whole as well as enough for the public services that are needed but not met by market demand alone. Smith also identifies landed property, capital, and labour as the three great classes of industrializing Europe. These remain the central issues of political economy from Ferguson, Smith, and Sismondi through to Ricardo and the work of Marx.

Positive philosophy: See *positivism*.

Positivism: Positivism, according to Auguste Comte (1798–1857), requires the "necessary and permanent subordination of imagination to observation which constitutes the scientific spirit, as opposed to the theological or metaphysical spirit" (Comte 1974: 139). It is an epistemology that rejects speculation or metaphysical principles as the basis for true knowledge, arguing that careful, systematic observation and measurement are the basis for knowledge. Knowledge is built on propositions that must be tested to see if they might be falsified (disproven) by empirical observations. As data are gathered and propositions tested, new, more complex relationships and propositions can be formulated and tested, leading, ultimately, to a comprehensive theory. For positivism, knowledge is cumulative. Finally, positivism advocates integrating all the sciences—natural and social.

Postman, Neil (1931–2003): Postman is the author of more than 18 books, including *Teaching as a Subversive Activity* (with Charles Weingartner); *Teaching as a Conserving Activity*; *Amusing Ourselves to Death: Public Discourse in the Age of Show Business*; *Conscientious Objections: Stirring up Trouble about Language, Technology, and Education*; *Technopoly: The Surrender of Culture to Technology*; and *The End of Education: Redefining the Value of School*. His books are provocative yet entertaining and informed analyses of the impact of technology on education and culture as a whole. His main message is that despite the enormous power and influence of information technology, humans must control and use technology to empower themselves rather than being dominated by it. To do this requires deeper insight into the history of technology and the manner in which it shapes decision-making processes.

Postmodernism: In the *Blackwell Encyclopedia of Sociology*, Albright (2007) writes that postmodernism embodies a shift in sensibility from concern with form to a concern with skill and craftsmanship, from structure to surface, from purity to pastiche, and from substance to image or simulation. Postmodernists reject the Enlightenment belief in reason, nature, and progress and are concerned with "undecidables," the limits of precise knowledge, conflicts created by incomplete information, fractals (or never ending, repeating patterns), catastrophes, and paradoxes. Postmodernism revels in playfulness, irony, ornamentation, and a pastiche of styles.

Print culture: Print culture is both a technological and a social phenomenon. It emerged in the mid-1400s with Gutenberg's creation of moveable type, which allowed for the widespread printing of documents. Gutenberg's technology and the emergent print culture initiated and encouraged a linear, contemplative, analytic, reflective, and literary mind. It is a mind that promotes an individualist approach to the world, which is consistent with the mechanistic and scientific worldview of the Enlightenment period, a perspective that remained dominant throughout what McLuhan terms the "typographic and mechanical era."

Proletariat: This term is derived from the Latin noun *"proles"* meaning "offspring." Collectively referred to as the proletariat, the proles were members of an impoverished, subordinate class in ancient Rome; they had no economic assets other than their sons. Socialists and communists used the term to identify the working class in early industrial Europe as the most impoverished, immiserated, exploited class under capitalist relations of production. Marx first identifies the proletariat in his critique of Hegel's *Philosophy of Law*. He calls them a class weighed down in bourgeois society with "radical chains"; in breaking these chains, the proletariat would emancipate all the other spheres of society. Marx describes the objective and subjective conditions and revolutionary potential of the proletariat more elaborately in the *Communist Manifesto*.

Public issues of social structure: Mills (1959) uses this term to describe issues that transcend a person's immediate social setting. These issues, such as discrimination or economic disparity, have to do with "the organization of many milieu into the institutions of an historical society as a whole, with the ways in which various milieu overlap and interpenetrate to form the larger structure of social and historical life. An issue is a public matter: some value cherished by publics is felt to be threatened" (p. 8).

Pure type: In his methodological analyses, Weber argues that sociologists should move away from the infinite complexity of reality to more clearly defined, conceptual understandings or "pure types" (also translated as "ideal types"). A pure type is an intellectual construct that sharply and precisely identifies the key characteristics that are pertinent to the social structure or action under study (for example, goal-rational action). The pure type brings to conscious awareness all aspects of the phenomenon under study and serves as a reference point or comparator for those phenomena as they take place in the real world. See also *abstraction*.

Rate of profit: Marx argued that the profit motive in capitalist production led capitalists to compete with one another by either undercutting their competitors and accepting a lower rate of profit while gaining a larger mass of profit or by using technology to replace workers and gain a competitive edge even though labour-power is the source of surplus value (profit). This meant that competition would create a tendency for the rate of profit to fall and would lead to periodic economic crises of overproduction and underconsumption (goods produced but not sold accumulating in warehouses). Such crises could lead to the revolutionary transformation of the economy, but Marx also recognized that this tendency could be offset by the discovery of new markets, the development of new consumer needs, or the creation of monopoly or oligopoly control of the market, which would allow for the sale of commodities above their expected market value. Because it was a tendency that could be potentially offset, the falling rate of profit in itself would not guarantee an economic crisis that would lead to revolutionary change.

Recipe knowledge: Schutz uses this term to describe the type of knowledge that individuals use in their everyday interactions within the life-world. Recipe knowledge generally allows one to know what to do next, even though such knowledge is not extensive or free from contradictions.

Repressive law: Durkheim used different types of law to serve as empirical indicators for the *conscience collective*. Repressive law was common among face-to-face societies in which punishment expressed the anger of the community avenging a transgression that was seen to harm the social whole.

Restitutive law: Durkheim used different types of law to serve as empirical indicators for the *conscience collective*. Restitutive law is a legal system consistent with complex societies characterized by organic solidarity—that is, societies in which individuals are increasingly dependent upon other individuals carrying out specialized social functions due to the presence of an advanced division of labour. Rather than seeking to punish transgressions against the social whole, restitutive law is designed to return things to the way they were prior to the transgression.

Saint-Simon (1760–1825): Claude Henri de Rouvroy, comte de Saint-Simon was a French political and social theorist and an early champion of sociology as an empirical science. He used the structure of medieval society as his enduring reference point to describe progress in history. All stable societies consisted of three orders—a spiritual elite, a governing or temporal elite, and the productive classes. This template informed Saint-Simon's conception of both social structure and the evolutionary development of societies through history. He saw history moving from classical Greece and Rome (polytheistic theology, ruling class, and slave production) to medieval society (Catholicism, kings and lords, and serf labour) and finally to industrial society based on scientific knowledge, governance by technocrats, and industrial production.

Smith, Adam (1723–90): A central figure in the Scottish Enlightenment, Smith was a moral philosopher who is best known for his treatise in political economy— *An Inquiry into the Nature and Causes of the Wealth of Nations* (1776), which begins with the premises of utilitarian philosophy. Smith notes that individuals pursuing their own interest end up pursuing the interests of all, which led to the idea that such action produces the "unseen hand" of the market and that a market left to its own devices (laissez-faire capitalism) will meet most of a society's needs. Through his famous pin-making example, Smith champions the productive power of an increasing division of labour to generate greater wealth in a nation. However, Smith also recognized that not all social needs would be met by the market and supported political interventions into the economy to ensure the welfare of all members of a society.

Social action—affective, goal-rational, traditional, and value-rational: Weber argues that sociology involves the systematic, interpretive understanding of "social action." All action for Weber involves subjective meaning—that is, meaning for the person carrying out the action. Action is *social* when the agent's subjective meaning takes into account the understanding or behaviour of others as the action is carried out.

Weber identifies four pure types of social action. *Affective action* is guided by desires or emotions (fear, anger, hate, vengeance, lust, or love, for example). *Goal-rational action* is mentally calculated action aimed at achieving a particular goal. *Traditional action* is guided by the dictates of tradition, and *value-rational action* stems from a particular value or belief.

Social facts: In *The Rules of Sociological Method*, Durkheim ([1895] 1982) states that one must determine what facts are "social" and to be studied by sociology as a unique discipline. "A social fact is identifiable through the power of external coercion which it exerts or is capable of exerting upon individuals. The presence of this power is in turn recognisable because of the existence of some pre-determined sanction, or through the resistance that the fact opposes to any individual action that may threaten it" (pp. 56–57). Social facts are external to the individual and are internalized through socialization.

Social facts as things: Durkheim ([1895] 1982) argues that social facts are not things but still must be treated as if they were things. Things are the opposite of ideas; they are external objects that can only be known by observation and experimentation. To treat social facts as things is not the same as categorizing them as things; rather, it is observing them with a particular frame of mind and "adopting the principle that one is entirely ignorant of what they are, that their characteristic properties, like the unknown causes upon which they depend, cannot be discovered by even the most careful form of introspection" (pp. 35–36). They can only be known through systematic data collection and observation.

Social relations of production: These relations form one of the two elements making up the mode of production or the economic base, as described by Marx in the preface to *Towards the Critique of Political Economy*. The social relations of production are property relations—the type of property that individuals own determines their objective position in the class structure of a society. See also *material forces of production*.

Social solidarity—mechanical and organic: Among the major questions in sociology are questions of social order—how is it established, how does it remain, and how does it change? Social order requires social integration or the creation of social solidarity. Durkheim ([1893] 1933) believed that all societies have a natural social order or form of social solidarity, although this form would differ among different societies or at different points in historical time. Durkheim uses *mechanical solidarity* to express the type of social order found in traditional, face-to-face societies. Within mechanical solidarity, "the individual personality is absorbed under the collective personality." The term creates an analogy between a simple society and a simple organism, both of which have a simple, mechanical unity. If one part fails, the society

or organism will die. Durkheim uses the term *organic solidarity* to describe the type of social order found in societies characterized by a complex division of social labour. Under organic solidarity, each individual is dependent on the society as a whole because it consists of so many integrated parts. The term suggests a complex organism where each organ "has its special physiognomy, its autonomy." Furthermore, "the unity of the organism is as great as the individuation of the parts is more marked" (Durkheim [1893] 1933:131).

Social statics and *social dynamics*: Comte argued that sociology involved two undertakings: "social statics" and "social dynamics." *Social statics* assessed a society at a particular point in time. The concept of social statics was analogous to the fixed, structural "anatomy" of a society; *social dynamics*, on the other hand, could be thought analogous to the moving physiology of a society. With the knowledge gained in the study of social statics, progressive, evolutionary change could take place within the processes of social dynamics.

Socialization: This is the process through which individuals are "associated" with others in a group, community, or society. It is the process through which individuals learn and internalize the dominant, socially accepted behaviours, attitudes, and beliefs. Through this internalization process, the relationship of personal biography, history, and social structure is established—although it remains dynamic and changing throughout one's life.

The sociological imagination: Mills (1959) coined this term to describe the "quality of mind" that enables one "to grasp history and biography and the relations between the two within society." It represents sociology's "task and its promise" (p. 6).

Socratic method: The classical Greek philosopher Socrates advanced knowledge through the process of dialogue—the continuous posing of questions to expose an idea's limitations or a proponent's errors in thought and understanding, which led to revised, more complete knowledge. This method is one of the origins of the idea of the dialectic and dialectical method.

Stahlhartes Gehäuse (steel-hard casing): At the end of *The Protestant Ethic and the Spirit of Capitalism*, Weber ([1920] 2002) pessimistically maintains that, in the modern era, humankind is locked inside the *stahlhartes Gehäuse* (steel-hard casing) of goal-rational action, a circumstance that creates "narrow specialists without mind, pleasure-seekers without heart" (p. 37). Once translated as "iron cage," steel-hard casing or steel-hard housing is a superior definition because steel is an alloy of iron and carbon, which is far stronger than iron alone, and steel is a modern product resulting from scientific, goal-rational action.

Sui generis: This Latin term means "unique" or "in a class or group of its own." Durkheim believed

that society was an entity different from all other objects of science, so it had to be understood within its own discipline—sociology— which necessitated a specific methodology aimed at gathering specific data for analysis and study—that is, social facts.

Suicide—altruistic, anomic, egoistic, and fatalistic: *Altruistic suicide*, Durkheim ([1897] 1951) argues, results from an individual's intense integration into the social system for religious, occupational, or other existential reasons. In these circumstances, one's life is seen as less significant than the importance of the group or society as a whole. *Anomic suicide* results from a lack of social integration and regulation, and is therefore particularly acute in episodes or periods of rapid social change—that is, in conditions of "anomie." Durkheim believed that, as religion declined in significance and the world became increasingly commercialized, individuals would feel directionless and insecure, bringing the purpose of their lives into question and predisposing some to suicide. *Egoistic suicide* results from a low level of integration into the social system for religious, occupational, gender, family, or other existential reasons. In such circumstances, the individual must rely on his or her own resources and is left in a position of "ego vulnerability" and predisposed to suicide. Durkheim ([1897] 1951) identifies *fatalistic suicide* in a footnote as a minor type of suicide with "little contemporary importance." Fatalistic suicide occurs under conditions of excessive regulation where "futures [are] pitilessly blocked and passions violently choked by oppressive discipline" (p. 276).

Superstructure: See *base*.

Technological determinism: In describing the dynamics of social change in the preface to *Towards the Critique of Political Economy*, Marx ([1859] 2005) writes, "At a certain stage of their development, *the material productive forces of society* come into contradiction with the existing relations of production [emphasis added]" (p. 61–62). This suggests that it is the material productive forces—or technology—that is the source of change. Statements such as "the hand-mill gives you society with the feudal lord; the steam-mill, society with the industrial capitalist" (Marx [1847] 1950:127) seem to suggest that it is technology that determines social change.

This-worldly asceticism: Ascetic Protestants believed that a small number of individuals—the "Elect"—were predestined to everlasting life. In glorifying God on earth, individuals were expected to rise above their natural condition—to tame and control all of their natural desires—and conduct their lives in a strictly disciplined manner. Without being able to know who was among the Elect, all devout, ascetic Protestants tried to live their lives in this manner, believing that if they could, it would confirm to themselves and others that they were part of the Elect. The result was an ascetic lifestyle that Weber termed a "this-worldly asceticism." Weber uses it

to demonstrate the elective affinity between ascetic Protestantism and the spirit of modern capitalism.

Thompson, Denys: See Leavis, F.R. (1895–1978) and Denys Thompson (1907–88)

Total living: Following all the deprivations of World War II, political and business leaders, academics, the film industry, and the popular press drew links between the benefits of mass production, mass consumption, and an expanding economy. Mass consumption became a civic responsibility that would ensure full employment, expand the economy, and confront and quash Soviet aspirations to spread communism around the globe. See also *consumers' republic*.

Traditional action: See *social action*.

Typographic and mechanical era: This era, according to McLuhan, began with Gutenberg's invention of moveable type in the middle of the fifteenth century, which led to the emergence of print culture. This culture initiated and encouraged a linear, analytic, reflective, and individualist approach to the world that was consistent with the mechanistic and scientific worldview of the Enlightenment period. The typographic and mechanical era extends into the middle of the twentieth century.

Value relevance: Weber argues that scholars choose their topics of research on the basis of their relevance to particular value systems that they hold. Though it is appropriate, Weber maintains, to pursue research on the basis of one's sense of value relevance, once the research process begins, the researcher must suspend his or her value system and approach the subject in as objective a manner as possible. See also *objectivity*.

Value-rational action: See *social action*.

Verstehende Soziologie: This is the German designation for Weber's methodological approach to sociology—that is, a sociology based on the interpretive understanding of social action. See also *deutend verstehen* and *social action*.

Weber, Max (1864–1920): Born in Erfurt, Germany, on April 21, 1864, Weber became a scholar whose ideas profoundly shaped social theory and research. Weber's father was a prominent attorney, and his mother was a devout Protestant who deeply influenced Weber's outlook on the world. Weber was an extremely disciplined, principled, politically engaged scholar with a highly developed work ethic and a deep commitment to scholarship of the highest standard. His vast corpus of work centres on studies in methodology; he advocates for an interpretive (*verstehende*) approach to the understanding of social action, economic history, and comparative religion. He left an unfinished general treatise on sociology entitled *Economy and Society*, but he is best known for *The Protestant Ethic and the Spirit of Capitalism*, which brings together all of the main themes in Weber's work.

Wesch, Michael (b. 1975): Currently the Coffman Chair for Distinguished Teaching Scholars at Kansas State University, Wesch (2015) embraces the challenges and opportunities to use the interactive potential of the Internet and YouTube to engage with his students. Wesch produced and posted his 2007 "A Vision of Students Today" and a more ambitious 2011 project "'a few ideas …' (Visions of Students Today)" along with videos such as "Information R/evolution" and "The Machine is Us/ing Us (Final Version)" to the Internet to demonstrate the nature, strengths, and limitations of digital information. Although Wesch recognizes the significance of print culture, his main objective is to encourage professors and students to embrace all of the potential of digital information because it represents the greatest promise for the further development of a knowledge-based society.

Williams, Raymond (1921–88): A novelist and academic, Williams was one of the foremost cultural critics, cultural historians, and cultural and political theorists of the latter half of the twentieth century. Two works, *Culture and Society, 1780–1950* and *Keywords: A Vocabulary of Culture and Society* established his reputation. One of the leading figures in the British New Left, Williams was most interested in the relationships between language, literature, and society. Williams's work spurred the development of "cultural studies," although he referred to his own position as "cultural materialism."

BIBLIOGRAPHY

ABC News. 2013. "Beyoncé National Anthem at Presidential Inauguration Ceremony 2013." Retrieved May 24, 2016 (https://www.youtube.com/watch?v=qGDH18R7GfA).

Adele. 2009. "Fool That I Am (Etta James Cover) Live at North Sea Jazz." Retrieved February 21, 2016 (https://www.youtube.com/watch?v=cjhycVMeaQw).

Adoratsky, V., ed. 1934. *Karl Marx: Chronik seines Lebens in Einzeldaten* (*Karl Marx: A Chronology of His Life in Single Dates*). Moscow: Marx-Engels-Verlag.

Adorno, Theodor and Max Horkheimer. [1944] 1972. *Dialectic of Enlightenment*. Translated by John Cumming. New York: Herder and Herder.

The Adventures of Ozzie and Harriet. 1952–66. New York: ABC.

Agee, James and Walker Evans. 1941. *Let Us Now Praise Famous Men*. Boston: Houghton Mifflin.

Aguilera, Christina. 2012. "At Last Sung at Etta James Funeral." Retrieved February 18, 2016 (https://www.youtube.com/watch?v=dOWpZtnoVZI).

Albright, Julie. 2007. "Postmodernism." *Blackwell Encyclopedia of Sociology*, edited by George Ritzer. Retrieved December 16, 2009 (http://www.blackwellreference.com/subscriber/tocnode. html?id=g9781405124331_chunk_g978140512433119_ss1-117).

Alexander, Jeffrey. 1982. *Theoretical Logic in Sociology*. Vol. 1, *Positivism, Presuppositions, and Current Controversies*. Berkeley: University of California Press.

Alexander, Jeffrey. 1986. "Rethinking Durkheim's Intellectual Development I: 'Marxism' and the Anxiety of Being Misunderstood." *International Sociology* 1:91–107.

Althusser, Louis. 1977a. "The '1844 Manuscripts' of Karl Marx." Pp. 153–60 in *For Marx*, translated by Ben Brewster. London: New Left Books.

Althusser, Louis. 1977b. "On the Young Marx." Pp. 49–86 in *For Marx*, translated by Ben Brewster. London: New Left Books.

Anderson, Stacey. 2011. "When Elvis Presley Scandalized America and MC Hammer Topped the Charts." *Rolling Stone*, June 7 (http://www.rollingstone.com/music/news/when-elvis-presley-scandalized-america-and-mc-hammer-topped-the-charts-20110607).

Andréas, Bert. 1963. *Le Manifeste Communiste de Marx et Engels: Histoire et bibliographie, 1848–1918* (*The Communist Manifesto of Marx and Engels: History and Bibliography, 1848–1918*). Milan: Feltrinelli.

Anka, Paul. [1960] 2012. "Puppy Love." Retrieved February 19, 2016 (https://www.youtube.com/watch?v=RR89JVJqBYg).

Apple. 2015a. "iPhone 6s and iPhone 6s Plus—Reveal." Retrieved November 28, 2015 (https://www.youtube.com/watch?v=Ar2wuOxBpDw).

Apple. 2015b. "iPhone 6s—The Only Thing That's Changed …" Retrieved November 28, 2015 (https://www.youtube.com/watch?v=aBYWGjIzvyw).

Arnold, Matthew. [1868] 1932. *Culture and Anarchy: An Essay in Political and Social Criticism*. Cambridge: Cambridge University Press.

Aron, Raymond. 1961. *Sociologie des societes industrielles: Esquisse d'une theorie des regimes politiques* (*Sociology of Industrial Societies: Outline of a Theory of Political Regimes*). Paris: Centre de documentation universitaire.

Aron, Raymond. 1962. *Dix-huit leçons sur la société industrielle* (*Eighteen Lectures on Industrial Society*). Paris: Gallimard.

Aron, Raymond. 1964. *German Sociology*. Translated by Mary and Thomas Bottomore. New York: The Free Press of Glencoe.

Avineri, Shlomo. 1967. "From Hoax to Dogma: A Footnote on Marx and Darwin." *Encounter* 28:30–32.

Bacon, Francis. 1864. *The Physical and Metaphysical Works of Lord Bacon, Including His Dignity and Advancement of Learning and His Novum Organum; Or, Precepts for the Interpretation of Nature*, edited by Joseph Devey. London: H.G. Bohn.

Baher, Peter. 2001. "The 'Iron Cage' and the 'Shell as Hard as Steel': Parsons, Weber, and the *Stahlhartes Gehäuse* Metaphor in the Protestant Ethic and the Spirit of Capitalism." *Theory and History* 40:153–69.

Bauldie, John. 1991. "Liner Notes." *Bob Dylan: The Bootleg Series*. Vols. 1–3, *Rare & Unreleased, 1961–1991*. New York: Sony Music Entertainment Inc.

Beamish, Rob. 1992. *Marx, Method, and the Division of Labor*. Chicago: University of Illinois Press.

Beamish, Rob. 1998. "The Making of the Manifesto." *Socialist Register* 34:218–39.

Beamish, Rob and Ian Ritchie. 2006. *Highest, Fastest, Strongest: A Critique of High-Performance Sport*. New York: Routledge.

Beloit College. 2015a. "2012 List." Retrieved May 22, 2015 (https://www.beloit.edu/mindset/previouslists/2012/).

Beloit College. 2015b. "2013 List." Retrieved May 22, 2015 (https://www.beloit.edu/mindset/previouslists/2013/).

Beloit College. 2015c. "2014 List." Retrieved May 22, 2015 (https://www.beloit.edu/mindset/previouslists/2014/).

Beloit College. 2015d. "2015 List." Retrieved May 22, 2015 (https://www.beloit.edu/mindset/previouslists/2015/).

Beloit College. 2015e. "2017 List." Retrieved May 22, 2015 (https://www.beloit.edu/mindset/previouslists/2017/).

Beloit College. 2015f. "2018 List." Retrieved May 22, 2015 (https://www.beloit.edu/mindset/previouslists/2018/).

Beloit College. 2015g. "2019 List." Retrieved August 18, 2015 (https://www.beloit.edu/mindset/).

Bell, Daniel. 1960a. *The End of Ideology: On the Exhaustion of Political Ideas in the Fifties*. Glencoe, IL: Free Press.

Bell, Daniel. 1960b. "Two Roads from Marx." Pp. 335–68 in *The End of Ideology: On the Exhaustion of Political Ideas in the Fifties*. Glencoe, IL: Free Press.

Bell, Daniel. 1973. *The Coming of Post-Industrial Society: A Venture in Social Forecasting*. New York: Basic Books.

Bell, Daniel. 1976. *The Cultural Contradictions of Capitalism*. New York: Basic Books.

Benjamin, Walter. 1968. "The Work of Art in the Age of Mechanical Reproduction." Pp. 217–52 in *Illuminations: Essays and Reflections*, edited by Hannah Arendt. New York: Schocken Books.

Bensaïd, Daniel. 2002. *Marx for Our Times*. Translated by Gregory Elliott. New York: Verso Books.

Bentham, Jeremy. 1948. *Fragment on Government and an Introduction to the Principles of Morals and Legislation*. Oxford: Blackwell Books. (Written in 1776 and 1789 respectively.)

Berg, Maxine. 1986. *The Age of Manufactures: Industry, Innovation, and Work in Britain, 1700–1820*. New York: Oxford University Press.

Berger, Peter. 1963. *Invitation to Sociology*. New York: Anchor Books.

Berman, Marshall. 1988. *All That Is Solid Melts Into Air: The Experience of Modernity*. Markham: Penguin Books.

Bernstein, Eduard. [1899] 1909. *Evolutionary Socialism: A Criticism and Affirmation*. Translated by Edith Harvey. London: Independent Labour Party.

Berry, Wendell. 1987. *Home Economics*. New York: North Point Press.

Best, Joel. 2011. *The Stupidity Epidemic: Worrying about Students, Schools, and America's Future*. New York: Routledge.

The Bill Haley Tapes [DVD]. 1995. Seattle: Jerden Records.

Bloom, Allan. [1966] 1990. "The Crisis of Liberal Education." Pp. 348–64 in *Giants and Dwarfs: Essays 1960–1990*. Toronto: Simon and Schuster.

Bloom, Allan. 1987. *The Closing of the American Mind: How Higher Education Has Failed Democracy and Impoverished the Souls of Today's Students*. Toronto: Simon and Schuster.

Böhm-Bawerk, Eugen. [1896] 1949. *Karl Marx and the Close of His System*. New York: Augustus M. Kelley.

Bourdieu, Pierre. [1980] 1990. *The Logic of Practice*. Translated by Richard Nice. Stanford, CA: Stanford University Press.

Bourdieu, Pierre. [1984] 1988. *Homo Academicus*. Translated by Peter Collier. Stanford, CA: Stanford University Press.

Bozarth, Nate. 2011. "Question Life." Retrieved August 5, 2015 (https://youtu.be/ozzz9fWhNDM).

Brenston, Jackie and His Delta Cats. [1951] 2013. "Rocket 88." Retrieved February 3, 2016 (https://www.youtube.com/watch?v=ZdnZ36F5n5c).

Broadbent Institute. 2015. *The Millennial Dialogue Report*. Retrieved July 19 (http://www.broadbentinstitute.ca/the_millennial_dialogue_report).

Brooks, Richard (Director). 1955. *Blackboard Jungle*. Hollywood, CA: Metro-Goldwyn-Mayer.

Bumstead, J.F. 1841. *The Blackboard in the Primary Schools*. Boston: Perkins & Marvin.

Bunz, Mercedes. 2014. *The Silent Revolution: How Digitalization Transforms Knowledge, Work, Journalism, and Politics without Making Too Much Noise*. New York: Palgrave Macmillan.

Burnett, Judith. 2010. *Generations: The Time Machine in Theory and Practice*. Farnham, UK: Ashgate.

Bury, John. 1920. *The Idea of Progress: An Inquiry into Its Origin and Growth*. London: Macmillan.

Cantril, Hadley. 1966. *The Pattern of Human Concerns*. New Brunswick, NJ: Rutgers University Press.

Carr, Edward. 1961. *What Is History?* New York: St. Martin's Press.

Carr, Nicholas. 2011. *The Shallows: What the Internet Is Doing to Our Brains*. New York: W.W. Norton & Company.

Carver, Terrell. 1998. *The Postmodern Marx*. Manchester: Manchester University Press.

Cassirer, Ernst. 1951. *The Philosophy of the Enlightenment*. Princeton: Princeton University Press.

Castells, Manuel. 1999. *Information Technology, Globalization and Social Development*. United Nations Research Institute for Social Development Discussion Paper No. 114. Geneva: UN Research Institute for Social Development. Retrieved October 31, 2015 (http://www.unrisd.org/unrisd/website/document.nsf/70870613ae33162380256b5a004d932e/f270e0c066f3de778 0256b67005b728c/$FILE/dp114.pdf).

Castells, Manuel. 2000. "Materials for an Exploratory Theory of the Network Society." *British Journal of Sociology* 51(1):5–24.

Castells, Manuel. 2010. *The Information Age: Economy, Society and Culture*. 2nd ed. 3 vols. West Sussex, UK: Wiley-Blackwell.

Clark, Ian, Greg Moran, Michael Skolnik, and David Trick. 2009. *Academic Transformation: The Forces Reshaping Higher Education in Ontario*. Montreal: McGill-Queen's University Press.

Cohen, Gerald. 1978. *Karl Marx's Theory of History: A Defence*. New York: Oxford University Press.

Cohen, Lizabeth. 2003. *A Consumers' Republic: The Politics of Mass Consumption in Postwar America*. New York: Knopf.

Cohen, Ronald. 2002. *Rainbow Quest: The Folk Music Revival in America, 1940–1970*. Amherst: University of Massachusetts Press.

Cohler, Anne. 1989. "Introduction." Pp. xi–xxviii in *The Spirit of the Laws*, edited by A. Cohler, B. Miller, and H. Stone. Cambridge: Cambridge University Press.

Cohn, Nik. 1969. *Rock from the Beginning*. New York: Stein and Day.

Cole, G.D.H. 1934. *What Marx Really Meant*. London: Victor Gollancz.

Cole, G.D.H. 1954. *Socialist Thought: Marxism and Anarchism, 1850–1890*. London: Macmillan & Co.

Collingwood, R.G. 1962. *The Idea of History*. Oxford: Clarendon Press.

Comte, Auguste. 1974. *The Essential Comte: Selected from Cours de philosophie positive*. Edited by Stanislav Andreski. New York: Barnes and Noble.

Côté, James and Anton Allahar. 2007. *Ivory Tower Blues: A University System in Crisis*. Toronto: University of Toronto Press.

Coupland, Douglas. 1991. *Generation X: Tales for an Accelerated Culture*. New York: St. Martin's Press.

Coyle, Karen. 2006. "Mass Digitization of Books." *The Journal of Academic Librarianship* 32:641–45.

Crowe, Cameron. 1985. "Liner Notes and Text for *Biograph*." *Bob Dylan: Biograph* [CD recording]. New York: Columbia.

D'Souza, Dinesh. 1992. *Illiberal Education*. New York: Vintage Books.

Dahrendorf, Ralf. 1959. *Class and Class Conflict in Industrial Society*. Stanford, CA: Stanford University Press.

Dahrendorf, Ralf. 1967. *Society and Democracy in Germany*. Garden City, NY: Doubleday.

Dawson, Jim. 2005. *Rock Around the Clock: The Record That Started the Rock Revolution*. San Francisco: Backbeat Books.

ddavies315. 2011. "The Millennials: The Next Best Thing." Retrieved August 14, 2015 (https://www.youtube.com/watch?v=5MQF4UTTL3Y).

Deane, Phyllis. 1979. *The First Industrial Revolution*. 2nd ed. Cambridge: Cambridge University Press.

Delanty, Gerard. 2007. "Modernity." *Blackwell Encyclopedia of Sociology*, edited by George Ritzer. Retrieved October 2, 2007 (http://www.blackwellreference.com/subscriber/tocnode.html?id=g9781405124331_chunk_g978140512433119_ss1-117).

Derrida, Jacques. 1994. *Specters of Marx*. Translated by Peggy Kamuf. London: Routledge.

Descartes, René. 1911. *The Philosophical Works of Descartes*. Vol. 1. Translated by E.S. Haldane and G.R.T. Ross. Cambridge: Cambridge University Press.

Deutscher, Isaac. 1971. "Discovering *Das Kapital*." Pp. 255–64 in *Marxism in Our Time*, edited by Tamara Deutscher. San Francisco: Ramparts Press.

Dijksterhuis, E.J. [1959] 1986. *The Mechanization of the World Picture*. Princeton, NJ: Princeton University Press.

Dobb, Maurice. 1947. *Studies in the Development of Capitalism*. New York: International Publishers.

Dos Passos, John. 1932. *Nineteen Nineteen*. London: Constable.

Dos Passos, John. 1936. *Big Money*. New York: Harcourt, Brace.

Dos Passos, John. 1937. *U.S.A.* New York: Modern Library.

Duggan, Maeve, Nicole Ellison, Cliff Lampe, Amanda Lenhart, and Mary Madden. 2015. "Social Media Update 2014" *Pew Research Center: Internet, Science & Tech*, January 9. Retrieved August 5, 2015 (http://www.pewinternet.org/2015/01/09/social-media-update-2014/).

Durkheim, Émile. [1892] 1960. *Montesquieu and Rousseau: Forerunners of Sociology*. Translated by R. Manheim. Ann Arbor: University of Michigan Press.

Durkheim, Émile. [1893] 1933. *The Division of Labor in Society*. Translated by G. Simpson. New York: The Free Press of Glencoe.

Durkheim, Émile. [1895] 1982. *The Rules of Sociological Method and Selected Texts on Sociology and Its Method*. Translated by W.D. Halls. New York: The Free Press.

Durkheim, Émile. [1897] 1951. *Suicide: A Study in Sociology*. Translated by J. Spaulding and G. Simpson. New York: The Free Press of Glencoe.

Durkheim, Émile. [1897] 1982. "Marxism and Sociology: The Materialist Conception of History." Pp. 167–74 in *The Rules of Sociological Method and Selected Texts on Sociology and Its Method*. Translated by W.D. Halls. New York: The Free Press.

Durkheim, Émile. [1901] 1982. "Preface to the Second Edition." Pp. 34–47 in *The Rules of Sociological Method and Selected Texts on Sociology and Its Method*. Translated by W.D. Halls. New York: The Free Press.

Durkheim, Émile. [1907] 1982. "Influences upon Durkheim's View of Sociology." Pp. 257-60 in *The Rules of Sociological Method and Selected Texts on Sociology and Its Method*. Translated by W.D. Halls. New York: The Free Press.

Durkheim, Émile. [1908] 1982. "Method of Sociology." Pp. 245–47 in *The Rules of Sociological Method and Selected Texts on Sociology and Its Method*. Translated by W.D. Halls. New York: The Free Press.

Durkheim, Émile. [1909] 1982. "The Contribution of Sociology to Psychology and Philosophy." Pp. 236–40 in *The Rules of Sociological Method and Selected Texts on Sociology and Its Method*. Translated by W.D. Halls. New York: The Free Press.

Durkheim, Émile. [1912] 1915. *The Elementary Forms of the Religious Life: A Study in Religious Sociology*. Translated by Joseph Swain. New York: The Macmillan Company.

Durkheim, Émile. [1924] 1953. *Sociology and Philosophy*. Translated by D.F. Pocock. London: Cohen & West.

Durkheim, Émile. [1925] 1973. *Moral Education*. Translated by Everett K. Wilson and Herman Schnurer. New York: Free Press.

Durkheim, Émile. [1928] 1958. *Socialism and Saint-Simon*. Edited by Marcel Mauss, translated by Charlotte Sattler. Yellow Springs, OH: The Antioch Press.

Durkheim, Émile. [1938] 1977. *The Evolution of Educational Thought: Lectures on the Formation and Development of Secondary Education in France*. Boston: Routledge & Kegan Paul.

Durkheim, Émile. 1950. *Leçons de sociologie: Physique des moeurs et du droit (Sociology Lessons: The Physics of Morals and the Law)*. Paris: Presses universitaires de France. (Unpublished lectures delivered at Bordeaux between 1896 and 1900 and at the Sorbonne in Paris between 1902 and 1915.)

Durkheim, Émile. [1955] 1983. *Pragmatism and Sociology*. New York: Cambridge University Press.

Durkheim, Émile. 1972. *Emile Durkheim: Selected Writings*. Edited by Anthony Giddens. Cambridge: Cambridge University Press.

Durkheim, Émile. 2004. *Durkheim's Philosophy Lectures*. Edited and translated by Neil Gross and Robert Alun Jones. Cambridge: Cambridge University Press.

Dylan, Bob. 1962a. "My Life in a Stolen Moment." Retrieved January 24, 2016 (https://beatpatrol.wordpress.com/2010/03/05/bob-dylan-my-life-in-a-stolen-moment-1962/).

Dylan, Bob. 1962b. "Song to Woody." Retrieved January 24, 2016 (http://bobdylan.com/songs/hard-times-new-york-town/).

Dylan, Bob. 1962c. "Talking New York." Retrieved January 24, 2016 (http://bobdylan.com/songs/talkin-new-york/).

Dylan, Bob. 1963a. "A Hard Rain's A-Gonna Fall." Retrieved January 24, 2016 (http://bobdylan.com/songs/hard-rains-gonna-fall/).

Dylan, Bob. 1963b. "I Shall Be Free." January 24, 2016 (http://bobdylan.com/songs/i-shall-be-free-no-10/).

Dylan, Bob. 1963c. "Last Thoughts on Woody Guthrie." Retrieved January 24, 2016 (http://bobdylan.com/songs/last-thoughts-woody-guthrie/).

Dylan, Bob. 1964a. *Another Side of Bob Dylan*. Retrieved January 24, 2016 (http://bobdylan.com/albums/another-side-of-bob-dylan/).

Dylan, Bob. 1964b. "Ballad of Hollis Brown." Retrieved January 24, 2016 (http://bobdylan.com/songs/ballad-hollis-brown/).

Dylan, Bob. 1964c. "Chimes of Freedom." Retrieved January 24, 2016 (http://bobdylan.com/songs/chimes-freedom/).

Dylan, Bob. 1964d. "My Back Pages." Retrieved January 24, 2016 (http://bobdylan.com/songs/my-back-pages/).

Dylan, Bob. 1964e. "Only a Pawn in Their Game." Retrieved January 24, 2016 (http://bobdylan.com/songs/only-pawn-their-game/).

Dylan, Bob. 1964f. "Restless Farewell." Retrieved January 24, 2016 (http://bobdylan.com/songs/restless-farewell/).

Dylan, Bob. 1964g. *The Times They Are A-Changin'*. Retrieved January 24, 2016 (http://bobdylan.com/albums/the-times-they-are-a-changin/).

Dylan, Bob. 1964h. "The Times They Are A-Changin'." Retrieved January 24, 2016 (http://bobdylan.com/songs/times-they-are-changin/).

Dylan, Bob. 1964i. "With God on Our Side." Retrieved January 24, 2016 (http://bobdylan.com/songs/god-our-side/).

Dylan, Bob. 2004. *Chronicles: Volume One*. Toronto: Simon & Schuster Paperbacks.

Dylan, Bob. 2006. *Dylan on Dylan: The Essential Interviews*. Edited by Jonathan Cott. London: Hodder & Stoughton.

Eagan, Kevin, Ellen Stolzenberg, Joseph Ramirez, Melissa Aragagon, Maria Suchard, and Sylvia Hurtado. 2014. *The American Freshman: National Norms Fall 2014*. Los Angeles: Higher Education Research Institute.

Eagan, Kevin, Ellen Bara Stolzenberg, Abigail K. Bates, Melissa C. Aragon, Maria Ramirez Suchard, Cecilia Rios-Aguilar. 2015. *The American Freshman: National Norms Fall 2015*. Los Angeles: Higher Education Research Institute.

Eisenstein, Elizabeth. 1979. *The Printing Press as an Agent of Change: Communications and Cultural Transformations in Early Modern Europe*. 2 vols. Cambridge: Cambridge University Press.

Elliot, Charles, ed. 1909–17. *Harvard Classics*. 51 vols. New York: P.F. Collier & Son.

"Elvis Presley Dokumentation Karriere 1956 [Elvis Presley Documentation of a Career]." 2010. Retrieved February 11, 2016 (https://www.youtube.com/watch?v=BxRH5BdSJqo).

Emberley, Peter and Waller Newell. 1994. *Bankrupt Education: The Decline of Liberal Education in Canada*. Toronto: University of Toronto Press.

Engels, Frederick. [1844] 1975. *Outlines of a Critique of Political Economy*. Pp. 418–31 in *Karl Marx and Frederick Engels: Collected Works*. Vol. 3. New York: International Publishers.

Engels, Frederick. [1845] 1975. *The Condition of the Working-Class in England*. Translated by Florence Kelly-Wischnewetzky. Pp. 295–596 in *Karl Marx and Frederick Engels: Collected Works*. Vol. 4. New York: International Publishers.

Engels, Frederick. [1878] 1939. *Anti-Dühring: Herr Eugen Dühring's Revolution in Science*. Edited by Clemens Dutt, translated by Emile Burns. New York: International Publishers. (First published in serial form in *Vorwärts* in 1877–78.)

Engels, Frederick. [1883] 1958. "Speech at the Graveside of Karl Marx." Pp. 167–69 in *Karl Marx and Frederick Engels: Selected Works*. Vol. 2. Moscow: Foreign Languages Publishing House.

Engels, Frederick. [1886] 1935. *Socialism: Utopian and Scientific*. Translated by Edward Aveling. New York: International Publishers.

Engels, Frederick. 1940. *Dialectics of Nature*. Translated and edited by Clemens Dutt. New York: International Publishers. (Written between 1873 and 1883.)

Fallis, George. 2007. *Multiversities, Ideas, and Democracy*. Toronto: University of Toronto Press.

Father Knows Best. 1954–60. New York: CBS.

Fay, Margaret. 1978. "Did Marx Offer to Dedicate Capital to Darwin? A Reassessment of the Evidence." *Journal of the History of Ideas* 39:133–46.

Febvre, Lucien and Henri-Jean Martin. [1958] 1976. *The Coming of the Book: The Impact of Printing 1450–1800*. Translated by David Gerard. London: New Left Books.

Ferguson, Adam. [1767] 1971. *An Essay on the History of Civil Society*. New York: Garland Publishers.

Ferguson, Niall. 2001. *The Cash Nexus: Money and Power in the Modern World, 1700–2000*. New York: Basic Books.

Fetscher, Iring. 1985. *Karl Marx und der Marxismus: Von der Ökonomiekritik zur Weltanschauung (Karl Marx and Marxism: From the Critique of Political Economy to Worldview)*. 4th ed. Munich: Piper Verlag.

Fichte, Johann Gottlieb. 1834–46. *Sämmtliche Werke* (Collected Works). 11 vols. Berlin: Veit und Comp.

Fiske, John. 1989. *Reading the Popular*. Boston: Unwin Hyman.

Fitch, Sir Joshua Girling. 1898. *Thomas and Matthew Arnold and Their Influence on English Education*. New York: Scribner's Sons.

Flexner, Abraham. [1930] 1994. *Universities: American, English, German*. New Brunswick, NJ: Transaction Publishers.

Foot, David. 1996. *Boom, Bust & Echo: How to Profit from the Coming Demographic Shift*. Toronto: Macfarlane, Walter & Ross.

Ford, Larry. 1971. "Geographic Factors in the Origin, Evolution, and Diffusion of Rock and Roll Music." *The Journal of Geography* 70:455–64.

Foucault, Michel. [1966] 1970. *The Order of Things: An Archaeology of the Human Sciences*. New York: Random House.

Foucault, Michel. [1975] 1995. *Discipline and Punish: The Birth of the Prison*. Translated by Alan Sheridan. New York: Vintage Books.

Foucault, Michel. 2008. *The Birth of Biopolitics*. Edited by Michel Senellart, translated by Graham Burchell. New York: Palgrave Macmillan. (Lectures given at the Collège de France, 1978–79.)

Free the Children. 2014. "We Day: We Act." Retrieved April 10, 2016 (http://www.weday.com/files/2014/10/WE-DAY-1-PAGER-CA.pdf).

Free the Children. 2016. "ME to WE." Retrieved April 10, 2016 (http://www.weday.com/what-is-we-day/).

Freire, Paulo. [1968] 1970. *Pedagogy of the Oppressed*. Translated by Myra Ramos. New York: Seabury Press.

Frieden, Jeffry. 2006. *Global Capitalism: Its Fall and Rise in the Twentieth Century*. New York: W.W. Norton & Company.

Gabler, Neal. 1998. *Life: The Movie—How Entertainment Conquered Reality*. New York: Vintage Books.

Galilei, Galileo. 1967. *Dialogue Concerning the Two Chief World Systems: Ptolemaic and Copernican*. Translated by Stillman Drake. Berkeley: University of California Press.

Gardner, Howard and Katie Davis. 2014. *The App Generation*. New Haven: Yale University Press.

Garofalo, Reebee and Steve Chapple. 1978. "From ASCAP to Alan Freed: The Pre-history of Rock 'n' Roll." *Popular Music and Society* 6:72–80.

Gatehouse, Jonathon. 2014. "Why We Need to Clear Our Cluttered Minds." *Maclean's*, September, 5. Retrieved November 26, 2015 (http://www.macleans.ca/society/science/why-we-need-to-clear-our-cluttered-minds/).

Gehlen, Arnold. [1957] 1980. *Man in the Age of Technology*. New York: Columbia University Press.

Giddens, Anthony. 1971. *Capitalism and Modern Social Theory: An Analysis of the Writings of Marx, Durkheim, and Max Weber*. New York: Cambridge University Press.

Giddens, Anthony. 1972. "Introduction: Durkheim's Writings in Sociology and Social Philosophy." Pp. 1–50 in *Emile Durkheim: Selected Writings*, edited by Anthony Giddens. New York: Cambridge University Press.

Giddens, Anthony. 1976. "Classical Social Theory and the Origins of Modern Sociology." *American Journal of Sociology* 81:703–29.

Giddens, Anthony. 1984. *The Constitution of Society*. Berkeley: University of California Press.

Gill, Andy. 1998. *My Back Pages: Classic Bob Dylan, 1962–69*. London: Carleton Books.

Goldthorpe, John. 1968. *The Affluent Worker: Industrial Attitudes and Behaviour*. London: Cambridge University Press.

Goldthorpe, John. 1969. *The Affluent Worker in the Class Structure*. London: Cambridge University Press.

Golub, Adam. 2009. "'They Turned the School into a Jungle! How *The Blackboard Jungle* Redefined the Education Crisis in Postwar America." *Film and History* 39:21–30.

Google. n.d. "Google Books Library Project—An Enhanced Card Catalog of the World's Books." Retrieved November 18, 2015 (http://www.google.ca/googlebooks/library/).

Gouldner, Alvin. 1958. "Introduction." Pp. v–xxvii in *Socialism and Saint-Simon*, by Émile Durkheim, edited by Marcel Mauss. Yellow Springs, OH: The Antioch Press.

Gouldner, Alvin. 1970. *The Coming Crisis of Western Sociology*. New York: Basic Books.

Green Day. 2004a. "American Idiot [Official Video]." Retrieved February 3, 2016 (https://www.youtube.com/watch?v=Ee_uujKuJMI).

Green Day. 2004b. "Boulevard of Broken Dreams [Official Video]." Retrieved February 3, 2016 (https://www.youtube.com/watch?v=S0a3gO7tL-c).

Grossmann, Henryk. 1929. *Das Akkumulations- und Zusammenbruchsgesetz des kapitalistischen Systems* (*The Law of Accumulation and Collapse of the Capitalist System*). Leipzig: Verlag von C. L. Hirschfeld

Gulbenkian Commission on the Restructuring of the Social Sciences. 1996. *Open the Social Sciences: Report of the Gulbenkian Commission on the Restructuring of the Social Sciences*. Stanford, CA: Stanford University Press.

Guralnick, Peter. 1994. *Last Train to Memphis: The Rise of Elvis Presley*. Boston: Little, Brown, and Company.

Guthrie, Woody. 1943. *Bound for Glory*. New York: E.P. Dutton.

Guthrie, Woody. 1971. *Bound for Glory*. New York: Penguin Books.

Habermas, Jürgen. [1968] 1971. *Knowledge and Human Interests*. Boston: Beacon Press.

Habermas, Jürgen. 1970. "Technology and Science as 'Ideology.'" Pp. 81–122 in *Toward a Rational Society*, translated by Jeremy Shapiro. Boston: Beacon Press.

Habermas, Jürgen. 1976. *Legitimation Crisis*. London: Heinemann.

Habermas, Jürgen. [1981] 1984. *Theory of Communicative Action*. Vol 1, *Reason and the Rationalization of Society*. Translated by Thomas McCarthy. Boston: Beacon Press.

Habermas, Jürgen. [1985] 1987. *Theory of Communicative Action*. Vol. 2, *Lifeworld and System: A Critique of Functionalist Reason*. Translated by Thomas McCarthy. Boston: Beacon Press.

Halberstam, David. 1993. *The Fifties*. New York: Villard Books.

Halévey, Elie. [1928] 1972. *The Growth of Philosophic Radicalism*. London: Faber and Faber.

Haley and the Saddlemen. [1951] 2009a. "Rock the Joint." Retrieved February 6, 2016 (https://www.youtube.com/watch?v=44YjmMKQTDU).

Haley and the Saddlemen. [1951] 2009b. "Rocket 88." Retrieved February 6, 2016 (https://www.youtube.com/watch?v=TPLS2i9dSy0).

Haley with Haley's Comets. [1953] 2012. "Crazy Man, Crazy." Retrieved February 6, 2016 (https://www.youtube.com/watch?v=HiOd4yXrBLc).

Haley with His Comets. [1954] 2012a. "Thirteen Women (And Only One Man)." Retrieved February 3, 2016 (https://www.youtube.com/watch?v=tvS-vQkLZrk).

Haley with His Comets. [1954] 2012b. "(We're Gonna) Rock Around the Clock." Retrieved February 3, 2016 (https://www.youtube.com/watch?v=sGPz5ewB75M).

Hall, Stuart. 1964. *The Popular Arts*. London: Hutchinson Educational Books.

Hallinan, Blake. 2011a. "Cracks and Fissures." Retrieved August 5, 2015 (https://youtu.be/4U-i_s22_Hc).

Hallinan, Blake. 2011b. "Standardized Education." Retrieved August 12, 2015 (https://www.youtube.com/watch?v=4U-i_s22_Hc&feature=youtu.be).

Harris, Sharon. 2007. "Slam Dances Tonight." *Torontoist*, April 14 (https://www.youtube.com/watch?v=Qn5vJBWgCLU&feature=youtu.be).

Harris, Sharon. 2014. "The Contradictions of Capitalism," *RSA: 21st Century Enlightenment*, April 9. Retrieved November 28, 2015 (https://www.thersa.org/events/2014/04/the-contradictions-of-capitalism-/).

Harvey, David. 2005. *A Brief History of Neoliberalism*. New York: Oxford University Press.

Haupt, Georges. 1982. "Marx and Marxism." Pp. 265–89 in *The History of Marxism: Marxism in Marx's Day*, edited by Eric Hobsbawm. Bloomington: Indiana University Press.

Hayek, Friedrich von. 1931. *Prices and Production*. London: G. Routledge and Sons.

Hayek, Friedrich von. 1934. *Monetary Theory and the Trade Cycle*. London: Cape Editions.

Hechinger, Grace. 2003. "Clark Kerr, Leading Public Educator and Former Head of California's Universities, Dies at 92." *New York Times*, December 2 (http://www.nytimes.com/2003/12/02/us/clark-kerr-leading-public-educator-former-head-california-s-universities-dies-92.html?pagewanted=all).

Hegel, Georg Wilhelm Friedrich. [1807] 1977. *The Phenomenology of Spirit*. Translation of the 5th edition by A.V. Miller. Oxford: Clarendon Press.

Hegel, Georg Wilhelm Friedrich. [1830] 1983. *Enzyklopädie der philosophischen Wissenschaften (Encyclopaedia of Philosophical Sciences)*. 3rd ed. 3 vols. Frankfurt: Suhrkamp.

Hegel, Georg Wilhelm Friedrich. 1840. *Georg Wilhelm Friedrich Hegel's Vorlesungen über die Geschichte der Philosophie (Hegel's Lectures on the History of Philosophy)*. Vol. 1. Edited by Carl Michelet. Berlin: Duncker and Humbolt.

Hegel, Georg Wilhelm Friedrich. 1841. *Wissenschaft der Logik (The Science of Logic)*. 2nd ed. Berlin: Duncker.

Hegel, Georg Wilhelm Friedrich. 1844. *Georg Wilhelm Friedrich Hegel's Vorlesungen über die Geschichte der Philosophie (Hegel's Lectures on the History of Philosophy)*. Vol. 2. Edited by Carl Michelet. Berlin: Duncker and Humbolt.

Hilferding, Rudolf. [1904] 1949. *Böhm-Bawerk's Criticism of Marx*. New York: Augustus M. Kelley.

Hill, Christopher. 1961. *Century of Revolution: 1603–1714*. Edinburgh: T. Nelson.

Hill, Christopher. 1972. *The World Turned Upside Down: Radical Ideas during the English Revolution*. London: Temple Smith.

Hobbes, Thomas. [1651] 1968. *Leviathan*. Edited by C.B. Macpherson. Toronto: Penguin Books.

Hobsbawm, Eric. 1962. *The Age of Revolution: 1789–1848*. London: Weidenfeldand Nicolson.

Hobsbawm, Eric. 1964. *Labouring Men: Studies in the History of Labour*. London: Weidenfeld and Nicolson.

Hobsbawm, Eric. 1969. *Industry and Empire: 1750 to the Present Day*. Harmondsworth, UK: Penguin Books.

Hobsbawm, Eric. 1994. *The Age of Extremes: The Short Twentieth Century, 1914–1991*. London: Michael Joseph.

Hobsbawm, Eric. 1999. *Industry and Empire: The Birth of the Industrial Revolution*. New York: The New Press.

Hoggart, Richard. 1958. *The Uses of Literacy: Aspects of Working-Class Life, with Special Reference to Publications and Entertainment*. Harmondsworth: Pelican Books.

Hoggart, Richard. 1970. "Why I Value Literature." Pp. 11–18 in *Speaking to Each Other*, by Richard Hoggart. Vol. 2. Harmondsworth: Penguin Books.

Hollingdale, Reginald. 1970. "Introduction." Pp. 9–38 in *Schopenhauer: Essays and Aphorisms*, translated and edited by Reginald Hollingdale. Markham, ON: Penguin Books.

Holly, Buddy. [1958] 2009. "The Apartment Tapes." Retrieved February 20, 2016 (http://edsel.myrmid.com/buddy/buddy.html).

Hook, Sidney. 1987. *Out of Step: An Unquiet Life in the 20th Century.* New York: Harper and Row.

Horkheimer, Max. 1947. *Eclipse of Reason.* New York: Oxford University Press.

Horkheimer, Max. 1974. *The Critique of Instrumental Reason.* Translated by Matthew O'Connell. New York: Seabury Press.

Horkheimer, Max and Theodor Adorno. [1944] 1972. *Dialectic of Enlightenment.* Translated by John Cumming. New York: Seabury Press.

Howe, Neil and William Strauss. 1991. *Generations: The History of America's Future, 1584 to 2069.* New York: William Morrow and Company.

Howe, Neil and William Strauss. 1992. "The New Generation Gap." *Atlantic Monthly*, December 1. Retrieved August 2, 2015 (https://www.theatlantic.com/past/docs/issues/92dec/9212genx.htm).

Howe, Neil and William Strauss. 2000. *Millennials Rising: The Next Great Generation.* New York: Vintage Books.

Hughes, H. Stuart. 1958. *Consciousness and Society: The Reorientation of European Social Thought, 1890–1930.* New York: Alfred A. Knopf.

Hughes, Thomas. 1857. *Tom Brown's Schooldays.* London: George Routledge.

Humboldt, Wilhelm von. 1963. *Humanist without Portfolio: An Anthology of the Writings of Wilhelm von Humboldt.* Translated by Marianne Cowan. Detroit: Wayne State University Press.

Hume, David. [1739–40] 1941. *A Treatise on Human Nature.* 3 vols. Edited by L.A. Selby-Bigge. Oxford: The Clarendon Press.

Hume, David. [1748] 1966. *Enquiry Concerning Human Understanding.* La Salle, IL: Open Court Classics.

Hunter, Evan. 1954. *Blackboard Jungle.* New York: Simon and Schuster.

Huxley, Aldous. 1932. *Brave New World.* Garden City, NY: Garden City Publishing Company.

Illich, Ivan. 1971. *Deschooling Society.* New York: Harper and Row.

Iman, Lindsey. 2011a. "Choices." Retrieved August 12, 2015 (https://www.youtube.com/watch?v=ktOv6V8wc-A).

Iman, Lindsey. 2011b. "Generation Me." Uploaded May 11, 2011. Retrieved August 5, 2015 (https://www.youtube.com/watch?v=Dof-D5KWIPc&feature=youtu.be).

Iman, Lindsey. 2011c. "What Affects My Learning." Retrieved August 12, 2015 (https://www.youtube.com/watch?v=XEvTyOCP-hQ).

Inglehart, Ronald and Christian Welzel. 2007. "Modernization." *Blackwell Encyclopedia of Sociology*, edited by George Ritzer. Retrieved October 2, 2007 (http://www.blackwellreference.com/subscriber/tocnode.html?id=g9781405124331_chunk_g978140512433119_ss1-118).

Jackson, Jaoab. 2010. "Google: 129 Million Different Books Have Been Published." *PCWorld*, August 6. Retrieved November 18, 2015 (http://www.pcworld.com/article/202803/google_129_million_different_books_have_been_published.html#comments).

"James Dean Dancing in the TV Show 'Glory in the Flower'." [1953] 2015. Retrieved February 3, 2016 (https://www.facebook.com/15AndInLoveWithTheLateJamesDean/videos/838584912849295/).

James, Etta and David Ritz. 1995. *Rage to Survive: The Etta James Story.* Cambridge, MA: Da Capo Press.

Jarboe, Greg. 2014. "What 300 Hours of Video Uploaded to YouTube Every Minute Means for Advertisers." *reelseo*, December 1. Retrieved August 14, 2015 (http://www.reelseo.com/300-hours-video-youtube-advertisers/).

Jenkins, Henry. 2009. *Confronting the Challenges of Participatory Culture: Media Education for the 21st Century.* Retrieved August 12, 2015 (https://mitpress.mit.edu/sites/default/files/titles/free_download/9780262513623_Confronting_the_Challenges.pdf).

"Jimmie Rogers Snow Joins Kerry Pharr on In Your Corner," 2014. Retrieved February 21, 2016 (https://www.youtube.com/watch?v=Hz4dYTKgOXM).

Johansson, Charity and Peter Felten. 2014. *Transforming Students: Fulfilling the Promise of Higher Education.* Baltimore: Johns Hopkins University Press.

Jones, Garth Stedman. 1982. "Engels and the History of Marxism." Pp. 290–326 in *The History of Marxism: Marxism in Marx's Day*, edited by Eric Hobsbawm. Bloomington: Indiana University Press.

Jones, Quincy, Bob Meyrowitz, and David Salzman (Producers). 1995. *History of Rock and Roll.* Burbank, CA: Warner Home Video.

JSTOR. n.d. "JSTOR to Offer DRM-Free, Unlimited-User Access for All eBooks." Retrieved November 19, 2015 (http://about.jstor.org/news/unlimited-drm-free-ebook-access).

JWT. 2012. *Gen Z: Digital in Their DNA*. April. Retrieved August 5, 2015 (http://www.slideshare.net/jwtintelligence/f-external-genz041812-12653599).

Kallan, Horace. 1957. "Modernism." Pp. 564–69 in *Encyclopaedia of the Social Sciences*. Vol. 10, edited by Edwin Seligman and Alvin Johnson. New York: The Macmillan Company.

Kant, Immanuel. [1783] 1968. *Prolegomena zu einer jeden künftigen Metaphysik die als Wissenschaft wird auftreten können* (*Prolegomena to Any Future Metaphysics That Can Qualify as a Science*). Pp. 113–264 in *Werke* (*Collected Works*). Vol. 5. Darmstadt: Wissenschaftlighe Buchgeselschaft.

Kautsky, Karl. [1887] 1925. *The Economic Doctrines of Karl Marx*. Translated by H.J. Stenning. London: A. & C. Black.

Kautsky, Karl. 1898–1903. *Karl Kautsky Papers*. D XIV 123–28. International Institute for Social History, Amsterdam, Netherlands.

Kautsky, Karl. 1927a. *Die materialistische Geschichtsaufassung* (*The Materialist Conception of History*). Bd. 1, *Natur und Gesellschaft* (Vol. 1, *Nature and Society*). Berlin: J.H.W. Dietz.

Kautsky, Karl. 1927b. *Die materialistische Geschichtsaufassung* (*The Materialist Conception of History*). Bd. 2, *Der Staat und die Entwicklung der Menscheit* (Vol. 2, *The State and the Development of Humankind*). Berlin: J.H.W. Dietz.

Kautsky, Karl. 1935. *Aus der Frühzeit des Marxismus: Engels' Briefwechsel mit Kautsky* (*From the Early Period of Marxism: Engels's Correspondence with Kautsky*), edited and elucidated by Karl Kautsky. Prague: Orbis Verlag.

Kelly, Steven. 2011a. "Mediated Learning?" Uploaded January 23. Retrieved August 12, 2015 (https://www.youtube.com/watch?v=dh2LBe325-8).

Kelly, Steven. 2011b. "An Ode to Tradition." Uploaded February 7. Retrieved August 12, 2015 (https://www.youtube.com/watch?v=Yn3H-KWs84U).

Kelly, Steven. 2011c. "The Old Future of Ed Reform." Uploaded May 11. Retrieved August 5, 2015 (https://www.youtube.com/watch?t=29&v=Xwn1QJyUPxA).

Kerr, Clark. 1963. *The Uses of the University*. Cambridge, MA: Harvard University Press.

Keynes, John Maynard. 1936. *The General Theory of Employment, Interest, and Money*. New York: Harcourt, Brace.

Kingston, Anne. 2014. "Get Ready for Generation Z." *Maclean's*, 127:42–45.

Knowles, Beyoncé. 2013. "Super Bowl 2013 Halftime Show." Retrieved February 17, 2016 (https://www.youtube.com/watch?v=kKVorba5GLs).

Kocka, Jürgen. 2016. *Capitalism: A Short History*. Princeton: Princeton University Press.

Kolodny, Annette. 1998. *Failing the Future: A Dean Looks at Higher Education in the Twenty-First Century*. Durham: Duke University Press.

Korsch, Karl. 1922. *Kernpunkte der materialistischen Geschichtsauffassung* (*Principles of the Materialist Conception of History*). Leipzig: C.L. Hirschfeld.

Korsch, Karl. [1923] 1970. *Marxism and Philosophy*. Translated by Fred Halliday. London: New Left Books.

Korsch, Karl. 1929. *Die materialistische Geschichtsauffassung: Eine Auseinandersetzung mit Karl Kautsky* (*The Materialist Conception of History: A Dispute with Karl Kautsky*). Leipzig: C.L. Hirschfeld.

Korsch, Karl. 1971. *Die materialistische Geschichtsauffasung und andere Schriften* (*The Materialist Conception of History and Other Writings*), edited by Erich Gerlach. Frankfurt: Europäische Verlagsanstalt.

Kranzberg, Melvin. 1985. "The Information Age: Evolution or Revolution?" Pp. 35–53 in *Information Technologies and Social Transformation*, edited by Bruce Guile. Washington, DC: National Academy Press.

Kuhn, Thomas. 1957. *The Copernican Revolution: Planetary Astronomy in the Development of Western Thought*. Cambridge, MA: Harvard University Press.

Kuhn, Thomas. 1962. *The Structure of Scientific Revolutions*. Chicago: University of Chicago Press.

Labriola, Antonio. 1904. "Historical Materialism." Pp. 95–246 in *Essays on the Materialistic Conception of History*, translated by Charles H. Kerr. New York: Charles H. Kerr.

Lasswell, Harold. 1965. "The Policy Sciences of Development." *World Politics* 17:286–309.

Latour, Bruno. 2005. *Reassembling the Social*. New York: Oxford University Press.

Lauper, Cyndi. 2014. "The Story Behind 'Money Changes Everything'." Retrieved February 21, 2016 (https://www.youtube.com/watch?v=i80d1vsa2BI).

Leave It to Beaver. 1957–58. New York: CBS.

Leave It to Beaver. 1958–63. New York: ABC.

Leavis, F.R. and Denys Thompson. 1933. *Culture and Environment: The Training of Critical Awareness*. London: Chatto & Windus.

Left, Sarah, Simon Jeffery, and Jane Perrone. 2001. "Violence Erupts in Central London." *The Guardian* (May 1). Retrieved February 20, 2016 (http://www.theguardian.com/world/2001/may/01/mayday.immigrationpolicy1).

Lenhart, Amanda. 2015. "Teens, Social Media & Technology Overview 2015." *Pew Research Center: Internet, Science & Tech*, April 9. Retrieved August 5, 2015 (http://www.pewinternet.org/files/2015/04/PI_TeensandTech_Update2015_0409151.pdf).

Lenin, Vladimir. 1927. *Materialism and Empirio-Criticism*. New York: International Publishers.

Lenin, Vladimir. 1943. "The Proletarian Revolution and the Renegade Kautsky." Pp. 113–217 in *V. I. Lenin Selected Works*. Vol. 7. New York: International Publishers. (First published in *Pravda* on October 11, 1918.)

Lenin, Vladimir. 1972. *Philosophical Notebooks*. London: Lawrence and Wishart. (Written between 1895 and 1916 with the bulk written between 1915–16.)

Lerner, Daniel. 1958. *The Passing of Traditional Society: Modernizing the Middle East*. Glencoe, IL: The Free Press.

Lerner, Daniel. 1968. "Modernization." Pp. 386–95 in *International Encyclopedia of the Social Sciences*. Vol. 10, edited by David Sills. New York: Crowell Collier and Macmillan.

Lerner, Murray (Producer). 2007. *The Other Side of the Mirror: Bob Dylan Live at Newport Folk Festival 1963–1965*. New York: Columbia.

Levine, Melvin. 2005. *Ready or Not, Here Life Comes*. New York: Simon & Schuster.

Levit, Alexandra. 2015. "Make Way for Generation Z." *New York Times*, March 28. Retrieved July 13, 2015 (http://www.nytimes.com/2015/03/29/jobs/make-way-for-generation-z.html).

Levitin, John. 2014. *The Organized Mind: Thinking Straight in an Age of Information Overload*. Toronto: Penguin Canada.

Levitt, Cyril. 1984. *Children of Privilege: Student Revolt in the Sixties*. Toronto: University of Toronto Press.

Lewis, Clive Staples. 2001. *Mere Christianity*. New York: HarperCollins.

Lichtheim, George. 1965. *Marxism: An Historical and Critical Study*. New York: Frederick A. Praeger.

Lichtman, Richard. 1979. *An Outline of Marxism*. Toronto: Coles Publishing.

Lilienfeld, Paul von. 1873. *Die menschliche Gesellschaft als Realer Organismus (Human Society as a Real Organism)*. Hamburg: E. Behre Verlag.

Locke, John. [1694] 1967. *Two Treatises on Government*. London: Cambridge University Press.

Lovejoy, Arthur. 1936. *The Great Chain of Being: A Study of the History of an Idea*. Cambridge, MA: Harvard University Press.

Lovejoy, Arthur. 1948. *Essays in the History of Ideas*. Baltimore: Johns Hopkins Press.

Luhmann, Niklas. [1984] 1995. *Social Systems*. Translated by John Bednarz Jr. and Dirk Baecker. Stanford, CA: Stanford University Press.

Lukács, Georg. [1923] 1970. *History and Class Consciousness*. Translated by Rodney Livingstone. London: Merlin Books.

Lukes, Stephen. 1973. *Emile Durkheim, His Life and Work: An Historical and Critical Study*. New York: Harper and Row.

Lukes, Stephen. 1982. "Introduction." Pp. 1–27 in *The Rules of Sociological Method and Selected Texts on Sociology and Its Method*. New York: The Free Press.

Luxemburg, Rosa. 1951. *The Accumulation of Capital*. Translated by Agnes Schwarzschild. London: Routledge and Kegan Paul.

Lyotard, Jean-François. 1984. *The Postmodern Condition: A Report on Knowledge*. Translated by Geoff Bennington and Brian Massumi. Minneapolis: University of Minnesota Press.

MadV. 2006a. "One World." Retrieved August 14, 2015 (https://www.youtube.com/watch?v=FHcoxjRGI60).

MadV. 2006b. "The Message." Retrieved August 14, 2015 (https://www.youtube.com/watch?v=Z-BzXpOch-E).

Malthus, Thomas. 1827. *Definitions in Political Economy*. London: Murray.

Mandel, Ernest. [1972] 1975. *Late Capitalism*. Translated by Joris De Bres. London: New Left Books.

Mangen, Anne, Bente Walgermo, and Kolbjørn Brønnick. 2013. "Reading Linear Tests on Paper versus Computer Screens: Effects on Reading Comprehension." *International Journal of Educational Research* 58:61–68.

Marceau, Haley. 2011. "Unbinding Education." Retrieved August 5, 2015 (http://visionsofstudents.org/).

Marcus, Greil. 1997. *Mystery Train: Images of America in Rock 'n' Roll Music.* 4th revised ed. New York: Plume Books.

Marcus, Greil. 2006. "Elvis Presley: The Ed Sullivan Shows." Liner notes for *Elvis Presley: The Ed Sullivan Shows* [DVD]. Chatsworth, CA: Image Entertainment. Retrieved February 15, 2016 (http://www.elvis.com.au/presley/dvd/dvd_ed_sullivan_shows_set.shtml).

Marcus, Greil. 2014. *The History of Rock 'n' Roll in Ten Songs.* New Haven: Yale University Press.

Marcuse, Herbert. [1941] 1954. *Reason and Revolution: Hegel and the Rise of Social Theory.* New York: Humanities Press.

Marcuse, Herbert. 1955. *Eros and Civilization.* Boston: The Beacon Press.

Marcuse, Herbert. 1958. *Soviet Marxism: A Critical Analysis.* London: Routledge and Kegan Paul.

Marcuse, Herbert. 1964. *One-Dimensional Man: Studies in the Ideology of Advanced Industrial Society.* Boston: Beacon Press.

Markham, Felix. 1964. "Introduction." Pp. xxxiii–xliv in *Social Organization, The Science of Man, and Other Writings*, by Henri de Saint-Simon. Edited and translated by F. Markham. New York: Harper Torchbooks.

Martin, Darnell (Director). 2008. *Cadillac Records.* New York: Sony Music Entertainment.

Marx, Karl. [1841] 1968. "Differenz der demokritischen und epikureischen Naturphilosophie nebst einem Anhange von Karl Heinrich Marx, Doktor der Philosophie" (The Difference between the Democritean and Epicurean Philosophy of Nature with an Appendix by Karl Marx, Doctor of Philosophy). Pp. 257–308 in *Werke* (*Collected Works*). Supplementary volume, pt. 1. Berlin: Dietz Verlag.

Marx, Karl. [1843] 1927. "Zur Kritik der Hegelschen Rechtsphilosophie" (Towards the Critique of the Hegelian Philosophy of Law). Pp. 607–21 in *Historisch-kritische Gesamtausgabe* (*Historical and Critical Complete Works*). Pt. 1, vol. 1.1, edited by D. Ryazanov. Frankfurt: Marx-Engels-Archiv Verlagsgesellschaft M.B.H.

Marx, Karl. [1844] 1932. *Ökonomisch-philosophische Manuskripte aus dem Jahre 1844* (*Economic and Philosophical Manuscripts of 1844*). Pp. 29–172 in *Historisch-kritische Gesamtausgabe* (*Historical and Critical Complete Works*). Pt. 1, vol. 3, edited by V. Adoratsky. Berlin: Marx-Engels Verlag. (Written in 1844.)

Marx, Karl. [1844] 1975. "Contribution to the Critique of Hegel's Philosophy of Law: Introduction." Pp. 175–86 in *Collected Works.* Vol. 3. New York: International Publishers.

Marx, Karl. [1845] 1982. *Exzerpte über Arteitsteilng, Maschinerie und Industrie* (*Excerpts on the Division of Labour, Machinery, and Industry*). Transcribed and edited by Rainer Winkelmann. Frankfurt/M: Ullstein Verlag.

Marx, Karl. [1847] 1950. *Misère de la Philosophie en Réponse à la Philosophie de la Misère de M. Proudhon* (*The Poverty of Philosophy: A Response to the Philosophy of Poverty by Proudhon*). Paris: Alfred Costes.

Marx, Karl. [1849] 1933. *Wage-Labour and Capital; Value, Price, and Profit.* New York: International Publishers.

Marx, Karl. [1850] 1935. *Class Struggles in France.* Edited by Clemens Dutt. New York: International Publishers.

Marx, Karl. [1851] 1981. *Die technologisch-historischen Exzerpte* (*The Technological-Historical Excerpts*). Transcribed and edited by Hans-Peter Müller. Frankfurt: Ullstein Verlag.

Marx, Karl. [1852] 1937. *The Eighteenth Brumaire of Louis Bonaparte.* Edited by Clemens Dutt. New York: International Publishers.

Marx, Karl. [1857–58] 1953. *Grundrisse der Kritik der politischen Ökonomie: Rohentwurf* (*Foundations for the Critique of Political Economy: Rough Draft*). Berlin: Dietz Verlag.

Marx, Karl. [1859] 1980. *Zur Kritik der politischen Ökonomie* (*Towards the Critique of Political Economy*). Pp. 95–245 in *Gesamtausgabe* (*Complete Works*). Part II, vol. 2. Berlin: Dietz Verlag.

Marx, Karl. [1859] 2005. "Preface to *Towards the Critique of Political Economy*." Pp. 55–66 in *Intersections: Readings in Sociology's Task and Promise*, edited by Rob Beamish. Boston: Pearson Custom Publishing.

Marx, Karl. [1860] 1982. *Herr Vogt: A Spy in the Workers' Movement.* Translated by R.A. Archer. London: New Park Publications.

Marx, Karl. [1861–63] 1921a. *Theorien über den Mehrwert* (*Theories of Surplus Value*). Vol. 1. Edited by Karl Kautsky. Stuttgart: Verlag von J.H. Dietz. (Written between 1861 and 1863.)

Marx, Karl. [1861–63] 1921b. *Theorien über den Mehrwert* (*Theories of Surplus Value*). Vol. 2, pt. 1. Edited by Karl Kautsky. Stuttgart: Verlag von J.H. Dietz. (Written between 1861 and 1863.)

Marx, Karl. [1861–63] 1921c. *Theorien über den Mehrwert* (*Theories of Surplus Value*). Vol. 2, pt. 2. Edited by Karl Kautsky. Stuttgart: Verlag von J.H. Dietz. (Written between 1861 and 1863.)

Marx, Karl. [1861–63] 1921d. *Theorien über den Mehrwert* (*Theories of Surplus Value*). Vol. 3. Edited by Karl Kautsky. Stuttgart: Verlag von J.H. Dietz. (Written between 1861 and 1863.)

Marx, Karl. [1867] 1983. *Das Kapital* (*Capital*). 1st ed. Vol. 1. Pp. 1–651 in *Gesamtausgabe* (*Complete Works*). Part II, vol. 5. Berlin: Dietz Verlag.

Marx, Karl. [1872] 1914. *Das Kapital: Kritik der politischen Ökonomie* (*Capital: Critique of Political Economy*). Vol. 1. Edited by Karl Kautsky. Berlin: J.H.W. Dietz.

Marx, Karl. [1872] 1987. *Das Kapital* (*Capital*). 2nd ed. Vol. 1. Pp. 57–719 in *Gesamtausgabe* (*Complete Works*). Part II, vol. 6. Berlin: Dietz Verlag.

Marx, Karl. [1875] 1989. *Le capital* (*Capital*). Vol. 1. Pp. 1–699 in *Gesamtausgabe* (*Complete Works*). Part II, vol. 7. Berlin: Dietz Verlag.

Marx, Karl. [1881] 1975. "Marx's Notes (1879–1880) on Adolph Wagner." Pp. 161–219 in *Karl Marx: Texts on Method*, translated by Terrell Carver. Oxford: Basil Blackwell.

Marx, Karl. [1885] 1926. *Das Kapital: Kritik der politischen Ökonomie* (*Capital: Critique of Political Economy*). Vol. 2. Arranged by Karl Kautsky with the assistance of Benedikt Kautsky. Berlin: J.H.W. Dietz.

Marx, Karl. [1890] 1976. *Capital*. 4th ed. Vol. 1. Translated by Ben Fowkes. Markham: Penguin Books.

Marx, Karl. [1894] 1929a. *Das Kapital: Kritik der politischen Ökonomie* (*Capital: Critique of Political Economy*). Vol. 3, pt. 1. Arranged by Benedikt Kautsky with the assistance of Karl Kautsky. Berlin: J.H.W. Dietz.

Marx, Karl. [1894] 1929b. *Das Kapital: Kritik der politischen Ökonomie* (*Capital: Critique of Political Economy*). Vol. 3, pt. 2. Arranged by Benedikt Kautsky with the assistance of Karl Kautsky. Berlin: J.H.W. Dietz.

Marx, Karl and Friedrich Engels. [1845] 1932. *Die deutsche Ideologie* (*The German Ideology*). Pp. 1–528 in *Historischkritische Gesamtausgabe* (*Historical and Critical Complete Works*). Pt. 1, vol. 5, edited by V. Adoratsky. Berlin: Marx-Engels Verlag.

Marx, Karl and Friedrich Engels. [1845] 1975. *The Holy Family*. Pp. 1–211 in *Collected Works*. Vol. 4. New York: International Publishers.

Marx, Karl and Friedrich Engels. 1848. *Manifest der kommunistischen Partei* (*Manifesto of the Communist Party*). London: Bildungs-Gesellschaft für Arbeiter.

Marx, Karl and Friedrich Engels. [1848] 1934. *Manifesto of the Communist Party*. London: Martin Lawrence.

Marx, Karl and Friedrich Engels. 1955. *Selected Correspondence*. Moscow: Progress Publishers.

Marx, Karl and Friedrich Engels. 1957. *Werke* (*Collected Works*). Vol. 2. Berlin: Dietz Verlag.

Marx, Karl and Friedrich Engels. 1963. *Werke* (*Collected Works*). Vol. 24. Berlin: Dietz Verlag.

Marx, Karl and Friedrich Engels. 1964. *Werke* (*Collected Works*). Vol. 25. Berlin: Dietz Verlag.

Marx, Karl and Friedrich Engels. 1965. *Werke* (*Collected Works*). Vol. 26.1. Berlin: Dietz Verlag.

Marx, Karl and Friedrich Engels. 1967. *Werke* (*Collected Works*). Vol. 26.2. Berlin: Dietz Verlag.

Marx, Karl and Friedrich Engels. 1968. *Werke* (*Collected Works*). Vol. 26.3. Berlin: Dietz Verlag.

Marx, Karl and Friedrich Engels. 1976–91. *Gesamtausgabe* (*Complete Works*). Pt. IV. Berlin: Dietz Verlag.

Marx, Karl and Friedrich Engels. 1992–2015. *Gesamtausgabe* (*Complete Works*). Pt. IV. Berlin: Akademie Verlag.

Marx, Karl and Friedrich Engels. 1999. *Gesamtausgabe* (*Complete Works*). Pt. IV, vol. 32. Berlin: Akademie Verlag.

Masnick, George. 2012. "Defining Generations." *Housing Perspectives*, November 28. Retrieved August 2, 2015 (http://housingperspectives.blogspot.ca/2012/11/defining-generations.html).

McCarthy, Caroline. 2007. "Amazon Enters Book Digitization Jungle with Rare-Book Project." *Tech Culture*, June 21. Retrieved November 18, 2015 (http://www.cnet.com/news/amazon-enters-book-digitization-jungle-with-rare-book-project/).

McCarthy, Kevin. 2007. "Juvenile Delinquency and Crime Theory in *Blackboard Jungle*." *Journal of Criminal Justice and Popular Culture* 14:317–29.

McClelland, David. 1961. *The Achieving Society*. Princeton, NJ: Van Nostrand.

McKinnon, Margaret, Daniela Palombo, Anthony Nazarov, Namita Kumar, Wayne Khuu, and Brian Levine. 2014. "Threat of Death and Autobiographical Memory: A Study of Passengers from Flight AT236." *Clinical Psychological Science* 4(2):312–19. Retrieved November 26, 2015 (http://cpx.sagepub.com/content/early/2014/08/16/2167702614542280).

McLellan, David. 1973. *Karl Marx: His Life and Thought*. London: Macmillan.

McLuhan, Marshall. N.d. "Marshall McLuhan Quotes/Quotations." Retrieved May 1, 2009 (http://www.icelebz.com/quotes/marshall_mcluhan/).

McLuhan, Marshall. 1962. *The Gutenberg Galaxy: The Making of Typographic Man*. Toronto: University of Toronto Press.

McLuhan, Marshall. 1964. *Understanding Media: The Extensions of Man*. New York: Mentor.

McLuhan, Marshall. 1967. "Marshall McLuhan: The World Is Show Business." Retrieved August 13, 2015 (https://www.youtube.com/watch?v=9P8gUNAVSt8).

McLuhan, Marshall and Quentin Fiore. 1967. *The Medium Is the Massage: An Inventory of Effects*. Toronto: Bantam Books.

McLuhan, Marshall and Eric McLuhan. 1988. *Laws of Media: The New Science*. Toronto: University of Toronto Press.

Medovoi, Leerom. 2005. *Rebels: Youth and the Cold War Origins of Identity*. Durham, NC: Duke University Press.

Meštrović, Stjepan. 1988. *Émile Durkheim and the Reformation of Sociology*. Totawa, NJ: Rowman & Littlefield.

Mészáros, István. 1975. *Marx's Theory of Alienation*. 4th ed. London: Merlin Press.

Meyer, Eduard. 1902. *Zur Theorie und Methodik der Geschichte (On Theory and Methods in History)*. Halle: S.M. Niemeyer.

Meyer, Eduard. 2015. "Introducing the New Microsoft Surface 3." Retrieved November 28, 2015 (https://www.youtube.com/watch?v=sJxghgy70Qo&feature=youtu.be).

Microsoft. 2014. "Surface Pro 3—Head to Head." Retrieved November 28, 2015 (https://www.youtube.com/watch?v=1jP4O7rEHQ8).

Miliband, Ralph. 1968. "C. Wright Mills." Pp. 3–11 in *C. Wright Mills and the Power Elite*, edited by William Domhoff and Hoyt Ballard. Boston: Beacon Press.

Mill, James. [1821] 1844. *Elements of Political Economy*. London: Henry G. Bohn.

Mill, John Stuart. 1848. *Principles of Political Economy, With Some of Their Applications to Social Philosophy*. London: J.W. Parker.

Miller, Jon. 2011. *The Generation X Report* 1(1). Retrieved August 2, 2015 (http://lsay.org/GenX_Rept_Iss1.pdf).

Mills, C. Wright. 1948. *New Men of Power: America's Labor Leaders*. New York: Harcourt Brace.

Mills, C. Wright. 1951. *White Collar: The American Middle Classes*. New York: Oxford University Press.

Mills, C. Wright. 1956. *The Power Elite*. New York: Oxford University Press.

Mills, C. Wright. 1958. *The Causes of World War Three*. New York: Ballantine Books.

Mills, C. Wright. 1959. *The Sociological Imagination*. New York: Oxford University Press.

Mills, C. Wright. 1960. *Images of Man: The Classic Tradition in Sociological Thinking*. New York: George Braziller.

Mills, C. Wright. 1962. *The Marxists*. New York: Dell Publishing.

Mills, C. Wright. 1963. *Power, Politics, and People: The Collected Essays of C. Wright Mills*. Edited by Irving Louis Horowitz. New York: Ballantine Books.

Mills, C. Wright. 2000. *C. Wright Mills: Letters and Autobiographical Writings*. Edited by Kathryn Mills with Pamela Mills. Berkeley: University of California Press.

Mills, Kathryn. 2000. "Remembrance." Pp. xvii–xx in *C. Wright Mills: Letters and Autobiographical Writings*, edited by Kathryn Mills with Pamela Mills. Berkeley: University of California Press.

Mills, Pamela. 2000. "My Father Haunts Me." Pp. xxi–xxiv in *C. Wright Mills: Letters and Autobiographical Writings*, edited by Kathryn Mills with Pamela Mills. Berkeley: University of California Press.

Mises, Ludwig von. 1934. *The Theory of Money and Credit*. London: Cape Editions.

Mitchell, Amy, Jeffrey Gottfried and Katerina Matsa. 2015. *Millennials and Political News: Social Media—the Local TV for the Next Generation?* Washington, DC: Pew Research Center. Retrieved August 5, 2015 (http://www.journalism.org/files/2015/06/Millennials-and-News-FINAL-7-27-15.pdf).

Montchréstien, Antoine de. [1615] 1889. *Traicté de l'économie politique, dédié au Roy et à la Reyne mère du Roy (Treatise on Political Economy, dedicated in 1615 to the King and the Queen Mother)*. Paris: Plon.

Montesquieu, Charles de Secondat, baron de. [1721] 1972. *Persian Letters*. 2 vols. Translated by John Ozell. New York: Garland Publishers.

Montesquieu, Charles de Secondat, baron de. [1734] 1968. *Considerations on the Causes of the Greatness of the Romans and Their Decline*. Translated by David Lowenthal. Ithaca: Cornell University Press.

Montesquieu, Charles de Secondat, baron de. [1748] 1989. *The Spirit of the Laws*. Translated and edited by A.M. Cohler, B.C. Miller, and H.S. Stone. Cambridge: Cambridge University Press.

Münch, Richard. 1987. *Theory of Action: Towards a New Synthesis Going Beyond Parsons*. London: Routledge & Kegan Paul.

Nachman, Gerald. 2009. *Right Here on Our Stage Tonight! Ed Sullivan's America*. Berkley: University of California Press.

New York Times. 1931. "Yale Long Debated Dropping Classics." May 13:18.

Newman, John Henry Cardinal. [1852] 1886. *The Idea of a University Defined and Illustrated*. 6th ed. London: Longman's, Green, and Co.

Newton, Isaac. 1953. *Newton's Philosophy of Nature: Selections from His Writings*. Edited by H.S. Thayer. New York: Hafner Press.

Nietzsche, Friedrich. [1882] 1974. *The Gay Science*. Translated by Walter Kaufmann. New York: Vintage Books.

Norman, Rebecca. 2011a. "Education Story." Retrieved August 12, 2015 (https://www.youtube.com/watch?t=10&v=2WsS9G5UwOQ).

Norman, Rebecca. 2011b. "How I Learn." Retrieved August 12, 2015 (https://www.youtube.com/watch?v=wBa5tNjVSQE).

Norman, Rebecca. 2011c. "Learning." Retrieved August 12, 2015 (https://www.youtube.com/watch?v=BQJoZzkviSs).

Norman, Rebecca. 2011d. "My Story." Retrieved August 12, 2015 (https://www.youtube.com/watch?v=x_dqwiDEi4Q).

Orwell, George. 1949. *Nineteen Eighty-Four*. New York: Harcourt, Brace.

Owen, Robert. [1814] 1927. *A New View of Society and Other Writings*. Toronto: J.M. Dent & Sons.

Owram, Doug. 1996. *Born at the Right Time: A History of the Baby Boom Generation*. Toronto: University of Toronto Press.

Page, Charles. 1959. "Sociology as a Teaching Enterprise." Pp. 579–99 in *Sociology Today*. Vol. 2, edited by Robert Merton, Leonard Broom, and Leonard Cottrell Jr. New York: Basic Books.

Palmer, Bryan. 2009. *Canada's 1960s: The Ironies of Identity in a Rebellious Era*. Toronto: University of Toronto Press.

Palmer, Tony (Director). 2008. *All You Need is Love: The Story of Popular Music* [DVD]. London: Isolde Films.

Parsons, Talcott. 1949. *The Structure of Social Action*. 2nd ed. Glencoe, IL: The Free Press.

Parsons, Talcott. 1968. "Emile Durkheim." Pp. 311–20 in *International Encyclopedia of the Social Sciences*, edited by David Sills. New York: Macmillan Publishing.

Perlman, Freddy. 1970. *The Incoherence of the Intellectual: C. Wright Mills's Struggle to Unite Knowledge and Action*. Detroit: Black and Red.

Persails, Dave. 1996. "Beatles: What's in a Name?" Retrieved February 3, 2016 (http://abbeyrd.best.vwh.net/named.htm).

Peterson, Richard. 1990. "Why 1955? Explaining the Advent of Rock Music." *Popular Music* 9:97–116.

Peterson, Richard and David Berger. 1975. "Cycles in Symbol Production: The Case of Popular Music." *American Sociological Review* 40:158–73.

Peyre, Henri. 1960. "Foreward." Pp. v–xvi in *Montesquieu and Rousseau: Forerunners of Sociology*, translated by Ralph Mannheim. Ann Arbor: University of Michigan Press.

Polanyi, Karl. 1944. *The Great Transformation*. Toronto: Farrar and Rinehart.

popopopopo159. 2011. "Visions of Minecrafters Today." Retrieved August 5, 2015 (https://www.youtube.com/watch?v=lWTOXJ3fHLk).

Posnick-Goodwin, Sherry. 2010. "Meet Generation Z." *California Educator* 14(5):8–16, 38.

Postman, Neil. 1985. *Amusing Ourselves to Death: Public Discourse in the Age of Show Business*. New York: Viking Press.

Postman, Neil. 1988. *Conscientious Objections: Stirring up Trouble about Language, Technology, and Education.* New York: Knopf.

Postman, Neil. 1992. *Technopoly: The Surrender of Culture to Technology.* New York: Alfred A Knopf

Postman, Neil. 1995. *The End of Education: Redefining the Value of School.* New York: Vintage Books.

Postman, Neil and Charles Weingartner. 1969. *Teaching as a Subversive Activity.* New York: Dell Publishing Company.

Prensky, Marc. 2001. "Digital Natives, Digital Immigrants." *On the Horizon* 9(5):1–6.

Presley, Elvis. [1954] 2014. "First Appearance on the Louisiana Hayride." Retrieved February 11, 2016 (https://www.youtube.com/watch?v=bLaPnpjw-pc&list=RD1Smo HU4_eY8&index=6).

Presley, Elvis. [1956a] 2012. "Dorsey Brothers Stage Show-1." Retrieved February 19, 2016 (http://www.dailymotion.com/video/xu6tjv_19560128-elvis-presley-dorsey-brothers-stage-show-1_music).

Presley, Elvis. [1956b] 2012. "Dorsey Brothers Stage Show-2." Retrieved February 19, 2016 (http://www.dailymotion.com/video/xu6tmn_19560204-elvis-presley-dorsey-brothers-stage-show-2_music).

Presley, Elvis. [1956c] 2012. "Dorsey Brothers Stage Show-3." Retrieved February 19, 2016 (http://www.dailymotion.com/video/xu6tob_19560211-elvis-presley-dorsey-brothers-stage-show-3_music).

Presley, Elvis. [1956d] 2012. "Dorsey Brothers Stage Show-4." Retrieved February 19, 2016 (http://www.dailymotion.com/video/xu6tr1_19560218-elvis-presley-dorsey-brothers-stage-show-4_music).

Presley, Elvis. [1956e] 2012. "Dorsey Brothers Stage Show-5." Retrieved February 19, 2016 (http://www.dailymotion.com/video/xu6tsl_19560317-elvis-presley-dorsey-brothers-stage-show-5_music).

Presley, Elvis. [1956f] 2012. "Dorsey Brothers Stage Show-6." Retrieved February 19, 2016 (http://www.dailymotion.com/video/xu6tt8_19560324-elvis-presley-dorsey-brothers-stage-show-6_music).

Presley, Elvis. [1956g] 2011. "I Want You, I Need You, I Love You." Retrieved February 11, 2016 (https://www.youtube.com/watch?v=IZSr30yQ8Ts).

Presley, Elvis. [1956h] 2009. "Hound Dog (Live on Milton Berle Show)." Retrieved February 11, 2016 (https://www.youtube.com/watch?v=zU4i5gyFK1s).

Presley, Elvis. [1956i] 2015. "Elvis Presley on the Steve Allen Show." Retrieved February 11, 2016 (https://www.youtube.com/watch?v=0MN-1nSQv3U&index=2&list=RD1SmoHU4_eY8).

Presley, Elvis. [1957] 2015. "Peace in the Valley (Sullivan)." Retrieved February 15, 2016 (https://www.youtube.com/watch?v=6nodeNzrQ_Y).

Preston, Jimmy and His Prestonians. [1949] 2015. Retrieved February 3, 2016 (https://www.youtube.com/watch?v=HOW0OrZR3sk).

Pryor, John, Linda DeAngelo, Laura Blake, Sylvia Hurtado, and Serge Tran. 2011. *The American Freshman: National Norms Fall 2011.* Los Angeles: Higher Education Research Institute.

Pryor, John, Sylvia Hurtado, Victor Saenz, José Santos, and William Korn. 2007. *The American Freshman: Forty Year Trends, 1966–2006.* Los Angeles: Higher Education Research Institute.

Project Gutenberg. N.d. "Free ebooks by Project Gutenberg." Retrieved November 18, 2015 (https://www.gutenberg.org/wiki/Main_Page).

Raymond, Alan and Susan Raymond (Directors). [1987] 2000. *Elvis '56* [DVD]. Studio City, CA: Lightyear Entertainment.

Readings, Bill. 1996. *The University in Ruins.* Cambridge, MA: Harvard University Press.

Reynolds, Caitlin. 2011a. "RE:Birth of Education." Retrieved August 5, 2015 (https://www.youtube.com/watch?v=vVhNoiSqvOk&feature=youtu.be).

Reynolds, Caitlin. 2011b. "We Are Not Mediated Enough." Retrieved August 12, 2015 (https://www.youtube.com/watch?v=K8bwa309Ewc).

Ricardo, David. [1817] 1891. *Principles of Political Economy and Taxation.* London: G. Bell and Sons.

Riesman, David. 1950. *The Lonely Crowd: A Study of Changing American Character.* New Haven: Yale University Press.

Riesman, David. 1960. "The Oral and Written Traditions." Pp. 109–16 in *Explorations in Communication*, edited by Marshall McLuhan and Edmund Carpenter. Boston: Beacon Press.

Rihanna. 2015. "American Oxygen." Retrieved February 20, 2016 (https://www.youtube.com/watch?v=Ao8cGLIMtvg).

Ritzer, George, ed. 2007. *Blackwell Encyclopedia of Sociology*. 11 vols. Oxford: Blackwell.

Rius. 1976. *Marx for Beginners*. Translated by Richard Appignanesi. New York: Pantheon Books.

Roberts, James, Luc Yaya, and Chris Manolis. 2014. "The Invisible Addiction: Cell-phone Activities and Addiction among Male and Female College Students." *Journal of Behavioral Addictions* 3:254–65.

Robertson, Mark. 2014. "300⁺ Hours of Video Uploaded to YouTube Every Minute" *reelse*, November 21. Retrieved August 14, 2015 (http://www.reelseo.com/youtube-300-hours/).

Robinson, Ken. 2010. "Changing Education Paradigms," *RSA Animate*, October. Retrieved November 28, 2015 (https://www.ted.com/talks/ken_robinson_changing_education_paradigms).

Rock and Roll Hall of Fame. 2016. "All Rock Hall Inductees." Retrieved January 31, 2016 (http://www.rockhall.com/inductees/).

Rojahn, Jürgen. 1998. "Publishing Marx and Engels after 1989: The Fate of the MEGA." *Critique* 31:196–207.

Rose, Ellen. 2013. *On Reflection: An Essay on Technology, Education, and the Status of Thought in the Twenty-First Century*. Toronto: Canadian Scholar's Press.

Rosenberg, Max and Milton and Subotsky (Directors). 1956. *Rock, Rock, Rock*. Culver City, CA: Vanguard Films.

Rousseau, Jean-Jacques. [1762] 1963. *The Social Contract and Discourses*. Translated by G.D.H. Cole. New York: Dutton.

Rubel, Maximilien. 1968. "Introduction." Pp. xvii-cxxxii in *Karl Marx Oeuvres Économique* (*Karl Marx, Economic Works*). Vol. 2. Paris: Gallimard.

Rubel, Maximilien. 1981a. "A History of Marx's 'Economics.'" Pp. 82–189 in *Rubel on Marx: Five Essays*, edited by Joseph O'Malley and Keith Algozin. New York: Cambridge University Press.

Rubel, Maximilien. 1981b. "The Plan and Method of the 'Economics.'" Pp. 190–229 in *Rubel on Marx: Five Essays*, edited by Joseph O'Malley and Keith Algozin. New York: Cambridge University Press.

Ruskin, John. 1885. *Modern Painters*. Vol. 3. New York: John Wiley & Sons.

Ryan, John. 1985. *The Production of Culture in the Music Industry: The ASCAP-BMI Controversy*. Lanham, MD: University Press of America.

Ryazanov, David. 1930. "Siebzig Jahre *Zur Kritik der politischen Ökonomie*" (On the 70th Anniversary of *Towards the Critique of Political Economy*). *Archiv für die Geschichte des Sozialismus und der Arbeiterbewegung* (*Archive for the History of Socialism and the Workers' Movement*) 15:1–31.

Sagolla, Lisa Jo. 2011. *Rock 'n' Roll Dances of the 1950s*. Santa Barbara, CA: Greenwood Press.

Saint-Simon, Henri. [1825] 1964. *Social Organization, The Science of Man, and Other Writings*. Edited and translated by F. Markham. New York: Harper Torchbooks.

Saint-Simon, Henri. 1975. *Selected Writings on Science, Industry, and Social Organization*. Translated and edited by K. Taylor. New York: Holmes and Meier Publishers.

Savage, Joseph. 2011a. "Ignoring and Watching." Uploaded January 22, 2011. Retrieved August 12, 2015 (https://www.youtube.com/watch?v=wIvQuWKCML8).

Savage, Joseph. 2011b. "RoughFirstDraft." Uploaded April 18, 2011. Retrieved August 12, 2015 (https://www.youtube.com/watch?v=ndvnLv30GV4).

Savage, Joseph. 2011c. "SecondDraftAudio." Uploaded February 6, 2011. Retrieved August 12, 2015 (https://www.youtube.com/watch?v=ZwJFe_Z_ixo).

Savage, Joseph. 2011d. "Students vs. Teachers in Classroom." Uploaded April 25, 2011. Retrieved August 12, 2015 (https://www.youtube.com/watch?v=b4YospwEFlQ).

Savage, Joseph. 2011e. "Understanding the Vision of Students Today." Uploaded May 27, 2011. Retrieved August 5, 2015 (https://www.youtube.com/watch?v=GyIyZDsEn3g&feature=youtu.be).

Say, Jean-Baptiste. 1817. *Traité d'économie politique* (*Treatise on Political Economy*). 3rd ed. Paris: Déterville.

Schäffle, Albert. 1896. *Bau und Leben des Socialen Körpers* (*The Structure and Life of the Social Body*). 2nd ed. Tübingen: Verlag der H. Laupp'schen Buchhandlung.

Schelling, Friedrich von. 1856–61. *Sämmtliche Werke* (*Collected Works*). Stuttgart: Cota Verlag.

Schiller, Herbert. 1973. *Mind Managers*. Boston: Beacon Press.

Schiller, Herbert. 1989. *Culture Inc.: The Corporate Takeover of Public Expression*. New York: Oxford University Press.

Schmidt, Alfred. 1972. "Henri Lefèbvre and Contemporary Interpretations of Marx." Pp. 322–41 in *The Unknown Dimension: European Marxism since Lenin*, edited by Dick Howard and Karl Klare. New York: Basic Books.

Schneweis, Derek. 2011. "Academic Vaccination." Retrieved August 5, 2015 (https://www.youtube.com/watch?v=OEDbrkUszLc&feature=youtu.be).

Schouls, Peter. 1989. *Descartes and the Enlightenment*. Montreal: McGill-Queen's University Press.

Schutz, Alfred. [1932] 1967. *The Phenomenology of the Social World*. Evanston, IL: Northwestern University Press.

Scorsese, Martin (Director). 2005. *No Direction Home: Bob Dylan*. Hollywood, CA: Paramount.

Seeger, Pete. 1971. "So Long, Woody, It's Been Good to Know Ya." Pp. vii–ix in *Bound for Glory*. New York: Penguin Books.

Seligman, Edwin and Alvin Johnson, eds. 1957. *Encyclopaedia of the Social Sciences*. 15 vols. New York: The Macmillan Company.

Sennett, Richard. 2008. *The Craftsman*. New Haven: Yale University Press.

Sesame Street. 1969–70. New York: National Educational Television (NET).

Sesame Street. 1970–present. Arlington, VA: PBS.

Shaw, George Bernard. 1889. *Fabian Essays on Socialism*. London: The Fabian Society.

Shaw, George Bernard. 1912. *The Intelligent Woman's Guide to Socialism and Capitalism*. London: Constable and Company.

Sigurdson, Kristjan. 2013. "Clark Kerr's Multiversity and Technology Transfer in the Modern American Research University." *College Quarterly* 16. Retrieved December 12, 2015 (http://collegequarterly.ca/2013-vol16-num02-spring/sigurdson.html).

Sills, David, ed. 1968. *International Encyclopedia of the Social Sciences*. 17 vols. New York: Crowell Collier and Macmillan.

Sismondi, Simonde de. [1815] 1966. *Political Economy*. New York: Augustus M. Kelley.

Smith, Adam. [1776] 1976. *An Inquiry into the Nature and Causes of the Wealth of Nations*. 2 vols. Edited by R.H. Campbell and A.S. Skinner. Indianapolis: Liberty Press.

Smith, David and Phil Evans. 1982. *Marx's Kapital for Beginners*. New York: Pantheon Books.

Smith, Wilson and Thomas Bender, eds. 2008. *American Higher Education Transformed, 1940–2005: Documenting the National Discourse*. Baltimore: Johns Hopkins University Press.

Snow, Jimmy. [1958] 2009. "Preaching Against Rock and Roll (1950s)." Retrieved May 2, 2016 (https://www.youtube.com/watch?v=9gQV15DPvyE).

Snyder, Timothy. 1997. *Nationalism, Marxism, and Modern Central Europe. A Biography of Kazimierz Kelles-Krauz (1872–1905)*. Cambridge, MA: Harvard University Press.

Sohn-Rethel, Alfred. [1971] 1978. *Intellectual and Manual Labour: A Critique of Epistemology*. Translated by Martin Sohn-Rethel. London: Macmillan.

Sombart, Werner. 1991. *The Economics and Sociology of Capitalism*. Edited by Richard Swedberg. Princeton, NJ: Princeton University Press.

Sparks & Honey. 2014. "Meet Generation Z: Forget Everything You Learned about Millennials," June 12. Retrieved August 3, 2015 (http://www.slideshare.net/sparksandhoney/generation-z-final-june-17).

SparkNotes Editors. 2007. *Karl Marx, 1818–1883*. SparkNotes Philosophy Guide. Retrieved December 14, 2009 (http://www.sparknotes.com/philosophy/marx).

Spence, Richard (Director). [1991] 2004. *The Real Buddy Holly Story* [DVD]. West Long Branch, NJ: White Star.

Spitz, Bob. 1989. *Dylan: A Biography*. New York: McGraw-Hill.

Stammler, Rudolf. [1894] 1924. *Wirtschaft und Recht nach der materialistischen Geschichtsauffassung: eine sozialphilosophische Untersuchung* (*Economy and Law According to the Materialist Conception of History: A Socio-Philosophical Investigation*). Berlin: de Gruyter.

Steinbeck, John. 1937. *Of Mice and Men*. New York: Covici.

Steinbeck, John. 1939. *The Grapes of Wrath*. New York: Viking Press.

Steinbeck, John. 1952. *East of Eden*. New York: Viking Press.

Stewart, Dugald. 1968. *Lectures on Political Economy*. New York: A.M. Kelley.

Stewart, James. [1770] 1776. *An Inquiry into the Principles of Political Economy: Being an Essay on the Science of Domestic Policy in Free Nations, in Which Are Particularly Considered Population, Agriculture, Trade, Industry, Money*. 2 vols. London: A. Millar and T. Cadell.

Stutz, Colin. 2015. "How 'Born in the U.S.A.' Inspired Rihanna's American Oxygen." *Billboard*, September 4. Retrieved February 20, 2016 (http://www.billboard.com/articles/columns/the-juice/6524518/how-born-in-the-usa-inspired-rihannas-american-oxygen).

Summers, John. 2008. *The Politics of Truth: Selected Writings of C. Wright Mills*. New York: Oxford University Press.

Tapscott, Don. 2008. *Grown Up Digital: How the Net Generation Is Changing Your World*. New York: McGraw-Hill.

Tawney, Richard. 1926. *Religion and the Rise of Capitalism*. New York: Harcourt, Brace and Company.

Taylor, Keith. 1975. "Introduction." Pp. 13–61 in *Henri Saint-Simon (1760–1825)*. Translated and edited by K. Taylor. New York: Holmes and Meier Publishers.

Terkel, Studs. 1967. *Division Street: America*. New York: Pantheon Books.

Terkel, Studs. 1970. *Hard Times: An Oral History of the Great Depression*. New York: Pantheon Books.

Terkel, Studs. 1974. *Working: People Talk about What They Do All Day and How They Feel about What They Do*. New York: Pantheon Books.

Thomas, Douglas and John Brown. 2011. *A New Culture of Learning: Cultivating the Imagination for a World of Constant Change*. Lexington: CreateSpace.

Thompson, E.P. 1970. *The Making of the English Working Class*. Markham: Penguin Books Canada.

Tindal, Gerald, Jan Hasbrouck, and Christopher Jones. 2005. *Oral Reading Fluency: 90 Years of Measurement*. Eugene, OR: Behavioural Research and Teaching.

Tocqueville, Alexis de. [1856] 1955. *The Old Regime and the French Revolution*. Translated by Stuart Gilbert. Garden City, NY: Doubleday.

Tönnies, Ferdinand. [1887] 1957. *Community and Society*. Translated and edited by Charles Loomis. East Lansing: Michigan State University Press.

Toobin, Jeffrey. 2007. "Google's Moon Shot: The Quest for the Universal Library." *The New Yorker* (February 5):30–35.

United States Senate. 1954 (April–June). Senate Subcommittee to Investigate Juvenile Delinquency of the Committee on the Judiciary. *Juvenile Delinquency* (Comic Books: Hearings. 83rd Congress, 2nd Session. Washington: United States Government Printing Office.

United States Senate. 1955 (June). Senate Subcommittee to Investigate Juvenile Delinquency of the Committee on the Judiciary. *Juvenile Delinquency (Motion Pictures)*: Hearing. 84th Congress, 1st Session. Washington: United States Government Printing Office.

Unterberger, Richie. 2002. *Turn! Turn! Turn! The '60's Folk-Rock Revolution*. San Francisco: Backbeat Books.

Usher, Abbott Payson. 1929. *A History of Mechanical Inventions*. New York: McGraw-Hill.

Wakefield, Dan. 2000. "Introduction." Pp. 1–18 in *C. Wright Mills: Letters and Autobiographical Writings*, edited by Kathryn Mills with Pamela Mills. Berkeley: University of California Press.

Wald, Alan. 1987. *The New York Intellectuals: The Rise and Decline of the Anti-Stalinist Left from the 1930s to the 1980s*. Chapel Hill: University of North Carolina Press.

Weber, Max. [1891] 1976. *The Agrarian Sociology of Ancient Civilizations*. Translated by R.I. Frank. London: New Left Books.

Weber, Max. [1903, 1905, 1906] 1975. *Roscher and Knies: The Logical Problems of Historical Economics*. Translated by Guy Oakes. New York: The Free Press.

Weber, Max. [1905] 1949. "Critical Studies in the Logic of the Cultural Sciences: A Critique of Eduard Meyer's Methodological Views." Pp. 113–88 in *The Methodology of the Social Sciences*, translated and edited by Edward Shils and Henry Finch. New York: The Free Press.

Weber, Max. [1905] 1968. "*Zur Auseinandersetzung mit Eduard Meyer*" ("A Dispute with Eduard Meyer"). Pp. 215–65 in *Gesammelte Aufsätze zur Wissenschaftslehre von Max Weber (Max Weber's Collected Essays in the Philosophy of Science)*, edited by Johannes Winckelmann. Tübingen: J.C.B. Mohr.

Weber, Max. [1907] 1977. *Critique of Stammler*. Translated by Guy Oakes. New York: The Free Press.

Weber, Max. [1919] 1946a. "Politics as a Vocation." Pp. 77–128 in *From Max Weber: Essays in Sociology*, translated and edited by Hans Gerth and C. Wright Mills. New York: Oxford University Press.

Weber, Max. [1919] 1946b. "Science as a Vocation." Pp. 129–58 in *From Max Weber: Essays in Sociology*, translated and edited by Hans Gerth and C. Wright Mills. New York: Oxford University Press.

Weber, Max. [1920] 1958. *The Protestant Ethic and the Spirit of Capitalism*. Translated by Talcott Parsons. New York: Charles Scribner's Sons.

Weber, Max. [1920] 2002. *The Protestant Ethic and the Spirit of Capitalism*. 3rd ed. Translated by Stephen Kalberg. Los Angeles: Roxbury.

Weber, Max. 1922. *Gesammelte Aufsätze zur Religionssoziologie* (*Collected Essays on the Sociology of Religion*). Vol. 1. Tübingen: Verlag J.C.B. Mohr.

Weber, Max. [1923] 1927. *General Economic History*. Translated by Frank Knight. Glencoe, IL: The Free Press.

Weber, Max. 1923a. *Gesammelte Aufsätze zur Religionssoziologie* (*Collected Essays on the Sociology of Religion*). Vol. 2. Tübingen: Verlag J.C.B. Mohr.

Weber, Max. 1923b. *Gesammelte Aufsätze zur Religionssoziologie* (*Collected Essays on the Sociology of Religion*) Vol. 3. Tübingen: Verlag J.C.B. Mohr.

Weber, Max. 1949. *The Methodology of the Social Sciences*. Translated and edited by Edward Shils and Henry Finch. New York: The Free Press.

Weber, Max. 1956. *Wirtschaft und Gesellschaft: Grundriss der verstehenden Soziologie* (*Economy and Society: An Outline of Interpretive Sociology*). 2 vols. Tübingen: J.C.B. Mohr.

Weber, Max. 1968a. *Economy and Society: An Outline of Interpretive Sociology*. 3 vols. Translated by Gunether Roth and Claus Wittich. New York: Bedminster Press.

Weber, Max. 1968b. *Gesammelte Aufsätze zur Wissenschaftslehre von Max Weber* (*Collected Essays in the Philosophy of Science*). Edited by Johannes Winckelmann. Tübingen: J.C.B. Mohr.

Weber, Max. 2012. *Max Weber: Collected Methodological Writings*. Edited by Hans Bruun and Sam Whimster and translated by Hans Brunn. New York: Routledge.

Webster, Frank. 1995. *Theories of the Information Society*. London: Routledge.

Wells, Herbert George. 1914. *The World Set Free: A Story of Mankind*. New York: E.P. Dutton & Company.

Wells, Herbert George. 1923. *Men Like Gods: A Novel*. New York: The Macmillan Company.

Wesch, Michael. 2007a. "A Vision of Students Today." Retrieved August 5, 2015 (https://www.youtube.com/watch?v=dGCJ46vyR9o).

Wesch, Michael. 2007b. "Information R/evolution." Retrieved August 5, 2015 (https://www.youtube.com/watch?v=-4CV05HyAbM).

Wesch, Michael. 2007c. "The Machine is Us/ing Us (Final Version)." Retrieved August 5, 2015 (https://www.youtube.com/watch?v=NLlGopyXT_g).

Wesch, Michael. 2008a. "A Portal to Media Literacy." Lecture presentation at the University of Manitoba, June 17, 2008. Retrieved August 6, 2015 (https://www.youtube.com/watch?v=J4yApagnros&list=PL01C06F0B5E2B9EE4&index=10).

Wesch, Michael. 2008b. "Anti-Teaching: Confronting the Crisis of Significance." *Education Canada* 48(2):4–7. Retrieved August 5, 2015 (http://www.cea-ace.ca/sites/cea-ace.ca/files/EdCan-2008-v48-n2-Wesch.pdf).

Wesch, Michael. 2009. "The Machine Is (Changing) Us: YouTube and the Politics of Authenticity." Presented at Personal Democracy Forum at Jazz at Lincoln Center. Retrieved August 6, 2015 (https://www.youtube.com/watch?v=09gR6VPVrpw&list=PL01C06F0B5E2B9EE4&index=8&feature=plcp).

Wesch, Michael. 2010. "From Knowledgeable to Knowledge-Able." *TED*[x]. Retrieved August 5, 2015 (https://www.youtube.com/watch?t=242&v=LeaAHv4UTI8).

Wesch, Michael. 2011a. "'a few ideas ...' (Visions of Students Today)." Retrieved August 5, 2015 (https://www.youtube.com/watch?v=jrXpitAlvao&list=PLBC8D1D92A2F2FB36&index=2).

Wesch, Michael. 2011b. "An Inside Look at the 'Visions of Students Today 2011.'" Retrieved August 5, 2015 (https://www.youtube.com/watch?v=HPs1SZoQ6NE&feature=youtu.be).

Wesch, Michael. 2011c. "Call for Submissions." Retrieved August 5, 2015 (https://www.youtube.com/watch?v=KUMWEmeFlyU&feature=youtu.be).

Wesch, Michael. 2011d. "Visions of Students Today." Retrieved August 5, 2015 (http://visionsofstudents.org/).

Wesch, Michael. 2011e. "'The Visions of Students Today' 2011 Remix One." Retrieved August 5, 2015 (https://www.youtube.com/watch?v=-_XNG3Mndww&feature=youtu.be).

Wesch, Michael. 2011f. "Visionsofstudents.org Video Collage." Retrieved August 14, 2015 (http://mediatedcultures.net/videos/visionsofstudents-org-video-collage/).

Wesch, Michael. 2015. "Michael Wesch Homepage, Kansas State University, Department of Sociology, Anthropology and Social Work." Retrieved August 5, 2015 (http://www.k-state. edu/sasw/faculty/wesch.html).

Whaite, Phil and Pete Doherty. 2004. "This Charming Man: An Interview with Pete Doherty." *Socialist Review* 284. Retrieved May 10, 2016 (http://socialistreview.org.uk/284/charming-man-interview-pete-doherty).

Whitburn, Joel. 2004. *Top Pop Singles: 1955-2002.* 10th ed. Menomonee Falls, WI: Record Research.

White, Charles. 1984. *The Life and Times of Little Richard: The Quasar of Rock.* New York: Harmony Books.

White, Shelley. 2014. "Generation Z: The Kids Who'll Save the World?" *The Globe and Mail,* September 26: E1, E5.

Wikipedia. 2016. "List of Rock Genres." Retrieved January 31, 2016 (https://en.wikipedia.org/wiki/ List_of_rock_genres).

Wikitubia. 2015. "MadV." Retrieved August 14, 2015 (http://youtube.wikia.com/wiki/Madv).

Williams, Raymond. 1961. *Culture and Society, 1780-1950.* Harmondsworth: Penguin Books.

Williams, Raymond. 1983. *Keywords: A Vocabulary of Culture and Society.* 2nd ed. London: Fontana Paperbacks.

Wolf, Maryanne. 2011. "Learning How to Think in a Digital World." Pp. 34-37 in *The Digital Divide: Arguments For and Against Facebook, Google, Texting, and the Age of Social Networking,* edited by Mark Bauerlein. New York: Penguin Group.

Woller, Gary. 1997. "Public Administration and Postmodernism: Editor's Introduction." *American Behavioral Scientist* 41:9-11.

Wu, Tim. 2015. "What Ever Happened to Google Books?" *The New Yorker,* September 11. Retrieved November 18, 2015 (http://www.newyorker.com/business/currency/what-ever-happened-to-google-books).

Zamiatin, Eugene. [1924] 1952. *We.* Translated by Gregory Ziboorg. New York: E.P. Dutton.

INDEX

Figures are indicated by page numbers in italics

abstraction, 191, 192. *See also* pure types (ideal types)
academic freedom, 64
Academic Transformation (Clark et al.), 63
acquired attention deficit disorder, 16
action, *see* social action
Adele, 307, 310–11, 318
Adorno, Theodor
    on culture industry, 248–50, 264, 317
    on "enlightenment," 249n89
    on ideal cultural forms, 257
    on mass deception from mass culture, 250, 289
    reasons for commentary on culture, 245, 324
adult education, 245n87
affective action, 192. *See also* social action
agency, human, 32, 42, 69, 133–34
Aguilera, Christina, 307, 309–10, 318–19
Albright, Julie, 224, 225
Alexander, Jeffrey, 140
Allahar, Anton
    Ivory Tower Blues, 10, 60
Allen, Steve, 302, 304
Almanac Singers, 275
altruistic suicide, 175–76
Amazon, 44–45
American Bandstand (TV show), 271n97, 318
The American Freshman (CIRP), 10, 14
American Idiot (Green Day), 313–14

"American Oxygen" (Rihanna), 314–16, 318
American Society of Composers, Authors, and Publishers (ASCAP), 264
Amusing Ourselves to Death (Postman), 252, 253. *See also* Postman, Neil
Anka, Paul, 306
anomic suicide, 176–77
anomie, 176, 176n63
Another Side of Bob Dylan (Dylan), 287
app-dependent, 51, 255, 257
app-enabled, 51
The App Generation (Gardner and Davis), xxi. *See also* Davis, Katie; Gardner, Howard
app mentality, 50
argumentation, 78–80
Arnold, Matthew
    on culture, 62, 72, 245, 256, 257, 317
    Culture and Anarchy, 62
    Dylan as meeting Arnold's standard, 288
    reasons for commentary on culture, 324
Arnold, Thomas, 62n20
art, 219–20
ASCAP (American Society of Composers, Authors, and Publishers), 264
ascetic Protestantism, *see* Protestantism
ascetic rationalism, 211
Atlantic Records, 269–70
Austrian school, 111n41

Baby Boomers, 8, 65, 262, 271
Baby Bust Generation, *see* Generation X
Bacon, Francis, 85, 178, 191
Baez, Joan, 282
"Ballad of Hollis Brown" (Dylan), 285
Bankrupt Education (Emberley and
    Newell), 60–61
base, 102–3, 104, 116–17. *See also*
    infrastructure; superstructure
Bauer, Bruno, 89, 89n26, 106
Bauer, Edgar, 106
Bauldie, John, 282n107
Beatles, 311–12, 317
Bebel, August, 95, 186
Beloit College Mindset List, 4–7, 4n1, 25, 30
Benjamin, Walter, 245
Berger, Peter, 178
Berle, Milton, 300, 302, 304
Bernstein, Eduard, 95, 100n37, 186
Berry, Chuck, 305, 317
Berry, Wendell
    "The Loss of the University," 61
Beruf (calling), 209–10
Beyoncé, 307, 308–9, 310
bidirectional communication, 45–46
Billboard (magazine), 269
Bill Haley and the Comets, 296–97,
    296n111, 300, 317
biology, 146, 154, 166, 179
Blackboard Jungle (film), 297–98, 299–300
Blackwell Encyclopedia of Sociology (2007),
    217, 224, 224n79, 225
Bloom, Allan, 60, 65, 67–68, 70, 71–72
"Blowin' in the Wind" (Dylan), 280, 282,
    282n107
blues shouters, 269
BMI (Broadcast Music Incorporated), 265
Bob Dylan (Dylan), 281
"Bo Diddley" (Diddley), 300
Bono, 295–96
BookSurge (CreateSpace), 44
Boomers, 8, 65, 262, 271
bourgeoisie, 125–27, 131, 214
Bozarth, Nate, 22
Brave New World (Huxley), 254, 254n93
broadcast industry, 265–67, 271
Broadcast Music Incorporated (BMI), 265

Broadside (magazine), 275n101, 282
Buddy Holly and the Crickets, 305, 311. *See
    also* Holly, Buddy
Bumstead, Josiah F., 52–53

calling (*Beruf*), 209–10
Calvin, John, 208
Canada, *see* North America
canon, 227n81
Capital (Marx), 87, 97–98, 108, 110, 187n64,
    243–44. *See also* Marx, Karl
capitalism
    ascetic Protestantism and, 208, 210–11
    division of labour, 91–92, 93
    economic determinism in, 108
    economic rationalism in, 206
    ethic of, 207
    Franklin's maxims on, 206, 210
    as ideology, 243–44
    key elements of, 194n71
    Marx's study of, 96–97, 101, 106, 107, 111,
        114, 118, 123, 134
    overproduction by, 108–11
    production in, 104, 128–29, 133
    property relations in, 103
    proving exploitation, 239–41
    Weber on spirit of, 205–6
    See also industrialization
capitalist society, *see* capitalism
Carr, Nicholas
    approach to, xxi
    Dylan's work and, 291
    on ideal cultural form, 257–58
    on Internet culture, 42, 255, 318
    on print culture, 54, 290
    reasons for commentary on culture, 324
    The Shallows, xxi, 42
Castells, Manuel, xxi, 10, 33–35, 36, 42,
        235–36
Catholicism, 174–75, 207
Chess Records, 270
children, 168
Christianity, muscular, 62n20. *See also*
        Catholicism; Protestantism; religion
Chudd, Lew, 269
civil rights movement, 282, 287
civil society, 91, 92, 115, 118

Clark, Ian
 Academic Transformation, 63
class, 90
class consciousness
 introduction to, 111–12
 basis in human consciousness, 113
 for class struggle, 123, 133, 137
 development of, 116, 236
 political action from, 114–15
classical sociology, *see* sociology
class struggle, 112, 123, 125, 132, 136–38, 325
The Closing of the American Mind (Bloom),
 60, 72. *See also* Bloom, Allan
Cohen, Gerald, 112
Cohen, Lizabeth, 262, 263
collective conscience/consciousness, *see*
 conscience collective
collective representations
 advantages over conscious collective,
  172–73
 definition of, 172, 237
 development of concept, 322
 Durkheim's emphasis on, xxii, 142
 in healthy societies, 177
 importance of term, 325
 influence on individuals, 179
 legal code as, 170
 parallels to Marx and Weber, 181
 problem with, 230
 of Protestants and Catholics, 174
 social solidarity from, 181
 sources of, 175
 suicide and, 174–77
 worldview from, 177, 178
 See also conscience collective
Collingwood, R.G., 186
commodification, of culture, 245–46,
 248–50, 251–54, 255–56, 257
commodity, 243, 243n86, 294
commodity-based economies, 243n85
Communist League, 121, 123–24, 132
Communist Manifesto (Marx), see *Manifesto
 of the Communist Party* (Marx)
Comte, Auguste
 introduction to, 150
 on absolute *vs.* relative truth, 153
 contributions to sociology, xvii, 154

on division of labour, 158
empirical inquiry, 152–53, 178
influence on Durkheim, xxiii
law of three stages, 149, 150–51
naming of sociology by, 139, 151n54, 154
positivism, 86, 87, 151, 15-2–54
power focus, 115
on rational prediction, 153–54
Saint-Simon and, 150
social stability and change focus, 151–52
on social statics and dynamics, 154
on sociology, xii
on transition to modernity, 155–56
Congress of Vienna, 124n46
conscience collective (collective conscience/
 consciousness)
 overview, 159–60
 vs. collective representations, 172–73
 development of concept, 156
 in *The Division of Labor*, 146, 155
 Durkheim's emphasis on, 142
 vs. individual consciousness, 171, 179
 individuals in, 179
 meaning and translation of term, 155n55
 mechanical solidarity and, 161
 Montesquieu's influence on, 147
 parallels to Marx and Weber, 181
 positive future from, 163
 problem with, 230
 repressive law and, 160
 social solidarity from, 181
 See also collective representations
consciousness, 187–88
consumers' republic, 263
consumption, mass, 262–63
continuous partial attention, 46–47
cool media, 40, 55, 291, 318–19
Cooper, Alice, 310
Cooperative Institutional Research Program
 The American Freshman, 10, 14
copyright law, American, 264
Côté, James
 Ivory Tower Blues, 10, 60
Coupland, Douglas
 Generation X, 8, 9
Coyle, Karen, 43, 44
The Craftsman (Sennett), 75–76

craftsmanship, 75–77. *See also* intellectual
craftsmanship
"Crazy Man, Crazy" (Haley and the
Comets), 296–97
CreateSpace, 44
Cuban Missile Crisis, 283
cultural products, *see* culture
culture
approach to, xxiii–xxiv, 323–24
Adorno and Horkheimer on, 248–50,
257, 264, 317
Arnold on, 62, 72, 245, 256, 257, 317
commodification of, 245–46, 248–50,
251–54, 255–56, 257
culture industry, 248–50, 257, 264, 317
digital media, 255, 257
entertainment-driven, 252–53, 254
Gabler on, 254–55, 257
history of concept, 238–39
Hoggart on, 246–48, 256–57, 288, 289
Huxleyan decline, 254
Leavis and Thompson on, 245–46,
256, 288
live literature example, 247–48
Marcuse on, 250–52, 257
Marx on production of, 243–44
Orwellian decline, 253–54
popular *vs.* high, 246
Postman on, 252–54, 257
postwar lack of criticism, 250–51
pure (ideal) type, xxiii, 256–58
ranking societies by, 241
of reality *vs.* entertainment, 254–55
as rooted in community, 256
as social product, 242
sociological study of, 241
as study of perfection, 245, 256
urbanization of, 246–47, 288
use of term, 238, 241–42
as way of life, 241–42
Weber on, 244
Williams on, 238–39
See also Dylan, Bob; folk music; mass
culture; popular culture; popular
music; rock and roll
Culture and Anarchy (Arnold), 62. *See also*
Arnold, Matthew

Culture and Environment (Leavis and
Thompson), 245n87
Culture and Society, 1780–1950 (Williams), 238
culture industry, 248–50, 257, 264, 317
Curtis, Sonny, 319

Darwin, Charles, 99, 100n36, 101n38
Das Kapital (Marx), see *Capital* (Marx);
Marx, Karl
Daszynski, Ignacy, 87, 87n25
David, Jacques-Louis, 219
Davis, Katie, xxi, 50–51, 255, 257, 318, 324
Dawson, Jim, 296, 297
Dean, James, 297
Delmore Brothers, 275
Depression, 261–62, 274
Descartes, René, 85, 143–44, 165, 169, 178
deutend verstehen, *see* interpretive
understanding
Deutscher, Isaac, 87
deviance, 159n58, 174. *See also* suicide
dialectic, 97–98
Diddley, Bo, 270, 300
difference, 157–58
digital media
approach to, xxiii, xxiv, 235
adoption and integration of, 6
App Generation, 50–51
bidirectional communication, 45–46
continuous partial attention from,
46–47
education and, 21–24, 30–31, 45, 53–54
as hot and cold media, 49
ideal cultural form and, 257
impact of, 31, 42–43, 45, 49–50, 51–52, 255
snack media, 16, 47–48
Wesch on, 49, 50
See also "Visions" project (Wesch)
digital natives, 6, 11–12, 14–16, 42–43
digitization projects, 43–45
Dilthey, Wilhelm, 86, 323
disk jockeys (DJs), 266–67
dissemination, of research, 78
The Division of Labor in Society
(Durkheim)
overview, 147, 162–63
conscience collective, 146, 155, 159–60

development of Durkheim's thought
    from, 155, 156–57
deviance, 159n58
division of labour, 157–58
impetus for, 155
law as social fact, 170–71
methodological focus, 156, 165, 173
repressive law, 160–61
restitutive law, 161, 161n59
social solidarity, 158–59, 160–62
subtitle of first edition, 155n56
See also Durkheim, Émile
division of labour, 91–92, 93, 156–57,
    157–58, 161, 162
DJs (disk jockeys), 266–67
Doherty, Pete, 312
domination, typology of, 192n68
doo-wop, 269
D'Souza, Dinesh
    Illiberal Education, 60
Durkheim, Émile
    approach to sociology, xxii–xxiii, 142–43,
        178–80, 237, 322
    background, 140–41
    demarcation of sociology, 166–68,
        173, 179
    Descartes's influence, 144, 165, 169
    deviance, 159n58
    division of labour, 157–58
    empirical inquiry focus, 143, 144, 147,
        148, 156, 169–70, 177, 178–79, 322
    on history, 172
    impact on sociology, 139
    on institutions, 173
    intellectual development, xxiii, 141–43,
        155, 156–57
    on marital status, 175
    on Marxism, 142, 187n65
    Mills on, 136
    Montesquieu's influence, 145, 147
    on objectivity, 169–71
    Parsons on, 141
    in positivist tradition, xxiii, 86, 87, 322
    problem with methodology, 230
    reasons for commentary on culture, 324
    repressive law, 160–61
    restitutive law, 161, 161n59

Saint-Simon's influence, 148
scientific realism of, 159
similarities with Marx and Weber,
    237–38
social change, 180
social order, 179–80
social solidarity, 155, 158–59, 160–62, 181
on society, 142, 146, 171–72, 177
on sociology, 177
on suicide, 173, 174–77
terms for culture, 238
use of language by, 156n57
vocabulary from, 180–81, 325
writings by, 141, 154–55
See also collective representations;
    conscience collective; The Division
    of Labor in Society (Durkheim);
    The Rules of Sociological Method
    (Durkheim); social facts; Suicide
    (Durkheim)
Dylan, Bob
    approach to, xxiii–xxiv, 236, 272, 281,
        291–92
    background, 272
    civil rights movement and, 282, 287
    complexity of music, 279–80, 289–90
    as cool media, 291
    Cuban Missile Crisis and, 283
    Guthrie and, 277–78, 277n103, 278n104
    lyrics, 288–89
    mass culture and, 287–88, 290–91
    move to New York, 272–73, 278
    musical apprenticeship, 278, 281, 288
    on politics, 286n110
    pure type construct of culture analysis,
        288–92
    shift in emphasis, 282, 287
    songwriting, 279, 280–81, 288–89
    Tom Paine Award, 285–86
    See also Dylan, Bob, music; folk music
Dylan, Bob, music
    Another Side of Bob Dylan, 287
    "Ballad of Hollis Brown," 285
    "Blowin' in the Wind," 280, 282,
        282n107
    Bob Dylan, 281
    The Freewheelin' Bob Dylan, 282–83, 284

"A Hard Rain's A-Gonna Fall," 283–84, 288, 289, 290
"Iron Ore Blues," 290
"I Shall Be Free," 284
"Only a Pawn in Their Game," 285, 287
"Restless Farewell," 287
"The Times They Are A-Changin'" (song), 284, 291
The Times They Are A-Changin' (album), 284–85, 287
"With God on Our Side," 285
See also Dylan, Bob

e-books, *see* digitization projects
Echo Boom Generation, *see* Generation Y (Millennials)
economic determinism, 108–11, 112
economic infrastructure
    as basis for critique, 105, 117, 132, 137
    Durkheim on, 142
    as important term, 136
    revolutionary change and, 106, 133, 215
    Weber on, 215
economic rationalism, 206
economics
    state intervention, 111n41
    See also political economy
Economy and Sociology (Weber), 184. *See also* Weber, Max
e-culture, *see* digital media
The Ed Sullivan Show (TV show), *see* Sullivan, Ed
education
    adult, 245n87
    British public school system, 62n20
    See also undergraduate students; university
egoistic suicide, 174–75
elective affinity, 205, 209, 237
electric age
    Carr on, 42
    digital information in, 49, 291
    education in, 54
    impact of, 36, 37–38, 41–42
    medium is the message and, 38, 236
Elliot, Charles, 227n82
embedded liberalism, 111n41

Emberley, Peter
    Bankrupt Education, 60–61
Emergency Civil Liberties Committee, 285–86
emotional action, 192. *See also* social action
empirical inquiry
    Comte on, 152–53, 178
    Descartes on, 143–44
    Durkheim on, 143, 144, 147, 148, 156, 169–70, 177, 178–79, 322
    Marx on, 131–32
    Montesquieu on, 147
    purpose of, 78, 179
    Suicide (Durkheim) as proof for, 177
    Weber on, 204
    See also methodology
Encyclopaedia of the Social Sciences (1957), 217–20, 218n76
encyclopedias, of sociology, 217
The End of Education (Postman), 25, 25n12
Engels, Friedrich, 90, 95, 99–100, 100n36, 186, 187n64
Enlightenment
    Adorno and Horkheimer on, 249, 249n89
    German idealism and, 94
    impact on Marx, 134, 138, 213
    importance for sociology, 85, 118
    modernist thought and, 220, 224
    overview of, 86
    postmodernist thought on, 226–27
    romanticism as reaction to, 219
    Weber and, 216
entertainment culture, 252–53, 254
Ertegun, Ahmet, 269, 270
ethical conduct, 195, 196–97, 198–99, 240–41
Evers, Medgar, 286n109
everyday stocks of knowledge at hand, 28, 63
exploitation, 116, 118, 126, 226, 239–41

Facebook, 12, 15, 20, 46
Failing the Future (Kolodny), 60
Fallis, George, 59, 61–62
fatalistic suicide, 174, 174n62
Federal Communications Commission (FCC), 265

Felten, Peter
  Transforming Students, 60, 61
Ferguson, Adam, 86, 91–92, 94, 111
feudal production, 127–28
Fichte, Johann Gottlieb, 94
"Fighter" (Aguilera), 309, 318–19
files, 80–81
film industry, 299–300
First International, 122n44
Fiske, John, 245
Flexner, Abraham, 64–65, 66
folk music
  approach to, xxiii–xxiv, 236
  Broadside (magazine), 275n101
  centres of, 273n100
  Depression and, 274
  essential elements of, 276
  in New York City, 273, 275, 276
  origins, 261, 273–74
  political activism and, 275–76, 276n102
  popularity of, 276–77
  record industry and, 274–75
  See also Dylan, Bob; Dylan, Bob, music;
    Guthrie, Woody; popular music
45-rpm vinyl records, 268, 268n95, 269
Foster, Stephen, 279n105
frames of mind, 181, 230, 237, 291, 323
France, 152, 219
Frankfurt school, 248. *See also* Adorno,
  Theodor; Horkheimer, Max;
  Marcuse, Herbert
Franklin, Benjamin, 206, 210
Freed, Alan, 267, 306–7
freedom
  academic, 64
  in Enlightenment thought, 86
  Hegel on, 94
  Marx on, 118, 134, 138
  sociology and, xi–xii
The Freewheelin' Bob Dylan (Dylan),
  282–83, 284

Gabler, Neal, 245, 254–55, 257, 293, 318, 324
Galilei, Galileo, 178, 191, 321
Gallic tradition, *see* positivism
Gardner, Howard, xxi, 50–51, 255, 257,
  318, 324

Gatehouse, Jonathan
  "Why We Need to Clear Our Cluttered
    Minds," 46–47
Geist (mind/spirit/intellect), 205, 238
Geisteswissenschaften (humanities), 185, 188,
  189, 190, 230, 323
geistig (mental, intellectual, spiritual), 238
gender-inclusive language, 29n13
generalizations, 186, 188, 192–93. *See also*
  pure types (ideal types); universally
  valid truth
generational cohorts, 7–8. *See also* Baby
  Boomers; Generation X; Generation Y
  (Millennials); Generation Z
generation lap, 15
Generation X, 8–10, 12
Generation X (Coupland), 8, 9
Generation Y (Millennials)
  introduction, 8
  attention spans, 46–47
  characteristics, 10–11
  as digital natives, 11–12, 45–46, 50–51
  education, 10–11, 14, 48, 54
  information processing by, 12, 49–50
  terms for, 10
  See also undergraduate students
Generation Z
  introduction, 8
  attention spans, 16, 46–47
  characteristics of, 7, 12–13, 14, 18
  as confident and motivated, 17
  consumption of snack media, 47–48
  as digital natives, 14–16, 45–46, 50–51
  education, 14, 48, 54
  expectations for, 13–14
  information processing by, 49–50
  need for grand narrative, 25
  stresses of, 17
  See also undergraduate students
"Generation Z" (White), 13
Gen Z (JWT), 13, 16, 17
German idealism, 94–95, 323
German tradition, *see* interpretive sociology
"Get Ready for Generation Z"
  (Kingston), 13
Giddens, Anthony, 160
Gilbert, James, 299

Gill, Andy, 282

Ginsberg, Allan, 287, 288

Gleason, Jackie, 301

The Globe and Mail, 13

goal-rational action
  commodification of culture from, 257
  definition, 192
  dominance in industrial societies, 200–
    201, 206, 211, 214, 231, 241
  problems from dominance of, 204, 239,
    240, 248
  scholarly action as, 195, 196
  Weber on, 200–201, 204, 205, 206, 214,
    231, 323
  See also social action

Google Books Library Project, 43, 44

governments
  economic intervention, 111n41
  Montesquieu on, 145–46

grade inflation, 11, 14

grand narrative, 25, 27–28

Great Depression, 261–62, 274

Green Day, 313–14, 317

Grown Up Digital (Tapscott), 15

Grundrisse (Marx), 95n28, 96n32, 106, 214.
  See also Marx, Karl

The Gutenberg Galaxy (McLuhan), xxi, 36, 37,
  38, 40, 235. *See also* McLuhan, Marshall

Gutenberg's bible, 44

Guthrie, Woody
  Dylan and, 272, 273, 277–78, 277n103,
    278n104
  folk music and, 274
  influence on 1960s music, 276n102
  life of, 274
  in New York City, 274, 275, 278

Halberstam, David, 298–99, 303

Haley and the Comets, 296–97, 296n111,
  300, 317

Hall, Stuart, 245

Hallinan, Blake, 21–22, 23, 24

"A Hard Rain's A-Gonna Fall" (Dylan),
  283–84, 288, 289, 290

Harris, Sam, 315

Hart, Michael
  Project Gutenberg, 43

Harvard Classics, 227n82

Harvard University, 64n21

Harvey, David, 70

Hayek, Friedrich von, 111n41

Hegel, Georg Wilhelm Friedrich
  on civil society, 115
  dialectical logic, 97, 98
  Durkheim on, 142
  on historical change, 105
  on human freedom, 94–95
  Marx and, xix, 88–89, 90, 105, 114,
    114n42, 115
  popularity of, 89

helicopter parents, 10

Hentoff, Nat, 280

Hess, Moses, 90, 106

Hilburn, Robert, 279, 283, 290

Hinduism, 175–76

historical materialism, 100n36, 185, 186–88,
  189, 197, 211–12

historical school, 185–86, 187, 188, 197, 211

history, 172, 213–14

Hobbes, Thomas, 86, 91, 115

Hoggart, Richard
  class-based analysis, 256–57, 274
  concerns about culture, 245, 246–47,
    248, 264
  ideal cultural forms, 256–57, 280, 285,
    289, 318
  live literature, 247–48
  reasons for commentary on culture, 324
  urbanization of culture, 246–47, 288

Holly, Buddy, 293, 305, 311, 317, 318, 319

Holmes, Odetta (Odetta), 272n98, 282n107

Horkheimer, Max
  on culture industry, 248–50, 264, 317
  on "enlightenment," 249n89
  on ideal cultural forms, 257
  on mass deception from mass culture,
    250, 289
  reasons for commentary on culture,
    245, 324

hot media, 39–40, 48

"The House of the Rising Sun" (song), 281,
  281n106

Howe, Neil, 8–9, 10

human agency, 32, 42, 69, 133–34

humanities, see *Geisteswissenschaften*
human reason, 63, 86, 94, 219, 220, 321
Humboldt, Wilhelm von, 63–64
Hume, David, 86, 91, 94
Huxley, Aldous, 247n88, 254, 254n93
hyper attention, 46–47
hyperlinks, 46–47

idealism, German, 94–95, 323
ideal types, *see* pure types
*The Idea of a University Defined and
    Illustrated* (Newman), 62
idea of the university, 65. *See also* university
identities, personal, 51
ideology, 188, 215, 237, 238, 244
Illiberal Education (D'Souza), 60
Iman, Lindsey, 22, 23
Imperial Records, 269
impressionism, 219
industrialization
    argument against exploitation, 239–41
    ascetic Protestantism and, 240
    impact on culture, 246, 247
    Manifesto of the Communist Party (Marx)
        and, 122–23
    modernization and, 221, 223
    Saint-Simon on, 148, 149–50
    See also capitalism
information age, 34. *See also* digital media
The Information Age (Castells), xxi, 33. *See
    also* Castells, Manuel
information revolution, 50. *See also* digital
    media; "Visions" project (Wesch)
infrastructure, 102–3, 106, 113–14, 116–17.
    See also economic infrastructure
Inglehart, Ronald, 224n80
Instagram, 15, 46
institutions, 173
intellectual craftsmanship, xxi, 75, 77–79,
    80, 81–82, 325. *See also* scholarship
intellectual production, 243–44
*International Encyclopedia of the Social
    Sciences* (1968), 217, 220–24, 220n77
International Working Men's Association,
    122n44
Internet, 9–10, 42, 45–46, 47. *See also*
    digital media

interpretive sociology *(verstehende
    Soziologie)*, 86–87, 230
interpretive understanding *(deutend
    verstehen)*
    explanation of, 185, 189, 229–31
    implications for sociology, 190–91, 215, 325
    typology of social action and, 192
    Weber and, 204
introductory texts, xvi–xvii
iron cage of reason *(stahlhartes Gehäuse)*,
    200–201, 200n74, 204, 211, 237, 257
"Iron Ore Blues" (Dylan), 290
"I Shall Be Free" (Dylan), 284
Ivory Tower Blues (Côté and Allahar), 10, 60

James, Etta, 307–8, 308–9, 309–10
Jarboe, Greg, 18
Johansson, Charity
    Transforming Students, 60, 61
Johnson, Robert, 275
JSTOR, 11
judgement of value, 196–97, 215
jukeboxes, 268, 268n95
jump blues, 269
juvenile delinquency, 299
J. Walter Thompson (JWT)
    Gen Z, 13, 16, 17

Kallan, Horace, 217–20
Kant, Immanuel, 63, 94, 142, 322, 323
Kautsky, Karl, 95, 186–87, 187n64
Kelles-Krauz, Kazimierz, 87n25
Kelly, Steven, 22, 23
Kennedy, John F., 283
Kerr, Clark, 66–67
Keynes, John Maynard, 111n41
Khanna, Sanjay, 17
Kindle Convert, 44–45
Kingston, Anne
    "Get Ready for Generation Z," 13
Knies, Karl, 187, 189n66
knowledge
    everyday stocks of knowledge at hand,
        28, 63
    Lyotard on, 224–25, 229
    objective, 170
    recipe, 28

Kolodny, Annette
   Failing the Future, 60
Korsch, Karl, 187, 214

labour, division of, 91–92, 93, 156–57,
   157–58, 161, 162
labour market, 55
labour-power, 110, 112–15, 116, 128
Labriola, Antonio, 187, 214
Lafargue, Laura Marx, 95
Lafargue, Paul, 95
Laski, Harold, 64n
Lauper, Cyndi, 307, 309, 310
law of three stages, 149, 150–51
Lead Belly (Huddie William Ledbetter),
   272n98, 275
League of the Just, 123–24. *See also*
   Communist League
Leavis, F.R.
   community roots needed for culture,
      246, 256, 288, 317
   concerns about culture, 245–46, 248,
      264
   Culture and Environment, 245n87
   reasons for commentary on culture, 324
Ledbetter, Huddie William (Lead Belly),
   272n98, 275
Lee, Julian, 312, 313
legal code, 170–71
legal-rational authority, 214, 231, 249
Lerner, Daniel, 220, 221–23, 224n80
Levine, Melvin
   Ready or Not, Here Life Comes, 11
Levitt, Cyril, 68
Lewis, Jerry Lee, 305
liberalism, embedded, 111n41
Libertines, 312, 317, 318
Liebknecht, Wilhelm, 95
Lilienfeld, Paul von, 156
literature, live, 247–48
Little Richard, 269n96, 305, 317
live literature, 247–48
Locke, John, 115
Lomax, John, 275
"The Loss of the University" (Berry), 61
Luce, Claire Boothe, 298
Lukács, Georg, 187, 188, 214

Lukes, Stephen, 140, 166
Lyotard, Jean-François, 224–25, 229

Madonna, 309
MadV, 18–19
Mallarmé, Stéphane, 252n91
Malthus, Thomas, 94, 105
Manifesto of the Communist Party (Marx)
   approach to, 119
   bourgeoisie, 125–27, 131
   class struggle, 112, 123, 125, 132, 136
   as compromise document, 123–24
   contested views on, 122
   on dialectic of progress, 134
   economic infrastructure focus, 132
   English translation, 124n45
   Enlightenment influence on, 134
   as high-water mark for Marx, 123
   human agency, 133–34
   impact of, 121–22
   on market societies, 122–23
   opening section, 124–25, 124n45
   production, 126–27, 127–29
   proletariat, 129–31
   publication history, 121n43
   revolution, 131, 214
   sociology contributions from, 131–33
   See also Marx, Karl
Marceau, Haley, 23
Marcus, Greil, 294, 304–5, 306
Marcuse, Herbert
   concerns about culture, 245, 248,
      250–52, 257
   on ideal cultural forms, 257
   on lack of criticism, 250–51, 288
   One-Dimensional Man, 250, 250n90, 288
   reasons for commentary on culture, 324
   on Soviet Union, 250n90
marital status, 175
Marx, Eleanor, 95
Marx, Karl
   approach to, 88
   approach to sociology, xxii–xxiii,
      236–37, 323
   background of, 88–90, 134–35
   Bauer and, 89n26
   bourgeoisie, 125–27, 131

on capitalist society, 114, 118, 122–23
class struggle, 112, 123, 125, 132, 136–38, 325
commentary on, 87, 96, 96nn30–31
conceptual framework of social whole,
102–5, 116–*17*
contemporary relevance, 119, 127
contributions to sociology, 87–88, 118,
131–33, 135–36
critiques by, 97, 97n33
on culture, 244
on dialectic, 97–98
difficulty organizing thoughts, xviii,
96–97, 96n32, 101
economic infrastructure focus, 105, 132
Enlightenment influence on, 134, 138, 213
Hegel and, xix, 88–89, 90, 105, 114,
114n42, 115
on history, 213–14
human agency, 133–34
on ideology, 237, 238, 244
intellectual development of, 89–90, 95,
105, 123, 214
on intellectual production, 243–44
intricacy of thought, 99, 106
labour-power, 112–15
later career, 122
materialist approach, 98–99, 115–16
Mills on, 135–36, 137
mode of production, 103–4, 236
on overproduction, 108–11, 128–29
on power, 115
presentation of ideas, 99
production, 102, 126–27, 127–29, 243–44
reasons for commentary on culture, 324
reputation of, 87
revolution, 90, 105–6, 112, 131, 132, 133,
213–14
similarities with Durkheim and Weber,
237–38
sociological imagination and, 134, 135
as sociologist, 95
study of, 87, 97
surplus value, 100n35, 110, 112–13, 128
terms for culture, 238
unfinished nature of work, 95–96, 137
vocabulary from, 136–38, 325
Weber and, xxiii, 213–15, 230–31

writings by, 95, 95nn28–29, 187n64
See also *Capital* (Marx); class
consciousness; economic
infrastructure; historical
materialism; *Manifesto of the
Communist Party* (Marx);
Marxism; material forces of
production; proletariat; social
relations of production; *Towards
the Critique of Political Economy*,
1859 preface (Marx)
Marxism
basis in 1859 preface, 100–101, 102–3
development and promotion of, 186–87,
187n64
Durkheim on, 142, 187n65
Engel's summary of, 99–100
historical materialism, 100n36, 185,
186–88, 189, 197, 211–12
as ideological system, 101
on Marx as sociologist, 95
on materialism, 115
orthodox, 100n37
See also Marx, Karl
mass consumption, 262–63. *See also* popular
culture
mass culture
critiques of, 247, 247n88, 248, 249–50,
257, 289
Dylan and, 287–88, 290–91
See also popular culture
mastery, 86, 118, 134
material forces of production
conflict with social relations of
production, 106, 264
definition, 103–4, 112
effect of industrialization on, 239
human workers as, 113, 116–17
within totality of relations of
production, 116, *117*
materialism, 98n34
materialist, 98–99, 98n34, 115–16
mature students, xi
McJob, 9
McLuhan, Marshall
introduction, xxi, 36, 236
cool media, 40, 55, 291, 318–19

on entertainment and education, 54
file system, 80–81
hot media, 39–40, 48
medium is the message, 38–39, 236, 291,
    301, 305, 318–19
on new mediums, 52
overextension of senses, 40
print culture, 36–37, 40–41
on reading, 48
in "Visions" project (Wesch), 19–20, 24
See also electric age
meaning, 33–34, 57, 189–90, 229, 230
mechanical solidarity, 161
medieval society, 149
medium is the message, 38–39, 236, 291,
    301, 305, 318–19
Mehring, Franz, 95
"The Message" (MadV), 19
metaphysics, 322
methodology
    discarding preconceptions, 169
    historical materialism, 100n36, 185,
        186–88, 189, 197, 211–12
    historical school, 185–86, 187, 188,
        197, 211
    objectivity, 169–70
    single-factor analyses, 212–13
    Weber's critique of Stammler on, 188–89,
        189n66
    See also empirical inquiry; interpretive
        understanding; pure types
        (ideal types); social action;
        social facts
Metternich, Klemens von, 124n46
Meyer, Eduard, 186, 187, 189, 189n66
Mies van der Rohe, Ludwig, 225
Miliband, Ralph, 78, 81
Mill, James, 92n27, 94, 111
Mill, John Stuart, 94, 115
Millennials, *see* Generation Y
Mills, C. Wright
    approach to, 73
    background of, 74–75, 135
    on craftsmanship, 76–77
    on disciplines and interests, 72
    on Durkheim, 136
    on human agency, 42, 69

on individual's view of world, 29
intellectual craftsmanship, xxi, 75,
    77–79, 80, 81–82, 325
letters to Tovarich, 69n22
on Marxist thought, 135–36, 137
memories about, 73–74, 75n23
"On Intellectual craftsmanship,"
    69–70
on sociology, xix–xx, 321
vocabulary for clear social reflection,
    136, 324
work process of, 78, 80–81
on writing, 78–80
See also sociological imagination
Mintz, Leo, 267
Mises, Ludwig von, 111n41
mode of production, 103–4, 236–37.
    See also economic infrastructure;
        infrastructure; Marx, Karl; material
        forces of production; social relations
        of production; superstructure
modern art, 219
modern era, *see* modernity
modernism
    art and, 219–20
    as breaking free of tradition, 219–20
    critiques of, 224
    definition, 217–18
    emphasis of, 215, 216, 225
    Enlightenment and, 220
    ideal types (pure types), 215–16
    transition to postmodernism, 228–29
    Weber and, 215, 216
    as worldview, 227–28
    See also modernity; modernization;
        postmodernism
modernist art, 219–20
modernity
    Enlightenment and, 220
    goal-rational action in, 200–201
    Marx on, 126, 127, 128–29
    production in, 128–29
    religion in, 194–95
    scholarship on, 155–56
    in sociology encyclopedias, 217
    See also modernism; modernization;
        postmodernism

modernization
  overview, 223–24
  Blackwell Encyclopedia of Sociology on,
    224n80
  development of concept, 220–21
  meaning of, 221–22
  process of, 222–23
  See also modernism; modernity;
    postmodernism
Modern Painters (Ruskin), 41
Modovoi, Leerom, 305
monopoly, 193n70, 266, 267–68
monopsony, 193n70
Monroe, Bill, 275
Montesquieu, 86, 115, 144–47, 155, 178, 321
"The Moondog Coronation Ball" (concert), 267
Moore, William Lewis, 286n109
Mooring, William, 299
Moran, Greg
  Academic Transformation, 63
movies, 299–300
multi-tasking, 12, 20, 46, 49
multiversity, 66–67, 72. *See also* university
muscular Christianity, 62n20. *See also*
    Protestantism; religion; Roman
    Catholicism

Nachman, Gerald, 301
Napoleonic Empire, 219
natural attitude, 28
nature, 239n84
nature, state of, 91
neoliberalism, 70–71, 111n41
network societies, 34, 38. *See also* electric age
Newell, Waller
  Bankrupt Education, 60–61
Newman, John Henry, 62, 66
Newton, Isaac, 85
New York City, 273, 275, 276, 278
Nietzsche, Friedrich, 195, 324
Nineteen Eighty-Four (Orwell), 253–54
No Doubt (band), 309
Norman, Rebecca, 22
norms, 179
North America
  education postwar, 65
  images of life in postwar, 298–99
  juvenile delinquency fears, 299
  mass consumption in postwar, 262–63
  postwar optimism, 261–62
  See also folk music; popular music
note taking, 80–81

objectivity, 169–70
Odetta (Odetta Holmes), 272n98, 282n107
oligopoly, 266
one-dimensional man, 248
One-Dimensional Man (Marcuse), 250,
    250n90, 288. *See also* Marcuse,
    Herbert
"One World" (MadV), 18–19
"On Intellectual craftsmanship" (Mills),
    69–70. *See also* Mills, C. Wright
"Only a Pawn in Their Game" (Dylan),
    285, 287
On Theory and Methods in History (Meyer),
    186
organic solidarity, 161–62
orthodox Marxism, 100n37. *See also*
    Marxism
Orwell, George
  Nineteen Eighty-Four, 253–54
overproduction, 108–11, 128–29
Owen, Robert, 94

Page, Charles, x
Parker, Tom, 301
Parsons, Talcott, 141, 155n55, 200n74
passion, sociological, xviii–xix
People's Songs, 275–76
personal trouble of milieu, 29–30, 31, 69,
    71, 255, 324
Peter, Paul, and Mary, 282
Peterson, Richard, 263–64, 265, 268
Pew Research Centre, 15
Phillips, Dewey, 266–67, 301, 302n112
Phillips, Sam, 266, 270, 296
philosophy, 64, 72, 144
Philosophy of Right (Hegel), xix
physicalism, 98n34
Pink (musician), 314, 317, 318
Pinterest, 15, 46
poetry slams, 22n9
political consciousness, 114

political economy
    central issues of, 92n27
    economy as basis for analysis, 94, 105
    exploitation and, 240
    Ferguson on, 91–92
    first use of term, 92n27
    influence on sociology, 90–91
    Marx and, 90, 95, 105, 115
    roots of, 91
    Smith on, 92–93
pop rock, 305–6
popular culture
    approach to, xxiv, 236, 263
    on generational cohorts, 8, 13
    vs. high culture, 246
    homogenous vs. complex debate, 263
    inability of to critique, 248
    See also folk music; mass culture; popular
        music; rock and roll
popular music
    American Society of Composers,
        Authors, and Publishers (ASCAP),
        264
    Broadcast Music Incorporated (BMI),
        265
    copyright law, 264
    disk jockeys (DJs), 266–67
    45-rpm vinyl records, 268, 268n95, 269
    jukeboxes, 268, 268n95
    origins, 261
    pre-WWII uniformity, 264
    radio, 265–67, 271
    record industry, 267–69, 269–70
    rhythm and blues (R & B), 269–70
    sociological approach to, 271
    transistor radio, 270
    transition to rock and roll, 263–64
    See also Dylan, Bob; Dylan, Bob, music;
        folk music; rock and roll
positive philosophy, see positivism
positivism, xxiii, 86, 87, 151, 152–54. See also
    empirical inquiry
Posnick-Goodwin, Sherry, 12–13
Postman, Neil, 252–54
    concerns about culture, 245, 252–54,
        253n92, 291, 318
    Dylan and, 291

The End of Education, 25, 25n12
    Generation X and, 10
    on ideal cultural forms, 257
    on print culture, 252
    reasons for commentary on culture,
        324
    on television, 290
    in "Visions" project (Wesch), 23–24, 25
postmodernism
    approach to, 324
    Blackwell Encyclopedia of Sociology and,
        224
    Encyclopaedia of the Social Sciences and,
        218n76
    International Encyclopedia of the Social
        Sciences and, 220n77
    on knowledge, 224–25
    overview, 224, 225–27
    transition to, 228–29
    Weber as bridge to, 216, 229
    worldview of, 228–29
    See also modernism; modernity;
        modernization
postsecondary education, see undergraduate
    students; university
power, 115, 238
prediction, rational, 153–54
Prensky, Marc, 11–12
Presley, Elvis, 267, 295–96, 301–5, 302n112,
    317, 318
print culture, 36–37, 40–41, 43, 52, 53, 54–55
production
    capitalist, 104, 128–29, 133
    culture and, 242
    feudal, 127–28
    intellectual, 243–44
    overproduction, 108–11, 128–29
    rate of profit and, 110
    society changed through changes in,
        126–27
    See also economic infrastructure;
        material forces of production;
        social relations of production;
        Towards the Critique of Political
        Economy, 1859 preface (Marx)
progress, 86, 118, 134
Project Gutenberg, 43

proletariat
  creation of, 129–31
  etymology of term, 125n47
  importance of term, 136
  opposition to exploitation, 239–41
  revolution from, 90, 112, 131, 133, 214
  use of term, 124n46
property relations, *see* social relations of
    production
*The Protestant Ethic and the Spirit of
    Capitalism* (Weber)
  introduction, 204
  ascetic Protestantism, 207–9, 210
  on calling, 209–10
  on capitalism and Protestantism,
    210–11, 240
  ethic of capitalism, 207
  on historical materialism, 211–12
  on historical school, 211
  objectives, 204–5, 230
  publication history, 204
  on single-factor analyses, 212–13
  spirit of capitalism, 205–7
  See also Weber, Max
Protestantism
  ascetic, 207–9, 210
  calling and, 209–10
  Calvinism, 208
  capitalism and, 210–11, 240
  Puritans, 209, 210
  suicide and, 174–75
psychology, 167, 167n60, 171
public issues of social structure, 29–30, 30–31,
    71, 255, 324. *See also* social structure
"Puppy Love" (Anka), 306
pure types (ideal types)
  introduction, xxiii, 193
  of culture, 256–58
  of Dylan, 288–92
  purpose of, 193–94, 205–6, 215–16
  of rock and roll, 295, 317–19
  Weber and, 204
Puritans, 209, 210

radio, 265–67, 271
radio, transistor, 270
Raley, John, 16

rate of profit, 110, 111, 112
rationalism, ascetic, 211
rational prediction, 153–54
R & B (rhythm and blues), 269–70
reading, 12, 47, 48
Ready or Not, Here Life Comes (Levine), 11
Reagan, Ronald, 299–300
reason
  absolute, 98
  human, 63, 86, 94, 219, 220, 321
  iron cage of reason (*stahlhartes Gehäuse*),
    200–201, 200n74, 204, 211, 237,
    257
recipe knowledge, 28
record industry, 267–69, 269–70, 274–75.
    See also popular music
record players, 270
Reign of Terror, 148n53
relevance, 197–98, 198n73, 199
religion
  capitalist production and, 243–44
  continued relevance, 212
  in modern era, 194–95
  muscular Christianity, 62n20
  Roman Catholicism, 174–75, 207
  suicide and, 174–75
  See also Protestantism
repressive law, 147, 160–61
research-oriented education, 63–64
restitutive law, 147, 161, 161n59
"Restless Farewell" (Dylan), 287
revolution, *see* social change
Reynolds, Caitlin, 22
rhythm and blues (R & B), 269–70
Ricardo, David, 94, 105, 133n48
Rickert, Heinrich, 86, 188
Rihanna, 314–16, 317, 318
Rimbaud, Arthur, 290
rock and roll
  approach to, xxiv, 236, 293–94
  for addressing issues, 317
  Adele, 310–11
  amalgamation of sounds, 306–7, 306–11,
    310–11
  American Bandstand (TV show),
    271n97, 318
  Beatles, 311–12

Beyoncé, 308–9, 310
Blackboard Jungle (film), 297–98, 299–300
Buddy Holly, 305, 311, 319
Christina Aguilera, 309–10, 318–19
as commodity, 294, 316–17
complexity of, 294
concerns about, 316
defining, 294
dialectic of emotions, 311–16
Ed Sullivan and, 300, 301, 302, 303–4, 305, 311
Elvis Presley, 267, 295–96, 301–5, 302n112, 318
Etta James, 307–8, 308–9, 309–10
Green Day, 313–14
human experience expressed by, 318
Libertines's "Time for Heroes," 312, 318
longevity of, 319
"The Moondog Coronation Ball" (concert), 267
as music of the people, 317
origins, 296–97, 300–301
physicality, 295–96, 297, 304, 305, 306
Pink, 314
pop rock, 305–6
pure type construct analysis of, 295, 317–19
Rihanna's "American Oxygen," 314–16
"Rock Around the Clock," 297–98, 300
sexual explicitness, 309
social forces in, 298
as teenage music, 267, 316, 317
visual aspect, 318–19
See also popular music
Rock and Roll Hall of Fame, 294
"Rock Around the Clock" (Haley and the Comets), 297–98, 300
"Rocket 88" (song), 296
"Rock the Joint" (song), 296
Roman Catholicism, 174–75, 207
Roscher, Wilhelm, 187, 189n66
Rose, Ellen, 46, 255, 257, 318, 324
Rousseau, Jean-Jacques, 86, 91, 115, 156
rules, xii
The Rules of Sociological Method (Durkheim)
introduction, 139, 165–66
collective representations, 172–73, 237

demarcation of sociology, 166–68, 173
on history, 172
on institutions, 173
methodological proposal, 156, 169–70, 178
on objectivity, 169–71
purpose of, 165
social facts, 156n57, 166, 168–69
on society, 146, 171–72
use of language in, 156n57
See also Durkheim, Émile
Ruskin, John, 41, 319

Saint-Simon, Henri de
background, 147–48
empirical focus, 148–49
influence of, 150
as positivist, xxiii, 86, 87, 178
on power, 115
on society, 149–50
on transition to modernity, 156
works of, 148
Savage, Joseph, 22, 23, 23n11
Say, Jean-Baptiste, 105
Schäffle, Albert, 156
Schary, Dore, 299
Schelling, Friedrich Wilhelm Joseph von, 89, 94
Schiller, Herbert, 245
Schneweis, Derek, 22
scholarship, xvii–xviii, 78–80, 191, 197–98, 198n73. *See also* intellectual craftsmanship; science
Schutz, Alfred, 28
science
as basis for ethics, 196–97, 198–99
as goal-rational action, 195, 196, 200
postmodernism and, 225
universal truths and, 199
as value-rational action, 196, 199
Weber on, 195–96
scientific action, *see* science
scientific method, 144, 169, 178. *See also* empirical inquiry; methodology
screen life, 45
Seeger, Pete, 274, 275, 275n101

Sennett, Richard
  The Craftsman, 75–76
senses, 36, 40
The Shallows (Carr), xxi, 42. *See also* Carr,
    Nicholas
Silverberg, David, 22n9
Simmel, Georg, 86, 188
single-factor analyses, 212–13
Sismondi, Simonde de, 111
Skolnik, Michael
  Academic Transformation, 63
slam poetry, 22n9
smartphones, 16, 20n7
Smith, Adam, 86, 91, 92–93, 94, 105, 111
snack media, 16, 47–48
Snow, Jimmy Rogers, 295, 304, 306
social action
  impact of frames of mind on, 237
  importance for Weber, 185, 229
  interpretive understanding approach to,
      190–91, 192
  meaning and, 189–90, 229
  science as, 195–96, 198–99
  typology of, 192
  See also goal-rational action
social change
  class consciousness for, 90, 133
  class struggle and, 137
  Comte on, 154
  Durkheim and, xxii–xxiii, 180
  Hegel on, 105
  labour-power and, 112, 131
  Manifesto of the Communist Party (Marx)
      and, 122
  Marx and, xxii–xxiii, 90, 105–6, 132,
      213–14
  technological determinism, 107–8
  Weber and, 213–14
  See also modernization
social cohesiveness, *see* social solidarity
social currents, 168
social dynamics, 154
social facts
  overview, 142–43, 180–81
  definition, 166–68, 173
  problem in approach to, 230
  as things, 156n57, 168–69

social history, xi
socialization, 179–80
social order, 179–80
social relationships, 32
social relations of production
  conditions of, 102
  conflict with material forces of
      production, 106, 264
  definition, 103
  effect of industrialization on, 239
  Marx's emphasis on, xxii
  popular culture and, 248
  profit generation and, 107, 112–13
  within totality of relations of
      production, 116, *117*
social solidarity, 155, 156, 158–59, 160–62,
    181
social statics, 154
social structure, 33–35, 42. *See also* public
    issues of social structure
society, 142, 146, 171–72, 177, 178
sociological imagination
  approach to, xvi, xxi, 4, 235, 236
  as important term, 325
  intersection of personal and public in,
      29–30, 31, 116
  Marx's influence on, 116, 134, 135
  purpose of, xix–xx, 29, 324
  questions for successful use of, 31–33
  transition to, 28
  Weber's influence on, 185
sociology
  assumptions about, 28
  benefits of, xv, xix–xx, 324
  classical tradition, xx–xxi, xxi–xxii,
      81–82, 237–38, 321, 324
  encyclopedias on, 217
  freedom and, xi–xii
  introductory texts on, xvi–xvii
  naming of discipline, 139, 151n54
  as passion, xviii–xix
  promise of, 325
  relativity of concepts, 191, 191n67
  study of, xv–xvi, xvii–xviii, 73
  teaching, x–xi
  See also Comte, Auguste; culture;
      digital media; Durkheim, Émile;

Marx, Karl; Mills, C. Wright;
    Montesquieu; Saint-Simon, Henri
    de; sociological imagination;
    Weber, Max
Socratic method, 98
Sombart, Werner, 194n71
songwriting, 279, 280
Soviet Union, 250n90, 283
Sparks & Honey
    "Meet Generation Z," 13, 15, 18
Spencer, Herbert, 151n54
Spice Girls, 309
The Spirit of the Laws (Montesquieu),
    145–47, 145n51
Springsteen, Bruce, 315, 317
Sputnik, 65
Stage Show (TV show), 301–2
stahlhartes Gehäuse (iron cage of reason),
    200–201, 200n74, 204, 211, 237, 257
Stammler, Rudolf, 187, 188–89
state intervention, in economy, 111n41
state of nature, 91
Stewart, Dugald, 91, 92, 94
Stewart, James, 92n27
Strauss, William, 8–9, 10
structure, 32n14. *See also* public issues of
    social structure; social structure
The Structure of Social Action (Parsons), 141
student movements, 67–68
students, *see* undergraduate students
suicide
    introduction, 173
    altruistic, 175–76
    anomic, 176–77
    egoistic, 174–75
    fatalistic, 173n62
    social integration for prevention, 177
    types of, 174
Suicide (Durkheim)
    overview, 173, 178
    collective representations, 174–75, 177
    implications of study, 177
    importance of, 173–74
    on marital status, 175
    methodological focus, 177, 178
    social integration, 177
    on society, 177

on sociology, 177
    See also Durkheim, Émile; suicide
Sullivan, Ed, 300, 301, 302, 303–4, 305, 311
Sun Records, 270
superstructure, 102–3, 104, 105, 106, 113–14,
    116–17. *See also* infrastructure
surplus value, 100n35, 110, 112–13, 128
Swados, Harvey, 79

Tapscott, Don
    Grown Up Digital, 15
technological determinism, 107–8
technology, 33–34, 34–35
teen culture, 267, 300, 317. *See also* rock
    and roll
television
    Elvis Presley, 301–4
    juvenile delinquency and, 299
    Postman on, 252, 253n92, 254, 290
    radio and, 265, 266, 271
    rock and roll on, 297, 298, 300, 318
Terkel, Studs, 277, 283
texting, 6, 16
theorizations, 227
this-worldly asceticism, 208, 209, 210
Thompson, Denys
    community roots needed for culture,
        246, 256, 288, 317
    concerns about culture, 245–46, 248,
        264
    Culture and Environment, 245n87
    reasons for commentary on culture,
        324
"Time for Heroes" (Libertines),
    312, 318
"The Times They Are A-Changin'" (Dylan),
    284, 291
The Times They Are A-Changin' (Dylan),
    284–85, 287
Tin Pan Alley, 263n94, 264
Tom Paine Award, 285–86, 286n108
Tönnies, Ferdinand, 156
total living, 262
Towards the Critique of Political Economy
    (Marx), 101, 122. *See also* Marx, Karl;
    *Towards the Critique of Political
    Economy*, 1859 preface (Marx)

Towards the Critique of Political Economy,
    1859 preface (Marx)
    approach to, 88, 101
    base and superstructure conception,
        102–3
    class consciousness reading of, 111–15
    conceptual framework of social whole,
        102–5, 116–17
    economic determinism reading, 108–11
    economic infrastructure focus, 105, 132
    final challenge in, 118
    interpretation of, 106, 107
    labour-power, 112–15
    mode of production, 103–4, 236
    orthodox Marxism use of, 100–101
    on overproduction, 108–11
    overview of, 118
    production, 102
    purpose of, 101–2
    revolution, 105–6, 214
    superstructure, 106
    technological determinism reading,
        107–8
    See also Marx, Karl
traditional action, 192. *See also* social action
Transforming Students (Johansson and
    Felten), 61
transistor radio, 270
Trick, David
    Academic Transformation, 63
truth
    relative *vs.* absolute, 153
    universally valid, 195–96, 195n72, 197,
        198, 198n73, 216
"Tutti Frutti" (Little Richard), 269n96, 301
12-inch LP records, 268
Twitter, 15, 46
typographic and mechanical era, 36, 37,
    39, 40–41. *See also* electric age; print
    culture

undergraduate students
    approach to, xvi, xxi, 4, 55–56
    adjustment to print culture, 52, 54–55, 63
    app-dependence and, 51
    barriers facing, 59, 63
    Beloit College Mindset List on, 4–7, 30
    changes across generations, 3–4
    continuous partial attention, 45–47
    digital media and, 6, 45
    e-culture of, 42–43
    educational opportunity for, 72
    expectations by, 60
    information processing, 7, 47, 48, 49–50,
        51–52
    mature students, xi
    Millennials, 10–11
    personal identities, 51
    personal impact on education
        experience, 70
    stresses facing, 6–7
    teaching, x–xi
    See also Generation Y (Millennials);
        Generation Z; university;
        "Visions" project (Wesch)
Understanding Media (McLuhan), xxi, 38,
    40, 80, 81, 235. *See also* McLuhan,
    Marshall
United States of America, *see* North
    America
unity of the sciences, 154, 178–79,
    180, 323
universally valid truth, 195–96, 195n72, 197,
    198, 198n73, 216
university
    approach to, xxi, 31
    as apprenticeship, 73
    Boomers and, 65
    careerist focus, 67
    coexistence of research and liberal
        focuses, 64
    contemporary approach, 64–65
    criticisms of, 60, 68–69
    in digital age, 21–24, 30–31, 53–56
    digitization of printed material, 43
    grand narrative needed, 25
    improvement of, 72–73
    liberal education approach, 62, 72
    as multiversity, 65–67, 72
    neoliberalism and, 70, 71
    print culture in, 43, 52
    purpose of, 59, 60–61
    research-oriented approach, 63–64
    student movements, 67–68

See also education; undergraduate
    students
University of Virginia, 44
Unterberger, Richie, 273, 275
utilitarian philosophy, 142, 240

value, judgement of, 196–97, 215
value-rational action, 192, 196, 199. *See also*
    social action
value-relevant action, 197–98, 198n73, 199
van Dyke, Henry, 64n
Van Ronk, Dave, 281n106
Venturi, Robert, 225
verstehende Soziologie (interpretive
    sociology), 86–87, 230
"Visions of Minecrafters Today"
    (popopopopo159), 23
"Visions" project (Wesch)
    introduction to, 19
    "a few ideas…" video (2011), 21–24
    "A Vision of Students Today" video
        (2007), 19–21, 48, 52–53
    Bumstead error, 52–53
    on digital information, 49, 50
    on education in digital age, 21–24, 31
    goal of, 53
    "Information R/evolution" video (2007), 50
    insight from, 24–25
    number of videos in, 21n8
vocabulary, for clear social reflection
    approach to, 136, 324–25
    from Durkheim, 180–81
    from Marx, 136–38
    Weber, 229–31

Wage-Labour and Capital (Marx), 108, 110.
    See also Marx, Karl
The Wealth of Nations (Smith), 92–93. *See
    also* Smith, Adam
Weber, Max
    approach to, 184–85, 201, 203, 217
    approach to sociology, xxii–xxiii, 185,
        190–91, 191–92, 215, 229, 237, 323
    ascetic rationalism and, 211
    background of, 183–84, 194–95
    on calling, 209–10
    capitalism, 205–7, 210–11, 240

classical tradition and, 216–17
complexity of thought, 200
critique of Stammler on methodology,
    188–89, 189n66
critiques by, 189n66
culture, 244
Durkheim and, 237–38
economic rationalism, 206
elective affinity, 205, 209, 237
on ethical conduct, 195, 196–97, 198–99
frames of mind, 181, 230, 237, 291, 323
on generalizations, 192–93
on historical materialism, 188, 211–12
on historical progression, 213–14
on historical school, 188, 211
ideal types (pure types), xxiii, 193–94,
    205–6
interpretive sociology (*verstehende
    Soziologie*), 86–87, 230
iron cage of reason (*stahlhartes Gehäuse*),
    200–201, 200n74, 204, 211,
    237, 257
on knowledge in sociology, 192
Marx and, xxiii, 213–15, 230–31, 237–38
methodology, 188, 204, 205
modernism and, 215, 216
postmodernism and, 216, 229
reasons for commentary on culture, 324
on relativity of concepts, 191n67
on scientific action, 195–96, 198–99, 200
on single-factor analyses, 212–13
terms for culture, 238
typology of domination, 192n68
on universal laws, 191
on value relevance, 197–98
vocabulary from, 229–31, 325
work of, 184, 189n66
See also interpretive understanding;
    social action; *The Protestant
    Ethic and the Spirit of Capitalism*
    (Weber)
We Day, 13n6
Weitling, Wilhelm, 106
Welzel, Christian, 224n80
Wesch, Michael, 19, 25. *See also* "Visions"
    project (Wesch)
Western canon, 226–27, 227nn81–82

White, Shelly
  "Generation Z," 13
"Why We Need to Clear Our Cluttered
  Minds" (Gatehouse), 46–47
Wiley-Blackwell Encyclopedia of Sociology,
  224n79. See also *Blackwell
  Encyclopedia of Sociology*
Williams, Raymond
  on culture, 238–39, 238n83, 241–42, 245,
    323, 324
  Marx's influence on, 242
  on nature, 239n84
Wills, Bob, 275

"With God on Our Side" (Dylan), 285
Woller, Gary, 224
World War I, 140, 194, 217, 261–62
World War II, 140n49, 261–62
writing, 78–80. *See also* intellectual
  craftsmanship; scholarship

Yale University, 64n21
Young, Izzy, 278
YouTube, 15, 18–19. *See also* "Visions"
  project (Wesch)

Zimmerman, Robert, *see* Dylan, Bob